MARKET
SHARE
REPORTER

ISSN 1052-9578

MARKET SHARE REPORTER

AN ANNUAL COMPILATION

OF REPORTED MARKET SHARE

DATA ON COMPANIES,

PRODUCTS, AND SERVICES

2003

ROBERT S. LAZICH, Editor

GALE®

Detroit • New York • San Diego • San Francisco • Cleveland • New Haven, Conn. • Waterville, Maine • London • Munich

Market Share Reporter 2003

Robert S. Lazich

Project Editor
Amanda Quick

Editorial
Joyce Piwowarski, Susan Turner

Imaging and Multimedia
Michael Logusz

Manufacturing
NeKita McKee

ISBN 0-7876-3349-6
ISSN 0071-0210

Printed in the United States of America
10 9 8 7 6 5 4 3 2 1

TABLE OF CONTENTS

TABLE OF TOPICS

The *Table of Topics* lists all topics used in *Market Share Reporter* in alphabetical order. One or more page references follow each topic; the page references identify the starting point where the topic is shown. The same topic name may be used under different SICs; therefore, in some cases, more than one page reference is provided.

INTRODUCTION

Market Share Reporter (MSR) is a compilation of market share reports from periodical literature. The thirteenth edition covers the period 1998 through 2002; while dates overlap slightly with the twelfth edition, the thirteenth edition of *MSR* has completely new and updated entries. As shown by reviews of previous editions plus correspondence and telephone contact with many users, this is a unique resource for competitive analysis, diversification planning, marketing research, and other forms of economic and policy analysis. Features of the 2003 edition include—

- More than 2,000 entries, all new or updated.
- SIC classification, with entries arranged under 511 SIC codes.
- Corporate, brand, product, service and commodity market shares.
- Coverage of private and public sector activities.
- North American coverage.
- Comprehensive indexes, including products, companies, brands, places, sources, and SICs.
- Table of Topics showing topical subdivisions of chapters with page references.
- Graphics.
- Annotated source listing—provides publishers' information for journals cited in this edition of *MSR*.

MSR is a one-of-a-kind resource for ready reference, marketing research, economic analysis, planning, and a host of other disciplines.

Categories of Market Shares

Entries in *Market Share Reporter* fall into four broad categories. Items were included if they showed the relative strengths of participants in a market or provided subdivisions of economic activity in some manner that could assist the analyst.

- *Corporate market shares* show the names of companies that participate in an industry, produce a product, or provide a service. Each company's market share is shown as a percent of total industry or product sales for a defined period, usually a year. In some cases, the company's share represents the share of the sales of the companies shown (group total)—because shares of the total market were not cited in the source or were not relevant. In some corporate share tables, brand information appears behind company names in parentheses. In these cases, the tables can be located using either the company or the brand index.

- *Institutional shares* are like corporate shares but show the shares of other kinds of organizations. The most common institutional entries in *MSR* display the shares of states, provinces, or regions in an activity. The shares of not-for-profit organizations in some economic or service functions fall under this heading.

- *Brand market shares* are similar to corporate shares with the difference that brand names are shown. Brand names include equivalent categories such as the names of television programs, magazines, publishers' imprints, etc. In some cases, the names of corporations appear in parentheses behind the brand name; in these cases, tables can be located using either the brand or the company index.

- *Product, commodity, service, and facility* shares feature a broad category (e.g. household appliances) and show how the category is subdivided into components (e.g. refrigerators, ranges, washing machines, dryers, and dishwashers). Entries under this category cover products (autos, lawnmowers, polyethylene, etc.), commodities (cattle, grains, crops), services (telephone, child care), and facilities (port berths, hotel suites, etc.). Subdivisions may be products, categories of services (long-distance telephone, residential phone service, 800-service), types of commodities (varieties of grain), size categories (e.g., horsepower ranges), modes (rail, air, barge), types of facilities (categories of hospitals, ports, and the like), or other subdivisions.

- *Other shares.* MSR includes a number of entries that show subdivisions, breakdowns, and shares that do not fit neatly into the above categorizations but properly belong in such a book because they shed light on public policy, foreign trade, and other subjects of general interest. These items include, for instance, subdivisions of governmental expenditures, environmental issues, and the like.

Coverage

The thirteenth edition of *Market Share Reporter* covers essentially the same range of industries as previous editions. However, all tables are *new* or represent *updated* information (more recent or revised data). Also, coverage in detail is different in certain industries, meaning that more or fewer SICs are covered or product details *within* SICs may be different. For these reasons, it is recommended that previous editions of *MSR* be retained rather than replaced.

Coverage. Beginning with the fifth edition, MSR's geographic area of coverage became North America—Canada, the United States, and Mexico. As in all past editions, the vast majority of entries are for the United States. In the first four editions of MSR, international data were included at greater or lesser intensity depending on availability of space. This necessitated, among other things, frequent exclusion of data organized by states or regions of the United States—which are popular with users.

In order to provide better service to users, a companion publication, called *World Market Share Reporter* (*WMSR*), is available. *WMSR* features global market share information as well as country-specific market share and/or market size information outside North America. At the same time, *MSR* features more geographical market shares in the North American area.

MSR reports on *published* market shares rather than attempting exhaustive coverage of the market shares, say, of all major corporations and of all products and services. Despite this limitation, *MSR* holds share information on nearly 3,600 companies, more than 1,800 brands, and more than 2,100 product, commodity, service, and facility categories. Several entries are usually available for each industry group in the SIC classification; omitted groups are those that do not play a conventional role in the market, e.g., Private Households (SIC 88).

Variation in coverage from previous editions is due in part to publication cycles of sources and a different mix of brokerage house reports for the period covered (due to shifting interests within the investment community).

As pointed out in previous editions, *MSR* tends to reflect the current concerns of the business press. In addition to being a source of market share data, it mirrors journalistic preoccupations, issues in the business community, and events abroad. Important and controversial industries and activities get most of the ink. Heavy coverage is provided in those areas that are—

- large, important, basic (autos, chemicals)
- on the leading edge of technological change (computers, electronics, software)
- very competitive (toiletries, beer, soft drinks)
- in the news because of product recalls, new product introductions, mergers and acquisitions, lawsuits, and for other reasons
- relate to popular issues (environment, crime), or have excellent coverage in their respective trade press.

In many cases, several entries are provided on a subject each citing the same companies. No attempt was made to eliminate such seeming duplication if the publishing and/or original sources were different and the market shares were not identical. Those who work with such data know that market share reports are often little more than the "best guesses" of knowledgeable observers rather than precise measurements. To the planner or analyst, variant reports about an industry's market shares are useful for interpreting the data.

Publications appearing in the September 2000 to June 2002 period were used in preparing *MSR*. As a rule, material on market share data for 2002 were used by preference; in response to reader requests, we have included historical data when available. In some instances, information for earlier years was included if the category was unique or if the earlier year was necessary for context. In a few other cases, projections for 2003 and later years were also included.

"Unusual" Market Shares

Some reviewers of the first edition questioned—sometimes tongue-in-cheek, sometimes seriously—the inclusion of tables on such topics as computer crime, endangered species of fish, children's allowances, governmental budgets, and weapons system stockpiles. Indeed, some of these categories do not fit the sober meaning of "market share." A few tables on such subjects are present in every edition—because they provide market information, albeit indirectly, or because they are the "market share equivalents" in an industrial classification which is in the public sector or dominated by the public sector's purchasing power.

Organization of Chapters

Market Share Reporter is organized into chapters by 2-digit SIC categories (industry groups). The exception is the first chapter, entitled *General Interest and Broad Topics*; this chapter holds all entries that bridge two or more 2-digit SIC industry codes (e.g. retailing in general, beverage containers, building materials, etc.) and cannot, therefore, be classified using the SIC system without distortion. Please note, however, that a topic in this chapter will often have one or more additional entries later—where the table could be assigned to a detailed industry. Thus, in addition to tables on packaging in the first chapter, numerous tables appear later on glass containers, metal cans, etc.

Within each chapter, entries are shown by 4-digit SIC (industry level). Within blocks of 4-digit SIC entries, entries are sorted alphabetically by topic, then alphabetically by title.

SIC and Topic Assignments

MSR's SIC classifications are based on the coding as defined in the *Standard Industrial Classification Manual* for 1987, issued by the Bureau of the Census, Department of Commerce. This 1987 classification system introduced significant revisions to the 1972 classification (as slightly modified in 1977); the 1972 system is still in widespread use (even by the Federal government); care should be used in comparing data classified in the new and in the old way.

The closest appropriate 4-digit SIC was assigned to each table. In many cases, a 3-digit SIC had to be used because the substance of the table was broader than the nearest 4-digit SIC category. Such SICs always end with a zero. In yet other cases, the closest classification possible was at the 2-digit level; these SICs terminate with double-zero. If the content of the table did not fit the 2-digit level, it was assigned to the first chapter of *MSR* and classified by topic only.

Topic assignments are based on terminology for commodities, products, industries, and services in the SIC Manual; however, in many cases phrasing has been simplified, shortened, or updated; in general, journalistically succinct rather than bureaucratically exhaustive phraseology was used throughout.

Organization of Entries

Entries are organized in a uniform manner. A sample entry is provided below. Explanations for each part of an entry, shown in boxes, are provided below the sample.

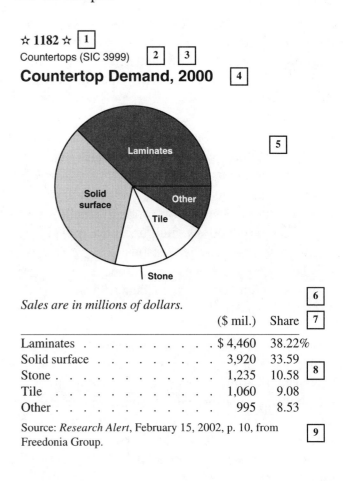

☆ 1182 ☆ 1
Countertops (SIC 3999) 2   3

Countertop Demand, 2000 4

5

Sales are in millions of dollars. 6

	($ mil.)	Share 7
Laminates	$ 4,460	38.22%
Solid surface	3,920	33.59
Stone	1,235	10.58 8
Tile	1,060	9.08
Other	995	8.53

Source: *Research Alert*, February 15, 2002, p. 10, from Freedonia Group. 9

1 *Entry Number.* A numeral between star symbols. Used for locating an entry from the index.

2 *Topic.* Second line, small type. Gives the broad or general product or service category of the entry. The topic for Countertop Demand, 2000 is Countertops.

3   *SIC Code.* Second line, small type, follows the topic. General entries in the first chapter do not have an SIC code.

4   *Title.* Third line, large type. Describes the entry with a headline.

5   *Graphic.* When a graphic is present, it follows the title. Some entries will be illustrated with a pie or bar chart. The information used to create the graphic is always shown below the pie or bar chart.

6   *Note Block.* When present, follows the title and is in italic type. The note provides contextual information about the entry to make the data more understandable. Special notes about the data, information about time periods covered, market totals, and other comments are provided. Self-explanatory entries do not have a note block.

7   *Column headers.* Follow the note block. Some entries have more than one column or the single column requires a header. In these cases, column headers are used to describe information covered in the column. In most cases, column headers are years (2000) or indicators of type and magnitude ($ mil.). Column headers are shown only when necessary for clarity of presentation.

8   *Body.* Follows the note block or the column header and shows the actual data in two or more columns. In most cases, individual rows of data in the body are arranged in descending order, with the largest market share holder heading the list. Collective shares, usually labelled "Others" are placed last.

9   *Source.* Follows the body. All entries cite the source of the table, the date of publication, and the page number (if given). In many cases, the publisher obtained the information from another source (original source); in all such cases, the original source is also shown.

Continued entries. Entries that extend over two adjacent columns on the same page are not marked to indicate continuation but continue in the second column. Entries that extend over two pages are marked *Continued on the next page.* Entries carried over from the previous page repeat the entry number, topic (followed by the word *continued*), title, and column header (if any).

Use of Names

Company Names. The editors reproduced company names as they appeared in the source unless it was clearly evident from the name and the context that a name had been misspelled in the original. Large companies, of course, tend to appear in a large number of entries and in variant renditions. General Electric Corporation may appear as GE, General Electric, General Electric Corp., GE Corp., and other variants. No attempt was made to enforce a uniform rendition of names in the entries. In the Company Index, variant renditions were reduced to a single version or cross-referenced.

Use of Numbers

Throughout *MSR*, tables showing percentage breakdowns may add to less than 100 or fractionally more than 100 due to rounding. In those cases where only a few leading participants in a market are shown, the total of the shares may be substantially less than 100.

Numbers in the note block showing the total size of the market are provided with as many significant digits as possible in order to permit the user to calculate the sales of a particular company by multiplying the market total by the market share.

In a relatively small number of entries, actual unit or dollar information is provided rather than share information in percent. In such cases, the denomination of the unit (tons, gallons, $) and its magnitude (000 indicates multiply by 1,000; mil., multiply by 1,000,000) are mentioned in the note block or shown in the column header.

Data in some entries are based on different kinds of currencies and different weight and liquid measures. Where necessary, the unit is identified in the note block or in the column header. Examples are long tons, short tons, metric tons or Canadian dollars, etc.

Graphics

Pie and bar charts are used to illustrate some of the entries. The graphics show the names of companies, products, and services when they fit on the charts. When room is insufficient to accommodate the label, the first word of a full name is used followed by three periods (…) to indicate omission of the rest of the label.

In the case of bar charts, the largest share is always the width of the column, and smaller shares are drawn in proportion. Two bar charts, consequently, should not be compared to one another.

Sources

The majority of entries were extracted from newspapers and from general purpose, trade, and technical periodicals normally available in larger public, special, or university libraries. All told, 1,009 sources were used; of these, 542 were primary print sources, Many more sources were reviewed but lacked coverage of the subject. These primary sources, in turn, used 467 original sources.

In many cases, the primary source in which the entry was published cites another source for the data, the original source. Original sources include other publications, brokerage houses, consultancies and research organizations, associations, government agencies, special surveys, and the like.

Many sources have also been used from the World Wide Web. The citation includes the Web address, the date the article was retrieved, and, if possible, the title of the article or report. In many cases Web pages have no title or author name. As well, it is not uncommon for Web pages to be moved or temporarity out of operation.

Since many primary sources appear as original sources elsewhere, and vice-versa, primary and original sources are shown in a single Source Index under two headings. Primary sources included in *MSR* almost always used the market share data as illustrative material for narratives covering many aspects of the subject. We hope that this book will also serve as a guide to those articles.

Indexes

Market Share Reporter features five indexes and three appendices.

- Source Index. This index holds 1,009 references in two groupings. *Primary sources* (542) are publications where the data were found. *Original sources* (467) are sources cited in the primary sources. Each item in the index is followed by one or more entry numbers arranged sequentially, beginning with the first mention of the source.

- Place Names Index. This index provides references to cities, states, parks and regions in North America. More than 310 are included. References are to entry numbers.

- Products, Services, Names and Issues Index. This index holds more than 2,170 references to products, personal names and services in alphabetical order. The index also lists subject categories that do not fit the definition of a product or service but properly belong in the index. Examples include *aquariums*, *counties*, *crime*, *defense spending, economies, lotteries*, and the like. Some listings are abbreviations for chemical substances, computer software, etc. which may not be meaningful to those unfamiliar with the industries. Wherever possible, the full name is also provided for abbreviations commonly in use. Each listing is followed by one or more references to entry numbers.

- Company Index. This index shows references to nearly 3,600 company names by entry number. Companies are arranged in alphabetical order. In some cases, the market share table from which the company name was derived showed the share for a combination of two or more companies; these combinations are reproduced in the index.

- Brand Index. The Brand Index shows references to more than 1,880 brands by entry number. The arrangement is alphabetical. Brands include names of publications, computer software, operating systems, etc., as well as the more conventional brand names (Coca Cola, Maxwell House, Budweiser, etc.)

- Appendix I - SIC Coverage. The first appendix shows SIC's covered by *Market Share Reporter*. The listing shows major SIC groupings at the 2-digit level as bold-face headings followed by 4-digit SIC numbers, the names of the SIC, and a *page* reference (rather than a reference to an entry number, as in the indexes). The page shows the first occurrence of the SIC in the book. *MSR*'s SIC coverage is quite comprehensive, as shown in the appendix. However, many 4-digit SIC categories are further divided into major product groupings. Not all of these have corresponding entries in the book.

- Appendix II - NAICS/SIC Conversion Guide. The SIC system is presently being revised, with SIC codes being replaced with North American Industry Classification System (NAICS) codes. NAICS is a six digit classification system that covers 20 sectors and 1,170 industries. The first two digits indicate the sector, the third indicates the subsector, the fourth indicates the industry group, the fifth indicates the NAICS industry, and the sixth indicates the national industry. This book is organized around the "old" SIC system because so many still use it. The appendix has both a SIC to NAICS and a NAICS to SIC look-up facility. More information on NAICS can be obtained form the Census Bureau Web site at: http://www.census.gov/naics.

- Appendix III - Annotated Source List. The third appendix provides publisher names, addresses, telephone and fax numbers, and publication frequency of primary sources cited in *Market Share Reporter*, 13th Edition.

What's New

Several recent changes have been made to *Market Share Reporter*. Personal names have been moved to the *Products, Services, Names and Issues Index*. Amusement parks and state parks will now be found in the *Place Names Index*. Titles of television shows, periodicals and music albums are now rendered in italics. We hope readers find these additions of use.

Available in Electronic Formats

Licensing. *Market Share Reporter* is available for licensing. The complete database is provided in a fielded format and is deliverable on such media as disk, CD-ROM or tape. For more information, contact Gale's Business Development Group at 1-800-877-GALE or visit us on our web site at www.galegroup.com/bizdev.

Online. *Market Share Reporter* is accessible online as File MKTSHR through LEXIS-NEXIS and as part of the MarkIntel service offered by Thomson Financial Securities Data. For more information, contact LEXIS-NEXIS, P.O. Box 933, Dayton, OH 45401-0933, phone (937)865-6800, toll-free (800)227-4908, website: http://www.lexis-nexis.com; or Thomson Financial Securities Data, Two Gateway Center, Newark, NJ 07102, phone: (973)622-3100, toll-free: (888)989-8373, website: www.tfsd.com.

Acknowledgements

Market Share Reporter is something of a collective enterprise which involves not only the editorial team but also many users who share comments, criticisms, and suggestions over the telephone. Their help and encouragement is very much appreciated. *MSR* could not have been produced without the help of many people in and outside of The Gale Group. The editors would like to express their special appreciation to Amanda Quick (Coordinating Editor, Gale Group) and to the staff of Editorial Code and Data, Inc.

Comments and Suggestions

Comments on *MSR* or suggestions for improvement of its usefulness, format, and coverage are always welcome. Although every effort is made to maintain accuracy, errors may occasionally occur; the editors will be grateful if these are called to their attention. Please contact:

Editors
Market Share Reporter
The Gale Group
27500 Drake Road
Farmington Hills, Michigan 48331-3535
Phone:(248)699-GALE
or (800)347-GALE
Fax: (248) 699-8069

General Interest and Broad Topics

★ 1 ★
Consumer Spending

Spending by Grandparents, 2002

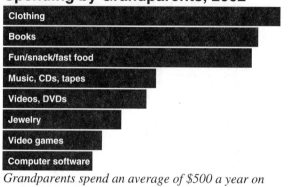

Grandparents spend an average of $500 a year on their grandchildren, up from $320 in 1992. They constitute a $35 billion annual market. Figures show what items they purchased for their grandkids over the last year.

Clothing	87.0%
Books	80.0
Fun/snack/fast food	78.0
Music, CDs, tapes	48.0
Videos, DVDs	45.0
Jewelry	37.0
Video games	31.0
Computer software	28.0

Source: *American Demographics*, April 2002, p. 42, from American Association of Retired Persons.

★ 2 ★
Consumer Spending

Tween Buying Power

Tweens (kids 8-12) spent $21.7 billion and influenced $170 billion of their parents' money, according to the source.

	($ bil.)	Share
Food and beverages (mostly snacks)	$ 9.0	41.28%
Apparel	5.0	22.94
Trading cards/board games	3.2	14.68
Gifts/room décor/misc.	1.8	8.26
Movie and sports	1.6	7.34
Pay-as-you-play parlor games . . .	1.2	5.50

Source: *Research Alert*, September 7, 2001, p. 12, from McNeal & Kids.

★ 3 ★
General Merchandise

Best-Selling General Merchandise Categories

Sales are shown in millions of dollars for the year ended May 20, 2001.

Batteries	$ 2,599.6
Film	1,561.6
Socks	1,524.1
Light bulbs	1,046.6
Candles	933.6
Disposable cameras	875.9
Cleaning tools/mops/brooms	858.9
Pantyhose/nylons	808.1
Motor oil	768.7
Blank audio/video cassettes	598.7

Source: *Grocery Headquarters*, August 2001, p. 5, from Information Resources Inc.

★ 4 ★

Homefurnishings

Gift and Decorative Accessory Industry

| Home decorative accessories |
| Stationery and paper products |
| General gifts |
| Collectibles |
| Seasonal decorations |

Market shares are shown in percent. General gifts included baby/child items ($1.9 billion), desk accessories ($1.6 billion), novelties ($1.6 billion) and wedding items ($1.3 billion).

Home decorative accessories	30.0%
Stationery and paper products	25.0
General gifts	25.0
Collectibles	16.0
Seasonal decorations	7.0

Source: *Research Alert*, November 16, 2001, p. 1, from Unity Marketing.

★ 5 ★

Homefurnishings

U.S. Housewares Industry

Market shares of the $67 billion industry.

Electrics	21.0%
Tabletop	16.1
Cook & bakeware	12.6
Space organizers	9.4
Kitchen tools	7.8
Cleaning products	7.1
Bathroom products	3.9
Promotional goods	2.7
Home office	1.4
Juvenile products	1.3

Source: *Modern Plastics*, January 2001, p. 51, from *State of the Industry Report* and National Houseware Manufacturers Association.

★ 6 ★

Licensed Merchandise

Licensed Merchandise Industry

Market is shown by segment.

Entertainment/character licensing	44.3%
Trademarks/brands/fashion	16.8
Other	38.9

Source: *Playthings*, August 2001, p. 43, from International Licensing Industry Merchandising.

★ 7 ★

Licensed Merchandise

Licensed Merchandise Sales, 2001

Retail sales are shown in billions of dollars. Apparel grew 13% over the previous year. Data are for both the U.S. and Canada.

	($ bil.)	Share
Apparel	$ 9.2	13.09%
Toys/games	8.0	11.38
Food/beverage	7.3	10.38
Accessories	6.1	8.68
Gifts/novelties	5.6	7.97
Publishing	4.7	6.69
Domestics	4.4	6.26
Health/Beauty	4.1	5.83
Video games/software	4.0	5.69
Stationery/paper	3.4	4.84
Other	13.5	19.20

Source: *Research Alert*, January 18, 2002, p. 1, from *Licensing Letter*.

★ 8 ★
Lifestyles

Health & Sustainability Market

Ecological lifestyles includes recycled and environmentally friendly products; Sustainable economy includes green buildings, renewable energy, and environmental management. Personal development includes CDs, yoga, fitness.

Ecological lifestyles	35.0%
Sustainable economy	33.0
Healthy living	14.0
Alternative health care	13.0
Personal development	5.0

Source: *Investor's Business Daily*, August 10, 2001, p. A8, from Salomon Smith Barney, *Natural Business*, First Call, and *LOHAS Journal*.

★ 9 ★
Luxury Goods

Luxury Goods Industry

The industry is shown in percent.

Clothing	28.0%
Fragrances and cosmetics	24.0
Shoes and leather goods	21.0
Wine and champagne	15.0
Jewelry and watches	7.0
Home accessories	5.0

Source: *New York Times*, November 18, 2001, p. 8.

★ 10 ★
Media

Largest Entertainment Firms

Firms are ranked by media revenue in billions of dollars.

AOL Time Warner	$ 36.2
Walt Disney	25.4
Vivendi Universal	24.3
Viacom	20.0
News Corp.	13.8

AT&T Broadband	.$ 9.6
Sony	9.0
Comcast	8.2
NBC	6.8

Source: *Broadcasting & Cable*, August 27, 2001, p. 17.

★ 11 ★
Natural Products

Best-Selling Natural Products, 2001

Sales are shown by outlet for the year ended August 2001.

Vitamins & minerals	$ 231.8
Frozen entrees, pizza & convenience foods . .	121.6
Milk, half & half, cream	113.5
Produce, fresh	111.5
Refrigerated juices & functional beverages . .	108.0
Chips, pretzels & snacks	104.0
Beverages, non-dairy	98.7
Yogurt & kefir	95.7
Supplements	92.2
Condiments	91.7

Source: *Grocery Headquarters*, December 2001, p. 48, from SPINscan.

★ 12 ★
Packaging

Cap and Closure Shipments

The market should see annual growth of 3%. Advances in the market will be fueled by plastic packaging at the expense of metal drink cases. Shipments are shown in billions of units.

	2000	2005	Share
Plastic	91.5	114.4	72.82%
Metal & other	44.6	42.7	27.18

Source: *Research Studies - Freedonia Group*, April 30, 2001, p. 1, from Freedonia Group.

★ 13 ★
Packaging

Flexible Food Packaging Indsutry

The industry had total sales of $5.149 billion.

Refrigerated meat	$ 1,308
Confections	900
Salty snacks	754

Continued on next page.

★ 13 ★ *Continued*

Packaging

Flexible Food Packaging Indsutry

The industry had total sales of $5.149 billion.

Produce	$ 730
Baked goods	320
Cookies/crackers	182
Beverages	155
Breakfast products	120
Baking needs/mixes	100
Dinner products	95
Frozen novelties	90

Source: *Packaging Digest*, November 2001, p. 12, from Esse Technologies.

★ 14 ★

Packaging

Food Packaging Market

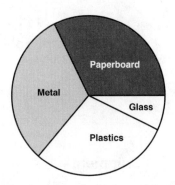

Sales are shown in millions of dollars.

	2000	2005	Share
Paperboard	$ 3,590	$ 4,075	32.44%
Metal	3,500	3,930	31.29
Plastics	2,790	3,640	28.98
Glass	920	915	7.29

Source: *Research Studies - Freedonia Group*, January 28, 2002, p. 5, from Freedonia Group.

★ 15 ★

Packaging

High Visibility Packaging Demand, 2006

Sales are shown in millions of dollars.

	($ mil.)	Share
Carded blister packs	2,325	29.85%
Windowed	1,895	24.33
Clamshell	1,730	22.21
Skin	1,340	17.20
Other	500	6.42

Source: *Research Studies - Freedonia Group*, March 15, 2002, p. 3, from Freedonia Group.

★ 16 ★

Packaging

Packaging Coatings and Additives Demand

The industry is expected to grow 5% annually. The growth is largely going to take place because of the switch to more expensive, high end coatings.

	($ mil.)	Share
Plastic	802	59.19%
Metal	280	20.66
Paper/paperboard	229	16.90
Glass & other	44	3.25

Source: *Research Studies - Freedonia Group*, October 29, 2001, p. 1, from Freedonia Group.

★ 17 ★

Packaging

Printed Packaging Market

The total market hit $70 billion.

	($ mil.)	Share
Corrugated	$ 27.39	38.82%
Flex packs	26.56	37.65
Cartons	9.13	12.94
Labels	7.47	10.59

Source: *Converting*, September 2001, p. 3, from IT Strategies.

★ 18 ★
Packaging

Rigid Packaging Sales

Sales are shown in millions of dollars. Changes foreseen in the market include reusable and more environmentally friendly products.

	2000	2005	Share
Drums	$ 1,400	$ 1,610	24.86%
Pails	1,245	1,595	24.63
Rigid intermediate bulk containers	830	1,315	20.31
Materials handling containers	891	1,110	17.14
Bulk boxes	724	845	13.05

Source: *Research Studies - Freedonia Group*, September 11, 2001, p. 3, from Freedonia Group.

★ 19 ★
Packaging

Soft Drink Packaging

Can's share has fallen after holding at 48.3% for 1998-99. 20oz PET has been rising over the last three years.

Cans	47.8%
2 liter PET	19.1
20 oz PET	18.0
1 liter PET	5.3
3 liter PET	4.2
24 oz PET	2.5
Other	3.1

Source: *Beverage Aisle*, September 2001, p. 82, from Container Consulting.

★ 20 ★
Payments

Value of Checks Written

Annual value is shown in trillions of dollars.

	($ bil.)	Share
Business to business	$ 20.4	42.77%
Business to consumer	6.9	14.47
Consumer to business	4.9	10.27
Other	15.5	32.49

Source: *Bank Systems & Technology*, January 2002, p. 30, from Federal Reserve Check and Electronic Payments Research Project.

★ 21 ★
Promotional Products

Promotional Products Industry

The industry hit $17.8 billion in 2000.

Wearables	29.1%
Writing instruments	10.5
Bags	10.5
Desk	7.0
Calendars	5.3
Glassware	4.7
Games	4.4
Recognition	4.1
Sporting goods	4.0
Other	20.4

Source: *Wearables Business*, August 2001, p. 8.

★ 22 ★
Self Improvement Industry

Self Improvement Market Segments

Figures are in millions of dollars for 2000.

	($ mil.)	Share
General motivational, new age, spiritual	$ 1,833	32.1%
Exercise	1,473	25.8
Business/financial	1,199	21.0
Weight loss	914	16.0
Stress management	291	5.1

Source: *Research Alert*, December 7, 2001, p. 5, from Marketdata Enterprises.

★ 23 ★
Water

U.S. Water Industry

Market shares are shown in percent.

Tap	35.0%
Bottled	34.0
Treated	31.0

Source: *Beverage World*, March 15, 2002, p. 16.

★ 24 ★

Weddings

U.S. Wedding Industry

The wedding industry reached $25.3 billion. The median cost for a wedding gown is $552 and a tux rental is $114.

	($ bil.)	Share
Receptions	$ 10.8	42.69%
Wedding expenses	4.3	17.00
Rings	3.8	15.02
Honeymoons	3.6	14.23
Wedding attire	2.8	11.07

Source: *Detroit Free Press*, June 25, 2001, p. 2F, from *Bride's Magazine*.

★ 25 ★

Weight Loss Industry

Weight Loss Market, 2001

Figures are in billions.

	($ bil.)	Share
Diet soft drinks	$ 14.40	38.51%
Health clubs revenue	12.52	33.48
Retail/multi-level meal replacement	2.27	6.07
Medically supervised diet programs	1.98	5.30
Low-calorie/diet entrees	1.91	5.11
Artificial sweeteners	1.74	4.65
Commercial weight loss centers . .	1.31	3.50
Diet books, cassettes, exercise videos	1.26	3.37

Source: *Research Alert*, May 17, 2002, p. 10, from Marketdata Enterprises.

★ 26 ★

Windows and Doors

Window and Door Market

Figures are in millions of units.

	2000	2002	Share
Vinyl	23.7	24.3	44.18%
Wood	23.1	22.7	41.27
Aluminum	7.7	7.3	13.27
Other	0.6	0.7	1.27

Source: "Window Market Slipping." Retrieved September 21, 2001 from the World Wide Web: http://www. windowanddoornet, from Ducker Research.

★ 27 ★

Windows and Doors

Window Market by Type

The nonresidential window segment of the building & construction market represents 492 million feet. Aluminum is estimated to hold 90% in the window segment. Figures are for the nonresidential market.

Commercial windows	50.0%
Store fronts	34.0
Curtainwall	16.0

Source: *Aluminum Today*, December 2001, p. 37.

SIC 01 - Agricultural Production - Crops

★ 28 ★
Crops (SIC 0100)

What Gets the Most Acreage

This was another disappointing year for farmers. Yields were high, particularly surprising considering the droughts and floods that hit the nation's farmland. Prices remained stubbornly low. Figures are in millions of acres.

	2000	2001	2002
Corn	79.5	76.0	77.7
Soybeans	74.5	75.2	75.9
Wheat	62.5	59.6	60.8
Cotton	15.5	16.2	16.0

Source: *Ag Lender*, December 2001, p. 10.

★ 29 ★
Produce (SIC 0100)

Fresh Produce Sales

Sales are shown in millions of dollars for the year ended January 26, 2002. Sales at Wal-mart are not included.

Salad mixes	$ 1,879.5
Potatoes	1,330.1
Carrots	916.6
Strawberries	754.4
Lettuce	555.1
Tomatoes	482.8
Mushrooms	473.4
Apples	399.9
Onions	325.1
Oranges	263.0
Celery	206.1

Source: *Grocery Headquarters*, April 2002, p. 70, from A. C. Nielsen.

★ 30 ★
Wheat (SIC 0111)

Top Wheat Producing States

Figures show millions of bushels.

Kansas	494.9
North Dakota	310.7
Oklahoma	198.9
Montana	168.8
Washington	157.4
Texas	136.5
South Dakota	120.8
Colorado	103.7
Idaho	102.4

Source: "Top Wheat Producing States." Retrieved June 27, 2002 from the World Wide Web: http://wbc.agr.state.mt.us.

★ 31 ★

Rice (SIC 0112)

Top Rice Producing States

Data share of total production. Mississippi and Texas have between 8-9% shares.

Arkansas	45.0%
California	20.0
Louisiana	15.0
Texas	9.0
Mississippi	9.0
Other	2.0

Source: "Rice: Questions and Answers." Retrieved June 25, 2002 from the World Wide Web: http://www.ers.usda.gov, from United States Department of Agriculture.

★ 32 ★

Corn (SIC 0115)

How Corn is Used, 2001

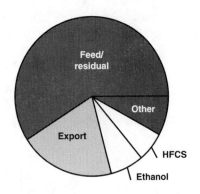

Corn is one of the most versatile crops in the United States. While much of it is used as feed, new markets keep developing. The ethanol sector had a 7% share, but was virtually nonexistant 15 years ago.

Feed/residual	59.0%
Export	20.0
Ethanol	7.0
HFCS	6.0
Other	8.0

Source: "The World of Corn." Retrieved June 25, 2002 from the World Wide Web: http://www.nega.com.

★ 33 ★

Corn (SIC 0115)

Top Corn Producing States

Data show millions of bushels.

Iowa	1,769.0
Illinois	1,473.4
Nebraska	1,239.7
Minnesota	1,032.7
Indiana	760.3
Ohio	470.9
South Dakota	429.5
Kansas	418.9
Wisconsin	404.1
Missouri	285.0

Source: "Corn in the Classroom." Retrieved June 25, 2002 from the World Wide Web: http://www.kycorn.org.

★ 34 ★

Beans (SIC 0119)

Top Navy Bean Producing States

Production is shown in hundredweight.

	(000)	Share
Michigan	2,320	43.04%
North Dakota	1,878	34.84
Minnesota	891	16.53
Nebraska	117	2.17
New Mexico	92	1.71
Idaho	92	1.71

Source: "U.S. Crops Data Rankings." Retrieved June 27, 2002 from the World Wide Web: http://nnas.usda.gov, p. NA, from National Agricultural Statistics.

★ 35 ★
Cotton (SIC 0131)

Top Cotton Producing States

Production of cotton (upland) is shown in thousands of bales.

	(000)	Share
Texas	5,300	28.74%
California	2,200	11.93
Georgia	1,900	10.30
Mississippi	1,810	9.82
Arkansas	1,730	9.38
Other	5,500	29.83

Source: "U.S. Crops Data Rankings." Retrieved June 27, 2002 from the World Wide Web: http://nnas.usda.gov, from National Agricultural Statistics.

★ 36 ★
Sugar Cane (SIC 0131)

Top Sugar Cane Producing States

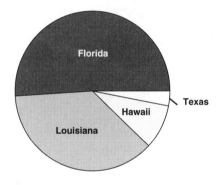

Production of sugar cane (for sugar) is shown in thousands of tons.

	(000)	Share
Florida	14,946	50.68%
Louisiana	10,906	36.98
Hawaii	2,784	9.44
Texas	856	2.90

Source: "U.S. Crops Data Rankings." Retrieved June 27, 2002 from the World Wide Web: http://nnas.usda.gov, p. NA, from National Agricultural Statistics.

★ 37 ★
Tobacco (SIC 0132)

Top Tobacco Producing States

Figures show total acreage harvested.

North Carolina	320,599
Kentucky	255,053
Tennessee	59,427
South Carolina	54,660
Virginia	54,035
Georgia	41,083
Ohio	11,457
Indiana	8,507
Pennsylvania	7,953
Maryland	7,939

Source: "Harvested Tobacco." Retrieved June 27, 2002 from the World Wide Web: http://www.ces.ncsu.edu.

★ 38 ★
Potatos (SIC 0134)

Top Potato Producing States

Production is shown in billions of pounds.

Idaho	15.2
Washington	10.3
Wisconsin	3.4
Colorado	2.8
Oregon	2.7

Source: *Quick Frozen Foods International*, April 2001, p. 93.

★ 39 ★
Vegetables (SIC 0161)

Largest Vegetable Growers in the North

Companies are ranked by acreage devoted to vegetable production.

R.D. Offutt Co.	65,000
Hartung Brothers Inc.	23,195
Fairbult Foods Inc.	14,700
Heartland Farms Inc.	9,997
Tri-Campbell Farms	9,600
Wysocki Produce Farm Inc.	9,100

Continued on next page.

★ 39 ★ *Continued*
Vegetables (SIC 0161)

Largest Vegetable Growers in the North

Companies are ranked by acreage devoted to vegetable production.

Black Gold Farms	8,500
Paramount Farms Inc.	7,648
Walther Farms	7,340
Okray Family Farms Inc.	6,893

Source: *AVG*, October 2001, p. 12.

★ 40 ★
Vegetables (SIC 0161)

Largest Vegetable Growers in the Southeast

Companies are ranked by acreage devoted to vegetable production.

A. Duda & Sons Inc.	22,000
Pacific Tomato Growers/Triple E Produce	17,874
Thomas Produce Co.	14,250
Hundley Farms Inc.	13,694
Six L's Packing Co.	11,500
Gargiulo Inc.	9,700
Pero Family Farms Inc.	7,038
Suwannee Farms/Eagle Island Farms	6,950
West Coast Tomato/McClure Farms	6,000
DiMare Homestead	6,000

Source: *AVG*, October 2001, p. 12.

★ 41 ★
Vegetables (SIC 0161)

Largest Vegetable Growers in the West

Companies are ranked by acreage devoted to vegetable production.

Grimmway Farms	43,400
Tanimura & Antle	39,730
Larsen Farms	28,000
D'Arrigo Bros. Co. of California	26,628
Ocean Mist Farms/Boutonnet Farms	16,342
P.J. Taggares Co.	15,950
Nunes Vegetables	15,160
Rio Farms	14,430

Boskovich Farms Inc.	13,500
Dresick Farms Inc.	13,393

Source: *AVG*, October 2001, p. 12.

★ 42 ★
Vegetables (SIC 0161)

Pumpkin Production by State

Figures are in millions of pounds.

	(mil.)	Share
Illinois	364	40.67%
California	180	20.11
New York	114	12.74
Pennsylvania	109	12.18
Other	128	14.30

Source: *USA TODAY*, November 19, 2001, p. A1, from *Census 2000*.

★ 43 ★
Vegetables (SIC 0161)

Top Baby Carrot Processors

Market shares are shown in percent.

Grimmway Farms/Bolthouse Farms	85.0%
Other	15.0

Source: *Food Institute Report*, October 22, 2001, p. 3.

★ 44 ★
Fruit (SIC 0170)

Retail Fruit Market

Less than 2% of the $15.5 billion retail fruit market is made up of pre-cut fruit. Less than 1% of the $17.7 billion vegetable industry is packaged.

Whole 98.4%
Pre-cut 1.6

Source: *Knight-Ridder/Tribune Business News*, November 12, 2001, p. NA.

★ 45 ★
Fruit (SIC 0171)

Largest Berry Growers

Companies are ranked by acreage devoted to berry production.

Cherryfield Foods 10,710
Jasper Wyman & Son 6,421
Northland Cranberries 2,524
Merrill Blueberry Farms 2,450
A.D. Makepeace Co. 1,798
Atlantic Blueberry Co. 1,320
Haines & Haines 1,212
Guptill Farms 1,176
Coastal Berry 1,100
Sunrise Growers 1,097

Source: *Fruit Grower*, August 2001, p. 6.

★ 46 ★
Fruit (SIC 0171)

Who Produces Raspberries?

The state's roughly 160 growers turned out about 69 million pounds. Market shares are shown in percent.

Washington 90.0%
Other 10.0

Source: *Knight-Ridder/Tribune Business News*, June 19, 2001, p. NA.

★ 47 ★
Fruit (SIC 0172)

Largest Grape Growers

Companies are ranked by acreage devoted to grape production.

E&J Gallo Winery 12,851
Michael Hat Farming 12,000
Beringer Wine Estates 10,212
Giumarra Vineyards 10,210
Delicate Vineyards 9,600
Golden State Vintners 7,883
Vino Farms 7,353
Sun World International 7,086
Monterey Pacific 6,720
Sunmet 6,375

Source: *Fruit Grower*, August 2001, p. 6.

★ 48 ★
Fruit (SIC 0172)

Top Grape Producing States

Production is shown in thousands of tons.

	(000)	Share
California	6,196	90.64%
Washington	319	4.67
New York	139	2.03
Michigan	61	0.89
Pennyslvania	58	0.85
Other	63	0.92

Source: "U.S. Crops Data Rankings." Retrieved June 27, 2002 from the World Wide Web: http://nnas.usda.gov, p. NA, from National Agricultural Statistics.

★ 49 ★

Nuts (SIC 0173)

Largest Nut Growers

Companies are ranked by acreage devoted to nut production.

Paramount Farming Co./Paramount Farming	48,077
Farmland Management Services	14,726
Golden Valley	10,800
Premiere Partners c/o Westchester Group	9,094
Chico Nut	8,619
Braden Farms	8,019
Lassen Land Co.	7,317
ML Macadamia Orchard	6,474
Jack Mariani Co.	6,000
Capital Agricultural Property Services	5,097

Source: *Fruit Grower*, August 2001, p. 6.

★ 50 ★

Nuts (SIC 0173)

Pecan Industry in Louisiana

The company estimates it has 85%-90% of the market that reaches from Baton Rouge to New Orleans. Nearly 23 million pounds are expected to be harvested in the state.

Bergeron	85.0%
Other	15.0

Source: *Greater Baton Rouge Business Report*, December 18, 2001, p. 14.

★ 51 ★

Nuts (SIC 0173)

Top Peanut Producers in Georgia

Figures are in millions of pounds.

	(mil.)	Share
Decatur	71.9	5.41%
Worth	70.9	5.34
Mitchell	69.0	5.19
Miller	68.8	5.18
Early	68.4	5.15

	(mil.)	Share
Irwin	54.2	4.08%
Baker	48.4	3.64
Seminole	46.8	3.52
Other	830.0	62.48

Source: *Knight-Ridder/Tribune Business News*, February 16, 2002, p. NA.

★ 52 ★

Fruit (SIC 0174)

U.S. Citrus Crop

Florida's citrus crop is 12.9 million tons, up 4%. Oranges make up 80% of the entire citrus crop.

Florida	77.0%
California/Arizona	20.0
Other	3.0

Source: *Frozen Fruit Digest*, February-March 2002, p. 26.

★ 53 ★

Fruit (SIC 0175)

Banana Market Industry in North America

The $4.5 billion market is shown in percent.

Dole Fresh Fruit	32.0%
Chiquita Fresh North America	26.0
Other	42.0

Source: *Advertising Age*, March 5, 2001, p. 8.

★ 54 ★

Fruit (SIC 0175)

Largest Stone Fruit Growers

Companies are ranked by acreage devoted to stone fruit production.

Gerawan Farming	5,858
Fowler Packing Co.	3,935
ITO Packing Co.	3,586
Taylor Orchards	3,510
Southern Orchard/Lane Packing	3,500
California Prune Packing	3,097
Thiara Brothers Orchards	2,700
Titan Peach Farms	2,600

Continued on next page.

★ **54** ★ *Continued*
Fruit (SIC 0175)

Largest Stone Fruit Growers

Companies are ranked by acreage devoted to stone fruit production.

Sun World International 2,532
Simonian Fruit 2,011

Source: *Fruit Grower*, August 2001, p. 6.

★ **55** ★
Fruit (SIC 0175)

Top Apple Producing States

Washington
New York
Michigan
California
        Pennsylvania
Other

Production is shown in millions of pounds.

	(mil.)	Share
Washington	4,900	47.92%
New York	1,120	10.95
Michigan	1,050	10.27
California	975	9.53
Pennsylvania	475	4.65
Other	1,706	16.68

Source: "U.S. Crops Data Rankings." Retrieved June 27, 2002 from the World Wide Web: http://nnas.usda.gov, p. NA, from National Agricultural Statistics.

★ **56** ★
Fruit (SIC 0175)

Top Pear Producing States

Production is shown in thousands of tons.

	(000)	Share
Washington	455	43.58%
California	312	29.89
Oregon	255	24.43
New York	9	0.86
Pennsylvania	4	0.38
Michigan	4	0.38
Other	5	0.48

Source: "U.S. Crops Data Rankings." Retrieved June 27, 2002 from the World Wide Web: http://nnas.usda.gov, p. NA, from National Agricultural Statistics.

★ **57** ★
Flowers (SIC 0181)

Flower and Plant Households

Data show millions of households that purchased greenery goods.

Flower transplants (annual) 35
Flower transplants (perennials) 29
Vegetable garden transplants 22
Flowering trees/shrubs 13
Herb transplants 10
Evergreen or leafy shrubs 7

Source: *American Demographics*, April 2002, p. 56, from National Gardening Association.

★ **58** ★
Flowers (SIC 0181)

Flower and Plant Sales

Data show share of consumer spending.

	2000	2001
Fresh cut flowers	39.1%	38.8%
Outdoor bedding plants	34.3	35.8
Potted plants	11.2	10.8
Artificial/dried flowers & plants	8.4	8.0
Foliage (green plants)	7.0	6.6

Source: *Business Wire*, March 19, 2002, p. 2362, from Ipsos-NPD Inc. and American Floral Endowment.

★ 59 ★

Flowers (SIC 0181)

Poinsettia Sales by Type

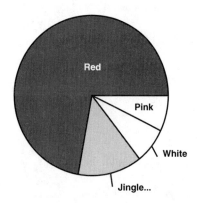

The flowers have become very popular lately. It has brought a gut in supply, keeping prices low for buyers and profits low for growers. Market shares are shown in percent.

Red 70.0%
Jingle Bells/Plum Pudding 13.0
White 7.0
Pink 7.0

Source: *Capper's*, November 27, 2001, p. 33.

★ 60 ★

Mushrooms (SIC 0182)

Agaricus Mushroom Sales

Sales hit 839 million pounds and was valued at $820 million. Production has fallen slightly over the last few years.

Pennsylvania 53.0%
California 15.0
Other 32.0

Source: *Utah Agriculture*, September 5, 2001, p. NA.

SIC 02 - Agricultural Production - Livestock

Pork (SIC 0213)

Largest Pork Processors

Companies are ranked by number of sows.

Smithfield Foods 710
Premium Standard Farms 211
Seaboard Farms 185
Triumph Pork Group 140
Prestage Farms 122
SMS of Pipestone 120
Cargill 109
Tyson Foods 108
Iowa Select Farms 100

Source: *Successful Farming*, October 2001, p. 19.

Pork (SIC 0213)

Largest Pork Processors in Canada

Companies are ranked by thousands of sows.

Maple Leaf Foods 90.0
Premium Pork 32.0
F. Menard 32.0
Isoporc 30.3
Hytek 30.0

Source: *Successful Farming*, October 2001, p. 19.

Pork (SIC 0213)

Largest Pork Processors in Mexico

Companies are ranked by thousands of sows.

Grupo Porcicola Mexicano 64.0
Proan (Proteina Animal) 35.0
Smithfield Foods 32.5

Source: *Successful Farming*, October 2001, p. 19.

Poultry (SIC 0250)

Largest Poultry Firms in Mexico

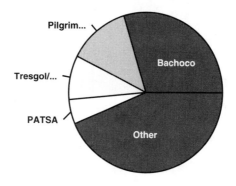

The industry has been growing for the last seven years. The rates: 5.8% for chickens, 4.8% for eggs and 10% for turkeys. 90% of all chicken is sold fresh. Market shares are shown in percent.

Bachoco 30.3%
Pilgrim Pride Mexico 12.7
Tresgol/Tyson 8.5
PATSA 5.0
Other 43.5

Source: *World Poultry*, no. 1, 2002, p. 14.

★ 65 ★
Poultry (SIC 0250)

Largest Poultry Producing States, 2000

States are ranked by billions of pounds in live weight.

Georgia	6.2
Arkansas	5.8
Alabama	5.3
North Carolina	4.1
Mississippi	3.7

Source: *Atlanta Journal-Constitution*, March 14, 2002, p. H1.

★ 66 ★
Broilers (SIC 0251)

Top Broiler Firms

Firms are ranked by average weekly ready-to-cook production in millions of pounds. Figures are based on the total of the top 42 companies, which was 648.61 million pounds.

	(mil.)	Share
Tyson Foods Inc.	$146.43	22.58%
Gold Kist Inc.	60.28	9.29
Pilgrim's Pride Corporation	56.70	8.74
ConAgra Poultry	48.37	7.46
Perdue Farms	46.48	7.17
Wayne Farms, ContiGroup	27.48	4.24
Sanderson Farms Inc.	22.83	3.52
Cagle's Inc.	21.88	3.37
Foster Farms	19.90	3.07
Mountain Farms Inc.	18.62	2.87
Other	179.64	27.70

Source: *WATT PoultryUSA*, January 2002, p. 26C.

★ 67 ★
Eggs (SIC 0252)

Largest Egg Producers

Companies are ranked by millions of layers in production at the end of the year. Shares are shown based on the top 40 firms.

	(mil.)	Share
Cal-Maine Foods Inc.	20.4	10.50%
Rose Acre Farms	16.0	8.23
Michael Foods Egg Products Co.	14.0	7.21
DeCoster Egg Farms	12.8	6.59

	(mil.)	Share
Buckeye Egg Farm	10.5	5.40%
Sparboe Companies	8.0	4.12
Dutchland Farms L.P.	7.3	3.76
Moark L.L.C.	6.4	3.29
Fort Recovery Equity	6.3	3.24
Midwest Poultry Services	5.9	3.04
Other	86.7	44.62

Source: *Egg Industry*, January 2002, p. 16.

★ 68 ★
Turkeys (SIC 0253)

Largest Turkey Processors

Firms are ranked by millions of pounds processed.

Jennie-O Turkey Store	1,250
Cargill	1,205
Butterball Turkey Co.	805
Carolina Turkeys	550
Pilgrim's Pride	536
Louis Rich Brand	290
Bil Mar	256
House of Raeford	255
Foster Farms	229

Source: *WATT PoultryUSA*, January 2002, p. 70.

★ 69 ★
Dogs (SIC 0271)

Top Dog Registrations, 2001

The top registered breeds for man's best friends are shown for the year.

Retrievers, labrador	165,970
Retrievers, Golden	62,497
German Shepard dogs	51,625
Dachshunds	50,478

Continued on next page.

★ **69** ★ *Continued*

Dogs (SIC 0271)

Top Dog Registrations, 2001

The top registered breeds for man's best friends are shown for the year.

Beagles	50,419
Yorkshire Terriers	42,025
Poodles	40,550
Boxers	37,035
Chihuahuas	36,627

Source: ''2001 Registration Statistics.'' Retrieved June 26, 2002 from the World Wide Web: http://www.aakc.org, from American Kennel Association.

★ **70** ★

Horses (SIC 0272)

Wild Horse Populations

Nevada	24,321
Wyoming	7,615
California	3,492
Utah	3,420
Colorado	943
Idaho	669
Arizona	275
Montana	189
New Mexico	70

Source: *Science World*, April 8, 2002, p. 6, from U.S. Bureau of Land Management.

SIC 08 - Forestry

★ 71 ★

Tree Farms (SIC 0811)

Christmas Tree Production in California

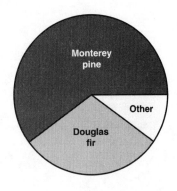

California leads the nation in Christmas tree consumption, with at least 3 million trees brought into the state annually, in addition to those grown in state. Live tree production is roughly valued at $10-12 million. Data show types of trees grown. Other includes red and white firs, cedars and Sierra redwoods.

Monterey pine	60.0%
Douglas fir	30.0
Other	10.0

Source: *Fresno Bee*, December 15, 2001, p. C1.

SIC 09 - Fishing, Hunting, and Trapping

★ 72 ★

Fisheries (SIC 0910)

Largest Commercial Fishery Landings, 2000

The largest commercial landings are shown in millions of dollars by port.

New Bedford, MA . . . . $ 146.3
Dutch Harbor-Unalaska, AK 124.9
Kodiak, AK 94.7
Dulac-Chauvin, LA 68.1
Empire-Venice, LA 61.6
Honolulu, HI 56.0
Hampton Roads, VA 52.8
Key West, FL 50.6
Port Arthur, TX 49.3
Bayou La Batre, AL 48.9

Source: ''Leading Ports by Dollars.'' Retrieved June 27, 2002 from the World Wide Web: http://www.st.nmfs.gov, from National Marine Fisheries Association.

SIC 10 - Metal Mining

★ 73 ★

Iron Ore (SIC 1011)

Iron Ore Shipments

Market shares are shown in percent. CCI stands for Cleveland-Cliffs Inc.

	2000	2001
CCI	57.74%	47.55%
USX	22.33	27.91
National	8.77	10.59
EVTAC	6.54	8.47
Inspat-In	4.53	5.49

Source: *E& MJ*, September 2001, p. 49.

★ 74 ★

Gold (SIC 1041)

How Gold Is Used

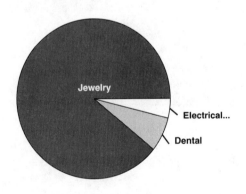

Market shares are shown in percent. Jewelry also refers to art products.

Jewelry	89.0%
Dental	7.0
Electrical and electronics	4.0

Source: ''Gold.'' Retrieved June 10, 2002 from the World Wide Web: http://www.usgs.gov.

★ 75 ★

Gold (SIC 1041)

Top Gold Producers in Canada

Firms are ranked by revenue in thousands of dollars.

Placer Dome	$ 1,565,000
Barrick Gold	1,357,000
Teck Corp.	1,224,000
Kinross Gold	284,600
Echo Bay Mines	284,392
Franco-Nevada Mining Corp.	218,236
Cambior Inc.	210,641
TVX Gold	179,533

Source: *Report on Business Magazine*, Annual 2000, p. 1.

★ 76 ★

Gold (SIC 1041)

Top Gold Producers in North America, 2000

Production is shown in thousands of ounces.

Anglo Gold	7,243
Newmont Mining	4,880
Barrick Gold Corporation	3,744
Placer Dome Inc.	2,984
Homestake Mining Company	2,206
Kinross Gold Corporation	944
Echo Bay Mines	695
Cambior	613
Meridian Gold Inc.	456
Glamis Gold	218

Source: ''Statistics.'' Retrieved June 10, 2002 from the World Wide Web: http://nma.org, from Gold Institute and Dr. John Dobra.

★ 77 ★

Silver (SIC 1044)

Top Silver Producers in North America, 2000

Production is shown in millions of ounces.

Industrias Penoles 44.7
Grupo Mexico 23.2
Homestake Mining 14.7
Cominco Ltd. 13.3
Echo Bay Mines Ltd. 12.3
Coeur d'Alene Mines Corp. . . . . . . , , . 11.7
Noranda Inc. 9.7
Hecla Mining Company 8.0
Placer Dome Inc. 6.3

Source: ''Statistics.'' Retrieved June 10, 2002 from the World Wide Web: http://nma.org, from Silver Institute.

SIC 12 - Coal Mining

★ 78 ★

Coal (SIC 1220)

Top Coal Producers in North America, 1999

The Peabody Group	
Arch Coal Inc.	
Kennecott Energy Company	
CONSOL Energy	
	RAG American Coal Holding
	AEI Resources Inc.
	A.T. Massey Coal Company
	The North American Coal Corporation
	Texas Utilities Mining Corporation
	Triton Coal Company

Production is shown in millions of short tons.

	Tons	Share
The Peabody Group	179.2	16.4%
Arch Coal Inc.	121.4	11.1
Kennecott Energy Company . . .	120.1	11.0
CONSOL Energy	73.1	6.7
RAG American Coal Holding . . .	59.2	5.4
AEI Resources Inc.	47.4	4.3
A.T. Massey Coal Company	38.8	3.5
The North American Coal Corporation	31.2	2.9
Texas Utilities Mining Corporation .	28.6	2.6
Triton Coal Company	23.8	2.2

Source: ''Statistics.'' Retrieved June 10, 2002 from the World Wide Web: http://nma.org, from *National Mining Association 1999 Coal Producer Survey*.

SIC 13 - Oil and Gas Extraction

★ 79 ★

Natural Gas (SIC 1311)

Largest Gas Producers

Companies are ranked by production in billions of cubic feet.

BP	1,174.0
ExxonMobil Corp.	1,157.0
Shell Oil Co.	616.0
Chevron Corp.	570.0
El Paso Corp.	550.0
Burlington Resources Inc.	527.0
Texaco Inc.	478.2
Devon Energy Corp.	426.1
Phillips Petroleum Co.	386.0

Source: *Oil & Gas Journal*, October 1, 2001, p. 76.

★ 80 ★

Oil (SIC 1311)

Crude and Condesate Production

Data show barrels annually.

	Barrels	Share
Louisiana	569,300	26.79%
Texas	527,465	24.82
Alaska	352,259	16.58
California	291,211	13.70
Oklahoma	67,577	3.18
New Mexico	65,907	3.10
Wyoming	58,305	2.74
Kansas	33,215	1.56
North Dakota	31,899	1.50
Other	128,064	6.03

Source: *World Oil*, February 2002, p. 48.

★ 81 ★

Oil (SIC 1311)

Largest Oil Refiners

Market shares are shown in percent.

Conoco-Phillips	13.7%
ExxonMobil	11.7
Valero	11.4
Shell	6.3
Chevron-Texaco	6.3
Other	41.0

Source: *Wall Street Journal*, January 24, 2002, p. A6, from Energy Department.

★ 82 ★

Oil (SIC 1311)

Largest U.S. Oil Fields

Data show size of recoverable resources, in billions of barrels.

Prudhoe Bay, Alaska	13.0
East Texas	5.4
Wilmington, CA	2.8
Midway-Sunset, CA	2.7
Kuparuk River, Alaska	2.6
Wasson, TX	2.1
Kern River, CA	2.1
Yates, TX	2.0
Panhandle, TX	1.5
Elk Hills, CA	1.4

Source: *Christian Science Monitor*, June 20, 2001, p. 24, from Energy Information Administration.

★ 83 ★

Oil (SIC 1311)

Leading Oil & Gas Producers in North America

Figures are in millions of metric tons.

United States	360
Mexico	163
Canada	114

Source: *Investor's Business Daily*, April 3, 2002, p. A16, from OECD.

★ 84 ★

Oil (SIC 1311)

Who Supplies the U.S. With Oil, 2001

Canada
Saudi Arabia
Venezuela
Mexico
Nigeria
Iraq
Norway
Great Britain
Colombia
Algeria

Data show millions of barrels per day.

Canada	1.79
Saudi Arabia	1.66
Venezuela	1.54
Mexico	1.42
Nigeria	0.85
Iraq	0.78
Norway	0.33
Great Britain	0.31
Colombia	0.28
Algeria	0.28

Source: *New York Times*, April 9, 2002, p. C4, from Energy Information Administration.

★ 85 ★

Natural Gas Liquids (SIC 1321)

Largest Gas Liquid Producers

Companies are ranked by reserves in millions of barrels.

BP	3,193
ExxonMobil	2,986
Phillips Petroleum Co.	2,010
Texaco Inc.	1,560
Occidental Petroleum Corp.	1,346
Chevron Corp.	1,054
Shell Oil Co.	1,052
Devon Energy Corp.	521
Anadarko Petroleum Corp.	458

Source: *Oil & Gas Journal*, October 1, 2001, p. 76.

★ 86 ★

Oil Wells (SIC 1381)

Oil Producing Wells, 2001

Data include flowing and artificial lifts.

	No.	Share
Texas	159,240	30.02%
Oklahoma	84,252	15.88
California	43,078	8.12
Kansas	42,350	7.98
Kentucky	29,557	5.57
Ohio	29,087	5.48
Louisiana	27,250	5.14
New Mexico	18,158	3.42
Illinois	17,912	3.38
Other	79,608	15.01

Source: *World Oil*, February 2002, p. 48.

SIC 14 - Nonmetallic Minerals, Except Fuels

★ 87 ★

Mining (SIC 1400)

Largest Mining Companies in Canada

Noranda Inc.
Inco Ltd.
Suncor Energy
Potash Corp. of Sas.
Syncrude
Agrium Inc.
Falconbridge
Placer Dome Ltd.
Cominco Ltd.
Teck Corp.

Firms are ranked by revenue in millions of dollars.

Noranda Inc.	$ 6,957.0
Inco Ltd.	4,331.7
Suncor Energy	3,388.0
Potash Corp. of Sas.	3,313.9
Syncrude	3,300.0
Agrium Inc.	2,781.4
Falconbridge	2,614.5
Placer Dome Ltd.	2,098.3
Cominco Ltd.	2,015.1
Teck Corp.	1,877.0

Source: *Canadian Mining Journal*, August 2001, p. 10.

★ 88 ★

Crushed Stone (SIC 1411)

Crushed Stone Industry

Areas are shown by production in millions of metric tons. Figures are for the second quarter.

	(mil.)	Share
South Atlantic	104.0	22.8%
East North Central	85.9	18.8
West South Central	62.5	13.7

Source: *Pit & Quarry*, December 1, 2001, p. 36, from U.S. Department of the Interior.

★ 89 ★

Sand and Gravel (SIC 1440)

Sand and Gravel Industry, 2002

Areas are shown by production in millions of metric tons for the second quarter.

	(mil.)	Share
East North Central	67.3	20.3%
Pacific	59.6	18.0
Mountain	51.6	15.6

Source: *Pit & Quarry*, December 1, 2001, p. 36, from U.S. Department of the Interior.

★ 90 ★

Clays (SIC 1455)

Ball Clay Consumption by Market

Market shares are shown in percent.

Floor and wall tile	36.0%
Sanitaryware	22.0
Exports	14.0
Refractories	6.0
Pottery	2.0
Other	20.0

Source: *Ceramic Industry*, January 2002, p. 18.

★ 91 ★

Diamonds (SIC 1499)

Polished Diamond Imports, 1999

Market shares are shown in percent.

India 69.0%
Israel 17.0
Belgium 9.0
Other 5.0

Source: *New York Times*, February 13, 2002, p. C2, from
Indo Argyle Diamond Council.

SIC 15 - General Building Contractors

★ 92 ★
Construction (SIC 1520)

Construction Industry Revenues

The industry is shown in percent.

New construction 58.1%
Modernization/upgrade/reconstruction 32.9
Maintenance/service 9.0

Source: *Contractor's Business Management Report*, April 2002, p. 1.

★ 93 ★
Residential Construction (SIC 1521)

Largest Builders

Firms are ranked by housing revenues in billions of dollars.

Lennar Corp. . . . . $ 5.46
Pulte Corp. 5.36
Centex Corp. 4.99
D.R. Horton Inc. 4.55
KB Home 4.36
The Ryland Group 2.63
NVR Inc. 2.55
Toll Brothers 2.18
M.D.C. Holdings Inc. 2.07

Source: *Professional Builder*, April 2002, p. 42.

★ 94 ★
Residential Construction (SIC 1521)

New Housing Construction

Figures are in thousands.

	1999	2001	2003
Single family	1,306	1,227	1,324
Mobile homes	348	178	243
Multifamily	341	327	360

Source: *Wood & Wood Products*, October 2001, p. 75, from National Association of Home Builders.

★ 95 ★
Residential Construction (SIC 1521)

Top Builders in Atlanta, GA

Market shares are shown in percent.

Pulte Corp. 4.3%
D.R. Horton 3.4
Colony Homes 2.1
Centex Corp. 1.8
Bowen Builders Group 1.7
Ryland Homes 1.6
Other 85.1

Source: *Builder*, May 2001, p. 223, from The Meyers Group.

★ 96 ★
Residential Construction (SIC 1521)

Top Builders in Chicago, IL

Market shares are shown in percent.

D.R. Horton 3.8%
Concord Homes 3.7
Ryland Homes 3.5
Neumann Homes 3.5
Lakewood Homes 3.3
Kimball Hill Homes 2.7
Centex Corp. 2.7
Other 76.8

Source: *Builder*, May 2001, p. 223, from The Meyers Group.

★ 97 ★

Residential Construction (SIC 1521)

Top Builders in Cincinnati, OH

Market shares are shown in percent.

Fischer Homes	10.6%
The Drees Co.	10.5
Crossman Communities	6.1
Erpenbeck Co.	5.8
Ryland Homes	3.5
Other	63.5

Source: *Builder*, May 2001, p. 223, from The Meyers Group.

★ 98 ★

Residential Construction (SIC 1521)

Top Builders in Cleveland/Lorain/ Elyria, OH

Market shares are shown in percent.

Ryan Homes	5.4%
Pulte Corp.	4.5
Unmistakably Premier Homes	2.6
Gross Builders	2.4
Zaremba Contractors	2.2
Whitlatch & Co.	2.2
Other	80.7

Source: *Builder*, May 2001, p. 223, from Realty One Builder Marketing.

★ 99 ★

Residential Construction (SIC 1521)

Top Builders in Columbus, OH

Market shares are shown in percent.

M/I Schottenstein Homes	21.1%
Dominion Homes	17.9
Rockford Homes	5.3
Centex Corp.	4.6
Maronda Homes	3.6
Other	46.7

Source: *Builder*, May 2001, p. 223, from The Meyers Group.

★ 100 ★

Residential Construction (SIC 1521)

Top Builders in Dallas, TX

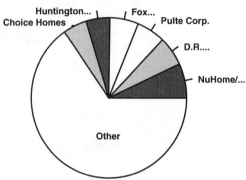

Market shares are shown in percent.

NuHome/U.S. Home Corp./Lennar Corp.	6.9%
D.R. Horton	6.3
Pulte Corp.	5.5
Fox & Jacobs Homes/Centex Corp.	5.5
Huntington Homes/Highland Homes	5.1
Choice Homes	4.8
Other	65.8

Source: *Builder*, May 2001, p. 223, from The Meyers Group.

★ 101 ★

Residential Construction (SIC 1521)

Top Builders in Denver, CO

Market shares are shown in percent.

Richmond Am Homes	12.3%
D R Horton/Continental/Trimark	8.5
K B Home (Kaufman & Broad)	7.9
US Home	5.1
Melody	4.8
Village Homes	3.6
Oakwood Homes	3.4
Shea Homes	2.3
Pulte	2.3
Other	49.8

Source: *Denver Business Journal*, July 27, 2001, p. 24B, from Home Builders Research.

★ 102 ★

Residential Construction (SIC 1521)

Top Builders in Detroit, MI

Market shares are shown in percent.

Pulte Corp.	7.6%
Toll Brothers	2.6
Tri-Mount Development	1.9
The Selective Group	1.5
Moceri Development	1.5
S.R. Jacobson Development	1.4
Robertson Brothers Co.	1.4
Other	82.1

Source: *Builder*, May 2001, p. 223, from The Meyers Group.

★ 103 ★

Residential Construction (SIC 1521)

Top Builders in Ft. Lauderdale, FL

Market shares are shown in percent.

Arvida/JMB Partners	18.9%
Lennar Corp.	9.1
Engle Homes	6.7
WCI Communities	5.5
Century Builders Group	4.4
Other	55.4

Source: *Builder*, May 2001, p. 223, from The Meyers Group.

★ 104 ★

Residential Construction (SIC 1521)

Top Builders in Ft. Worth/Arlington, TX

Market shares are shown in percent.

Choice Homes	12.3%
KB Homes	8.7
Centex Corp.	8.0
David Weekley Homes	4.1
Village Builders/Lennar Corp.	3.7
Goodman Family of Builders	3.3
Other	59.9

Source: *Builder*, May 2001, p. 223, from The Meyers Group.

★ 105 ★

Residential Construction (SIC 1521)

Top Builders in Grand Rapids/ Muskegon/ Holland, MI

Market shares are shown in percent.

Eastbrook Co.	5.2%
Pulte Corp.	1.8
Holwerda Builders	1.6
Bosgraaf Builders	1.4
Justin Zylstra, Builder	1.1
Other	88.9

Source: *Builder*, May 2001, p. 223.

★ 106 ★

Residential Construction (SIC 1521)

Top Builders in Hampton Roads VA/ NC

Market shares are shown in percent.

Terry Peterson Residential	4.0%
Affordable Homes	3.3
Napolitano Enterprises	3.0
Centex Corp.	2.7
Boyce/Ainslie/Cohen/Widener Ltd.	2.4
Other	84.6

Source: *Builder*, May 2001, p. 223, from The Meyers Group.

★ 107 ★
Residential Construction (SIC 1521)

Top Builders in Indianapolis, MD

Data show number of permits filed in 2000.

Crossman Communities	1,987
C.P. Morgan Co. Inc.	1,508
Davis Homes	950
Dura Cos.	701
Ryland Homes	681

Source: *Indianapolis Business Journal*, October 29, 2001, p. 24B.

★ 108 ★
Residential Construction (SIC 1521)

Top Builders in Las Vegas, NV

Market shares are shown in percent.

KB Home	13.8%
Del Webb Corp./Coventry Homes	8.2
Pardee Construction Co./Weyerhaeuser Real Estate	4.2
Pulte Corp.	3.7
Richmond American/M.D.C. Holdings	3.2
American West Homes	3.1
Other	36.2

Source: *Builder*, May 2001, p. 223, from The Meyers Group.

★ 109 ★
Residential Construction (SIC 1521)

Top Builders in Los Angeles/Long Beach, CA

Market shares are shown in percent.

Pardee Construction Co.	6.4%
KB Home	3.9
Centex Corp.	3.6
John Laing Homes	3.3
Beazer Homes USA	3.1
Other	79.7

Source: *Builder*, May 2001, p. 223, from The Meyers Group.

★ 110 ★
Residential Construction (SIC 1521)

Top Builders in Minneapolis/St. Paul, MN

Market shares are shown in percent.

Rottlund Homes	4.7%
Lundgren Bros./Orrin Thompson	4.5
Centex Corp.	3.7
Pulte Corp.	3.0
D.R. Horton	3.0
Ryland Homes	2.4
Other	78.7

Source: *Builder*, May 2001, p. 223, from The Meyers Group.

★ 111 ★
Residential Construction (SIC 1521)

Top Builders in Monmouth/Ocean Counties, NJ

Market shares are shown in percent.

U.S. Home Corp.	7.7%
Calton Homes/Centex Corp.	6.5
The Kokes Organization	4.3
K. Hovnanian Enterprises	3.7
D.R. Horton	3.6
Other	74.2

Source: *Builder*, May 2001, p. 223, from The Meyers Group.

★ 112 ★

Residential Construction (SIC 1521)

Top Builders in Nashville, TN

Market shares are shown in percent.

Flournoy Construction	4.6%
Pulte Corp.	3.9
Phillips Builders/Beazer Homes	3.8
Fox Ridge Homes/NVR	3.7
The Jones Co.	2.0
Other	82.0

Source: *Builder*, May 2001, p. 223, from The Meyers Group.

★ 113 ★

Residential Construction (SIC 1521)

Top Builders in Orange County, CA

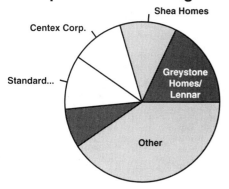

Market shares are shown in percent.

Greystone Homes/Lennar Corp.	18.2%
Shea Homes	11.7
Centex Corp.	10.8
Standard Pacific Corp.	10.7
John Laing Homes	7.7
Other	40.9

Source: *Builder*, May 2001, p. 223, from The Meyers Group.

★ 114 ★

Residential Construction (SIC 1521)

Top Builders in Orlando, FL

Market shares are shown in percent.

The Villages	12.0%
U.S. Home Corp./Lennar Corp.	8.8
Maronda Homes	6.2
Centex Corp.	5.8
Pulte Corp.	4.9
Engle Homes	4.7
Other	57.6

Source: *Builder*, May 2001, p. 223, from The Meyers Group.

★ 115 ★

Residential Construction (SIC 1521)

Top Builders in Philadelphia, PA

Market shares are shown in percent.

Orleans Homebuilders	5.8%
Pulte Corp.	5.1
Toll Brothers	4.1
David Cutler Group	2.8
Ryan Homes/NVR	2.7
Gambone Brothers	2.7
Other	76.8

Source: *Builder*, May 2001, p. 223, from The Meyers Group.

★ 116 ★

Residential Construction (SIC 1521)

Top Builders in Phoenix/Mesa, AZ

Market shares are shown in percent.

Del Webb Corp./Coventry Homes	7.3%
Shea Homes	6.4
D.R. Horton	5.9
KB Home	5.8
Greystone Homes/U.S. Home Corp.	4.2
Richmond American/M.D.C. Holdings	4.1
Other	66.3

Source: *Builder*, May 2001, p. 223, from The Meyers Group.

★ 117 ★

Residential Construction (SIC 1521)

Top Builders in Pittsburgh, PA

Data show number of permits filed in 2000.

Ryan Homes	667
A.R. Building Co.	110
Heartland Homes Inc.	106
All Star Homes Inc.	72
Hawthorne Homes Co.	57

Source: *Pittsburgh Business Times*, October 19, 2001, p. 46.

★ 118 ★

Residential Construction (SIC 1521)

Top Builders in Portland, OR/ Vancouver

Market shares are shown in percent.

Arbor Custom Homes	5.7%
D.R. Horton	3.1
Schuler Homes	2.7
Holt Homes	2.4
AHO Construction	2.3
Legend Homes	1.9
Other	81.9

Source: *Builder*, May 2001, p. 223, from The Meyers Group.

★ 119 ★

Residential Construction (SIC 1521)

Top Builders in Riverside/San Bernadino, CA

Market shares are shown in percent.

KB Homes	10.7%
The Forecast Group	4.2
Centex Corp.	3.8
U.S. Home Corp./Lennar Corp.	3.7
Richmond American/M.D.C. Holdings . . .	3.4
Other	25.8

Source: *Builder*, May 2001, p. 223, from The Meyers Group.

★ 120 ★

Residential Construction (SIC 1521)

Top Builders in Sacramento, CA

Market shares are shown in percent.

Lennar	14.2%
Beazer Homes	8.8
Pulte	7.4
Elliott Homes	6.0
Other	63.6

Source: *Sacramento Business Journal*, December 21, 2001, p. 1, from *Builder*.

★ 121 ★

Residential Construction (SIC 1521)

Top Builders in St. Louis, MO

Market shares are shown in percent.

McBride & Son	6.1%
The Jones Co.	5.5
MLP Multifamily	5.4
Whittaker Homes/Fortress Co.	4.3
Mayer Homes	3.6
Taylor-Morley Homes	2.5
Other	72.6

Source: *Builder*, May 2001, p. 223, from The Meyers Group.

★ 122 ★
Residential Construction (SIC 1521)

Top Builders in Salt Lake City/Ogden, Utah

Market shares are shown in percent.

Salisbury Homes	7.7%
Ivory Homes	6.9
John Laing Homes	3.8
Woodside Homes Corp.	3.7
Hamlet Homes	3.4
Other	74.5

Source: *Builder*, May 2001, p. 223, from The Meyers Group.

★ 123 ★
Residential Construction (SIC 1521)

Top Builders in San Diego, CA

Market shares are shown in percent.

KB Home	10.5%
Shea Homes	8.8
D.R. Horton	8.4
William Lyon Homes	7.6
Pardee Construction Co./Weyerhaeuser	6.9
Western Pacific Housing	6.4
Other	51.4

Source: *Builder*, May 2001, p. 223, from The Meyers Group.

★ 124 ★
Residential Construction (SIC 1521)

Top Builders in Tampa Bay, FL

Market shares are shown in percent.

Rutenberg Homes/U.S. Home/Lennar Corp.	10.2%
Ryland Homes	7.0
Pulte Corp.	4.4
Westfield Homes USA	4.2
M/I Schottenstein Homes	4.2
Inland Homes	3.3
Other	66.7

Source: *Builder*, May 2001, p. 223, from The Meyers Group.

★ 125 ★
Residential Construction (SIC 1521)

Top Builders in the Bay Area

Data show number of homes sold.

Western Pacific Housing	419
Shea Homes	396
Standard Pacific	366
Toll Brothers Inc.	350
KB Home	342

Source: *San Francisco Business Times*, July 20, 2001, p. 28.

SIC 16 - Heavy Construction, Except Building

★ 126 ★

Contracting Work (SIC 1600)

Leading Contracting Firms in Canada

Firms are ranked by revenue in thousands of dollars.

PCL Construction Group	$ 2,789,534
SNC Lavalin Group	1,740,406
Bechtel Canada	1,600,000
Agra Inc.	1,293,683
Armbro Enterprises	1,014,549
Ledcor Inc.	891,000

Source: *Report on Business Magazine*, Annual 2000, p. 1.

★ 127 ★

Heavy Construction - Highways (SIC 1611)

Largest Highway Contractors in the Puget Sound Area

Wilder Construction

Lakeside Industries

Tucci & Sons Inc.

Woodworth & Co. Inc.

Kiewit Pacific Co.

Firms are ranked by billings in millions of dollars.

Wilder Construction	$ 101.0
Lakeside Industries	98.0
Tucci & Sons Inc.	37.9
Woodworth & Co. Inc.	31.0
Kiewit Pacific Co.	20.0

Source: *Puget Sound Business Journal*, November 16, 2001, p. 22B.

SIC 17 - Special Trade Contractors

★ 128 ★

Contracting Work - Piping (SIC 1711)

Top Piping Contractors

Firms are ranked by sales in millions of dollars.

Kinetics Group	$ 601.52
Comfort Systems USA	159.10
Bracknell Corp.	135.00
EMCOR Group	132.88
Williams Power Inc.	132.50
MMC Corp.	122.40
Harder Mechanical Contractors	115.83
Enron Facility Services	114.82

Source: *Contractor*, May 2001, p. 22.

★ 129 ★

Contracting Work - Plumbing (SIC 1711)

Top Plumbing Contractors

Firms are ranked by sales in millions of dollars.

American Plumbing and Mechanical	$ 470.36
EMCOR Group Inc.	332.20
Encompass Services Corp.	309.70
Roto-Rooter/Service America	280.69
American Residential Services/Rescue Rooter	200.00
Bracknell Corp.	120.00
Comfort Systems USA	95.46
TDIndustries	61.50

Source: *Contractor*, May 2001, p. 22.

★ 130 ★

Contracting Work - Painting (SIC 1721)

Top Painting Contractors

Firms are ranked by 2000 revenue in millions of dollars.

Kenny Industrial Services	$ 150.0
Protherm Services Group	37.5
Robison-Prezioso Inc.	$ 32.0
Swanson & Youngdale Inc.	31.9
Techno Coatings Inc.	30.8
Ascher Brothers Co. Inc.	26.6
Avalotis Corp.	23.5
Fine Painting & Decorating Co. Inc.	22.1

Source: *ENR*, October 7, 2001, p. 56.

★ 131 ★

Contracting Work - Electrical (SIC 1731)

Leading Markets for Electrical Contracting

Regions are ranked by potential electrical contracting sales, in millions.

New York City, NY	$ 944.2
Chicago, IL	869.1
Atlanta, GA	629.5
Los Angeles-Long Beach, CA	609.6
Boston, MA	586.3
Dallas, TX	511.0
Philadelphia, PA	449.3
Detroit, MI	444.6
Phoenix-Mesa, AZ	398.3

Source: *Electrical Wholesaling*, November 2001, p. 1.

★ 132 ★

Contracting Work - Masonry (SIC 1741)

Top Masonry Contractors

Firms are ranked by 2000 revenue in millions of dollars.

McGee Brothers Co. Inc.	$ 74.5
The Western Group	50.1
Dee Brown Inc.	44.1
Seedorff Masonry Inc.	40.6
Pyramid Masonry Contractors	40.6
Leonard Masonry Inc.	39.5
Caretti Inc.	35.8
Sun Valley Masonry Inc.	34.6
J.D. Long Masonry	33.5

Source: *ENR*, October 7, 2001, p. 56.

★ 133 ★

Contracting Work - Roofing (SIC 1761)

Top Roofing Contractors

Firms are ranked by 2000 revenue in millions of dollars.

General Roofing	$ 253.4
Centimark Corp.	216.6
Tecta America Corp.	174.8
The Hartford Roofing Group	68.0
Birdair Inc.	60.0
W.R. Kelso Inc.	45.2
Latite Roofing & Sheet Metal Co.	45.1

Source: *ENR*, October 7, 2001, p. 56.

★ 134 ★

Contracting Work - Sheet Metal (SIC 1761)

Top Sheet Metal Contractors

Firms are ranked by sales in millions of dollars.

Comfort Systems USA	$ 302.29
EMCOR Group Inc.	166.10
Enron Facility Services	114.62
PSEG Energy Technologies	75.00
Kirk & Blum	71.08
Hill Mechanical Group	59.85
FirstEnergy Facilities Services Group	56.80
Kinetics Group	45.11

Source: *Contractor*, May 2001, p. 22.

★ 135 ★

Contracting Work - Concrete (SIC 1771)

Top Concrete Contractors

Firms are ranked by 2000 revenue in millions of dollars.

Baker Concrete Construction	$ 365.0
Miller & Long Co. Inc.	246.8
Ceco Concrete Construction	175.5
Structural Group	134.0
Suncoast Post-Tension Inc.	113.0
Colasanti Corp.	105.5
Capform Inc.	98.0
Largo Concrete Inc.	96.6

Source: *ENR*, October 7, 2001, p. 56.

★ 136 ★

Contracting Work - Steel Erection (SIC 1791)

Top Steel Erection Contractors

Firms are ranked by 2000 revenue in millions of dollars.

Schuff International Inc.	$ 278.1
Midwest Steel Inc.	249.3
SMI-Owen Steel Co.	177.0
The Williams Group	71.0
Steel City	56.0
J.L. Davidson Co. Inc.	51.8
Sowles Co.	51.0
Area Erectors Inc.	47.7

Source: *ENR*, October 7, 2001, p. 56.

★ 137 ★

Contracting Work - Glazing/Curtain Wall (SIC 1793)

Top Glazing/Curtain Wall Contractors

Firms are ranked by 2000 revenue in millions of dollars.

Walters & Wolf	$ 185.1
Harmon Inc.	125.4
Harmon Ltd.	108.0
Flour City Architectural Metals	70.3
Trainor Glass	63.4
W&W Glass Systems Inc.	42.3
Masonry Arts Inc.	41.2
Architectural Glass & Aluminum Co. Inc.	40.9

Source: *ENR*, October 7, 2001, p. 56.

★ 138 ★

Contracting Work - Excavation/Foundation (SIC 1794)

Top Excavation/Foundation Contractors

Firms are ranked by 2000 revenue in millions of dollars.

Manafort Brothers Inc.	$ 145.8
Hayward Baker Inc.	110.0
Ryan Inc. Central	94.6
Condon-Johnson	83.2
McKinney Drilling Co.	78.0
Berkel & Co. Contractors Inc.	74.3
AGRA Foundations	71.0
Borderland Construction Co.	70.5

Source: *ENR*, October 7, 2001, p. 56.

★ 139 ★

Saunas (SIC 1799)

U.S. Sauna Market

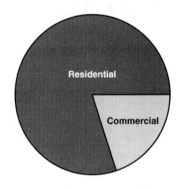

The average sauna buyer is 42, married with two kids and has an income of $60,000-$80,000.

Residential	80.0%
Commercial	20.0

Source: *Swimming Pool/Spa Age*, June 2001, p. NA, from Saunatec Inc.

SIC 20 - Food and Kindred Products

★ 140 ★
Food (SIC 2000)

Best-Selling Deli Items

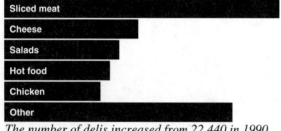

The number of delis increased from 22,440 in 1990 to 25,000 in 1999.

Sliced meat	28.6%
Cheese	13.8
Salads	12.4
Hot food	10.8
Chicken	10.3
Other	24.1

Source: *Dairy Herd Management*, July 2001, p. 6, from International Dairy Deli Bakery Association.

★ 141 ★
Food (SIC 2000)

Best-Selling Packaged Deli Items, 2001

Sales are shown by outlet for the year ended September 2001.

Remaining ready made salads	$ 1,887.0
Entrees, refrigerated	879.4
Combination lunches	785.1
Sandwiches, refrigerated/frozen	769.5
Gelatin salads, refrigerated	195.2
Fruit, refrigerated	168.8

Pasta, refrigerated	$ 146.7
Pizza, refrigerated	135.0
Salad dressing, refrigerated	130.3
Fruit salads, refrigerated	54.0

Source: *Grocery Headquarters*, December 2001, p. 48, from A.C. Nielsen.

★ 142 ★
Food (SIC 2000)

Best-Selling Perishable Food Items

Sales are shown in millions of dollars.

Ground beef, bulk	$ 3,861.1
Bananas	1,636.3
Chicken breast, boneless	1,601.7
Pork loin chop	1,435.8
Cold cuts, ham	1,156.0
Grapes	1,120.6
Prepared foods, pizza	940.1
Prepared foods, combo meal	919.8
Cold cuts, turkey	903.3
Chicken breast, bone-in	757.2

Source: *Food Institute Report*, January 7, 2002, p. 8, from *Supermarket Business* and A.C. Nielsen.

★ 143 ★
Food (SIC 2000)

Ethical Nutrition Market

Sales are shown in millions of dollars.

	2000	2006	Share
Infant nutrition . . .	$ 3,569.3	$ 4,870.0	38.84%
Ethical nutrition supplies/equipment . .	2,701.3	3,370.0	26.87
Adult nutrition	1,268.6	2,159.1	17.22
Parenteral nutrition . . .	1,592.6	2,140.8	17.07

Source: *Research Studies - Business Communications Inc.*, November 27, 2001, p. 1, from Business Communications Inc.

★ 144 ★

Food (SIC 2000)

Largest Food Firms in Canada, 2000

Firms are ranked by sales in millions of dollars.

McCain Foods 5.25
Maple Leaf Foods 3.94
George Weston Ltd. 2.77
Molson Canada 2.37
Parmalat Canada 2.20
Cooperative Federee de Quebec 2.00
Kraft Canada 1.97
Saputo Inc. 1.86
Nestle Canada 1.57

Source: *Food in Canada*, September 2001, p. NA.

★ 145 ★

Food (SIC 2000)

Largest Functional Food Producers, 2000

Firms are ranked by functional food sales in millions of dollars.

	($ mil.)	Share
PepsiCo.	$ 3,530	0.82%
General Mills	1,400	0.33
Kellogg	1,370	0.32
Kraft	780	0.18
Coca-Cola	650	0.15
Red Bull	600	0.14
Ocean Spray	460	0.11
Campbell Soup	460	0.11
Ferolito, Vultaggio & Sons . . .	380	0.09
Groupe Danone	270	0.06
Other	419,740	97.70

Source: *Food Institute Report*, November 19, 2001, p. 3, from *Nutrition Business Journal*.

★ 146 ★

Food (SIC 2000)

Leading Dry Food Categories

Sales are shown in billions of dollars.

Carbonated beverages . . . . $ 12.9
Bread & baked goods 12.1
Snacks 8.8
Cereal 8.0
Juices, drinks 6.6

Pet food . . . .$ 5.5
Condiments/gravy/sauce 5.5
Candy 4.3
Cookies 4.1
Soup 3.8

Source: *Food Institute Report*, August 6, 2001, p. 3, from *Progressive Grocer A.C. Nielsen 2001 Sales Manual.*

★ 147 ★

Food (SIC 2000)

Prepared Food Industry

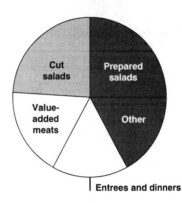

Supermarket sales of prepared refrigerated foods reached $7.1 billion in 2000 and should hit $9 billion in 2005.

Prepared salads 25.0%
Cut salads 24.0
Value-added meats and poultry 18.0
Entrees and dinners 16.0
Other 17.0

Source: *Food Institute Report*, November 12, 2001, p. 5, from Food Spectrum.

★ 148 ★

Food (SIC 2000)

Prepared Food Sales

Data show supermarket sales in millions of dollars.

Dry dinners, pasta . . . . $ 1,449.02
Mexican tortillas 791.68
Rice mixes 544.48
Potatoes, mashed, dry 195.59
Mexican shells 167.57
Potatoes, specialty, dry 132.81
Mexican dinners, dry/kit 118.00

Continued on next page.

★ 148 ★ *Continued*
Food (SIC 2000)
Prepared Food Sales

Data show supermarket sales in millions of dollars.

Dry dinners, rice	$ 62.73
Pizza pie & crust mixes	41.64
Mixes, ethnic specialties	38.64

Source: *Supermarket Business*, September 15, 2001, p. 36, from A.C. Nielsen.

★ 149 ★
Food (SIC 2000)
Top Food Companies

Companies are ranked by sales in millions of dollars.

Philip Morris	$ 31,200.0
ConAgra Inc.	25,385.8
Coca-Cola Co.	20,458.0
PepsiCo.	20,438.0

Source: *Food Processing*, May 2001, p. 20.

★ 150 ★
Food (SIC 2000)
Top Food Categories in Canada

Sales are shown for the year ended December 30, 2000.

Milk	$ 1,501
Flavored soft drinks	1,433
Frozen dinners/entrees/meat pies/egg rolls . .	923
Prepackaged bread	768
RTC cereals	740
Shelf stable juices/drink/nectars/iced tea . . .	726
Snack foods	651
Cookies/grahams	548
Chilled juices/drinks/nectars/iced tea	511
Refrigerated yogurt	486
Prepackaged cheddar cheese	446

Source: "Food Processing Ingredients." Retrieved May 1, 2002 from the World Wide Web: http://ffas.usda.gov, from A.C. Nielsen.

★ 151 ★
Food (SIC 2000)
Top Produce Items, 2000

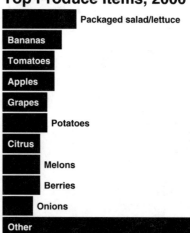

Fruit has 53.17% of sales, with vegetables holding the rest.

Packaged salad/lettuce	10.40%
Bananas	7.85
Tomatoes	7.05
Apples	6.88
Grapes	6.46
Potatoes	5.52
Citrus	5.43
Melons	4.64
Berries	4.56
Onions	3.70
Other	37.51

Source: *Progressive Grocer*, September 2001, p. 49, from Perishables Group.

★ 152 ★
Food (SIC 2000)
U.S. Food Sales, 2000

Total sales reached $79.8 billion.

Dairy	20.5%
Beverages	14.3
Confectionery	13.8
Meat/poultry	13.7
Seafood	11.1
Grains/cereal	9.3
Condiments	9.1
Produce	8.2

Source: *Presentations*, July 2001, p. 16.

★ 153 ★

Beef (SIC 2010)

Largest Meat/Poultry Processors

Firms are ranked by gross revenue in billions of dollars.

IBP	$ 16.9
ConAgra Foods Inc.	12.5
Excel Corp./Cargill Inc.	10.5
Tyson Foods	7.1
Smithfield Foods	5.1
Sara Lee Meat Group	4.5
Farmland Refrigerated Foods	4.0
Hormel Foods Corp.	3.6
Perdue Farms	2.5
Oscar Mayer/Kraft	2.5

Source: *Food Institute Report*, July 2, 2001, p. 7.

★ 154 ★

Beef (SIC 2011)

Leading Beef Packers

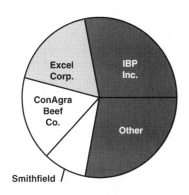

Market shares are shown in percent.

IBP Inc.	28.0%
Excel Corp.	18.0
ConAgra Beef Co.	17.0
Smithfield	9.0
Other	28.0

Source: *Feedstuffs*, November 5, 2001, p. 3, from *Cattle Buyers Weekly*.

★ 155 ★

Bacon (SIC 2013)

Top Refrigerated Bacon Brands, 2001

Shares are shown based on supermarket sales for the year ended June 17, 2001.

Oscar Mayer	17.5%
Hormel Black Label	6.4
Bar-S	4.2
Farmland	3.6
Gwaltney	2.8
Wright	2.6
Smithfield	2.5
Louis Rich	2.2
Farmer John	2.0
Private label	18.6
Other	37.6

Source: *National Provisioner*, August 2001, p. 56, from Information Resources Inc.

★ 156 ★

Bacon (SIC 2013)

Top Refrigerated Bacon Producers, 2001

Shares are shown based on supermarket sales for the year ended June 17, 2001.

Oscar Mayer	17.6%
Hormel Foods	10.5
Bar-S Foods Co.	4.4
Farmland Foods Inc.	3.7
Gwaltney of Smithfield	3.6
Wright Meat Packaging	2.8
Thorn Apple Valley	2.8
Smithfield Packaging	2.8
John Morrell & Co.	2.6
Other	49.2

Source: *National Provisioner*, August 2001, p. 56, from Information Resources Inc.

★ 157 ★
Hot Dogs (SIC 2013)

Leading Hot Dog Brands, 2001

Brands are for the year ended February 25, 2001.
Figures are for supermarkets $2 million and over.

	($ mil.)	Share
Oscar Mayer	$ 306.6	18.43%
Hygrade	261.3	15.71
Bar S	105.1	6.32
Hebrew National	56.3	3.38
Bryan	54.0	3.25
Eckrich	44.6	2.68
Armour	41.0	2.46
Nathan's	40.7	2.45
Kahn's	35.4	2.13
Private label	105.0	6.31
Other	613.7	36.89

Source: *Refrigerated & Frozen Foods*, June 2001, p. 40,
from A.C. Nielsen.

★ 158 ★
Hot Dogs (SIC 2013)

Top Hot Dog Makers

Market shares are shown in percent.

Sara Lee	25.0%
Kraft	21.0
ConAgra	12.0
Other	42.0

Source: *New York Times*, July 15, 2001, p. 6, from Information Resources Inc.

★ 159 ★
Lunch Meat (SIC 2013)

Top Refrigerated Non-Sliced Lunch Meat Brands, 2000

Market shares are shown in percent.

Hickory Farms	6.2%
Oscar Mayer	5.8
Hillshire Farm	5.1
Hebrew National	4.9
Scbweigert	4.5
Kahn	4.3
Gallo Salame	3.5
Old Wisconsin	3.2
Klement	3.1
Private label	3.3
Other	56.1

Source: *Food Institute Report*, April 9, 2001, p. 17, from
Information Resources Inc.

★ 160 ★
Lunch Meat (SIC 2013)

Top Refrigerated Sliced Lunch Meat Brands, 2001

Brands are for the year ended February 25, 2001.
Figures are for supermarkets $2 million and over.

	($ mil.)	Share
Oscar Mayer	$ 676.7	23.45%
Butterball	132.1	4.58
Hillshire Farm Deli Select	131.9	4.57
Louis Rich	110.1	3.82
Buddig	105.9	3.67
Healthy Choice	78.9	2.73
Bryan	75.8	2.63
Land O Frost	74.7	2.59
Bar S	71.6	2.48
Private label	407.7	14.13
Other	1,020.5	35.36

Source: *Refrigerated & Frozen Foods*, June 2001, p. 40,
from A.C. Nielsen.

★ 161 ★

Meat (SIC 2013)

Pre-Packaged Meat Sales in Canada, 2001

Sales are shown in millions of dollars for the year ended December 1, 2001.

Frozen dinners and entrees (chicken, beef) .	$ 1,008
Bacon and bacon substitutes	275
Wieners	264
Luncheon meats	264
Frozen meat patties/steakettes	94
Frozen & refrigerated sausages	84
Canned meat	56
Remaining frozen meat	30
Refrigerated entrees	30
Beef jerky	20
Meat sticks	19

Source: *Food in Canada*, March 2002, p. 22, from A.C. Nielsen.

★ 162 ★

Meat (SIC 2013)

Top Uncooked Meat Brands

Brands are ranked by sales in millions of dollars for the 12 weeks ended December 20, 2001.

Gold n Plump	$ 19.9
Moran	10.9
The Turkey Store	9.4
Perdue	4.8
Private label	36.9

Source: *Frozen Food Age*, April 2002, p. 14, from Information Resources Inc.

★ 163 ★

Meat Snacks (SIC 2013)

Top Meat Snack Suppliers, 2001

Companies are ranked by sales for the year ended August 12, 2001.

	($ mil.)	Share
GoodMark Foods	$ 99.59	29.37%
Link Snacks Inc.	56.89	16.78
Oberto Sausage Co.	53.20	15.69
Bridgford Foods Corp.	44.54	13.14
Curtice-Burns	12.07	3.56
The Dial Corp.	10.24	3.02

	($ mil.)	Share
Mirab USA	$ 9.08	2.68%
Tillamook Country Smoker	5.82	1.72
Snackmasters Marketing	4.50	1.33
Carl Budding Co.	4.42	1.30
Other	38.71	11.42

Source: *Professional Candy Buyer*, November-December 2001, p. 18, from Information Resources Inc.

★ 164 ★

Sausage (SIC 2013)

Top Breakfast Sausage/Ham Brands, 2001

Shares are shown based on supermarket sales for the year ended June 17, 2001.

Jimmy Dean	21.3%
Bob Evans	12.9
Tennessee Pride	6.2
Johnsonville	4.5
Owens	3.4
Farmer John	3.4
Hormel Little Sizzler	2.9
Purnell Old Folks	2.7
Rudy's Farm	2.0
Other	40.7

Source: *National Provisioner*, August 2001, p. 56, from Information Resources Inc.

★ 165 ★

Sausage (SIC 2013)

Top Dinner Sausage Brands, 2000

Market shares are shown in percent based on supermarket sales.

Hillshire Farm	29.5%
Eckrich	8.2
Johnsonville	4.0
Bryan	2.8
Thorn Apple Valley	2.1
Bryan Smoky Hollow	1.6
Bar-S	1.6
John Morrell	1.4
Bob Evans	1.3
Private label	6.9
Other	40.6

Source: *Food Institute Report*, April 16, 2001, p. 17, from Information Resources Inc.

★ 166 ★

Sausage (SIC 2013)

Top Refrigerated Dinner Sausage Makers, 2001

Market shares are shown for the year ended December 2, 2001. Data exclude Wal-Mart.

Hillshire Farm & Kahn's	28.5%
Johnsonville Foods Inc.	11.9
Armour Swift-Eckrich Inc.	11.1
Bryan Foods Inc.	4.4
Private label	6.9
Other	37.2

Source: *Grocery Headquarters*, April 2002, p. 14, from Information Resources Inc.

★ 167 ★

Poultry (SIC 2015)

Leading Frozen Poultry Brands, 2001

Brands are for the year ended February 25, 2001. Figures are for supermarkets $2 million and over.

	($ mil.)	Share
Tyson	$ 307.6	17.82%
Banquet	215.1	12.46
Barber	43.4	2.51
Cagle's	40.8	2.36
Pilgrim's Pride	35.4	2.05
Advance Fast Fixins	34.7	2.01
Tender Bird	34.5	2.00
Weaver	33.8	1.96
Private label	440.2	25.51
Other	540.2	31.30

Source: *Refrigerated & Frozen Foods*, June 2001, p. 40, from A.C. Nielsen.

★ 168 ★

Poultry (SIC 2015)

Top Frozen Poultry Vendors, 2001

Shares are shown based on supermarket sales for the year ended June 17, 2001.

Tyson Foods	23.3%
ConAgra Inc.	15.2
Pilgrims Pride	2.9
Gold Kist	2.7
Barber Foods	2.5
Advance Food Co.	2.4
OK Foods Inc.	2.0
Rosina Brand Sausage Co.	1.8
On-Cor Frozen Foods Inc.	1.7
Other	45.5

Source: *National Provisioner*, August 2001, p. 56, from Information Resources Inc.

★ 169 ★

Dairy Foods (SIC 2020)

Best-Selling Dairy Products, 2001

Sales are shown by outlet for the year ended September 2001.

Milk, refrigerated	$ 10,886.6
Orange juice, refrigerated	3,133.0
Eggs, fresh	2,396.7
Yogurt, refrigerated	2,311.2
Cheese, shredded	1,845.7
Cheese, processed slices, American . . .	1,731.0
Margarine and spreads	1,412.4
Butter	1,300.9
Cheese, natural, American cheddar . . .	1,087.2
Cottage cheese	970.2

Source: *Grocery Headquarters*, December 2001, p. 48, from A.C. Nielsen.

★ 170 ★

Dairy Foods (SIC 2020)

Largest Dairy Processors, 2000

Firms are ranked by dairy sales in millions of dollars. Some figures have been estimated.

Suiza Foods Corp.	$ 5,364.6
Kraft Foods North America	4,000.0
Dean Foods Co.	3,255.0
Land O'Lakes Inc.	2,700.0
Kroger Co.	2,660.0

Continued on next page.

★ 170 ★ *Continued*

Dairy Foods (SIC 2020)

Largest Dairy Processors, 2000

Firms are ranked by dairy sales in millions of dollars. Some figures have been estimated.

Schreiber Foods Inc.	$ 2,000.0
Dairy Farmers of America	1,704.0
Leprino Foods	1,501.0
Prairie Farms Dairy Inc.	1,452.0
Unilever	1,373.9

Source: *Dairy Field*, July 2001, p. 34.

★ 171 ★

Butter (SIC 2021)

Top Butter Brands, 2001

Market shares are shown based on supermarket sales of March 25, 2001.

Land O'Lakes	34.2%
Challenge	4.2
Crystal Farms	1.8
Breakstone	1.8
Tillamook	1.6
Kellers	1.6
Hotel bar	1.5
Land O'Laes Light	1.1
Cabot	1.0
Private label	43.7
Other	7.5

Source: *Dairy Field*, June 2001, p. 16, from Information Resources Inc.

★ 172 ★

Butter (SIC 2021)

Top Butter Vendors

Land O'Lakes
Challenge Dry Products
Kraft Foods
Crystal Farms
Tillamook County Creamery
Kellars Creamery
Hotel Bar Foods
Cabot Creamery
Private label
Other

Sales are for the year ended June 15, 2001.

	($ mil.)	Share
Land O'Lakes	$ 411	17.13%
Challenge Dry Products	55	2.29
Kraft Foods	22	0.92
Crystal Farms	22	0.92
Tillamook County Creamery	21	0.88
Kellars Creamery	17	0.71
Hotel Bar Foods	15	0.63
Cabot Creamery	13	0.54
Private label	518	21.58
Other	1,306	54.42

Source: *Dairy Foods*, October 2001, p. 18, from Information Resources Inc.

★ 173 ★

Butter (SIC 2021)

Top Margarine/Spread/Butter Blend Brands, 2001

Market shares are shown for the year ended December 2, 2001. Figures are for supermarkets only.

I Can't Believe It's Not Butter	16.2%
Shedd's Country Crock	13.9
Parkay	8.9
Blue Bonnet	8.2
Imperial	5.2
Fleischmann's	5.1
I Can't Believe It's Not Butter Light	4.9

Continued on next page.

★ 173 ★ *Continued*

Butter (SIC 2021)

Top Margarine/Spread/Butter Blend Brands, 2001

Market shares are shown for the year ended December 2, 2001. Figures are for supermarkets only.

Land O'Lakes	4.8%
Brummel & Brown	3.5
Private label	8.8
Other	20.5

Source: *Grocery Headquarters*, April 2002, p. 14, from Information Resources Inc.

★ 174 ★

Butter (SIC 2021)

Top Margarine/Spread/Butter Blend Makers, 2001

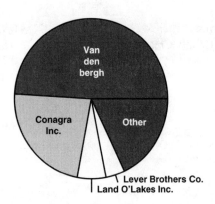

Market shares are shown for the year ended December 2, 2001. Figures are for supermarkets only.

Van den bergh Foods Co.	49.1%
Conagra Inc.	23.0
Land O'Lakes Inc.	5.5
Lever Brothers Co.	4.2
Other	18.2

Source: *Grocery Headquarters*, April 2002, p. 14, from Information Resources Inc.

★ 175 ★

Cheese (SIC 2022)

Cheese Sales by Type

Supermarket sales are shown in millions of dollars.

	($ mil.)	Share
Natural	$ 4,973.1	68.4%
Processed	2,188.0	30.1
Imitation	109.1	1.5

Source: *Dairy Foods*, March 2002, p. C4, from Information Resources Inc.

★ 176 ★

Cheese (SIC 2022)

Top American Cheese Brands

Brands are ranked by sales in millions of dollars.

	($ mil.)	Share
Kraft Single Slice	$ 552.7	29.22%
Kraft Velveeta	337.8	17.86
Borden	143.3	7.57
Kraft Deli Deluxe	104.1	5.50
Kraft Deluxe	58.6	3.10
Kraft Free	45.5	2.41
Land O'Lakes	39.2	2.07
Kraft Velveeta Light	35.0	1.85
Crystal Farms	20.9	1.10
Private label	446.6	23.61
Other	108.1	5.71

Source: *Dairy Field*, March 2002, p. 36, from Information Resources Inc.

★ 177 ★

Cheese (SIC 2022)

Top American Cheese Makers, 2001

Market shares are shown for the year ended December 2, 2001. Data exclude Wal-Mart.

Kraft Foods Inc.	61.1%
American Dairy Brands	8.2
Land O'Lakes Inc.	2.0
Crystal Farms Inc.	1.1
Private label	23.4
Other	4.2

Source: *Grocery Headquarters*, April 2002, p. 14, from Information Resources Inc.

★ 178 ★
Cheese (SIC 2022)

Top Cheese Making States, 2000

8.25 million pounds of cheese were produced during the year. Data exclude cottage cheese.

Wisconsin	27.0%
California	18.0
New York	9.0
Minnesota	8.0
Idaho	7.0
Pennsylvania	5.0
Other	26.0

Source: *New York Times*, June 28, 2001, p. C1, from Department of Agriculture.

★ 179 ★
Cheese (SIC 2022)

Top Natural Cheese Vendors, 2001

Market shares are shown for the year ended December 2, 2001. Data exclude Wal-Mart and does not include shredded.

Kraft Foods Inc.	17.0%
Tillamook County Creamery	6.1
Sorrento Cheese Co. Inc.	4.5
Kraft/Pollio Dairy	3.3
Private label	34.9
Other	34.2

Source: *Grocery Headquarters*, April 2002, p. 14, from Information Resources Inc.

★ 180 ★
Cheese (SIC 2022)

Top Shredded Cheese Brands, 2001

Brands are ranked by sales in millions of dollars.

	($ mil.)	Share
Kraft	$ 477.8	27.34%
Sargento	87.7	5.02
Crystal Farms	$ 66.8	3.82%
Sargento Fancy	66.4	3.80
Borden	54.6	3.12
Sargento Chefstyle	51.1	2.92
Kraft Classic Melts	34.4	1.97
Sargento Light	29.6	1.69
Di Giorno	24.6	1.41
Private label	732.0	41.89
Other	122.4	7.00

Source: *Dairy Foods*, March 2002, p. 20, from Information Resources Inc.

★ 181 ★
Cheese (SIC 2022)

Top Shredded Cheese Vendors

Vendors are ranked by sales in millions of dollars for the ended November 4, 2001.

	($ mil.)	Share
Kraft Foods	$ 551.0	32.05%
Sargento	239.0	13.90
Crystal Farms	67.0	3.90
American Dairy Brands	54.0	3.14
Sorrento	27.0	1.57
Saputo USA	7.9	0.46
Kraft/Polli O	7.5	0.44
Meixelsperger	6.6	0.38
Dutch Farms	5.6	0.33
Other	753.4	43.83

Source: *Dairy Foods*, January 2002, p. 20, from Information Resources Inc.

★ 182 ★
Infant Formula (SIC 2023)

Top Baby Formula/Powder Brands, 2001

Market shares are shown for the year ended December 2, 2001. Data exclude Wal-Mart.

Enfamil	44.3%
Similac	18.2
Prosobee	8.1
Isomil	6.6
Carnation Good Start	5.4
Enfamil Lactofree	3.5
Nutramigen	3.4

Continued on next page.

★ 182 ★ *Continued*

Infant Formula (SIC 2023)

Top Baby Formula/Powder Brands, 2001

Market shares are shown for the year ended December 2, 2001. Data exclude Wal-Mart.

Carnation Follow Up	2.8%
Other	7.7

Source: *Grocery Headquarters*, April 2002, p. 14, from Information Resources Inc.

★ 183 ★

Infant Formula (SIC 2023)

Top Baby Formula/Powder Makers, 2001

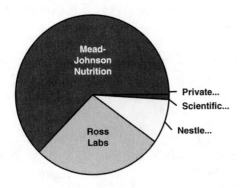

Market shares are shown for the year ended December 2, 2001. Data exclude Wal-Mart.

Mead-Johnson Nutrition	62.0%
Ross Labs	27.2
Nestle USA	9.3
Scientific Hospital Supplies	0.1
Private label	1.4

Source: *Grocery Headquarters*, April 2002, p. 14, from Information Resources Inc.

★ 184 ★

Frozen Desserts (SIC 2024)

Top Frozen Novelty Brands, 2001

Brands are ranked by supermarket sales in millions of dollars.

	($ mil.)	Share
Klondike	$ 143.0	7.37%
Nestle Drumstick	105.0	5.42
Popsicle	91.5	4.72
Haagen Dazs	52.4	2.70
Well's Blue Bunny	48.1	2.48
Dole Fruit and Juice	43.6	2.25
Silouette	42.7	2.20
Fudgesicle	42.6	2.20
Blue Bell Novelties	42.1	2.17
Private label	337.0	17.38
Other	991.0	51.11

Source: *Dairy Foods*, February 2002, p. 18, from Information Resources Inc.

★ 185 ★

Ice Cream (SIC 2024)

Ice Cream Market by Segment

Sales are shown in millions of dollars.

	($ mil.)	Share
Ice cream bulk	$ 4,549.6	92.02%
Frozen yogurt	246.0	4.98
Sherbert	147.8	2.99
Ice milk	0.9	0.02

Source: *Frozen Food Age*, December 2001, p. 21, from A. C. Nielsen.

★ 186 ★

Ice Cream (SIC 2024)

Ice Cream Sales by Region

Supermarket sales of ice cream and sherbert are shown in millions of dollars.

	($ mil.)	Share
Northeast	$ 862	18.43%
Great Lakes	704	15.06
Mid-South	627	13.41
Southeast	601	12.85

Continued on next page.

★ 186 ★ *Continued*
Ice Cream (SIC 2024)

Ice Cream Sales by Region

Supermarket sales of ice cream and sherbert are shown in millions of dollars.

	($ mil.)	Share
California	$ 564	12.06%
West	541	11.57
South Central	456	9.75
Plains	321	6.86

Source: *Dairy Foods*, March 2002, p. 18, from Information Resources Inc.

★ 187 ★
Ice Cream (SIC 2024)

Ice Cream Sales by Type

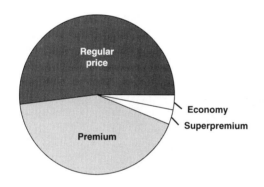

Market shares are shown in percent.

Regular price	51.8%
Premium	41.7
Superpremium	3.3
Economy	3.2

Source: *Supermarket News*, May 14, 2001, p. 44, from International Ice Cream Alliance.

★ 188 ★
Ice Cream (SIC 2024)

Soft Ice Cream Market in Utah, 2000

Market shares are shown in percent.

Asael Farr and Sons Co.	90.0%
Other	10.0

Source: *Knight-Ridder/Tribune Business News*, May 26, 2002, p. NA.

★ 189 ★
Ice Cream (SIC 2024)

Top Flavors for Ice Cream

Market shares are shown in percent.

Vanilla	27.3%
Chocolate	7.7
Neapolitan	6.8
Butter pecan/pecan	4.6
Chocolate chip	3.4
Other	50.2

Source: *Dairy Foods*, May 2002, p. 15, from Information Resources Inc., International Dairy Foods Association, and International Ice Cream Association.

★ 190 ★
Ice Cream (SIC 2024)

Top Ice Cream Brands, 2001

Brands are ranked by supermarket sales in millions of dollars.

	($ mil.)	Share
Breyers	$ 520.0	12.36%
Dreyers/Edy's Grand	367.0	8.72
Blue Bell	229.0	5.44
Haagen Dazs	190.0	4.52
Ben & Jerry's	160.0	3.80
Well's Blue Bunny	113.0	2.69
Healthy Choice	97.6	2.32
Turkey Hill	96.4	2.29
Dreyer's Edy's	94.4	2.24
Other	2,340.6	55.62

Source: *Dairy Foods*, February 2002, p. 18, from Information Resources Inc.

★ 191 ★
Ice Cream (SIC 2024)

Top Ice Cream Makers, 2001

Market shares are shown for the year ended December 2, 2001. Figures are for supermarkets only.

Dreyer's Grand	18.2%
Good Humor-Breyers	15.2
Blue Bell Creameries Inc.	5.9
Ben & Jerry's Homemade Inc.	4.6
Private label	23.6
Other	32.5

Source: *Grocery Headquarters*, April 2002, p. 14, from Information Resources Inc.

★ 192 ★

Ice Cream (SIC 2024)

Top Sherbert/Sorbet/Ice Brands

Sales are shown in thousands of dollars for the year ended December 2, 2001.

	($000)	Share
Dreyers'Edy's Whole Fruit . . .	$ 30,069	22.16%
Haagen Dazs	20,951	15.44
Dreyers/Edys	16,838	12.41
Blue Bell	9,824	7.24
Other	57,986	42.74

Source: *Frozen Food Age*, March 2002, p. S8, from ACNielsen.

★ 193 ★

Pudding (SIC 2024)

Top Refrigerated Pudding/Mousse/Parfait Brands, 2001

Brands are ranked by sales in millions of dollars for the year ended July 15, 2001.

	($ mil.)	Share
Jell-O	$ 140.0	26.91%
Jell-O Gelatin Snacks	89.0	17.11
Kozy Shack	71.7	13.78
Jell-O Free	66.6	12.80
Swiss Miss	50.1	9.63
Jolly Rancher	21.4	4.11
Lulu's	7.0	1.35
Reser's	6.9	1.33
Swiss Miss Pie Lovers	6.4	1.23
Private label	27.0	5.19
Other	34.1	6.56

Source: *Dairy Field*, October 2001, p. 12, from Information Resources Inc.

★ 194 ★

Pudding (SIC 2024)

Top Shelf-Stable Pudding/Gelatin Brands, 2001

Brands are ranked by sales in millions of dollars for the year ended July 15, 2001.

	($ mil.)	Share
Hunt's Snack Pack	$ 122.8	43.4%
Kraft Handi-Snacks	70.6	24.9

	($ mil.)	Share
Hunt's Snack Pack Puddin' Pies . .	$ 22.8	8.1%
Hunt's Snack Pack Juicy Gels . . .	13.8	4.9
Kraft Handi-Snacks Gels	9.1	3.2
Hunt's Snack Pack Swirl	7.4	2.6
Thank You	3.2	1.1
Hunt's Snack Pack Puddin' Cakes	3.2	1.1
Mini Fruity Gels	3.1	1.1
Private label	19.9	7.1
Other	7.0	2.5

Source: *Dairy Field*, October 2001, p. 12, from Information Resources Inc.

★ 195 ★

Cottage Cheese (SIC 2026)

Top Cottage Cheese Brands

Market shares are shown in percent.

Knudsen	8.0%
Breakstone	8.0
Deans	2.9
Breakstone Doubles	2.8
Friendship	2.5
Light N Lively	2.3
Hiland	2.3
Kemps	1.8
Prairie Farms	1.7
Private label	39.1
Other	28.6

Source: *Dairy Foods*, March 2002, p. 20, from Information Resources Inc.

★ 196 ★

Cream Cheese (SIC 2026)

Cream Cheese Market

Market shares are shown in percent. Kraft makes Kraft Philadelphia Original.

Kraft	67.0%
Other	33.0

Source: *Forbes*, April 15, 2002, p. 138.

★ 197 ★
Milk (SIC 2026)

Dairy Free Milk Market

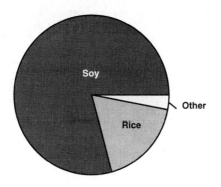

Market shares are shown in percent.

Soy 80.0%
Rice 17.5
Other 2.5

Source: *Washington Post*, January 2, 2002, p. 4, from SPINS.

★ 198 ★
Milk (SIC 2026)

Flavored Milk Sales by Region, 2002

Total non-flavored sour cream sales hit $705 million for the year ended January 27, 2002. Figures include buttermilk and eggnog.

Great Lakes . . . . $ 132
Southeast 108
Mid-South 101
West 86
Northeast 83
South Central 69
Plains 66
California 59

Source: *Dairy Foods*, April 2002, p. 10, from Information Resources Inc.

★ 199 ★
Milk (SIC 2026)

Largest Milk Processors

Firms are ranked by sales in millions of dollars.

Suiza Foods . . . . $ 4,600
Dean Foods 3,100
Kroger Co., Dairy Div. 1,400
Prairie Farms Cooperative 1,200
Dairy Farms of America 800
Wessanen USA 750

Source: *Dairy Foods*, July 2001, p. 7, from Beverage Marketing Corp.

★ 200 ★
Milk (SIC 2026)

Milk Market in Minneapolis, MN

Shares are for the year ended October 21, 2001.

Kemps 59.0%
Land O'Lakes 26.0
Private label 11.4
Other 3.2

Source: *Star Tribune*, December 2, 2001, p. 1D, from Information Resources Inc.

★ 201 ★
Milk (SIC 2026)

Milk Sales by Region

Supermarket sales are shown in millions of dollars for the year ended August 12, 2001.

	($ mil.)	Share
Northeast	$ 1.620	15.53%
Great Lakes	1.543	14.79
Southeast	1.400	13.42
Mid South	1.320	12.65
California	1.310	12.56
West	1.200	11.50
South Central	1.190	11.41
Plains	0.850	8.15

Source: *Dairy Foods*, November 2001, p. 20, from Information Resources Inc.

★ 202 ★

Milk (SIC 2026)

Organic Milk Sales

Market shares are shown in percent.

Horizon Organic Dairy 70.0%
Other 30.0

Source: *Health Products Business*, July 2001, p. 48.

★ 203 ★

Milk (SIC 2026)

Top Flavored Milk/Buttermilk/Eggnog Brands, 2001

Market shares are shown in percent for the year ended November 4, 2001.

Nestle Nesquik 14.5%
Borden 2.7
Meadow Gold 1.9
Dairy Fresh 1.9
Pet 1.3
Prairie Farms 1.2
Hood 1.2
Hiland 1.2
Dairyland 1.2
Private label 23.6
Other 49.3

Source: *Dairy Field*, February 2002, p. 16, from Information Resources Inc.

★ 204 ★

Milk (SIC 2026)

Top Flavors for Milk

Other includes banana, vanilla, orange and milk.

Chocolate 95.0%
Strawberry 4.0
Other 1.0

Source: *Dairy Foods*, September 2001, p. 52, from Milk Processors Education Program.

★ 205 ★

Milk (SIC 2026)

Top Refrigerated Skim/Lowfat Milk Brands, 2001

Brands are ranked by sales in millions of dollars for the year ended June 20, 2001.

	($ mil.)	Share
Lactaid	$ 139	2.15%
Kemps	117	1.81
Dean's	117	1.81
Mayfield	78	1.21
Prairie Farms	48	0.74
Land O'Lakes	47	0.73
Anderson Erickson	44	0.68
Sunnyside Farms	43	0.67
Horizon Organic Inc.	43	0.67
Private label	4,100	63.47
Other	1,684	26.07

Source: *Dairy Foods*, August 2001, p. 4, from Information Resources Inc.

★ 206 ★

Milk (SIC 2026)

Top Soy Milk Producers, 2000

The leaders of the $390 million wholesale market are shown in percent. Data comes from a survey done by the source.

White Wave 21.0%
The Hain Celestial Group 13.0
Eden Foods Inc. 11.0
Vitasoy USA Inc. 10.0
Imagine Foods Inc. 10.0
Other 35.0

Source: *Natural Foods Merchandiser*, April 2002, p. 24.

★ 207 ★

Milk (SIC 2026)

Top Soy Milk (Refrigerated) Makers

Market shares are shown in percent.

White Wave 76.5%
Other 23.5

Source: *Knight-Ridder/Tribune Business News*, March 18, 2002, p. NA.

★ 208 ★

Milk (SIC 2026)

Top Whole Milk Brands, 2001

Brands are ranked by sales in millions of dollars for the year ended May 2001.

	($ mil.)	Share
Bordon	$ 49	1.60%
Swiss	35	1.14
Mayfield	35	1.14
Dean's	33	1.07
Lehigh Valley	27	0.88
Farmland Dairies	24	0.78
Prairie Farms	22	0.72
Hiland	22	0.72
Private label	2,000	65.15
Other	823	26.81

Source: *Dairy Foods*, August 2001, p. 4, from Information Resources Inc.

★ 209 ★

Milkshakes (SIC 2026)

Top Refrigerated Milkshake Drinks, 2001

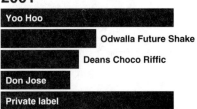

Market shares are for the year ended November 4, 2001.

Yoo Hoo	19.5%
Odwalla Future Shake	11.2
Deans Choco Riffic	8.6
Don Jose	8.4
Private label	20.0
Other	32.2

Source: *Beverage Industry*, December 2001, p. 14, from Information Resources Inc.

★ 210 ★

Sour Cream (SIC 2026)

Sour Cream Sales by Region, 2002

Total non-flavored sour cream sales hit $636million for the year ended January 27, 2002.

	($ mil.)	Share
Great Lakes	$ 106	16.75%
California	100	15.80
West	90	14.22
Northeast	90	14.22
Mid-South	66	10.43
Southeast	65	10.27
South Central	59	9.32
Plains	57	9.00

Source: *Dairy Foods*, April 2002, p. 10, from Information Resources Inc.

★ 211 ★

Sour Cream (SIC 2026)

Sour Cream Sales by Type, 2000

Total non-flavored sour cream sales hit $586.9 million for the year, up 3.3% over 1999.

	($ mil.)	Share
Full-fat	$ 427.7	72.87%
Low-fat	104.0	17.72
Nonfat	55.2	9.41

Source: *Dairy Foods*, July 2001, p. 14, from A.C. Nielsen and International Dairy Foods Association.

★ 212 ★

Sour Cream (SIC 2026)

Top Sour Cream Brands, 2001

Brands are ranked by sales in millions of dollars for the year ended July 15, 2001.

	($ mil.)	Share
Breakstone	$ 88.3	14.73%
Daisy	52.0	8.67
Knudsen Hampshire	45.3	7.56
Daisy Light	19.2	3.20
Land O'Lakes	13.3	2.22
Dean's	10.7	1.78

Continued on next page.

★ 212 ★ *Continued*

Sour Cream (SIC 2026)

Top Sour Cream Brands, 2001

Brands are ranked by sales in millions of dollars for the year ended July 15, 2001.

	($ mil.)	Share
Friendship	$ 10.1	1.68%
Knudsen Nice n' Light	9.6	1.60
Private label	189.3	31.57
Other	161.8	26.98

Source: *Food Institute Report*, October 8, 2001, p. 4, from *Dairy Field* and Information Resources Inc.

★ 213 ★

Yogurt (SIC 2026)

Top Yogurt Makers

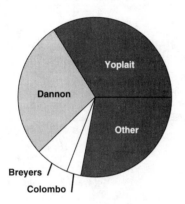

Market shares are shown in percent.

Yoplait	34.0%
Dannon	28.0
Breyers	7.0
Colombo	3.0
Other	28.0

Source: *New York Times*, April 18, 2002, p. C8, from Information Resources Inc.

★ 214 ★

Baby Food (SIC 2032)

Top Baby Food Makers

Market shares are shown in percent.

Gerber	73.8%
Heinz	12.2
Beech-Nut	11.4
Other	2.6

Source: *St. Louis Post-Dispatch*, May 20, 2001, p. E1, from Information Resources Inc.

★ 215 ★

Canned Food (SIC 2032)

Private Label Canned Goods

Sales are shown in millions of dollars. Other refers to beans.

	($ mil.)	Share
Mushrooms, canned or bottled	$ 94.1	52.5%
Green beans, canned or bottled	160.5	35.1
Corn, canned or bottled	171.6	33.6
Green peas, canned or bottled	65.8	30.8
Other	109.6	22.4

Source: *Private Label Buyer*, November 2001, p. 66, from Information Resources Inc.

★ 216 ★

Canned Food (SIC 2032)

Who Eats The Most Baked Beans

Figures show consumption, in tons.

Detroit, MI	722,282
Washington D.C.	346,715
Buffalo, NY	319,486
New York City, NY	294,666
Philadelphia, PA	279,997

Source: *USA TODAY*, October 4, 2001, p. D1, from AC Nielsen for Bush's Baked Beans.

★ 217 ★

Canned Fruit (SIC 2033)

Retail Canned Fruit Sales

Data show supermarket sales in millions of dollars.

Pineapple	$ 264.61
Peaches, cling	262.30

Continued on next page.

★ 217 ★ *Continued*
Canned Fruit (SIC 2033)

Retail Canned Fruit Sales

Data show supermarket sales in millions of dollars.

Apple sauce	$ 222.16
Fruit cocktail	125.51
Pears	122.12
Pie & pastry filling	115.22
Cranberries	103.36
Fruit mixes & salad	88.92
Oranges	84.72

Source: *Supermarket Business*, September 15, 2001, p. 42, from A.C. Nielsen Homescan.

★ 218 ★
Canned Vegetables (SIC 2033)

Canned Vegetable Sales, 2001

Sales are for the third quarter.

	($ mil.)	Share
Corn	$ 94.3	20.17%
Green beans	86.5	18.50
Peas	39.4	8.43
Mushrooms	36.5	7.81
Mixed vegetables	22.6	4.83
Potatoes/sweet potatoes	15.8	3.38
Sauerkraut	11.3	2.42
Spinach	9.2	1.97
Carrots	7.4	1.58

Source: *Food Institute Report*, November 12, 2001, p. 14, from Information Resources Inc.

★ 219 ★
Juices (SIC 2033)

Leading Fresh-Packed Single-Serve Juices

Market shares are shown in percent.

Snapple	10.0%
Minute Maid	8.5
Tropicana	7.5
Dole	7.5
Veryfine	5.6
Other	60.9

Source: *Beverage Industry*, March 15, 2002, p. 35, from Beverage Marketing Corp.

★ 220 ★
Juices (SIC 2033)

Real Lemon Juice Sales

Market shares are shown in oercent.

ReaLemon	48.0%
Other	52.0

Source: "Cadbury Schweppes Acquires ReaLemon." Retrieved January 8, 2002 from the World Wide Web: http://www.bevnet.com, from A.C. Nielsen.

★ 221 ★
Juices (SIC 2033)

Refrigerated Juice Sales, 2001

Sales are shown based on sales for the year ended April 22, 2001.

	($ mil.)	Share
Orange juice	$ 3,075.4	68.5%
Fruit drink	684.5	15.2
Blended fruit juice	315.2	7.0
Grapefruit juice	130.0	2.9
Teas	97.3	2.2
Lemonade	73.8	1.6
Cider	44.5	1.0
Fruit nectar	23.4	0.5
Apple juice	11.6	0.3

Source: *Beverage Industry*, June 2001, p. 38, from Information Resources Inc.

★ 222 ★
Juices (SIC 2033)

Retail Grapefruit Juice Sales

Sales are shown for the four weeks ended April 14, 2001.

	(mil.)	Share
Gallons	3.4	94.44%
Frozen	0.2	5.56

Source: *Food Institute Report*, April 14, 2001, p. 10, from A.C. Nielsen.

★ 223 ★
Juices (SIC 2033)

Top Orange Juice Firms in the West

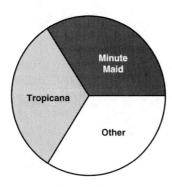

Market shares are shown in percent.

Minute Maid	34.0%
Tropicana	32.1
Other	33.9

Source: *Sarasota Herald Tribune*, February 25, 2002, p. 10.

★ 224 ★
Juices (SIC 2033)

Top Refrigerated Orange Juice Brands, 2001

Market shares are for the year ended December 2, 2001. Sales are at all food, drug and mass merchandisers, except Wal-Mart.

Tropicana Pure Premium	40.1%
Minute Maid Premium	19.1
Florida's Natural	8.6
Tropicana Season's Best	2.1
Tropicana	0.7
Simply Orange	0.7
Citrus World Donald Duck	0.7
Florida's Natural Grower's Pride	0.5
Deans	0.5
Private label	20.5
Other	6.5

Source: *Beverage Industry*, January 2002, p. 18, from Information Resources Inc.

★ 225 ★
Juices (SIC 2033)

Top Refrigerated Orange Juice Firms, 2001

Market shares are for the year ended December 2, 2001. Sales are at all food, drug and mass merchandisers, except Wal-Mart.

Tropicana Dole Beverages	43.0%
Minute Maid Co.	19.8
Dean Foods Co.	0.7
Citrus World Inc.	0.7
Johanna Foods Inc.	0.5
Hiland Dairy	0.4
Marigold Foods Inc.	0.3
Land-O-Sun Dairies	0.3
Odwella Inc.	0.2
Other	34.1

Source: *Beverage Industry*, January 2002, p. 18, from Information Resources Inc.

★ 226 ★
Juices (SIC 2033)

Top Refrigerated Smoothie Drinks, 2001

Market shares are for the year ended November 4, 2001.

Odwalla	38.4%
Fresh Samantha	23.5
Tropicana	15.6
Fantasia	9.3
Naked Food Naked Juice	8.3
Other	4.9

Source: *Beverage Industry*, December 2001, p. 14, from Information Resources Inc.

★ 227 ★
Ketchup (SIC 2033)

Ketchup Market Shares

Sales are shown for the year ended August 2001.

Heinz	58.6%
Other	41.4

Source: *Brandweek*, October 15, 2001, p. 38, from Information Resources Inc.

★ 228 ★

Spreads (SIC 2033)

Retail Jam/Jelly Sales

Data show supermarket sales in millions of dollars.

	($ mil.)	Share
Peanut butter	$ 817.65	49.10%
Preserves	217.21	13.04
Honey	162.25	9.74
Jams	145.75	8.75
Jelly	140.69	8.45
Fruit spreads	120.42	7.23
Marmalade	35.63	2.14
Butter, fruit & honey	20.27	1.22
Garlic spreads	5.46	0.33

Source: *Supermarket Business*, September 15, 2001, p. 42, from A.C. Nielsen Homescan.

★ 229 ★

Dry Dinners (SIC 2034)

Boxed Macaroni & Cheese Sales

Market shares are shown in percent.

Kraft Macaroni & Cheese	82.0%
Other	18.0

Source: *Forbes*, April 15, 2002, p. 138.

★ 230 ★

Dry Dinners (SIC 2034)

Dinner Kit Market Shares

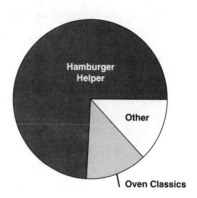

Market shares are shown in percent.

Hamburger Helper	74.5%
Oven Classics	12.6
Other	12.9

Source: *Knight-Ridder/Tribune Business News*, September 21, 2001, p. NA, from Information Resources Inc.

★ 231 ★

Dry Dinners (SIC 2034)

Top Dry Dinner Mixes, 2001

Market shares are shown in percent.

Betty Crocker	58.7%
Banquet Homestyle Bakes	16.8
Kraft Stove Top Oven Classics	8.9
Campbell's Souper Bakes	5.1
Lipton Sizzle & Stir	4.1
Chef Boyardee	0.7
Other	1.1

Source: *Advertising Age*, June 24, 2002, p. B12, from Information Resources Inc.

★ 232 ★

Soup (SIC 2034)

Top Soup Brands, 2001

Market shares are shown for the year ended December 2, 2001. Data exclude Wal-Mart.

Campbell's	78.7%
Campbell's Healthy Request	6.2
Snows	0.5

Continued on next page.

★ 232 ★ *Continued*

Soup (SIC 2034)

Top Soup Brands, 2001

Market shares are shown for the year ended December 2, 2001. Data exclude Wal-Mart.

Herb Ox	0.2%
Campbell's Select	0.2
Pepperidge Farm	0.1
Kitchen Basics	0.1
College Inn	0.1
Bookbinders	0.1
Private label	12.7
Other	8.9

Source: *Grocery Headquarters*, April 2002, p. 14, from Information Resources Inc.

★ 233 ★

Soup (SIC 2034)

Top Soup Makers, 2001

Market shares are shown for the year ended December 2, 2001. Data exclude Wal-Mart.

Campbell Soup Co.	85.1%
Castlebury Foods	0.5
Hormel Foods	0.2
Kitchen Basics Inc.	0.1
Private label	12.7

Source: *Grocery Headquarters*, April 2002, p. 14, from Information Resources Inc.

★ 234 ★

Dips (SIC 2035)

Top Refrigerated Dips, 2000

Shares are shown based on sales for the year ended December 30, 2000.

T. Marzetti	17.7%
Dean Foods Co.	16.1
Kraft Foods Inc.	9.1
Heluva Good Cheese Inc.	5.4
Avomex Inc.	2.6
Rod's Food Products Inc.	2.4
Pancho's Mexicna Foods Inc.	1.7
Biscon Foods Co.	1.6
Private label	15.9
Other	27.5

Source: *Snack Food & Wholesale Bakery*, June 2001, pp. SI-69, from Information Resources Inc.

★ 235 ★

Dips (SIC 2035)

Top Shelf Stable Dips, 2000

Shares are shown based on sales for the year ended December 30, 2000.

Frito Lay Fritos	49.1%
Frito Lay	16.8
Kraft Cheez Whiz	7.8
Ruffles	7.2
Utz	1.6
Kraft	1.4
Herrs	1.2
Golden Flake	1.1
Old Dutch	0.9
Private label	2.2
Other	10.7

Source: *Snack Food & Wholesale Bakery*, June 2001, pp. SI-69, from Information Resources Inc.

★ 236 ★

Marinades (SIC 2035)

Top Sauce/Marinade Brands

Shares are shown of the $185 million market.

	($ mil.)	Share
Kikkoman	$ 82	44.32%
La Choy Oriental Sauces . . .	24	12.97
Other	79	42.70

Source: *Brandweek*, May 20, 2002, p. 1, from Information Resources Inc.

★ 237 ★

Mayonnaise (SIC 2035)

Top Mayonnaise Brands

The market is valued at $1 billion.

Hellmann's	23.3%
Miracle Whip	20.5
Other	56.2

Source: *Brandweek*, April 29, 2002, p. 4, from Information Resources Inc.

★ 238 ★
Mustard (SIC 2035)

Mustard Sales by Type

Market shares are shown in percent.

Traditional yellow	40.0%
Dijon	19.3
Brown or deli	15.2
Specialty	11.3
Honey	10.3
Other	3.9

Source. *DSN Retailing Today*, April 8, 2002, p. 21, from Information Resources Inc.

★ 239 ★
Mustard (SIC 2035)

Top Mustard Brands, 2001

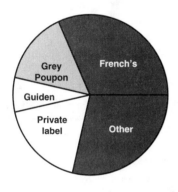

Market shares are shown in percent.

French's	31.7%
Grey Poupon	14.9
Guiden	6.6
Private label	17.6
Other	29.2

Source: *New York Times*, June 11, 2002, p. C6, from Information Resources Inc.

★ 240 ★
Pasta Sauce (SIC 2035)

Top Pasta Sauce Brands, 2001

Market shares are shown for the year ended December 2, 2001. Figures exclude Wal-Mart.

Prego	17.3%
Classico	10.6
Ragu	7.8

Ragu Old World Style	7.4%
Ragu Chunky Gardenstyle	7.2
Hunts	7.0
Five Brothers	6.1
Ragu Hearty	4.4
Private label	4.4
Other	27.8

Source: *Grocery Headquarters*, April 2002, p. 14, from Information Resources Inc.

★ 241 ★
Pasta Sauce (SIC 2035)

Top Pasta Sauce Makers, 2001

Market shares are shown for the year ended December 2, 2001. Figures exclude Wal-Mart.

Ragu Foods Co.	37.8%
Campbell Soup Co.	21.3
H.J. Heinz Co.	11.6
Conagra Grocery Products	7.2
Private label	4.4
Other	17.7

Source: *Grocery Headquarters*, April 2002, p. 14, from Information Resources Inc.

★ 242 ★
Pickles and Relish (SIC 2035)

Pickles and Relish Sales, 2000

Sales are shown in millions of dollars.

	($ mil.)	Share
Pickles	$ 639.2	54.21%
Olives	422.1	35.80
Relish	117.9	10.00

Source: *Supermarket News*, October 8, 2001, p. 74, from Information Resources Inc.

★ 243 ★
Salad Dressing (SIC 2035)

Top Salad Dressing Brands, 2001

Market shares are shown for the year ended December 2, 2001. Figures exclude Wal-Mart.

Kraft	21.8%
Wishbone	14.3
Hidden Valley	6.7
Kens Steak House	6.6

Continued on next page.

★ 243 ★ *Continued*
Salad Dressing (SIC 2035)

Top Salad Dressing Brands, 2001

Market shares are shown for the year ended December 2, 2001. Figures exclude Wal-Mart.

Kraft Free	6.4%
Hidden Valley Ranch	6.1
Newman's Own	3.4
Wishbone Just 2 Good	3.2
Kraft Light Done Right	3.2
Private label	6.9
Other	21.4

Source: *Grocery Headquarters*, April 2002, p. 14, from Information Resources Inc.

★ 244 ★
Salad Dressing (SIC 2035)

Top Salad Dressing Makers, 2001

Market shares are shown for the year ended December 2, 2001. Figures exclude Wal-Mart.

Kraft Foods Inc.	33.1%
Lipton	17.4
Clorox Co.	12.7
Kens Food Inc.	6.6
Private label	6.9
Other	23.3

Source: *Grocery Headquarters*, April 2002, p. 14, from Information Resources Inc.

★ 245 ★
Frozen Vegetables (SIC 2037)

Frozen Vegetable Sales, 2001

Data show thousands of pounds.

Potatoes/fries/hashbrowns	419.4
Corn on cob	263.0
Mixed vegetables	167.1
Corn	81.0
Peas	74.0

Beans	69.0
Broccoli	63.5
Spinach	37.8
Prepared vegetables	22.3
Carrots	12.2

Source: *Food Institute Report*, September 17, 2001, p. 15, from Information Resources Inc. InfoScan.

★ 246 ★
Frozen Vegetables (SIC 2037)

Top Fruit & Vegetable Processors

Firms are ranked by sales in millions of dollars.

Lamb-Weston Inc.	$ 1,500.0
Simplot Food Group	1,300.0
McCain Foods	850.0
Heinz Frozen Foods	784.2
Agrilink Foods	653.0
Pillsbury Co.	650.0
Fresh Express Inc.	520.0
Dole Foods	470.0
Hanover Foods	300.3
Ready Pac Foods	240.0

Source: *Refrigerated & Frozen Foods*, February 2001, p. 32.

★ 247 ★
Frozen Dinners (SIC 2038)

Leading Frozen Dinner/Entree Makers, 2001

Shares are for the year ended February 25, 2001. Figures are for supermarkets $2 million and over.

Nestle Prepared Food Division	34.6%
ConAgra Foods	23.9
Luiginos	8.6
Vlasic Foods	7.7
Heinz Frozen Food	6.1
Mars/Uncle Ben's	3.1
Agrilink Foods	2.6
Other	13.4

Source: *Refrigerated & Frozen Foods*, June 2001, p. 40, from Information Resources Inc. InfoScan.

★ 248 ★
Frozen Dinners (SIC 2038)

Top Frozen Dinner Brands, 2001

Market shares are shown for the year ended December 2, 2001. Data exclude Wal-Mart.

Healthy Choice	17.3%
Swanson Hungryman	12.4
Swanson Traditional Favorites	9.5
Banquet Select Menu	9.1
Banquet Value Menu	8.0
Kid Cuisine	7.5
Marie Callenders Comp. Dinners	5.3
Marie Callenders	4.6
Banquet the Hearty One	2.5
Other	23.8

Source: *Grocery Headquarters*, April 2002, p. 14, from Information Resources Inc.

★ 249 ★
Frozen Dinners (SIC 2038)

Top Frozen Entree Makers, 2001

Market shares are shown for the year ended December 2, 2001. Data are for supermarkets only.

Nestle USA Inc.	42.1%
Luigino's Inc.	9.5
Weight Watchers Co.	9.4
Armour Swift-Eckrich Inc.	7.0
Uncle Ben's Inc.	5.2
Other	26.8

Source: *Grocery Headquarters*, April 2002, p. 14, from Information Resources Inc.

★ 250 ★
Frozen Foods (SIC 2038)

Frozen Breakfast Food Market, 2000

Sales are for the year ended January 31, 2000.

	($ mil.)	Share
Swanson Great Starts	$ 78.5	9.20%
Pillsbury Toaster Scrambles	52.1	6.11
Aunt Jemima	34.0	3.99
Pillsbury Hungry Jack	32.1	3.76
Red Baron Breakfast Pizza	22.8	2.67
Jimmy Dean	18.2	2.13
Eggo Toaster Muffins	18.1	2.12
Aunt Jemima	18.1	2.12
Krusteaz	10.7	1.25
Other	568.5	66.64

Source: *Frozen Food Age*, April 2001, p. 20, from Information Resources Inc.

★ 251 ★
Frozen Foods (SIC 2038)

Frozen Organic Market Shares

The market for "all natural" frozen entrees is shown.

Amy's Kitchen	70.0%
Other	30.0

Source: *Pittsburgh Business Times*, August 24, 2001, p. 1.

★ 252 ★
Frozen Foods (SIC 2038)

Leading Frozen Meat/Meat Substitute Makers, 2001

Shares are for the year ended February 25, 2001. Figures are for supermarkets $2 million and over.

Morningstar Farms	9.9%
Gardenburger	7.0
Boca Burger	5.0
Others	78.1

Source: *Refrigerated & Frozen Foods*, June 2001, p. 40, from Information Resources Inc. InfoScan.

★ 253 ★

Frozen Foods (SIC 2038)

Leading Hand-Held Entrée Leaders, 2001

Shares are for the year ended February 25, 2001.
Figures are for supermarkets $2 million and over.

Chef America	45.5%
Camino Real	6.2
Ruiz Food Products	5.8
Schwan's/Tony's	4.6
Delimex	4.6
Other	33.3

Source: *Refrigerated & Frozen Foods*, June 2001, p. 40, from Information Resources Inc. InfoScan.

★ 254 ★

Frozen Foods (SIC 2038)

Top Frozen Appetizer Brands

Shares are for the year ended July 15, 2001.

Bagel Bites	17.7%
Totino's Pizza Rolls	13.6
Totino's Appetizers/Snack Rolls	11.4
T.G.I. Friday's	10.8
Poppers	6.9
Farm Rich Dippers	2.4
Chung's	2.3
Jose Ole Mexi Minis	1.9
Hot Pockets	1.6
Delimex	1.6
Other	29.8

Source: *Quick Frozen Foods International*, October 2001, p. 59, from Information Resources Inc.

★ 255 ★

Frozen Foods (SIC 2038)

Top Frozen Appetizer Makers, 2001

Shares are shown for the year ended January 28, 2001.

Pillsbury	26.3%
Ore-Ida Foods Inc.	20.9
Anchor Food Products	16.7
ConAgra Inc.	3.0
Rich-SeaPak Corp.	2.8
Chung's Gourmet Foods	2.5
Ligino's Inc.	2.3
Chef America	2.2
Other	23.3

Source: *Quick Frozen Foods International*, April 2001, p. 78, from Information Resources Inc.

★ 256 ★

Frozen Foods (SIC 2038)

Top Frozen Food Categories in Canada, 2000

Sales are shown in millions of Canadian dollars.

Frozen dinners/entrees	$ 838.1
Ice cream/related products	381.2
Frozen fruit beverages (inc iced tea)	299.0
Frozen seafood	294.6
Frozen confections	246.2
Frozen/ref. pizza, bread, subs	192.7
Frozen regular vegetables	158.9
Frozen french fries	99.0
Frozen meat patties/steakettes	85.4
Frozen pizza snacks	82.2

Source: *Frozen Food Age*, October 2001, p. 1, from A.C. Nielsen Market Track.

★ 257 ★

Frozen Foods (SIC 2038)

Top Frozen Pizza Brands

Market shares are shown for the year ended July 15, 2001.

	($ mil.)	Share
DiGiorno	$358.7	14.29%
Tombstone	357.1	14.23
Red Baron	208.3	8.30
Totino's Party Pizza	185.7	7.40
Tony's	180.3	7.18
Freschetta	176.7	7.04
Jack's Original	99.4	3.96
Stouffer's	98.3	3.92
Celeste	76.5	3.05
Red Baron BTR	65.9	2.63
Red Baron Super Single	65.4	2.61
Other	637.1	25.39

Source: *Quick Frozen Foods International*, October 2001, p. 18, from Information Resources Inc.

★ 258 ★

Frozen Foods (SIC 2038)

Top Frozen Pizza Vendors, 2001

Market shares are shown for the year ended July 15, 2001.

Tombstone Pizza Corp.	31.3%
Tony's Pizza Service	29.0
Pillsbury Co.	9.7
Jack's Frozen Pizza Inc.	6.7
Stouffer Foods Corp.	4.7
Van de Kamps	3.4
Private label	5.8
Other	9.4

Source: *Snack Food & Wholesale Bakery*, September 2001, p. 18, from Information Resources Inc.

★ 259 ★

Frozen Foods (SIC 2038)

Top Frozen Potato Brands

Brands are ranked by sales in millions of dollars for the year ended February 25, 2001.

	($ mil.)	Share
Ore-Ida	$155.1	0.0%
Ore-Ida Golden Crinkles	79.7	0.0
Ore-Ida Tater Tots	60.4	0.0
Inland Valley	33.8	0.0
Private label	242.8	0.0
Other	276.9	0.0

Source: *Frozen Food Age*, June 2001, p. 28, from Information Resources Inc.

★ 260 ★

Frozen Foods (SIC 2038)

Top Frozen Poultry Makers, 2001

Market shares are shown for the year ended December 2, 2001. Data are for supermarkets only.

Tyson Foods Inc.	23.9%
Conagra Inc.	12.2
Gold Kist	2.9
Armour Swift-Eckrich Inc.	2.7
Private label	26.2
Other	32.1

Source: *Grocery Headquarters*, April 2002, p. 14, from Information Resources Inc.

★ 261 ★

Frozen Foods (SIC 2038)

Top Frozen Waffle Brands, 2000

Market shares are shown based on supermarket sales for the year ended November 5, 2000.

Kellogg's Eggo	55.3%
Pillsbury Hungry Jack	15.9
Aunt Jemima	8.1
Kellogg's NutriGrain Eggo	5.0
Kellogg's Special K Eggo	2.2
Kellogg's Eggo Minis	1.9
Vans	0.5
Other	11.1

Source: *Milling & Baking News*, February 13, 2001, p. NA, from Information Resources Inc.

★ 262 ★

Frozen Foods (SIC 2038)

Top Meat/Poultry/Seafood Processors

Firms are ranked by sales in billions of dollars.

ConAgra	$ 25.0
IBP	14.1
Cargill Meat Sector	9.0
Tyson Foods	7.1
Smithfield Foods	5.4
Farmland Industries	4.4
Sara Lee US Foods	4.0
Hormel Foods Group	3.6
Perdue Farms	2.5
Pilgrim's Pride Inc.	2.3

Source: *Refrigerated & Frozen Foods*, February 2001, p. 32.

★ 263 ★

Frozen Foods (SIC 2038)

Top Meatless Product Makers

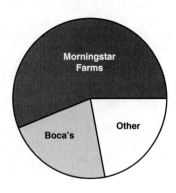

Market shares are shown in percent.

Morningstar Farms	56.1%
Boca's	22.0
Other	21.9

Source: *Knight-Ridder/Tribune Business News*, May 7, 2002, p. NA, from Information Resources Inc.

★ 264 ★

Cereal (SIC 2043)

Cereal Sales by Type

Figures are in millions of dollars.

	2001	2002	2003
Cold	$ 7,673	$ 7,864	$ 8,108
Hot	786	809	827

Source: *Prepared Foods*, February 2002, p. 13, from Mintel.

★ 265 ★

Cereal (SIC 2043)

Retail Cereal Sales

Data show supermarket sales in millions of dollars.

	($ mil.)	Share
Ready to eat	$ 6,945.55	87.23%
Hot	841.37	10.57
Granola & natural types	160.05	2.01
Wheat germ	15.30	0.19

Source: *Supermarket Business*, September 15, 2001, p. 42, from A.C. Nielsen Homescan.

★ 266 ★

Cereal (SIC 2043)

Top Cereal Brands, 2001

Market shares are shown in percent for the year ended April 22, 2001.

General Mills Cheerios	4.9%
Kellogg's Frosted Flakes	4.5
General Mills Honey Nut Cheerios	3.0
Kellogg's Frosted Mini Wheat's	2.8
Kellogg's Raisin Bran	2.7
General Mills Lucky Charms	2.4
General Mills Cinnamon Toast Crunch	2.4
Kellogg's Corn Flakes	2.3
Kellogg's Rice Krispies	2.1
Other	72.9

Source: *Milling & Baking News*, July 30, 2001, p. 3, from Information Resources Inc.

★ 267 ★

Cereal (SIC 2043)

Top Cereal Makers, 2001

Market shares are shown for the year ended December 2, 2001. Figures exclude Wal-Mart.

Kellogg Co.	31.9%
Kraft Foods Inc.	15.2
Quaker Oats Co.	8.8
Private label	7.7
Other	36.4

Source: *Grocery Headquarters*, April 2002, p. 14, from Information Resources Inc.

★ 268 ★

Baking Mixes (SIC 2045)

Muffin and Biscuit Mix Market

Shares are shown based on unit sales.

Jiffy	55.3%
Other	44.7

Source: *FSB*, December 1, 2001, p. 56, from Information Resources Inc.

★ 269 ★

Baking Supplies (SIC 2045)

Baking Supply Sales

Data show supermarket sales in millions of dollars.

Stuffing products	$ 280.50
Frosting, ready-to-spread	261.15
Breading products	247.83
Chocolate chips & morsels	220.36
Croutons	140.63
Cake decorations & icing	124.99
Pie & pastry shells	75.41
Yeast, dry	70.85
Baking chips, non-chocolate	61.61
Baking chocolate	49.01
Baking soda	46.48

Source: *Supermarket Business*, September 15, 2001, p. 42, from A.C. Nielsen Homescan.

★ 270 ★

Dough (SIC 2045)

Refrigerated Biscuit Dough Market

Market shares are shown in percent.

Pillsbury	78.0%
Earthgrains	1.0
Private label	21.0

Source: *Crain's Chicago Business*, July 9, 2001, p. 4.

★ 271 ★

Dough (SIC 2045)

Refrigerated Bread/Bun/Roll Dough Category

Market shares are shown in percent.

Pillsbury	80.7%
Other	19.3

Source: "News in Baking." Retrieved January 4, 2002 from the World Wide Web: http://www.bakery-net.com, from Information Resources Inc.

★ 272 ★

Dough (SIC 2045)

Refrigerated Dough Companies

Market shares are shown in percent.

General Mills	80.0%
Earthgrains	17.0
Other	3.0

Source: *Milling & Baking News*, April 23, 2002, p. 24.

★ 273 ★

Dough (SIC 2045)

Refrigerated Dough Sales, 2000

Supermaket sales are shown in millions of dollars.

	($ mil.)	Share
Biscuits	$ 476.8	34.72%
Bread/buns/rolls	356.6	25.97
Pastries/dumplings	264.2	19.24
Cookies/brownies	239.8	17.46
Pizza crust	35.9	2.61

Source: *Snack Food & Wholesale Bakery*, June 2001, pp. S-31, from Information Resources Inc.

★ 274 ★

Dough (SIC 2045)

Top Frozen Dough Brands

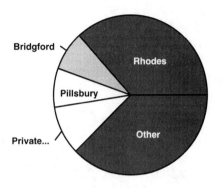

Brands are ranked by sales in millions of dollars.

	($ mil.)	Share
Rhodes	$ 43.0	37.04%
Bridgford	9.1	7.84
Pillsbury	9.0	7.75
Private label	11.3	9.73
Other	43.7	37.64

Source: *Frozen Food Age*, April 2001, p. 18, from Information Resources Inc.

★ 275 ★

Pet Food (SIC 2047)

Pet Food Market Leaders

Total cat and dog food sales are expected to grow from $18.4 billion in 2000 to $19.5 billion in 2001. Grocery stores still have the largest part of sales.

	Sales ($ bil.)	Share
Ralston Purina	$ 2.2	20.0%
Friskies Pet Care	1.5	13.2
Kal Kan	1.2	11.0

Source: *Food Institute Report*, December 24, 2001, p. 3, from *Petfood Industry*.

★ 276 ★

Pet Food (SIC 2047)

Top Dry Dog Food Brands, 2001

Market shares are shown for the year ended December 2, 2001. Data exclude Wal-Mart.

Pedigree Mealtime	13.4%
Iams	12.8
Purina One	11.0
Purina Dog Chow	8.8
Purina Puppy Chow	4.3
Ken-L Ration Kibbles 'n Bits	4.3
Purina Dog Chow Little Bites	3.0
Private label	8.8
Other	33.6

Source: *Grocery Headquarters*, April 2002, p. 14, from Information Resources Inc.

★ 277 ★

Pet Food (SIC 2047)

Top Dry Dog Food Makers, 2001

Market shares are shown for the year ended December 2, 2001. Data exclude Wal-Mart.

Ralston Purina Co.	39.6%
Kal Kan Foods Inc.	15.1
The Iams Co.	12.8
Heinz Pet Products Co.	10.1
Private label	8.8
Other	13.6

Source: *Grocery Headquarters*, April 2002, p. 14, from Information Resources Inc.

★ 278 ★

Pet Food (SIC 2047)

Top Pet Food Makers

Market shares are shown in percent.

Ralston Purina	26.9%
Nestle	18.6
M&M/Mars	14.9
H.J. Heinz Co.	12.2
Procter & Gamble Co.	4.8
Private label	16.6
Other	5.0

Source: *Food Processing*, June 2001, p. 49, from Information Resources Inc.

★ 279 ★
Bagels (SIC 2051)

Top Frozen Bagel Brands, 2001

Market shares are shown in percent for the year ended January 7, 2001.

Lenders	49.6%
Lenders Big N Crusty	25.7
Pillsbury Toaster Bagel	6.0
Sara Lee	2.8
Private label	13.1
Other	2.8

Source: *Snack Food & Wholesale Bakery*, June 2001, p. S1, from Information Resources Inc.

★ 280 ★
Bread (SIC 2051)

Top Fresh Bread Makers, 2001

Market shares are shown in percent for the year ended May 27, 2001. Figures are for food stores only.

Interstate Brands	11.1%
Arnold-Orowheat	10.9
Earthgrains	8.1
Flowers	6.0
Pepperidge Farm	4.5
Merita	2.7
Stroehmann's	2.3
Roush	2.2
American Bakers Co-op	2.0
Private label	26.6
Other	23.6

Source: *USA TODAY*, July 3, 2001, p. 3B, from Information Resources Inc.

★ 281 ★
Buns and Rolls (SIC 2051)

Top Fresh Bun and Roll Brands, 2001

Market shares are shown based on supermarket sales for the year ended May 27, 2001. Data include bagels, croissants, english muffins, hot dogs and hamburger buns.

Thomas	16.5%
Sara Lee	3.3
Martins	2.8
Wonder	2.4
Pepperidge Farm	2.2
Earth Grains	1.7

Lenders	1.6%
Oroweat	1.5
Francisco	1.5
Private label	31.4
Other	35.1

Source: *Milling & Baking News*, July 10, 2001, p. NA, from Information Resources Inc.

★ 282 ★
Buns and Rolls (SIC 2051)

Top Fresh Roll/Biscuit Brands, 2001

Market shares are shwon based on supermarket sales for the year ended January 7, 2001.

Francisco	7.0%
Martins	6.9
King's Hawaiian	6.2
Sister Schuberts	4.4
Private label	26.9
Other	48.6

Source: *Snack Food & Wholesale Bakery*, June 2001, pp. S-31, from Information Resources Inc.

★ 283 ★
Buns and Rolls (SIC 2051)

Top Hamburger Bun Brands, 2001

Market shares are shown based on supermarket sales for the year ended January 7, 2001.

Wonder	6.6%
Sunbeam	2.8
Colonial	2.6
Mrs. Baird's	2.4
Private label	47.8
Other	37.8

Source: *Snack Food & Wholesale Bakery*, June 2001, pp. S-31, from Information Resources Inc.

★ 284 ★
Buns and Rolls (SIC 2051)

Top Hot Dog Bun Brands, 2001

Market shares are shown based on supermarket sales for the year ended January 7, 2001.

Wonder	3.7%
Rainbo	3.3
Merita	2.6
Sunbeam	2.3
Private label	52.6
Other	35.5

Source: *Snack Food & Wholesale Bakery*, June 2001, pp. S-31, from Information Resources Inc.

★ 285 ★
Coffee Cake (SIC 2051)

Top Fresh Coffee Cake Brands, 2001

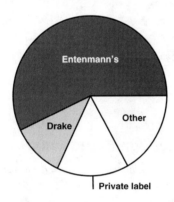

Market shares are shown based on supermarket sales for the year ended January 7, 2001.

Entenmann's	56.8%
Drake	10.9
Private label	15.2
Other	17.1

Source: *Snack Food & Wholesale Bakery*, June 2001, pp. S-31, from Information Resources Inc.

★ 286 ★
Muffins (SIC 2051)

Top Fresh Muffin Brands, 2001

Market shares are shown based on supermarket sales for the year ended January 7, 2001.

Otis Spunkmeyer	18.4%
Little Debbie	6.9
Private label	52.8
Other	21.9

Source: *Snack Food & Wholesale Bakery*, June 2001, pp. S-26, from Information Resources Inc.

★ 287 ★
Pies (SIC 2051)

Leading Pie Brands

Market shares are shown in percent for the year ended June 17, 2001. Figures do not include snack pies.

Entenmann's	7.8%
Our Special Touch	7.6
Private label	54.9
Other	29.7

Source: *Snack Food & Wholesale Bakery*, August 2001, p. 20, from Information Resources Inc.

★ 288 ★
Pies (SIC 2051)

Leading Snack Pie Brands

Market shares are shown in percent for the year ended June 17, 2001.

Hostess	13.0%
Tastykake	9.7
J.J.'s	9.2
Home Run	7.5
Private label	13.1
Other	47.5

Source: *Snack Food & Wholesale Bakery*, August 2001, p. 20, from Information Resources Inc.

★ 289 ★
Cookies (SIC 2052)

Top Biscuit Makers in Mexico

Market shares are shown in percent.

Grupo Gamesa 52.0%
Bimbo 20.0
Other 28.0

Source: *South American Business Information*, August 27, 2001, p. NA.

★ 290 ★
Cookies (SIC 2052)

Top Cookie Brands, 2001

Brands are ranked by sales in millions of dollars for the year ended August 12, 2001.

	($ mil.)	Share
Nabisco Oreo	$ 610.7	11.31%
Nabisco Chips Ahoy	404.6	7.50
Keebler Chips Deluxe	176.8	3.28
Nabisco Newtons	156.3	2.90
Keebler Fudge Shoppe	132.9	2.46
Nabisco Snackwells	118.5	2.20
Nabisco Teddy Grahams	113.6	2.10
Pepperidge Farm Distinctive . . .	112.4	2.08
Nabisco Nilla	90.2	1.67
Other	3,481.3	64.50

Source: *Baking & Snack*, October 1, 2001, p. NA, from Information Resources Inc.

★ 291 ★
Cookies (SIC 2052)

Top Cookie Makers, 2001

Market shares are shown in percent.

Nabisco 37.7%
Keebler 14.3
Parmalat 8.4
Pepperidge Farm 6.3
Little Debbie 5.0
Murray Biscuit Co. 4.8
Voortman 1.5
Stella D'Oro 1.1
Private label 8.5
Other 12.4

Source: *Snack Food & Wholesale Bakery*, January 2002, p. 15, from Information Resources Inc.

★ 292 ★
Cookies (SIC 2052)

Top Cookie Makers in Mexico

Market shares are shown in percent, based on a $475 million market.

Gamesa 52.0%
Lara 20.0
Other 28.0

Source: *InfoLatina S.A. de C.V.*, August 24, 2001, p. NA.

★ 293 ★
Cookies (SIC 2052)

Who Makes Girl Scout Cookies

The 3 firms make 2.4 billion cookies annually, or 200 million boxes.

Consolidated Biscuit/Little Brownie Bakers . . 60.0%
ABC Bakers 40.0

Source: *BusinessWeek*, April 15, 2002, p. 12.

★ 294 ★
Crackers (SIC 2052)

Retail Cracker Sales

Data show supermarket sales in millions of dollars.

Flavored snack . . . . $ 900.94
Cheese 560.89

Continued on next page.

★ 294 ★ *Continued*
Crackers (SIC 2052)

Retail Cracker Sales

Data show supermarket sales in millions of dollars.

Flaked soda	$ 455.00
Sprayed butter	400.31
Graham	277.18
Sprayed flake	121.86
Wafers/toast & bread sticks	114.17
Oyster	44.41
Matzo	26.55

Source: *Supermarket Business*, September 15, 2001, p. 42, from A.C. Nielsen Homescan.

★ 295 ★
Frozen Bakery Products (SIC 2053)

Leading Frozen Pie Makers, 2001

Market shares are shown in percent for the year ended June 17, 2001.

Mrs. Smith's	47.7%
Sara Lee	21.1
Edward's Baking Co.	13.4
Marie Callender's	8.2
Other	9.6

Source: *Snack Food & Wholesale Bakery*, August 2001, p. 20, from Information Resources Inc.

★ 296 ★
Frozen Bakery Products (SIC 2053)

Top Frozen Sweet Goods Brands, 2000

Market shares are shown in percent for the year ended December 31, 2000.

Pillsbury Toaster Strudel	41.1%
Pepperidge Farm	29.8
Sara Lee	14.5
Other	14.6

Source: *Snack Food & Wholesale Bakery*, June 2001, p. S1, from Information Resources Inc.

★ 297 ★
Sugar Substitutes (SIC 2061)

Top Sugar Substitute Brands

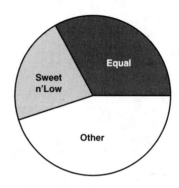

The market is valued at sales of $300 million.

	($ mil.)	Share
Equal	$ 99	33.0%
Sweet n'Low	66	22.0
Other	135	45.0

Source: *Crain's New York Business*, July 2, 2001, p. 1, from Information Resources Inc.

★ 298 ★
Sugar Substitutes (SIC 2062)

Sugar and Sweetener Sales

Data show supermarket sales in millions of dollars.

	($ mil.)	Share
Granulated	$ 1,002.04	68.89%
Substitutes	239.38	16.46
Brown	118.31	8.13
Powdered	76.09	5.23
Remaining sugar products	18.77	1.29

Source: *Supermarket Business*, September 15, 2001, p. 36, from A.C. Nielsen.

★ 299 ★
Breath Fresheners (SIC 2064)

Top Breath Freshener Brands, 2001

Market shares are shown for the year ended October 7, 2001.

Altoids	32.5%
Tic Tac	21.2
BreathSavers	12.5
Certs Cool Mint Drops	7.3

Continued on next page.

★ 299 ★ *Continued*
Breath Fresheners (SIC 2064)

Top Breath Freshener Brands, 2001

Market shares are shown for the year ended October 7, 2001.

Certs Powerful Mints	6.3%
BreathSavers Ice Breakers	5.3
Van Melle's Mentos	2.3
Smint	2.0
Certs	2.0
BreathSavers Cool Blast	1.6
Other	7.0

Source: *Professional Candy Buyer*, November-December 2001, p. 18, from Information Resources Inc.

★ 300 ★
Breath Fresheners (SIC 2064)

Top Breath Freshener Makers

Market shares are shown in percent for the year ended June 24, 2001.

Philip Morris Co. Inc.	32.8%
Ferrero USA Inc..	23.3
RJR Nabisco Inc..	20.4
Warner Lambert	17.0
Chupa Chups USA	1.8
Ragold Inc..	1.2
Blitz Design Corp.	1.2
Brown & Haley	0.7
Other	1.6

Source: *Manufacturing Confectioner*, September 2001, p. 25, from Information Resources Inc.

★ 301 ★
Confectionery Products (SIC 2064)

Candy and Gum Industry

Sales are shown in millions of dollars.

	2000	2001
Chocolate	$ 12.9	$ 13.3
Non-chocolate	7.5	7.5
Gum	2.2	2.4

Source: *Candy Industry*, March 2002, p. 14, from National Confectioners Association.

★ 302 ★
Confectionery Products (SIC 2064)

Candy Sales in Convenience Stores

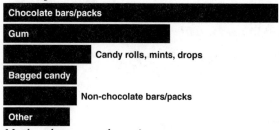

Market shares are shown in percent.

Chocolate bars/packs	37.5%
Gum	22.8
Candy rolls, mints, drops	11.5
Bagged candy	10.2
Non-chocolate bars/packs	9.5
Other	8.5

Source: *USA TODAY*, August 16, 2001, p. D1, from National Association of Convenience Stores.

★ 303 ★
Confectionery Products (SIC 2064)

Halloween Candy Sales, 2001

Sales are shown, in millions, for the four weeks ended November 4, 2001.

	($ mil.)	Share
Chocolate candy snack size	$ 532.8	22.90%
Choc. candy box/bag/bar > 3.5 oz .	386.8	16.63
Gum	254.8	10.95
Non-chocolate chewy candy . . .	227.3	9.77
Chocolate candy bar < 3.5 oz . . .	196.1	8.43
Novelty non-chocolate candy . . .	155.2	6.67
Hard sugar candy/package & roll candy	142.5	6.13
Breath fresheners	83.3	3.58
Non-chocolate Halloween candy . .	69.8	3.00
Other	277.9	11.94

Source: *Professional Candy Buyer*, January-February 2002, p. 30, from National Confectioners Association and Information Resources Inc.

★ 304 ★

Confectionery Products (SIC 2064)

Private Label Candy Segments, 2001

Sales are shown in millions of dollars for the year ended March 25, 2001.

Non-chocolate chewy (box/bag > 3.5 oz) . .	$ 60.5
Chocolate candy (box/bag > 3.5 oz)	28.8
Hard sugar candy	17.5
Plain mints	16.1
Diet candy	9.0
Novelty candy	8.9
Specialty nut/coconut candy	4.5
Licorice box/bag (> 3 oz)	2.7

Source: *Confectioner*, June 2001, p. 102, from Information Resources Inc.

★ 305 ★

Confectionery Products (SIC 2064)

Top Diet Candy Brands

Shares are for the year ended February 25, 2001.

Russell Stover	27.9%
Sweet n'Low	11.1
Estee	8.1
Lifesavers Delites	7.5
Fifty 50	5.6
Go Lightly	4.4
Bob's	3.2
Sweet n'Low Patteez	2.2
Square Shooters	2.1
Private label	9.6
Other	18.3

Source: *Candy Industry*, April 2001, p. 50, from Information Resources Inc.

★ 306 ★

Confectionery Products (SIC 2064)

Top Fruit Roll/Bar Makers, 2001

Companies are ranked by sales in millions of dollars for the year ended November 4, 2001.

	($ mil.)	Share
General Mills	$ 346.9	63.36%
Kraft Foods	80.9	14.78
Brach's	49.3	9.00
McKee Foods	10.1	1.84
Private label	45.5	8.31
Other	14.8	2.70

Source: *Candy Industry*, January 2002, p. 30, from Information Resources Inc.

★ 307 ★

Confectionery Products (SIC 2064)

Top Hard Candy Brands, 2001

Brands are ranked by sales in millions of dollars for the year ended May 20, 2001.

	($ mil.)	Share
Lifesavers Crème Savers	$ 92.3	19.91%
Hershey Jolly Rancher	57.2	12.34
Lifesavers Lifesavers	50.6	10.91
Storck Werther's Original	32.5	7.01
Nestle Pearson Nips	19.5	4.21
M&M/Mars Starburst	16.7	3.60
Hershey's Tastetations	14.2	3.06
Farley's	7.6	1.64
Private label	17.6	3.80
Other	155.5	33.53

Source: *Professional Candy Buyer*, July 2001, p. 54, from Information Resources Inc.

★ 308 ★

Confectionery Products (SIC 2064)

Top Hard Candy Producers

Market shares are shown in percent.

Kraft Nabisco	32.4%
Hershey Chocolate	15.9
Storck USA	9.3
Tootsie Roll Industry	8.5
Charms Inc.	6.8
Nestle USA Inc.	5.6
Mars Inc.	3.9
Spangler Candy Co.	2.6

Continued on next page.

★ 308 ★ *Continued*
Confectionery Products (SIC 2064)

Top Hard Candy Producers

Market shares are shown in percent.

Brach & Brock Confections	2.6%
Private label	3.0
Other	9.4

Source: *Candy Industry*, February 2002, p. 36.

★ 309 ★
Confectionery Products (SIC 2064)

Top Licorice Brands

Data do not include Wal-Mart.

Twizzlers	60.6%
American Licorice	21.1
Good & Plenty	6.3
Kenny's	3.1
Bassett's	2.0
Twizzlers Twist-N-Fill	1.3
Starburst Fruit Twists	1.2
Other	4.4

Source: *Professional Candy Buyer*, March 2002, p. 18, from Information Resources Inc.

★ 310 ★
Confectionery Products (SIC 2064)

Top Licorice Makers, 2001

Companies are ranked by sales in millions of dollars for the year ended November 4, 2001.

	($ mil.)	Share
Twizzlers	$ 109.9	61.53%
American Licorice	33.5	18.76
Good & Plenty	12.5	7.00
Kenny's	4.7	2.63
Bassett's	3.1	1.74
Starburst	2.5	1.40
Twizzlers Twist-N-Fill	2.3	1.29
Panda	0.9	0.50
Crows	0.9	0.50
Other	8.3	4.65

Source: *Candy Industry*, January 2002, p. 30, from Information Resources Inc.

★ 311 ★
Confectionery Products (SIC 2064)

Top Marshmallow Brands

Market shares are shown in percent for the year ended June 24, 2001.

Jet Puffed	46.6%
Campfire	4.6
Jet Puffed Funmallows	4.1
Fireside	2.0
Private label	40.5
Other	2.2

Source: *Manufacturing Confectioner*, September 2001, p. 25, from Information Resources Inc.

★ 312 ★
Confectionery Products (SIC 2064)

Top Marshmallow Makers

Market shares are shown in percent for the year ended June 24, 2001.

Favorite Brands	52.0%
Campfire	4.9
Clown Confections Inc.	2.0
Private label	40.5

Source: *Manufacturing Confectioner*, September 2001, p. 25, from Information Resources Inc.

★ 313 ★
Confectionery Products (SIC 2064)

Top Nonchocolate Chewy Candy Bar (< 3.5 oz) Brands

Market shares are shown in percent for the year ended June 24, 2001.

Skittles	17.8%
Van Melles Mentos	12.4
Starburst	12.0
LifeSavers GummiSavers	8.7
Reese's Pieces	3.5
Van Melles Air Heads	2.9
Sathers	2.9
Y&S Twizzler	2.7
Zero	2.5
Trolli Brite Crawlers	2.5
Other	32.1

Source: *Manufacturing Confectioner*, September 2001, p. 25, from Information Resources Inc.

★ 314 ★
Confectionery Products (SIC 2064)

Top Nonchocolate Chewy Candy Bar (< 3.5 oz) Makers

Market shares are shown in percent for the year ended June 24, 2001.

Mars Inc.	31.5%
Van Melle	15.4
Hershey Foods Corp.	12.3
RJR Nabisco Inc.	11.7
Tootsie Roll Industries	3.9
Favorite Brands Intl.	3.2
Other	22.0

Source: *Manufacturing Confectioner*, September 2001, p. 25, from Information Resources Inc.

★ 315 ★
Confectionery Products (SIC 2064)

Top Nonchocolate Chewy Candy Makers

Market shares are shown in percent. Figures exclude Wal-Mart.

Masterfoods	21.1%
Kraft Confections	15.6
Hershey Foods	10.5
Tootsie Roll Inds.	6.9
Brach's Confections	6.0
Van Melee	5.4
Private label	6.4
Other	28.0

Source: *Candy Industry*, May 2002, p. 34, from Information Resources Inc.

★ 316 ★
Confectionery Products (SIC 2064)

Top Novelty Candy Brands, 2001

Brands are ranked by sales in millions of dollars for the year ended December 2, 2001.

	($ mil.)	Share
Tootsie Roll Child's Play	$ 18.1	6.89%
Sweet Tarts	15.2	5.79
Pez	14.1	5.37
Willy Wonka Nerds	11.9	4.53
Hot Tamales	10.6	4.04
Topps Baby Bottle Pop	10.4	3.96
Sunmark Spree	10.4	3.96
Ce De Smarties	9.2	3.50
Topps Ring Pop	8.5	3.24
Other	154.3	58.74

Source: *MMR*, January 28, 2002, p. 21, from Information Resources Inc.

★ 317 ★
Confectionery Products (SIC 2064)

Top Specialty Nut/Coconut Brands

Market shares are shown in percent for the year ended June 24, 2001.

Leaf Pay Day	39.4%
Brach's	11.3
Sophie Mae	3.8
Pearsons	3.5
Planters	3.2
Brach's Maple Nut Goodies	3.0
Lance	2.2
Russell Stover	2.0
Annabelle Big Hunk	1.6
Other	30.0

Source: *Manufacturing Confectioner*, September 2001, p. 25, from Information Resources Inc.

★ 318 ★

Confectionery Products (SIC 2064)

Top Specialty Nut/Coconut Makers

Market shares are shown in percent for the year ended June 24, 2001.

Hershey Foods Corp.	40.1%
Brach's Confections	14.3
Fine Products Co. Inc.	3.8
Pearson Candy Co.	3.5
RJR Nabisco	3.2
Private label	4.6
Other	30.5

Source: *Manufacturing Confectioner*, September 2001, p. 25, from Information Resources Inc.

★ 319 ★

Confectionery Products (SIC 2064)

Top Sugarless Candy Makers

Market shares are shown in percent for the year ended June 24, 2001.

Russell Stover Candies Inc.	31.5%
Simply Lite	13.2
Hain Food Group	7.7
RJR Nabisco Inc.	7.2
Fifty 50	5.4
GoLightly Candy Co.	3.9
Private label	10.5
other	20.6

Source: *Manufacturing Confectioner*, September 2001, p. 25, from Information Resources Inc.

★ 320 ★

Cough Drops (SIC 2064)

Top Cough Drop Brands

Brands are ranked by sales for the year ended January 28, 2001.

	($ mil.)	Share
Halls	$ 115.5	28.27%
Ricola	41.3	10.11
Cold Eeze	30.4	7.44
Ludens	29.0	7.10
Halls Defense	22.1	5.41
Robitussin	15.6	3.82
Robitussin Honey	14.2	3.48
Halls Plus	14.0	3.43
Sucrets	13.2	3.23

	($ mil.)	Share
Private label	$ 48.9	11.97%
Other	64.3	15.74

Source: *MMR*, April 16, 2001, p. 67, from Information Resources Inc.

★ 321 ★

Cough Drops (SIC 2064)

Top Cough Drop Makers

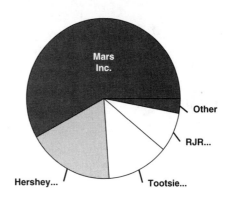

Market shares are shown in percent for the year ended June 24, 2001.

Mars Inc.	57.7%
Hershey Foods Corp.	18.3
Tootsie Roll Industries	13.0
RJR Nabisco	7.7
Other	3.3

Source: *Manufacturing Confectioner*, September 2001, p. 25, from Information Resources Inc.

★ 322 ★

Mints (SIC 2064)

Top Mint Brands, 2001

Market shares are shown for the year ended October 7, 2001.

LifeSavers	40.5%
Van Melle's Mentos	13.4
Brach's Star Brites	8.6
Farley's	5.7
Tic Tac Silvers	3.9
Brach's Plain Mints	3.6
Sathers	2.6
Richardson After Dinner Plain Mints	1.8
Primrose Plain Mints	1.6

Continued on next page.

★ 322 ★ *Continued*
Mints (SIC 2064)

Top Mint Brands, 2001

Market shares are shown for the year ended October 7, 2001.

Private label	9.4%
Other	8.9

Source: *Professional Candy Buyer*, November-December 2001, p. 18, from Information Resources Inc.

★ 323 ★
Mints (SIC 2064)

Top Mint Makers

Market shares are shown in percent for the year ended June 24, 2001.

RJR Nabisco	40.0%
Van Melle NV	16.3
Brach's Confections	15.0
Favorite Brands Intl.	6.0
Bob Candies Inc.	3.4
Agrolimen	3.4
Private label	9.0
Other	6.9

Source: *Manufacturing Confectioner*, September 2001, p. 25, from Information Resources Inc.

★ 324 ★
Snack Bars (SIC 2064)

Top Granola Bars, 2001

Brands are ranked by sales in millions of dollars for the year ended October 7, 2001.

	($ mil.)	Share
Quaker Chewy	$ 154.70	11.68%
Kellogg's Nutri-Grain	124.60	9.41
Nature Valley	89.70	6.77
Kellogg's Rice Krispies Treats . .	89.20	6.73
Slim Fast	70.70	5.34
Quaker Fruit & Oatmeal	60.90	4.60
Sunbelt Snacks	50.50	3.81
General Mills Milk 'n Cereal . . .	40.40	3.05
Kudos granola bars	39.60	2.99
Private label	70.80	5.35
Other	533.38	40.27

Source: *Baking & Snack*, December 1, 2001, p. NA, from Information Resources Inc.

★ 325 ★
Snack Bars (SIC 2064)

Top Snack Bar Makers, 2001

Companies are ranked by sales in millions of dollars for the year ended November 4, 2001.

	($ mil.)	Share
Kellogg's	$ 297.3	18.72%
Quaker Oats	249.0	15.68
Slim Fast Foods	157.0	9.88
General Mills	150.0	9.44
McKee Foods	129.9	8.18
Rexall Sundown	89.1	5.61
Kraft Foods	85.1	5.36
Nestle	72.7	4.58
Clif Bar	58.3	3.67
Private label	91.5	5.76
Other	208.6	13.13

Source: *Candy Industry*, January 2002, p. 30, from Information Resources Inc.

★ 326 ★
Snack Bars (SIC 2064)

Top Snack/Energy Bar Brands, 2001

Sales are for the year ended February 25, 2001.

	($ mil.)	Share
Slim-Fast	$ 79.7	22.57%
PowerBar	41.5	11.75
Balance	40.1	11.36
Slim-Fast	37.4	10.59
Advantage	24.4	6.91
Eclif	21.5	6.09
Luna	20.0	5.66
Other	88.5	25.06

Source: *Professional Candy Buyer*, May 2001, p. 80, from Information Resources Inc.

★ 327 ★

Chocolate (SIC 2066)

Top Boxed/Bagged (< 3.5 oz) Chocolate Candy Producers

Market shares are shown in percent for the year ended June 24, 2001.

Hershey Foods Corp.	40.7%
Mars Inc.	34.2
Nestle SA	14.7
Ferrero USA Inc.	2.4
Russell Stover Candies	2.2
Tootsie Roll Industries	1.2

Source: *Manufacturing Confectioner*, September 2001, p. 25, from Information Resources Inc.

★ 328 ★

Chocolate (SIC 2066)

Top Boxed/Bagged (> 3.5 oz) Chocolate Candies

Market shares are shown in percent for the year ended June 24, 2001.

M&Ms	14.4%
Hershey's	11.4
Hershey's Kisses	6.5
Hershey's Nuggets	6.0
Snickers	4.7
Reese's	4.7
York Peppermint Patty	2.8
Nestle Treasures	2.6
Ferrero Rocher	2.0
Private label	1.8
Other	43.1

Source: *Manufacturing Confectioner*, September 2001, p. 25, from Information Resources Inc.

★ 329 ★

Chocolate (SIC 2066)

Top Boxed/Bagged (> 3.5 oz) Chocolate Candy Producers

Market shares are shown in percent for the year ended June 24, 2001.

Hershey Foods Corp.	45.6%
Mars Inc.	23.9
Nestle SA	7.0
Brach's Confections	3.3
Philip Morris Co. Inc.	2.6
Ferrero USA	2.2
Other	15.4

Source: *Manufacturing Confectioner*, September 2001, p. 25, from Information Resources Inc.

★ 330 ★

Chocolate (SIC 2066)

Top Chocolate Bar Brands in Canada, 2001

Reese Brand
Kit Kat
Caramilk
Oh Henry
Hershey Milk Chocolate
M&Ms
Coffee Crisp
Cadbury Milk Chocolate
Smarties
Mars
Other

Market shares are shown in percent for the year ended December 29, 2001. Total sales hit $749.3 million.

Reese Brand	6.3%
Kit Kat	5.4
Caramilk	4.9
Oh Henry	4.7
Hershey Milk Chocolate	4.6
M&Ms	4.5
Coffee Crisp	4.2

Continued on next page.

★ 330 ★ *Continued*
Chocolate (SIC 2066)

Top Chocolate Bar Brands in Canada, 2001

Market shares are shown in percent for the year ended December 29, 2001. Total sales hit $749.3 million.

Cadbury Milk Chocolate	4.0%
Smarties	3.8
Mars	3.7
Other	53.9

Source: *Marketing Magazine*, May 27, 2002, p. 1, from industry sources.

★ 331 ★
Chocolate (SIC 2066)

Top Chocolate Candy Bars < 3.5 oz.

Market shares are shown in percent for the year ended February 24, 2002.

M&Ms	12.5%
Hershey's	10.5
Reeses	7.0
Snickers	6.9
Kit Kat	4.9
Twix	4.2
York Peppermint Patty	3.3
Peter Paul Almond Joy	3.1
Nestle Butterfinger	3.0
Three Musketeers	2.7
Other	49.1

Source: *Candy Industry*, April 2002, p. 44, from Information Resources Inc.

★ 332 ★
Chocolate (SIC 2066)

Top Chocolate Candy Brands (Snacks/ Fun Size)

Market shares are shown in percent for the year ended June 24, 2001.

Snickers	15.7%
Reese's	13.8
Kit Kat	10.9
M&Ms	6.5
Milky Way	6.4
Three Musketeers	5.6

Butterfinger	5.2%
Nestle Crunch	4.8
Other	31.1

Source: *Manufacturing Confectioner*, September 2001, p. 25, from Information Resources Inc.

★ 333 ★
Chocolate (SIC 2066)

Top Chocolate Candy Makers, 2001

Companies are ranked by sales in millions of dollars for the year ended November 4, 2001.

	($ mil.)	Share
Hershey	$ 2,116.1	40.71%
Mars	1,372.0	26.39
Nestle	414.1	7.97
R.M. Palmer	93.9	1.81
Kraft Foods	74.7	1.44
Ferrero	61.7	1.19
Tootsie Roll	51.3	0.99
Brach's	40.7	0.78
Private label	48.5	0.93
Other	925.2	17.80

Source: *Candy Industry*, January 2002, p. 30, from Information Resources Inc.

★ 334 ★
Chocolate (SIC 2066)

Top Chocolate Candy Makers (Snacks/ Fun Size)

Market shares are shown in percent for the year ended June 24, 2001.

Hershey Foods Corp.	42.2%
Mars Inc.	40.2
Nestle SA	16.3
Tootsie Roll Industries	0.6
Russell Stover Candies	0.6
Other	9.9

Source: *Manufacturing Confectioner*, September 2001, p. 25, from Information Resources Inc.

★ 335 ★
Chocolate (SIC 2066)

Top Chocolate Covered Cookies/ Wafers

Market shares are shown in percent for the year ended June 24, 2001.

Reese's Sticks	27.1%
Twix	27.0
Kit Kat	23.7
Kit Kat Big Kat	8.2
Kit Kat Bites	5.9
Russell Stover	2.9
Other	5.2

Source: *Manufacturing Confectioner*, September 2001, p. 25, from Information Resources Inc.

★ 336 ★
Gum (SIC 2067)

Chewing Gum Market

Market shares are shown in percent.

Wrigley	53.5%
Pfizer	25.5
Hershey	13.5
Other	7.5

Source: *New York Times*, August 28, 2001, p. C1, from Information Resources Inc. and Prudential Securities.

★ 337 ★
Gum (SIC 2067)

Top Chewing Gum Brands

Brands are ranked by sales in millions of dollars for the year ended November 4, 2001.

	($ mil.)	Share
Wrigley's Winterfresh	$ 56.6	11.81%
Wrigley's Double Mint	49.0	10.23
Wrigley's Big Red	46.7	9.75
Wrigley's Juicy Fruit	40.9	8.54
Freedent	39.5	8.24
Wrigley's Spearmint	28.4	5.93
Bubble Tape	23.9	4.99
Bubblicious	23.5	4.90
Bubble Yum	20.8	4.34
Everest	11.8	2.46
Other	138.1	28.82

Source: *Professional Candy Buyer*, January-February 2002, p. 36, from Information Resources Inc.

★ 338 ★

Gum (SIC 2067)

Top Gum Brands in Canada

Market shares are shown in percent for the year ended December 29, 2001. Total sales hit $334 million.

Dentyne	21.9%
Excel	20.8
Trident	18.6
Extra	10.9
Clorets	6.3
Juicy Fruit	3.1
Bubblicious	2.8
Freedent	2.3
Other	13.3

Source: *Marketing Magazine*, May 27, 2002, p. 1, from industry sources.

★ 339 ★

Gum (SIC 2067)

Top Sugarless Gum Brands, 2001

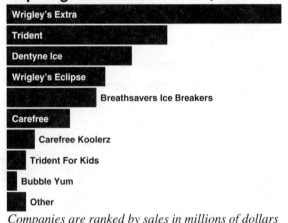

Companies are ranked by sales in millions of dollars for the year ended November 4, 2001.

	($ mil.)	Share
Wrigley's Extra	$ 192.0	31.14%
Trident	109.3	17.73
Dentyne Ice	88.2	14.30
Wrigley's Eclipse	70.2	11.39
Breathsavers Ice Breakers	64.4	10.44
Carefree	42.7	6.93

	($ mil.)	Share
Carefree Koolerz	$ 21.4	3.47%
Trident For Kids	11.5	1.87
Bubble Yum	6.7	1.09
Other	10.2	1.65

Source: *Candy Industry*, January 2002, p. 30, from Information Resources Inc.

★ 340 ★

Gum (SIC 2067)

Top Sugarless Gum Firms

Market shares are shown in percent.

William W. Wrigley Jr.	42.3%
Pfizer	35.3
Kraft Foods	22.0
The Topps Company	0.2
Lacleded Prof. Prods.	0.1

Source: *New York Times*, August 7, 2001, p. C8, from Information Resources Inc.

★ 341 ★

Nuts (SIC 2068)

Nut Sales in Supermarkets

Data show supermarket sales in millions of dollars.

	($ mil.)	Share
Bags	$ 537.09	40.55%
Cans	492.58	37.19
Jars	182.50	13.78
Unshelled	112.20	8.47

Source: *Supermarket Business*, September 15, 2001, p. 36, from A.C. Nielsen.

★ 342 ★

Nuts (SIC 2068)

Snack Nuts Market in Omaha, NE

Market shares are shown in percent for supermarkets.

Herman Nut & Supply Co.	95.0%
Other	5.0

Source: *Knight-Ridder/Tribune Business News*, October 10, 2001, p. NA.

★ 343 ★

Nuts (SIC 2068)

Top Snack Nut Brands, 2000

Market shares are shown for the year ended December 31, 2000.

Planters	43.6%
Nutcracker	2.8
Sunkist	2.1
Mauna Loa	1.8
Planters Sweet Roast	1.6
Ann's House of Nuts	1.5
Fisher	1.3
Blue Diamond	1.3
Private label	22.9
Other	21.1

Source: *Snack Food and Wholesale Bakery*, June 2001, p. S54, from Information Resources Inc.

★ 344 ★

Fats and Oils (SIC 2079)

Top Cooking/Salad Oil Brands, 2001

Crisco
Wesson
Mazola
Crisco Puritan
Lou Ana
Mazola Right Blend
Wesson Best Blend
Hollywood
Private label

Brands are ranked by sales in millions of dollars for the year ending July 15, 2001.

	($ mil.)	Share
Crisco	$ 168.93	19.2%
Wesson	155.84	17.7
Mazola	122.91	13.9
Crisco Puritan	42.25	4.8
Lou Ana	40.01	4.5
Mazola Right Blend	16.05	1.8
Wesson Best Blend	11.41	1.3
Hollywood	6.78	0.8
Private label	272.72	31.0

Source: *Chemical Market Reporter*, September 3, 2001, p. 2, from Information Resources Inc.

★ 345 ★

Alcoholic Beverages (SIC 2080)

Alcoholic Beverage Sales in Alberta, Canada

Market shares are shown in percent.

Beer	51.6%
Spirits	25.9
Wine	22.5

Source: *Calgary Sun*, July 6, 2001, p. 8.

★ 346 ★

Alcoholic Beverages (SIC 2080)

Alcoholic Beverage Sales in Canada

Sales are shown in millions of dollars.

	1997-8	1998-9	1999-00
Beer	$ 6,204	$ 6,501	$ 6,723
Spirits	3,098	3,236	3,367
Wine	2,411	2,638	2,931

Source: "Wine." Retrieved November 19, 2001 from the World Wide Web: http://ffas.usda.gov.

★ 347 ★

Beverages (SIC 2080)

Best-Selling Beverages at Grocery Stores, 2002

Sales are shown in millions of dollars for the year ended January 27, 2002.

Carbonated beverages	$ 13,072.4
Milk	10,565.6
Beer/ale/alcoholic cider	7,057.4
Juice	4,334.0
Wine	3,661.2
Bottled juices	3,281.0
Coffee	2,651.0
Bottled water	2,146.5
Liquor	1,566.9

Source: *Beverage Industry*, March 2002, from 54.

★ 348 ★

Beverages (SIC 2080)

Beverage Market, 2000

Market shares are shown based on receipts.

Beer	28.1%
Soft drinks	27.9
Spirits	18.8
Fruit beverages	9.5
Wine	9.4
Bottled water	3.4
Sports drinks	1.6
RTD tea	1.4

Source: *Beverage Aisle*, June 15, 2001, p. 36.

★ 349 ★

Beverages (SIC 2080)

Beverage Market in Canada

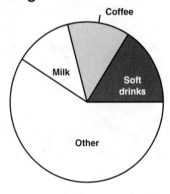

Coffee

Milk

Soft drinks

Other

Market shares are shown in percent.

Soft drinks	16.2%
Coffee	13.2
Milk	11.7
Other	58.9

Source: *Beverage World*, December 15, 2001, p. 20, from Beverage Marketing Corp.

★ 350 ★

Beverages (SIC 2080)

Beverage Market in Mexico

Market shares are shown by category.

	2000	2005
Carbonated soft drinks	21.4%	23.7%
Milk	8.7	9.4
Beer	7.2	7.5

	2000	2005
Coffee	4.0%	3.9%
Bottled water	1.8	3.1
Fruit beverages	0.9	1.3
Distilled spirits	0.1	0.1
Wine	0.0	0.1
Other	55.8	51.0

Source: *Beverage World International*, September-October 2001, p. 8, from Beverage Marketing Corp.

★ 351 ★

Beverages (SIC 2080)

Largest Beverage Firms

Largest North American based films are ranked by sales in millions of dollars.

Coca-Cola Company	$ 20,458.0
Coca-Cola Enterprises	14,750.0
Anheuser-Busch	10,103.5
Pepsi Bottling Group	7,982.0
PeisCo.	7,557.0
Seagram Co.	5,108.0
Philip Morris	4,375.0
FEMSA	4,023.0
Southern Wine & Spirits of America	3,440.0
Panamerican Beverages Inc.	2,599.4

Source: *Beverage Aisle*, August 2001, p. 42.

★ 352 ★

Beverages (SIC 2080)

Private Label Beverage Industry in Canada

Cott's has a 60% share in the U.S.

Cott's	90.0%
Other	10.0

Source: *Report on Business Magazine*, November-December 2001, p. 22.

★ 353 ★

Beer (SIC 2082)

Beer Consumption by State

Figures are in thousands of 2.25 gallon cases.

	(000)	Share
California	293,075	10.64%
Texas	246,567	8.95
Florida	173,295	6.29
New York	141,951	5.15
Pennsylvania	127,500	4.63
Illinois	125,417	4.55
Ohio	118,764	4.31
Michigan	94,013	3.41
North Carolina	78,268	2.84
Other	1,356,710	49.24

Source: *Beer Handbook*, Annual 2001, p. 1.

★ 354 ★

Beer (SIC 2082)

Beer Sales by Type

Over the last ten years consumers have increasingly gravitated to domestic light beers and a wide range of imports. Light beer claimed less than 14% of the market twenty years ago. Market shares are shown by class.

Light	45.2%
Premium	20.4
Popular	11.4
Imports	10.9
Superpremium & micro/specialty	5.4
Ice	3.7
Malt liquor	2.9

Source: *Cheers*, March 2002, p. 35, from *Adams Beer Handbook*.

★ 355 ★

Beer (SIC 2082)

Top Beer Brands, 2001

Market shares are shown in percent.

Bud Light	17.8%
Budweiser	16.8
Coors Light	8.6
Miller Lite	8.2
Busch	4.1
Natural Light	4.0
Corona Extra	3.2

Miller High Life	2.8%
Miller Genuine Draft	2.8
Busch Light	2.7
Other	29.0

Source: *Beverage World*, April 15, 2002, p. 48, from Beverage Marketing Corp.

★ 356 ★

Beer (SIC 2082)

Top Beer Makers in Texas

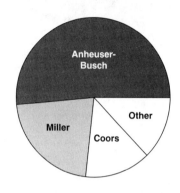

Market shares are shown in percent.

	1999	2001
Anheuser-Busch	48.5%	52.0%
Miller	24.6	21.5
Coors	14.1	13.8
Other	12.8	12.7

Source: *Knight-Ridder/Tribune Business News*, May 31, 2002, p. NA, from Beer Marketer's Insights.

★ 357 ★

Beer (SIC 2082)

Top Brewers, 2001

Market shares are shown in percent.

Anheuser-Biusch	48.6%
Miller	19.6
Coors	11.0
Pabst	4.5
Heineken	2.4
Other	13.9

Source: *USA TODAY*, April 19, 2002, p. 10B, from Beer Marketer's Insights.

★ 358 ★

Beer (SIC 2082)

Top Imported Beer Brands

Sales are shown based on 2.25 gallon cases.

	(000)	Share
Corona Extra	85,061	28.25%
Heineken	58,000	19.26
Labatt Blue	15,269	5.07
Tecate	12,026	3.99
Guinness Stout	10,690	3.55
Foster's Lager	10,196	3.39
Beck's	8,135	2.70
Amstel Light	8,000	2.66
Bass Ale	7,690	2.55
Modelo Especial	6,656	2.21
Other	79,427	26.37

Source: *Beverage Dynamics*, March 2002, p. 36, from *Adams Handbook Advance 2002*.

★ 359 ★

Malt Beverages (SIC 2082)

Top Malt Beverage Brands, 2001

Market shares are shown in percent.

Smirnoff Ice	40.8%
Mike's Hard Lemonade/Ice Tea	20.5
Zima	12.5
Tequiza	6.8
Doc's Hard Lemon	5.4
Hooper's Hooch	4.9
Rick's	2.6
Bacardi Silver	1.7
Other	4.8

Source: *Advertising Age*, June 24, 2002, p. S20, from Information Resources Inc.

★ 360 ★

Wine (SIC 2084)

California Table Wine Shipments

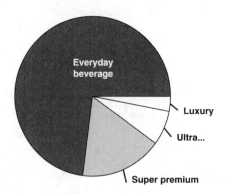

Market shares are shown in percent.

Everyday beverage	73.0%
Super premium	17.0
Ultra premium	7.0
Luxury	3.0

Source: *Beverage Dynamics*, September-Ocotber 2001, p. 30.

★ 361 ★

Wine (SIC 2084)

Largest Vintners in Silicon Valley

Companies are ranked by number of cases sold in 2000.

J. Lohr Winery	626,000
Bonny Doon Vineyard	194,000
Emilio Guglielmo Winery Inc.	150,000
Mirassou Vineyards	105,000
David Bruce Winery Inc.	60,000
Thomas Fogerty Winery and Vineyards	15,500
Byington Winery & Vineyards Inc.	15,255
Clos LaChance Wines Inc.	13,500

Source: *Silicon Valley/San Jose Business Journal*, November 2, 2001, p. 22.

★ 362 ★

Wine (SIC 2084)

Top Metro Areas for Wine Sales, 2000

Shares are shown based on sales of thousand 9-liter cases.

Los Angeles-Long Beach	5.6%
New York City	4.1
Chicago	3.4
Boston-Lawrence-Lowell-Brockton	2.8
Washington D.C.	2.3
Orange County	1.9
San Diego	1.7
Riverside-San Bernadino	1.7
Philadelphia	1.7
Other	74.8

Source: *Wine Handbook*, Annual 2001, p. 25.

★ 363 ★

Wine (SIC 2084)

U.S. Wine Sales

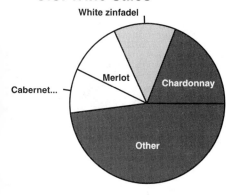

Sales are at supermarkets.

Chardonnay	19.0%
White zinfadel	13.0
Merlot	11.0
Cabernet sauvignon	9.0
Other	48.0

Source: *Wines & Vines*, May 2001, p. 81, from A.C. Nielsen and Adams.

★ 364 ★

Liquor (SIC 2085)

Largest Spirits Suppliers, 2000

Total spirits consumption rose 2.6% in 2000 and reached a consumption total of 148.1 million 9-liter cases. Premium blends continue to be very popular, enjoying high growth rates. Market shares are shown based on dollar sales.

UDV North America Diageo	13.9%
Seagram Americas	12.3
Brown-Forman Beverages	8.2
Schieffelin & Somerset Diageo	7.7
Bacardi USA	7.7
Allied Domecq Spirits USA	7.5
Jim Beam Brands	7.3
Constellation Brands	6.1
Heaven Hill Distilleries	2.8
E&J Gallo Winery	1.7
Other	24.8

Source: *Beverage Industry*, May 2001, p. 14, from *Adams Handbook*.

★ 365 ★

Liquor (SIC 2085)

Top Bourbon Brands, 2000

Market shares are shown based on sales of cases.

Jack Daniels	28.0%
Jim Beam	23.1
Evan Williams	6.9
Early Times	6.7
Wild Turkey	3.8
Ten High	3.8
Old Crow	3.6
Ancient Age	3.6
Maker's Mark	2.5
Heaven Hill	2.1
Other	15.8

Source: *Research Alert*, October 19, 2001, p. 8, from Impact Databank.

★ 366 ★

Liquor (SIC 2085)

Top Cocktail Mixers, 2001

Shares are shown based on a $107 million market for the year ended September 9, 2001.

Mrs. & Mrs. T	27.2%
Jose Cuervo	20.1
Holland House	6.3
Finest Call	5.9
Daily's	5.6
Master of Mixes	4.7
Coco Lopez	4.4
Roses Liquid	3.8
Major Peters	2.3
Sauza Liquid	1.8
Other	17.9

Source: *Beverage Industry*, November 2001, p. 11, from Information Resources Inc.

★ 367 ★

Liquor (SIC 2085)

Top Cognac Brands

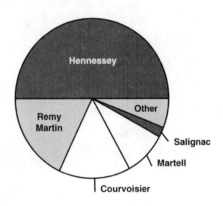

Market shares are shown in percent.

Hennessey	50.0%
Remy Martin	18.0
Courvoisier	15.0
Martell	9.0
Salignac	2.0
Other	6.0

Source: *Research Alert*, October 5, 2001, p. 7, from Impact Databank.

★ 368 ★

Liquor (SIC 2085)

Top Frozen Cocktail Brands, 2001

Shares are shown based on a $43.3 million market for the year ended September 9, 2001.

Bacardi	99.3%
Mrs. Bowens	0.4
Goya	0.1
Flaherty's	0.1

Source: *Beverage Industry*, November 2001, p. 11, from Information Resources Inc.

★ 369 ★

Liquor (SIC 2085)

Top Gin Brands, 2001

Brands are ranked by sales of nine-liter cases.

	(000)	Share
Seagram's	2,900	27.19%
Tanqueray	1,445	13.55
Gordon's	1,015	9.52
Gilbey's	660	6.19
Beefeater	650	6.09
Bombay	625	5.86
Fleischmann's	380	3.56
Barton	350	3.28
Burnett's	325	3.05
Other	2,315	21.71

Source: *Research Alert*, January 18, 2002, p. 5, from Impact Databank.

★ 370 ★

Liquor (SIC 2085)

Top Rum Brands, 2000

Americans consumed 14.8 million nine liter cases, up 7.3% over the previous year. Market shares are shown in percent.

Bacardi	50.5%
Captain Morgan	19.3
Castillo	7.5
Ronrico	3.4
Myer's	2.1
Other	17.3

Source: *Research Alert*, March 1, 2002, p. 8, from Impact Databank.

★ 371 ★

Liquor (SIC 2085)

Top Scotch Brands

Brands are ranked by sales in thousands of nine-liter cases.

	1999	2000	Share
Dewar's	1,400	1,415	17.21%
Johnnie Walker Red	700	675	8.21
Clan MacGregor	640	600	7.30
Johnnie Walker Black	505	560	6.81
Chivas Regal	495	520	6.33
Other	4,480	4,450	54.14

Source: *Research Alert*, August 17, 2001, p. 8, from Impact Databank.

★ 372 ★

Liquor (SIC 2085)

Top Vodka Brands, 2000

Brands are ranked by sales of 9-liter cases.

	Cases (000)	Share
Smirnoff	5,900	15.97%
Absolut	4,650	12.59
Popov	1,950	5.28
Gordon's	1,800	4.87
McCormick	1,595	4.32
Other	21,045	56.97

Source: *Research Alert*, November 2, 2001, p. 10, from Impact Databank.

★ 373 ★

Bottled Water (SIC 2086)

Single-Serve Water Leaders, 2001

Figures are estimated based on 515 million cases.

Nestle	58.0%
Aquafina	9.0
Dasani	8.0
Other	25.0

Source: *Beverage World*, April 2002, p. 37, from Goldman Sachs Global Equity Research.

★ 374 ★

Bottled Water (SIC 2086)

Top Bottled Water Brands, 2001

Market shares are shown in percent.

Aquafina	13.8%
Dasani	12.0
Poland Spring	11.2
Arrowhead	6.6
Aberfoyle	5.6
Crystal Geyser	5.5
Evian	3.8
Other	41.5

Source: *Wall Street Journal*, April 18, 2002, p. A8, from *Beverage Digest* and Beverage Marketing Corp.

★ 375 ★

Bottled Water (SIC 2086)

Top Bottled Water Firms

Market shares are shown in percent.

Nestle/Perrier Group	37.5%
Danone	16.2
Pepsico	12.5
Coca-Cola	8.1
CG Roxanne	6.4
Other	19.3

Source: *Atlanta Journal-Constitution*, February 24, 2002, p. G1, from *Beverage Digest*.

★ 376 ★

Energy Drinks (SIC 2086)

Energy Drink Market Shares

Market shares are shown in percent.

Red Bull	65.0%
Hansen	20.0
Other	15.0

Source: *Advertising Age*, December 31, 2001, p. 22, from Beverage Marketing Corp.

★ 377 ★

Powdered Drinks (SIC 2086)

Powdered Drink Market

Market shares are shown in percent.

Kraft Kool-Aid	85.0%
Other	15.0

Source: *Forbes*, April 15, 2002, p. 138.

★ 378 ★

Powdered Drinks (SIC 2086)

Top Powdered Fruit Drinks

Market shares are shown in percent. Kraft Foods holds 88% of the market.

Kool Aid	31.5%
Crystal Light Fruit	13.6
Country Time	11.8
Crystal Light Teas	9.4
Kool Aid Mega Mountain Twists	4.1
Kool Aid Magic Twists	3.9
Crystal Light Tropical Passions	3.9
Kool AId Island Twists	3.1
Private label	5.8
Other	12.9

Source: *Beverage Industry*, February 2002, p. 8, from Information Resources Inc.

★ 379 ★

Soft Drinks (SIC 2086)

Fountain Drink Market Shares

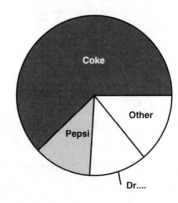

Market shares are shown in percent.

Coke	62.0%
Pepsi	12.0
Dr. Pepper/Seven Up	12.0
Other	14.0

Source: *Beverage World*, November 15, 2001, p. 52, from Beverage Marketing Corp.

★ 380 ★

Soft Drinks (SIC 2086)

Isontonic Drink Sales, 2001

Sales are shown by category for the year ended July 15, 2001.

Non-aseptic, shelf stable	$ 995.2
Apple juice, shelf stable bottled	589.6
Canned vegetable juice/cocktail	211.0
Cranberry juice/cocktail, shelf stable bottled	205.1
Mixes, shelf stable	52.5
Aseptic, shelf stable	12.1

Source: *Beverage Aisle*, October 15, 2001, p. 22, from Information Resources Inc.

★ 381 ★

Soft Drinks (SIC 2086)

Leading Carbonated Beverage Brands in Drug Stores

Market shares are shown in percent.

Coke Classic	20.9%
Pepsi	15.3

Continued on next page.

★ 381 ★ *Continued*
Soft Drinks (SIC 2086)

Leading Carbonated Beverage Brands in Drug Stores

Market shares are shown in percent.

Diet Coke	10.7%
Sprite	7.0
Diet Pepsi	6.2
Mountain Dew	5.8
Dr. Pepper	4.1
Caffeine-free Diet Coke	3.1
7Up	2.7
Private label	1.6

Source: *Drug Store News*, July 23, 2001, p. 37, from A.C. Nielsen.

★ 382 ★
Soft Drinks (SIC 2086)

Lemon Lime Beverage Market

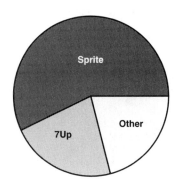

The $6.5 billion market is shown in percent.

Sprite	57.0%
7Up	22.0
Other	21.0

Source: *New York Times*, March 28, 2002, p. C6, from Beverage Marketing Corp.

★ 383 ★
Soft Drinks (SIC 2086)

New Age Beverage Market, 2001

Market shares are shown in percent for the year ended April 22, 2001.

Snapple	39.8%
SoBe	17.0

Arizona	10.3%
Lipton	6.4
Fruitopia	5.8
Nestea	4.3
Red Bull	3.9
V8 Splash	3.4
Mistic	3.2
Other	5.7

Source: *Beverage Industry*, June 2001, p. 22, from Information Resources Inc.

★ 384 ★
Soft Drinks (SIC 2086)

New Age Beverage Sales, 2001

Data show wholesale dollar sales, in millions.

	2000	2001
Retail PET waters	$ 2,674.2	$ 3,530.0
Single-serve fruit beverages	2,470.7	2,548.0
RTD tea	1,395.6	1,495.6
Sparkling water	498.0	495.0
Premium soda	290.0	305.0
Vegetable/fruit juice blends	235.0	225.0
RTD coffee	232.0	289.7
New Age Dairy	205.5	223.8
Energy drinks	130.0	275.0
Other nutrient-enhanced	10.0	10.5

Source: *Beverage Aisle*, January 15, 2002, p. 22, from Beverage Marketing Corp.

★ 385 ★
Soft Drinks (SIC 2086)

Private Label Beverage Sales

Unit shares are shown in percent. Private label's share of carbonated soft drinks fell from 5% in 1993 to 4.3% in 1998 and then rose to 4.7% in 2000.

Bottled water	32.7%
Bottled juices	20.7
Canned juices	17.3
Carbonated beverages	12.5
Ready-to-drink tea	2.2
Isotonics	2.1
Other	12.5

Source: *Progressive Grocer*, February 15, 2002, p. 14, from Private Label Manufacturers Association.

★ 386 ★
Soft Drinks (SIC 2086)

Top Diet Soda Brands

Market shares are shown in percent.

	Market Share	Diet Share
Diet Coke	8.7%	33.6%
Diet Pepsi	5.0	19.1
Caffeine Free Diet Coke	1.7	6.5
Diet Dr. Pepper	1.0	4.0
Diet Mountain Dew	0.9	3.5
Caffeine Free Diet Ppepsi	0.9	3.6
Pepsi One	0.5	2.0
Diet Sprite	0.5	2.0
Diet 7 Up	0.5	2.1
Fresca	0.3	1.0
Other	5.9	22.7

Source: *Beverage Industry*, March 15, 2002, p. 35, from Beverage Marketing Corp.

★ 387 ★
Soft Drinks (SIC 2086)

Top Instant Tea Drinks, 2001

Market shares are shown in percent.

Lipton	37.0%
Nestea	20.7
4C	6.2
Country Time	3.6
Nestea Decaf	2.9
Tetley	1.5
Nestea Free	1.1
Private label	25.3
Other	1.7

Source: *Beverage Industry*, February 2002, p. 8, from Information Resources Inc.

★ 388 ★
Soft Drinks (SIC 2086)

Top Refrigerated Tea Vendors, 2001

Shares are for the year ended April 22, 2001.

Turkey Hill Dairy Inc.	19.0%
Nestle USA Inc.	14.4
Coca Cola Co.	7.9
Milo Restaurant Servicing	7.2
Ferolito Vultaggio & Sons	5.8
Donovan Coffee Co. Inc.	4.9
General Mills	4.6
Citrus World	4.1
Wengert's Dairy Inc.	2.8
Private label	14.4
Other	14.6

Source: *Dairy Field*, August 2001, p. 50, from Information Resources Inc.

★ 389 ★
Soft Drinks (SIC 2086)

Top Soft Drink Brands, 2001

Market shares are shown in percent.

Coke Classic	19.9%
Pepsi-Cola	13.2
Diet Coke	8.8
Mountain Dew	6.9
Sprite	6.5
Dr. Pepper	6.2
Diet Pepsi	5.3
7Up	1.9
Caffeine Free Diet Coke	1.7
Barq's root beer	1.1
Other	28.5

Source: *Atlanta Journal-Constitution*, March 1, 2002, p. F1, from Beverage Digest/Maxwell.

★ 390 ★
Soft Drinks (SIC 2086)

Top Soft Drink Flavors, 2000

Distribution is shown in percent.

Cola	60.5%
Lemon lime	10.5
Pepper-type	10.1
Citrus	10.1
Other	10.4

Source: *Atlanta Journal-Constitution*, November 29, 2001, p. G1, from *Beverage Digest*.

★ 391 ★
Soft Drinks (SIC 2086)

Top Soft Drink Makers, 2001

| Coca-Cola Co. |
| Pepsi-Cola Co. |
| Dr. Pepper/Seven Up |
| Cott Corp. |
| Private label/other |
| National Beverage |
| Big Red |
| Seagram |
| Red Bull |
| Monarch |

Market shares are shown in percent.

Coca-Cola Co.	43.7%
Pepsi-Cola Co.	31.6
Dr. Pepper/Seven Up (Cadbury)	15.6
Cott Corp.	3.8
Private label/other	2.2
National Beverage	2.2
Big Red	0.4
Seagram	0.3
Red Bull	0.1
Monarch	0.1

Source: *PR Newswire*, March 4, 2002, from Beverage Digest/Maxwell.

★ 392 ★
Soft Drinks (SIC 2086)

Top Soft Drink Makers in Drug Stores

Corporate shares are shown in percent.

Coke	43.0%
Pepsi	35.6
Dr. Pepper/Seven Up Corp.	18.3
Private label	1.9
Other	1.3

Source: *Beverage Industry*, March 2002, p. 3, from Information Resources Inc. and A.C. Nielsen.

★ 393 ★
Soft Drinks (SIC 2086)

Top Soft Drink Makers in Mass Merchandisers

Corporate shares are shown in percent.

Pepsi	43.2%
Coke	37.1
Dr. Pepper/Seven Up Corp.	15.7
Private label	1.9

Source: *Beverage Industry*, March 2002, p. 3, from Information Resources Inc. and A.C. Nielsen.

★ 394 ★
Soft Drinks (SIC 2086)

Top Soft Drink Makers in Mexico

Market shares are shown in percent.

Coke	70.0%
Pepsi	16.5
Other	13.5

Source: *Business Mexico*, February 2002, p. 51, from *Beverage Digest*.

★ 395 ★
Sports Drinks (SIC 2086)

Sports Drink Market

Market shares are shown in percent.

Gatorade	78.0%
Powerade	15.0
All Sport	4.0
Other	3.0

Source: *Crain's Chicago Business*, June 25, 2001, p. 3.

★ 396 ★
Seafood (SIC 2091)
Canned Salmon Market

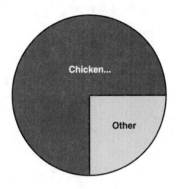

Market shares are shown in percent.

Chicken of the Sea 75.0%
Other 25.0

Source: "Industry Strives for Continued Innovation."
Retrieved May 16, 2002 from the World Wide Web: http://
www.chickenofthesea.com.

★ 397 ★
Seafood (SIC 2091)
Canned Seafood Sales

Data show supermarket sales in millions of dollars.

	($ mil.)	Share
Tuna	$ 1,093.00	70.33%
Salmon	152.51	9.81
Sardines	75.35	4.85
Oysters	48.71	3.13
Clams	43.15	2.78
Crab	36.80	2.37
Shrimp	30.17	1.94
Anchovies	13.81	0.89
Other	60.60	3.90

Source: *Supermarket Business*, September 15, 2001, p. 36,
from A.C. Nielsen.

★ 398 ★
Seafood (SIC 2091)
Salmon Import Shares

Market shares are shown in percent.

Chile 48.0%
Canada 37.0
Norway 6.3
U.K. 5.1
Faroe Islands 2.0
Other 1.6

Source: *Seafood Business*, June 2001, p. 1, from National
Marine Fisheries Service.

★ 399 ★
Seafood (SIC 2092)
Top Frozen Fish Brands, 2001

*Brands are ranked by sales in millions of dollars for
the year ended June 17, 2001.*

	($ mil.)	Share
Gorton's	$ 167.7	14.55%
Van de Kamps	113.3	9.83
Mrs. Pauls	56.6	4.91
Seapack	48.7	4.22
Singleton	39.4	3.42
Contessa	32.4	2.81
Mrs. Pauls Select Cuts . . .	30.1	2.61
Aqua Star	22.0	1.91
Van de Kamps Crispy & Healthy .	19.8	1.72
Private label	275.7	23.92
Other	347.0	30.10

Source: *Food Institute Report*, September 17, 2001, p. 22,
from Information Resources Inc.

★ 400 ★
Seafood (SIC 2092)
Top Frozen Seafood Suppliers, 2001

*Firms are ranked by sales in millions of dollars for
the year ended September 9, 2001.*

Gorton Corp. 15.7%
Pet Inc. 11.0
Mrs. Paul's Kitchens Inc. 7.7
Rich-SeaPak Corp. 4.0
Singleton Seafood Corp. 3.5
Z.B. Industries 2.7
Booth Products Corp. 2.5

Continued on next page.

★ 400 ★ *Continued*

Seafood (SIC 2092)

Top Frozen Seafood Suppliers, 2001

Firms are ranked by sales in millions of dollars for the year ended September 9, 2001.

Aqua Star Inc.	2.1%
Private label	25.1
Other	25.7

Source: *Frozen Food Age*, November 2001, p. 26, from Information Resources Inc.

★ 401 ★

Seafood (SIC 2092)

Top Seafood Brands

Brands are ranked by sales in millions of dollars for the 12 weeks ended December 20, 2001.

Louis Kemp Crab Delight	$ 7.4
Vita	5.9
Lascco	3.0
Phillips	2.5
Private label	9.1

Source: *Frozen Food Age*, April 2002, p. 14, from Information Resources Inc.

★ 402 ★

Coffee (SIC 2095)

Top Ground Coffee Brands, 2001

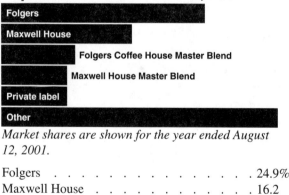

Market shares are shown for the year ended August 12, 2001.

Folgers	24.9%
Maxwell House	16.2
Folgers Coffee House Master Blend	8.6
Maxwell House Master Blend	8.4
Private label	7.6
Other	34.3

Source: *Beverage Industry*, October 2001, p. 14, from Information Resources Inc.

★ 403 ★

Coffee (SIC 2095)

Top Ground Coffee Makers, 2001

Market shares are shown for the year ended December 2, 2001. Figures exclude Wal-Mart and the decaf segment.

Procter & Gamble	33.2%
Kraft Foods Inc.	29.2
Starbucks Coffee Co.	6.0
Sara Lee Corp.	5.4
Private label	8.2
Other	18.0

Source: *Grocery Headquarters*, April 2002, p. 14, from Information Resources Inc.

★ 404 ★

Coffee (SIC 2095)

Top Ground Decaffeinated Coffee Brands, 2001

Market shares are shown for the year ended August 12, 2001.

Folgers	31.2%
Maxwell House	17.4
Starbucks	5.2
Folgers Coffee Singles	4.1
Private label	17.8
Other	24.3

Source: *Beverage Industry*, October 2001, p. 14, from Information Resources Inc.

★ 405 ★

Coffee (SIC 2095)

Top Instant Coffee Brands, 2001

Market shares are shown for the year ended August 12, 2001.

Folgers	20.9%
General Foods International Coffee	19.1
Tasters Choice Original Blend	14.3
Maxwell House	13.4
Private label	6.2
Other	26.1

Source: *Beverage Industry*, October 2001, p. 14, from Information Resources Inc.

★ 406 ★

Coffee (SIC 2095)

Top Whole Coffee Brands, 2001

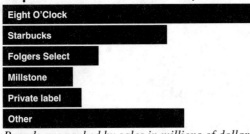

Brands are ranked by sales in millions of dollars for the year ended August 12, 2001.

Eight O'Clock 31.9%
Starbucks 19.1
Folgers Select 11.0
Millstone 8.4
Private label 9.1
Other 20.5

Source: *Beverage Industry*, October 2001, p. 14, from Information Resources Inc.

★ 407 ★

Coffee Drinks (SIC 2095)

Best-Selling Coffee Drinks

Brands are ranked by sales in millions of dollars for the year ended February 24, 2002. Sales are for supermarkets, drug stores and mass merchandisers, but not Wal-Mart.

Frappuccino . . . . $ 96,578.8
Arizona 2,167.2
Planet Java 1,316.0
Blue Luna 810.9
Havana 614.5
Kogee 486.0
Coffee House 403.2
Main St. Cafe 386.0

Source: *Tea & Coffee Trade Journal*, May 20, 2002, p. 15, from Information Resources Inc.

★ 408 ★

Coffee Drinks (SIC 2095)

Bottled Coffee Drink Market

Market shares are shown in percent.

Starbucks 90.0%
Other 10.0

Source: *Wall Street Journal*, February 2, 2001, p. B4.

★ 409 ★

Snacks (SIC 2096)

Largest Snack/Bakery Goods Makers

Firms are ranked by snack and bakery sales in millions of dollars.

Frito-Lay Inc. . . . . $ 7,865
Kraft Foods Inc. 4,300
Sara Lee Bakery Group 3,400
George Weston Bakeries Inc. 3,200
General Mills Inc. 3,100
Keebler Co. 2,700
Flowers Foods 1,619
Pepperidge Farm Inc. 1,000
McKee Foods Corp. 930

Source: *Snack Food & Wholesale Bakery*, December 2001, p. 20.

★ 410 ★

Snacks (SIC 2096)

Leading Snack Mixes

Market shares are shown in percent.

Frito Lay 17.5%
General Mills Chex Mix 9.2
Sunshine Cheez-It Mix 2.7
Gardetto's Snack-ens 2.0
Other 68.6

Source: *Snack Food & Wholesale Bakery*, February 2001, p. 18, from Information Resources Inc.

★ 411 ★
Snacks (SIC 2096)

Private Label Snack Sales

Figures are in millions of dollars.

	($ mil.)	Share
Snack nuts	$ 287.9	35.29%
Potato chips	149.1	18.28
Tortilla/tostada chips	83.6	10.25
Popcorn, microwave	74.7	9.16
Snack bars/granola bars	70.9	8.69
Pretzels	59.7	7.32
Cheese snacks	41.6	5.10
Dry fruit snacks	34.3	4.20
Corn snacks (not tortilla)	14.0	1.72

Source: *Private Label Buyer*, January 2002, p. 22, from Information Resources Inc.

★ 412 ★
Snacks (SIC 2096)

Snack Food Sales in Convenience Stores

Data are for 2000.

Salty/nuts/rice	33.0%
Candy/gum/mint	17.0
Cookies	16.0
Crackers	13.0
Bakery snacks	8.0
Snack/granola/energy	5.0
Snack kits	3.0
Toaster pastry	2.0
Other	3.0

Source: *National Petroleum News*, January 2002, p. 15, from Information Resources Inc. and Snack World 2000.

★ 413 ★
Snacks (SIC 2096)

Snacks and Sweets Sales in Canada

Sales are shown in millions of dollars for the year ended October 10, 2000.

Snack foods	$ 593
Cookies & grahams	498
Confectionery	394
Baked desserts, prepackaged frozen	351
Snack crackers	268
Microwave popcorn	57
Frozen desserts, prepackaged	57

Source: *Food in Canada*, November 2001, p. NA, from A. C. Nielsen MarketTrack.

★ 414 ★
Snacks (SIC 2096)

Top Corn Chip Brands, 2001

Market shares are shown in percent.

Frito Lay Fritos	42.0%
Fritos Scoops	24.9
Doritos 3D's	12.1
Bugles	7.3
Fritos Chilis and Scoops	3.1
Fritos Sloppy Joe and Scoops	2.7
Sabrositas	1.7
Other	6.2

Source: *Snack Food & Wholesale Bakery*, June 2001, p. S1, from Information Resources Inc.

★ 415 ★
Snacks (SIC 2096)

Top Frozen Pretzel Brands, 2001

Market shares are shown in percent.

Super Pretzel	67.2%
Super Pretzel Softstix	13.1
Private label	9.5

Source: *Snack Food & Wholesale Bakery*, June 2001, p. S1, from Information Resources Inc.

★ 416 ★

Snacks (SIC 2096)

Top Potato Chip Brands

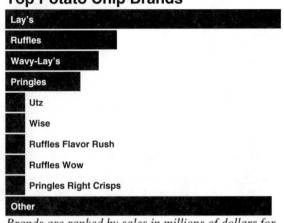

Brands are ranked by sales in millions of dollars for the year ended December 2, 2001.

	($ mil.)	Share
Lay's	$ 835.6	29.95%
Ruffles	337.9	12.11
Wavy-Lay's	283.9	10.18
Pringles	223.8	8.02
Utz	67.8	2.43
Wise	60.1	2.15
Ruffles Flavor Rush	59.0	2.11
Ruffles Wow	50.2	1.80
Pringles Right Crisps	49.7	1.78
Other	822.0	29.46

Source: *MMR*, January 28, 2002, p. 21, from Information Resources Inc.

★ 417 ★

Snacks (SIC 2096)

Top Potato Chip Brands in Drug Stores

Brands are ranked by sales in millions of dollars.

	($ mil.)	Share
Lays	$ 17.4	41.04%
Ruffles	5.2	12.26
Herrs	2.9	6.84
Ruffles Flavor Rush	2.7	6.37
Utz	2.4	5.66
Wavy Lays	1.9	4.48
Jay's	1.0	2.36
Cape Cod	0.8	1.89
Ruffles Wow	0.7	1.65

	($ mil.)	Share
Lays Wow	$ 0.7	1.65%
Other	6.7	15.80

Source: *Drug Store News*, May 21, 2001, p. 82, from Information Resources Inc.

★ 418 ★

Snacks (SIC 2096)

Top Potato Chip Makers

Firms are ranked by sales in millions of dollars for the year ended April 22, 2001.

Frito-Lay	$ 1,700.0
Wise Foods	83.5
Utz Potato Chip Co. Inc.	75.6
Jays Foods Inc.	52.6
Herr Foods	45.3
Cape Cod Potato Chips	39.8
Old Dutch Foods Inc.	39.1
Golden Flake Snack Foods	32.6
Mike Sells Potato Chip Co.	22.2

Source: *Food Institute Report*, August 13, 2001, p. 4, from Information Resources Inc.

★ 419 ★

Snacks (SIC 2096)

Top Pretzel Brands, 2001

Market shares are shown in percent.

Rold Gold	30.0%
Snyders of Hanover	21.1
Snyders of Hanover Olde Tyme	4.0
Combos	3.1
Bachman	2.8
Herrs	2.2
Utz	2.1
Utz Specials	1.5
Jays	1.4
Other	31.8

Source: *Snack Food & Wholesale Bakery*, June 2001, p. S1, from Information Resources Inc.

★ 420 ★

Snacks (SIC 2096)

Top Refrigerated Appetizer/Snack Roll Brands, 2001

Market shares are shown in percent.

AFC	29.0%
Sushi House	14.4
Kikka	11.8
Holly Farms	8.0
Ace Inc.	6.5
Fuji Food Products	5.0
Atheons	5.0
Nobrand	2.0
Other	18.3

Source: *Snack Food & Wholesale Bakery*, June 2001, p. S1, from Information Resources Inc.

★ 421 ★

Snacks (SIC 2096)

Top Salty Snack Brands in Drug Stores

Brands are ranked by sales in millions of dollars.

	($ mil.)	Share
Pringles	$ 29.0	16.55%
General Mills Chex Mix	9.6	5.48
Pringles Right Crisps	5.8	3.31
Pringles Cheezums	3.0	1.71
Funyuns	2.2	1.26
Sunshine Chez It	2.1	1.20
Gardetto's Snak Ens	2.1	1.20
Sunchips	1.9	1.08
Baken Ets	1.3	0.74
Other	118.2	67.47

Source: *Drug Store News*, May 21, 2001, p. 82, from Information Resources Inc.

★ 422 ★

Snacks (SIC 2096)

Top Snacks Processors

Firms are ranked by sales in millions of dollars.

Anchor Food Products	$ 503.0
Kraft Foods Ijnc.	368.0
SCIS Food Services	350.0
McCain Food Services	300.0
ConAgra Inc.	300.0

Reser's Fine Foods	$ 285.0
Murry's Inc.	200.0
Pillsbury Co.	188.2
Rich-SeaPak Corp.	170.0
J&J Snack Foods Corp.	165.0

Source: *Refrigerated & Frozen Foods*, February 2001, p. 32.

★ 423 ★

Snacks (SIC 2096)

Top Tortilla Chip Brands, 2001

Market shares are shown in percent.

Doritos	38.8%
Tostitos	34.2
Santitas	3.4
Baked Tostitos	2.8
Mission	2.7
Tostitos Wow	1.5
Doritos Wow	1.2
Padrinos	0.9
Old Dutch	0.8
Other	13.7

Source: *Snack Food & Wholesale Bakery*, June 2001, p. S1, from Information Resources Inc.

★ 424 ★

Snacks (SIC 2096)

U.S. Snacking Industry

Figures are in billions of dollars.

	($ bil.)	Share
Salty snacks	$ 13.6	27.36%
Candy	12.8	25.75
Cookies/crackers	10.1	20.32
Bakery snacks	4.6	9.26
Breakfast snacks	3.2	6.44
Nuts	2.7	5.43
Gum	1.9	3.82
Other	0.8	1.61

Source: *Candy Industry*, November 2001, p. 35.

★ 425 ★

Pasta (SIC 2098)

Leading Frozen Pasta/Noodle Brands, 2001

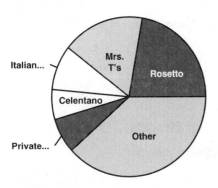

Brands are ranked by sales for the year ended February 25, 2001. Figures are for supermarkets $2 million and over.

	($ mil.)	Share
Rosetto	$ 53.2	22.05%
Mrs. T's	40.9	16.95
Italian Village	21.9	9.08
Celentano	14.7	6.09
Private label	17.8	7.38
Other	92.8	38.46

Source: *Refrigerated & Frozen Foods*, June 2001, p. 40, from Information Resources Inc. InfoScan.

★ 426 ★

Pasta (SIC 2098)

Leading Refrigerated Pasta Brands, 2001

Nestle
Kraft
Private label
Other

Brands are ranked by sales for the year ended February 25, 2001. Figures are for supermarkets $2 million and over.

	($ mil.)	Share
Nestle	$ 77.1	52.59%
Kraft	35.6	24.28
Private label	18.7	12.76
Other	15.2	10.37

Source: *Refrigerated & Frozen Foods*, June 2001, p. 40, from Information Resources Inc. InfoScan.

★ 427 ★

Pasta (SIC 2098)

Microwavable Pasta Market, 2002

Sales are shown for the year ended February 24, 2002. The market could be as high as $2.2 billion.

Easy Mac	$ 58.2
Ragu Express	20.7

Source: *Wall Street Journal*, April 8, 2002, p. A21, from Information Resources Inc.

★ 428 ★

Pasta (SIC 2098)

Pasta Sales in Supermarkets

Data show supermarket sales in millions of dollars.

Macaroni	$ 568.69
Spaghetti	456.20
Noodles & dumplings	205.70
Oriental noodles	35.23

Source: *Supermarket Business*, September 15, 2001, p. 36, from A.C. Nielsen.

★ 429 ★

Pasta (SIC 2098)

Top Dry Pasta Makers, 2001

Market shares are shown in percent for North America.

New World Pasta	24.0%
Borden Inc.	17.0
Barilla	11.0
Bestfoods Inc.	8.0
Private label	20.0
Other	20.0

Source: *Milling & Baking News*, August 14, 2001, p. NA, from Information Resources Inc.

★ 430 ★
Pasta (SIC 2098)

U.S. Dry Pasta Market Segments

Five billion pounds were consumed in 2000.

Ingredients	43.0%
Private and brand label retail	37.0
Government bids	10.0
Foodservice	10.0

Source: *Rural Cooperatives*, July 2001, p. 4.

★ 431 ★
Chilled Foods (SIC 2099)

Leading Breakfast Entrees, 2001

Shares are shown based on supermarket sales for the year ended June 17, 2001.

Jimmy Dean	30.0%
Rudys Farm	16.6
Bob Evans	8.8
Tennessee Pride	8.2
Mama Marys	7.7
Owens	7.3
Owens Border	3.3
Webber Farms	2.3
Bob Evans Farms Sandwiches	2.3
Private label	1.7
Other	11.8

Source: *National Provisioner*, August 2001, p. 56, from Information Resources Inc.

★ 432 ★
Chilled Foods (SIC 2099)

Leading Refrigerated Breakfast Entrees, 2001

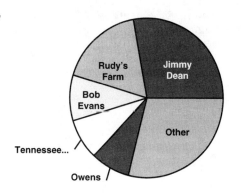

Brands are ranked by sales for the year ended February 25, 2001. Figures are for supermarkets $2 million and over.

Jimmy Dean	$ 26.8
Rudy's Farm	16.5
Bob Evans	9.0
Tennessee Pride	8.0
Owens	7.9
Other	28.2

Source: *Refrigerated & Frozen Foods*, June 2001, p. 40, from Information Resources Inc. InfoScan.

★ 433 ★
Chilled Foods (SIC 2099)

Leading Refrigerated Dinners/ Entrees, 2001

Shares are shown based on supermarket sales for the year ended June 17, 2001.

Lloyds	18.0%
Louis Rich Carving Board	13.5
Tyson	8.7
Perdue Short Cuts	6.3
Perdue Done It	5.3
Hormel	5.2
On Cor Redi Serve	2.0
El Monterey	2.0
Ed & Joan Deluca	1.1
Private label	25.4
Other	12.5

Source: *National Provisioner*, August 2001, p. 56, from Information Resources Inc.

★ 434 ★

Chilled Foods (SIC 2099)

Leading Refrigerated Entrée Makers, 2001

Vendors are ranked by sales for the year ended February 25, 2001. Figures are for supermarkets $2 million and over.

	($ mil.)	Share
Intl. Fish & Meat/Lloyd's	$ 88.3	17.91%
Kraft/Louis Rich	66.1	13.41
Perdue Farms	60.6	12.29
Tyson Foods	46.1	9.35
Hormel Foods	19.6	3.98
On-Cor	10.4	2.11
Ruiz Food Products	9.7	1.97
DeLuca's	6.0	1.22
Don Miguel	4.2	0.85
Private label	126.4	25.64
Other	55.6	11.28

Source: *Refrigerated & Frozen Foods*, June 2001, p. 40, from Information Resources Inc. InfoScan.

★ 435 ★

Chilled Foods (SIC 2099)

Leading Refrigerated Meal/Lunch Combos, 2001

Vendors are ranked by sales for the year ended February 25, 2001. Figures are for supermarkets $2 million and over.

	($ mil.)	Share
Kraft/Oscar Mayer	$ 621.8	89.39%
ASE Consumer Products	61.9	8.90
Private label	11.4	1.64
Other	0.5	0.07

Source: *Refrigerated & Frozen Foods*, June 2001, p. 40, from Information Resources Inc. InfoScan.

★ 436 ★

Chilled Foods (SIC 2099)

Leading Refrigerated Pizza/Pizza Kit Brands, 2001

Shares are for the year ended February 25, 2001. Figures are for supermarkets $2 million and over.

	($ mil.)	Share
Mama Rosa	$ 73.8	61.86%
Stephano's	4.2	3.52
Pizzeria Uno	3.7	3.10
Reno's	3.3	2.77
Private label	15.0	12.57
Other	19.3	16.18

Source: *Refrigerated & Frozen Foods*, June 2001, p. 40, from Information Resources Inc. InfoScan.

★ 437 ★

Chilled Foods (SIC 2099)

Leading Refrigerated Pizza/Pizza Kit Leaders, 2001

Shares are for the year ended February 25, 2001. Figures are for supermarkets $2 million and over.

Gilardi Foods	64.9%
Stephano's	3.5
Uno Restaurants	3.1
I&K/SCIS Food Services	2.8
Nardone Bros. Baking	2.6
Piazza Enterprises	2.2
Reser's	1.5
Private label	12.6
Other	6.8

Source: *Refrigerated & Frozen Foods*, June 2001, p. 40, from Information Resources Inc. InfoScan.

★ 438 ★

Chilled Foods (SIC 2099)

Leading Refrigerated Potato Brands, 2001

Brands are for the year ended April 7, 2001. Figures are for supermarkets $2 million and over.

	($ mil.)	Share
Northern Star	$ 34.6	54.92%
Bob Evans	8.4	13.33
Yoder's	4.1	6.51
Reser's	3.6	5.71
Private label	6.2	9.84
Other	6.1	9.68

Source: *Refrigerated & Frozen Foods*, June 2001, p. 40, from A.C. Nielsen.

★ 439 ★

Desserts (SIC 2099)

Our Favorite Desserts

Figures show what people have for dessert, based on a survey.

	1990	2000
Fruit	24.1%	23.3%
Frozen desserts	17.1	21.0
Cake	12.8	11.5
Dessert salads	12.1	1.7
Pie	11.1	8.8
Gelatin	3.6	2.7
Pudding	3.3	3.9

Source: *DSN Retailing Today*, May 21, 2001, p. 8, from NPD Group's National Eating Trends Service.

★ 440 ★

Salad (SIC 2099)

Leading Fresh Cut Salad Processors, 2001

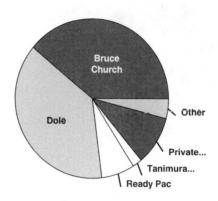

Shares are for the year ended February 25, 2001. Figures are for supermarkets $2 million and over.

Bruce Church	39.1%
Dole	38.1
Ready Pac	7.0
Tanimura & Antle	2.2
Private label	10.0
Other	3.6

Source: *Refrigerated & Frozen Foods*, June 2001, p. 40, from Information Resources Inc. InfoScan.

★ 441 ★

Salad (SIC 2099)

Top Salad Brands, 2001

Market shares are shown for the year ended December 2, 2001. Data exclude Wal-Mart.

Fresh Express	36.8%
Dole	30.9
Ready Pac	8.3
Dole Greener Selection	5.9
Earthbound Farm	3.3
Salad Time	2.3
Noreast	0.4
Private label	10.3
Other	1.8

Source: *Grocery Headquarters*, April 2002, p. 14, from Information Resources Inc.

★ 442 ★

Sports Nutrition (SIC 2099)

Sports Nutrition Market, 1999

Market shares are shown in percent.

Drinks 50.6%
Bars 18.1
Other 31.3

Source: Nutraceuticals World, November 2001, p. 74, from Euromonitor.

★ 443 ★

Sports Nutrition (SIC 2099)

Sports Nutrition Market in Canada, 1999

Market shares are shown in percent.

Drinks 95.5%
Bars 1.5
Other 3.0

Source: Nutraceuticals World, November 2001, p. 74, from Euromonitor.

★ 444 ★

Sports Nutrition (SIC 2099)

Sports Nutrition Market in Mexico, 1999

Market shares are shown in percent.

Drinks 95.1%
Bars 1.4
Other 3.5

Source: Nutraceuticals World, November 2001, p. 74, from Euromonitor.

★ 445 ★

Tea (SIC 2099)

U.S. Tea Industry, 2000

The retail tea market was valued at $4.2 billion. RTD, specialty and herbal have all shown double digit growth rates.

RTD 61.5%
Regular tea 13.0
Specialty 10.8
Herbal 7.6
Instant/mix 7.1

Source: Gourmet Retailer, November 2001, p. 44, from Packaged Facts.

★ 446 ★

Tortillas (SIC 2099)

Top Tortilla/Taco Kit Brands, 2001

Shares are shown based on sales for the year ended September 9, 2001.

Mission 25.0%
Old El Paso 15.3
Guerrero 13.7
Taco Bell 4.2
Tia Rosa 4.0
Ortega 3.7
Dianes 2.8
Albuquerque 2.0
Mission Estilo Caesero 1.6
Private label 5.7
Other 22.0

Source: Snack Food & Wholesale Bakery, November 2001, p. 13, from Information Resources Inc.

SIC 21 - Tobacco Products

★ 447 ★
Tobacco (SIC 2100)

Sales of Cigarettes and Tobacco Products, 2001

Sales are at food stores for the year ended November 4, 2001.

	($ mil.)	Share
Cigarettes	$ 6,067.3	85.30%
Tobacco products	522.8	7.35
Chewing tobacco and snuff	355.3	5.00
Cigars	109.4	1.54
Pipe tobacco	24.2	0.34
Roll your own tobacco	21.2	0.30
Smoking accessories (pipes.etc...) .	12.7	0.18

Source: *Grocery Headquarters*, February 2002, p. 45, from Information Resources Inc.

★ 448 ★
Cigarettes (SIC 2111)

Leading Cigarette Producers, 2000

Total unit sales hit 416.3 billion in 2000. Market shares are shown in percent.

Philip Morris	50.4%
R.J. Reynolds	23.6
Brown & Williamson	11.5
Lorillard	8.8
Liggett	1.6
Other	4.1

Source: *Grocery Headquarters*, June 2001, p. 81, from Information Resources Inc.

★ 449 ★
Cigarettes (SIC 2111)

Top Cigarette Brands, 2001

Market shares are shown in percent.

Marlboro	38.8%
Newport	7.8
Doral	5.8
Camel	5.6
Basic	5.0
Winston	4.8
GPC	3.2
Kool	2.8
Salem	2.6
Virginia Slims	2.4
Other	78.9

Source: *Advertising Age*, June 24, 2002, p. S20, from Information Resources Inc.

SIC 22 - Textile Mill Products

★ 450 ★

Fabrics (SIC 2200)

Largest Fabric Exporters to the U.S.

Data do not include apparel.

China	13.7%
Canada	11.2
Mexico	8.7
India	6.6
Pakistan	6.4
Korean Republic	5.6
Italy	5.1
Taiwan	4.8
Thailand	4.4

Source: *InFurniture*, July 2001, p. 21, from U.S. Department of Commerce.

★ 451 ★

Fabrics (SIC 2211)

Coated Fabric Industry

Demand is shown in millions of square yards.

	2000	2005	Share
Motor vehicles & other transport	$ 192	$ 239	37.94%
Furniture	90	100	15.87
Industrial	70	80	12.70
Awnings, tents & other	67	77	12.22
Protective clothing	54	64	10.16
Wallcoverings	42	41	6.51
Book coverings	30	29	4.60

Source: *Research Studies - Freedonia Group*, September 21, 2001, p. 3, from Freedonia Group.

★ 452 ★

Upholstery (SIC 2211)

Top Upholstery Companies

Firms are ranked by annual sales in millions of dollars.

La-Z-Boy Inc.	$ 1,050
Furniture Brands International	960
Klaussner Furniture Industries	840
The Global Group	640
LifeStyle Furnishings Ltd.	480
The Rowe Companies	348
Ashley Furniture Industries Inc.	304
Flexsteel Industries	287
Ethan Allen Interiors	240
The Falcon Companies	180

Source: *Upholstery Design & Management*, May 2001, p. 11.

★ 453 ★

Hosiery (SIC 2250)

Top Hosiery Brands

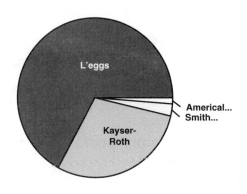

Brands are ranked by sales in millions of dollars.

	($ mil.)	Share
L'eggs	$ 292.7	54.5%
Kayser-Roth	127.5	23.8
Smith Hosiery	10.6	2.0
Americal Corp.	6.6	1.2

Source: *Progressive Grocer*, February 1, 2002, p. 44, from Information Resources Inc.

★ 454 ★

Carpets (SIC 2273)

Carpet Fiber Market

Total production is 3.5 million pounds.

Nylon	55.0%
Polypropylene	37.0
Polyester	8.0

Source: *C&EN*, July 23, 2001, p. 17, from Fiber Economics Bureau.

★ 455 ★

Carpets (SIC 2273)

Top Carpet Makers

Firms are ranked by 2000 sales in millions of dollars. Total specialized carpet sales hit $3.08 billion.

	($ mil.)	Share
Shaw	$ 690	22.71%
Interface	399	13.13
Mohawk	395	13.00
C&A	308	10.14

	($ mil.)	Share
Lees	$ 296	9.74%
Milliken	175	5.76
Beaulieu	171	5.63
J&J Industries	137	4.51
Mannington Carpet	131	4.31
Masland	74	2.44
Other	262	8.62

Source: *Floor Focus*, June 2001, p. 1.

★ 456 ★

Rugs (SIC 2273)

Top Area Rug Makers

Companies are ranked by sales in millions of dollars.

Mohawk Home	$ 245
Maples Industries	132
Beaulieu Homes	125
Shaw Rugs	115
Oriental Weavers	74

Source: *Home Textiles Today*, January 7, 2002, p. 34.

SIC 23 - Apparel and Other Textile Products

★ 457 ★

Apparel (SIC 2300)

Activewear Market by Segment, 2001

Market shares are shown in percent.

Tees	37.5%
Polo/golf/rugby	12.6
Swimwear	8.7
Tanks/sleeveless	7.5
Sweatshirts	5.0
Shorts	3.8
Outerwear	3.8
Pants/slacks	2.7
Socks	2.6
Sweatpants	2.3
Other	13.5

Source: *Sporting Goods Business*, May 2002, p. 18, from NPD Fashionworld.

★ 458 ★

Apparel (SIC 2300)

Apparel Sales by Category

Sales are shown in millions of dollars.

	1999	2000	Share
Women	$ 94.6	$ 96.6	52.99%
Men	63.5	63.3	34.72
Children	20.9	22.4	12.29

Source: *Children's Business*, May 2001, p. 24, from NPD Group.

★ 459 ★

Apparel (SIC 2300)

Best-Selling Sports Apparel Categories, 2000

Sales are shown in millions of dollars.

	($ mil.)	Share
Camping	$ 1,964.1	17.74%
Golf	1,835.3	16.58
Swimming	1,469.6	13.27
Hunting	1,284.9	11.60
Fishing	882.5	7.97
Bicycling	742.0	6.70
Aerobics	725.3	6.55
Running/jogging	652.3	5.89
Bowling	600.4	5.42
Other	915.9	8.27

Source: *Research Alert*, July 6, 2001, p. 5, from National Sporting Goods Association.

★ 460 ★

Apparel (SIC 2300)

Best-Selling Sports Logos for Apparel

Dallas Cowboys
Los Angeles Lakers
New York Yankees
San Francisco 49ers
Chicago Bulls

Figures are based on a survey.

Dallas Cowboys	15.0%
Los Angeles Lakers	9.3
New York Yankees	8.5
San Francisco 49ers	7.6
Chicago Bulls	6.8

Source: *USA TODAY*, November 23, 2001, p. C1, from ESPN Sports Poll.

★ 461 ★
Apparel (SIC 2300)

Jeans Sales by Color

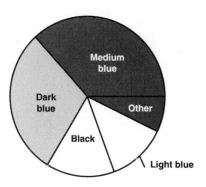

Sales are shown by segment.

Medium blue 36.0%
Dark blue 29.0
Black 14.0
Light blue 12.0
Other 7.0

Source: *WWD*, May 9, 2002, p. 6B.

★ 462 ★
Apparel (SIC 2300)

Jeans Sales by Price Range

Sales are shown by segment.

	2000	2001
$25-$49.99	46.0%	43.7%
Jeans below $25	42.7	45.2
$50 and over	11.3	11.1

Source: *WWD*, May 9, 2002, p. 6B.

★ 463 ★
Apparel (SIC 2300)

Popular Brands of Golf Apparel

Figures are based on a survey.

Cutter & Buck 34.0%
Ashworth 22.0
Tommy Bahama 19.0

Source: *Golf World Business*, January 2002, p. 17.

★ 464 ★
Apparel (SIC 2300)

Preferred Brands of Children's Apparel

The table shows the brands shoppers would select when shopping at a discount store or superstore. Figures show the results of a survey and are not market shares.

OshKosh 10.0%
Levi's 10.0
Hanes 9.0

Source: *DSN Retailing Today*, October 22, 2001, p. 24, from Lee J. Shapiro.

★ 465 ★
Apparel (SIC 2300)

Swimwear Sales by Segment

Swimwear was a $2.9 billion market for the year ended August 2001.

	Sales ($000)	Share
Women's	$ 1,827,657	61.67%
Men's	515,176	17.38
Girl's	371,241	12.53
Boy's	131,174	4.43
Infant/toddler	118,381	3.99

Source: "NPDFashionworld." Retrieved April 3, 2002 from the World Wide Web: http://www.npd.com, from NPD.

★ 466 ★
Apparel (SIC 2300)

Top Apparel Firms

Firms are ranked by 2000 sales in billions of dollars.

Gap Inc. . . . . $ 13.6
The Limited 10.1
Nike 8.9
Sara Lee Branded Apparel 7.5
VF Corp. 5.7
Levi Strauss & Co. 4.6
Jones Apparel Group inc. 4.1
Spiegel Inc. 3.7
Liz Claiborne 3.1
Reebok International 2.8

Source: *Bobbin*, June 2001, p. 62.

★ 467 ★

Apparel (SIC 2300)

Top Underwear Brands in Canada

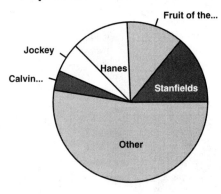

Market shares are shown in percent.

Stanfields	13.5%
Fruit of the Loom	12.1
Hanes	11.7
Jockey	6.0
Calvin Klein	4.0
Other	53.4

Source: *Marketing Magazine*, March 25, 2002, p. 9, from Canadian Soft Goods Index.

★ 468 ★

Apparel (SIC 2300)

Underwear Sales at the Holidays

Figures are in millions of pieces.

	(mil.)	Share
Men's	140	50.00%
Women's	92	32.86
Boy's/girl's	48	17.14

Source: *PR Newswire*, February 8, 2002, p. NA, from NPD.

★ 469 ★

Apparel (SIC 2320)

Boy's Apparel Sales

Sales are shown in millions of dollars at mass merchandisers.

	($ mil.)	Share
Tops	$ 1,694	36.77%
Bottoms	1,035	22.47
Furnishings	720	15.63
Activewear	638	13.85
Outerwear	339	7.36
Suits, sportscoats	43	0.93
Other	138	3.00

Source: *Retail Merchandiser*, July 2001, p. 21.

★ 470 ★

Apparel (SIC 2320)

Men's Apparel Sales

Sales are shown in millions of dollars at mass merchandisers.

	($ mil.)	Share
Tops	$ 4,444	32.41%
Bottoms	3,499	25.52
Furnishings	2,359	17.21
Activewear	1,220	8.90
Suits, sportscoats	890	6.49
Outerwear	886	6.46
Other	412	3.01

Source: *Retail Merchandiser*, July 2001, p. 21.

★ 471 ★

Apparel (SIC 2321)

Men's Dress Shirt Market

Selected shares are shown in percent.

Arrow	25.0%
Van Heusen	2.0
Other	73.0

Source: "To Our Fellow Shareholders." Retrieved January 22, 2002 from the World Wide Web: http://www.pvh.com.

★ 472 ★

Apparel (SIC 2322)

Top Men's/Boy's Underwear Makers

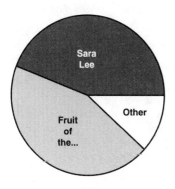

Market shares are shown in the mass merchant channel.

Sara Lee	44.8%
Fruit of the Loom	44.6
Other	11.6

Source: *Crain's Chicago Business*, November 12, 2001, p. 4.

★ 473 ★

Apparel (SIC 2325)

Jeans Market for Men

The top brand shares are for men 15-49.

	Q1 2000	Q1 2001
Levi's	24.5%	23.1%
Wrangler	12.9	14.7
Collections	12.8	9.2
Rustler	0.9	3.5
Other	51.1	50.5

Source: *Textile World*, August 2001, p. NA, from STS Market Research.

★ 474 ★

Apparel (SIC 2330)

Girl's Apparel Sales

Sales are shown in millions of dollars at mass merchandisers.

	($ mil.)	Share
Tops	$ 908	23.96%
Bottoms	724	19.11
Intimate apparel	584	15.41
Dresses, skirts	533	14.07
Activewear	445	11.74
Outerwear	279	7.36
Other	316	8.34

Source: *Retail Merchandiser*, July 2001, p. 21.

★ 475 ★

Apparel (SIC 2330)

Women's Apparel Sales

Sales are shown in millions of dollars at mass merchandisers.

	($ mil.)	Share
Tops	$ 7,617	33.79%
Dresses, skirts, shoes	4,408	19.55
Bottoms	4,136	18.35
Intimate apparel	3,620	16.06
Activewear	1,431	6.35
Outerwear	552	2.45
Other	778	3.45

Source: *Retail Merchandiser*, July 2001, p. 21.

★ 476 ★

Apparel (SIC 2341)

Top Women's/Girl's Underwear Makers

Market shares are shown in the mass merchant channel.

Sara Lee	43.1%
Fruit of the Loom	13.1
Other	43.8

Source: *Crain's Chicago Business*, November 12, 2001, p. 4.

★ 477 ★
Hats (SIC 2353)

Popular Brands of Golf Hats

Figures are based on a survey.

Ahead Headgear	74.0%
Other	26.0

Source: *Golf World Business*, January 2002, p. 17.

★ 478 ★
Curtains (SIC 2391)

Top Curtain/Drapery Makers

S. Lichtenberg
Burlington Industries
CHF Corp.
Croscill Home Fashions
Miller Curtain

Companies are ranked by sales in millions of dollars.

S. Lichtenberg	$ 125
Burlington Industries	113
CHF Corp.	109
Croscill Home Fashions	80
Miller Curtain	68

Source: *Home Textiles Today*, January 7, 2002, p. 34.

★ 479 ★
Homefurnishings (SIC 2392)

Bath Product Sales, 2000

Total sales rose from $2.7 billion in 1999 to $2.9 billion in 2000. Most items were purchased in discount stores (44% share). Most towels were solids rather than patterned (85% to 15%); consumers were more interested in shower curtains with a print than a solid color (73% to 27%). Most bath accessories were ceramic or plastic (40% and 23% shares).

Bath towels	55.0%
Bath/scatter rugs	23.0
Bath accessories	11.0
Shower curtains	9.0
Tank sets	2.0

Source: *Home Textiles Today*, May 28, 2001, p. 10.

★ 480 ★
Homefurnishings (SIC 2392)

Largest Bedding Markets, 2001

Markets are ranked by sales in millions of dollars.

Chicago, IL	$ 3,383.0
New York City, NY	3,228.1
Los Angeles-Long Beach	2,460.9
Washington D.C.-MD-VA-WV	2,335.1
Atlanta, GA	1,814.9
Philadelphia, PA-NJ	1,710.4
Houston, TX	1,704.3
Boston, MA-New Hampshire	1,578.9
Dallas, TX	1,512.8

Source: *Furniture Today*, December 31, 2001, p. 14.

★ 481 ★
Homefurnishings (SIC 2392)

Largest Home Textile Makers

Firms are ranked by estimated sales in millions of dollars.

Springs Industries	$ 1,801
Westpoint Stevens	1,752
Pillowtex	1,114
Mohawk Home	600
Dan River	482
Pacific Coast Feather	318
Croscill Home Fashions	315
Gleniot Corp.	252
Burlington Industries	249
Hollander Home Fashions	203

Source: *Home Textiles Today*, January 7, 2002, p. 32.

★ 482 ★
Homefurnishings (SIC 2392)

Preferred Brands of Bed/Bath Linens

The table shows the brands shoppers would select when shopping at a discount store or superstore. Figures show the results of a survey.

Cannon	33.0%
Martha Stewart	13.0
Polo/Ralph Lauren	9.0

Source: *DSN Retailing Today*, October 22, 2001, p. 24.

★ **483** ★
Homefurnishings (SIC 2392)
Slip Cover Market

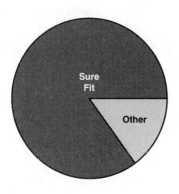

Market shares are shown in percent.

Sure Fit 85.0%
Other 15.0

Source: *Bobbin*, December 1, 2001, p. 32.

★ **484** ★
Homefurnishings (SIC 2392)
Top Bath Accessory Makers

Companies are ranked by sales in millions of dollars.

Springs Industries . . . . $ 70
Allure Home Creation 60
Croscill Home 45
Creative Bath Products 45
Ex-Cell Home 5

Source: *Home Textiles Today*, January 7, 2002, p. 34.

★ **485** ★
Homefurnishings (SIC 2392)
Top Bath Towel Makers

Companies are ranked by sales in millions of dollars.

WestPoint Stevens . . . . $ 500
Pillowtex 495
Springs Industries 221
Santens 50
1888 Mills 29

Source: *Home Textiles Today*, January 7, 2002, p. 34.

★ **486** ★
Homefurnishings (SIC 2392)
Top Bedding Makers, 2000

Firms are ranked by sales in millions of dollars.

	($ mil.)	Share
Sealy	$ 1,035	22.50%
Serta	729	15.85
Simmons	720	15.65
Spring Air	420	9.13
Orth-A-Pedic	180	3.91
King Koil	157	3.41
Restonic	152	3.30
Enfglander	137	2.98
Kingsdown	117	2.54
Springwall	90	1.96
Other	863	18.76

Source: *Furniture Today*, December 31, 2001, p. 68.

★ **487** ★
Homefurnishings (SIC 2392)
Top Blanket Makers

Companies are ranked by sales in millions of dollars.

WestPoint Stevens . . . . $ 140
Sunbeam 110
Charles D. Owen 95
Pillowtex 32
Beacon Blankets 29

Source: *Home Textiles Today*, January 7, 2002, p. 34.

★ **488** ★
Homefurnishings (SIC 2392)
Top Decorative Pillow Makers

Companies are ranked by sales in millions of dollars.

Brentwood Originals . . . . $ 111
Arlee 63
Mohawk Home 24
Newport 23
Fashion Pillows 21

Source: *Home Textiles Today*, January 7, 2002, p. 34.

★ 489 ★
Homefurnishings (SIC 2392)

Top Down Comforter Makers

Companies are ranked by sales in millions of dollars.

Pacific Coast Feather	$ 111
Pillowtex	70
Hollander Home Fashions	52
Phoenix Down	43
Down Lite International	40

Source: *Home Textiles Today*, January 7, 2002, p. 34.

★ 490 ★
Homefurnishings (SIC 2392)

Top Kitchen Textile Makers

Companies are ranked by sales in millions of dollars.

Barth & Dreyfuss	$ 60
Franco Mfg.	51
Cecil Saydah	51
John Ritzenthaler Co.	32
Charles Craft	20

Source: *Home Textiles Today*, January 7, 2002, p. 34.

★ 491 ★
Homefurnishings (SIC 2392)

Top Sheet/Pillowcase Makers

Springs Industries

WestPoint Stevens

Dan River

Pillowtex

Thomaston Mills

Companies are ranked by sales in millions of dollars.

Springs Industries	$ 650
WestPoint Stevens	600
Dan River	238
Pillowtex	200
Thomaston Mills	80

Source: *Home Textiles Today*, January 7, 2002, p. 34.

★ 492 ★
Homefurnishings (SIC 2392)

Top Shower Curtain Makers

Companies are ranked by sales in millions of dollars.

Springs Industries	$ 71
Allure Home Creation	69
Ex-Cell Home Fashions	65
Maytex Mills	33
Creative Bath Products	30

Source: *Home Textiles Today*, January 7, 2002, p. 34.

★ 493 ★
Homefurnishings (SIC 2392)

U.S. Bedding Market, 2001

Market shares are shown in percent.

Sheets/pillowcases	35.0%
Comforters	23.0
Bed pillows	10.0
Bed-in-the-bag	7.0
Blankets	6.0
Mattress pads	4.0
Decorative pillows	4.0
Bedspreads	4.0
Duvet covers	3.0
Throws	2.0
Quilts	2.0
Other	10.0

Source: *Home Textiles Today*, March 4, 2002, p. 8.

SIC 24 - Lumber and Wood Products

★ 494 ★
Decking (SIC 2426)

U.S. Decking Demand

Demand is shown in millions of board feet.

	2000	2005
Wood	4,366	4,470
Wood-plastic	236	488
Plastic & other	75	117

Source: *Wood & Wood Products*, April 2002, p. 54.

★ 495 ★
I-Joists (SIC 2430)

I-Joist Market Shares

Share is somewhere between 50-60%.

Trus Joist	60.0%
Other	40.0

Source: *Builder*, September 2001, p. 91.

★ 496 ★
Millwork (SIC 2431)

Leading Millwork Firms in Washington State

Firma are ranked by revenue in millions of dollars.

Jefferson Millwork & Design	$ 12.0
Specified Woodworking	6.0
Wood Alive Woodworks	3.7
Galliher & Huguely Associates	2.5
Brunswick Woodworking	2.4

Source: *Washington Business Journal*, Annual 2002, p. 77.

★ 497 ★
Pallets (SIC 2448)

U.S. Pallet Market

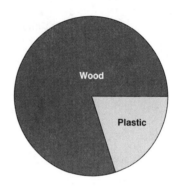

The $9 billion industry is shown by type. The market is shifting from wood to plastic at a rate of 2% to 4% a year.

Wood	80.0%
Plastic	20.0

Source: *PR Newswire*, March 14, 2002, p. NA.

★ 498 ★
Manufactured Homes (SIC 2450)

Prefabricated Home Shipments

Shipments are shown in millions of dollars.

	2000	2005	Share
Manufactured housing . .	$ 251	$ 300	52.63%
Panelized, modular, other . .	260	270	47.37

Source: *Research Studies - Freedonia Group*, August 8, 2001, p. 5, from Freedonia Group.

★ 499 ★
Manufactured Homes (SIC 2450)

Top Manufactured Home Builders, 2001

Data show number of units shipped.

Champion Enterprises 36,851
Fleetwood Enterprises 30,482
Clayton Homes 19,200
Oakwood Homes 18,604
Cavalier Homes 12,669
Horton Homes 10,900
Palm Harbor Homes 10,829
Skyline Corp. 10,000
Patriot Homes 5,192

Source: *Builder*, May 2002, p. 177.

★ 500 ★
Log Homes (SIC 2452)

Top Log Home Builders, 2001

Data show number of units constructed.

Honka Log Homes 3,500
Jim Barna Log Systems 475
Log Homes of America 150
Gastineau Log Homes 142
Hearthstone 102
Wholesale Log Homes 88
Fall Clerk Housing 67
Town & Country Cedar Homes 65
Mountaineer Log & Siding 64

Source: *Builder*, May 2002, p. 177.

★ 501 ★
Hospital Beds (SIC 2499)

Medical/Surgical Bed Market

Market shares are shown in percent.

Hill-Rom 90.0%
Other 10.0

Source: *Modern Healthcare*, June 18, 2001, p. 80, from Salomon Smith Barney.

★ 502 ★
Washboards (SIC 2499)

U.S. Washboard Market

Market shares are shown in percent.

Bron-Shoe 90.0%
Other 10.0

Source: *Business First-Columbus*, June 8, 2001, p. B1.

SIC 25 - Furniture and Fixtures

★ 503 ★
Furniture (SIC 2500)

RTA Furniture Market Shares, 1999

RTA stands for ready-to-asssemble. Figures are based on retail sales.

Sauder Woodworking Co.	25.0%
Bush Industries	18.0
O'Sullivan Furniture	16.0
Dorel Industries Inc.	10.0
Mills Pride L.P. (Masco Corp.)	7.0
Other	24.0

Source: *HFN*, October 15, 2001.

★ 504 ★
Furniture (SIC 2500)

Top Furniture Makers, 2000

Firms are ranked by shipments in millions of dollars.

La-Z-Boy	$ 2,232.0
Furniture Brands International	2,116.2
LifeStyle Furnishings International	1,780.0
Ashley	952.0
Klaussner	931.0
Ethan Allen	760.2
Sauder Woodworking	552.0
Bush Furniture	419.7
O'Sullivan	397.5
Bassett	344.6

Source: *Furniture Today*, December 31, 2001, p. 68.

★ 505 ★
Furniture (SIC 2500)

Top Furniture Makers in Canada, 2000

Firms are ranked by sales in millions of dollars.

Dorel Inds.	$ 620.1
Palliser Furniture	438.4
Shermag	$ 162.2
South Shore Inds.	150.0
Simmons Canada	122.5
Canadel Furniture	118.0
Sealy Canada	103.0
La-Z-Boy Canada	94.0
Bestar	76.8
El Ran Furniture	75.0

Source: *Furniture Today*, December 31, 2001, p. 68.

★ 506 ★
Furniture (SIC 2511)

Wood Household Furniture Imports

Figures are in thousands of dollars.

	($ 000)	Share
China	$ 1,650,728	26.23%
Canada	1,368,514	21.75
Italy	460,384	7.32
Malaysia	399,483	6.35
Mexico	392,802	6.24
Other	2,020,730	32.11

Source: *Wood Digest*, October 2001, p. 74, from U.S. Department of Commerce.

★ 507 ★
Mattresses (SIC 2515)

Mattress Sales by Size

Sales are shown by size.

Queen	33.0%
Twin (including XL)	32.0
Full (including XL)	23.0
King (including California King)	9.0
Odd sizes	3.0

Source: *HFN*, July 16, 2001, p. 34, from International Sleep Products Association.

★ 508 ★

Office Furniture (SIC 2520)

Contract Furniture Shipments

Shipments are shown by category.

	1998	2000
Systems	36.8%	35.7%
Seating	24.5	25.0
Files	12.9	10.9
Deks	10.2	11.1
Tables	5.5	7.0
Storage	5.3	5.8
Other	3.8	4.5

Source: *Wood & Wood Products*, May 2001, p. 69, from Business & Institutional Furniture Manufacturers Association.

★ 509 ★

Office Furniture (SIC 2520)

Top Office Furniture Purchasers in the Federal Government

Herman Miller
Krueger International
Cramer Inc.
Haworth Inc.
Steelcase Inc.
Knoll Inc.
Kimball International Mfg. Inc.
Other

Market shares are shown based on value of purchases.

Herman Miller	12.01%
Krueger International	11.88
Cramer Inc.	7.75
Haworth Inc.	4.57
Steelcase Inc.	4.56
Knoll Inc.	4.30
Kimball International Mfg. Inc.	3.99
Other	50.94

Source: *Government Executive*, August 1, 2001, p. NA.

★ 510 ★

Lockers (SIC 2542)

U.S. Lockers Market

Company has over 50% of the market.

Hollman Inc.	50.0%
Other	50.0

Source: *Club Management*, December 2001, p. 83.

SIC 26 - Paper and Allied Products

★ 511 ★
Paper (SIC 2600)

Recycled Paper Market

Data show the leading end markets.

Exports	27.6%
Recycled paperboard	20.4
Tissue	20.1
Printing and writing	14.9
Newsprint	5.2
Other	11.8

Source: *Waste Age*, November 2001, p. 26.

★ 512 ★
Paper (SIC 2621)

Paper Industry by Segment

Production is shown in thousands of tons for the year ended April.

	1999	2001	Share
Printing/writing	8,819	8,378	43.94%
Uncoated freesheet	4,661	4,429	23.23
Newsprint	2,355	2,310	12.12
Coated freesheet	1,656	1,484	7.78
Coated groundwood	1,400	1,493	7.83
Uncoated groundwood . . .	600	503	2.64
Other	502	470	2.46

Source: *American Printer*, September 2001, p. 9.

★ 513 ★
Paper (SIC 2621)

Top Newsprint Producers

Market shares are shown based on capacity in North America.

Abitibi-Consolidated	28.5%
Bowater	17.1
NorskeCanada	10.9
Kruger	7.2
SP Newsprint	5.1
North Pacific Paper	5.1
Enron Corp.	4.0
Tembec	3.5
Store Enso	3.3
Other	15.3

Source: *Pulp & Paper*, December 2001, p. 9.

★ 514 ★

Paper (SIC 2621)

Top Uncoated Groundwood Producers

Market shares are shown based on capacity in North America.

	(000)	Share
Abitibi-Consolidated	1,725	27.38%
Norske Skog	982	15.59
Bowater Inc.	690	10.95
Stora Enso	625	9.92
Daishowa N. America	320	5.08
Inexcon Maine Inc.	277	4.40
J.D. Irving	250	3.97
Madison	228	3.62
Kruger	220	3.49
St. Marys	210	3.33
Other	773	12.27

Source: *Pulp & Paper*, September 2001, p. 9.

★ 515 ★

Corrugated Boxes (SIC 2650)

Corrugated Box Market

| Food and kindred products |
| Paper and allied products |
| Chemicals and allied products |
| Rubber and misc. |
| Printing & publishing |
| Apparel and other |
| Textile mill products |
| Other |

Market shares are shown in percent.

Food and kindred products	41.3%
Paper and allied products	21.0
Chemicals and allied products	5.7
Rubber and misc.	5.0
Printing & publishing	1.1
Apparel and other	1.0
Textile mill products	1.0
Other	1.1

Source: *Paperboard Packaging*, January 2002, p. 18, from Fibre Box Association.

★ 516 ★

Paperboard (SIC 2650)

Largest Linerboard Producers

Market shares are shown in percent.

Smurfit-Stone	19.0%
International Paper	16.0
Weyerhaeuser	11.0
Georgia-Pacific	10.0
Inland	7.0
Other	37.0

Source: *Paperboard Packaging*, January 2002, p. 18, from Jacobs-Sirrine Consultants.

★ 517 ★

Paperboard (SIC 2650)

Top Bleached Paperboard Producers

Market shares are shown based on capacity in North America.

International Paper	36.6%
Westvaco	22.2
Potlatch	8.5
Georgia-Pacific	4.6
Smurfit-Stone	4.3
Blue Ridge Paper	3.7
Gulf States Paper	3.6
Fort James	3.1
Weyerhaeuser	3.0
Other	10.4

Source: *Pulp & Paper*, September 2001, p. 9.

★ 518 ★

Boxboard (SIC 2652)

Folding Boxboard Market Shares, 2000

Market shares are shown in percent.

Recycled	41.0%
Solid bleached	33.0
Unbleached kraft	26.0

Source: *Paperboard Packaging*, March 2002, p. 28, from American Forest & Paper Association.

★ 519 ★
Folding Cartons (SIC 2657)

Folding Carton Sales

Sales are shown in millions of tons.

	(mil.)	Share
Beverages and beverage carriers . .	1,048	15.03%
Dry food and produce	1,041	14.93
Hardware and household supplies . .	579	8.31
Frozen foods	523	7.50
Medicinal	507	7.27
Retail food carry out boxes and trays	497	7.13
Paper goods	418	6.00
Soaps and detergents	334	4.79
Tobacco	310	4.45
Other	1,714	24.59

Source: *Paperboard Packaging*, January 2002, p. 18, from Paperboard Packaging Council.

★ 520 ★
Plastic Bags (SIC 2672)

Top Garbage Bags, 2001

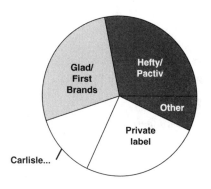

Sales are shown in millions of dollars.

	1999	2001	Share
Hefty/Pactiv	$ 288.3	$ 311.1	28.28%
Glad/First Brands	314.0	299.0	27.18
Carlisle Plastics	137.5	145.2	13.20
Private label	245.0	271.3	24.66
Other	85.2	73.4	6.67

Source: *Investor's Business Daily*, September 24, 2001, p. A8, from Information Resources Inc. and J.P. Morgan Chase & Co.

★ 521 ★
Plastic Bags (SIC 2672)

Top Sandwich/Freezer/Storage Bags, 2001

Sales are shown in millions of dollars.

	1999	2001	Share
Ziploc/DowBrands . . .	$ 310.7	$ 329.2	32.27%
Glad/First Brands	179.1	181.1	17.75
Baggies/Pactiv	148.3	151.0	14.80
Private label	218.7	299.4	29.35
Other	55.2	59.3	5.81

Source: *Investor's Business Daily*, September 24, 2001, p. A8, from Information Resources Inc. and J.P. Morgan Chase & Co.

★ 522 ★
Baby Wipes (SIC 2676)

Top Baby Wipe Brands, 2001

Brands are ranked by unit sales for the year ended December 2, 2001.

	(mil.)	Share
Huggies Natural Care	26.6	20.14%
Pampers Baby Fresh One Ups . . .	20.1	15.22
Huggies Supreme Care	10.7	8.10
Huggies	7.0	5.30
Luvs	3.9	2.95
Pampers One Ups	2.8	2.12
Other	61.0	46.18

Source: *MMR*, February 11, 2002, p. 20, from Information Resources Inc.

★ 523 ★
Diapers (SIC 2676)

Private Label Diaper Sales

Total category sales reached $629.1 million.

	($ mil.)	Share
Diapers, disposable	$ 390.6	62.08%
Baby wipes	122.3	19.44
Disposable training pants	109.0	17.32
Moist towelettes	7.3	1.16

Source: *Private Label Buyer*, January 2002, p. 32, from Information Resources Inc.

★ 524 ★
Diapers (SIC 2676)

Top Diaper Brands

Brands are ranked by sales in millions of dollars for the year ended October 7, 2001.

	($ mil.)	Share
Huggies Ultratrim	$ 648.5	27.60%
Pampers Baby Dry	458.0	19.49
Pampers Premium	226.1	9.62
Luvs Ultra Leakguards	209.6	8.92
Huggies Supreme	185.8	7.91
Drypers	53.7	2.29
Luvs Ultra Leakguards Stretch	41.0	1.74
Huggies	35.9	1.53
Huggies Overnites	31.7	1.35
Other	459.7	19.56

Source: *MMR*, December 17, 2001, p. 38, from Information Resources, Inc.

★ 525 ★
Diapers (SIC 2676)

Top Diaper/Training Pants Makers, 2001

Market shares are shown in percent.

Kimberly-Clark Corp.	45.40%
Procter & Gamble	33.60
Drypers Corp.	2.00
Associated Hyenic Products	0.90
Jettar	0.08
United Colors of Benetton	0.07
Universal Converter	0.06
Absormex	0.06
Paragon Trade Brands	0.04
Private label	17.80

Source: *Advertising Age*, June 24, 2002, p. S20, from Information Resources Inc.

★ 526 ★
Feminine Hygiene Products (SIC 2676)

Top Pantyliner Brands in Canada

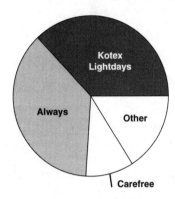

Market shares are shown in percent for the year ended February 28, 2002. Total sales hit $65 million.

Kotex Lightdays	37.4%
Always	37.2
Carefree	9.7
Other	15.8

Source: *Marketing Magazine*, May 27, 2002, p. 1, from industry sources.

★ 527 ★
Feminine Hygiene Products (SIC 2676)

Top Sanitary Napkin/Liner Brands, 2001

Market shares are shown in percent.

Always	29.5%
Kotex	16.1
Stayfree	14.6
Carefree	8.0
Kotex Lightdays	6.7
Always All Days	6.7
Kotex Overnight	4.2
Kotex Freedom	1.5
Kotex Lightdays Long	1.2
Other	11.5

Source: *Chain Drug Review*, January 7, 2002, p. 83, from Information Resources Inc.

★ 528 ★

Feminine Hygiene Products (SIC 2676)

Top Tampon Brands, 2001

Market shares are shown in percent.

Tampax	32.8%
Playtex Gentle Glide	21.7
Kotex Security	12.7
O.B.	11.1
Tampax Satin	2.9
Playtex Silk Glide	2.9
Tampax Compak	2.8
Playtex	2.1
Playtex Slimfits	1.8
Other	9.2

Source: *Chain Drug Review*, January 7, 2002, p. 83, from Information Resources Inc.

★ 529 ★

Sanitary Paper Products (SIC 2676)

Away From Home Tissue Industry

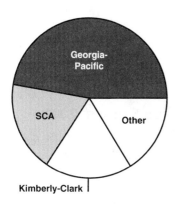

Market shares are shown in percent.

Georgia-Pacific	44.0%
SCA	17.0
Kimberly-Clark	17.0
Other	15.0

Source: *Knight-Ridder/Tribune Business News*, December 3, 2001, p. NA.

★ 530 ★

Sanitary Paper Products (SIC 2676)

Top Adult Incontinence Brands, 2001

Market shares are shown in percent.

Depend	31.1%
Depend Poise	21.5
Serenity	9.1
Sure Care Slip-On	0.8
Attends	0.7
Other	36.8

Source: *Chain Drug Review*, January 7, 2002, p. 58, from Information Resources Inc.

★ 531 ★

Sanitary Paper Products (SIC 2676)

Top Moist Towelette Brands, 2001

Market shares are shown for the year ended May 20, 2001.

Huggies Natural Care	19.0%
Pampers Baby One-Up	15.2
Huggies Supreme	8.2
Kleenex Cottonelle	5.7
Wet Ones	5.3
Huggies	5.3
Luvs	3.1
Pampers Baby Fresh	2.1
Chubs	1.9
Private label	20.3
Other	13.9

Source: *Grocery Headquarters*, August 2001, p. 12, from Information Resources Inc.

★ 532 ★

Sanitary Paper Products (SIC 2676)

Top Paper Towel Brands, 2001

Market shares are shown for the year ended December 2, 2001. Data exclude Wal-Mart.

Bounty	35.1%
Brawny	11.1
Kleenex Viva	8.2
Sparkle	8.1
Scott	7.9
Mardi Gras	3.0
Bounty Medleys	2.2
Coronet	1.8
Marcal	1.7

Continued on next page.

★ 532 ★ *Continued*
Sanitary Paper Products (SIC 2676)

Top Paper Towel Brands, 2001

Market shares are shown for the year ended December 2, 2001. Data exclude Wal-Mart.

Private label 17.0%
Other 3.9

Source: *Grocery Headquarters*, April 2002, p. 14, from Information Resources Inc.

★ 533 ★
Sanitary Paper Products (SIC 2676)

Top Paper Towel Vendors, 2001

Market shares are shown for the year ended December 2, 2001. Data exclude Wal-Mart.

Procter & Gamble 37.9%
Georgia-Pacific Corp. 26.0
Kimberly-Clark Corp. 16.8
Marcal Paper Mills Inc. 1.7
Private label 17.0
Other 0.6

Source: *Grocery Headquarters*, April 2002, p. 14, from Information Resources Inc.

★ 534 ★
Sanitary Paper Products (SIC 2676)

Top Toilet Paper Makers

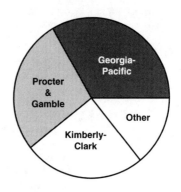

Market shares are shown in percent.

	($ mil.)	Share
Georgia-Pacific	$ 1,200	33.33%
Procter & Gamble	969	26.92
Kimberly-Clark	917	25.47
Other	514	14.28

Source: *Brandweek*, March 11, 2002, p. 6, from Information Resources Inc.

★ 535 ★
Sanitary Paper Products (SIC 2676)

Top Toilet Tissue Brands, 2001

Market shares are shown for the year ended December 2, 2001. Figures exclude Wal-Mart.

Charmin 15.2%
Quilted Northern 12.9
Angel Soft 10.3
Kleenex Cottonelle 9.8
Charmin Ultra 9.3
Scott 5.9
Scottissue 5.8
Soft 'n Gentle 3.5
Quilted Northern Ultra 2.5
Other 24.8

Source: *Grocery Headquarters*, April 2002, p. 14, from Information Resources Inc.

★ 536 ★

Stationery (SIC 2678)

Preferred Brands of Stationery

Bic
Hallmark
Mead

The table shows the brands shoppers would select when shopping at a discount store or superstore. Figures show the results of a survey and are not market shares.

Bic	21.0%
Hallmark	20.0
Mead	13.0

Source: *DSN Retailing Today*, October 22, 2001, p. 24, from Lee J. Shapiro.

★ 537 ★

Stationery (SIC 2678)

Retail Stationery Sales

Data show supermarket sales in millions of dollars.

School paper/forms	$ 155.37
Pens & pencils	106.43
Artist/hobby paint/supply	53.57
Planners/binders/folders	46.96
Glue	43.28
Markers	35.64
Scissors	16.54
Mailing supplies	15.78
Crayons	15.72
Corrective fluid & erasers	11.82

Source: *Supermarket Business*, September 15, 2001, p. 42, from A.C. Nielsen Homescan.

SIC 27 - Printing and Publishing

★ 538 ★
Publishing (SIC 2700)

Largest Business to Business Communications Firms

Firms are ranked by revenues in millions of dollars.

Reed Elsevier	$ 2,500
United Business Media	1,400
McGraw-Hill	1,000
Primedia	518
Ziff Davis Media	471

Source: *Business Publisher*, October 31, 2001, p. 5, from Veronis, Suhler & Associates.

★ 539 ★
Publishing (SIC 2700)

Largest Professional Education And Training Media Firms

Firms are ranked by revenues in billions of dollars.

Pearson Education	$ 3.1
Harcourt General	2.4
Thomson Corp.	2.1
McGraw Hill and Wolters Kluwer	1.0

Source: *Business Publisher*, October 31, 2001, p. 5.

★ 540 ★
Newspapers (SIC 2711)

Largest Newspapers in the Bay Area

Data show circulation.

San Francisco Chronicle	527,466
San Jose Mercury News	283,757
Contra Costa Times	183,725
San Francisco Examiner	97,000
The Press Democrat	91,179

Source: *San Francisco Business Times*, November 2, 2001, p. 25.

★ 541 ★
Newspapers (SIC 2711)

Leading Daily Newspaper Markets

Figures show the areas with the highest percentage of readers.

Hartford/New Haven, CT	65.3%
West Palm Beach, FL	63.8
Boston, MA	63.6
Cleveland, OH	62.2
New York City, NY	62.1
Providence/New Bedford	62.0
Tampa/St. Petersburg/Sarasota, FL	61.7
Harrisburg/Lancaster/Lebanon/York, PA	61.0
Philadelphia, PA	60.4
Pittsburgh, PA	60.3

Source: *PR Newswire*, October 31, 2001, p. NA, from Scarborough Research.

★ 542 ★
Newspapers (SIC 2711)

Top Newspapers, 2001

Data show circulation for the six months ended September 30, 2001.

USA Today	2,241,677
Wall Street Journal	1,780,605
New York Times	1,109,371
Los Angeles Times	972,957
Washington Post	759,864
New York Daily News	734,473
Chicago Tribune	621,305
Newsday of New York's Long Island	577,354
Houston Chronicle	551,854
New York Post	533,860

Source: *Detroit Free Press*, October 31, 2001, p. 6E, from Audit Bureau of Circulations.

★ 543 ★

Comic Books (SIC 2721)

Comic Book Industry Shares

The sales of products are shown for January 2002.

Comics	63.76%
Toys & models	10.50
Graphic novels/trade paperbacks	10.36
Magazines	4.41
Videos	2.79
Apparel	1.58
Books	1.27
Novelties/comics	1.22
Games	0.98
Diamond pubs	0.81
Cards	0.79
Other	1.53

Source: *Comic Buyer's Guide*, February 15, 2002, p. 13, from Diamond Comics Distributors.

★ 544 ★

Comic Books (SIC 2721)

Top Comic Book Publishers, 2001

Shares are for June 2001, and include all products (figures, graphic novels, etc.).

Marvel Comics	24.20%
DC Comics	23.88
Image Comics	7.14
Dark Horse Comics	5.09
Wizard Entertainment	2.56
Dynamic Forces	2.22
Chaos Comics	1.52
Viz Communications	1.47
Crossgen Comics	1.34
The Upper Deck Company	0.93
Other	29.65

Source: "Comic Book Network Emag." Retrieved September 1, 2001 from the World Wide Web: http://www.yahoo.com.

★ 545 ★

Comic Books (SIC 2721)

Top Comic Book Publishers, 2002

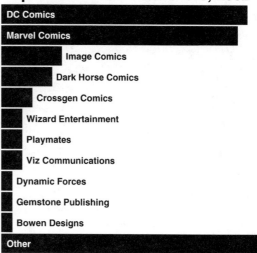

Market shares are shown for February 2002, based on sales of comics, magazines and graphic novels.

DC Comics	25.03%
Marvel Comics	24.42
Image Comics	6.19
Dark Horse Comics	5.13
Crossgen Comics	2.67
Wizard Entertainment	1.99
Playmates	1.63
Viz Communications	1.50
Dynamic Forces	1.41
Gemstone Publishing	1.37
Bowen Designs	1.13
Other	27.53

Source: "Top 100 Comics." Retrieved February 26, 2002 from the World Wide Web: http://www.digitalwebbing.com.

★ 546 ★

Comic Books (SIC 2721)

Top Selling Comics, 2002

Sales of books are shown for February 2002. Figures are in thousands.

Dark Knight Strikes Again 3	185
Ultimates 2	116
New X-Men 123	114
Uncanny X-Men 403	105
Ultimate X-Men 15	102
Amazing Spiderman 40	93
Ultimate Spiderman 19	84

Continued on next page.

★ 546 ★ *Continued*

Comic Books (SIC 2721)

Top Selling Comics, 2002

Sales of books are shown for February 2002. Figures are in thousands.

Ultimate Spiderman 18	84
X-Treme X-Men 10	80
Green Arrow 13	79

Source: *Comic Buyer's Guide*, March 8, 2002, p. 13, from *Comics & Games Retailers Market Beat.*

★ 547 ★

Comic Books (SIC 2721)

Top Selling Graphic Novels, 2002

Sales of books are shown by comics shops for February 2002. Figures are in thousands.

Lone Wolf & Cub Vol. 19: Moon In Our Hearts	14
Wolverine: The Origin	13
History of the DC Universe	12
Akira Book 6	9
Ultimate Spiderman: HC	7
Image Comics 10th Anniversary	7
Astro Boy: Vol. 1	7
Essential Spiderman: Vol. 5	6
Complete Frank Miller: Spiderman	5

Source: *Comic Buyer's Guide*, March 8, 2002, p. 13, from *Comics & Games Retailers Market.*

★ 548 ★

Magazines (SIC 2721)

Largest Average Single-Copy Sellers, 2000

Figures show average circulation

Cosmopolitan	1,844,726
Family Circle	1,802,235
Woman's Day	1,748,765
National Enquirer	1,706,367
TV Guide	1,611,628
Woman's World	1,528,298

People Weekly	1,392,046
Star	1,356,636
First For Women	1,286,139
O, the Oprah Magazine	1,242,076

Source: *Grocery Headquarters*, September 2001, p. 48, from Magazine Publishers of America.

★ 549 ★

Magazines (SIC 2721)

Largest Magazine Publishers

Companies are ranked by share of ad revenue for the first ten months of the year.

Time Inc.	$ 22.1
Hearst	8.9
Conde Nast	8.2
Hachette Filipacchi	5.7
Meredith	5.1
Gruner & Jahr	4.3
Primedia	3.8
Parade	3.2
McGraw-Hill	2.3
Gemstar-TV Guide	2.3

Source: *New York Times*, December 6, 2001, p. C7, from Publishers Information Bureau.

★ 550 ★

Magazines (SIC 2721)

Magazine Revenue Leaders, 2000-01

Figures are in millions of dollars.

People Weekly	$ 668.9
Sports Illustrated	521.1
TV Guide	493.8
Time	459.4
BusinessWeek	307.2
Better Homes & Gardens	303.8
Reader's Digest	301.7
Newsweek	294.3
Fortune	253.1
Forbes	223.2

Source: *Folio*, September 15, 2001, p. 21.

★ 551 ★
Books (SIC 2731)

Best-Selling Bibles, 2001

| New International Version |
| King James Version |
| New King James |
| New Living |
| Other |

Market shares are shown in percent.

New International Version 32.1%
King James Version 22.0
New King James 10.0
New Living 8.0
Other 27.9

Source: ''Five Days Early.'' Retrieved May 2, 2002 from the World Wide Web: http://www.worldmag.com.

★ 552 ★
Books (SIC 2731)

Books Sales in Oprah's Book Club

Data show trade paperback sales, in millions, for date.

The Pilot's Wife 2.80
The Poisonwood Bible 2.30
House of Sand and Fog 2.20
Where the Heart Is 2.00
Here on Earth 1.95
We Were the Mulvaneys 1.60
The Reader 1.50
Midwives 1.35
While I Was Gone 1.30

Source: *The Economist*, April 13, 2002, p. 80, from *Publishers Weekly*.

★ 553 ★
Books (SIC 2731)

Children's Book Market

Consumers purchased $1.9 billion in children's books, or 469 million units. Figures are based on dollar sales.

Picture/story books 25.0%
Nonfiction 15.6
Color and activity 14.2
Series/chapter books 9.4
Novelty 6.5
Other 29.3

Source: *BP Report*, April 8, 2002, p. NA.

★ 554 ★
Books (SIC 2731)

Christian Book Buying Preferences

54% of the books were bought at Christian book stores. Market shares are shown in percent.

Christian fiction 19.0%
Inspirational 18.0
Bible studies 17.0
Devotionals 14.0
Reference 8.0
Bibles 7.0
Children's 6.0
Other 11.0

Source: *Publishers Weekly*, November 26, 2001, p. 14.

★ 555 ★
Books (SIC 2731)

Favorite Genres for Men

Figures are based on a survey.

Espionage 7.1%
History 5.6
Science fiction 5.1
Computers 4.6
Mystery 4.4

Source: *USA TODAY*, December 26, 2001, p. D1, from Ipsos-Booktrends.

★ 556 ★
Books (SIC 2731)

Favorite Genres for Women

Figures are based on a survey.

Romance 25.6%
General fiction 7.6
Mystery 7.3
Religious fiction 4.2
Cooking/wine 4.0

Source: *USA TODAY*, December 26, 2001, p. D1, from
Ispos Booktrends.

★ 557 ★
Books (SIC 2731)

Romance Novel Sales, 2000

*2,289 romance titles were released: 2,056 print
romances, 172 e-books and 61 audiobooks.*

Contemporary 58.0%
Historicals 28.5
Inspirational 6.1
Young adult 3.5
Paranormal 3.5
Other 0.4

Source: *Library Journal*, August 2001, p. 86, from
ROMSTAT.

★ 558 ★
Books (SIC 2731)

Strategy Book Publishing

*The company holds the lead in video game strategy
manuals.*

Prima Games 45.0%
Other 55.0

Source: *Business Wire*, June 4, 2002, p. NA, from
NPDFunworld.

★ 559 ★
Books (SIC 2731)

Top Trade Book Publishers, 2000

Marke shares are shown based on revenues.

Random House 25.8%
Penguin 12.5
HarperCollins 12.1
Simon & Schuster 8.8
Scholastic 5.0
St. Martin's/Holt/FSG 4.3
Warner/Little Brown 4.2
Thomas Nelson 3.1
Hungry Minds 3.1
Houghton Mifflin 1.5
Other 19.6

Source: *New York Times*, March 11, 2002, p. C13, from
Subtext.

★ 560 ★
Textbooks (SIC 2731)

K-12 Textbook Adoptions

*Market shares are shown in percent. Textbook adop-
tions were mostly in the field of reading and language arts.*

Pearson Education 5.7%
McGraw-Hill Reading 4.2
Other 91.1

Source: *Educational Marketer*, December 10, 2001, p. NA,
from Simba Information.

★ 561 ★
Textbooks (SIC 2731)

Textbook Adoptions in Alabama

*Data are for grades 6-8. The source states that
school purchasing was about one-third lower than
normal, no doubt from belt tighening in districts.
Harcourt led with a 42.2% market share.*

Timeless Voices, Timeless Themes 36.0%
The Readers Choice 27.0
Elements of Literature 26.0
Other 11.0

Source: *Educational Marketer*, October 1, 2001, p. NA.

★ 562 ★
Textbooks (SIC 2731)

Top College Publishers

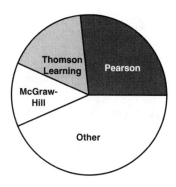

Market shares are shown in percent.

Pearson	.26.7%
Thomson Learning	16.6
McGraw-Hill	13.1
Other	43.6

Source: *Educational Marketer*, August 20, 2001, p. NA, from Simba Information.

★ 563 ★
Textbooks (SIC 2731)

Top College Publishers

Market shares are shown based on revenues.

Pearson Education	.26.7%
Thomson Learning	16.6
McGraw-Hill	13.1
Other	43.6

Source: *Educational Marketer*, August 20, 2001, p. NA.

★ 564 ★
Textbooks (SIC 2731)

Top Educational Publishers

Market shares are shown based on revenues.

Pearson Education	.20.3%
McGraw-Hill	16.1
Harcourt	9.7
Houghton Mifflin	9.6
Thomson Learning	6.3
WRC Media	2.3

Scholastic	2.3%
Other	33.4

Source: *Educational Marketer*, September 3, 2001, p. NA.

★ 565 ★
Textbooks (SIC 2731)

U.S. School Book Fair Market, 2000

Market shares are shown in percent.

Scholastic	.80.0%
Other	.20.0

Source: *Educational Marketer*, August 6, 2001, p. NA.

★ 566 ★
Book Printing (SIC 2732)

Largest Book Printers

Companies are ranked by segment sales in millions of dollars.

R.R. Donnelley & Sons	$ 788
Quebecor World	.780
Banta Corp.	.384
Von Hoffmann Corp.	.318
Courier Corp.	.208
Bertelsmann Arvato	.195
Phoenix Color	.155
Taylor Publishing	.110
Hess Management	90

Source: *Printing Impressions*, December 2001, p. NA.

★ 567 ★
Directories (SIC 2741)

Leading Directory Printers in Canada

Market shares are shown in percent.

Quebecor World	.90.0%
Other	.10.0

Source: *Business Wire*, September 6, 2001, p. NA.

★ 568 ★
Directories (SIC 2741)

Leading Directory Printers in Mexico

Market shares are shown in percent.

Quebecor World	75.0%
Other	25.0

Source: *Business Wire*, September 6, 2001, p. NA.

★ 569 ★
Yearbooks (SIC 2741)

Top Yearbook Publishers

Market shares are estimated in percent.

Josten	50.0%
Taylor Publishing Co.	20.0
Herff Jones Inc.	20.0
Walsworth Publishing	10.0

Source: *Education Week*, May 16, 2001, p. 1.

★ 570 ★
Printing (SIC 2750)

Largest Catalog Printers

Companies are ranked by segment sales in millions of dollars.

Quebecor World	$ 1,105
Quad/Graphics	900
R.R. Donnelley & Sons	840
Banta Corp.	246
Arandell Corp.	196

Perry Judd's Inc.	$ 102
Spencer Press	94
Continental Web Press	73
Consolidated Graphics	68

Source: *Printing Impressions*, December 2001, p. NA.

★ 571 ★
Printing (SIC 2750)

Largest Financial Printers

Companies are ranked by segment sales in millions of dollars.

Bowne & Co.	$ 847
R.R. Donnelley & Sons	525
Merrill Corp.	260
Cunningham Graphics	120
IKON Office Solutions	45
Burrups Packard	30
Applied Printing Technologies	25
Henry Wurst Inc.	21
Scott Printing	16

Source: *Printing Impressions*, December 2001, p. NA.

★ 572 ★
Printing (SIC 2750)

Top Printers

Companies are ranked by most recent year fiscal sales, in billions of dollars.

Quebecor World	$ 6.5
R.R. Donnelley & Sons	5.7
Mail-Well Inc.	2.4
Moore Corporation	2.2
Vertis	1.9
Quad Graphics	1.8
Wallace Computer Sciences	1.7
Banta Corporation	1.5

Source: *Graphic Arts Monthly*, November 2001, p. 43.

★ 573 ★

Printing (SIC 2752)

Flexo Printing Market, 2002

Nearly 90% of flexographic printing is for packaging applications.

Corrugated/preprint production 34.0%
Flexible-film packaging 24.0
Folding cartons 19.3
Labels 12.3
Envelopes 4.5
Paper bags & multi-wall sacks 3.5
Newspapers 2.4

Source: *Converting Magazine*, April 2002, p. 46.

★ 574 ★

Printing (SIC 2752)

Largest Publication Printers

Companies are ranked by segment sales in millions of dollars.

Quebecor World . . . . $ 1,885
R.R. Donnelley & Sons 1,208
Quad/Graphics 684
Cadmus Communications 416
Brown Printing 304
Perry Judd's Inc. 206
Banta Corp. 200
Vertis Inc. 199
Publishers Printing/Publishers Press 186

Source: *Printing Impressions*, December 2001, p. NA.

★ 575 ★

Business Forms (SIC 2761)

IP Electronic Law Forms

IP stands for intellectual property.

LegalStar Inc. 90.0%
Other 10.0

Source: *Business First of Buffalo*, May 7, 2001, p. C14.

★ 576 ★

Business Forms (SIC 2761)

Largest Business Form Distributors

Firms are ranked by form sales in millions of dollars.

American Business Forms . . . . $ 102.5
SFI 85.2
Proforma 75.6
Data Supplies 58.6
Global DocuGraphix 48.3
GBS 35.7
Source4 . . . . 27.7
FISERV Document Solutions 18.9
Data Source 15.4
Graphic Services Group 12.2

Source: *Business Forms, Labels & Systems*, November 2001, p. 26.

★ 577 ★

Business Forms (SIC 2761)

Largest Tag and Label Distributors

Firms are ranked by label sales in millions of dollars.

SFI . . . . $ 26.1
Proforma 22.0
American Business Forms 18.0
GBS 16.9
Source4 . . . . 8.3
Global DocuGraphix 7.7
AFE Industries 7.3
Allied Office Products 5.2
Great American Business Products 4.6
The Shamrock Companies 4.1

Source: *Business Forms, Labels & Systems*, November 2001, p. 26.

★ 578 ★

Greeting Cards (SIC 2771)

Everyday Card Sales by Occasion

By holiday, Christmas and Valentine's Day are the top occasions.

Birthdays	60.0%
Anniversaries	8.0
Get well/feel better	7.0
Sympathy	6.0
Friendship/encouragement	6.0
Other	13.0

Source: *Drug Store News*, May 21, 2001, p. 76, from Greeting Card Association.

★ 579 ★

Greeting Cards (SIC 2771)

Greeting Card Industry

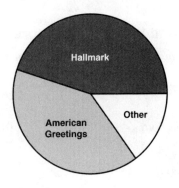

Market shares are shown in percent.

Hallmark	45.0%
American Greetings	40.0
Other	15.0

Source: *Columbus Dispatch*, December 23, 2001, p. 1E.

★ 580 ★

Greeting Cards (SIC 2771)

Top Holidays for Greeting Cards

Total dollar sales were $7.5 billion on 7 billion cards sold.

Christmas	61.0%
Valentine's Day	25.0
Mother's Day	4.0
Easter	3.0
Father's Day	2.5
Other	4.5

Source: *Chain Drug Review*, September 24, 2001, p. 61, from American Greeting Association.

SIC 28 - Chemicals and Allied Products

★ 581 ★
Chemicals (SIC 2800)

Disinfectant/Antimicrobial Chemical Sales, 2005

The $700 million is shown in percent.

Paints & coatings 32.7%
Plastics 21.0
Consumer products 13.5
Food processing 8.4
Medical & healthcare 8.0
Other 16.4

Source: *Chemical Week*, August 29, 2001, p. 24, from Freedonia Group.

★ 582 ★
Chemicals (SIC 2800)

Largest Chemical Producers, 2000

Firms are ranked by chemical sales in billions of dollars.

DuPont . . . . $ 28.4
Dow Chemical 23.0
ExxonMobil 21.5
Huntsman Corp. 8.0
General Electric 7.7
BASF 7.7
Chevron Phillips 7.6
Equistar 7.4
Union Carbide 6.5
PPG Industries 6.2

Source: *C&EN*, May 7, 2001, p. 28.

★ 583 ★
Chemicals (SIC 2800)

Mexico's Chemical Industry

Output is shown in tons.

	Tons	Share
Basic petrochemicals	7,310,002	36.47%
Basic inorganics	6,847,627	34.16
Other petrochemicals	2,360,582	11.78
Synthetic resins	2,219,575	11.07
Artificial and synthetic fibers . .	629,215	3.14
Nitrogen fertilizers	393,247	1.96
Carbon black and synthetic rubber	283,968	1.42

Source: *Chemical Engineering*, April 2002, p. 44, from ANIQ and Pemex.

★ 584 ★
Chemicals (SIC 2800)

Top Flurocarbon Makers, 2001

Market shares are shown in percent.

DuPont 34.0%
Honeywell 28.0
Atofina 19.0
Other 19.0

Source: *Chemical Week*, August 8, 2001, p. 27, from SRI Consulting.

★ 585 ★

Chemicals (SIC 2812)

Oil Field Chemicals

Demand will grow nearly 3% a year through 2005 to $2.3 billion. Advances will be driven by gains in natural gas production. Demand is shown in millions of dollars.

	2000	2005	Share
Commodity chemicals . . .	$ 620	$ 665	28.48%
Specialty chemicals	600	695	29.76
Gases	490	610	26.12
Polymers	240	270	11.56
Other	85	95	4.07

Source: *Research Studies - Freedonia Group*, March 8, 2002, p. 1, from Freedonia Group.

★ 586 ★

Chemicals (SIC 2812)

Pulp and Paper Chemicals Demand

Growth in the market will be driven by a shift to higher value chemicals. Demand is shown in millions of dollars.

	2001	2006	Share
Specialty additives . . .	$ 3,032	$ 3,855	50.46%
Filler & coating pigments . .	1,350	1,650	21.60
Pulping & deinking chemicals	930	1,065	13.94
Bleaching chemicals	831	1,070	14.01

Source: *Research Studies - Freedonia Group*, April 5, 2002, p. 3, from Freedonia Group.

★ 587 ★

Industrial Gases (SIC 2813)

Cylinder Gas Market in Alaska

Cylinder gases are used by hospitals, the mining and construction industry.

Air Liquide America Corp./Airgas Inc. 90.0%
Other 10.0

Source: *Knight-Ridder/Tribune Business News*, August 3, 2001, p. NA.

★ 588 ★

Industrial Gases (SIC 2813)

Industrial Gas Shipments

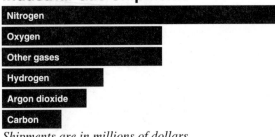

Shipments are in millions of dollars.

	1999	2004	Share
Nitrogen	$ 1,236	$ 2,090	33.15%
Oxygen	975	1,180	18.72
Other gases	740	1,225	19.43
Hydrogen	505	750	11.90
Argon dioxide	475	650	10.31
Carbon	310	410	6.50

Source: *Gases & Welding Distributor*, November-December 2001, p. 28, from Freedonia Group.

★ 589 ★

Industrial Gases (SIC 2813)

U.S. Helium Market

The total market in 2000 reached 3.4 billion cubic feet.

Cryogenics 24.0%
Pressure/purge 20.0
Welding 18.0
Controlled atmosphere 16.0
Leak detection 6.0
Breathing mixtures 3.0
Other 13.0

Source: *C&EN*, December 10, 2001, p. 19, from Bureau of Land Management.

★ 590 ★
Inorganic Chemicals (SIC 2819)

Activated Carbon Sales

Calgon Carbon	
Norit Americas	
Westvaco	
Barnebay & Sutcliffe	

Producers are ranked by capacity in millions of pounds per year.

Calgon Carbon	180
Norit Americas	135
Westvaco	100
Barnebay & Sutcliffe	30

Source: *Chemical Market Reporter*, April 23, 2001, p. 31.

★ 591 ★
Inorganic Chemicals (SIC 2819)

Hydrochloric Acid Market by End Use

The 7.5 million metric ton market is shown in percent.

Ethylene dichloride	64.0%
TDI/MDI	8.0
Food grade HCl	4.0
Steel picking	3.0
Calcium chloride	3.0
Oil well acidizing	2.0
Brine treating	2.0
Chlorine	1.0
Other	13.0

Source: *Chemical Week*, December 5, 2001, p. 50, from CMAI.

★ 592 ★
Inorganic Chemicals (SIC 2819)

Sodium Silicate Market

PQ Corp. is the top producer. The market is mature, with demand at 1.2 million short tons.

Detergents	38.0%
Catalysts	15.0
Pulp & paper	12.0
Elastomers	7.0
Food and health care	5.0
Coatings	3.0

Agriculture	3.0%
Other	17.0

Source: *Chemical Market Reporter*, December 24, 2001, p. 23.

★ 593 ★
Inorganic Chemicals (SIC 2819)

Sodium Sulfate Sales

End market is shown in percent. Top producers include Penoles, OxyChem and Cooper Resources.

Detergents	46.0%
Kraft pulping	13.0
Textiles	12.0
Glass	11.0
Carpet fresheners	7.0
Other	14.0

Source: *Chemical Market Reporter*, August 6, 2001, p. 39.

★ 594 ★
Inorganic Chemicals (SIC 2819)

Top Sodium Sulfite Producers

Producers are ranked by capacity in thousands of short tons. The top end uses were for pulp and paper 55% and water treatment 20%.

Southern Ionics	75
Indspec Chemical	70
Solvay Minerals	55
General Chemical Corp.	36
Calabrian Corp.	15
Olympic Chemical	7

Source: *Chemical Market Reporter*, January 7, 2002, p. 31.

★ 595 ★
Plastics (SIC 2821)

Automotive Plastics Industry in North America

The major drive in growth for the category is expected to be "modular marketing", according to the source, a term that refers to a supplier using the "freedom of plastics to combine adjacent parts in order to increase market share." Figures are in billions of pounds.

	2001	2011
Interior segment	1.64	2.00
Exterior body segment	1.29	1.58
Powertrain & chassis segment	1.00	1.41
Underhood/engine segment	0.41	0.63

Source: *Advanced Materials & Composites News*, June 18, 2001, p. NA, from Market Search Inc.

★ 596 ★
Plastics (SIC 2821)

Biodegradable Polymer Market

Figures are for North America, in millions of pounds.

	2000	2005	Share
Loose-filled packaging	20	25	71.43%
Compost bags	5	8	22.86
Other	1	2	5.71

Source: *Chemical Market Reporter*, August 6, 2001, p. 6, from Business Communications Company.

★ 597 ★
Plastics (SIC 2821)

Ethylene Glycol Sales

End market is shown in percent. Dow and Shell are the top producers. Total demand stands at 5.4 billion pounds.

PET bottle-grade resin	34.0%
Antifreeze	26.0
Polyester fibers	24.0
Other	16.0

Source: *Chemical Market Reporter*, September 3, 2001, p. 39.

★ 598 ★
Plastics (SIC 2821)

Foamed Plastics Demand

The market is expected to grow 3%, with construction driving foamed plastic demand. Figures are in kilotons.

	2000	2005	Share
Urethane	1,579	1,802	50.96%
Polystyrene	869	991	28.03
Vinyl, RIM & other	651	743	21.01

Source: *Urethanes Technology*, August 2001, p. 50, from Freedonia Group.

★ 599 ★
Plastics (SIC 2821)

Injection Molded Plastics Demand

The market is expected to increase 3.5% annually to 16.1 billion pounds in 2005. Figures are in millions of pounds.

	2000	2005	Share
Packaging	4,373	5,310	33.08%
Consumer	4,080	4,880	30.40
Motor vehicles	1,428	1,656	10.32
Electrical & electronic	1,368	1,582	9.86
Other	2,281	2,622	16.34

Source: *Research Studies - Freedonia Group*, October 8, 2001, p. 3, from Freedonia Group.

★ 600 ★
Plastics (SIC 2821)

Largest Injection Molders in North America

Companies are ranked by injecting molder sales in millions of dollars (for the most recent year).

Textron Automotive Co.	$ 1,500.0
Visteon Corp.	1,300.0
Lear Corp.	980.0
Newell Rubbermaid	900.0
Delphi Automotive Systems	675.0
Guide Corp.	520.0
Venture	487.0
Nypro Inc.	478.1

Source: *Plastics News*, December 31, 2001, p. 77.

★ 601 ★
Plastics (SIC 2821)

Largest Plastics Recyclers/Brokers in North America

Companies are ranked by recycling sales in millions of dollars (for the most recent year).

KW Plastics/Recycling Division . . . . . $ 122.0
Rapid Industrial Plastics Co. 60.0
Martin Color Fl Inc. 45.0
B. Schoenberg & Co. Inc. 42.7
Champion Polymer Recycling 32.6
Clean Tech Inc. 30.0
American Environmental Corp. 28.7

Source: *Plastics News*, December 31, 2001, p. 77.

★ 602 ★
Plastics (SIC 2821)

Natural Polymer Industry

Demand is shown in millions of dollars.

	2000	2005	Share
Cellulose ethers	$ 707	$ 870	30.53%
Starch & fermentation products	330	595	20.88
Protein-based polymers . . .	414	567	19.89
Other	636	818	28.70

Source: *Research Studies - Freedonia Group*, September 21, 2001, p. 3, from Freedonia Group.

★ 603 ★
Plastics (SIC 2821)

Plasticizer Demand in North America

The top producers include ExxonMobil, Sterling and Sunoco.

Phthalates 69.0%
Aliphatics 8.0
Epoxies 7.0
Trimellitates 4.0
Other 12.0

Source: *Chemical Market Reporter*, November 5, 2001, p. 22, from Chemical Market Resources Inc.

★ 604 ★
Plastics (SIC 2821)

Reinforced Plastics Demand

Figures are based on 4.18 billion pounds.

Construction 34.3%
Automotive 29.4
Producer durable equipment 14.4
Marine 8.4
Other 13.5

Source: *Reinforced Plastics*, July/August 2001, p. 1, from Freedonia Group.

★ 605 ★
Plastics (SIC 2821)

Top Polyurethane Markets, 2000

Figures are in millions of pounds.

	(mil.)	Share
Construction	1,380	25.91%
Transportation	1,197	22.47
Furniture	515	9.67
Carpet cushions	513	9.63
Appliance	265	4.97
Packaging	234	4.39
Bedding	205	3.85
Textiles & fibres	177	3.32
Other	841	15.79

Source: *Adhesives & Sealants Industry*, February 2002, p. 18.

★ 606 ★

Plastics (SIC 2821)

Transparent Plastics Market, 2006

The average annual growth rate for the market is 6%, driven by sales for the home entertainment sector (CDs and DVDs). Figures are for North America.

Polycarbonates	32.3%
Acrylics	24.8
Polystyrene	23.9
SBCs	5.4
SAN	4.8
Cellulosics	3.3
Other	5.4

Source: *Chemical Market Reporter*, November 26, 2001, p. 6, from Business Communications Co.

★ 607 ★

Plastics (SIC 2821)

U.S. Composite Sales

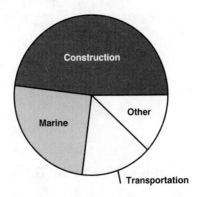

Distribution is shown in percent.

Construction	48.0%
Marine	25.0
Transportation	15.2
Other	11.8

Source: *Reinforced Plastics*, June 2001, p. 12.

★ 608 ★

Fibers (SIC 2824)

U.S. Fiber Shipments, 2001

Market shares are shown in percent for the first six months.

Olefin	63.0%
Polyester	29.0
Other	18.0

Source: *Nonwovens Industry*, December 2001, p. 26.

★ 609 ★

Supplements (SIC 2833)

Leading Herbal Supplements, 2001

Brands are ranked by sales in millions of dollars for the year ended July 22, 2001.

	($ mil.)	Share
Sundown Herbals	$ 81.7	15.42%
Nature's Resource	35.8	6.76
Sundown	20.1	3.79
Healthy Woman	18.8	3.55
One-A-Day	18.6	3.51
Estroven	17.3	3.26
Sundown Herbals Extra	13.3	2.51
Ginkoba	12.4	2.34
Nature Made	11.9	2.25
Other	300.0	56.61

Source: *MMR*, September 3, 2001, p. 22, from Information Resources Inc.

★ 610 ★

Supplements (SIC 2833)

U.S. Nutrition Industry

The $47.6 billion market is shown in percent.

Functional foods	35.7%
Dietary supplements	34.1
Natural foods	21.9
Natural personal care	8.3

Source: *Chemical Market Reporter*, August 27, 2001, p. 3, from Health Business Partners and *Nutrition Business Journal*.

★ 611 ★
Supplements (SIC 2833)

U.S. Supplement Sales

Sales are shown in millions of dollars for the year ended April 2001.

Vitamins and minerals	$ 220.6
Meal replacements/supplements	162.2
Diet formulas	140.2
Herbal singles	124.6
Herbal formulas	73.8
Food supplements	48.0
Digestive aids and enzymes	28.5
Other	260.9

Source: *Drug Store News*, August 6, 2001, p. 23, from SPINS and ACNielsen ScanTrack.

★ 612 ★
Vitamins (SIC 2833)

Top Adult Multivitamin Brands in Canada

Market shares are shown in percent for the year ended December 29, 2001. Total sales hit $84.5 million.

Centrum	39.3%
Jamieson	10.0
One-A-Day	7.5
Paramettes	0.9
Private label	28.6
Other	13.8

Source: *Marketing Magazine*, May 27, 2002, p. 1, from industry sources.

★ 613 ★
Vitamins (SIC 2833)

Top Children's Multivitamin Brands

Brands are ranked by sales for the year ended January 28, 2001.

	($ mil.)	Share
Flintstones	$ 37.0	27.86%
Sundown Pokemon	15.3	11.52
Centrum Kids	14.4	10.84
Poly Vi Sol	12.5	9.41
Bugs Bunny	8.6	6.48
Sesame Street	5.1	3.84
One-A-Day Kids Complete	4.5	3.39
Lil Critters Gummy Bites	2.2	1.66
Flintstones Complete	2.2	1.66
Other	31.0	23.34

Source: *MMR*, April 16, 2001, p. 67, from Information Resources Inc.

★ 614 ★
Vitamins (SIC 2833)

Top Multivitamin Brands, 2001

Market shares are shown in percent.

Centrum	14.7%
Centrum Silver	12.4
One-A-Day	7.4
Flintstones	4.4
Centrum Performance	3.8
Bausch & Lomb Ocuvite	2.1
Centrum Kids	2.0
Theragran M	1.9
Geritol Complete	1.1
Private label	31.0
Other	19.2

Source: *Chain Drug Review*, January 7, 2002, p. 64, from Information Resources Inc.

★ 615 ★
Vitamins (SIC 2833)

Top Vitamin/Mineral Supplement Brands, 2001

Market shares are shown in percent.

Osteo-Bi-Flex	5.8%
Sundown Herbals	4.9
Sundown	4.8

Continued on next page.

139

★ 615 ★ *Continued*

Vitamins (SIC 2833)

Top Vitamin/Mineral Supplement Brands, 2001

Market shares are shown in percent.

Nature Made	4.4%
Citracal	2.7
Os-Cal	2.5
Nature's Resource	2.3
Nature's Bounty	2.3
Natrol	2.2
Viactiv	1.9
Private label	28.0
Other	38.2

Source: *Chain Drug Review*, January 7, 2002, p. 64, from Information Resources Inc.

★ 616 ★

Analgesics (SIC 2834)

Digestive Remedies Market, 2000

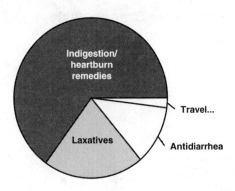

The market was valued at $3.2 billion in 2000.

Indigestion/heartburn remedies	64.9%
Laxatives	21.3
Antidiarrhea	11.5
Travel sickness	2.3

Source: *Datamonitor Industry Market Research*, Annual 2001, p. NA, from Datamonitor.

★ 617 ★

Analgesics (SIC 2834)

Flu Season Sales

Sales are shown in millions of dollars for the 12 weeks ended December 2, 2001.

Sinus tabs/packets	$ 147.9
Sinus liquid/powder	73.4
Sore throat drops	47.0
Nasal spray/drops/inhaler	42.5
Cough syrup	33.6
Nasal strips	5.5
Sore throat liquids	5.3

Source: *Drug Store News*, February 18, 2002, p. 27, from Information Resources Inc.

★ 618 ★

Analgesics (SIC 2834)

Top Acne Remedy Brands

Market shares are shown in percent.

Clean & Clear	9.8%
Neutrogena acne wash	9.3
Clearasil	8.8
Oxy Balance	6.8
Stri-Dex	6.2
Clearsil StayClear	6.2
Neutrogena On-the-Spot	4.9
Oxy 10 Balance	4.8
Nature's Cure	3.8
Neutrogena acne treatment	3.3
Other	36.1

Source: *Chain Drug Review*, January 7, 2002, p. 64, from Information Resources Inc.

★ 619 ★

Analgesics (SIC 2834)

Top Acne Remedy Brands in Drug Stores

Brands are ranked by drug store sales in millions of dollars.

	($ mil.)	Share
Clearasil	$ 14.2	13.16%
Neutrogena Acne Wash	7.3	6.77
Johnson & Johnson's Clean & Clear	5.9	5.47
Oxy Balance	5.6	5.19

Continued on next page.

★ 619 ★ *Continued*
Analgesics (SIC 2834)

Top Acne Remedy Brands in Drug Stores

Brands are ranked by drug store sales in millions of dollars.

	($ mil.)	Share
Oxy 10 Balance	$ 5.6	5.19%
Neutrogena On the Spot	5.4	5.00
Neutrogena Acne Treatment . .	4.9	4.54
Clearasil StayClear	4.2	3.89
Stridex	4.1	3.80
Other	50.7	46.99

Source: *Drug Store News*, May 21, 2001, p. 60, from Information Resources Inc.

★ 620 ★
Analgesics (SIC 2834)

Top Antacid Brands (Liquid/Powder), 2001

Market shares are shown in percent.

Mylanta	23.6%
Maalox	19.5
Mylicon	12.3
Mylanta Supreme	10.2
Gaviscon	5.7
Beano	2.2
Gerber	1.6
Tagamet HB 200	1.5
Maalox Maximum	1.5
Private label	17.1
Other	4.8

Source: *Chain Drug Review*, January 7, 2002, p. 60, from Information Resources Inc.

★ 621 ★
Analgesics (SIC 2834)

Top Antacid Brands (Tablet), 2001

Market shares are shown in percent.

Pepcid AC	14.3%
Zantac 75	10.6
Tums Extra	9.1
Gas X	5.1
Rolaids	4.9
Tums	4.3

Tums Ultra	3.8%
Pepcid Complete	3.8
Tagamet HB 200	3.2
Private label	19.1
Other	21.3

Source: *Chain Drug Review*, January 7, 2002, p. 60, from Information Resources Inc.

★ 622 ★
Analgesics (SIC 2834)

Top Antacid (Tablet) Brands in Drug Stores, 2000

Brands are ranked by drug store sales in millions of dollars.

	$ mil.)	Share
Pepcid AC	$ 56.0	24.52%
Zantac 75	42.0	18.39
Tums EX	26.1	11.43
Gas X	17.9	7.84
Tagamet HB 200	14.4	6.30
Tums	14.1	6.17
Rolaids	10.7	4.68
Phazyme	10.5	4.60
Tums Ultra	9.1	3.98
Other	27.6	12.08

Source: *Drug Store News*, May 21, 2001, p. 46, from IMS Health.

★ 623 ★
Analgesics (SIC 2834)

Top Antacid Vendors, 2001

Market shares are shown for the year ended May 20, 2001.

Smithkline Beecham	24.1%
Johnson & Johnson	22.3
Warner-Lambert	17.5
Novartis	7.9
Private label	16.6
Other	11.6

Source: *Grocery Headquarters*, August 2001, p. 12.

★ 624 ★

Analgesics (SIC 2834)

Top Cold/Allergy/Sinus Brands in Drug Stores

Brands are ranked by sales in millions of dollars. Figures refer to tablets or packets.

	($ mil.)	Share
Benadryl	$ 53.0	12.73%
Alka Seltzer Plus	29.2	7.01
Theraflu	27.1	6.51
Sudafed	26.5	6.36
Tylenol Cold	23.2	5.57
Tylenol Sinus	22.8	5.47
Tylenol Allergy Sinus	17.8	4.27
Advil Cold & Sinus	15.8	3.79
Other	201.1	48.28

Source: *Drug Store News*, May 21, 2001, p. 38, from Information Resources Inc.

★ 625 ★

Analgesics (SIC 2834)

Top Cold/Allergy (Tablet/Packet) Vendors, 2001

Market shares are shown for the year ended May 20, 2001.

McNeil	15.8%
Warner Wellcome	12.6
Parke-Davis	9.7
Novartis	8.0
Private label	23.7
Other	30.2

Source: *Grocery Headquarters*, August 2001, p. 12.

★ 626 ★

Analgesics (SIC 2834)

Top Cold/Sinus Remedy Brands

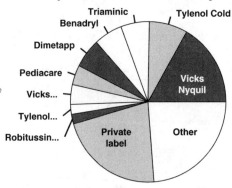

Brands are ranked by sales for the year ended January 28, 2001.

	($ mil.)	Share
Vicks Nyquil	$ 106.6	16.80%
Tylenol Cold	51.2	8.07
Triaminic	37.1	5.85
Benadryl	36.9	5.81
Dimetapp	35.6	5.61
Pediacare	28.1	4.43
Vicks Dayquil	22.8	3.59
Tylenol Flu	13.5	2.13
Robitussin Pediatric	13.4	2.11
Private label	138.3	21.79
Other	151.1	23.81

Source: *MMR*, April 16, 2001, p. 67, from Information Resources Inc.

★ 627 ★

Analgesics (SIC 2834)

Top External Analgesic Brands, 2001

Brands are ranked by sales in millions of dollars for the year ended December 2, 2001.

	($ mil.)	Share
Bengay	$ 35.4	16.78%
Joint-Ritis	23.5	11.14
Icy Hot	21.0	9.95
Aspercreme	14.0	6.64
Flex All 454	9.4	4.45
Mineral Ice	7.1	3.36
Salonpas	6.5	3.08
Absorbine Jr.	5.9	2.80

Continued on next page.

★ 627 ★ *Continued*
Analgesics (SIC 2834)

Top External Analgesic Brands, 2001

Brands are ranked by sales in millions of dollars for the year ended December 2, 2001.

	($ mil.)	Share
Sportscreme	$ 5.6	2.65%
Other	82.6	39.15

Source: *MMR*, January 2/, 202, p. 18, from Information Resources Inc.

★ 628 ★
Analgesics (SIC 2834)

Top First Aid Ointment Brands

Brands are ranked by sales for the year ended January 28, 2001.

	($ mil.)	Share
Neosporin Plus	$ 50.2	12.77%
Neosporin	46.0	11.70
Solarcaine	14.6	3.71
Betadine	10.7	2.72
Becton Dickinson	10.1	2.57
Polysporin	9.5	2.42
A and D	9.2	2.34
Fruit of the Earth	8.1	2.06
Aquaphor	7.4	1.88
Other	227.3	57.82

Source: *MMR*, April 16, 2001, p. 67, from Information Resources Inc.

★ 629 ★
Analgesics (SIC 2834)

Top Internal Analgesic (Tablet) Brands in Drug Stores

Brands are ranked by sales in millions of dollars.

	($ mil.)	Share
Tylenol	$ 152.5	17.76%
Advil	113.0	13.16
Aleve	57.2	6.66
Bayer	45.3	5.28
Tylenol PM	38.3	4.46

	($ mil.)	Share
Excedrin	$ 31.0	3.61%
Motrin IB	28.9	3.37
Ecotrin	23.2	2.70
Other	369.2	43.00

Source: *Drug Store News*, May 21, 2001, p. 38, from Information Resources Inc.

★ 630 ★
Analgesics (SIC 2834)

Top Laxative Brands, 2001

Market shares are shown in percent.

Dulcolax	8.6%
Ex-Lax	8.5
Fibercon	7.3
Senokot	6.2
Correctol	5.8
Senokot S	4.9
Colace	4.8
Fleet	3.7
Fiber Choice	3.2
Private label	31.5
Other	15.5

Source: *Chain Drug Review*, January 7, 2002, p. 64, from Information Resources Inc.

★ 631 ★
Analgesics (SIC 2834)

Top Laxative (Stimulant/Powder) Brands in Drug Stores, 2000

Brands are ranked by drug store sales in millions of dollars.

	($ mil.)	Share
Metamucil	$ 38.4	42.76%
Citrucel	18.9	21.05
Fleet	12.7	14.14
Fleet Phospho Soda	7.0	7.80
Perdiem	4.6	5.12
Other	8.2	9.13

Source: *Drug Store News*, May 21, 2001, p. 46, from IMS Health.

★ 632 ★
Analgesics (SIC 2834)

Top Lice Treatment Brands

Total sales reached $134.9 million.

Rid	30.2%
Nix	22.0
Pronto	4.4
Lice Free	4.4
Acumed	2.6
Clear	2.4
Lice Guard Robi Comb	2.1
A-200	1.3
Other	30.4

Source: *Chain Drug Review*, January 7, 2002, p. 78, from Information Resources Inc.

★ 633 ★
Analgesics (SIC 2834)

Top Nasal Spray Brands

Brands are ranked by sales in millions of dollars for the year ended June 17, 2001.

	($ mil.)	Share
Afrin	$ 73.9	18.46%
Primatene Mist	36.8	9.19
Nasalcrom	30.5	7.62
Vicks Sinex	25.0	6.25
Four Way	23.9	5.97
Zicam	21.7	5.42
Vicks Vapo Stream	14.8	3.70
Vicks	14.1	3.52
Neo Synephrine	14.0	3.50
Other	145.6	36.37

Source: *MMR*, August 20, 2001, p. 40, from Information Resources Inc.

★ 634 ★
Analgesics (SIC 2834)

Top Nasal Spray/Inhaler Brands in Drug Stores

Brands are ranked by sales in millions of dollars.

	($ mil.)	Share
Afrin	$ 29.3	23.96%
Nasalcrom	15.2	12.43
Primatene Mist	14.5	11.86
Vicks Sinex	8.9	7.28

	($ mil.)	Share
Zicam	$ 8.2	6.70%
Neosynephrine	7.5	6.13
Vicks	6.1	4.99
4 Way	5.7	4.66
Vicks Vapo Steam	5.4	4.42
Other	21.5	17.58

Source: *Drug Store News*, May 21, 2001, p. 38, from Information Resources Inc.

★ 635 ★
Analgesics (SIC 2834)

Top Pain Reliever Vendors

Market shares are shown for the year ended May 20, 2001.

McNeil Consumer	30.6%
Whitehall-Robins	15.3
Bayer Consumer	13.5
Bristol-Myers	9.0
Private label	24.1
Other	7.5

Source: *Grocery Headquarters*, August 2001, p. 12.

★ 636 ★
Drugs (SIC 2834)

Cardiac Anti-Clogging Agents

Market shares are shown in percent.

Integrilin	50.0%
Other	50.0

Source: *San Francisco Business Times*, August 3, 2001, p. 23.

★ 637 ★

Drugs (SIC 2834)

Drug Delivery Systems

The market is expected to increase 9% annually to hit $67 billion in 2005. Market includes specialized drug dosage formulations, medial supplies, devices and equipment. Demand is shown in millions of dollars.

	2000	2005	Share
Oral	$ 22,030	$ 33,300	49.59%
Parenteral	12,585	19,805	29.49
Inhalation	7,400	11,385	16.95
Transdermal & implantable	1,427	2,665	3.97

Source: *Research Studies - Freedonia Group*, August 8, 2001, p. 3, from Freedonia Group.

★ 638 ★

Drugs (SIC 2834)

Drug Delivery Systems (Inhaled), 2000

The market was valued at $3.8 billion in 2000.

Servent	10.7%
Flonase	9.1
Flovent	8.2
Proventil HFA	7.9
Vancenase	7.8
Atrovent	5.3
Vancenase Pocket	4.3
Ventolin	2.5
Pumicort	1.4
Beclovent	1.3
Other	41.5

Source: *Datamonitor Industry Market Research*, Annual 2001, p. NA, from Datamonitor.

★ 639 ★

Drugs (SIC 2834)

Erectile Dysfunction Market

Sales of erectile dysfuntion medication should reach $2 billion in 2002. Pfizer makes Viagra.

Pfizer	90.0%
Other	10.0

Source: *Fortune*, February 18, 2002, p. 28.

★ 640 ★

Drugs (SIC 2834)

Leading Health Care Firms

Firms are ranked by revenue in millions of dollars.

Merck & Co.	$ 40.3
McKesson HBOC Inc.	36.7
Cardinal Health	29.8
Pfizer Inc.	29.5
Johnson & Johnson	29.1
GlaxoSmithKline	27.4
Aetna U.S. Healthcare	26.8
UnitedHealth Group	21.1
Aventis Pharmaceuticals	21.0
Bristol-Myers Squibb	18.2

Source: *H&HN*, May 2001, p. 38.

★ 641 ★
Drugs (SIC 2834)

Leading Pharamcy Benefit Managers, 2001

Data show share of annual prescription claims processed.

Merck-Medco	28.7%
Advance PCS	19.8
Express Scripts	14.1
Caremark	7.3
Wellpoint	5.1
Other	25.0

Source: *New York Times*, January 30, 2002, p. C5, from IMS Health and Deutsche Bank Alex. Brown.

★ 642 ★
Drugs (SIC 2834)

Most Advertised Drugs, 2001

Spending is shown in millions of dollars.

Vioxx	$ 135.43
Celebrex	130.36
Nexium	126.14
Viagra	90.63
Allegra	89.09
Zocor	85.64
Glucophage XR	79.72
Imitrex	70.60
Flonase	68.99
Paxil	65.12

Source: *Wall Street Journal*, March 13, 2002, p. B1, from Competitive Media Reporting.

★ 643 ★
Drugs (SIC 2834)

Multiple Scherosis Drugs

Market shares are shown in percent.

	2002	2005
Avonex	58.0%	45.0%
Copaxone	25.0	25.0
Betaseron	17.0	15.0
Rebif	0.0	15.0

Source: *Wall Street Journal*, March 22, 2002, p. B4, from SG Cowan Securities.

★ 644 ★
Drugs (SIC 2834)

Top Branded Drugs, 2000

Market shares are shown in percent.

Prilosec	3.7%
Lipitor	3.4
Prevacid	2.6
Prozac	2.3
Zocor	2.0
Celebrex	1.8
Zoloft	1.7
Paxil	1.6
Other	80.9

Source: *Chain Drug Review*, June 4, 2001, p. RX18, from Scott-Levin SPA.

★ 645 ★
Drugs (SIC 2834)

Top Drug Classes in Canada

Market shares are shown in percent.

Cardiovasculars	13.1%
Psychotherapeutics	11.2
Hormones	8.8
Anti-infectives	8.2
Analgesics	6.4
Other	52.3

Source: *Chain Drug Review*, January 7, 2002, p. 10.

★ 646 ★
Drugs (SIC 2834)

Top Generic Drugs, 2000

Market shares are shown in percent.

Hydrocodone/APAP	4.2%
Ranitidine HCI	3.1
Lorazepam	2.4
Atenolol	2.4
Albuterol aerosol	2.3
Alprazelam	2.2
Propoxyphene-N/APAP	2.1
Tamoxifen	1.8
Cephalexin	1.8
Other	77.7

Source: *Chain Drug Review*, June 4, 2001, p. RX18, from Scott-Levin SPA.

★ 647 ★
Drugs (SIC 2834)

Top Prescription Drug Firms, 2000

Firms are ranked by drug sales in billions of dollars.

	($ bil.)	Share
Pfizer	$ 15.3	10.6%
GlaxoSmithKline	13.0	8.9
Merck and Co.	10.8	7.4
Bristol-Myers Squibb	9.0	6.2
AstraZeneca	8.5	5.9
Johnson & Johnson	7.9	5.4
Pharmacia	6.3	4.3
Lilly	6.1	4.2
American Home Products	6.0	4.2
Schering Plough	5.8	3.4

Source: *Business Wire*, June 15, 2001, p. NA, from IMS Health.

★ 648 ★
Drugs (SIC 2834)

Top Prescription Drugs, 2001

Sales are shown in billions of dollars. Figures include cholesterol reducers, antiulcerants and antidepressants. Spending increased 17% over 2000, rising to $154 billion. The average cost of a prescription at a pharmacy rose to $49.84.

	($ bil.)	Share
Lipitor	$ 4.52	2.90%
Prilosec	4.00	2.56
Prevacid	$ 3.20	2.05%
Zocor	2.74	1.76
Celebrex	2.39	1.53
Zoloft	2.15	1.38
Paxil	2.12	1.36
Vioxx	2.03	1.30
Prozac	1.99	1.28
Other	130.86	83.88

Source: *Wall Street Journal*, March 29, 2002, p. A3, from National Institute for Health Care Management Foundation.

★ 649 ★
Drugs (SIC 2834)

U.S. Cholesterol Reducing Statins

Shares are shown for the year ended June 2001.

Lipitor	46.4%
Zocor	30.9
Pravachol	13.9
Baycol	3.7
Mevacor	2.7
Other	2.4

Source: *Wall Street Journal*, August 9, 2001, p. A3, from IMS Health.

★ 650 ★
Ear Care (SIC 2834)

Top Ear Drop Brands in Drug Stores

Brands are ranked by drug store sales in millions of dollars. Figures include wax removal, swimmer's ear and earaches.

Murine Ear	$ 4.7
Debrox	4.5
Auro-Dri	1.7
Swim Ear	1.1
Ototek Loop	0.7
Similasan	0.6
Flents	0.6
Bausch & Lomb	0.5
Private label	6.7
Other	2.1

Source: *Drug Store News*, February 18, 2002, p. 29, from Information Resources Inc.

★ 651 ★
Smoking Cessation Products (SIC 2834)

Top Smoking Relief Brands, 2001

Market shares are shown in percent.

Nicorette 78.0%
Other 22.0

Source: *Chain Drug Review*, January 7, 2002, p. 64, from
Information Resources Inc.

★ 652 ★
Weight Control Products (SIC 2834)

Top Diet Aid Brands in Drug Stores

*Brands are ranked by sales in millions of dollars for
the year ended November 4, 2001.*

	($ mil.)	Share
Metabolife 356 (tablet)	$ 74.1	14.91%
Ultra Slim Fast (liquid/powder) . .	46.1	9.28
Ensure (liquid/powder)	29.1	5.86
Ensure Plus (liquid/powder) . . .	20.3	4.08
Private label (liquid/powder) . . .	20.1	4.04
Private label (tablet)	18.9	3.80
Metab O Lite (tablet)	14.3	2.88
Slim Fast	13.0	2.62
Boost	11.5	2.31
Dexatrim	9.9	1.99
Other	239.7	48.23

Source: *Drug Store News*, January 21, 2002, p. 42, from
Information Resources Inc.

★ 653 ★
Weight Control Products (SIC 2834)

Top Meal Replacement Brands, 2001

Market shares are shown in percent.

Ultra Slim-Fast 45.9%
Ensure 11.0
Boost 6.2
Ensure Plus 6.1
PediaSure 5.6
Slim-Fast 2.3
Carb Solutions 1.4
Ensure Light 1.3
Boost Plus 1.2
Other 19.0

Source: *Chain Drug Review*, January 7, 2002, p. 64, from
Information Resources Inc.

★ 654 ★
Weight Control Products (SIC 2834)

Top Weight Control (Candy/Tablet) Brands in Drug Stores, 2000

*Brands are ranked by drug store sales in millions of
dollars.*

	($ mil.)	Share
Metabolife 356	$ 30.8	26.37%
Metab-O-Lite	21.8	18.66
Enforma Fat Trapper	9.6	8.22
Metabolize	8.9	7.62
Dexatrim	8.2	7.02
Enforma Exercise in a Bottle . . .	6.3	5.39
Twinlab Diet Fuel	4.0	3.42
Dexatrim Natural	4.0	3.42
Other	23.2	19.86

Source: *Drug Store News*, May 21, 2001, p. 46, from Information Resources Inc.

★ 655 ★
Weight Control Products (SIC 2834)

Top Weight Control (Liquid/Powder) Brands in Drug Stores, 2000

*Brands are ranked by drug store sales in millions of
dollars.*

	($ mil.)	Share
Ultra Slim Fast	$ 42.1	31.82%
Ensure	30.3	22.90
Ensure Plus	21.5	16.25
Boost	10.8	8.16
Ensure Glucerna OS	7.5	5.67
Pedia Sure	6.7	5.06
Met-Rx	3.7	2.80
Boost Plus	2.7	2.04
Ensure Light	2.6	1.97
Other	4.4	3.33

Source: *Drug Store News*, May 21, 2001, p. 46, from Information Resources Inc.

★ **656** ★

Weight Control Products (SIC 2834)

Top Weight Control (Liquid/Powder) Vendors, 2001

Market shares are shown for the year ended May 20, 2001.

Slim-Fast	46.4%
Ross Labs	29.6
Mead-Johnson	8.0
Weider	1.1
Private label	6.1
Other	8.8

Source: *Grocery Headquarters*, August 2001, p. 12.

★ **657** ★

Breath Alcohol Testing (SIC 2835)

Breath Alcohol Testing Equipment

Market shares are shown in percent.

CMI	80.0%
Other	20.0

Source: *Medical Devices & Surgical Technology Week*, January 27, 2002, p. 16.

★ **658** ★

Diagnostics (SIC 2835)

Esoteric Testing Market

Market shares are estimated.

Quest Diagnostics	16.0%
Lab Corp.	12.0
Specialty Labs	5.0
AML	4.0
Impath	3.0
Esoterix	2.0
Other	58.0

Source: *Investor's Business Daily*, August 15, 2001, p. A8, from company reports, U.S. Bancorp. Piper Jaffray, Merrill Lynch & Co., and First Call.

★ **659** ★

Diagnostics (SIC 2835)

Medical Diagnostic Kit Sales, 2006

Sales are shown in millions of dollars.

	($ mil.)	Share
Clinical laboratory testing . . .	$ 1,808.5	35.11%
Home use	1,646.8	31.97
Research	1,368.2	26.56
Veterinary testing	327.0	6.35

Source: *Research Studies - Business Communications Inc.*, April 10, 2002, p. 3, from Business Communications Co.

★ **660** ★

Diagnostics (SIC 2835)

Top Glucometer Brands in Drug Stores, 2000

Brands are ranked by drug store sales in millions of dollars.

One Touch	$ 415.9
Accu-Chek Comfort	368.9
Clucometer Elite	235.0
Acc-Chek Advantage	187.1
Precision Q-I-D	125.8
Fast Take	90.9
Sure Step	89.0
Medicare	56.2
Glucometer DEX	55.2
One Touch Hospital	38.3

Source: *Drug Store News*, May 21, 2001, p. 46, from IMS Health.

★ **661** ★

Biotechnology (SIC 2836)

Contract Biologics Technologies

Market shares are shown in percent.

Microbial fermentation	46.0%
Mammalian cell culture	30.0
Biopharmaceutical fill and finish	12.0
Transgenics	4.0
Other	8.0

Source: *Chemical Week*, April 17, 2002, p. 25, from High-Tech Business Decisions.

★ 662 ★

Biotechnology (SIC 2836)

U.S. Biotechnology Industry

The industry had its start in San Francisco and Boston. The top nine areas accounted for more than 60% of the spending by the National Institute of Health, which funds medical research.

San Francisco, Oakland, San Jose	20.3%
Los Angeles, Riverside, Orange County . . .	20.2
Boston, Worcester, Lawrence	12.9
New York, Long Island, Northern New Jersey .	12.8
San Diego	6.2
Washington, Baltimore	5.6
Other	12.0

Source: *New York Times*, June 11, 2002, p. C4, from The Brookings Institution.

★ 663 ★

Detergents (SIC 2841)

Top Liquid Detergent Brands, 2001

Market shares are shown for the year ended October 7, 2001.

	($ mil.)	Share
Tide	$ 1,051.3	35.04%
All	317.7	10.59
Purex	279.1	9.30
Wisk	227.2	7.57
Xtra	168.5	5.62
Cheer	159.9	5.33
Era	145.8	4.86
Surf	127.2	4.24
Gain	126.1	4.20
Arm & Hammer	116.7	3.89
Other	280.7	9.36

Source: *Household & Personal Products Industry*, January 2002, p. 76, from Information Resources Inc.

★ 664 ★

Detergents (SIC 2841)

Top Liquid Detergent Makers, 2001

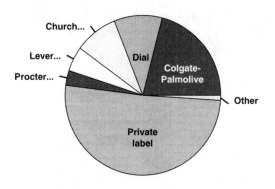

Market shares are shown for the year ended December 2, 2001.

Colgate-Palmolive	21.0%
Dial	10.0
Church Dwight	9.0
Lever Brothers	5.0
Procter & Gamble	3.0
Private label	51.0
Other	1.0

Source: *Chemical Week*, January 23, 2002, p. 24, from Information Resources Inc.

★ 665 ★

Detergents (SIC 2841)

Top Powder Detergent Brands, 2001

Market shares are shown for the year ended October 7, 2001.

	($ mil.)	Share
Tide	$ 806.2	44.79%
Gain	241.7	13.43
Cheer	134.9	7.49
Surf	128.1	7.12
Arm & Hammer Fabricare	111.3	6.18
Wisk	76.2	4.23
Purex	73.2	4.07
All	48.2	2.68
Dreft	34.2	1.90
Other	146.0	8.11

Source: *Household & Personal Products Industry*, January 2002, p. 76, from Information Resources Inc.

★ 666 ★

Detergents (SIC 2841)

Top Powder Detergent Makers, 2001

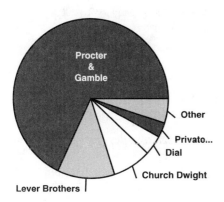

Market shares are shown for the year ended December 2, 2001.

Procter & Gamble	68.0%
Lever Brothers	12.0
Church Dwight	8.0
Dial	4.0
Private label	3.0
Other	5.0

Source: *Chemical Week*, January 23, 2002, p. 24, from Information Resources Inc.

★ 667 ★

Dry-Cleaning Kits (SIC 2841)

Home Dry-Cleaning Kits

Total sales reached $76.7 million for the year ended July 15, 2001. The industry was forecast to be much larger and so several companies are now leaving the market.

	($ mil.)	Share
Dryel	$ 50.6	65.97%
Custom Cleaner	12.0	15.65
Clorox Freshcare	11.6	15.12
Other	2.5	3.26

Source: *Advertising Age*, September 10, 2001, p. 4, from Information Resources Inc.

★ 668 ★

Soap (SIC 2841)

Top Bar Soap Brands in Drug Stores, 2000

Brands are ranked by sales in millions of dollars.

	($ mil.)	Share
Dove	$ 30.1	23.41%
Dial	12.5	9.72
Lever 2000	9.8	7.62
Irish Spring	9.8	7.62
Ivory	7.2	5.60
Caress	6.7	5.21
Olay	6.1	4.74
Cetaphil	4.4	3.42
Other	42.0	32.66

Source: *Drug Store News*, May 21, 2001, p. 51, from Information Resources Inc.

★ 669 ★

Soap (SIC 2841)

Top Bar Soaps, 2001

Brands are ranked by sales in millions of dollars for the year ended August 12, 2001.

	($ mil.)	Share
Dove	$ 323.2	23.76%
Dial	154.8	11.38
Lever 2000	128.7	9.46
Irish Spring	102.4	7.53
Zest	85.9	6.32
Caress	85.1	6.26
Oil of Olay	72.9	5.36
Ivory	69.5	5.11
Safeguard	37.7	2.77
Coast	31.6	2.32
Other	268.2	19.72

Source: *MMR*, October 29, 2001, p. 37, from Information Resources Inc.

★ 670 ★

Soap (SIC 2841)

Top Bath Product Brands, 2001

Market shares are shown in percent.

Vaseline Intensive Care	8.2%
Mr. Bubble	6.7
Calgon	6.6

Continued on next page.

★ 670 ★ *Continued*

Soap (SIC 2841)

Top Bath Product Brands, 2001

Market shares are shown in percent.

Village Naturals	6.2%
Lander	5.2
Kid Zone	3.4
Healing Garden	2.9
Kid Care Scooby Doo	2.7
Private label	11.2
Other	46.9

Source: *Chain Drug Review*, January 21, 2002, p. 17, from Information Resources Inc.

★ 671 ★

Soap (SIC 2841)

Top Liquid Soap Brands, 2001

Shares are shown based on sales for the year ended August 12, 2001.

Dial	11.5%
Soft Soap	10.1
Caress	7.0
Dove	6.7
Suave	5.5
Softsoap Herbal Essentials	5.0
Clairol Herbal Essences	4.1
Olay Complete	4.0
Oil of Olay	3.4
Private label	7.8
Other	34.9

Source: *Household & Personal Products Industry*, December 2001, p. 67, from Information Resources Inc.

★ 672 ★

Soap (SIC 2841)

Top Nondeodorant Bar Soap Brands, 2001

Market shares are shown in percent.

Dove	43.7%
Caress	11.8
Ivory	10.5
Olay	10.2
Dove Nutrium	4.5
Jergens	2.8
Tone	2.1

Tone Island Mist	1.5%
Aveeno	1.5
Other	11.4

Source: *Chain Drug Review*, January 21, 2002, p. 17, from Information Resources Inc.

★ 673 ★

Cleaning Products (SIC 2842)

Household Cleaner Sales

Categories are ranked by sales for the year ended August 2001.

	($ mil.)	Share
All purpose cleaners, disinfectants	$ 629.5	26.9%
Toilet bowl cleaners/disinfectants .	385.1	16.5
Nonabrasive tub/tile cleaners . . .	352.4	15.1
Glass cleaners/ammonia	275.7	11.8
Drain cleaners	204.5	8.7
Spray disinfectants	173.2	7.4
Abrasive tub/tile cleaners	133.3	5.7
Oven/appliance cleaners	65.6	2.8
Lime/rust removers	62.8	2.7
Specialty cleaners/polish	56.4	2.4

Source: *Household and Personal Products Industry*, December 2001, p. 53, from Information Resources Inc.

★ 674 ★

Cleaning Products (SIC 2842)

Industrial & Institutional Cleaning Business

The I&I segment is worth $15 billion.

Ecolab	20.0%
Johnson Wax/DiverseyLever	17.0
Other	63.0

Source: *Household & Personal Products Industry*, December 2001, p. 38.

★ 675 ★
Cleaning Products (SIC 2842)

Industrial & Institutional Cleaning Market Segments

Sales are shown in millions of dollars.

	($ mil.)	Share
Janitorial	$ 2,800	36.84%
Food processing/industrial cleaning	2,800	36.84
Foodservice	1,400	18.42
Laundry	600	7.89

Source: *Household & Personal Products Industry*, November 2001, p. 92, from Kline & Co.

★ 676 ★
Floor Polish (SIC 2842)

Top Floor Polish Brands, 2000

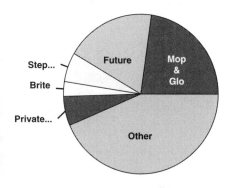

Market shares are shown in percent.

Mop & Glo	22.5%
Future	19.4
Step Saver	5.9
Brite	3.0
Private label	5.6
Other	43.6

Source: *Soap & Cosmetics*, September 2001, p. 22, from Euromonitor.

★ 677 ★
Furniture Polish (SIC 2842)

Top Furniture Polish Brands

Market shares are shown in percent.

Pledge	51.1%
Old English	14.4

Endust	10.6%
Scott's Liquid Gold	5.4
Behold	3.3
Favor	2.4
Klen Guard	1.5
Weiman Lemon Oil	0.5
Private label	2.4
Other	8.4

Source: *Soap & Cosmetics*, September 2001, p. 22, from Euromonitor.

★ 678 ★
Baby Care (SIC 2844)

Breastfeeding Pain Remedies

Market shares are shown in percent.

Lanolin	93.0%
Other	7.0

Source: *Washington Business Journal*, August 17, 2001, p. 25, from Information Resources Inc.

★ 679 ★
Baby Care (SIC 2844)

Top Baby Oil Brands, 2001

Market shares are shown in percent.

Johnson's	52.0%
Baby Magic	4.3
Johnson's Baby	4.2
Gerber	1.2
Lander	0.8
Private label	36.4

Source: *Chain Drug Review*, January 7, 2002, p. 58, from Information Resources Inc.

★ 680 ★
Baby Care (SIC 2844)

Top Baby Ointment/Cream Brands

Brands are ranked by sales in millions of dollars for the year ended October 7, 2001.

	$ mil.)	Share
Desitin	$ 28.7	39.32%
A&D	17.1	23.42
Balmex	10.9	14.93
Johnson's	2.6	3.56
Aveeno	2.3	3.15

Continued on next page.

★ 680 ★ *Continued*

Baby Care (SIC 2844)

Top Baby Ointment/Cream Brands

Brands are ranked by sales in millions of dollars for the year ended October 7, 2001.

	$ mil.)	Share
Johnson's Baby	$ 2.1	2.88%
Gerber	1.5	2.05
Dr. Smith's	1.4	1.92
Triple Paste	0.4	0.55
Other	6.0	8.22

Source: *MMR*, December 17, 2001, p. 38, from Information Resources, Inc.

★ 681 ★

Baby Care (SIC 2844)

Top Baby Powder Brands, 2001

Market shares are shown in percent.

Johnson's	55.6%
Johnson's Baby	4.3
Gold Bond	3.4
Caldesene	2.0
Gerber	1.6
Johnson & Johnson	1.3
Balmex	1.1
Destin	0.7
Other	30.0

Source: *Chain Drug Review*, January 7, 2002, p. 64, from Information Resources Inc.

★ 682 ★

Cosmetics (SIC 2844)

Ethnic Care Product Makers

Vendors are ranked by sales in millions of dollars for the year ended February 3, 2002.

	($ mil.)	Share
Pro-line International	$ 11.2	6.44%
Carson Products	9.0	5.17
Luster Products	7.3	4.20
Soft Sheen Products	6.3	3.62
Colomer	4.8	2.76
Wella/Johnson	4.7	2.70

	($ mil.)	Share
A.P. Products	$ 3.4	1.95%
Supreme Beauty	0.9	0.52
Gillette	0.4	0.23
Other	126.0	72.41

Source: *Household & Personal Products Industry*, April 2002, p. 50, from Information Resources Inc.

★ 683 ★

Cosmetics (SIC 2844)

Ethnic Product Market

Market shares are shown in percent.

Chemicals	23.7%
Hair coloring	16.1
Skin care products	13.6
Hair dressing	12.8
Styling	10.7
Conditioners	6.0
Curl/wave maintenance	5.7
Shaving products	3.9
Men's styling	3.2
Other	4.3

Source: *Chain Drug Review*, April 1, 2002, p. 19, from Information Resources Inc.

★ 684 ★

Cosmetics (SIC 2844)

Mass Market Cosmetics Sales

Market shares are shown in percent.

Face makeup	32.6%
Eye makeup	26.8
Lip makeup	22.7
Nail polish/treatments	12.1
Artificial nails	3.6
Makeup combos	2.2

Source: *Chain Drug Review*, March 4, 2002, p. 27, from Information Resources Inc.

★ 685 ★

Cosmetics (SIC 2844)

Top Eye Makeup Brands, 2001

Market shares are shown in percent.

Expert Eyes	8.3%
Great Lash	7.5

Continued on next page.

★ 685 ★ *Continued*
Cosmetics (SIC 2844)

Top Eye Makeup Brands, 2001

Market shares are shown in percent.

Cover Girl Eye Enhancers	4.3%
Almay One Coat	4.2
Voluminous	4.0
Volume Express	3.9
Full N'Soft	3.4
Cover Girl Professional	3.0
ColorStay	3.0
Other	58.4

Source: *Chain Drug Review*, January 21, 2002, p. 17, from Information Resources Inc.

★ 686 ★
Cosmetics (SIC 2844)

Top Eye Makeup Brands in Drug Stores

Brands are ranked by drug store sales in millions of dollars.

	($ mil.)	Share
Maybelline Expert Eyes	$ 29.7	8.34%
Maybelline Great Lash	20.4	5.73
Almay One Coat	19.1	5.36
L'Oreal Voluminous	16.3	4.58
Revlon ColorStay	15.2	4.27
Cover Girl Eye Enhancers	12.7	3.57
Maybelline Volume Express . . .	11.6	3.26
Other	231.2	64.91

Source: *Drug Store News*, May 21, 2001, p. 54, from Information Resources Inc.

★ 687 ★
Cosmetics (SIC 2844)

Top Facial Makeup Brands

■	Cover Girl
■	Revlon ColorStay
■	Revlon Age Defying
■	Revlon New Complexion
■	Cover Girl Smoothers
■	L'Oreal Feel Naturale
■	Cover Girl Ultimate Finish
■	L'Oreal Visible Lift
■	Cover Girl Simply Powder
■	Other

Brands are ranked by sales for the year ended January 28, 2001.

	($ mil.)	Share
Cover Girl	$ 96.6	8.33%
Revlon ColorStay	55.7	4.80
Revlon Age Defying	53.8	4.64
Revlon New Complexion	51.0	4.40
Cover Girl Smoothers	39.2	3.38
L'Oreal Feel Naturale	30.4	2.62
Cover Girl Ultimate Finish	30.0	2.59
L'Oreal Visible Lift	29.8	2.57
Cover Girl Simply Powder	28.5	2.46
Other	745.0	64.22

Source: *MMR*, April 16, 2001, p. 67, from Information Resources Inc.

★ 688 ★
Cosmetics (SIC 2844)

Top Facial Makeup Brands in Drug Stores

Brands are ranked by drug store sales in millions of dollars.

	($ mil.)	Share
Cover Girl Clean	$ 26.9	6.03%
Revlon Age Defying	25.8	5.79
Revlon New Complexion	24.9	5.59
Revlon ColorStay	24.5	5.50

Continued on next page.

★ 688 ★ *Continued*

Cosmetics (SIC 2844)

Top Facial Makeup Brands in Drug Stores

Brands are ranked by drug store sales in millions of dollars.

	($ mil.)	Share
L'Oreal Free Naturale	$ 13.0	2.92%
Neutrogena Healthy Skin	12.8	2.87
L'Oreal Visible Lift	12.3	2.76
Other	305.6	68.55

Source: *Drug Store News*, May 21, 2001, p. 54, from Information Resources Inc.

★ 689 ★

Cosmetics (SIC 2844)

Top Facial Makeup Vendors

Market shares are shown for the year ended May 20, 2001.

Noxell	28.2%
Revlon	17.8
Maybelline	12.5
L'Oreal	10.3
Almay	6.8
Other	24.4

Source: *Grocery Headquarters*, August 2001, p. 12.

★ 690 ★

Cosmetics (SIC 2844)

Top Lip Makeup Brands in Drug Stores

Brands are ranked by drug store sales in millions of dollars.

	($ mil.)	Share
Revlon Super Lustrous	$ 32.8	9.01%
Revlon ColorStay	27.0	7.42
Revlon Moondrops	16.8	4.62

	($ mil.)	Share
Maybelline Moisture Whip	$ 15.5	4.26%
L'Oreal Colour Riche	15.3	4.20
Cover Girl Continous Color . . .	15.0	4.12
Olay Color Moist	13.3	3.65
Other	228.2	62.71

Source: *Drug Store News*, May 21, 2001, p. 54, from Information Resources Inc.

★ 691 ★

Cosmetics (SIC 2844)

Top Lipstick Brands

Market shares are shown in percent.

Revlon	21.7%
L'Oreal	13.5
Maybelline	12.9
Cover Girl	12.3
Max Factor	5.0
Almay	3.8
Other	30.8

Source: *Chemical Market Reporter*, December 3, 2001, p. FR3, from Information Resources Inc. and Deutsche Banc Alex. Brown.

★ 692 ★

Denture Care (SIC 2844)

Top Dental Cleanser (Paste/Powder) Brands, 2001

Market shares are shown in percent.

Dentu-Crème	50.8%
Fresh n Brite	20.3
Dentu-Gel	9.6
Stain Away Plus	9.1
Ban A Stain	4.5
Kleenite	3.2
Polident	1.2
Other	1.3

Source: *Chain Drug Review*, January 7, 2002, p. 64, from Information Resources Inc.

★ 693 ★

Denture Care (SIC 2844)

Top Dental Cleanser (Tablet) Brands, 2001

Market shares are shown in percent.

Polident	23.2%
Efferdent	20.0
Efferdent Plus	13.9
Polident Overnight	9.8
Fixodent	5.1
Smokers Polident	4.9
Polident for Partials	3.0
Other	20.1

Source: *Chain Drug Review*, January 7, 2002, p. 64, from Information Resources Inc.

★ 694 ★

Denture Care (SIC 2844)

Top Denture Adhesive Brands, 2001

Market shares are shown in percent.

Fixodent	42.6%
Sea-Bond	11.7
Super Poligrip	11.3
Fixodent Free	9.7
Poligrap Free	8.1
Fixodent Fresh	3.5
Poligrap Ultra Fresh	3.3
Effergrip	2.5
Cushion Grip	2.1
Other	5.3

Source: *Chain Drug Review*, January 7, 2002, p. 58, from Information Resources Inc.

★ 695 ★

Deodorants (SIC 2844)

Top Deodorant Brands, 2001

Right Guard

Mennen Speed Stick

Degree

Secret

Secret Sheer Dry

Dove

Old Spice High Endurance

Ban

Other

Market shares are shown in percent.

Right Guard	7.2%
Mennen Speed Stick	7.0
Degree	7.0
Secret	5.2
Secret Sheer Dry	5.0
Dove	4.6
Old Spice High Endurance	4.3
Ban	3.9
Other	55.8

Source: *Chain Drug Review*, January 21, 2002, p. 17, from Information Resources Inc.

★ 696 ★

Deodorants (SIC 2844)

Top Deodorant Vendors

Market shares are shown for the year ended May 20, 2001.

Procter & Gamble	27.1%
Gillette	19.1
Mennen	14.3
Helene Curtis	11.7
Carter-Wallace	6.1
Other	16.7

Source: *Grocery Headquarters*, August 2001, p. 12.

★ 697 ★
Eye Care (SIC 2844)

Top Eye Care/Lens Solution Brands

Market shares are shown in percent.

Opti-Free	8.3%
Renu Multiplus	7.5
Renu	4.6
Aosept	3.8
Refresh Tears	2.9
Refresh Plus	2.5
Genteal	2.3
Boston	2.3
Sensitive Eye	2.2
Private label	11.7
Other	51.9

Source: *Chain Drug Review*, January 7, 2002, p. 74, from Information Resources Inc.

★ 698 ★
Eye Care (SIC 2844)

Top Eye Care Vendors, 2001

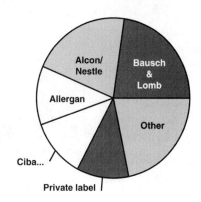

Market shares are shown for the year ended May 20, 2001.

Bausch & Lomb	23.3%
Alcon/Nestle	20.8
Allergan	12.0
Ciba Vision	11.5
Private label	10.5
Other	21.9

Source: *Grocery Headquarters*, August 2001, p. 12.

★ 699 ★
Feminine Hygiene Products (SIC 2844)

Top Feminine Hygiene Medicinal Brands, 2001

Market shares are shown in percent.

Monistat 3	13.9%
Summer's Eve	9.5
Massengill	7.5
Monistat 7	7.1
Monistat 1	6.2
Vagisil	5.1
Vagistat 1	4.6
K-Y	4.1
FDS	3.6
Gyne-Lotrimin 3	2.9
Other	35.5

Source: *Chain Drug Review*, January 7, 2002, p. 64, from Information Resources Inc.

★ 700 ★
Foot Care (SIC 2844)

Top Foot Care Brands, 2001

Brands are ranked by sales for the year ended January 28, 2001.

	($ mil.)	Share
Lotrimin	$ 51.1	16.33%
Lamisil	44.8	14.32
Tinactin	44.7	14.29
Desenex	21.6	6.90
Dr. Scholl's	21.1	6.74
Micatin	9.8	3.13
Johnson's Odor Eaters	9.0	2.88
Fungi Care	5.9	1.89
Dr. Scholl's Odor Destroyer	5.6	1.79
Other	99.3	31.74

Source: *MMR*, April 16, 2001, p. 67, from Information Resources Inc.

Foot Care (SIC 2844)

Top Foot Care Device Makers, 2001

Firms are ranked by sales for the year ended July 15, 2001.

	($ mil.)	Share
Schering-Plough	$ 245.9	69.29%
Implus	17.3	4.87
Profoot Care	14.3	4.03
Johnson & Johnson	11.0	3.10
Combe	9.3	2.62
Pedifix	7.8	2.20
Homemedics	5.6	1.58
W.E. Bassett	4.9	1.38
Spenco Medical	2.6	0.73
Other	36.2	10.20

Source: *MMR*, September 3, 2001, p. 25, from Information Resources Inc.

Foot Care (SIC 2844)

Top Foot Care Firms in Drug Stores, 2001

Companies are ranked by sales in millions of dollars for the year ended July 15, 2001.

	($ mil.)	Share
Schering-Plough	$ 88.3	42.43%
Profoot	9.4	4.52
PediFix	6.2	2.98
Implus	5.6	2.69
Johnson & Johnson	4.5	2.16
Combe	3.4	1.63
Spenco Medical	2.8	1.35
Private label	10.6	5.09
Other	77.3	37.15

Source: *Drug Store News*, September 10, 2001, p. 23, from Information Resources Inc.

Fragrances (SIC 2844)

Top Fragrance Brands for Men

Brands are ranked by sales for the year ended January 28, 2001.

	($ mil.)	Share
Stetson	$ 32.8	7.12%
Old Spice	32.1	6.97
Gillette Series	17.9	3.89
Drakkar Noir	16.2	3.52
Jovan Musk for Men	15.9	3.45
Aspen	14.7	3.19
Preferred Stock	14.6	3.17
Mennen Skin Bracer	13.9	3.02
Davidoff Cool Water	13.6	2.95
Other	288.7	62.71

Source: *MMR*, April 16, 2001, p. 67, from Information Resources Inc.

Fragrances (SIC 2844)

Top Fragrance Brands for Women

Brands are ranked by sales for the year ended January 28, 2001.

	($ mil.)	Share
Calgon	$ 30.8	4.77%
Shower to Shower	29.8	4.61
Body Fantasy	23.9	3.70
Elizabeth Taylor Whte Diamonds	22.0	3.40
Gold Bond	21.5	3.33

Continued on next page.

★ 704 ★　Continued
Fragrances (SIC 2844)

Top Fragrance Brands for Women

Brands are ranked by sales for the year ended January 28, 2001.

	($ mil.)	Share
Designer Imposters	$ 17.3	2.68%
Vanderbilt by Gloria Vanderbilt . .	14.6	2.26
Jovan Musk for Women	13.7	2.12
Other	472.6	73.14

Source: *MMR*, April 16, 2001, p. 67, from Information Resources Inc.

★ 705 ★
Fragrances (SIC 2844)

Top Fragrance Producers for Men

Vendors are ranked by sales in millions of dollars for the year ended January 27, 2002. Figures exclude Wal-Mart.

	($ mil.)	Share
Coty	$ 62.00	18.22%
Procter & Gamble	27.20	7.99
Unilever Prestige	21.90	6.44
J.B. Williams	15.10	4.44
The Gillette Co.	13.60	4.00
Other	200.48	58.92

Source: *Household & Personal Products Industry*, April 2002, p. 50, from Information Resources Inc.

★ 706 ★
Fragrances (SIC 2844)

Top Fragrance Producers for Women

Vendors are ranked by sales in millions of dollars for the year ended January 27, 2002. Figures exclude Wal-Mart.

	($ mil.)	Share
Coty	$ 85.6	20.20%
Elizabeth Arden	36.8	8.69
Parfums de Coeur	33.7	7.95
Revlon	26.3	6.21
New Dana	18.1	4.27
Other	223.2	52.68

Source: *Household & Personal Products Industry*, April 2002, p. 50, from Information Resources Inc.

★ 707 ★
Fragrances (SIC 2844)

Top Perfume/Cologne Brands in Drug Stores

Brands are ranked by drug store sales in millions of dollars.

	($ mil.)	Share
Calgon	$ 11.0	4.41%
Elizabeth Taylor's White Diamonds	10.6	4.25
Body Fantasy	8.6	3.44
Gold Bond	7.4	2.96
Jean Nate	6.8	2.72
Other	205.3	82.22

Source: *Drug Store News*, May 21, 2001, p. 54, from Information Resources Inc.

★ 708 ★
Fragrances (SIC 2844)

Top Shaving Lotion Brands in Drug Stores

Brands are ranked by drug store sales in millions of dollars.

	($ mil.)	Share
Old Spice	$ 10.2	8.21%
Stetson	9.1	7.32
Drakkar	7.6	6.11
Davidoff Cool Water	6.6	5.31
Fragrance Impressions	5.8	4.67
Other	85.0	68.38

Source: *Drug Store News*, May 21, 2001, p. 54, from Information Resources Inc.

★ 709 ★
Hair Care (SIC 2844)

Hair Care Industry

Sales are shown in millions of dollars for the year ended July 14, 2001.

Shampoo (aerosol, liquid, lotion, powder)	$ 1,850.0
Hair coloring, women	1,410.0
Cream rinses and conditioners	998.1
Wave setting products	808.1
Hair spray, women	435.9
Hair coloring, men	146.7

Continued on next page.

★ 709 ★ *Continued*
Hair Care (SIC 2844)

Hair Care Industry

Sales are shown in millions of dollars for the year ended July 14, 2001.

Hair preparations	$ 142.1
Hair growth products	118.3
Hair preparations, men	38.7
Home permanents	37.5

Source: *MMR*, September 3, 2001, p. 66, from A.C. Nielsen.

★ 710 ★
Hair Care (SIC 2844)

Top Ethnic Hair Dressing Brands

Brands are ranked by sales in millions of dollars for the year ended February 3, 2002.

	($ mil.)	Share
Luster Products	$ 5.0	17.01%
Pro-Line International	3.6	12.24
Namasday Laboratory	3.5	11.90
Wella/Johnson	3.1	10.54
Bronner Brothers	2.5	8.50
Soft Sheen	2.4	8.16
J. Strickland	2.4	8.16
A.P. Products	1.3	4.42
Imperial Dak	1.2	4.08
Other	4.4	14.97

Source: *Household & Personal Products Industry*, April 2002, p. 50, from Information Resources Inc.

★ 711 ★
Hair Care (SIC 2844)

Top Hair Coloring Brands, 2001

Brands are ranked by sales in millions of dollars for the year ended October 7, 2001. Data exclude Wal-Mart.

	($ mil.)	Share
L'Oreal Preference	$ 144.4	13.25%
Clairol Nice N Easy	97.9	8.98
L'Oreal Excellence	97.3	8.93
L'Oreal Feria	87.3	8.01
Clairol Natural Instincts	64.4	5.91
Just for Men	63.6	5.83
Clairol Hydrience	48.1	4.41
L'Oreal Casting Color Spa	33.9	3.11

	($ mil.)	Share
Clairol Ultress	$ 31.8	2.92%
Other	421.3	38.65

Source: *MMR*, December 17, 2001, p. 43, from Information Resources Inc.

★ 712 ★
Hair Care (SIC 2844)

Top Hair Coloring Vendors

Market shares are shown for the year ended May 20, 2001.

L'Oreal	41.4%
Clairol	36.9
Revlon	7.5
Combe	7.3
Garnier	4.3
Other	2.6

Source: *Grocery Headquarters*, August 2001, p. 12.

★ 713 ★
Hair Care (SIC 2844)

Top Hair Conditioner Brands, 2001

Market shares are shown in percent.

Herbal Essences	7.0%
Thermasilk	5.7
Infusium 23	4.9
Alberto VO5	4.9
Pantene Smooth and Sleek	3.6
Finesse	3.6
Suave	3.0
Pantene Sheer Volume	2.9
Pantene Hydrating Curls	2.6
Pantene Constant Care	2.6
Other	59.2

Source: *Chain Drug Review*, January 21, 2002, p. 17, from Information Resources Inc.

★ 714 ★
Hair Care (SIC 2844)

Top Hair Relaxer Kit Brands, 2001

Market shares are shown in percent.

Soft Sheen Optimum Care	10.6%
Dark & Lovely	7.7
Just For Me	6.8
Soft & Beautiful	6.7
Luster S-Curl	6.7
African Pride	6.6
Johnson's Gentle Treatment	6.3
Dark & Lovely Plus	5.6
Ogilvie	4.9
Other	38.1

Source: *Chain Drug Review*, January 21, 2002, p. 17, from Information Resources Inc.

★ 715 ★
Hair Care (SIC 2844)

Top Hair Spray Brands, 2001

Market shares are shown in percent.

Rave	10.4%
Pantene Pro V	7.3
Suave	6.8
Salon Selectives	4.8
White Rain Classic Care	4.4
Aqua Net	4.4
Herbal Essences	3.9
Consort	3.7
Thermasilk	3.5
Other	50.8

Source: *Chain Drug Review*, January 21, 2002, p. 17, from Information Resources Inc.

★ 716 ★
Hair Care (SIC 2844)

Top Hair Styling Gel/Mousse Brands

Brands are ranked by sales for the year ended January 28, 2001.

	($ mil.)	Share
Pantene Pro V	$ 42.1	7.02%
La Looks	39.7	6.62
Suave	34.3	5.72
Clairol Herbal Essences	28.0	4.67
Salon Selectives	23.5	3.92
Thermasilk	20.8	3.47
Dep	17.6	2.94
Vidal Sassoon	12.2	2.04
Vital Care	10.5	1.75
Frizz Ease	10.5	1.75
Other	360.3	60.10

Source: *MMR*, April 16, 2001, p. 67, from Information Resources Inc.

★ 717 ★
Hair Care (SIC 2844)

Top Shampoo Brands, 2001

Brands are ranked by sales in millions of dollars for the year ended December 30, 2001.

	($ mil.)	Share
Clairol Herbal Essences	$ 105.0	8.08%
Suave	49.0	3.77
Pantene Pro V	45.0	3.46
Thermasilk	43.1	3.32
Finesse	34.2	2.63
Pert Plus	32.7	2.52
Pert	32.6	2.51
Pantene Smooth and Sleek	30.3	2.33
Pantene Sheer Volume	29.1	2.24
Other	899.0	69.15

Source: *MMR*, February 25, 2002, p. 27, from Information Resources Inc.

★ 718 ★

Hair Care (SIC 2844)

Top Shampoo Brands in Canada, 2001

Market shares are shown in percent.

Colgate	40.8%
Crest	26.4
Sensodyne	11.0
Aquafresh	9.6
Arm & Hammer	6.5
Close-Up	1.3
Oral-B	0.9
Aim	0.6
Pepsodent	0.1
Other	3.1

Source: *Marketing Magazine*, May 27, 2002, p. 1, from industry sources.

★ 719 ★

Hair Care (SIC 2844)

Top Shampoo Vendors

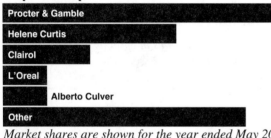

Market shares are shown for the year ended May 20, 2001.

Procter & Gamble	32.1%
Helene Curtis	19.9
Clairol	9.8
L'Oreal	5.2
Alberto Culver	4.6
Other	28.4

Source: *Grocery Headquarters*, August 2001, p. 12.

★ 720 ★

Lip Care (SIC 2844)

Lip Care Market Segments

Market shares are shown in percent.

	2000	2001
Traditional	51.2%	43.9%
Cold sore	15.7	24.0
Medicated	13.1	9.9
Style and flavored	10.8	11.7
Therapeutic features	4.4	5.9
Sun care	3.4	4.1
Other	1.3	0.5

Source: *Progressive Grocer*, April 15, 2002, p. S1, from Information Resources Inc.

★ 721 ★

Lip Care (SIC 2844)

Top Lip Care Brands, 2001

Market shares are shown in percent.

Chapstick	25.0%
Abreva	10.9
Blistex	10.0
Carmex	6.0
Mentholatum Soft Lips	4.1
Chapstick Flava Craze	2.8
Campho-Phenique	2.8
Blistex Herbal Answer	2.5
Herpecin L	2.4
Other	33.5

Source: *Chain Drug Review*, January 7, 2002, p. 64, from Information Resources Inc.

★ 722 ★

Nail Care (SIC 2844)

Nail Care Sales, 2001

Sales are shown for the year ended May 20, 2001.

	($ mil.)	Share
Nail polish/treatments	$ 190.4	54.17%
Nail accessories/treatments	79.6	22.65
Artificial nails & accessories	53.5	15.22
Nail polish removers	28.0	7.97

Source: *Drug Store News*, August 6, 2001, p. 25, from Information Resources Inc.

★ 723 ★
Nail Care (SIC 2844)

Top Artificial Nail Brands

Kiss
Broadway Nails
Nailene
Fing'rs
Sally Hansen Professional
Nailene Color Expressions
IBD 5 Second
Sally Hansen
Nailene Sculptuready
Other

Brands are ranked by sales in millions of dollars.

	($ mil.)	Share
Kiss	$ 17.9	14.52%
Broadway Nails	16.0	12.98
Nailene	14.5	11.76
Fing'rs	13.8	11.19
Sally Hansen Professional . . .	6.9	5.60
Nailene Color Expressions . .	6.6	5.35
IBD 5 Second	4.7	3.81
Sally Hansen	3.9	3.16
Nailene Sculptuready	3.4	2.76
Other	35.6	28.87

Source: *MMR*, August 20, 2001, p. 35, from Information Resources Inc.

★ 724 ★
Nail Care (SIC 2844)

Top Artificial Nails/Accessory Brands

Market shares are shown in percent.

Kiss	18.8%
Broadway Nails	14.9
Nailene	11.0
Sally Hansen Professional	5.1
IBD 5 Second	5.0
Fing'rs	4.6
Cosmar Press & Go	4.0
Nailene Color Express	3.7
Pro 10	3.3
Jonel	2.4
Other	27.2

Source: *Chain Drug Review*, March 18, 2002, p. 51, from Information Resources Inc.

★ 725 ★
Nail Care (SIC 2844)

Top Nail Polish Brands, 2002

Brands are ranked by sales in millions of dollars for the year ended March 24, 2002. Data do not include Wal-Mart.

	($ mil.)	Share
Maybelline Express Finish	$ 26.0	8.13%
Sally Hansen Hard As Nails . . .	21.7	6.78
Sally Hansen	20.2	6.31
Revlon	18.6	5.81
L'Oreal Jet Set	17.1	5.35
Cover Girl Nail Slicks	13.3	4.16
Wet n Wild	11.3	3.53
Sally Hansen Teflon Tuff	10.6	3.31
Sally Hansen Chrome Nail	10.4	3.25
Other	170.7	53.36

Source: *MMR*, May 13, 2002, p. 38, from Information Resources Inc.

★ 726 ★
Oral Care (SIC 2844)

Top Dental Floss Brands

Brands are ranked by sales in millions of dollars for the year ended December 2, 2001.

	($ mil.)	Share
Glide	$ 26.8	21.19%
Reach	24.1	19.05
Reach Easy Slide	8.3	6.56
Reach Dentotape	7.0	5.53
Reach Gentle Gum Care	5.9	4.66
J&J Reach Whitening	5.2	4.11
Oral B	4.6	3.64
Oral B Ultra Floss	4.4	3.48
Oral B Satinfloss	4.3	3.40
Private label	25.0	19.76
Other	10.9	8.62

Source: *MMR*, February 11, 2002, p. 26, from Information Resources Inc.

★ 727 ★
Oral Care (SIC 2844)

Top Oral Pain Relief Brands, 2001

Market shares are shown in percent.

Anbesol	18.9%
Orajel	14.6

Continued on next page.

★ 727 ★ *Continued*
Oral Care (SIC 2844)

Top Oral Pain Relief Brands, 2001

Market shares are shown in percent.

Baby Orajel	12.9%
Colgate Peroxyl	7.9
Glyoxide	4.0
Zilactin	3.9
Zilactin B	3.6
Orabase B	3.4
Other	30.8

Source: *Chain Drug Review*, January 7, 2002, p. 64, from Information Resources Inc.

★ 728 ★
Oral Care (SIC 2844)

Top Oral Rinse Brands, 2001

Market shares are shown in percent.

Listerine	42.8%
Scope	15.3
Plax	5.0
Act	4.0
Targon	2.1
Act for Kids	1.9
Capacol	1.3
Biotene	1.2
Other	26.4

Source: *Chain Drug Review*, January 7, 2002, p. 64, from Information Resources Inc.

★ 729 ★
Oral Care (SIC 2844)

Top Toothpaste Brands

Sales are shown for the year ended December 2, 2001.

	($ mil.)	Share
Crest	$ 252.5	21.04%
Colgate	187.6	15.63
Colgate Total	102.1	8.51
Aquafresh	95.7	7.97
Crest Multicare	72.5	6.04
Sensodyne	55.7	4.64
Mentadent	52.0	4.33
Colgate Total Fresh Stripe	41.7	3.47
Colgate 2 in 1	37.8	3.15

	($ mil.)	Share
Arm & Hammer Dental Care Advanced	$ 33.4	2.78%
Other	269.0	22.42

Source: *MMR*, February 11, 2002, p. 25, from Information Resources Inc.

★ 730 ★
Oral Care (SIC 2844)

Top Toothpaste Vendors

Market shares are shown for the year ended May 20, 2001.

Colgate	33.3%
Procter & Gamble	27.3
Smithkline Beecham	10.6
Chesebrough-Pond's	9.9
Church & Dwight	6.4
Other	12.5

Source: *Grocery Headquarters*, August 2001, p. 12.

★ 731 ★
Oral Care (SIC 2844)

Top Whitening Brands, 2001

Sales are at food stores for the year ended November 4, 2001.

	($ mil.)	Share
Crest Whitestraps	$ 69.12	61.18%
Rembrandt Dazzling White	11.91	10.54
Natural White 5 Minute	7.32	6.48
Natural White Rapid White	4.84	4.28
Plus White Ultra	4.30	3.81
Rembrandt Plus	4.03	3.57
Natural White Pro	3.40	3.01

Continued on next page.

★ 731 ★ *Continued*
Oral Care (SIC 2844)

Top Whitening Brands, 2001

Sales are at food stores for the year ended November 4, 2001.

	($ mil.)	Share
Plus White One Step	$ 3.08	2.73%
Biodent Oral Care	1.77	1.57
Dr. George's Dental White	1.25	1.11
Other	1.95	1.73

Source: *Grocery Headquarters*, February 2002, p. 45, from Information Resources Inc.

★ 732 ★
Personal Care Products (SIC 2844)

Cosmetics and Toiletry Sales, 2000

The industry had sales of $29 billion.

Hair care	21.0%
Cosmetics	20.0
Skin care	18.0
Perfume	9.0
Oral care	8.0
Personal soaps	7.0
Deodorants	7.0
Shaving	2.0
Other	8.0

Source: *Chemical Week*, December 5, 2001, p. 48, from Freedonia Group.

★ 733 ★
Personal Care Products (SIC 2844)

Personal Care Industry

Sales are shown in millions of dollars.

	2001	2003	2005
Hair care	$ 8,318	$ 8,315	$ 8,371
Color cosmetics	7,307	7,872	8,251
Skin care	6,916	7,705	8,312
Fragrances	6,019	6,002	5,889
Bath/shower	4,300	4,288	4,223
Oral hygiene	4,262	4,339	4,399
Men's grooming products . .	2,449	2,519	2,569
Deodorants	1,969	1,978	1,974
Sun care	1,115	1,211	1,306

Source: *Chemical Specialties*, November 2001, p. 18, from Euromonitor.

★ 734 ★
Personal Care Products (SIC 2844)

Top Brands of Depilatories in Drug Stores, 2001

Sales are for the year ended October 7, 2001.

	($ mil.)	Share
Aussie Nads	$ 33.9	24.69%
Nair	29.0	21.12
Sally Hansen	25.6	18.65
Epil Stop	13.9	10.12
Magic	6.0	4.37
Other	28.9	21.05

Source: *Drug Store News*, December 17, 2001, p. 74, from Information Resources Inc.

★ 735 ★
Personal Care Products (SIC 2844)

Top Health & Beauty Care Products

Sales are shown in millions of dollars for the year ended January 27, 2002.

Private label internal analgesic tablets . . .	$ 459.9
Ultra Slim Fast	375.7
Tylenol internal analgesic tablets	344.6
Private label cold/allergy/sinus	293.5
Advil internal analgesic tablets	291.2
Private label mineral supplements	287.4
Always sanitary napkins/liners	278.3
Gillette Mach3 refill razor blades	271.8
Crest toothpaste	254.0
Listerine mouthwash/dental rinse	237.3

Source: *Grocery Headquarters*, April 2002, p. 96.

★ 736 ★
Shaving Cream (SIC 2844)

Top Shaving Cream Brands, 2001

Market shares are shown in percent.

Skintimate	26.3%
Edge Pro Gel	12.6

Continued on next page.

★ 736 ★ *Continued*
Shaving Cream (SIC 2844)

Top Shaving Cream Brands, 2001

Market shares are shown in percent.

Edge	9.6%
Gillette Series	8.6
Foamy	7.5
Satin Care	6.9
Colgate	6.8
Barbasol	4.2
Edge Active Care	3.6
Other	13.9

Source: *Chain Drug Review*, January 21, 2002, p. 17, from Information Resources Inc.

★ 737 ★
Skin Care (SIC 2844)

Top Facial Cleanser Brands

Brands are ranked by sales for the year ended January 28, 2001.

	($ mil.)	Share
Ponds	$ 68.4	10.77%
Oil of Olay Daily	42.3	6.66
Johnson's Clean & Clear	38.0	5.98
Biore	36.1	5.68
Oil of Olay	35.1	5.53
Noxzema	32.2	5.07
St. Ives Swiss Formula	29.8	4.69
Neutrogena Deep Clean	25.1	3.95
Cetaphil	24.8	3.90
Other	303.4	47.76

Source: *MMR*, April 16, 2001, p. 67, from Information Resources Inc.

★ 738 ★
Skin Care (SIC 2844)

Top Facial Moisturizer Brands

Brands are ranked by sales for the year ended January 28, 2001.

	($ mil.)	Share
Oil of Olay	$ 72.5	20.17%
Oil of Olay Complete	42.1	11.71
Ponds	32.1	8.93
Neutrogena Moisture	24.5	6.82
Oil of Olay Provital	16.9	4.70
Neutrogena Healthy Skin	16.9	4.70
L'Oreal Plenitude Futu E	16.6	4.62
Neutrogena Pore Refining	14.0	3.89
Private label	11.4	3.17
Other	112.5	31.29

Source: *MMR*, April 16, 2001, p. 67, from Information Resources Inc.

★ 739 ★
Skin Care (SIC 2844)

Top Fade/Age/Bleach Creams

Sales are for the year ended March 25, 2001.

	($ mil.)	Share
L'Oreal Plentitude Revitalift	$ 35.3	9.10%
Oil of Olay Total Effects	33.1	8.53
Neutrogena Healthy Skin	30.4	7.84
Nive Visage Q10	27.5	7.09
ROC Actif Pur	27.1	6.98
L'Oreal Plentitude	17.8	4.59
L'Oreal Plentitude The Line Eraser	16.1	4.15
Ponds Dramatic Results	14.4	3.71
Night Of Olay	11.1	2.86

Continued on next page.

★ 739 ★ *Continued*

Skin Care (SIC 2844)

Top Fade/Age/Bleach Creams

Sales are for the year ended March 25, 2001.

	($ mil.)	Share
Sudden Change	$ 10.3	2.65%
Other	164.9	42.50

Source: *MMR*, May 14, 2001, p. 31, from Information Resources Inc.

★ 740 ★

Skin Care (SIC 2844)

Top Hand/Body Lotion Brands, 2001

Brands are ranked by sales for the year ended January 28, 2001.

	($ mil.)	Share
Vaseline Intensive Care	$ 129.2	8.07%
Jergens	77.5	4.84
Nivea	62.5	3.91
Lubriderm	61.0	3.81
Curel	53.8	3.36
Suave	52.1	3.26
Eucerin	48.6	3.04
Neutrogena Norwegian Formula	32.0	2.00
Keri	29.8	1.86
Other	1,053.5	65.84

Source: *MMR*, April 16, 2001, p. 67, from Information Resources Inc.

★ 741 ★

Skin Care (SIC 2844)

Top Hand/Body Lotion Brands in Drug Stores

Brands are ranked by drug store sales in millions of dollars.

	($ mil.)	Share
Vaseline Intensive Care	$ 31.0	9.34%
Nivea	22.1	6.66
Eucerin	19.6	5.90
Lubriderm	16.9	5.09
Cetaphil	13.0	3.92
Jergens	12.9	3.89
Neutrogena Norwegian Formula	12.5	3.77

	($ mil.)	Share
Curel	$ 12.4	3.73%
Other	191.6	57.71

Source: *Drug Store News*, May 21, 2001, p. 60, from Information Resources Inc.

★ 742 ★

Skin Care (SIC 2844)

Top Hand/Body Lotion Vendors, 2001

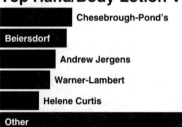

Market shares are shown for the year ended May 20, 2001.

Chesebrough-Pond's	12.9%
Beiersdorf	11.6
Andrew Jergens	9.8
Warner-Lambert	8.5
Helene Curtis	6.8
Other	50.4

Source: *Grocery Headquarters*, August 2001, p. 12.

★ 743 ★

Sun Care (SIC 2844)

Sun Care Sales by Type

Figures are in millions of dollars.

	1996	2000	Share
Sun protection	$ 653.9	$ 828.3	77.32%
Self tanning	147.1	220.6	20.59
After sun	18.8	22.4	2.09

Source: *Soap & Cosmetics*, December 2001, p. 34, from Euromonitor.

★ 744 ★

Sun Care (SIC 2844)

Top Sun Care Brands in Drug Stores

Brands are ranked by sales in millions of dollars.

	($ mil.)	Share
Neutrogena	$ 25.9	14.08%
Banana Boat	21.1	11.47
Coppertone	18.1	9.84
Coppertone Sport	9.5	5.17
Hawaiian Tropic	8.8	4.79
Coppertone Endless Summer	6.6	3.59
Coppertone Water Babies	5.8	3.15
Bain de Soleil	5.5	2.99
Private label	21.1	11.47
Other	61.5	33.44

Source: *Drug Store News*, September 10, 2001, p. 23, from Information Resources Inc.

★ 745 ★

Sun Care (SIC 2844)

Top Suntan Lotion Brands, 2001

Market shares are shown in percent.

Banana Boat	12.4%
Coppertone	11.0
Neutrogena	10.5
Hawaiian Tropic	6.1
Coppertone Endless Summer	5.4
Coppertone Sport	5.3
Coppertone Water Babies	4.3
No-Ad	4.2
Banana Boat Sport	3.5
Other	37.3

Source: *Chain Drug Review*, January 21, 2002, p. 17, from Information Resources Inc.

★ 746 ★

Paints and Coatings (SIC 2851)

Coatings Industry by Technology, 2001

Market shares are shown in percent.

Solvent-based	49.0%
Water-based	41.0
Powder	6.0
Rad-cure	2.0
Other	2.0

Source: *Chemical Specialties*, November 2001, p. 16, from Kusumager, Nerlfi & Growney.

★ 747 ★

Paints and Coatings (SIC 2851)

Coatings, Sealants and Adhesive Demand

Demand is shown in millions of square yards.

	2000	2005	Share
Coatings	$ 4,200	$ 4,940	72.43%
Adhesives	789	1,010	14.81
Selants	640	870	12.76

Source: *Research Studies - Freedonai Group*, September 21, 2001, p. 3, from Freedonia Group.

★ 748 ★

Paints and Coatings (SIC 2851)

Color Pigment Demand

Sales are shown in millions of dollars.

	2000	2005	Share
Organic	$ 1,340	$ 1,755	50.72%
Inorganic	1,025	1,210	34.97
Specialty	375	495	14.31

Source: *Research Studies - Freedonia Group*, September 14, 2001, p. 3, from Freedonia Group.

★ 749 ★

Paints and Coatings (SIC 2851)

Military Aircraft Coatings Market

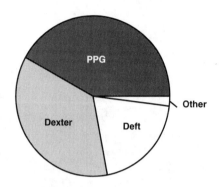

Market shares are shown in percent. The North American market had sales of $68.2 million.

PPG	42.0%
Dexter	36.0
Deft	20.0
Other	2.0

Source: *Chemical Market Reporter*, December 3, 2001, p. 14, from PG Phillips & Associates.

★ 750 ★

Paints and Coatings (SIC 2851)

Paint and Coatings Industry

Sales are shown in millions of dollars.

	1999	2004
Lithographic	$ 1,960	$ 2,405
Flexographic	960	1,250
Gravure	765	930
Digital	175	290
Letterpress	131	115
Other	464	650

Source: *Paint & Coatings Industry*, June 2001, p. 80, from Freedonia Group.

★ 751 ★

Paints and Coatings (SIC 2851)

Pigment Sales by Market, 2000

Demand is shown by segment.

Printing ink	29.0%
Paint and coatings	25.0
Plastics	15.0
Textile and leather	6.0
Paper and paperboard	3.0
Other	22.0

Source: *Chemical Week*, November 7, 2001, p. 30, from Freedonia Group.

★ 752 ★

Paints and Coatings (SIC 2851)

Popular Colors for Cars in North America

Figures are based on a survey. Silver was the top color in the sports utility, compact and medium-sized car segments.

	1999	2001
Neutral	12.0%	19.0%
White	16.0	16.0
Red	16.0	15.0
Silver/natural	12.0	14.0
Black	13.0	11.0
Blue	8.0	11.0
Green	15.0	10.0
Specialty	8.0	4.0

Source: *PR Newswire*, January 7, 2002, p. NA, from PPG Industries.

★ 753 ★

Paints and Coatings (SIC 2851)

Radiation Curable Industry by Segment

The $459 million market is shown in percent. The radicure market is also known as ultraviolet/electron beam, is estimated at $1.2 billion globally.

Overprint	44.0%
Plastic substrates	20.0
Fiber optics	13.0
Release	7.0
Hardwood flooring	4.0
Electronics	4.0

Continued on next page.

★ 753 ★ *Continued*
Paints and Coatings (SIC 2851)

Radiation Curable Industry by Segment

The $459 million market is shown in percent. The radicure market is also known as ultraviolet/electron beam, is estimated at $1.2 billion globally.

Wood furniture 3.0%
Autos 3.0

Source: *Chemical Market Reporter*, May 21, 2001, p. 3, from PG Phillips & Associates.

★ 754 ★
Paints and Coatings (SIC 2851)

Top Coatings Firms in North America

Firms are ranked by sales in billions of dollars.

Sherwin-Williams . . . . $ 3.874
PPG Industries 3.260
DuPont Performance Coatings 1.470
ICI Paints North America 1.450
RPM Inc. 1.040
Valspar Corp. 1.000
Benjamin Moore & Co. 0.820
Akzo Nobel 0.750

Source: *Paint & Coatings Industry*, July 2001, p. 38.

★ 755 ★
Paints and Coatings (SIC 2851)

Top Powder Coating Producers

Data are for North America.

Morton/Rohm and Haas 12.0%
DuPont 10.0
PPG 9.0
Lilly/Valspar 9.0
Ferro 9.0
HB Fuller 6.0
Other 45.0

Source: *Chemical Market Reporter*, June 25, 2001, p. 14, from PG Phillips & Associates.

★ 756 ★
Paints and Coatings (SIC 2851)

U.S. Coatings Market

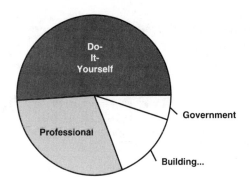

The market is based on 668 million gallons.

Do-It-Yourself (consumer) 51.0%
Professional 30.0
Building maintenance 14.0
Government 5.0

Source: *Chemical Market Reporter*, August 27, 2001, p. 4, from Impact Marketing Consultants.

★ 757 ★
Organic Chemicals (SIC 2865)

Largest Formaldehyde Makers

Firms are ranked by capacity in millions of pounds per year.

Borden Chemical 4,600
Georgia-Pacific 2,510
Celanese 1,730
Neste Resins 900
DuPont 900
Perstorp 450
Degussa 215
Solutia 200
ISP 200

Source: *Chemical Market Reporter*, May 21, 2001, p. 39.

★ 758 ★

Organic Chemicals (SIC 2865)

Oxygen Scavenger Market in North America

Scavengers are used in plastic containers to preserve the shelf life of packaged foods and beverages. Shares are shown based on 1.3 billion packages.

Meats 37.0%
Beer 30.0
Ketchup 11.0
Juices 11.0
Other 11.0

Source: *Chemical Week*, July 18, 2001, p. 27, from BRG Townsend.

★ 759 ★

Organic Chemicals (SIC 2865)

Paraxylene Market Sales

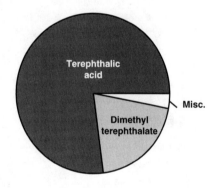

Market shares are shown in percent.

Terephthalic acid 77.0%
Dimethyl terephthalate 20.0
Misc. 3.0

Source: *Chemical Market Reporter*, November 12, 2001, p. 31.

★ 760 ★

Organic Chemicals (SIC 2865)

Top Isopropanol Producers

Producers are ranked by capacity in millions of pounds annually.

ExxonMobil 660
Shell 600
Dow 550
Equistar 65

Source: *Chemical Market Reporter*, November 12, 2001, p. 31.

★ 761 ★

Organic Chemicals (SIC 2869)

Carbon Dioxide Market, 2000

Total demand was 7.5 million tons.

Chilling 25.0%
Freezing 19.0
Carbonated beverages 17.0
Industrial 10.0
Oil recovery 7.0
Dry ice for food 6.0
Dry ice 3.0
Other 13.0

Source: *Chemical Week*, August 22, 2001, p. 32, from J.R. Campbell & Associates.

★ 762 ★

Organic Chemicals (SIC 2869)

Hydrofluoric Acid Market

The total market reached 350,000 metric tons annually. The U.S. has 19% of the world market.

Fluorcarbons 60.0%
Metal picking 5.0
Petroleum alkylation 3.0
Aluminum production 2.0
Other 30.0

Source: *Chemical Week*, August 22, 2001, p. 33, from SRI Consulting.

★ 763 ★

Organic Chemicals (SIC 2869)

Leading LAB Producers, 2000

LAB stands for linear alkybenzene. Figures are for North America.

Condea 45.0%
Hutsman 33.0
Petresa 22.0

Source: *Chemical Market Reporter*, June 25, 2001, p. 2, from CAHA.

★ 764 ★

Organic Chemicals (SIC 2869)

Top Propylene Oxide Producers

| Lyondell |
| Dow |
| Huntsman |

Producers are ranked by millions of pounds manufactured annually.

Lyondell 2,360
Dow 2,095
Huntsman 525

Source: *Chemical Market Reporter*, September 10, 2001, p. 4.

★ 765 ★

Agrichemicals (SIC 2879)

Lawn Care Market

Market shares are shown in percent.

Scotts 52.0%
Other 48.0

Source: *Fortune*, May 13, 2002, p. 179.

★ 766 ★

Agrichemicals (SIC 2879)

Preferred Brands of Lawn & Garden Chemicals

The table shows the brands shoppers would select when shopping at a discount store or superstore. Figures show the results of a survey.

Scott 24.0%
Miracle-Gro 12.0
Ortho 5.0

Source: *DSN Retailing Today*, October 22, 2001, p. 24, from Lee J. Shapiro.

★ 767 ★

Pesticides (SIC 2879)

Pesticide Sales by Type, 2010

Projected sales are shown in millions of dollars for the year.

	($ mil.)	Share
Herbicides	$ 5,500	66.67%
Insecticides	2,000	24.24
Fungicides	750	9.09

Source: *Industrial Bioprocessing*, November 16, 2001, p. 2.

★ 768 ★

Pesticides (SIC 2879)

Retail Insecticide Sales

Data show supermarket sales in millions of dollars.

Ant & roach, regular aerosol . . . . . . $ 61.17
Insect repellants 33.14
Indoor foggers 21.40
Rodenticides 15.56
Wasp & hornet 14.72
Flying insect, aerosol 11.57
Mouse, rat, mole traps 10.47
Flea & tick, aerosol 6.34
Ant traps 4.93

Source: *Supermarket Business*, September 15, 2001, p. 36, from A.C. Nielsen.

★ 769 ★

Adhesives (SIC 2891)

Adhesives Market in North America

Market shares are shown in percent.

Wood	29.0%
Metal	28.0
Plastics	24.0
Glass	19.0

Source: *Coatings World*, December 2001, p. 28, from PGPhillips.

★ 770 ★

Adhesives (SIC 2891)

Radiation-Cured Adhesive Sales, 2000

Sales are shown in millions of dollars.

	($ mil.)	Share
Dental	$ 125	62.5%
Assembly	45	22.5
Laminating	21	10.5
Pressure sensitive	9	4.5

Source: *Adhesives & Sealants Industry*, October-November 2001, p. 23.

★ 771 ★

Ink (SIC 2893)

Top Printing Ink Firms

Firms are ranked by sales in millions of dollars.

Sun Chemical	$ 3,300
Flint Ink	1,400
INX International	300
SICPA	110
Color Converting	108
Wikoff Color	81
Central Ink	73
Toyo Ink America	71
Superior	67

Source: *Ink World*, April 2002, p. 39.

★ 772 ★

Fireworks (SIC 2899)

Top Fireworks Makers in South Florida

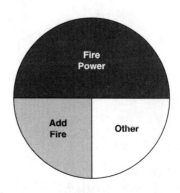

Market shares are estimated in percent.

Fire Power	50.0%
Add Fire	25.0
Other	25.0

Source: *Knight-Ridder/Tribune Business News*, July 4, 2001, p. NA.

SIC 29 - Petroleum and Coal Products

★ 773 ★
Gasoline (SIC 2911)

Gasoline Market in California

Market shares are shown in percent.

Chevron-Texaco	25.0%
Ultramar-Valero	20.0
Equilon	15.0
Other	40.0

Source: *North County Times (California)*, September 8, 2001, p. 1.

★ 774 ★
Gasoline (SIC 2911)

Top Gasoline Marketers

Market shares are shown based on gallons.

ExxonMobil	17.42%
BP	12.38
Citgo	10.27
Marathon	8.61
Chevron	7.70
Motiva	7.47
Equilon	6.72
Tosco	4.76
Sunoco	4.31
Phillips	3.63
Other	16.73

Source: *National Petroleum News*, July 15, 2001, p. 132.

★ 775 ★
Shingles (SIC 2952)

Shingel Market in California

Sales of asphalt shingles grow 8-11% a year, compared to 3-4% for the general shingle market.

Laminated	75.0%
Other	25.0

Source: *Investor's Business Daily*, June 11, 2002, p. A9.

★ 776 ★
Motor Oil (SIC 2992)

Top Motor Oils, 2001

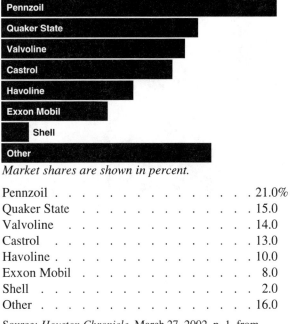

Market shares are shown in percent.

Pennzoil	21.0%
Quaker State	15.0
Valvoline	14.0
Castrol	13.0
Havoline	10.0
Exxon Mobil	8.0
Shell	2.0
Other	16.0

Source: *Houston Chronicle*, March 27, 2002, p. 1, from NPD Group.

SIC 30 - Rubber and Misc. Plastics Products

★ 777 ★
Tires (SIC 3011)

Light Truck Tire Market in Mexico

Market shares are shown based on 4 million units.

Goodyear	24.5%
Euzkadi	22.5
Firestone	17.0
General	9.5
Tornel	8.5
Uniroyal	4.5
B.F. Goodrich	4.0
Michelin	3.0
Other	6.5

Source: *Modern Tire Dealer*, Fact Book 2002, p. 1.

★ 778 ★
Tires (SIC 3011)

OEM Tire Market, 2001

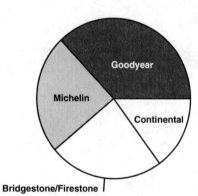

Bridgestone/Firestone

OEM stands for original equipment manufacturer.
Data are for North America.

Goodyear	37.0%
Michelin	24.0
Bridgestone/Firestone	24.0
Continental	15.0

Source: *Tire Business*, February 2, 2002, p. 3.

★ 779 ★
Tires (SIC 3011)

Replacement Light Truck Tire Market in Canada

Market shares are shown based on 2.2 million units.

Goodyear	14.5%
Motomaster	14.0
Michelin	11.0
BFGoodrich	11.0
Dayton	7.0
Bridgestone	7.0
Hankook	5.0
Kumho	4.5
Firestone	4.5
Other	21.5

Source: *Modern Tire Dealer*, Fact Book 2002, p. 1.

★ 780 ★
Tires (SIC 3011)

Replacement Tire Market, 2001

Figures are for passenger cars.

Goodyear	16.5%
Michelin	8.5
Firestone	7.5
Cooper	5.0
Bridgestone	5.0
BF Goodrich	5.0
Other	52.5

Source: *USA TODAY*, April 30, 2002, p. 3B, from *Modern Tire Dealer*.

★ 781 ★
Tires (SIC 3011)

Replacement Tire Market in Canada

Market shares are shown based on 15 million units.

Motomaster	18.5%
Goodyear	15.5
Michelin	10.0
Bridgestone	5.5
Kumho	5.0
BFGoodrich	5.0
Dayton	4.0
Uniroyal	3.5
Hankook	3.5
Other	29.5

Source: *Modern Tire Dealer*, Fact Book 2002, p. 1.

★ 782 ★
Tires (SIC 3011)

Replacement Tire Market in Mexico

Market shares are shown based on 6.7 million units.

Goodyear	22.0%
Euzkadi	21.0
Firestone	17.0
General	10.5
Uniroyal	7.0
Tornel	6.0
B.F. Goodrich	5.5
Michelin	4.0
Other	7.0

Source: *Modern Tire Dealer*, Fact Book 2002, p. 1.

★ 783 ★
Tires (SIC 3011)

Scrap Tire Market

Tires make up 2% of municipal solid waste annually. One scrap tire is generated per person per year.

Tire derived fuel	64.0%
Civil engineering applications	15.0
Ground rubber	9.0
Export	8.0
Cut/punched/stamped products	4.0

Source: *Waste Age*, March 2002, p. 20.

★ 784 ★
Footwear (SIC 3021)

Golf Shoe Market

Data are at sporting goods stores.

FootJoy/Nike	71.7%
Other	28.2

Source: *Golf World*, June 22, 2001, p. S6.

★ 785 ★
Footwear (SIC 3021)

Men's Footwear Market by Segment

Figures are for September - November 2001.

$50-$74.99	$ 31.5
$0-$49.99	27.1
$75-$99.99	20.8
$125 and above	12.2
$100-$124.99	8.6

Source: *Footwear News*, January 14, 2002, p. 7, from NPD Fashionworld - POS Department Stores.

★ 786 ★
Footwear (SIC 3021)

Sports Footwear Categories, 2000

Sales are shown in millions of dollars.

	($ mil.)	Share
Walking shoes	$ 3,317.4	25.47%
Gym shoes/sneakers	1,871.2	14.37
Jogging/running shoes	1,637.8	12.57
Cross-training shoes	1,528.2	11.73
Hiking boots	816.9	6.27

Continued on next page.

★ 786 ★ *Continued*
Footwear (SIC 3021)

Sports Footwear Categories, 2000

Sales are shown in millions of dollars.

	($ mil.)	Share
Basketball	$ 786.3	6.04%
Tennis	533.4	4.09
Sport sandals	467.8	3.59
Fitness	297.0	2.28
Aerobic shoes	292.0	2.24
Other	1,478.1	11.35

Source: *Research Alert*, July 6, 2001, p. 5, from National Sporting Goods Association.

★ 787 ★
Footwear (SIC 3021)

Sports Shoe Market, 2000

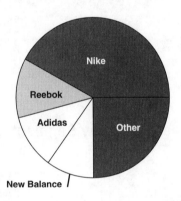

The $7.8 billion market is shown in percent.

Nike	42.3%
Reebok	11.9
Adidas	10.8
New Balance	9.6
Other	25.1

Source: "Adidas-Salomon." Retrieved Janaury 22, 2001 from the World Wide Web: http://www.bloomberg.com, from Sporting Goods Intelligence.

★ 788 ★
Footwear (SIC 3021)

Sports Shoe Sales by Segment

Retail sales are shown in billions of dollars.

	1999	2001	Share
Men's	$ 8.03	$ 8.54	55.42%
Women's	4.19	4.41	28.62
Children's	2.32	2.46	15.96

Source: "Athletic Footwear Sales Climb." Retrieved May 30, 2002 from the World Wide Web: http://www.sgma. com, from Sporting Goods Manufacturers Association.

★ 789 ★
Rubber Parts (SIC 3050)

Top Rubber Parts Makers

Firms are ranked by orginal equipment sales in millions of dollars.

Delphi Automotive	$ 21.5
Dana Corp.	7.1
Eaton Corp.	2.8
Federal-Mogul Corp.	2.0
Continental	1.6
Collins & Aikman	1.6
Bridgestone/Firestone	1.4
Goodyear	1.3

Source: *Rubber & Plastics News*, July 9, 2001, p. 15.

★ 790 ★
Gaskets and Seals (SIC 3053)

Gaskets and Seals Demand

Demand is expected to increase 5% annually. Slight improvements in motor vehicles will help drive growth. Sales are shown in millions of dollars.

	2000	2005	Share
Seals	$ 4,609	$ 5,820	43.02%
Gaskets	3,037	3,855	28.49
Nonmetallic	1,728	2,215	16.37
Metallic	1,309	1,640	12.12

Source: *Rubber World*, November 2001, p. 20, from Freedonia Group.

★ **791** ★

Personal Flotation Devices (SIC 3069)

Inflatable PFD Market

Market shares are shown in percent.

Watermark	.60.0%
Other	.40.0

Source: *Outdoor Retailer*, January 2002, p. 72.

★ **792** ★

Plastic Products (SIC 3081)

Largest Plastic Film/Sheet Makers in North America

Companies are ranked by film & sheet sales in millions of dollars (for the most recent year).

Bemis Co. Inc.	$ 1,658.6
DuPont	.1,412.0
Cryovac Inc.	.1,220.0
Tyco Plastics and Adhesives Group . . .	.1,200.0
Printpack Inc..	950.0
Pechiney Plastic Packaging Inc.	950.0
Pilant Corp.	915.0

Source: *Plastics News*, December 31, 2001, p. 77.

★ **793** ★

Plastic Bottles (SIC 3085)

PET Bottle Market by End Use

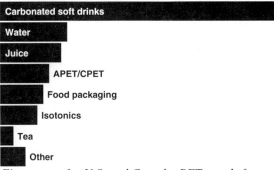

Figures are for U.S. and Canada. PET stands for polyethylene terephthalate.

Carbonated soft drinks	.46.0%
Water	.11.0
Juice	.10.0
APET/CPET	.8.0
Food packaging	.7.0
Isotonics	.6.0

Tea	.2.0%
Other	.4.0

Source: *Chemical Week*, September 12, 2001, p. 39.

★ **794** ★

Hot Tubs (SIC 3088)

Hot Tub/Spa Sales in Canada

22,690 units were sold during the year, worth $129.8 million in retail sales. Sales increased 12.8% from last year.

	units	Share
Acylic	20,450	90.13%
Soft sided tubs	1,600	7.05
Concrete spas	440	1.94
Wooden hot tubs	200	0.88

Source: *Pool & Spa Marketing*, Summer 2001, p. 32.

★ **795** ★

Condoms (SIC 3089)

Top Condom Brands

Brands are ranked by sales in millions of dollars for the year ended January 27, 2002. Figures exclude Wal-Mart.

	($ mil.)	Share
Trojan	$ 66.0	31.16%
Trojan Enz	39.9	18.84
Durex	31.7	14.97
LifeStyles	24.5	11.57
Trojan Ultra Pleasure	10.4	4.91
Trojan Magnum	8.5	4.01
Kling Tite Naturalamb	8.3	3.92
Trojan Supra	4.8	2.27
Trojan Extended Pleasure	3.3	1.56
Other	14.4	6.80

Source: *MMR*, March 25, 2002, p. 22, from Information Resources Inc.

★ 796 ★

Condoms (SIC 3089)

Top Condom Makers

Market shares are shown in percent.

Carter-Wallace 68.0%
Durex 15.9
Ansell 14.6
Other 1.5

Source: *Grocery Headquarters*, November 2001, p. 49, from A.C. Nielsen.

★ 797 ★

Plastic Handles (SIC 3089)

Plastic Handle Industry

Data refer to plastic binders that hold double, triple or four packs of juice, pasta sauce and other food products. Share is estimated.

Borg 95.0%
Other 5.0

Source: *Knight-Ridder/Tribune Business News*, November 12, 2001, p. NA.

SIC 31 - Leather and Leather Products

★ 798 ★
Footwear (SIC 3131)

Hiking Boot Market

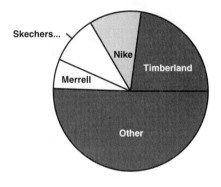

Sales are shown for July 2001- December 2001.

Timberland	23.1%
Nike	10.7
Skechers USA	9.5
Merrell	6.2
Other	50.5

Source: *Footwear News*, March 11, 2002, p. 9, from NPD FashionWorld.

★ 799 ★
Footwear (SIC 3131)

Hiking Boot Sales by Age

Sales are shown by age for July 2001- December 2001.

0-17	37.5%
30-44	29.1
18-24	10.8
45-54	9.3
25-29	8.5
55-64	2.9
65+	2.0

Source: *Footwear News*, March 25, 2002, p. 9, from NPD FashionWorld.

★ 800 ★
Footwear (SIC 3131)

Outdoor Footwear Market Shares

Market shares are shown in percent. Hunting had the top share by activity.

Timberland	33.2%
Merrell	10.7
Nike	9.8
Other	46.3

Source: *Sporting Goods Business*, December 2001, p. 47, from SPORTSCANInfo.

★ 801 ★
Footwear (SIC 3140)

Casual Lifestyle Market

Casual footwear grew more than 20% in 2001, and the lifestyle/fashion portion has increased more than 40% during the year. Dollar shares are shown in percent.

K-Swiss	20.2%
Skechers	19.6
Reebok	17.6
Nike	7.2
Other	35.4

Source: *Sporting Goods Business*, February 2002, p. 14, from Sportscaninfo.

★ 802 ★
Footwear (SIC 3140)

Leading Sandal Brands

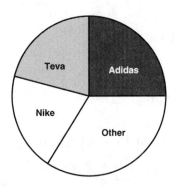

Dollar shares are shown in percent.

Adidas 24.9%
Teva 21.4
Nike 20.1
Other 33.6

Source: *Sporting Goods Business*, February 2002, p. 14, from Sportscaninfo.

★ 803 ★
Footwear (SIC 3144)

Women's Boot Sales byType

There were strong sales in July - October 2001 compared to the same period in 2000.

Ankle/bootie 49.0%
High shaft 25.5
Mid shaft 18.8
All weather 1.8
Hiking 1.7
Other 3.2

Source: *Footwear News*, December 17, 2001, p. 4, from NPD FashionWorld - POS Department Stores.

★ 804 ★
Footwear (SIC 3144)

Women's Shoe Sales

Shares are shown for sales from March 2001-February 2002. Figures are for department stores.

Tailored casual 34.1%
Casual 30.3
Dress 23.6
Active casual 7.1
Athletic 2.8
Evening 2.1

Source: *Footwear News*, May 27, 2002, p. 4, from NPDFashionworld.

★ 805 ★
Luggage (SIC 3161)

Luggage and Leather Goods Sales in Canada, 2001

Sales are shown in millions of Canadian dollars.

Handbags/evening . . . . $ 92,051
Wallets 24,552
Luggage 21,008
Belts 20,488
Briefcases 1,610
Backpacks 1,603
Credit card/key case 1,396
Sport bags 790

Source: "Luggage, Leathergoods, Accessories." Retrieved March 28, 2002 from the World Wide Web: http://www. llanda.com, from Luggage, Leathergoods & Accessories Association.

★ 806 ★
Luggage (SIC 3161)

U.S. Luggage Sales

Sales are for the direct market (catalogs, online and on television).

Badanco 75.0%
Other 25.0

Source: *The Record*, March 6, 2002, p. B3.

SIC 32 - Stone, Clay, and Glass Products

★ 807 ★
Glass (SIC 3221)

Glass Packaging Market Shares, 2001

Market shares are shown in percent.

Owens-Illinois	42.0%
Ball-Foster	32.0
Consumers Packaging/Anchor Glass	18.0
Other	8.0

Source: *Packaging Strategies*, November 15, 2001, p. 5, from Owens-Illinois.

★ 808 ★
Glassware (SIC 3229)

Preferred Brands of Glassware/ Dishware

The table shows the brands shoppers would select when shopping at a discount store or superstore. Figures show the results of a survey and are not market shares.

Corel	14.0%
Corning	13.0
Libbey	8.0

Source: *DSN Retailing Today*, October 22, 2001, p. 24, from Lee J. Shapiro.

★ 809 ★
Cement (SIC 3241)

Cement & Concrete Additive Demand

Sales are shown in millions of dollars. The industry should see 6% annual growth.

	2000	2005	Share
Chemicals	$ 469	$ 638	51.24%
Minerals	315	414	33.25
Fibers	117	193	15.50

Source: *Research Studies - Freedonia Group*, September 14, 2001, p. 3, from Freedonia Group.

★ 810 ★
Fiber Cement (SIC 3241)

Fiber Cement Building Products

Fiber-cement is a mixture of cement and sand with cellulose fibers to provide strength. Data show selected market shares (Hardie is the industry leader). Figures are for North America.

Hardie	13.0%
Cemplank	1.5
Other	85.5

Source: *Knight-Ridder/Tribune Business News*, April 20, 2001, p. NA.

★ 811 ★
Advanced Ceramics (SIC 3250)

Advanced Ceramics Industry

The $8.4 billion is expected to hit $11.1 billion.

	2000	2005
Electronic ceramics	64.7%	64.8%
Chemical processing and environmental-related	18.7	18.2
Ceramic coatings	10.2	10.4
Structural ceramics	6.4	6.6

Source: *Ceramic Industry*, August 2001, p. 24, from Business Communications Co.

★ 812 ★
Bricks (SIC 3250)

Brick Market in Colorado

Robinson Brick produced about 100 million bricks a year out of a national market of 8.5 billion. Shares are for the local single family residential market.

Robinson Brick	80.0%
Other	20.0

Source: *Denver Business Journal*, September 21, 2001, p. 23A.

★ 813 ★
Refractories (SIC 3250)

U.S. Refractories Demand

The principal factor in the improving market comes from gains in the primary metals industry. Demand is shown in millions of dollars.

	2000	2005	Share
Bricks & shapes	$ 1,311	$ 1,400	54.69%
Monlithics	658	715	27.93
Other	410	445	17.38

Source: *Research Studies - Freedonia Group*, August 20, 2001, p. 3.

★ 814 ★
Ceramic Tiles (SIC 3253)

Top Ceramic Tile Makers

Market shares are shown in percent.

Dal-Tile	25.0%
Florida Tile	6.0
Other	69.0

Source: *Floor Focus*, January/February 2002, p. 1.

★ 815 ★
Gypsum (SIC 3275)

Gypsum Product Demand in North America

Figures are in thousands of metric tons.

	2000	2005	Share
Gypsum board	29,913	32,300	71.68%
Other	11,362	12,760	28.32

Source: *Research Studies - Freedonia Group*, August 3, 2001, p. 3, from Freedonia Group.

★ 816 ★
Abrasives (SIC 3291)

Abrasive Product Shipments

Sales are shown in millions of dollars.

	1999	2004	Share
Nonmetallic	$ 4,205	$ 5,115	90.45%
Metallic	463	540	9.55

Source: *Industrial Ceramics*, September 2001, p. 122, from Freedonia Group.

★ 817 ★
Abrasives (SIC 3291)

Steel Wool Market

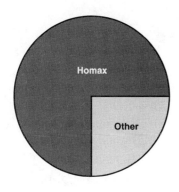

Market shares are shown in percent.

Homax 75.0%
Other 25.0

Source: *Bellingham Business Journal*, January 2002, p. A5.

★ 818 ★
Abrasives (SIC 3291)

Top Abrasive Markets in Northeast Central States

Sales are shown in millions of dollars.

Motor vehicles & car bodies . . . . . . $ 89.3
Internal combustion engines 86.7
Motor vehicle parts & accessories 85.7
Construction machinery 47.7
Gray & ductile iron foundries 36.2

Source: *Industrial Distribution*, January 2002, p. 63, from Industrial Market Information.

SIC 33 - Primary Metal Industries

★ 819 ★
Forgings (SIC 3312)

Forging Industry in North America

Data show number of plants for each process.

	No.	Share
Closed die	308	63.51%
Open die	125	25.77
Ring rolling	22	4.54
Other	30	6.19

Source: *Forging*, May 2001, p. 22.

★ 820 ★
Metals (SIC 3312)

Largest Ferrous Scrap Processors

Firms are ranked by gross tons processed.

Metal Management	4.1
OmniSource Corp.	4.0
Tube City Inc.	3.9
Philip Metals Inc.	3.6
Hugo Neu Corp.	3.1
Ferrous Processing & Trading Co.	2.8
Commercial Metals Co.	2.2
David J. Joseph Co.	2.1
Schnitzer Steel Products Co.	1.5

Source: *Recycling Today*, March 2002, p. 38.

★ 821 ★
Steel (SIC 3312)

Largest Steel Firms

Firms are ranked by production in net tons.

Nucor	12.3
USS	10.0
Bethlehem	8.7
LTV	6.5
AK	6.1
National	5.9
Stelco	4.9
Dofasco	4.5
Ahmsa	3.3
Rouge	2.8

Source: *American Metal Market*, March 11, 2002, p. 1.

★ 822 ★
Steel (SIC 3312)

Stainless Steel Imports

Figures are in tons.

Stainless sheet/strip	388,263
Stainless bar	125,725
Stainless rod	82,056
Stainless plate	65,622
Stainless wire	31,059

Source: *New Steel*, April 2001, p. 9, from Georgetown Economie Service and Specialty Steel Industry of North America.

★ 823 ★
Steel (SIC 3312)

U.S. Steel Imports, 2001

Over 30 millions tons were imported for the year. New tariffs have been put in place to help make U.S. companies more competitive. Other includes Non European Union countries, such as Russia.

Asia	21.3%
European Union	20.2
Canada	15.5
Central and South America	14.4
Mexico	9.9
Africa and Oceania	4.7
Other	13.9

Source: *New York Times*, March 6, 2002, p. C12, from American Steel and Iron Institute.

★ 824 ★

Pipe (SIC 3317)

Pipe Demand by Type

Pipe demand is expected to increase 2.5% annually through 2005. Shipments are shown in millions of feet.

	2000	2005	Share
Copper	$ 5,780	$ 6,507	40.30%
Plastic	5,596	6,401	39.65
Steel	2,218	2,381	14.75
Other	780	856	5.30

Source: *Research Studies - Freedonia Group*, October 29, 2001, p. 3, from Freedonia Group.

★ 825 ★

Pipe (SIC 3317)

Steel Pipe Market

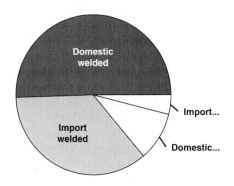

Data show percent of total shipments.

Domestic welded	51.4%
Import welded	35.7
Domestic seamless	10.1
Import seamless	4.3

Source: *Supply House Times*, November 2001, p. 16, from *Preston Pipe & Tube Report*.

★ 826 ★

Foundries (SIC 3320)

Foundry Product Shipments, 2000

Market shares are shown in percent.

Ohio	15.0%
Alabama	11.6
Wisconsin	11.4
Indiana	11.2
Michigan	8.0
Other	42.8

Source: *Recycling Today*, March 2002, p. 58, from American Foundry Society.

★ 827 ★

Aluminum (SIC 3334)

U.S. Aluminum Market, 2000

The market is shown in percent.

Transportation	32.5%
Containers & packaging	20.4
Building & construction	13.1
Exports	11.4
Electrical	6.9
Consumer durables	6.9
Other	8.7

Source: *Wall Street Journal*, September 26, 2001, p. B4, from Aluminum Association.

★ 828 ★

Copper (SIC 3351)

Copper Consumption by Market

The end market is shown in percent.

Building construction	40.0%
Electric products	25.0
Transportation equipment	13.0
Industrial machinery	12.0
Consumer & general products	10.0

Source: *Skillings Mining Review*, May 4, 2002, p. 4.

★ 829 ★

Castings (SIC 3360)

Metal Casting Shipments

The casting industry consists of 2,770 operations. Shipments, shown here in thousands of short tons, fell 10% in 2001 after several years of good growth.

	2000	2002	Share
Gray iron	5,631	4,967	36.92%
Ductile iron	4,321	4,080	30.32
Steel	1,364	1,257	9.34
Aluminum die casting . . .	1,210	1,196	8.89
Aluminum per. mold/sand . .	842	846	6.29
Zinc/lead	347	309	2.30
Copper base	325	303	2.25
Malleable iron	204	140	1.04
Investment cast	156	159	1.18
Magnesium	74	84	0.62
Other	115	114	0.85

Source: *Advanced Materials & Processes*, January 2002, p. 43.

SIC 34 - Fabricated Metal Products

★ 830 ★
Beverage Cans (SIC 3411)

U.S. Beverage Can Leaders

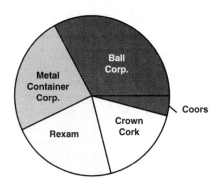

Market shares are shown in percent.

Ball Corp.	33.0%
Metal Container Corp.	24.0
Rexam	22.0
Crown Cork & Seal	17.0
Coors	4.0

Source: *Packaging Strategies*, October 31, 2001, p. 4, from *Beverage Digest's Fact Book, 2000.*

★ 831 ★
Cutlery (SIC 3421)

Swiss Army Knife Market Shares

Market shares are shown in percent.

Swiss Army	75.0%
Other	25.0

Source: "Oh Yeah, You and What Army?" Retrieved January 22, 2002 from the World Wide Web: http://www.outsidemag.

★ 832 ★
Razor Blades (SIC 3421)

Female Shaving Market

Market shares are shown in percent.

Mach3	24.0%
Venus	11.0
Other	65.0

Source: *New York Times*, October 31, 2001, p. C4.

★ 833 ★
Razor Blades (SIC 3421)

Retail Shaving Market

Figures are in millions of dollars.

	($ mil.)	Share
Disposable razors	$ 599.7	62.38%
Nondisposable razors	196.6	20.45
Depilatory (women)	157.2	16.35
Depilatory (men)	7.9	0.82

Source: *MMR*, September 3, 2001, p. 76, from A.C. Nielsen.

★ 834 ★
Razor Blades (SIC 3421)

Top Disposable Razor Blade Brands, 2001

Market shares are shown in percent.

Schick Slim Twin	15.2%
Schick Xtreme III	10.1
Custom Plus	9.1
Good News	8.6
Daisy Plus	7.0
Good News Plus	6.5

Continued on next page.

★ 834 ★ *Continued*

Razor Blades (SIC 3421)

Top Disposable Razor Blade Brands, 2001

Market shares are shown in percent.

Bic Softwin	5.8%
Bic	5.6
Custom Plus for Women	4.3
Other	27.8

Source: *Chain Drug Review*, January 21, 2002, p. 17, from Information Resources Inc.

★ 835 ★

Razor Blades (SIC 3421)

Top Razor Blade Brands, 2001

Market shares are shown in percent.

Venus	33.9%
Mach3	23.8
Schick Silk Effects Plus	8.2
Sensor Excel for Women	7.4
Sensor Excel	4.1
Mach3 Cool Blue	4.1
Sensor	2.7
Schick Silk Effects	2.3
Schick FX Diamond	2.0
Other	11.5

Source: *Chain Drug Review*, January 21, 2002, p. 17, from Information Resources Inc.

★ 836 ★

Razor Blades (SIC 3421)

Top Razor Refill Vendors, 2001

Market shares are shown for the year ended May 20, 2001.

Gillette	82.4%
Warner-Lambert	12.7
American Safety	1.5
Noxell	0.2
Private label	3.1
Other	10.1

Source: *Grocery Headquarters*, August 2001, p. 12, from Information Resources Inc.

★ 837 ★

Toilet Seats (SIC 3430)

Toilet Seat Sales by Type

Market shares are shown in percent.

Wood/composite	66.0%
Plastic	18.0
Soft	16.0

Source: *Do-It-Yourself Retailing*, April 2002, p. 64, from Vista Sales & Marketing.

★ 838 ★

Faucets (SIC 3432)

Leading Faucet Producers in North America

The market was valued at $2.5 billion.

Moen	30.0%
Delta Faucet	30.0
Other	40.0

Source: *BusinessWeek*, June 4, 2001, p. NA.

★ 839 ★
Guns (SIC 3482)

Top Handgun Makers, 1999

Makers are ranked by total production of 1,331,230 handguns.

	Units	Share
Ruger	312,731	23.49%
Smith & Wesson	279,435	20.99
Beretta	117,684	8.84
Other	621,380	46.68

Source: *Shooting Industry,* July 1, 2001, p. 32.

★ 840 ★
Guns (SIC 3482)

Top Rifle Makers, 1999

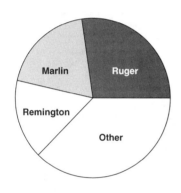

Makers are ranked by total production of 1,569,685 rifles.

	Units	Share
Ruger	428,329	27.29%
Marlin	301,874	19.23
Remington	252,776	16.10
Other	586,706	37.38

Source: *Shooting Industry,* July 1, 2001, p. 32.

★ 841 ★
Guns (SIC 3482)

Top Shotgun Makers, 1999

Makers are ranked by production of 1,106,995 shotguns.

	Units	Share
Remington	364,354	32.91%
Mossberg	329,829	29.79
H&R	187,562	16.94
Other	225,250	20.35

Source: *Shooting Industry,* July 1, 2001, p. 32.

★ 842 ★
Military Accessories (SIC 3489)

Military Holsters and Belts Market

Market shares are shown in percent.

Gregory Mountain Products	80.0%
Other	20.0

Source: *Outdoor Retailer,* January 2002, p. 1.

★ 843 ★
Body Armour (SIC 3499)

Body Armour Industry

Market shares are shown for high performance vest insert market.

Simula Inc.	80.0%
Other	20.0

Source: *Business Wire,* November 6, 2001, p. NA.

★ 844 ★
Locks (SIC 3499)

Automotive Lock Market in North America

Market shares are shown in percent.

Strattec	65.0%
Other	35.0

Source: *Knight-Ridder/Tribune Business News,* June 23, 2001, p. NA.

★ 845 ★

Toilet Repair Kits (SIC 3499)

Toilet Repair Kit Industry

Market shares are shown in percent.

Fluidmaster 80.0%
Other 20.0

Source: *Plumbing & Mechanical*, September 2001, p. 20.

SIC 35 - Industry Machinery and Equipment

★ 846 ★

Engines (SIC 3511)

U.S. Diesel Engine Demand

Sales are shown in millions of dollars.

	2000	2005	Share
Motor vehicles	$ 7,185	$ 8,945	51.17%
Construction equipment	2,334	2,960	16.93
Agricultural equipment	1,515	1,680	9.61
Other	2,791	3,895	22.28

Source: *Research Studies - Freedonia Group*, July 26, 2001, p. 3, from Freedonia Group.

★ 847 ★

Engines (SIC 3519)

Boat Engine Market Shares

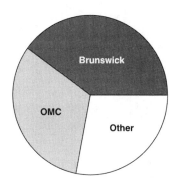

Market shares are shown in percent. Brunswick makes the Mercury brand.

Brunswick	40.0%
OMC	32.0
Other	28.0

Source: *Knight-Ridder/Tribune Business News*, January 2, 2001, p. NA.

★ 848 ★

Engines (SIC 3519)

Four-Cycle Gasoline Engine Market

Market shares are shown in percent. The company also has 45% of the global market.

Briggs	65.0%
Other	35.0

Source: *Milwaukee Journal Sentinel*, November 19, 2001, p. 3, from Robert W. Baird & Co.

★ 849 ★

Lawn & Garden Equipment (SIC 3524)

Largest Grill Makers, 2000

Shares are shown based on unit shipments for the year.

Bradley/Coleman	32.0%
Sunbeam Outdoor Products	21.0
Weber-Stephen	15.0
Ducane	4.0
Other	28.0

Source: *Appliance*, September 2001, p. 19.

★ 850 ★

Lawn & Garden Equipment (SIC 3524)

Largest Leaf Blower Makers, 2000

Shares are shown based on unit shipments for the year.

Toro	35.3%
Black & Decker	25.1
Frigidaire Hoem Products (Weed Eater)	12.6
Other	27.0

Source: *Appliance*, September 2001, p. 19.

★ 851 ★

Lawn & Garden Equipment (SIC 3524)

Largest Mower (Walk Behind, Gas) Makers, 2000

Shares are shown based on unit shipments for the year.

American Yard Products 31.5%
Murray 16.5
MTD Products 11.5
Toro 5.0
Snapper 1.5
Other 34.0

Source: *Appliance Manufacturer*, April 2001, p. 19.

★ 852 ★

Lawn & Garden Equipment (SIC 3524)

Largest String Trimmer Makers, 2000

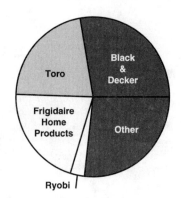

Shares are shown based on unit shipments for the year.

Black & Decker 27.5%
Toro 22.0
Frigidaire Home Products (Weed Eater) . . . 21.0
Ryobi 2.5
Other 27.0

Source: *Appliance Manufacturer*, April 2001, p. 19.

★ 853 ★

Lawn & Garden Equipment (SIC 3524)

Lawn and Garden Shipments

Shipments are shown in thousands of units.

	2001	2002
Walk-behind powered mowers . . .	5,646	5,797
Front-engine lawn tractors	1,189	1,212
Tillers	402	411
Riding garden tractors	181	183
Rear-engine riding mowers	133	135

Source: *Appliance Manufacturer*, January 2002, p. 76, from Outdoor Power Equipment Institute.

★ 854 ★

Drills (SIC 3531)

HDD Market in North America

HDD stands for horizontal directional drill. The market has been strong, although growth slowed last year. Market shares are shown in percent.

Vermeer/Charles Machine Works/Case . . . 87.0%
Other 13.0

Source: *Diesel Progress North American Edition*, September 2001, p. 12, from Yengst Associates.

★ 855 ★

Mining Equipment (SIC 3532)

Shipments of Mining Equipment, 2000

Value of shipments is shown in millions of dollars.

	($ mil.)	Share
Portable drilling rigs and parts . .	$ 387.2	30.71%
Crushing, pulverizing and screening (except portable) machinery	308.9	24.50
Underground mining machinery, except parts)	297.2	23.57
Portable crushing, screening, washing and combo. Plants . . .	134.5	10.67
Drills, other mining machinery . .	133.0	10.55

Source: "Statistics." Retrieved June 10, 2002 from the World Wide Web: http://nma.org, from U.S. Department of Commerce.

★ 856 ★

Wine Chillers (SIC 3532)

Refrigerated Wine Chiller Market

Market shares are shown in percent.

Haier 60.0%
Other 40.0

Source: *Forbes*, May 13, 2002, p. 74.

★ 857 ★

Lift Equipment (SIC 3536)

Lift Equipment Sales

Figures show unit sales.

	1999	2000
Scissor lifts	46,000	40,000
Boom lifts	17,000	13,000
Telescopic rough-terrain lifts . . .	15,000	12,000
Rough-terrain	1,300	1,000

Source: *Diesel Progress North American Edition*, September 2001, p. 8.

★ 858 ★

Machine Tools (SIC 3541)

Leading CNC Machinery Producers in Canada

A total of 1,036 machines were installed last year. Machining centers and turning technology have 80% of the market.

Haas 18.3%
Okuma 9.8
DMG 6.9
Mazak 5.8
Daewoo 5.2
Fadal 3.5
Other 50.5

Source: *Canadian Machinery and Metalworking*, March 2002, p. 16.

★ 859 ★

Machine Tools (SIC 3541)

Leading CNC System Suppliers

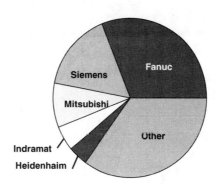

Market shares are shown in percent.

Fanuc 31.0%
Siemens 16.0
Mitsubishi 8.9
Indramat 4.8
Heidenhaim 4.1
Other 35.2

Source: *Design News*, October 15, 2001, p. 21, from ARC study.

★ 860 ★

Machine Tools (SIC 3541)

Leading Lathe/Turning Center Producers in Canada

Market shares are shown in percent.

Okuma 19.9%
Haas 12.0
Daewoo 9.8
Mazak 7.7
Mori Seiki 6.6
Nakamura-Tome 5.7
Other 38.3

Source: *Canadian Machinery and Metalworking*, March 2002, p. 16.

★ 861 ★

Machine Tools (SIC 3541)

Leading Milling Center Producers in Canada

Market shares are shown in percent.

Toshiba	30.4%
Nicolas Correa	13.0
TOS	11.6
Trak	8.7
Milltronics	8.7
Kurazi	8.7
Other	21.8

Source: *Canadian Machinery and Metalworking*, March 2002, p. 16.

★ 862 ★

Machine Tools (SIC 3541)

Metal Cutting Industry

Market shares are shown in percent.

Turning machines	27.8%
Horizontal turning machines	13.4
Other	58.8

Source: *Metalworking Marketer*, March 2002, p. 7, from Gardner Research.

★ 863 ★

Hardware (SIC 3546)

Preferred Brands of Hardware

The table shows the brands shoppers would select when shopping at a discount store or superstore. Figures show the results of a survey and are not market shares.

Craftsman	25.0%
Black & Decker	18.0
Stanley	7.0

Source: *DSN Retailing Today*, October 22, 2001, p. 24, from Lee J. Shapiro.

★ 864 ★

Power Tools (SIC 3546)

Power and Hand Tool Demand

Demand is expected to increase 4% annually, with growth coming in prt from new cordless products. Shipments are shown in millions of dollars.

	2000	2005	Share
Power tools, electric	$ 5,580	$ 7,160	47.48%
Hand tools	4,830	5,650	37.47
Power tools, other	1,840	2,270	15.05

Source: *Research Studies - Freedonia Group*, October 30, 2001, p. 3, from Freedonia Group.

★ 865 ★

Rapid Prototyping (SIC 3549)

Rapid Prototyping Market

Market shares are shown in percent.

3D Systems	50.0%
DTM	20.0
Other	30.0

Source: *Performance Materials*, June 25, 2001, p. 1, from U.S. Department of Justice.

★ 866 ★

Paper Machinery (SIC 3554)

Corrugated Paper Machinery Market

Market shares are shown for North America.

Forber SPA	70.0%
Other	30.0

Source: *Green Bay-Press Gazette*, May 16, 2002, p. 1.

★ 867 ★

Printing Equipment (SIC 3555)

Color Printing Industry

Market shares are shown in percent.

Xerox	85.0%
Other	15.0

Source: *M2 Presswire*, June 8, 2001, p. NA.

★ 868 ★
Food Processing Equipment (SIC 3556)

Mini Donut Machinery Industry

Data show the company's reported share of market.

Lil'Orbits 95.0%
Other 5.0

Source: *Minneapolis-St. Paul CityBusiness*, November 23, 2001, p. 10.

★ 869 ★
Sludge Equipment (SIC 3559)

U.S. Sludge Equipment Industry

The equipment market was expected to hit $47.2 million in 2000.

Dewatering 72.8%
Sludge digestion 16.0
Final treatment 11.1

Source: *Industrial Bioprocessing*, October 26, 2001, p. 3.

★ 870 ★
Stone Working Machinery (SIC 3559)

Stone Working Equipment Purchases, 2002

Figures show the types of items survey respondents planned to use.

Hand tools 83.2%
Polishing machines 45.0
Bridge saws 29.0
Shapecutting machines 22.1
Cranes 15.3
Quarrying equipment 11.5
Blockcutters 4.6
Gangsaws 3.8
Tile lines 2.3
Other 8.4

Source: *Stone World*, January 2002, p. 98.

★ 871 ★
Pumps (SIC 3561)

Fluid Handling Pump Sales, 2000

Sales are shown in millions of dollars. Growth will be driven by the extraction, food and beverage sectors.

	($ mil.)	Share
Process manufacturers	$ 2,275	36.96%
Utilities	1,690	27.46
Resource extraction industries . . .	870	14.13
Construction sector	567	9.21
Other	753	12.23

Source: *Research Studies - Freedonia Group*, December 19, 2001, p. 7, from Freedonia Group.

★ 872 ★
Packaging Equipment (SIC 3565)

U.S. Packaging Equipment Shipments

Market shares are shown in percent.

Food 38.5%
Beverages 18.0
Pharmaceuticals 8.9
Paper/consumer/non-durables 6.7
Household/agricultural chemicals 6.7
Hardware/auto/industrial 5.7
Personal care/toiletries/cosmetics 5.3
Converters/printers 3.2
Other 7.0

Source: *Packaging Digest*, December 2001, p. 44, from Packaging Machinery Manufacturers Institute.

★ 873 ★
Gas Pump Screens (SIC 3569)

Gas Pump Screens

Market shares are shown in percent.

Planar 80.0%
Other 20.0

Source: *Business Journal-Portland*, February 23, 2001, p. 17.

★ 874 ★
Hose and Cable (SIC 3569)

Hose and Cable Sector in the Fire/Rescue Industry

Fire and rescue sales reached $8 million in 2001, up 23% over the previous year.

Hannay Reels Inc.	95.0%
Other	5.0

Source: *Business Review - Serving New York's Capital Region*, March 8, 2002, p. 7.

★ 875 ★
Computers (SIC 3571)

Computer Market by Segment

Figures are shown based on unit sales.

	2000	2001	2002
Desktops	82.9%	77.5%	75.5%
Mobile PCs	17.1	22.5	24.5

Source: *Advertising Age*, March 25, 2002, p. 3, from NPD Techworld.

★ 876 ★
Computers (SIC 3571)

Computer Product Industry

Figures are for the first six months.

	2000	2001
Desktop PCs	26.2%	20.1%
Printing retail supplies	22.9	29.1
Printers	9.4	7.9
Cathode ray tube monitors	7.5	5.5
Other	34.0	37.4

Source: *Investor's Business Daily*, October 10, 2001, p. A6, from Intelectmt.com.

★ 877 ★
Computers (SIC 3571)

Handheld Applications for Physicians

Only 15% now use such devices, although that number is expected to increase dramatically. The market is expected to grow from $70 million to $834 in 2004.

Sales to physician practices	50.0%
Back-end advertising/sponsorships	43.0
Sales to hospitals	7.0

Source: *Healthcare Purchasing News*, July 2001, p. 11, from Frost & Sullivan.

★ 878 ★
Computers (SIC 3571)

Handheld Computer Market in Mexico

Market shares are shown in percent.

Palm	83.6%
Other	16.4

Source: "Palm and Lation Channels to Expand Distribution." Retrieved October 8, 2001 from http://www.palmos.com, from International Data Corp.

★ 879 ★
Computers (SIC 3571)

Handheld PC Market

Market shares are shown in percent.

	2000	2001
Palm	71.0%	58.0%
Handspring	14.0	15.0
Hewlett Packard	3.0	5.0
Compaq	2.0	7.0
Sony	1.0	6.0

Source: *Consumer Electronics*, February 4, 2002, p. NA.

★ 880 ★
Computers (SIC 3571)

Handhelds by Operating System

Market shares are shown in percent.

Palm 80.0%
Microsoft 16.0
Other 4.0

Source: *Wall Street Journal*, September 7, 2001, p. A4, from NPD Intelect.

★ 881 ★
Computers (SIC 3571)

Largest Desktop Makers, 2000

Shares are shown based on unit shipments for the year.

Dell 20.0%
Compaq 16.0
Hewlett-Packard 13.0
Gateway 10.0
Apple 4.0
IBM 4.0
eMachines 4.0
Acer 3.0
Micron 2.0
NEC 1.0
Other 23.0

Source: *Appliance*, September 2001, p. 19.

★ 882 ★
Computers (SIC 3571)

Top Laptop Makers, 2001

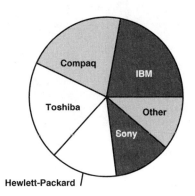

Shares are for the first ten months of the year.

IBM 21.9%
Compaq 21.1
Toshiba 19.6
Hewlett-Packard 14.3
Sony 12.4
Other 10.7

Source: *New York Times*, December 17, 2001, p. C19, from NPD Intelect.

★ 883 ★
Computers (SIC 3571)

Top Notebook Computers

Unit shares are shown in percent.

Compaq 30.0%
Toshiba 16.8
IBM 15.9
Hewlett-Packard 15.9
Sony 12.7
Other 8.7

Source: *New York Times*, June 4, 2001, p. C8, from NPD Intelect.

★ 884 ★

Computers (SIC 3571)

Top Notebook Makers in Canada

Market shares are shown in percent.

IBM	31.0%
Dell	17.0
Other	52.0

Source: *Computing Canada*, April 12, 2002, p. 16, from Evans Research.

★ 885 ★

Computers (SIC 3571)

Top PC Firms, 2001

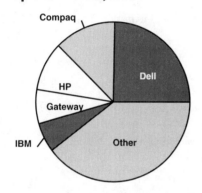

Market shares are estimated in percent.

	(000)	Share
Dell	10,750	24.5%
Compaq	5,472	12.5
HP	4,375	10.0
Gateway	3,235	7.4
IBM	2,496	5.7
Other	17,560	40.0

Source: *Business Wire*, January 26, 2001, p. NA, from Gartner Dataquest Inc.

★ 886 ★

Computer Disk Drives (SIC 3572)

CD Burner Sales

Sales are shown in millions of units. Consumers now purchase more blank CDs than recorded CDs. As more obtain broadband connections, downloading music is a snap, which has music executives very worried.

	1999	2001	Share
Internal PC drives	1.6	4.3	75.44%
External PC drives	0.3	1.1	19.30
Home decks	0.1	0.3	5.26

Source: *USA TODAY*, April 5, 2002, p. 2B, from NPDTechworld.com.

★ 887 ★

Computer Disk Drives (SIC 3572)

CD-Recordable/RW Drive Makers

Figures are for February 2002.

Sony	12.0%
Pacific Digital	10.0
I/O Magic	9.7
Cendyne	9.0
Iomega	7.8
Other	51.5

Source: "NPDTechworld." Retrieved April 18, 2002 from the World Wide Web: http://www.npdtechworld.com, from NPD.

★ 888 ★

Computer Disk Drives (SIC 3572)

Disk Drive Market

Market shares are shown in percent.

Seagate	21.5%
Quantum	16.4
Maxtor	13.5
IBM	13.1
Other	35.5

Source: *Investor's Business Daily*, April 18, 2001, p. A8, from Gartner Dataquest.

★ 889 ★
Computer Disk Drives (SIC 3572)

Top Home CD Recorders

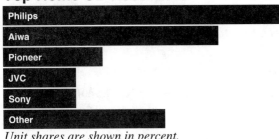

Unit shares are shown in percent.

Philips	30.9%
Aiwa	24.1
Pioneer	10.8
JVC	8.3
Sony	8.0
Other	17.9

Source: *New York Times*, June 18, 2001, p. C8, from NPD Intelect.

★ 890 ★
Computer Monitors (SIC 3575)

Computer Monitor Shipments in Canada

Shares are for the second quarter of 2001.

17 inch	71.5%
15 inch	13.3
19 inch	13.0
21 inch	1.6
Other	0.6

Source: "Monitor Market Second Quarter 2001." Retrieved November 15, 2001 from the World Wide Web: http://www.evansresearch.com, from Evans Research.

★ 891 ★
Computer Peripherals (SIC 3577)

Computer OEM Revenues, 2000

Firms are ranked by revenues in millions of dollars. OEM stands for original equipment manufacturers.

IBM	$ 37.2
Dell	22.4
Hewlett-Packard	21.1
Compaq	18.9
Gateway	8.2
Sun Micro	7.1

Source: *CircuiTree*, February 2002, p. 88.

★ 892 ★
Computer Peripherals (SIC 3577)

Digital Projector Market in Canada

Market shares are shown based on video graphics array.

XGA	62.0%
SVGA	36.0
SXGA	2.0

Source: *Computing Canada*, February 1, 2002, p. 16, from Evans Research.

★ 893 ★
Computer Peripherals (SIC 3577)

Top MP3 Player Makers

Shares are for November 2001.

Nike	20.8%
Rio	11.2
Archos	9.8
Samsung	9.6
Intel	8.7
Other	39.9

Source: *New York Times*, January 14, 2002, p. C8, from NPDTechworld.

★ 894 ★

Computer Peripherals (SIC 3577)

Whiteboard Industry

Whiteboards transfer information written on the board to a computer. Market shares are shown in percent.

PolyVision Corp.	80.0%
Other	20.0

Source: *Grand Rapids Press*, November 12, 2001, p. A7.

★ 895 ★

Computer Printers (SIC 3577)

Computer Printer Sales by Format

Revenue from inkjet printers and supplies is expected to grow at an annual rate of 8% between 2000 and 2005.

	2000	2005
Narrow format	86.4%	81.5%
Wide format	13.6	18.5

Source: *Investor's Business Daily*, October 16, 2001, p. A8, from I.T. Strategies.

★ 896 ★

Computer Printers (SIC 3577)

Digital Inkjet Printer Market

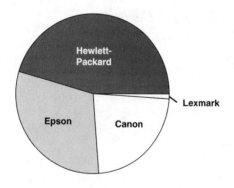

Market shares are shown in percent.

Hewlett-Packard	45.6%
Epson	30.8
Canon	23.1
Lexmark	0.5

Source: *Investor's Business Daily*, May 14, 2001, p. A6, from International Data Corp.

★ 897 ★

Automated Teller Machines (SIC 3578)

ATM Security Equipment

The company provides 51% of the devices to the 83,000 bank branches.

Diebold	51.0%
Other	49.0

Source: *American Banker*, September 27, 2001, p. 7.

★ 898 ★

Automated Teller Machines (SIC 3578)

Leading ATM Shippers

Firms are ranked by unit shipments.

	Units	Share
Diebold	13,634	22.41%
Tidel	12,723	20.91
NCR	10,400	17.10
Other	24,078	39.58

Source: *American Banker*, June 25, 2001, p. 17, from Nilson Report.

★ 899 ★

Mailing Equipment (SIC 3579)

Mailing Equipment Market

Market shares are shown in percent.

Pitney Bowes	80.0%
Other	20.0

Source: *San Diego Business Journal*, January 14, 2002, p. 16.

★ 900 ★

POS Terminals (SIC 3579)

Largest POS Terminal Shippers

Firms are ranked by units shipped.

	Units	Share
VeriFone	651,000	36.90%
Hypercom Corp.	513,894	29.13
IVI Checkmate	250,235	14.19
Other	348,882	19.78

Source: *Credit Card Management*, April 2001, p. 12, from *ATM & Debit News*.

★ 901 ★

POS Terminals (SIC 3579)

POS Terminals by Operating System

Market shares are shown in percent.

Microsoft	69.0%
Windows NT/200/XP	46.0
Windows 9x/CE	23.0

Source: *EDP Weekly's IT Monitor*, April 1, 2002, p. 3, from IHL Consulting Group.

★ 902 ★

POS Terminals (SIC 3579)

Top Terminal Firms in Canada

Market shares are shown in percent.

Ingenico	75.0%
Other	25.0

Source: *ATM Debit Card News*, December 20, 2001, p. 1.

★ 903 ★

Scanners (SIC 3579)

Self Scanning Market

Shares are estimated for 70%-80%.

U-Scan Express	80.0%
Other	20.0

Source: *Knight-Ridder/Tribune Business News*, January 15, 2002, p. NA.

★ 904 ★

Hearth Products (SIC 3585)

Hearth Unit Shipments

A total of 1.6 hearth appliances were shipped during the year. Cordwood (fireplaces, freestanding wood stoves and fireplace inserts) fell 23 percent, while gas units increased 8 percent.

Gas	62.0%
Cordwood	36.0
Pellet gas	2.0

Source: *Fuel Oil News*, July 2001, p. 42, from Hearth Products Association.

★ 905 ★

Heating and Cooling (SIC 3585)

Central Cooling Market

The chiller market is relatively stabile. The major groups are: reciprocating liquid chiller package (RLCP), large tonnage liquid cooled chillers (LTLC) and gas engine driven units. Shares are shown by technology.

RLCP	64.0%
LTLC	27.0
Absorption	8.0
GEO	1.0

Source: *Air Conditioning, Heating & Refrigeration News*, July 2, 2001, p. 1.

★ 906 ★

Heating and Cooling (SIC 3585)

Commercial HVAC Unit Shipments

	2000	2002
Split system	623,263	623,201
Gas electric	279,425	283,568
Packaged	156,010	156,782

Source: *Contracting Business*, January 2002, p. 32.

★ 907 ★

Heating and Cooling (SIC 3585)

Home Heating by Type

Market shares are shown in percent.

Forced air	97.0%
Radiant floor	3.0

Source: *Knight-Ridder/Tribune News Service*, August 2, 2001, p. NA.

★ 908 ★

Heating and Cooling (SIC 3585)

Largest Air Conditioner (Room) Makers, 2000

Shares are shown based on unit shipments for the year.

Fedders	18.0%
LG Electronics	15.5
Electrolux	13.0
Whirlpool	12.0

Continued on next page.

★ 908 ★ *Continued*

Heating and Cooling (SIC 3585)

Largest Air Conditioner (Room) Makers, 2000

Shares are shown based on unit shipments for the year.

Haier	6.0%
Goodman	6.0
Sharp	3.0
Samsung	3.0
Matsushita	3.0
Friedrich	3.0
Other	17.5

Source: *Appliance Manufacturer*, April 2001, p. 19.

★ 909 ★

Heating and Cooling (SIC 3585)

Largest Air Purifier (Portable) Makers, 2000

Shares are shown based on unit shipments for the year.

Honeywell	27.0%
Holmes/Duracraft	23.0
Sunbeam	8.0
Rival (Bionaire)	4.0
Duracraft	4.0
Oreck	3.0
Hunter	3.0
Other	32.0

Source: *Appliance Manufacturer*, April 2001, p. 19.

★ 910 ★

Heating and Cooling (SIC 3585)

Largest Central Air Makers, 2000

Shares are shown based on unit shipments for the year.

United Technologies	28.0%
Goodman	18.0
American Standard	13.0
Lennox	12.0
Rheem/Paloma Industries	11.0
York	7.0
Nortek	6.0
Other	5.0

Source: *Appliance Manufacturer*, April 2001, p. 19.

★ 911 ★

Heating and Cooling (SIC 3585)

Largest Commercial Refrigerator Makers, 2000

Shares are shown based on unit shipments for the year.

True	25.5%
UTC/Carrier (Beverage Air)	22.0
ITW	13.5
Glywed (Victory, Williams)	8.0
Enodis (Delfield)	7.0
Manitowoc (McCall)	6.5
Continental	5.5
Dover (Randell)	3.5
Other	8.5

Source: *Appliance Manufacturer*, April 2001, p. 19.

★ 912 ★

Heating and Cooling (SIC 3585)

Largest Dehumidifier Makers, 2000

Shares are shown based on unit shipments for the year.

Whirlpool	32.0%
Electrolux (Frigidaire)	31.0
Fedders	12.0
W.C. Wood	9.0
Samsung	4.0
Ebco	3.0
Other	9.0

Source: *Appliance*, September 2001, p. 19.

★ 913 ★

Heating and Cooling (SIC 3585)

Largest Furnace Makers, 2000

Shares are shown based on unit shipments for the year.

Carrier	32.0%
Goodman	17.0
Lennox	16.0
Rheem	12.0
American Standard (Trane)	12.0
York	5.0
Nordyne	5.0
Other	1.0

Source: *Appliance*, September 2001, p. 19.

★ 914 ★

Heating and Cooling (SIC 3585)

Largest Heat Pump Makers, 2000

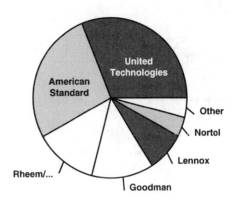

Shares are shown based on unit shipments for the year.

United Technologies	31.0%
American Standard	27.0
Rheem/Paloma Industries	13.0
Goodman	13.0
Lennox	8.0
Nortel	4.0
Other	4.0

Source: *Appliance Manufacturer*, April 2001, p. 19.

★ 915 ★

Heating and Cooling (SIC 3585)

Largest Heaters (Electric Room) Makers, 2000

Shares are shown based on unit shipments for the year.

Holmes (Patton)	56.0%
Honeywell/Duracraft	15.0
DeLonghi	7.0
Lakewood	6.0
Arvin (HeatStream)	6.0
Marvin	2.0
Other	8.0

Source: *Appliance Manufacturer*, April 2001, p. 19.

★ 916 ★

Heating and Cooling (SIC 3585)

Largest Refrigerated Display Case Makers, 2000

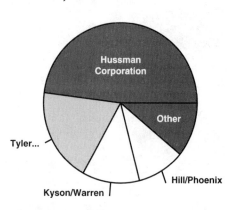

Shares are shown based on unit shipments for the year.

Hussman Corporation	48.0%
Tyler Refrigeration	19.0
Kyson/Warren	12.0
Hill/Phoenix	10.0
Other	11.0

Source: *Appliance*, September 2001, p. 19.

★ 917 ★

Heating and Cooling (SIC 3585)

Largest Water Heater Makers, 2000

Shares are shown based on unit shipments for the year.

Rheem Manufacturing	40.0%
State Industries	19.0
Bradford-White	14.0
American Water Heater	14.0
A.O. Smith	13.0

Source: *Appliance*, September 2001, p. 19.

★ 918 ★

Heating and Cooling (SIC 3585)

Leading HVAC Makers, 2000

Market shares are estimated in percent. HVAC stands for heating, ventilating and air conditioning.

Carrier	22.0%
Trane	15.0
AAON	12.0
Other	51.0

Source: *Investor's Business Daily*, September 7, 2001, p. A8, from company reports, Air Conditioning and Refrigeration Institute, and First Call.

★ 919 ★

Filter Pitchers (SIC 3599)

Flow-Through Pitcher Filter Category

Dollar sales rose slightly from $71.06 million to $71.77 million in 2000, although units fell from 4.18 million to 4.13 million.

Brita	80.0%
Other	20.0

Source: *WC&P Magazine*, November 2001, p. NA.

★ 920 ★

Filters (SIC 3599)

U.S. Filter Demand

Demand is shown in millions of dollars.

	2000	2005	Share
Motor vehicle filters	$ 2,758	$ 3,355	37.87%
Fluid filters	2,689	3,465	39.11
Air purification filters	1,565	2,040	23.02

Source: *Research Studies - Freedonia Group*, October 8, 2001, p. 5, from Freedonia Group.

SIC 36 - Electronic and Other Electric Equipment

★ 921 ★
Electronics (SIC 3600)

Largest Electronics Firms in North America

Firms are ranked by electronics revenue in billions of dollars.

IBM	$ 88.3
Hewlett-Packard	49.0
Compaq Computer	42.3
Motorola	37.5
Lucent Technologies	33.4
Dell Computer	31.8
Ingram Micro	30.7
Nortel Networks	30.2
Cisco Systems	23.9

Source: *Electronic Business*, August 2001, p. 33.

★ 922 ★
Household Appliances (SIC 3630)

U.S. Appliance Market

Market shares are shown in percent.

Whirlpool	33.10%
GE	26.60
Maytag	17.90
Electrolux (Frigidaire)	16.60
Goodman (Amana)	2.54
Other	3.26

Source: *Investor's Business Daily*, August 21, 2001, p. 1, from *Appliance Magazine*.

★ 923 ★
Household Appliances (SIC 3630)

U.S. Appliance Shipments

Shipments are shown in thousands of units.

	2001	2002
Microwave ovens	12,645	12,749
Refrigerators	9,053	9,263
Washers	7,275	7,400
Dishwashers	5,591	5,752
Air conditioners, room	5,575	5,500
Dryers, electric	5,040	5,080
Ranges, electric	4,937	5,011
Ranges, gas	3,020	3,103
Freezers	1,982	1,990
Dryers, gas	1,420	1,440
Dehumidifiers	966	978

Source: *Appliance Manufacturer*, January 2002, p. 76, from Association of Home Appliance Manufacturers.

★ 924 ★

Cooking Equipment (SIC 3631)

Largest Microwave Oven Makers, 2000

Shares are shown based on unit shipments for the year.

Sharp	29.0%
Samsung	25.0
LG Electronics/Goldstar	10.0
Whirlpool	9.0
Sanyo	8.0
Matsushita	8.0
Daewoo	5.0
Other	6.0

Source: *Appliance*, September 2001, p. 19.

★ 925 ★

Cooking Equipment (SIC 3631)

Largest Range (Electric) Makers, 2000

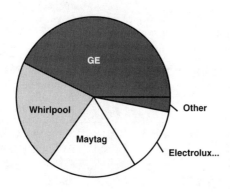

Shares are shown based on unit shipments for the year.

GE	43.0%
Whirlpool	22.0
Maytag	19.0
Electrolux (Frigidaire)	13.0
Other	3.0

Source: *Appliance*, September 2001, p. 19.

★ 926 ★

Cooking Equipment (SIC 3631)

Largest Range (Gas) Makers, 2000

Shares are shown based on unit shipments for the year.

GEA	38.0%
Maytag	26.0
Electrolux	19.0
Goodman	8.0
Whirlpool	4.0
Other	5.0

Source: *Appliance Manufacturer*, April 2001, p. 19.

★ 927 ★

Freezers (SIC 3632)

Largest Freezer Makers, 2000

Shares are shown based on unit shipments for the year.

Electrolux (Frigidaire)	69.0%
W.C. Wood	27.0
Haier	3.0
Sanyo	1.0

Source: *Appliance*, September 2001, p. 19.

★ 928 ★

Refrigerators (SIC 3632)

Largest Refrigerator (Built-In) Makers, 2000

Shares are shown based on unit shipments for the year.

U-Line	75.0%
Marvel Industries	14.0
Sub-Zero	10.0
Other	1.0

Source: *Appliance*, September 2001, p. 19.

★ 929 ★
Refrigerators (SIC 3632)

Refrigeration Product Sales

Data show unit shipments for year to date October.

	2000	2001
Refrigerators	7,884,400	7,867,200
Chest freezers	913,100	1,044,500
Upright freezers	759,500	748,200

Source: *Appliance*, January 2002, p. 30, from Air Conditioning and Refrigeration Institute.

★ 930 ★
Laundry Equipment (SIC 3633)

Largest Dryer Makers, 2000

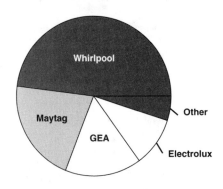

Shares are shown based on unit shipments for the year.

Whirlpool	48.0%
Maytag	21.0
GEA	16.0
Electrolux	10.0
Other	5.0

Source: *Appliance Manufacturer*, April 2001, p. 19.

★ 931 ★
Laundry Equipment (SIC 3633)

Largest Washer Makers, 2000

Shares are shown based on unit shipments for the year.

Whirlpool	46.0%
Maytag	26.0
Electrolux	14.0
GEA	13.0
Other	1.0

Source: *Appliance Manufacturer*, April 2001, p. 19.

★ 932 ★
Laundry Equipment (SIC 3633)

Washer and Dryer Sales

Data show unit shipments for year to date October.

	2000	2001
Automatic washers	6,230,300	6,068,200
Electric dryers	4,200,300	4,194,000
Gas dryers	1,214,800	1,120,600

Source: *Appliance*, January 2002, p. 30, from Association of Home Appliance Manufacturers.

★ 933 ★
Personal Care Appliances (SIC 3634)

Largest Beard/Mustache Trimmer Makers, 2000

Shares are shown based on unit shipments for the year.

Conair	35.8%
Remington	26.3
Wahl	22.0
Norelco Consumer Products	11.7
Other	4.2

Source: *Appliance*, September 2001, p. 19.

★ 934 ★

Personal Care Appliances (SIC 3634)

Largest Hair Dryer Makers, 2000

Shares are shown based on unit shipments for the year.

Conair	36.0%
Helen of Troy	31.0
Remington	8.0
Windmere	1.0
Other	24.0

Source: *Appliance Manufacturer*, April 2001, p. 19.

★ 935 ★

Personal Care Appliances (SIC 3634)

Largest Hair Setter Makers, 2000

Shares are shown based on unit shipments for the year.

Conair	48.0%
Helen of Troy	24.0
Remington	22.0
Other	6.0

Source: *Appliance Manufacturer*, April 2001, p. 19.

★ 936 ★

Personal Care Appliances (SIC 3634)

Largest Shaver (Men's) Makers, 2000

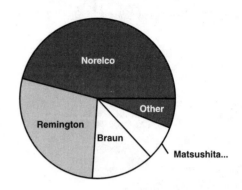

Shares are shown based on unit shipments for the year.

Norelco	46.0%
Remington	28.0
Braun	13.0
Matsushita (Panasonic)	7.0
Other	6.0

Source: *Appliance*, September 2001, p. 19.

★ 937 ★

Personal Care Appliances (SIC 3634)

Largest Shaver (Women's) Makers, 2000

Shares are shown based on unit shipments for the year.

Remington	47.0%
Matsushita (Panasonic)	38.0
Norelco Consumer Products	5.0
Conair	3.0
Emjoi	2.0
Wahl	1.0
Other	4.0

Source: *Appliance*, September 2001, p. 19.

★ 938 ★

Personal Care Appliances (SIC 3634)

Well-Care Product Sales

Sales are shown in millions of dollars for the year ended May 19, 2001.

Body massager appliance and accessory . . $ 145.0
Electric foot products 45.4

Source: *Drug Store News*, August 6, 2001, p. 23, from SPINS and ACNielsen ScanTrack.

★ 939 ★

Small Appliances (SIC 3634)

Bread Slicing Machines

Market shares are shown in percent.

Oliver Products Co. 80.0%
Other 20.0

Source: *Grand Rapids Press*, March 4, 2002, p. A8.

★ 940 ★

Small Appliances (SIC 3634)

Largest Blender Makers, 2000

Shares are shown based on unit shipments for the year.

Hamilton Beach/Proctor-Silex 56.0%
Sunbeam Corp. 27.0
Salton/Maxim Housewares 3.0
Appliance Corp. of America 3.0
Braun 2.0
Waring 1.0
Other 8.0

Source: *Appliance Manufacturer*, April 2001, p. 19.

★ 941 ★

Small Appliances (SIC 3634)

Largest Breadmaker Producers, 2000

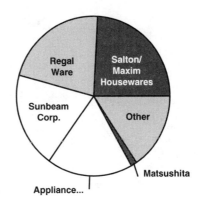

Shares are shown based on unit shipments for the year.

Salton/Maxim Housewares (Breadman/
  Toastmaster) 20.0%
Regal Ware 18.0
Sunbeam Corp. 16.0
Appliance Corp. of America 15.0
Matsushita 1.0
Other 13.0

Source: *Appliance Manufacturer*, April 2001, p. 19.

★ 942 ★

Small Appliances (SIC 3634)

Largest Can Opener Producers, 2000

Shares are shown based on unit shipments for the year.

Hamilton Beach/Proctor-Silex 28.0%
Applica (Windmere/Black & Decker) 23.0
The Holmes Group (Rival) 22.0
Oster/Sunbeam 9.0
Salton (Toastmaster) 3.0
Presto 3.0
Krups 2.0
Other 10.0

Source: *Appliance*, September 2001, p. 19.

★ 943 ★

Small Appliances (SIC 3634)

Largest Coffeemaker Producers, 2000

Shares are shown based on unit shipments for the year.

Hamilton Beach/Proctor-Silex	33.0%
Sunbeam/Oster (Mr. Coffee)	26.0
Applica (Windmere/Black & Deck)	13.0
Krups	4.0
Braun	4.0
West Bend	3.0
Other	17.0

Source: *Appliance*, September 2001, p. 19.

★ 944 ★

Small Appliances (SIC 3634)

Largest Food Processor Producers, 2000

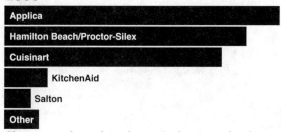

Shares are shown based on unit shipments for the year.

Applica (Windmere/Black & Decker)	33.0%
Hamilton Beach/Proctor-Silex	29.0
Cuisinart	26.0
KitchenAid	5.0
Salton (Toastmaster)	3.0
Other	4.0

Source: *Appliance*, September 2001, p. 19.

★ 945 ★

Small Appliances (SIC 3634)

Largest Iron Makers, 2000

Shares are shown based on unit shipments for the year.

Hamilton Beach/Proctor-Silex	40.0%
Applica Consumer Products	20.0
Sunbeam Corp.	10.0
Rowenta	5.0
Other	15.0

Source: *Appliance Manufacturer*, April 2001, p. 19.

★ 946 ★

Small Appliances (SIC 3634)

Largest Toaster Makers, 2000

Shares are shown based on unit shipments for the year.

Hamilton Beach/Proctor-Silex	60.0%
Salton/Maxim	16.0
Applica Consumer Products	10.0
Sunbeam Corp.	3.0
Holmes	2.0
Appliance Corp. of America	2.0
Other	7.0

Source: *Appliance Manufacturer*, April 2001, p. 19.

★ 947 ★

Vaccum Cleaners (SIC 3635)

Largest Vaccum Cleaner Makers, 2000

Shares are shown based on unit shipments for the year.

Hoover	29.0%
Eureka	25.5
Royal	16.5
Matushita	7.5
Bissell	7.0
Kirby	3.0
Iona	3.0
Electrolux	2.0
Other	6.5

Source: *Appliance Manufacturer*, April 2001, p. 19.

★ 948 ★

Vacuum Cleaners (SIC 3635)

Largest Wet/Dry Vac Makers, 2000

Shares are shown based on unit shipments for the year.

Shop Vac	51.0%
Sears/Kenmore	35.0
Genie	6.0
Eureka	5.0
Royal	1.0
Other	2.0

Source: *Appliance*, September 2001, p. 19.

★ 949 ★

Dishwashers (SIC 3639)

Dishwasher Shipments by Type

Data show unit shipments for year to date October.

	2000	2001	Share
Built-in	4,662,700	4,450,800	97.45%
Portable	130,700	116,500	2.55

Source: *Appliance*, January 2002, p. 30, from Association of Home Appliance Manufacturers.

★ 950 ★

Dishwashers (SIC 3639)

Largest Dishwasher Makers, 2000

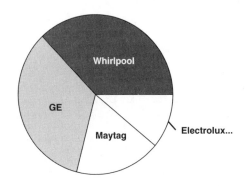

Shares are shown based on unit shipments for the year.

Whirlpool	37.0%
GE	34.0
Maytag	18.0
Electrolux (Frigidaire)	11.0

Source: *Appliance*, September 2001, p. 19.

★ 951 ★

Floor Care Equipment (SIC 3639)

Largest Floor Polisher Makers, 2000

Shares are shown based on unit shipments for the year.

Hoover	72.0%
Thorne Electric	19.0
Electrolux	9.0

Source: *Appliance Manufacturer*, April 2001, p. 19.

★ 952 ★

Floor Care Equipment (SIC 3639)

Largest Shampooers/Steam Cleaner Makers, 2000

Shares are shown based on unit shipments for the year.

Hoover	46.0%
Bissell	36.0
Royal	14.0
Eureka	3.0
Other	1.0

Source: *Appliance*, September 2001, p. 19.

★ 953 ★

Garbage Disposals (SIC 3639)

Largest Garbage Disposal Makers, 2000

Shares are shown based on unit shipments for the year.

In-Sink-Erator	72.0%
Anaheim/Watertown/Waste King	28.0

Source: *Appliance Manufacturer*, April 2001, p. 19.

★ 954 ★

Trash Compactors (SIC 3639)

Largest Trash Compactor Makers, 2000

Shares are shown based on unit shipments for the year.

Whirlpool	89.0%
Broan	11.0

Source: *Appliance Manufacturer*, April 2001, p. 19.

★ 955 ★

Lighting (SIC 3641)

Light Industry Leaders

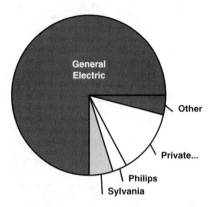

Market shares are shown for the year ended October 2001.

General Electric	75.0%
Sylvania	5.0
Philips	3.0
Private label	13.0
Other	4.0

Source: *Grocery Headquarters*, May 2002, p. 121, from CCITriad/Vista home center syndicated scanner data.

★ 956 ★

Consumer Electronics (SIC 3651)

Audio Equipment Sales

Sales are shown for year to date.

	2000	2001
Portable audio	1,350,098	1,188,686
Systems	1,297,435	1,283,158
Aftermarket autosound . .	1,297,435	1,283,158
Separate components . . .	839,345	732,175

Source: *Appliance*, December 2001, p. 15.

★ 957 ★

Consumer Electronics (SIC 3651)

Camcorder Market Shares, 2000

Shares are shown based on unit shipments for the year.

Sony	40.0%
JVC	25.0
Matsushita	23.0
Canon	2.0
Other	10.0

Source: *Appliance Manufacturer*, April 2001, p. 19.

★ 958 ★

Consumer Electronics (SIC 3651)

Camcorder Sales by Type

Sales are shown at electronics chains though November 2001.

Digital	50.0%
Hi8mm	34.0
VHS-C	27.3
Mini-DV	17.3
Digital 8	15.7
8mm	4.7
Full size	1.0

Source: *Consumer Electronics*, December 31, 2001, p. NA, from NPD Intelect.

★ 959 ★

Consumer Electronics (SIC 3651)

Home and Audio Shipments

Data are in thousands of units.

	2000	2001
CD players	54,374	52,200
Portable headset audio	34,865	32,775
Portable CD gear	32,161	33,125
Home radios	19,976	17,200
Compact systems	11,455	9,975
Tape/radio tape players	8,612	5,700
Tape/rad tape recorders	8,304	7,150
Home theater-in-box	1,157	2,250
MP3 players	510	625
Rack systems	151	80

Source: *Audio Week*, January 14, 2002, p. NA, from Consumer Electronics Association.

★ 960 ★
Consumer Electronics (SIC 3651)

Home Information Product Shipments

Shipments are shown in thousands of units.

	2001	2002
Telephones, wireless	53,400	57,000
Telephones, cordless	31,696	30,608
Telephones, corded	26,620	25,696
Telephones, answering devices	20,959	20,655
Computer printers	20,000	21,000
Caller ID devices	15,218	15,409
Computers, personal	13,900	13,900
Modems/fax modems	12,500	12,500
Word processors and electronic typewriters	868	434

Source: *Appliance Manufacturer*, January 2002, p. 76, from Outdoor Power Equipment Institute.

★ 961 ★
Consumer Electronics (SIC 3651)

Largest CD Player Makers, 2000

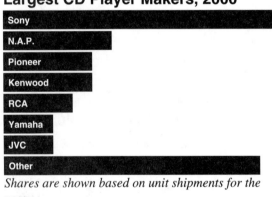

Shares are shown based on unit shipments for the year.

Sony	28.0%
N.A.P.	11.0
Pioneer	9.0
Kenwood	9.0
RCA	7.0
Yamaha	5.0
JVC	5.0
Other	26.0

Source: *Appliance*, September 2001, p. 19.

★ 962 ★
Consumer Electronics (SIC 3651)

Largest Cordless Telephone Makers, 2000

Shares are shown based on unit shipments for the year.

GE	23.0%
Vtech	17.0
Uniden	13.0
Sony	10.0
Panasonic	10.0
BellSouth	8.0
AT&T/Lucent	8.0
Other	11.0

Source: *Appliance*, September 2001, p. 19.

★ 963 ★
Consumer Electronics (SIC 3651)

Largest DVD Player Makers

Market shares are shown in percent.

Sony	20.0%
Apex Digital	14.0
Toshiba	12.0
Samsung Electronics	10.0
Pioneer	10.0
Panasonic	10.0
Other	24.0

Source: *Technology Advertising & Branding Report*, February 25, 2002, p. NA.

★ 964 ★
Consumer Electronics (SIC 3651)

Largest VCR Makers, 2000

Shares are shown based on unit shipments for the year.

Philips USA	13.0%
Matsushita	12.5
Thomson	8.5
Symphonic	7.0
Sony	7.0
Sanyo Fisher	5.5
JVC	5.5
Orion	5.0
Emerson	4.5

Continued on next page.

★ 964 ★ *Continued*
Consumer Electronics (SIC 3651)

Largest VCR Makers, 2000

Shares are shown based on unit shipments for the year.

Sharp 4.0%
Other 27.5

Source: *Appliance Manufacturer*, April 2001, p. 19.

★ 965 ★
Consumer Electronics (SIC 3651)

Leading Audio Brands

Market shares are estimated in percent.

Sony 20.75%
Bose 8.50
RCA 7.50
Pioneer 6.50
Aiwa 6.20
Yamaha 6.00
Philips/Magnavox 5.50
JVC 5.20
Other 33.85

Source: *Dealerscope*, August 2001, p. 1, from NPD Intelect.

★ 966 ★
Consumer Electronics (SIC 3651)

Leading Digital TV Brands

Market shares are shown in percent.

Sony 35.6%
Mitsubishi 13.1
Toshiba 11.9
Hitachi 9.0
RCA 8.0
Panasonic 7.0
Philips 5.4
Pioneer 4.1
Other 5.9

Source: *Dealerscope*, August 2001, p. 1, from NPD Intelect.

★ 967 ★
Consumer Electronics (SIC 3651)

Leading LCD Television Makers

LCD stands for liquid crystal displays.

Sharp 80.0%
Other 20.0

Source: *Wall Street Journal*, March 11, 2002, p. A3.

★ 968 ★
Consumer Electronics (SIC 3651)

Leading TV Brands (Direct View)

Market shares are shown in percent.

RCA/ProScan 15.3%
Sony 12.8
Philips/Magnavox 11.2
Zenith 7.9
Sanyo 7.8
Panasonic 7.2
Sharp 4.9
GE 4.4
Other 28.5

Source: *Dealerscope*, August 2001, p. 1, from NPD Intelect.

★ 969 ★
Consumer Electronics (SIC 3651)

Leading TV (Color) Makers, 2000

Shares are shown based on unit shipments for the year.

Thomson (RCA/GE) 22.0%
N.A.P. 11.0
Sony 10.0
Sanyo 8.0
LG Electronics/Zenith 8.0
Matsushita 7.0
Sharp 5.0
Toshiba 4.0
Samsung 3.0
Other 22.0

Source: *Appliance*, September 2001, p. 19.

★ 970 ★

Personal Electronics (SIC 3651)

PVR Market Shares

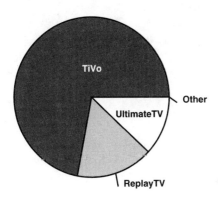

Market shares are shown in percent.

TiVo	.72.0%
ReplayTV	16.0
UltimateTV	11.8
Other	0.2

Source: *Audio Week*, October 1, 2001, p. NA, from NPD.

★ 971 ★

Personal Electronics (SIC 3651)

Web TV Market Shares

Market shares are shown in percent as of July 2001.

Philips	.52.0%
Sony	.41.0
Thomson	7.0

Source: *Audio Week*, October 1, 2001, p. NA, from NPD.

★ 972 ★

Music (SIC 3652)

Largest Independent Labels

Market shares are shown in percent.

Jive	6.7%
Arista	4.9
Def Jam	3.9
Other	84.5

Source: *Time*, September 15, 2001, p. 25.

★ 973 ★

Music (SIC 3652)

Leading Country Distributors, 2001

Market shares are shown in percent.

Universal	.28.8%
WEA	.21.7
BMG	.17.7
Sony	.13.4
EMD	.10.6
Indies	7.9

Source: *Billboard*, January 26, 2002, p. 51, from SoundScan.

★ 974 ★

Music (SIC 3652)

Leading Music Distributors

Shares are as of October 2001.

Universal	.26.9%
Warner	.16.3
Sony	.15.7
BMG	.13.6
EMI	.10.4
Other	.17.2

Source: *New York Times*, December 10, 2001, p. C1, from Sanford C. Bernstein.

★ 975 ★

Music (SIC 3652)

Leading R&B Distributors, 2001

Market shares are shown in percent.

Universal	.35.3%
Sony	.19.1
BMG	.16.7
EMD	.11.8
WEA	9.1
Indies	8.0

Source: *Billboard*, January 26, 2002, p. 51, from SoundScan.

★ 976 ★

Music (SIC 3652)

Music Sales by Format

Market shares are shown in percent.

	1987	2000
CDs	11.5%	89.3%
Cassettes	62.5	5.0
Vinyl	20.1	0.5

Source: *USA TODAY*, November 23, 2001, p. 2E, from Recording Industry Association of America.

★ 977 ★

Music (SIC 3652)

Popular Types of Music

Rock
Popular
Rap/hip-hop
R&B/urban
Country
Jazz
Classical
Other

Market shares are shown in percent.

Rock	24.0%
Popular	12.1
Rap/hip-hop	11.4
R&B/urban	10.6
Country	10.5
Jazz	3.4
Classical	3.2
Other	24.8

Source: *Audio Week*, May 6, 2002, p. NA, from Recording Industry Association of America.

★ 978 ★

Music (SIC 3652)

Top Albums, 2001

Sales are shown in millions of units.

Hybrid Theory	4.81
Hotshot	4.51
Celebrity	4.42
A Day Without Rain	4.41
Break the Cycle	4.24
Songs in A Minor	4.10
Survivor	3.72
Weathered	3.58
O Brother, Where Art Thou	3.46
Now 6 hits anthology	3.13

Source: *USA TODAY*, January 4, 2002, p. E1, from SoundScan.

★ 979 ★

Music (SIC 3652)

Top Albums in Detroit, MI

Unit sales are shown.

Celebrity	98,000
Hybrid Theory	86,000
A Day Without Rain	80,000
Songs in A Minor	79,000
Hotshot	75,000
Break the Cycle	75,000
Weathered	70,000
Survivor	70,000
All For You	62,000
Who is Jill Scott?	58,000

Source: *Detroit Free Press*, January 9, 2002, p. D1, from SoundScan.

★ 980 ★

Music (SIC 3652)

Top Music Producers in Canada

The industry is valued at $726 million.

Universal Music Canada	30.0%
Sony	15.0
Other	55.0

Source: *Macleans*, July 30, 2001, p. 36.

★ 981 ★

Music (SIC 3652)

Who Buys Music?

Adults are representing a larger share of music purchasers. Overall industry revenues have been stagnant lately.

	1991	2000
10-34	71.2%	54.7%
35+	28.3	44.0

Source: *USA TODAY*, February 18, 2002, p. 2B, from Recording Industry Association of America.

★ 982 ★

Broadcasting Equipment (SIC 3661)

Set-Top Digital Box Deployments

Market shares are shown for North America.

Motorola/Scientific-Atlanta	88.7%
Other	11.3

Source: *Business Wire*, October 1, 2001, p. NA, from Trace Strategies.

★ 983 ★

Cabling (SIC 3661)

Copper and Fiber Cabling Market

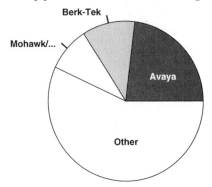

The $1.6 billion local network cabling industry is shown in percent.

Avaya	23.0%
Berk-Tek	11.0
Mohawk/CTD unit	9.0
Other	57.0

Source: *Mergers & Acquisitions*, February 18, 2002, p. NA.

★ 984 ★

Cellular Phones (SIC 3661)

Top Cell Phone Firms, 2001

Shares are for the first ten months of the year.

Nokia	41.7%
Motorola	19.6
Ericsson	10.1
Kyocera/Qualcomm	7.0
Audiovox	6.0
Other	15.6

Source: *New York Times*, December 17, 2001, p. C19, from NPD Intelect.

★ 985 ★

Fax Machines (SIC 3661)

Top Fax Machine Producers, 2002

Shares are for February 2002.

Panasonic	39.0%
Brother	36.7
Sharp	15.1
Hewlett-Packard	8.9
Canon	0.3

Source: *New York Times*, April 8, 2002, p. C10, from NPDTechworld.

★ 986 ★

Modems (SIC 3661)

Modem Market in North America, 2002

Market shares are shown for the first quarter.

Toshiba	29.3%
Motorola	22.5
Other	48.2

Source: *CableFAX*, May 3, 2002, p. NA.

★ 987 ★

Smart Tools (SIC 3663)

Smart Tool Market Shares, 2000

Market shares are shown in percent.

	1999	2004
Handhelds	69.0%	42.0%
Vertical application devices	22.0	10.0
Smart phones	9.0	48.0

Source: *Inside Business*, February 2001, p. 13.

★ 988 ★

Walkie Talkies (SIC 3663)

Walkie Talkie Market Shares

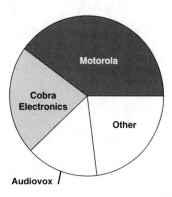

The "family services radio" niche recently hit $431 million. The market should see growth of 25% in 2001. Data are as of February 2001.

Motorola	40.0%
Cobra Electronics	21.7
Audiovox	15.2
Other	23.1

Source: *Crain's Chicago Business*, April 23, 2001, p. 3, from NPD Intelect Market Training.

★ 989 ★

Biometrics (SIC 3669)

Biometric Device Industry

Biometric revenues are expected to grow from $58.4 million in 1999 to $594 million in 2003.

Fingers	34.0%
Hand	26.0
Face	15.0
Voice	11.0
Iris	9.0
Signature	3.0
Retina	2.0

Source: *Employee Benefit News*, September 1, 2001, p. NA, from International Biometric Group.

★ 990 ★

Biometrics (SIC 3669)

Fingerprint Analysis Systems

Shares are for equipment used by law enforcement.

NEC	60.0%
Other	40.0

Source: *Houston Business Journal*, March 1, 2002, p. NA.

★ 991 ★

Biometrics (SIC 3669)

Voice Biometrics Market

Technology sales are shown in millions of dollars.

	2001	2003	Share
Phone-toll fraud prevention . .	$ 15	$ 28	20.00%
Call centers	15	40	28.57
Forensics	13	20	14.29
Corrections monitoring . . .	12	16	11.43
Data security	10	25	17.86
Physical access security . . .	4	8	5.71
Other future uses	1	3	2.14

Source: *Investor's Business Daily*, November 15, 2001, p. A8, from J. Markowitz Consultants.

★ 992 ★

Networking Equipment (SIC 3669)

Broadband DLC Market in North America, 2001

Shares are for the first six months of the year based on revenues. DLC stands for digital loop carrier.

Alcatel	40.0%
AFC	16.0
Nortel	13.0
Lucent	13.0
Other	18.0

Source: *XDSL News*, October 2001, p. 13, from RHK Inc.

★ 993 ★

Networking Equipment (SIC 3669)

IP Aggregation Routers

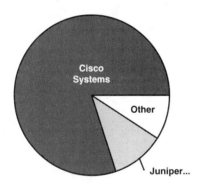

Market shares are shown in percent for North America. IP stands for Internet Protocol.

Cisco Systems	80.0%
Juniper Networks	11.0
Other	9.0

Source: *Investor's Business Daily*, December 24, 2001, p. A5, from International Data Corp.

★ 994 ★

Networking Equipment (SIC 3669)

IP Router Market Shares

Market shares are shown in percent.

Cisco	60.0%
Juniper	33.0
Other	7.0

Source: *Fiber Optics Business*, October 15, 2001, p. 3, from RHK.

★ 995 ★

Networking Equipment (SIC 3669)

Leading Networking Gear, 2001

Market shares are shown in percent for the fourth quarter 2001.

Cisco	17.7%
Agere	11.3
Linksys	11.1
D-Link	5.4
Other	54.5

Source: *Investor's Business Daily*, May 1, 2002, p. A6, from Synergy Researhc Group.

★ 996 ★

Networking Equipment (SIC 3669)

Optical Telecom Gear Market

Market shares are shown in percent.

	Q2 2001	Q3 2001
Lucent	22.8%	22.8%
Fujitsu	18.0	15.7
Nortel	15.6	11.1
Cisco	4.0	4.4
Other	39.6	46.0

Source: *Investor's Business Daily*, February 8, 2002, p. A8, from Dell'Oro Group and Communications Industry Researchers.

★ 997 ★
Networking Equipment (SIC 3669)

Wireless Handset Market

Shares are for new business users.

SpectraLink	38.0%
Nortel Networks	16.0
Avaya	16.0
Ericsson	7.0
Other	23.0

Source: *Investor's Business Daily*, September 6, 2001, p. A10, from company reports, Infotech, and First Call.

★ 998 ★
Networking Equipment (SIC 3669)

XDSL Market in North America, 2001

Shares are for the first six months of the year based on revenues.

Alcatel	49.0%
Lucent	19.0
Cisco	15.0
Fujitsu	6.0
Nortel	4.0
Other	7.0

Source: *XDSL News*, October 2001, p. 13, from RHK Inc.

★ 999 ★
Telematics (SIC 3669)

U.S. Telematics Revenues, 2006

Figures are in billions of dollars.

	($ bil.)	Share
Cellular charges	$ 10	50.0%
Hardware	6	30.0
Service revenues	4	20.0

Source: *Automotive News*, October 15, 2001, p. 1T.

★ 1000 ★
Energy Storage (SIC 3670)

Energy Storage Industry

The market is expected to more than double between 2000 and 2005. Sales are in millions of dollars.

	2000	2005	Share
Electronic, capacitive	$ 57	$ 196	61.44%
Superconducting, magnetic . .	36	80	25.08
Flywheel	25	43	13.48

Source: *American Ceramic Society Bulletin*, September 2001, p. 14, from Business Communications Co.

★ 1001 ★
Printed Circuit Boards (SIC 3672)

Printed Wiring Board Market in North America, 2001

Shares are estimated.

Communications	36.0%
Computers	20.0
Automotive	16.0
Instrumentation	11.0
Industrial electronics	6.0
Government/military	4.0
Consumer	4.0
Business/retail	3.0

Source: *CircuiTree*, January 2002, p. 28, from IPC/TMRC.

★ 1002 ★
Animal Tracking (SIC 3674)

Animal Tracking Technology

The animal tracking business uses electronic ear tags, or implantable chips, that can be tracked electronically. There is an infrastructure in 6,000 animal shelters that can read the frequencies. 66% of animal clinics use the patented system.

Applied Digital System	70.0%
Other	30.0

Source: *South Florida Business Journal*, April 20, 2001, p. 53.

★ 1003 ★
Microprocessors (SIC 3674)

Graphics Chip Market

Figures are for the third quarter of the year.

Nvidia Corp.	31.0%
Intel Corp.	26.0
ATI Technologies	17.0
Other	26.0

Source: *Investor's Business Daily*, November 12, 2001, p. A6, from Mercury Research.

★ 1004 ★
Semiconductors (SIC 3674)

Programmable DSP Chips

Market shares are shown in percent.

Texas Instruments	43.5%
Agere Systems	16.1
Motorola	12.0
Analog Devices	8.2
Other	20.2

Source: *Electronic News*, April 1, 2002, p. 24, from Forward Concepts.

★ 1005 ★
Semiconductors (SIC 3674)

Semiconductor End Markets

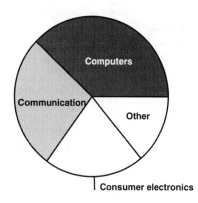

Data show percent of dollar sales.

	2000	2005
Computers	46.0%	38.0%
Communication	24.0	27.0
Consumer electronics	15.0	21.0
Other	15.0	14.0

Source: *Investor's Business Daily*, March 21, 2002, p. A1, from Cahners In-Stat.

★ 1006 ★
Load Leveling (SIC 3679)

U.S. Load Leveling Industry

The electric utility industry has seen demand spike, shortages grow, and new regulations knock at its door. One solution has involved storing the power produced at night to use during the day. Segments of the industry are in millions of dollars.

	2001	2006
Electrochemical batteries	$ 6	$ 40
Fuel cell	3	60
Flywheel energy storage	1	6
Capacitive energy storage	1	20
SMES	0	30
Pumped hydro	0	200
Compressed air	0	935

Source: *Research Studies - Business Communications Inc.*, October 1, 2001, p. 1, from Business Communications Co.

★ 1007 ★

Automotive Electronics (SIC 3690)

Automotive Electronics Demand

The North American market is expected to grow 7% annually. Advances will be driven by consumer demand for safer vehicles, such as airbags and tire pressure monitors. Sales are shown in millions of dollars.

	2001	2006	Share
Engine & drivetrain . .	$ 8,995	$ 10,530	33.32%
Safety & security	7,005	10,650	33.70
Navigation & instrumentation	3,475	6,230	19.72
Comfort/convenience/ entertainment	3,125	4,190	13.26

Source: *Research Studies - Freedonia Group*, March 15, 2002, p. 3, from Freedonia Group.

★ 1008 ★

Automotive Electronics (SIC 3690)

Mobile Video Package Market

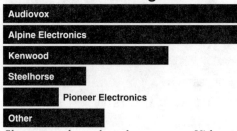

Shares are shown based on revenue. Video packages include DVD or VCR players, screens and speakers. Unit sales hit 334,000 in 2001, 454,000 are expected to be sold in 2003 and 472,000 in 2005.

Audiovox	30.0%
Alpine Electronics	26.0
Kenwood	18.0
Steelhorse	9.0
Pioneer Electronics	6.0
Other	11.0

Source: *The Register-Guard (Eugene, OR)*, May 25, 2002, p. A1, from Consumer Electronics Market Research and NPDTechworld.

★ 1009 ★

Batteries (SIC 3691)

Batteries for Mobile Technology

Market shares are shown for rechargable batteries for mobile information technology. The industry saw 27% growth in 2000 and roughly 2-3% in 2001, a probable reflection of the slowing economy.

	2001	2003
Lithium ion	81.6%	81.4%
Lithiumn polymer	10.7	12.3
NIMH	7.0	5.7
NICAD	0.7	0.5

Source: *Purchasing*, February 21, 2002, p. 26, from Freedonia Group.

★ 1010 ★

Batteries (SIC 3691)

Battery And Fuel Cell Material Demand

The market is expected to grow 6%, with lithium and fuel cells driving demand. Figures are in millions of dollars.

	2000	2005	Share
Metals	$ 1,320	$ 1,695	54.07%
Chemicals	570	805	25.68
Polymers	184	300	9.57
Carbon/graphite	76	117	3.73
Other	140	218	6.95

Source: *Research Studies - Freedonia Group*, October 2, 2001, p. 1, from Freedonia Group.

★ 1011 ★

Batteries (SIC 3691)

Rechargable Battery Market

Market shares are shown in percent.

Rayovac	75.0%
Other	25.0

Source: *Capital Times*, March 27, 2002, p. 8C.

★ **1012** ★

Batteries (SIC 3691)

Top Alkaline Battery Vendors, 2001

Market shares are shown based on mass market sales for the year ended November 4, 2001.

Duracell	44.2%
Energizer	31.9
Rayovac	14.3
Panasonic	0.5
Sony Tape	0.1
Red Cell Intl.	0.1
Fuji	0.1
Eastman Kodak	0.1
Atico	0.1
Private label	8.8

Source: *Grocery Headquarters*, February 2002, p. 54, from Information Resources Inc.

★ **1013** ★

Batteries (SIC 3691)

Top Batteries in Drug Stores, 2000

Brands are ranked by sales in millions of dolalrs.

	($ mil.)	Share
Duracell	$ 254.3	52.07%
Energizer	150.8	30.88
Duracell Ultra	63.6	13.02
Ray O Vac	5.7	1.17
Kodak Photolife	5.3	1.09
Eveready	2.8	0.57
Ray O Vac Loud N Clear	2.6	0.53
Panasonic	1.7	0.35
AT&T	1.6	0.33

Source: *Drug Store News*, August 6, 2001, p. 25, from Information Resources Inc.

★ **1014** ★

Batteries (SIC 3691)

Top Battery Brands, 2001

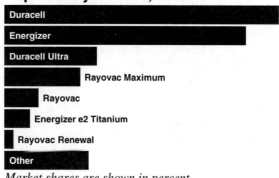

Market shares are shown in percent.

Duracell	33.0%
Energizer	28.7
Duracell Ultra	11.2
Rayovac Maximum	8.9
Rayovac	4.1
Energizer e2 Titanium	2.9
Rayovac Renewal	1.2
Other	10.0

Source: *Chain Drug Review*, January 7, 2002, p. 37, from Information Resources Inc.

★ **1015** ★

Batteries (SIC 3691)

U.S. Batteries Demand

Sales are shown in millions of dollars.

	2000	2005
Secondary	$ 6,755	$ 9,390
Primary	3,670	4,975

Source: *Research Studies - Freedonia Group*, August 3, 2001, p. 1, from Freedonia Group.

★ 1016 ★

Recording Media (SIC 3695)

Analog Cassette Sales

Figures are in millions of units. Data are for North America.

	2001	2002	2003
Spoken word cassettes	677	615	545
Blank audiocassettes	175	150	128
Music cassettes	60	50	40

Source: *Tape-Disc Business*, February 2002, p. 14, from Magnetic Media Information.

★ 1017 ★

Recording Media (SIC 3695)

Leading Blank Audio Tape Brands

Brands are ranked by sales in millions of dollars for the year ended November 4, 2001.

	($mil.)	Share
Maxell UR	$ 14.4	12.49%
TDK D	11.8	10.23
Sony HF	9.1	7.89
Maxell XLII	8.9	7.72
Sony	6.9	5.98
TDK CD Power	6.7	5.81
Sony MC	5.1	4.42
Fuji DR I	4.8	4.16
RCA	4.5	3.90
Sony CDIT	2.8	2.43
Other	40.3	34.95

Source: *MMR*, January 14, 2002, p. 33, from Information Resources Inc.

★ 1018 ★

Recording Media (SIC 3695)

Leading Blank Audio/Video Brands

Brands are ranked by sales in millions of dolalrs for the year ended July 15, 2001.

	($ mil.)	Share
Sony	$ 94.0	14.97%
RCA	49.2	7.84
Maxell	42.0	6.69
Memorex	36.8	5.86
Maxell HGX Gold	33.8	5.38
Maxell GX Silver	32.0	5.10
Fuji HQ	28.5	4.54
TDK	26.2	4.17

	($ mil.)	Share
TDK Revue	$ 20.6	3.28%
Other	264.8	42.17

Source: *Chain Drug Review*, September 24, 2001, p. 53, from Information Resources Inc.

★ 1019 ★

Recording Media (SIC 3695)

Leading Blank Video Tape Brands, 2001

Brands are ranked by sales in millions of dollars for the year ended November 4, 2001.

	($ mil.)	Share
RCA	$ 70.5	16.52%
Sony	63.9	14.97
Sony V	39.4	9.23
Maxell GX Silver	33.5	7.85
Fuji HQ	29.0	6.79
Maxell HGX Gold	28.0	6.56
TDK Revue	23.5	5.51
TDK HG Ultimate	12.0	2.81
Sony HMP	10.4	2.44
Fuji	10.0	2.34
Other	106.6	24.98

Source: *MMR*, January 14, 2002, p. 33, from Information Resources Inc.

★ 1020 ★

Electrical Power Devices (SIC 3699)

Power Quality Devices

Figures are in millions of dollars. UPS stands for uninterruptible power supply. TVSS stands for transient voltage surge suppressors.

	2000	2006	Share
UPS	$ 2,724.3	$ 5,150.9	72.06%
TVSS	767.2	1,374.0	19.22
Power conditioning . . .	230.7	436.2	6.10
Power monitoring . . .	90.0	187.4	2.62

Source: *Research Studies - Business Communications Inc.*, October 2, 2001, p. 4, from Business Communications Inc.

SIC 37 - Transportation Equipment

★ 1021 ★
Autos (SIC 3711)

Auto Auction Services

Figures are for North America.

Manheim Auctions 40.0%
Adesa 20.0
Other 40.0

Source: *Investor's Business Daily*, November 1, 2001, p. A10.

★ 1022 ★
Autos (SIC 3711)

Auto Industry in Chicago, IL

Market shares are shown in percent.

Sport utility vehicle 25.6%
Midsize car 23.7
Small car 15.8
Van/minivans 10.4
Luxury car 10.2
Pickup truck 8.3
Sports car 2.4
Other 1.4

Source: *PR Newswire*, February 11, 2001, p. NA.

★ 1023 ★
Autos (SIC 3711)

Best-Selling Autos in Los Angeles, CA

Data show unit sales.

Toyota Camry 21,404
Honda Accord 21,262
Honda Civic 18,123
Toyota Corolla 12,655
Ford Explorer 11,996
Ford Expedition 10,026
Ford F-150 9,795
Chevrolet Sivlerado 8,943
Toyota Tacoma 8,685

Source: *Los Angeles Business Journal*, October 8, 2001, p. 34.

★ 1024 ★
Autos (SIC 3711)

Light Vehicle Sales, 2001

Market shares are shown in percent.

GM 28.1%
Ford 21.9
Chrysler 13.2
Toyota 10.1
Honda 7.0
Nissan 4.1
Volkswagen 2.1
Hyundai 2.0
Mitsubishi 1.9
Other 9.6

Source: *Financial Times*, January 6, 2002, p. 9, from DRI WEFA and Reuters.

★ 1025 ★

Autos (SIC 3711)

Light Vehicles Sales by Origin

Market shares are shown in percent.

	1990	2001
Big three	72.0%	64.0%
Asian brands	25.0	30.0
Europe	3.0	6.0

Source: *Forbes*, September 17, 2001, p. 76, from WARD's AutoInforbank.

★ 1026 ★

Autos (SIC 3711)

Luxury Car Sales, 2001

Data are in thousands.

Lexus	223,638
BMW	213,127
Mercedes	206,638
Cadillac	172,083
Lincoln	158,934
Audi	83,283
Infinity	71,365
Jaguar	44,532

Source: *Wall Street Journal*, February 4, 2002, p. B1.

★ 1027 ★

Autos (SIC 3711)

New Car and Truck Registrations

Data show the states with the highest share of total registrations.

California	11.7%
Texas	8.5
Florida	6.8
New York	5.8
Michigan	4.7

Source: *Wall Street Journal*, May 3, 2002, p. A1, from R. L. Polk & Co.

★ 1028 ★

Autos (SIC 3711)

Popular Cars for Women

Data show the most popular types. 2001 data is for the first nine months.

Midsize car	24.1%
Sport utility	20.8
Small car	19.2
Pickup	14.0
Luxury car	7.9
Van/mini	7.4
Sport car	4.3
Large car	2.0
Other	0.2

Source: *PR Newswire*, January 25, 2002, p. NA, from R.L. Polk.

★ 1029 ★

Autos (SIC 3711)

Top Car and Light Truck Brands, 2001

Shares are shown based on unit sales.

Ford	19.2%
Chevrolet	15.6
Toyota	8.8
Dodge	7.3
Honda	6.0
Nissan	3.7
Pontiac	3.1
GMC	3.1
Chrysler	3.1
Jeep	2.7
Other	72.6

Source: *Advertising Age*, June 24, 2002, p. S10, from *Automotive News*.

★ 1030 ★

Autos (SIC 3711)

Top Cars and Trucks in Canada

Market shares are shown in percent.

Honda Civic Sedan Coupe	7.9%
Chevrolet Cavalier	5.9
Mazda Protege	5.5
Pontiac Sunfire	5.0
Ford Focus	5.0
Toyota Corolla	4.7
Honda Accord	3.4

Continued on next page.

★ 1030 ★ *Continued*
Autos (SIC 3711)

Top Cars and Trucks in Canada

Market shares are shown in percent.

Pontiac Grand Am	3.1%
Nissan Sentra Sedan	3.1
Other	56.4

Source: *Marketing Magazine*, May 27, 2002, p. 1, from Des Rosiers Automotive Consulting.

★ 1031 ★
Autos (SIC 3711)

Top Cars and Trucks in Mexico

Data show the top models for the 2002 model year through June.

Nissan Tsuru	71,054
Chevrolet Joy/Swing	55,127
Nissan Sentra	41,587
Volkswagen Pointer	37,365
Volkswagen Pentra	30,965
Volkswagen Beetle	29,980
Ford F-series	26,770
Dodge Stratus	26,680

Source: *Ward's Dealer Business*, August 2001, p. 13.

★ 1032 ★
Autos (SIC 3711)

Top Mid-Sized Car Makers

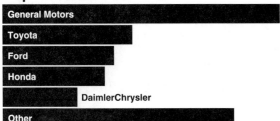

Market shares are shown in percent.

General Motors	30.0%
Toyota	14.0
Ford	12.0
Honda	11.0
DaimlerChrysler	8.0
Other	25.0

Source: *Motor Trend*, May 2002, p. 32.

★ 1033 ★
Autos (SIC 3711)

Top Minivans in Canada

Market shares are shown in percent.

Dodge Caravan	36.6%
GM Transport/Venture/Montana	25.9
Ford Windstar	17.5
Honda Odyssey	6.0
GM Astro/Safari	4.5
Toyota Sienna	4.1
Mazda MPV 4X2	3.7
Kia Sedona	0.8
Chrysler Town & Country	0.8
Nissan Quest	0.1

Source: *Marketing Magazine*, May 27, 2002, p. 1, from Des Rosiers Automotive Consulting.

★ 1034 ★
Autos (SIC 3711)

Top Pickups in Canada

Market shares are shown in percent.

GM Silverado/C/K/Sierra	36.7%
Ford F-Series	30.3
Chrysler Dodge Ram	12.0
Chrylser Dodge Dakota	7.2
GM Chevroler S10 Sonoma	4.3
Ford Ranger	4.1
Mazda B Series 4x2	1.3
GM Chevrolet Avalanche	1.1
Toyota Tundra	0.9
Toyota Tundra 4x4	0.8
Other	1.4

Source: *Marketing Magazine*, May 27, 2002, p. 1, from Des Rosiers Automotive Consulting.

★ 1035 ★
Trucks (SIC 3713)

Class 4 Truck Leaders

Sales are shown by company.

	Units	Share
Chevrolet	19,531	20.77%
International	10,201	10.85
Freightliner	6,715	7.14
Ford	3,501	3.72
Mack	1,471	1.56
Mitsubishi Faso	559	0.59
Other	52,037	55.35

Source: *Automotive News*, January 28, 2002, p. 80, from Automotive News Data Center.

★ 1036 ★
Trucks (SIC 3713)

Class 5 Truck Leaders

Sales are shown by company.

	Units	Share
Chevrolet	18,336	38.48%
International	2,130	4.47
Mack	849	1.78
Ford	808	1.70
Mitsubishi	630	1.32
Hino	485	1.02
Peterbilt	54	0.11
Other	24,362	51.12

Source: *Automotive News*, January 28, 2002, p. 80, from Automotive News Data Center.

★ 1037 ★
Trucks (SIC 3713)

Class 6 Truck Leaders

Sales are shown by company.

	Units	Share
Chevrolet	14,957	18.12%
Hino	10,587	12.82
Ford	10,371	12.56
Freightliner	2,170	2.63
Mack	716	0.87
GMC	669	0.81
Peterbilt	652	0.79
Other	42,435	51.40

Source: *Automotive News*, January 28, 2002, p. 80, from Automotive News Data Center.

★ 1038 ★
Trucks (SIC 3713)

Class 7 Truck Leaders

Sales are shown by company.

	Units	Share
Hino	41,575	23.61%
Ford	20,912	11.88
Freightliner	10,638	6.04
Peterbilt	4,722	2.68
Chevrolet	2,628	1.49
Nissan Diesel	2,228	1.27
Other	93,351	53.02

Source: *Automotive News*, January 28, 2002, p. 80, from Automotive News Data Center.

★ 1039 ★
Trucks (SIC 3713)

Class 8 Truck Leaders

Sales are shown by company.

	Units	Share
Ford	44,351	16.77%
Hino	21,895	8.28
Kenworth	20,351	7.70
Nissan Diesel	15,305	5.79
Isuzu Truck	12,190	4.61
Peterbilt	9,345	3.53
Sterling	1,354	0.51
Other	139,614	52.80

Source: *Automotive News*, January 28, 2002, p. 80, from Automotive News Data Center.

★ 1040 ★
Auto Parts (SIC 3714)

Custom Wheel Sales, 2000

Custom wheels make up about 7% of the total market for tire and wheels. Sales of custom wheels are shown by type.

Aluminum	75.0%
Steel	12.0
Wire	3.0

Source: *Tire Business*, December 3, 2001, p. 1.

★ 1041 ★
Auto Parts (SIC 3714)
Largest Auto Parts Suppliers

The top firms in North America are ranked by estimated revenue in millions of dollars.

Delphi Corp.	$ 18,867
Visteon Corp.	12,878
Johnson Controls	8,444
Lear Corp.	7,888
Magna International	7,140
Dana Corp.	5,553
TRW Automotive	4,992
Robert Bosch Corp.	4,140
Denso International America Inc.	3,721
ArvinMentor Inc.	3,299

Source: *Automotive News*, March 25, 2002, p. 1.

★ 1042 ★
Auto Parts (SIC 3714)
Leading Class 5-7 Truck Engine Makers, 1999

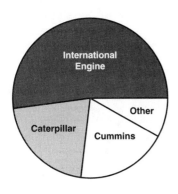

Data are for North America.

International Engine	52.0%
Caterpillar	21.0
Cummins	19.0
Other	8.0

Source: "1999 North American Diesel Engine Market Share." Retrieved November 7, 2001 from: http://www.corporate-ir.net.

★ 1043 ★
Auto Parts (SIC 3714)
Leading School Bus Engine Makers, 1999

Data are for North America.

International Engine	67.0%
Cummins	22.0
Caterpillar	11.0

Source: "1999 North American Diesel Engine Market Share." Retrieved November 7, 2001 from: http://www.corporate-ir.net, from Power Systems Research.

★ 1044 ★
Auto Parts (SIC 3714)
Preferred Brands of Automotive Brakes

Data show a survey of technicians of the brands they most often install.

Raybestos	25.0%
Bendix	16.0
Wagner	15.0
NAPA	10.0

Source: *Aftermarket Business*, October 2001, p. 28.

★ 1045 ★
Auto Parts (SIC 3714)
Preferred Brands of Automotive Clutches

Data show a survey of technicians of the brands they most often install.

Borg-Warner	16.0%
Luk	13.0
NAPA	9.0
Sachs	7.0

Source: *Aftermarket Business*, October 2001, p. 28.

★ 1046 ★
Auto Parts (SIC 3714)

Preferred Brands of Automotive Filters

Data show a survey of technicians of the brands they most often install.

NAPA 18.0%
Wix 12.0
ACDelco 11.0
Fram 10.0

Source: *Aftermarket Business*, October 2001, p. 28.

★ 1047 ★
Auto Parts (SIC 3714)

Preferred Brands of Automotive Spark Plugs

Data show a survey of technicians of the brands they most often install.

ACDelco 36.0%
Autolite 17.0
Champion 13.0
Bosch 10.0

Source: *Aftermarket Business*, October 2001, p. 28.

★ 1048 ★
Auto Parts (SIC 3714)

Sun Protection Category

This auto accessories category includes things such as seat covers, windshield covers, protective film and cushions.

Axius 95.0%
Other 5.0

Source: ''Pennzoil-Quaker State Company.'' Retrieved February 28, 2002 from the World Wide Web: http://www. pennzoil-quakerstate.com.

★ 1049 ★
Auto Parts (SIC 3714)

Top Brake Material Makers

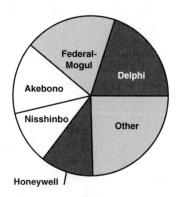

Market shares are shown in percent.

Delphi 22.0%
Federal-Mogul 21.0
Akebono 16.0
Nisshinbo 12.0
Honeywell 12.0
Other 27.0

Source: *Automotive News*, April 8, 2002, p. 3.

★ 1050 ★
Auto Parts (SIC 3714)

Transmission Sales by Type

Data are for cars and light trucks, both domestic and foreign.

	1998	1999	2000
Automatic	86.8%	88.8%	89.4%
Manual	13.2	11.2	10.6

Source: *Aftermarket Business*, January 2002, p. 8.

★ 1051 ★
Recreational Vehicles (SIC 3715)

RV and Motorhome Shipments

Shipments are shown by year.

	2001	2002
Towable RV	210,400	215,400
Motorhomes	48,300	47,800

Source: *RV Business*, January 2002, p. 7.

★ 1052 ★
Recreational Vehicles (SIC 3716)

Class A Market Shares, 2001

Market shares are shown in percent.

Monaco	20.4%
Fleetwood	18.7
Winnebago	16.6
Coachmen	7.5
National RV	6.7
Other	30.1

Source: *RV Business*, April 2002, p. 18.

★ 1053 ★
Recreational Vehicles (SIC 3716)

Fifth-Wheel Market Shares, 2001

Market shares are shown in percent.

Thor	28.7%
Forest River	14.0
Fleetwood	11.2
Jayco	8.5
Monaco	4.2
Other	33.4

Source: *RV Business*, April 2002, p. 18.

★ 1054 ★
Aircraft (SIC 3721)

Largest Jets and the Fractional Industry

The industry has seen some growth since 2001. Total unit sales grew 20% and share owners grew 30%.

NetJet's Falcon 2000	40.0%
Flexjet's Challenger 604	25.0
NetJet's Gulfstream IVSP	22.0
Other	13.0

Source: "ARG Releases Updated 5 Year Forecast." Retrieved May 2, 2002 from the World Wide Web: http://www.aviationresearch.com, from Aviation Research Group.

★ 1055 ★
Helicopters (SIC 3721)

Commercial Helicopter Shipments, 2000

Total shipments hit 532 craft, valued at $969 million.

	Units	Share
Robinson	390	73.31%
McDonnell Douglas	41	7.71
Sikorsky	40	7.52
Schweizer	36	6.77
Boeing	8	1.50
Enstrom	7	1.32
Brantly	6	1.13
Kaman	3	0.56
Hiller	1	0.19

Source: "Commerical Helicopter Shipments." Retrieved April 3, 2002 from the World Wide Web: http://www.aia-aerispace.org, from AIA.

★ 1056 ★
Autonomous Underwater Vehicles (SIC 3731)

How AUVs Are Used

The table shows how 174 vehicles are used.

Academic	41.0%
Military	39.0
Commercial	20.0

Source: *Offshore*, January 2002, p. 64.

★ 1057 ★
Shipbuilding (SIC 3731)

Shipbuilding and Repair Industry

Two companies own what is commonly referred to as "The Big Six": General Dynamics owns Electric Boat, Bath Iron Works and National Steel and Shipbuilding Co.; Northrop Grumman owns Newport News Shipbuilding and Ingalls and Avondale.

The Big Six	66.0%
Other	34.0

Source: *National Defense*, March 2002, p. 32.

★ 1058 ★

Boats (SIC 3732)

Boat Building Market Shares

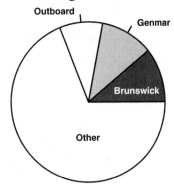

Market shares are shown in percent.

Brunswick	11.1%
Genmar	10.6
Outboard	9.1
Other	69.2

Source: *Knight-Ridder/Tribune Business News*, January 2, 2001, p. NA, from Statistical Surveys.

★ 1059 ★

Boats (SIC 3732)

Boat Industry Sales, 2001

Retail sales are shown in millions of dollars.

Inboard boats-cruisers	$ 2,769.7
Outboard motors	2,508.0
Outboard boats	2,338.0
Sterndrive boats	2,264.5
Personal watercraft	658.1
Inboard boats-runabouts	435.1
Boat trailers	179.9
Jet boats	110.4
Canoes	58.0

Source: "Statistics." Retrieved February 9, 2002 from the World Wide Web: http://www.nmma.org, from *2001 Annual Sailing Business Review*.

★ 1060 ★

Boats (SIC 3732)

Boat Registrations by State, 2000

	No.	Share
Michigan	1,000,049	7.82%
California	904,863	7.08
Florida	840,684	6.58
Minnesota	812,247	6.35
Texas	626,761	4.90
Wisconsin	573,920	4.49
New York	525,436	4.11
Ohio	416,798	3.26
South Carolina	383,734	3.00
Illinois	372,162	2.91
Other	6,325,489	49.49

Source: "Statistics." Retrieved February 9, 2002 from the World Wide Web: http://www.nmma.org, from U.S. Coast Guard and National Marine Manufacturers Association.

★ 1061 ★

Boats (SIC 3732)

Recreational Boat Shipments

Shipments are shown in millions of dollars. Figures are expected to grow 6% annually to $16.6 billion to the year 2005.

	2000	2005	Share
Boats	$ 7,363	$ 9,620	58.09%
Propulsion systems . . .	3,090	4,380	26.45
Accessories	2,000	2,560	15.46

Source: *Research Studies - Freedonia Group*, June 1, 2001, p. 5, from Freedonia Group.

★ 1062 ★

Boats (SIC 3732)

U.S. Sailboat Industry, 2001

Foreign sailboats are carving out a niche in the industry, particularly for larger yachts.

	Imports	Domestic
36 ft and longer	26.0%	74.0%
20 ft to 35 ft. sailboats	2.0	98.0

Source: *New York Times*, August 18, 2001, p. B1, from The Sailing Company.

★ 1063 ★

Railroad Equipment (SIC 3743)

Railroad Bearings Industry

Market shares are shown in percent.

Brencos	60.0%
Other	40.0

Source: "Welcome to the Brenco." Retrieved June 10, 2002 from http://www.brencoqbs.com.

★ 1064 ★

Bicycle Locks (SIC 3751)

Bike Lock Market

Market shares are shown in percent.

Kryptonite Corp.	60.0%
Other	40.0

Source: *BusinessWeek*, August 13, 2001, p. NA.

★ 1065 ★

Bicycles (SIC 3751)

Bicycle Sales by Segment

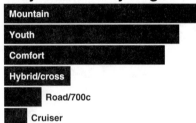

Unit shares are shown in percent.

	2000	2001
Mountain	42.77%	37.61%
Youth	25.66	23.75
Comfort	13.62	21.78
Hybrid/cross	11.29	9.29
Road/700c	3.91	4.55
Cruiser	2.63	2.89

Source: *Bicycle Retailer and Industry News*, December 1, 2001, p. 1, from National Bicycle Dealers Association.

★ 1066 ★

Bicycles (SIC 3751)

U.S. Bicycle Shipments, 2001

Shipments are shown through August 2001. The BMX segment continues to fall and is being replaced by road bikes.

	($ mil.)	Share
26 inch	251.1	61.85%
700c DB	54.9	13.52
20 inch	45.6	11.23
700c UB	37.7	9.29
24 inch	9.4	2.32
Other	7.3	1.80

Source: *Bicycle Retailer and Industry News*, November 1, 2001, p. 1, from Bicycle Products Suppliers Association.

★ 1067 ★

Motorcycles (SIC 3751)

Top Cruiser Brands

Data show sales.

	Units	Share
Harley	117,742	45.01%
Honda	61,091	23.35
Yamaha	35,318	13.50
Suzuki	23,052	8.81
Kawasaki	17,198	6.57
Indian	3,701	1.41
Polaris/Victory	1,948	0.74
Other	1,526	0.58

Source: *Dealernews*, January 2002, p. 26.

★ 1068 ★

Motorcycles (SIC 3751)

Top Dirtbike Makers

Market shares are shown in percent, based on total sales of 252,031 units.

Honda	42.69%
Yamaha	35.84
Kawasaki	9.64
Suzuki	6.66
KTM/Husaberg	4.81
Aprilia	0.05
Duceti	0.02

Source: *Dealernews*, October 2001, p. 66.

★ 1069 ★

Motorcycles (SIC 3751)

Top Motorcycle Makers, 2001

Data show shipments.

	Units	Share
Honda	232,053	29.77%
Harley-Davidson	173,893	22.31
Yamaha	160,798	20.63
Suzuki	90,858	11.65
Kawasaki	74,330	9.53
KTM/Husaberg	11,642	1.49

Source: *Dealernews*, August 2001, p. 94.

★ 1070 ★

Aerospace (SIC 3761)

Largest Missile Producers, 2000

Data show the largest contractors.

	($ mil.)	Share
Lockheed Martin	$ 1,752	48.34%
Raytheon	1,317	36.33
Northrop Grumman	150	4.13
General Dynamics	81	2.23
Motorola	48	1.31

Source: *Wall Street Journal*, October 3, 2001, p. B4, from *Government Executive*.

★ 1071 ★

Aerospace (SIC 3761)

Top Defense Contractors, 2002

The largest military contractors are ranked by contract value in billions of dollars.

Lockheed Martin	$ 14.69
Boeing	13.34
Newport News Shipbuilding	5.89
Raytheon	5.58
Northrop Grumman	5.15
General Dynamics	4.91
United Technologies	3.37
TRW	1.90
Science Applications International	1.75
General Electric	1.75

Source: *Wall Street Journal*, March 28, 2002, p. R4, from U.S. Department of Defense.

★ 1072 ★

Aerospace (SIC 3761)

Top States for Defense Contracts

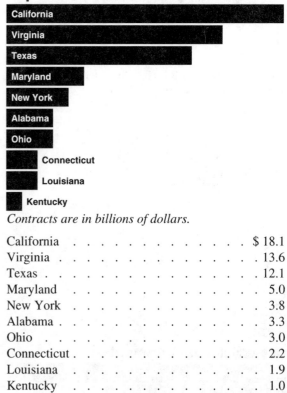

Contracts are in billions of dollars.

California	$ 18.1
Virginia	13.6
Texas	12.1
Maryland	5.0
New York	3.8
Alabama	3.3
Ohio	3.0
Connecticut	2.2
Louisiana	1.9
Kentucky	1.0

Source: *USA TODAY*, November 23, 2001, p. 7B, from U. S. Department of Defense.

★ 1073 ★

Travel Trailers (SIC 3792)

Camping Trailer Market, 2001

Market shares are shown in percent for the year ended April 2001.

Coleman	48.3%
Fleetwood	42.3
Other	9.4

Source: *RV Business*, October 2001, p. 25, from Statistical Surveys.

★ 1074 ★

Travel Trailers (SIC 3792)

Travel Trailer Market Shares, 2001

Market shares are shown in percent.

Thor	24.5%
Fleetwood	17.0
Forest River	12.7
Jayco	6.6
Coachmen	5.8
Other	33.4

Source: *RV Business*, April 2002, p. 18.

★ 1075 ★

Ski Lifts (SIC 3799)

Ski Lift Industry

Market shares are shown in percent.

Dopplemayr-CTEC Inc.	55.0%
Leitner Poma	45.0

Source: *Knight-Ridder/Tribune Business News*, August 25, 2001, p. NA.

★ 1076 ★

Snowmobiles (SIC 3799)

Top States for Snowmobiles, 2001

Figures show total registrations for the year.

	Units	Share
Michigan	357,033	21.69%
Minnesota	277,290	16.84
Wisconsin	214,331	13.02
New York	146,662	8.91
Maine	90,000	5.47
New Hampshire	66,000	4.01
Illinois	54,128	3.29
Pennsylvania	45,270	2.75%
Other	395,469	24.02

Source: "Snowmobile Statistics." Retrieved June 25, 2002 from the World Wide Web: http://www.snowmobile.org, from International Snowmobile Manufacturers Association.

SIC 38 - Instruments and Related Products

★ 1077 ★
Laboratory Instruments (SIC 3821)

Blood Gas and Electrolyte Market Shares, 2001

Market shares are shown in percent.

i-STAT	54.0%
IL	14.0
Radiometer	8.0
Diametrics	7.0
Roche	5.0
AVOX	4.0
NOVA	3.0
Bayer	3.0
Other	2.0

Source: *Clinical Lab Products*, December 2001, p. NA, from EAC.

★ 1078 ★
Laboratory Instruments (SIC 3821)

Needle Bearing Technology, 2001

Market shares are shown in percent.

BD	90.0%
Other	10.0

Source: *Clinical Lab Products*, January 2002, p. NA, from EAC.

★ 1079 ★
Laboratory Instruments (SIC 3821)

POC Cardiac Market Shares, 2001

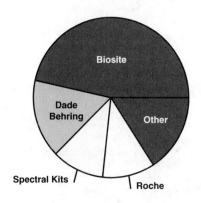

Market shares are shown in percent.

Biosite	47.0%
Dade Behring	16.0
Spectral Kits	11.0
Roche	11.0
Other	16.0

Source: *Clinical Lab Products*, December 2001, p. NA, from EAC.

★ 1080 ★
Motion Control Industry (SIC 3823)

Motion Control Industry in North America

The industry is expected to grow from $1.15 billion in 2000 to $1.39 billion in 2005.

	2000	2005
Servo systems	61.5%	61.7%
Position controllers	19.9	21.4
Stepper systems	18.6	16.9

Source: *Motion Systems Distributor*, January 2002, p. 20, from Intex Managment Services.

★ 1081 ★

Meter Readers (SIC 3824)

Automatic Meter Reader Industry, 2000

Data show shipments in North America.

	Units	Share
Schlumberger	2,003,524	57.09%
Itron	696,054	19.83
DCSI	451,599	12.87
Hunt	328,065	9.35
Utili-Link	16,546	0.47
ABB	10,835	0.31
Teldata Inc.	1,824	0.05
Comverge	477	0.01
Hexagram	300	0.01
Other	384	0.01

Source: *Utility Automation*, September 2001, p. 16.

★ 1082 ★

Thermometers (SIC 3824)

Thermometers for the Semiconductor Industry

Market shares are shwon in percent.

Sekidenko	50.0%
Other	50.0

Source: *Knight-Ridder/Tribune Business News*, March 21, 2002, p. NA.

★ 1083 ★

Explosion Detection Equipment (SIC 3827)

Explosive Detection System Industry

Market shares are shown in percent.

InVision Technologies	90.0%
Other	10.0

Source: *Airport Security Report*, January 16, 2002, p. NA.

★ 1084 ★

Explosive Detection Equipment (SIC 3827)

Explosive Residue Testing Equipment

Market shares are for the airport industry.

Barringer	70.0%
Other	30.0

Source: *USA TODAY*, April 9, 2002, p. 2E.

★ 1085 ★

Infrared Imaging (SIC 3827)

Infrared Imaging Industry in Law Enforcement

Share is for the airborne law enforcement systems. The company also has roughly 70% of the market for airborne imaging systems used by television and radio broadcasting stations.

Flir Systems	85.0%
Other	15.0

Source: *Business Journal-Portland*, July 13, 2001, p. 14.

★ 1086 ★

Lasers (SIC 3827)

Semiconductor Laser Market

Market shares are shown in percent.

Cymer	85.0%
Other	15.0

Source: *Knight-Ridder/Tribune Business News*, January 15, 2002, p. NA.

★ 1087 ★

Pavement Sensing Equipment (SIC 3827)

Roadway/Runway Information Systems

Market shares are shown in percent.

Surface Systems Inc.	90.0%
Other	10.0

Source: "Quixote Corp. Announces Acquisition."
Retrieved November 7, 2001 from the World Wide Web: http://www.itsa.org.

★ 1088 ★

Sensors (SIC 3827)

Oil Debris Monitoring Products

Market shares are shown in percent.

Engineered Sensors/Tedeco 80.0%
Other 20.0

Source: "Eaton Aerospace Cockpit Controls." Retrieved February 28, 2002 from the World Wide Web: http://www.aerospace.eaton.com.

★ 1089 ★

Sensors (SIC 3827)

Sensor Industry Technologies

Sales are shown in millions of dollars.

	2001	2006	Share
Active	$ 1,568	$ 1,933	28.32%
Semiconductive	1,345	2,119	31.05
Passive	1,174	1,583	23.19
Electromechanical	928	1,190	17.44

Source: *American Ceramic Society Bulletin*, May 2002, p. 15, from Business Communications Co.

★ 1090 ★

First Aid Products (SIC 3841)

Top First Aid Accessory Brands

Market shares are shown in percent.

Johnson & Johnson 17.5%
Band-Aid 12.3
Nexcare 3.3
Kling 2.1
Hurt Free 2.1
Spenco 2nd Skin 2.0
Nexcare Active Strips 1.9
New Skin 1.8
Curity Kerlix 1.8
Nexcare Comfort Strips 1.7
Private label 22.9
Other 30.6

Source: *Chain Drug Review*, February 18, 2002, p. 36, from Information Resources Inc.

★ 1091 ★

First Aid Products (SIC 3841)

Top First Aid Support/Brace Brands, 2001

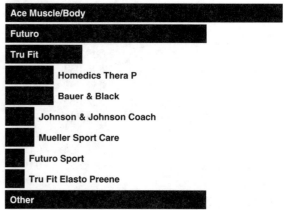

Brands are ranked by sales for the year ended January 28, 2001.

	($ mil.)	Share
Ace Muscle/Body	$ 69.8	28.87%
Futuro	51.6	21.34
Tru Fit	19.9	8.23
Homedics Thera P	12.6	5.21
Bauer & Black	12.6	5.21
Johnson & Johnson Coach	7.5	3.10
Mueller Sport Care	6.3	2.61
Futuro Sport	5.8	2.40
Tru Fit Elasto Preene	5.0	2.07
Other	50.7	20.97

Source: *MMR*, April 16, 2001, p. 67, from Information Resources Inc.

★ 1092 ★

Surgical Instruments (SIC 3841)

Vascular Closing Devices

Shares are shown bason on revenues in the $300 million (and still quite young) market.

St. Jude 44.0%
Abbott 36.0
Vascular Solutions 4.0
Other 16.0

Source: *Star Tribune*, May 6, 2002, p. 1A, from analyst estimates.

★ 1093 ★
Surgical Instruments (SIC 3841)

Ventricular Assist Devices

Market shares are estimated.

Thoratec 90.0%
Other 10.0

Source: *Modern Healthcare*, November 5, 2001, p. 30.

★ 1094 ★
Medical Supplies (SIC 3842)

Disposable Supplies Market, 2005

Figures are in billions of dollars.

	($ bil.)	Share
Catheters, infusion products	$ 27.3	42.00%
Diagnostic and laboratory	16.9	26.00
Wound management	6.5	10.00
Non-woven textiles	4.4	6.77
Other	9.9	15.23

Source: *Hospital Materials Management*, January 2002, p. 3, from Freedonia Group.

★ 1095 ★
Medical Supplies (SIC 3842)

Sterile Lap Sponges

Market shares are shown in percent.

Medical Action 85.0%
Other 15.0

Source: *LI Business News*, July 6, 2001, p. 5A.

★ 1096 ★
Medical Supplies (SIC 3842)

Top Suture Brands

Market shares are shown in percent.

Ethicon 75.0%
Other 25.0

Source: *Hospital Materials Management*, March 2002, p. 1.

★ 1097 ★
Medical Supplies (SIC 3842)

U.S. Blood Industry

Sales are shown in millions of dollars.

	2001	2006
Blood components & plasma products	$ 4,976.5	$ 7,259
Equipment, blood tests & other consumables	1,158.4	1,432

Source: *Biomedical Market Newsletter*, September 18, 2001, p. 31, from Business Communications Co.

★ 1098 ★
Medical Supplies (SIC 3842)

Urological Catheter Market

Market shares are estimated.

Bard 45.0%
Kendall 11.0
Other 44.0

Source: *Healthcare Purchasing News*, January 2002, p. 20.

★ 1099 ★
Orthopedic Appliances (SIC 3842)

Bone Graft Substitute Market, 2000

The market was valued at $157 million in 2000.

Osotech 37.0%
GenSci 16.0
Interpore 12.0
Medtronic/Danek 11.0
Wright 6.0
RTI 5.0
Other 13.0

Source: *Datamonitor Industry Market Research*, Annual 2001, p. NA, from Datamonitor.

★ 1100 ★

Orthopedic Appliances (SIC 3842)

Maxillofacial Implant Market, 2000

The market was valued at $126 million in 2000.

Plates & screws	86.0%
Specialty Instrumentation	8.3
Resorbables	5.7

Source: *Datamonitor Industry Market Research*, Annual 2001, p. NA, from Datamonitor.

★ 1101 ★

Orthopedic Appliances (SIC 3842)

Orthopedic Implant Market

Market shares are shown in percent.

Stryker	24.0%
Johnson & Johnson	24.0
Zimmer	19.0
Biomet	14.0
Smith & Nephew	8.0
Other	11.0

Source: *Investor's Business Daily*, September 25, 2001, p. A10, from company reports and Robert W. Baird & Co.

★ 1102 ★

Orthopedic Appliances (SIC 3842)

Shoulder Joint Market, 2000

The market was valued at $57 million in 2000.

Biomet	33.0%
DePuy	31.0
Tornier	13.0
Sulzer Orthopedics	9.0
Smith & Nephew	8.0
Other	6.0

Source: *Datamonitor Industry Market Research*, Annual 2001, p. NA, from Datamonitor.

★ 1103 ★

Orthopedic Appliances (SIC 3842)

Spinal Cord Stimulation Industry

The $250 million market is shown in percent.

Implantable	80.0%
Radio frequency devices	20.0

Source: *Investor's Business Daily*, February 12, 2002, p. A10.

★ 1104 ★

Orthopedic Appliances (SIC 3842)

Spinal Implant Leaders, 2000

The market was valued at $622 million in 2000.

Sofamor Danek	31.3%
Spine-Tech	27.6
US Surgical	21.9
Other	19.1

Source: *Datamonitor Industry Market Research*, Annual 2001, p. NA, from Datamonitor.

★ 1105 ★

Orthopedic Appliances (SIC 3842)

Spine Implant Market

The market was estimated at $1.1 billion in 2001.

	($ mil.)	Share
Plates, rods, screws	$ 475	43.18%
Allograft/bone substitutes	285	25.91
Fusion cages	185	16.82
Electrical stimulation	155	14.09

Source: "Market Review." Retrieved November 14, 2001 from the World Wide Web: http://www.biomet.com, from Biomet.

★ **1106** ★
Vaccines (SIC 3842)

Vaccine Market Segments, 2000

The market was valued at $822 million in 2000. VZV stands for Varicella Zoster Virus.

VZV	33.0%
Influenza	15.0
Haemophilus Influenza type b (Hib)	12.0
DTP	7.0
Lyme disease	5.0
Other	18.0

Source: *Datamonitor Industry Market Research*, Annual 2001, p. NA, from Datamonitor.

★ **1107** ★
Dental Equipment (SIC 3843)

Artificial Tooth Industry

Market shares are shown in percent.

Dentsply International's Trubyte	70.0%
Other	30.0

Source: *Wall Street Journal*, April 12, 2002, p. A13.

★ **1108** ★
Dental Equipment (SIC 3843)

Dental Chair Market Shares

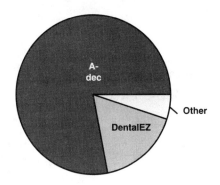

Market shares are shown in percent.

A-dec	78.0%
DentalEZ	17.0
Other	5.0

Source: "2000 DIS Equipment Survey." Retrieved February 15, 2002 from the World Wide Web: http://www. brooks.af.mil, from *DIS Equipment Survey*.

★ **1109** ★
Dental Equipment (SIC 3843)

Dental Operating Light Market Shares

Market shares are shown in percent.

A-dec	62.0%
Pelton & Crane	21.0
DentalEZ	11.0
Other	6.0

Source: "2000 DIS Equipment Survey." Retrieved February 15, 2002 from the World Wide Web: http://www. brooks.af.mil, from *DIS Equipment Survey.*

★ **1110** ★
Dental Equipment (SIC 3843)

Slow-Speed Handpieces Market Shares

Market shares are shown in percent. The devices are used in oral care, pin placement and chairside prosthetic adjustments.

Midwest	78.0%
Star	14.0
KaVo	8.0
Other	4.0

Source: "2000 DIS Equipment Survey." Retrieved February 15, 2002 from the World Wide Web: http://www. brooks.af.mil, from *DIS Equipment Survey*.

★ **1111** ★
Dental Equipment (SIC 3843)

U.S. Dental Industry

Market shares are estimated in percent.

Schein	27.0%
Patterson	27.0
Other	46.0

Source: *Investor's Business Daily*, November 29, 2001, p. A11.

★ 1112 ★
Imaging Equipment (SIC 3844)

Imaging Scans by Volume

The market has been growing slower than some analysts have expected. A great deal of attention is being paid to the digital radiography sector. About 70% of imaging procedures are general radiography.

X-ray	70.0%
Ultrasound	11.0
CT (cat scans)	8.0
MR	6.0
NM	3.0
Fluro	3.0

Source: *Diagnostics Imaging*, December 2001, p. 52, from Fuji Medical Systems.

★ 1113 ★
Ultrasound (SIC 3844)

U.S. Ultrasound Industry

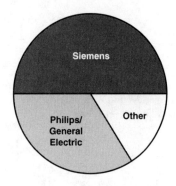

Industry revenues should hit $1.1 billion in 2001, with the top 3 firms having 84% of the market.

Siemens	50.0%
Philips/General Electric	34.0
Other	16.0

Source: *Business Wire*, June 11, 2002, p. NA, from Klein Biomedical Consultants.

★ 1114 ★
Defibrillators (SIC 3845)

Portable Defibrillator Market

Market shares are shown in percent.

Medtronic	40.0%
Cardiac Science	20.0
Other	40.0

Source: *Knight-Ridder/Tribune News Service*, February 18, 2002, p. NA.

★ 1115 ★
Hearing Aids (SIC 3845)

Hearing Aid Sales

Shares are shown for the first nine months. DSA - digital signal analog. DSP - digital signal processor.

Full-shell classic	15.3%
Full-shell DPA	10.8
Canal classic	8.6
Canal DPA	7.5
BTE DSP	6.7
Canal DSP	5.5
Full-shell DSP	5.1
CIC DPA	5.1
BTE DPA	4.6
Other	30.8

Source: *The Hearing Journal*, January 2002, p. 21, from Hearing Industries Association Statistical Reporting Program.

★ 1116 ★
Contact Lenses (SIC 3851)

Top Contact Lens Makers

Market shares are shown in percent.

Johnson & Johnson	32.0%
Ciba Vision Corp.	29.0
Bausch & Lomb	15.0
Other	24.0

Source: *Delaney Report*, April 15, 2002, p. 4.

★ 1117 ★
Optical Goods (SIC 3851)
Optical Goods Industry

The industry had sales of $16.5 billion.

Lenses	50.5%
Rx frames	32.8
Contact lenses	12.6
Plano sunglasses/clips	4.1

Source: *20/20 Magazine*, April 2002, p. 3.

★ 1118 ★
Cameras (SIC 3861)
Camera Sales by Type

Market shares are shown in percent.

	1998	2000
35mm lens shutter	58.6%	46.6%
Digital still	7.9	30.4
Instant	7.0	7.8
Advanced photo system	11.6	7.3
110	9.7	2.8

Source: *Photo Marketing*, August 2001, p. 17, from Photo Marketing Association Camera/Camcorder Surveys.

★ 1119 ★
Cameras (SIC 3861)
Top Digital Camera Brands, 2002

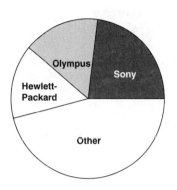

Market shares are shown in percent.

Sony	23.0%
Olympus	16.0
Hewlett-Packard	15.0
Other	46.0

Source: "Digital Camera Sales Shoot Up." Retrieved April 1, 2002 from the World Wide Web: http://www.news.com, from International Data Corp.

★ 1120 ★
Cameras (SIC 3861)
Top Digital Camera Makers in Canada

Shares are for the second quarter of 2001.

Kodak	22.0%
Sony	17.0
HP	14.5
Fuji	14.0
Other	32.5

Source: "Digital Cameras Second Quarter 2001." Retrieved November 15, 2001 from the World Wide Web: http://www.evansresearch.com, from Evans Research.

★ 1121 ★
Cameras (SIC 3861)
Top Disposable Camera Brands, 2001

Market shares are shown based on mass market sales for the year ended November 4, 2001.

Kodak Max Flash	33.2%
Fuji Quicksnap Flash	15.0

Continued on next page.

★ 1121 ★ *Continued*

Cameras (SIC 3861)

Top Disposable Camera Brands, 2001

Market shares are shown based on mass market sales for the year ended November 4, 2001.

Kodak Max HQ	7.0%
Kodak Max	5.4
Kodak Fun Saver	4.6
Jazz	3.9
Fuji Quicksnap	3.9
Kodak Advantix Switchable	2.8
Kodak Advantix Access	2.4
Private label	14.7

Source: *Grocery Headquarters*, February 2002, p. 54, from Information Resources Inc.

★ 1122 ★

Copiers (SIC 3861)

Color Laser Copier Market Shares, 2000

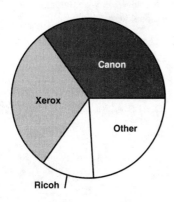

Market shares are shown in percent.

Canon	35.0%
Xerox	30.0
Ricoh	11.0
Other	24.0

Source: *Long Island Business News*, March 16, 2001, p. 25A, from Dataquest Inc.

★ 1123 ★

Copiers (SIC 3861)

Copy Machine Market Shares, 2000

Market shares are shown in percent.

Canon	32.0%
Xerox	25.0
Sharp	10.0
Other	33.0

Source: *Long Island Business News*, March 16, 2001, p. 25A, from Dataquest Inc.

★ 1124 ★

Copiers (SIC 3861)

High Speed Copiers and Print On Demand

The industry is shown by revenue segment for black and white high-speed copiers and Print on Demand Systems. Figures are in billions of dollars.

Segment 4, 5, 6 copiers	$ 9.2
POD systems (40 pages per minute)	3.2

Source: *Printing News*, August 13, 2001, p. 2, from CAP Ventures.

★ 1125 ★

Copiers (SIC 3861)

Top Duplicating Machine Purchasers in the Federal Government

Market shares are shown based on value of purchases.

De La Rue Giori SA	21.57%
Minolta Corp.	8.85
Bell & Howell	7.18
Xerox Corp.	4.90
Oce-Van der Grinten NV	4.86
Other	52.64

Source: *Government Executive*, August 1, 2001, p. NA.

★ 1126 ★

Film (SIC 3861)

Top Conventional Film Vendors, 2001

Market shares are shown based on mass market sales for the year ended November 4, 2001.

Eastman Kodak	70.1%
Fuji	22.2
Polaroid	3.2
Private label	4.5

Source: *Grocery Headquarters*, February 2002, p. 45, from Information Resources Inc.

★ 1127 ★

Film (SIC 3861)

Top Film Brands, 2001

Brands are ranked by sales in millions of dollars for the year ended June 17, 2001.

	($ mil.)	Share
Kodak Gold	$ 292.3	19.49%
Kodak Gold Max	275.4	18.36
Polaroid Platinum 600	230.7	15.38
Kodak Advantix	181.7	12.11
Fuji	134.8	8.99
Polaroid I-Zone	41.5	2.77
Kodak	33.7	2.25
Polaroid Spectra Platinum	28.4	1.89
Fuji Super HQ	28.1	1.87
Fuji APS Nexia	25.1	1.67
Other	228.3	15.22

Source: *MMR*, August 20, 2001, p. 43, from Information Resources Inc.

★ 1128 ★

Photographic Equipment (SIC 3861)

Amateur Photo Market, 2000

Market shares are shown in percent.

Photo processing	41.8%
Film sales	18.0
Digital imaging products/services	11.8
Conventional cameras	10.0
Portrait studio	3.9
Photo accessories	3.6
Albums	2.9
Video camcorders	2.0
Video accessories	2.0
Frames	1.7
Other	2.4

Source: *Research Alert*, January 18, 2002, p. 3, from Photo Marketing Association International.

★ 1129 ★

Photographic Equipment (SIC 3861)

Digital ICE Technology

According to the source, the company markets and licenses technologies to original equipment manufacturers in the image scanning and film processing industries. Share refers to the film scanning and digital mini-lab markets.

Applied Science Fiction	75.0%
Other	25.0

Source: *Austin Business Journal*, October 12, 2001, p. B20.

★ 1130 ★

Watches (SIC 3873)

Top Watch Makers

Timex's share is more than the next thirty firms combined. Market shares are estimated in percent.

Timex	30.0%
Seiko	6.0
Casio	6.0
Other	58.0

Source: *Knight-Ridder/Tribune Business News*, June 20, 2001, p. NA.

SIC 39 - Miscellaneous Manufacturing Industries

★ 1131 ★

Jewelry (SIC 3911)

Popular Types Of Wedding Bands

Figures are based on a survey of 650 respondents. One point made from the survey: wedding ring/band shoppers are looking for something that will stand out this year. Nearly a third planned to purchase a ring with a stone 1 carat or larger - suggesting the high end market is very strong.

Yellow gold	38.0%
Platinum	24.0
White gold	22.0
Other	16.0

Source: *National Jeweler*, March 1, 2002, p. 9.

★ 1132 ★

Jewelry (SIC 3911)

Retail Jewelry Sales

After record sales in the 1990s, sales have slipped slightly. Total sales reached $41.6 billion in 2000.

Diamond jewelry	30.0%
Loose diamonds	16.0
Karat gold	11.0
Colored stones	9.0
Watches	4.0
Platinum	3.0
Fashion jewelry	3.0
Tabletop gifts/silver	2.0
Estate jewelry	2.0
Cultured pearls	2.0
Other	18.0

Source: *National Jeweler*, August 1, 2001, p. 44, from Jewelers of America.

★ 1133 ★

Musical Instruments (SIC 3931)

Best-Selling School Instruments, 2001

Data show unit sales.

	Units	Share
Clarinets	131,197	19.57%
Trumpets	128,757	19.20
Violins/violas/cellos	127,500	19.02
Flutes	127,373	19.00
Trombones	59,133	8.82
Alto sax	58,055	8.66
Tenor sax	12,177	1.82
French horns	10,998	1.64
Euphoniums	9,410	1.40
Coronets	5,916	0.88

Source: *Music Trades*, April 2002, p. 66.

★ 1134 ★

Musical Instruments (SIC 3931)

Grand Piano Sales, 2001

Data show unit sales.

	Units	Share
5'-5'5"	10,439	28.48%
Grand player pianos	8,590	23.44
Under 5'	7,633	20.82
5'6"-5'10"	6,174	16.84
5'11"-6'4"	2,020	5.51
6'5"-7'10"	1,599	4.36
7'11" and over	199	0.54

Source: *Music Trades*, April 2002, p. 66.

★ 1135 ★

Musical Instruments (SIC 3931)

High-End Piano Market

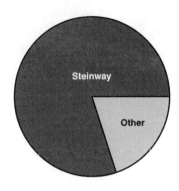

Market shares are shown in percent.

Steinway 80.0%
Other 20.0

Source: *Barron's*, April 22, 2002, p. 34.

★ 1136 ★

Musical Products (SIC 3931)

Largest Musical Product Markets

Sales are shown in millions of dollars.

California . . . . $ 1,052.2
New York 560.8
Texas 507.6
Florida 440.2
Illinois 326.6
New Jersey 257.7
Ohio 252.0
Pennsylvania 237.8
Maryland 220.1
Michigan 212.2

Source: *Music Trades*, August 2001, p. 186.

★ 1137 ★

Musical Products (SIC 3931)

Largest Musical Product Retailers

Firms are ranked by estimated revenue in millions of dollars.

Guitar Center Inc. . . . . $ 785.6
Sam Ash Music Corp. 325.0
Mars Inc. 305.0
Brook Mays/H&H 130.3

Hermes Music . . . . $ 82.0
Schmitt Music Company 62.5
Victor's House of Muisc 56.2
J.W. Pepper 53.9
Washington Music Center 52.4
Pro Sound & Stage Lighting 50.3

Source: *Music Trades*, August 2001, p. 84.

★ 1138 ★

Toys and Games (SIC 3940)

Retail Toy Sales, 2001

The total industry (including video games) jumped from $31.1 to $34.3 billion.

	2000	2001	Share
Video games	$ 6,581	$ 9,409	29.63%
Dolls/accessories	2,835	3,061	9.64
Infant/preschool	2,772	3,154	9.93
Vehicles	2,624	2,821	8.88
Games/puzzles	2,492	2,237	7.04
Plush	2,336	2,031	6.40
Sports	2,135	1,528	4.81
Action figures/accessories . .	1,187	1,618	5.09
Building/construction . . .	722	882	2.78
Ride-ons	664	773	2.43
Other	4,443	4,245	13.37

Source: *Research Alert*, February 15, 2002, p. 7, from NPD Group and Toy Industry Association.

★ 1139 ★

Toys and Games (SIC 3944)

Battery Powered Ride-Ons

Market shares are shown in percent. Power Wheel's share is higher than 80% of the industry.

Power Wheels (Fisher Price) 80.0%
Other 20.0

Source: "Mattel - About Us." Retrieved February 28, 2002 from the World Wide Web: http://www.mattel.com.

★ 1140 ★
Toys and Games (SIC 3944)
Pogo Stick Market

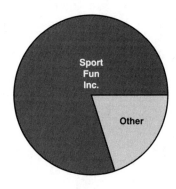

Market shares are shown in percent.

Sport Fun Inc. 80.0%
Other 20.0

Source: *Business Wire*, August 1, 2001, p. NA.

★ 1141 ★
Toys and Games (SIC 3944)
Table Based Role Playing Games

Market shares are shown in percent. There are an estimated 1.5 million people who play D&D every month in the United States between 12 and 35.

Dungeons & Dragons 60.0%
Other 40.0

Source: "Opening the Dungeon." Retrieved August 28, 2001 from the World Wide Web: http://www.salon.com/feature/2000/03/09/open_dungeon/print.html, from Wizards.

★ 1142 ★
Toys and Games (SIC 3944)
Toddler Playset Market

Market shares are shown in percent.

Little People (Fisher Price) 65.0%
Other 35.0

Source: "Mattel - About Us." Retrieved February 28, 2002 from the World Wide Web: http://www.mattel.com.

★ 1143 ★
Video Games (SIC 3944)
Popular Video Games, 2002

Data show rental revenue, in millions, for the week ended March 10, 2002.

State of Emergency . . . . $ 0.54
Grand Theft Auto 3 . . . . 0.42
Max Payne 0.20
Wreckless: Yakuza Missions 0.17
All Star Baseball 2003 . . . . 0.17

Source: *Video Business*, March 18, 2002, p. 30.

★ 1144 ★
Video Games (SIC 3944)
Sports Video Game Market

EA has roughly 35% of the entire PlayStation market, and 80% of the sports titles sold for them.

Electronic Arts 80.0%
Other 20.0

Source: *San Francisco Business Times*, November 16, 2001, p. 3.

★ 1145 ★
Video Games (SIC 3944)
Top Computer Game Publishers, 2001

Shares are from August 2000 - July 2001.

Electronic Arts 22.0%
Vivendi Universal Publishing 17.0
Infogrames Entertainment 17.0
Microsoft 9.0
Activision 5.0
Interplay 4.0
Ubisoft 3.0
Disney 3.0
Valusoft 2.0
Eidos 2.0
Other 16.0

Source: *New York Times*, August 27, 2001, p. C9, from Sanford C. Bernstein and Simba Information.

★ 1146 ★
Video Games (SIC 3944)

Top Video Game Publishers

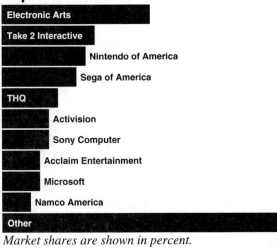

Market shares are shown in percent.

Electronic Arts	16.2%
Take 2 Interactive	9.8
Nintendo of America	9.0
Sega of America	8.2
THQ	5.8
Activision	5.4
Sony Computer	4.7
Acclaim Entertainment	4.4
Microsoft	3.5
Namco America	3.4
Other	29.6

Source: San Francisco Chronicle, May 19, 2002, p. G1, from Credit Suisse First Boston and NPD Funworld.

★ 1147 ★
Video Games (SIC 3944)

Top Video Game Titles

Data show unit sales, in millions, since 1992.

Myst	3.1
The Sims	2.3
MP Roller Coaster Tycoon	2.3
MS Flight Simulator	2.1
Who Wants to Be a Millionaire . . .	1.6
Riven: The Sequel to Myst	1.4
MS Age of Empires II	1.3
Monopoly Game	1.2
Diablo 2	1.2
Lego Island	1.1

Source: New York Times, July 9, 2001, p. B7, from NPD Intelect.

★ 1148 ★
Video Games (SIC 3944)

U.S. Console Games Market Shares

Market shares are shown in percent.

Sports	22.2%
Action	19.8
Strategy	17.6
Racing	16.7
Fighting	5.7
Family	3.6
Shooters	3.5
Child	3.4
Other	7.5

Source: Screen Digest, March 2002, p. 93, from NPDFunworld and Interactive Digital Software Association.

★ 1149 ★
Video Games (SIC 3944)

Video Game Console Market in North America

Figures are estimated.

	2000	2001	2002
Sony	55.0%	67.0%	43.0%
Nintendo	28.0	16.0	29.0
Microsoft	0.0	9.0	27.0
Other	17.0	8.0	0.0

Source: Wall Street Journal, November 9, 2001, p. B1, from International Data Corp.

★ 1150 ★
Video Games (SIC 3944)

Video Game Consoles, 2001

Market shares are shown in percent.

Sony Playstation 2	70.0%
Microsoft Xbox	16.0
Nintendo GameCube	14.0

Source: Advertising Age, May 20, 2002, p. 3, from NPD Funworld.

★ 1151 ★
Video Games (SIC 3944)

Video Game Ratings

Market shares are shown in percent.

Everyone	62.0%
Teen	25.0
Mature	10.0
Early childhood	3.0

Source: *Investor's Business Daily*, February 20, 2002, p. A5, from NPD Group.

★ 1152 ★
Exercise Equipment (SIC 3949)

Home Gym Sales

Sales show millions of units. Shares of the group are shown in percent.

	No.	% of Group
Total Gym	2,000,000	55.56%
Soloflex	1,000,000	27.78
Bowflex	600,000	16.67

Source: *Investor's Business Daily*, June 5, 2002, p. A7.

★ 1153 ★
Sporting Goods (SIC 3949)

Aluminum Bat Market

Eaton thinks it may be able to bring its share to as high as 60% of the market. It is the top aluminum bat maker. Wood bats are used primarily by professional players and make up only a small portion of bat sales. Bat sales made up 37% of all baseball equipment sales.

Eaton	45.0%
Other	55.0

Source: *Los Angeles Times*, May 27, 2002, p. C1.

★ 1154 ★
Sporting Goods (SIC 3949)

Baseball Bat (Wooden) Market

Market shares are shown in percent.

Louisville Slugger	75.0%
Other	25.0

Source: "Baseball Business." Retrieved August 28, 2001 from the World Wide Web: http://www.kybiz.com.

★ 1155 ★
Sporting Goods (SIC 3949)

Baseball Glove Market

Shares are for the week ended December 10, 2000.

Mizuno	35.12%
Rawlings	31.44
Other	33.44

Source: "Mizuno Rises to #1." Retrieved January 22, 2002 from the World Wide Web: http://www.mizunousa.com.

★ 1156 ★
Sporting Goods (SIC 3949)

Batter's Helmet Market

Market shares are shown in percent. The company holds 70% of the market for catcher's equipment.

Rawlings Sporting Goods Co. Inc.	91.0%
Other	9.0

Source: *St. Louis Business Journal*, May 14, 2001, p. 1.

★ 1157 ★
Sporting Goods (SIC 3949)

Cheerleading Industry Leaders

The industry is home to a number of companies, most of them quite small. Market shares are shown in percent.

Varsity Brands Inc.	50.0%
National Spirit Group	25.0
Other	25.0

Source: *USA TODAY*, April 26, 2002, p. 3D.

★ 1158 ★

Sporting Goods (SIC 3949)

Football Market Shares

The company's share of high school and college balls is between 70-80%.

Wilson Sporting Goods	80.0%
Other	20.0

Source: *Sporting Goods Dealer*, November-December 2001, p. 20.

★ 1159 ★

Sporting Goods (SIC 3949)

Golf Ball Sales

Market shares are shown for March 2001.

Titleist Pro VI	9.3%
Lady Precept	6.8
Top Flite XL	5.9
Titleist Tour Distance	4.5
Titleist Professional	3.4
Other	70.1

Source: *Chicago Tribune*, May 6, 2001, p. 10, from Datatech.

★ 1160 ★

Sporting Goods (SIC 3949)

Golf Industry Leaders

Firms are ranked by sales in millions of dollars.

Fortune Brands Golf Products Div.	$ 772.9
Callaway	710.8
Taylor-Made	394.0
Spaulding - Golf Div.	149.7
Adams Golf	46.1
Aldila	31.2

Source: *DSN Retailing Today*, January 21, 2002, p. 19.

★ 1161 ★

Sporting Goods (SIC 3949)

Golf Industry Sales, 2001

Sales are shown in millions of dollars. 2001 figures are through November.

	1999	2001
Woods	$ 532.8	$ 573.3
Balls	475.9	511.5
Irons	$ 408.4	$ 421.1
Footwear	187.5	197.1
Gloves	149.9	157.0
Putters	147.9	153.8
Bags	147.0	145.5
Wedges	60.1	64.0

Source: *Brandweek*, January 28, 2002, p. 16, from Golf Datatech.

★ 1162 ★

Sporting Goods (SIC 3949)

Golf's Off-Course Wood Market

Callaway leads in the $475 million irons market as well with a 17% share.

Callaway Golf	27.0%
TaylorMade	17.0
Other	56.0

Source: *Golf World Business*, May 2001, p. 25.

★ 1163 ★

Sporting Goods (SIC 3949)

Hunting Industry Sales

Rifles/shotguns/handguns	50.0%
Ammo	25.0
Accessories and clothing	25.0

Source: *Sporting Goods Business*, February 2002, p. 58.

★ 1164 ★

Sporting Goods (SIC 3949)

Largest Sports Equipment Categories

The category dropped slightly from $17.3 billion in 2000 to $17.27 billion in 2001.

	($ bil.)	Share
Exercise equipment	$ 3.61	20.90%
Golf	2.59	15.00
Firearms/hunting	1.80	10.42
Camping	1.69	9.79
Team/institutional	1.54	8.92
Fishing	1.00	5.79
Other	5.04	29.18

Source: "U.S. Sports Product Sales." Retrieved May 30, 2002 from the World Wide Web: http://www.sgma.com, from Sporting Goods Manufacturers Association.

★ 1165 ★

Sporting Goods (SIC 3949)

NBA Licensed Merchandise

Allen Iverson is the top selling player of the NBA (National Basketball Association).

Philadelphia Sixers	30.3%
Los Angeles Lakers	23.8
New York Knicks	13.1
Other	32.8

Source: *Knight-Ridder/Tribune Business News*, June 14, 2001, p. NA, from Sport Scan.

★ 1166 ★

Sporting Goods (SIC 3949)

Outdoor Industry, 2000

Total sales increased 20% over the last five years to $5.17 billion.

	($ mil.)	Share
Apparel/outerwear	$ 1,100.0	21.41%
Footwear	972.0	18.92

	($ mil.)	Share
Apparel accessories	$ 713.4	13.89%
Equipment accessories	573.9	11.17
Apparel/sportswear	573.9	11.17
Paddlesports equipment accessories	299.9	5.84
Backpacks/daypacks	294.7	5.74
Tents	201.6	3.92
Sleeping bags/pads	165.4	3.22
Rock/ice climbing equipment	108.4	2.11
Luggage/travel accessories	82.7	1.61
Camping accessories	51.7	1.01

Source: *Outdoor Retailer*, November 2001, p. 14, from Leisure Trends Group.

★ 1167 ★

Sporting Goods (SIC 3949)

Shoeshow Market Shares

Market shares are shown in percent.

Tubbs Snowshoe	80.0%
Other	20.0

Source: *Sacramento Business Journal*, April 6, 2001, p. 3.

★ 1168 ★

Sporting Goods (SIC 3949)

Ski Pole Sales

Sales are at chain stores.

Scott Co.	70.0%
Other	30.0

Source: "Scott, Leki, Ross Rake Ski Pole Market." Retrieved September 18, 2001 from the World Wide Web: http://www.snowtradenews.com.

★ 1169 ★
Sporting Goods (SIC 3949)

Ski Sales by Type

Skis have seen unit sales fall in recent years, offset by explosive growth in snowboarding. Figures are in millions of dollars.

Alpine skis, downhill	$ 241.0
Snowboards	112.7
Cross-country skis	12.5

Source: *Los Angeles Times*, February 9, 2001, p. C1, from SnowSports Industries America.

★ 1170 ★
Sporting Goods (SIC 3949)

Sporting Goods Industry

Sales are shown in billions of dollars.

	2000	2001	Share
Apparel	$ 21.8	$ 21.2	45.20%
Equipment	17.3	16.6	35.39
Footwear	9.0	9.1	19.40

Source: *DSN Retailing Today*, January 21, 2002, p. 6, from Sporting Goods Manufacturers Association.

★ 1171 ★
Sporting Goods (SIC 3949)

Table Tennis Table Market

The company is also the largest tennis table maker in the world.

Escalade Sports	85.0%
Other	15.0

Source: "Escalade Sports." Retrieved February 11, 2001 from the World Wide Web: http://www.tabletennis.se.

★ 1172 ★
Writing Instruments (SIC 3951)

Disposable Pen Market in Mexico

The market is valued at $70 million.

Bic Mexico	60.0%
Other	40.0

Source: *InfoLatina S.A. de C.V.*, August 30, 2001, p. NA.

★ 1173 ★
Writing Instruments (SIC 3952)

Children's Coloring and Writing Market

The children's coloring and writing market is valued at $800 million.

Crayola	75.0%
Rose Art Industries	13.0
Other	12.0

Source: *Crain's Chicago Business*, June 4, 2001, p. 3.

★ 1174 ★
Mops and Brooms (SIC 3991)

Top Mop/Broom/Cleaning Tool Brands, 2001

Shares are shown based on unit sales.

Swifter	18.8%
Pledge Grab It	11.6
Quickie	7.6
Libman	4.2
Rubbermaid	4.1
O Cedar Originals	2.6
Private label	6.0
Other	45.1

Source: *Advertising Age*, June 24, 2002, p. S10, from Information Resources Inc.

★ 1175 ★
Toothbrushes (SIC 3991)

Leading Power Toothbrush/Dental Device Makers

Sales are shown for the year ended June 17, 2001.

	($ mil.)	Share
Gillette (Braun Oral-B)	$ 130.2	24.7%
P&G (Credt Spinbrush)	68.0	14.5
Sonicare	67.6	14.4
Colgate (Actibrush)	37.3	8.0
Teledyne WaterPik	29.9	6.4
Bausch & Lomb (Interplak) . . .	20.9	4.5

Source: *Advertising Age*, August 6, 2001, p. 4, from Information Resources Inc.

★ 1176 ★
Toothbrushes (SIC 3991)

Top Toothbrush Brands, 2001

Market shares are shown in percent.

Oral B Advantage	7.6%
Oral B Cross Action	7.0
Oral B Indicator	6.3
Colgate Wave	5.6
Colgate Navigator	4.5
Reach Plaque Sweeper	3.8
Advanced Design Reach	3.7
Colgate Total	3.4
Aquafresh	3.2
Other	54.9

Source: *Chain Drug Review*, November 5, 2001, p. 48, from Information Resources Inc.

★ 1177 ★
Caskets (SIC 3995)

Top Casket Makers

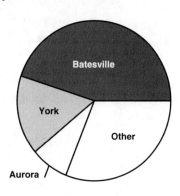

Market shares are shown in percent.

Batesville	45.0%
York	16.0
Aurora	8.0
Other	31.0

Source: *Mergers & Acquisitions Report*, May 21, 2001, p. NA.

★ 1178 ★
Flooring (SIC 3996)

Hard Flooring Shipments

Figures are in millions of square years. Hard flooring is expected to grow about 3 percent a year to 2005.

	1995	2000	2005
Resilient	441	518	545
Nonresilient	140	208	255

Source: *Research Studies - Freedonia Group*, June 5, 2001, p. 1, from Freedonia Group.

★ 1179 ★
Flooring (SIC 3996)

Top Floor Coverings Markets, 2000

The top categories of the $19 billion flooring industry are shown. Figures are in billions of dollars.

	($ bil.)	Share
Carpets and area rugs	$ 11.9	63.30%
Resilient/vinyl	2.3	12.23
Ceramic tile	2.2	11.70
Hardwood	1.6	8.51
Laminate	0.8	4.26

Source: *Wall Street Journal*, August 7, 2001, p. 32, from First Union Securities.

★ 1180 ★
Candles (SIC 3999)

Candle Sales by Type

Market shares are shown in percent.

Poured	54.0%
Pillers and tapers	31.0
Votives and tealights	15.0

Source: *WWD*, December 28, 2001, p. 4, from Unity Marketing.

★ 1181 ★
Candles (SIC 3999)

Top Candle Brands in Drug Stores

Brands are ranked by sales in millions of dollars for the year ended December 30, 2000.

American Greetings	$ 10.7
Candle Lite	9.9
Glade Candle Scents	9.7

Continued on next page.

★ 1181 ★ *Continued*
Candles (SIC 3999)

Top Candle Brands in Drug Stores

Brands are ranked by sales in millions of dollars for the year ended December 30, 2000.

Yankee Housewamer	$ 6.9
Modd Makers	6.4
Ambria	6.1
Country Air	4.9
Fragrance De Lite	4.4
Renuzit Longlast Aromasense	2.4

Source: *Drug Store News*, May 21, 2001, p. 76, from Information Resources Inc.

★ 1182 ★
Countertops (SIC 3999)

Countertop Demand, 2000

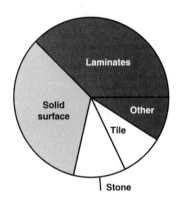

Sales are in millions of dollars.

	($ mil.)	Share
Laminates	$ 4,460	38.22%
Solid surface	3,920	33.59
Stone	1,235	10.58
Tile	1,060	9.08
Other	995	8.53

Source: *Research Alert*, February 15, 2002, p. 10, from Freedonia Group.

★ 1183 ★
Crash Cushions (SIC 3999)

Portable/Permanent Crash Cushion Market

Market shares are shown in percent. Padding barrel materials are highway barricades to protect cars from sliding off the embankment.

Quixote	90.0%
Other	10.0

Source: "Quixote: Barrels and a lot More." Retrieved January 28, 2002 from the World Wide Web: http://www.thestreet.com.

★ 1184 ★
Household Supplies (SIC 3999)

Retail Cleaning Item Sales

Data show supermarket sales in millions of dollars.

Scouring pads	$ 196.45
Brooms, mops & applicators	190.17
Cloth, polishing/cleaning	93.64
Sponges & squeegees	57.98
Brushes, kitchen & scrub	34.62
Brushes, bathroom	20.14
Dustpans	7.74
Feather dusters	4.66

Source: *Supermarket Business*, September 15, 2001, p. 42, from A.C. Nielsen Homescan.

★ 1185 ★
Pet Kennels (SIC 3999)

Pet Kennel and Shelter Market Shares

The company has a 50% or more in several niches.

Doskocil Manufacturing	50.0%
Other	50.0

Source: *Knight-Ridder/Tribune Business News*, February 14, 2002, p. NA.

★ 1186 ★

Playing Cards (SIC 3999)

Playing Card Market

Market shares refer to the casino industry. In Nevada, the company has an 89% share.

United States Playing Card Co. 72.0%
Other 28.0

Source: "Coinless Systems Inc." Retrieved April 23, 2002 from the World Wide Web: http://www.yahoo.com.

★ 1187 ★

Sewing Patterns (SIC 3999)

Who Makes Sewing Patterns

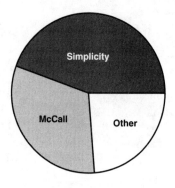

Market shares are shown in percent.

Simplicity 45.0%
McCall 31.5
Other 23.5

Source: "Conso International Corporation." Retrieved January 22, 2002 from the World Wide Web: http://www.ftc.gov.

SIC 40 - Railroad Transportation

★ 1188 ★

Railroads (SIC 4011)

Freight Transportation in Canada, 1999

Data show percent of total freight transported.

CN 55.0%
CP 45.0

Source: *American Shipper*, June 2002, p. 30, from Statistics Canada.

★ 1189 ★

Railroads (SIC 4011)

Largest Railroads in North America, 2000

Firms are ranked by revenue in billions of dollars.

UP . . . . $ 10.5
BNSF 9.2
NS 6.1
CSX 6.0
CN 3.6
CP 2.4
TFM 0.6
FXE 0.5

Source: ''Statistics.'' Retrieved June 10, 2002 from the World Wide Web: http://www.aar.org, from American Association of Railroads.

SIC 41 - Local and Interurban Passenger Transit

★ 1190 ★

Bus Fleets (SIC 4131)

Largest Bus Fleets in North America

Groups are ranked by fleet size.

MTA New York City Transit	4,560
New Jersey Transit Corp.	3,239
Los Angeles County MTA	2,437
Chicago Transit Authority	1,890
Montreal Urban Community Transit Corp.	1,686
Toronto Transit Commission	1,637
Washington Metropolitan Area Transit	1,516
Metropolitan Transit Authority of Harris County	1,495
Southeastern Pennsylvania Transportation Authority	1,384
New York City Dept. of Transportation	1,291

Source: *Metro Magazine*, September/October 2001, p. NA.

★ 1191 ★

Bus Fleets (SIC 4151)

Largest School Bus Fleets

Data show size of fleet.

Laidlaw Transit Inc.	40,167
First Student	12,000
Atlantic Express	6,498
National Express Corp.	5,769
School Services & Leasing	2,656
Stock Transportation	1,988
Student Transportation of America	1,400
Cardinal Coach Lines Ltd.	1,350
Cook-Illinois Corp.	1,200
WE Transport	1,048

Source: ''Top 50 Contractors.'' Retrieved June 5, 2001 from the World Wide Web: http://www.schoolbusfleet. com.

SIC 42 - Trucking and Warehousing

★ 1192 ★
Shipping (SIC 4210)

How Freight Is Transported, 1999

Market shares are shown in percent.

	Weight	Value
Truck	29.4%	82.4%
Rail	40.3	9.9
Air	0.4	3.5
Pipeline	16.8	2.7
Water	13.1	1.5

Source: *Wall Street Journal*, September 17, 2001, p. A10, from Enos Transportation Foundation.

★ 1193 ★
Shipping (SIC 4210)

How Goods Are Shipped

Data are by revenue-tons.

Motor carriers	63.3%
Carload rail	15.8
Intermodal rail	1.2
Other	19.7

Source: *Trains Magazine*, November 2001, p. 54.

★ 1194 ★
Trucking (SIC 4210)

Largest Less-then-Truckload Trucking Companies

Firms are ranked by revenue in billions of dollars.

Yellow Corp.	$ 3.23
Roadway Express	2.81
Consolidated Freightways	2.37
US Freightways	2.22
Con-Way Transportation Services	2.00
American Freightways	1.43
ABF Freight System	1.28
Overnite Transportation Co.	1.10

Watkins Motor Lines	$ 0.87
Vitran Express	0.50

Source: *Transportation & Distribution*, October 2001, p. 36.

★ 1195 ★
Trucking (SIC 4210)

Largest Trucking Companies

Firms are ranked by revenue in billions of dollars.

United Parcel	$ 20.0
Schneider National	3.0
Roadway Express	2.9
Yellow Freight Systems	2.7
Allied Worldwide	2.3
Fedex Ground	2.2
J.B. Hunt Transport	2.1
Consolidated Freightways	2.1
Con-Way Transportation	1.9
Ryder Integrated Logistics	1.6

Source: *Commercial Carrier Journal*, August 2001, p. 36.

★ 1196 ★
Warehousing (SIC 4222)

Largest Refrigerated Warehousing Firms

Companies are ranked by total refrigerated space, in cubic feet. Data are for North America.

AmeriCold Logistics	441.7
Millard Refrigerated Services	196.8
CS Integrated	175.9
Atlas Cold Storage	127.9
United States Cold Storage	105.7
P&O Cold Logistics	69.7
Versacold Group	57.6
Nordic Cold Storage	54.5

Continued on next page.

★ 1196 ★ *Continued*
Warehousing (SIC 4222)

Largest Refrigerated Warehousing Firms

Companies are ranked by total refrigerated space, in cubic feet. Data are for North America.

Columbia Colstor 44.5
Interstate Warehousing 39.3

Source: *Food Institute Report*, January 14, 2002, p. 3.

SIC 43 - U.S. Postal Service

★ 1197 ★

Postal Service (SIC 4311)

Leading Types of Mail

The Postal Service delivered 207.8 billion pieces of mail in 2000.

	(bil.)	Share
First class	103.5	50.00%
Priority	1.2	0.50
Express	0.7	0.03

Source: "United States Postal Service Comment." Retrieved April 3, 2002 from the World Wide Web: http://ntia.doc.gov.

★ 1198 ★

Postal Service (SIC 4311)

Postal Service Profile

The Postal Service lost volume in nearly every category of mail it carried in 2001. Data show the millions served by the U.S. Postal Service.

Residences	125.4
Businesses	12.2

Source: *Atlanta Journal-Constitution*, June 23, 2002, p. C1, from U.S. Postal Service.

SIC 44 - Water Transportation

★ 1199 ★
Shipping (SIC 4412)

Container Cargo Industry in Hawaii

The country imports 80% of its consumer goods and 97% comes through the commercial harbor system. Market shares are shown in percent.

Matson 70.0%
Other 30.0

Source: *Pacific Business News*, July 27, 2001, p. 51.

★ 1200 ★
Shipping (SIC 4412)

Trans-Atlantic Carrier Market Shares, 2001

Import shares are shown for the first six months of the year.

Maersk Sealand 13.5%
Hapag-Lloyd 9.2
Evergreen 7.1
P&O Nedlloyd 6.9
Mediterranean Shipping 6.8
Other 56.5

Source: *Journal of Commerce*, November 12, 2001, p. 14.

★ 1201 ★
Shipping (SIC 4412)

Trans-Pacific Carrier Market Shares, 2001

Import shares are shown for the first six months of the year.

Maersk Sealand 11.6%
Evergreen 9.0
Hanjin 8.3
Cosco 7.6
APL 7.0
Other 56.5

Source: *Journal of Commerce*, November 12, 2001, p. 14.

★ 1202 ★
Cruise Lines (SIC 4481)

Cruise Line Market

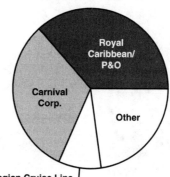

Market shares are shown in percent.

Royal Caribbean/P&O 36.7%
Carnival Corp. 31.7
Norwegian Cruise Line 8.8
Other 22.8

Source: *Knight-Ridder/Tribune News Service*, November 20, 2001, p. NA, from Travel Trade Publications.

★ 1203 ★
Cruise Lines (SIC 4481)

Who Visits Hawaii on Cruises

Figures show origin of tourists.

U.S. West	33.9%
Japan	27.2
U.S. East	23.7
International	11.5
Canada	3.7

Source: *Pacific Business News*, May 18, 2001, p. 9, from SMS Inc.

★ 1204 ★
Ports (SIC 4491)

Western Port Traffic

Volume is in thousands.

	2000	2001
Los Angeles	4,879	5,183
Long Beach	4,601	4,463
Oakland	1,777	1,644
Seattle	1,488	1,315
Tacoma	1,376	1,320

Source: *Los Angeles Business Journal*, February 4, 2002, p. 3.

SIC 45 - Transportation by Air

★ 1205 ★
Airlines (SIC 4512)

Top Airlines, 2001

Market shares are shown based on percentage of passengers in domestic market.

Delta	15.5%
Southwest	13.2
United	11.4
American	11.0
US Airways	9.4
Other	39.5

Source: *USA TODAY*, May 2, 2002, p. B1, from Bureau of Transportation Statistics.

★ 1206 ★
Airlines (SIC 4512)

Top Airlines by ASM

Market shares are shown in percent. ASM stands for available seat miles.

	(mil.)	Share
American	13.6	19.4%
United	11.6	16.6
Delta	10.7	15.3
Northwest	7.1	10.2
Continental	6.3	9.0
Southwest	5.6	8.0
US Airways	4.7	6.7
America West	2.0	2.9

Source: *Aviation Daily*, February 22, 2002, p. 8, from ECLAT Consulting.

★ 1207 ★
Airlines (SIC 4512)

Top Airlines by Passengers, 2001

Data show share of passengers.

Delta	14.1%
American	11.7
United	11.3
Southwest	11.1
US Airways	8.4
Other	44.4

Source: *USA TODAY*, April 29, 2002, p. B1, from Bureau of Transportation Statistics.

★ 1208 ★
Airlines (SIC 4512)

Top Airlines by RPM, 2001

Market shares are shown based on revenue passenger miles.

United	18.61%
American	17.30
Delta	15.54
Northwest	11.67
Continental	9.76
US Airways	7.33
Southwest	7.10
America West	3.04
Alaska	1.96
ATA	1.86
Other	5.83

Source: *Aviation Daily*, January 17, 2002, p. 8.

★ 1209 ★
Airlines (SIC 4512)

Top Airlines in Albuquerque, NM

Market shares are shown for airports, based on enplaned passengers in 2001.

Southwest	52.52%
Delta	8.57
American	7.60
America West	6.69
United	6.54
Other	18.08

Source: *Aviation Daily*, May 6, 2002, p. 7, from U.S. Department of Transportation.

★ 1210 ★
Airlines (SIC 4512)

Top Airlines in Austin, TX

Market shares are shown for airports, based on enplaned passengers in 2001.

Southwest	36.23%
American	23.70
Continental	11.30
Delta	9.88
United	5.83
Other	13.06

Source: *Aviation Daily*, May 6, 2002, p. 7, from U.S. Department of Transportation.

★ 1211 ★
Airlines (SIC 4512)

Top Airlines in Cincinnati, OH

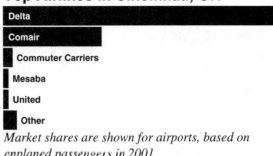

Market shares are shown for airports, based on enplaned passengers in 2001.

Delta	68.13%
Comair	24.09
Commuter Carriers	2.29
Mesaba	1.36
United	1.18
Other	2.95

Source: *Aviation Daily*, May 6, 2002, p. 7, from U.S. Department of Transportation.

★ 1212 ★
Airlines (SIC 4512)

Top Airlines in Columbus, OH

Market shares are shown for airports, based on enplaned passengers in 2001.

Delta	17.72%
Southwest	13.13
Commuter Carriers	12.62
America West	9.68
US Airways	9.50
Other	37.35

Source: *Aviation Daily*, May 6, 2002, p. 7, from U.S. Department of Transportation.

★ 1213 ★

Airlines (SIC 4512)

Top Airlines in Denver, CO

Market shares are shown for airports, based on enplaned passengers in 2001.

United	59.05%
Frontier	8.94
Air Wisconsin	6.00
Delta	4.84
American	4.71
Other	16.46

Source: *Aviation Daily*, May 6, 2002, p. 7, from U.S. Department of Transportation.

★ 1214 ★

Airlines (SIC 4512)

Top Airlines in Detroit, MI

Market shares are shown for airports, based on enplaned passengers in 2001.

Northwest	68.63%
Mesaba	8.50
Spirit	3.32
Southwest	3.29
American	2.81
Other	13.45

Source: *Aviation Daily*, May 6, 2002, p. 7, from U.S. Department of Transportation.

★ 1215 ★

Airlines (SIC 4512)

Top Airlines in Fort Lauderdale, FL

Market shares are shown for airports, based on enplaned passengers in 2001.

Delta	25.12%
US Airways	14.55
Southwest	13.12
Continental	9.49
American	7.08
Other	30.64

Source: *Aviation Daily*, May 6, 2002, p. 7, from U.S. Department of Transportation.

★ 1216 ★

Airlines (SIC 4512)

Top Airlines in Hartford, CT

Market shares are shown for airports, based on enplaned passengers in 2001.

Delta	24.12%
US Airways	21.29
American	12.92
Southwest	12.02
United	8.53
Other	22.12

Source: *Aviation Daily*, May 6, 2002, p. 7, from U.S. Department of Transportation.

★ 1217 ★
Airlines (SIC 4512)

Top Airlines in Indianapolis, MD

Market shares are shown for airports, based on enplaned passengers in 2001.

Southwest	12.98%
Northwest	12.54
US Airways	11.04
Delta	11.03
American Trans Air	10.82
Other	41.59

Source: *Aviation Daily*, May 6, 2002, p. 7, from U.S. Department of Transportation.

★ 1218 ★
Airlines (SIC 4512)

Top Airlines in Las Vegas, NV

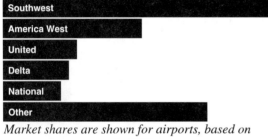

Southwest
America West
United
Delta
National
Other

Market shares are shown for airports, based on enplaned passengers in 2001.

Southwest	33.98%
America West	17.31
United	8.59
Delta	7.53
National	7.23
Other	25.36

Source: *Aviation Daily*, May 6, 2002, p. 7, from U.S. Department of Transportation.

★ 1219 ★
Airlines (SIC 4512)

Top Airlines in Milwaukee, MN

Market shares are shown for airports, based on enplaned passengers in 2001.

Midwest Express	30.48%
Northwest	18.96
Commuter Carriers	9.17
Delta	7.33
Sun Country Airlines	6.02
Other	28.04

Source: *Aviation Daily*, May 6, 2002, p. 7, from U.S. Department of Transportation.

★ 1220 ★
Airlines (SIC 4512)

Top Airlines in Nashville, TN

Market shares are shown for airports, based on enplaned passengers in 2001.

Southwest	51.86%
Delta	10.63
American	9.73
Northwest	7.33
US Airways	6.12
Other	14.33

Source: *Aviation Daily*, May 6, 2002, p. 7, from U.S. Department of Transportation.

★ 1221 ★
Airlines (SIC 4512)

Top Airlines in Portland, OR

Market shares are shown for airports, based on enplaned passengers in 2001.

Alaska	21.37%
United	17.29
Southwest	15.71
Horizon	12.80
Delta	10.58
Other	22.25

Source: *Aviation Daily*, May 6, 2002, p. 7, from U.S. Department of Transportation.

★ 1222 ★

Airlines (SIC 4512)

Top Airlines to the Federal Government

Market shares are shown based on expenses/charges put on government cards.

United Airlines	20.8%
Delta	19.5
U.S. Airways	14.1
American Airlines	13.9
Northwest	10.1
Continental	4.7
Trans World Airlines	4.1

Source: *Government Executive*, August 1, 2001, p. NA, from General Services Administration's Federal Supply Service.

★ 1223 ★

Airlines (SIC 4512)

Top Coast-to-Coast Flight Markets, 2001

Data show passengers, in millions.

Los Angeles-New York	1.9
Los Angeles-Atlanta	1.3
San Francisco-New York	1.2
Los Angeles-Newark, NJ	1.0
Los Angeles-Washington D.C.	0.9

Source: *USA TODAY*, April 30, 2002, p. B1, from Bureau of Transportation Statistics.

★ 1224 ★

Fractional Airline Industry (SIC 4512)

Fractional Ownership Market, 2001

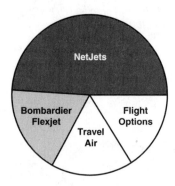

The industry is expected to be made up of over 1,600 aircraft and more than 13,500 owners by the end of 2006. Current shares are shown in percent.

NetJets	49.0%
Bombardier Flexjet	18.0
Travel Air	17.0
Flight Options	16.0

Source: *Flight International*, April 9, 2002, p. 25, from Aviation Research Group.

★ 1225 ★

Air Cargo (SIC 4513)

Largest Air Cargo Operators, 2000

Firms are ranked by freight ton miles, in thousands.

FedEx	7,401.9
UPS	4,339.1
Emery Worldwide	1,048.3
Polar Air Cargo	1,047.2
Evergreen Intl.	792.0
Airborne Express	648.2
DHL	452.4
Gemini	223.5
Arrow Air	154.1
Challenge Air Cargo	153.4

Source: *Air Cargo World*, August 2001, p. 55, from Air Transport Association of America.

★ 1226 ★

Air Cargo (SIC 4513)

Top Air Courier Purchasers in the Federal Government

Market shares are shown based on value of purchases.

Federal Express	39.31%
Flight Intternational Inc.	13.00
Lynden Air Cargo	7.86
K&K Aircraft Inc.	5.33
Canadian Commercial Corp.	5.19
Other	29.31

Source: *Government Executive*, August 1, 2001, p. NA.

★ 1227 ★

Airports (SIC 4513)

Top Cargo Airports, 2000

Airports are ranked by tonnage transported during the year.

Memphis Airport	2,489,070
Louisville Airport	1,519,558
Chicago O'Hare	1,463,941
Indianapolis Airport	1,173,967
Dallas/Ft. Worth	904,994
Dayton, OH	832,205
Toledo Airport	426,733
Cincinnati Airport	381,253
Minneapolis/St. Paul	369,888

Source: *Air Cargo World*, August 2001, p. 24, from Airports Council International, Hillwood Properties, and Greater Rockland Airport.

★ 1228 ★

Airports (SIC 4581)

Large Jet Departures

Figures show share of departures represented by large jets, such as Boeing and Airbus.

	May 2001	May 2002
Las Vegas	97.7%	97.0%
Honolulu	87.9	86.6
Phoenix	84.9	81.1
San Francisco	83.9	80.0
Atlanta	76.4	74.1
Orlando	76.0	77.3
New York (Kennedy) . . .	73.1	78.6

	May 2001	May 2002
Baltimore-Washington . . .	72.7%	77.1%
Tampa	70.6	74.2

Source: *USA TODAY*, May 7, 2002, p. 9B, from OAG.

★ 1229 ★

Airports (SIC 4581)

Market Shares at Baltimore-Washington Airport

Market shares are shown in percent.

Southwest Airlines	34.01%
US Airways	24.08
United Airlines	6.45
Delta Airlines	6.00
Northwest Airlines	4.64
US Airways Express	4.38
American Airlines	4.08
Continental Airlines	3.69
Other	12.67

Source: *Baltimore Business Journal*, July 20, 2001, p. 20.

★ 1230 ★

Airports (SIC 4581)

Market Shares at Chicago O'Hare International Airport, 2000

Shares are shown based on enplaned passengers.

United Airlines	47.0%
American Airlines	35.0
Delta Air Lines	3.0
Northwest Airlines	2.0
Continental Airlines	2.0
Other	11.0

Source: "U.S. Airlines Passenger Market." Retrieved December 1, 2001 from the World Wide Web: http://www.fitchratings.com, from Fitch Ratings.

★ 1231 ★

Airports (SIC 4581)

Market Shares at Cincinnati International Airport, 2000

Shares are shown based on enplaned passengers.

Delta Air Lines 62.0%
ComAir 31.0
Northwest Airlines 2.0
United Airlines 1.0
Other 4.0

Source: "U.S. Airlines Passenger Market." Retrieved December 1, 2001 from the World Wide Web: http://www.fitchratings.com, from Fitch Ratings.

★ 1232 ★

Airports (SIC 4581)

Market Shares at Dallas-Fort Worth International Airport, 2000

Shares are shown based on enplaned passengers.

American Airlines 70.0%
Delta Air Lines 17.0
United Airlines 2.0
Continental Airlines 2.0
Other 9.0

Source: "U.S. Airlines Passenger Market." Retrieved December 1, 2001 from the World Wide Web: http://www.fitchratings.com, from Fitch Ratings.

★ 1233 ★

Airports (SIC 4581)

Market Shares at Fairbanks (AK) International Airport, 2000

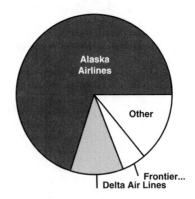

Shares are shown based on enplaned passengers.

Alaska Airlines 70.0%
Delta Air Lines 11.0
Frontier Flying Service 5.0
Other 14.0

Source: "U.S. Airlines Passenger Market." Retrieved December 1, 2001 from the World Wide Web: http://www.fitchratings.com, from Fitch Ratings.

★ 1234 ★

Airports (SIC 4581)

Market Shares at Honolulu International Airport, 2000

Shares are shown based on enplaned passengers.

Aloha Airlines 26.0%
Hawaiian Airlines 24.0
United Airlines 9.0
Japan Airlines 7.0
Northwest Airlines 5.0
Other 29.0

Source: "U.S. Airlines Passenger Market." Retrieved December 1, 2001 from the World Wide Web: http://www.fitchratings.com, from Fitch Ratings.

★ 1235 ★
Airports (SIC 4581)

Market Shares at JFK International Airport, 2000

Shares are shown based on enplaned passengers.

American Airlines 21.0%
Delta Air Lines 14.0
TWA 10.0
United Airlines 6.0
British Airways 6.0
Other 43.0

Source: "U.S. Airlines Passenger Market." Retrieved December 1, 2001 from the World Wide Web: http://www.fitchratings.com, from Fitch Ratings.

★ 1236 ★
Airports (SIC 4581)

Market Shares at Los Angeles International Airport, 2000

Shares are shown based on enplaned passengers.

United Airlines 23.0%
Southwest Airlines 11.0
American Airlines 11.0
Delta Air Lines 8.0
Alaska Airlines 3.0
Other 44.0

Source: "U.S. Airlines Passenger Market." Retrieved December 1, 2001 from the World Wide Web: http://www.fitchratings.com, from Fitch Ratings.

★ 1237 ★
Airports (SIC 4581)

Market Shares at Manchester (NH) National Airport, 2000

Shares are shown based on enplaned passengers.

US Airways 33.0%
Southwest Airlines 32.0
United Airlines 12.0
Northwest Airlines 8.0
Continental Airlines 7.0
Other 8.0

Source: "U.S. Airlines Passenger Market." Retrieved December 1, 2001 from the World Wide Web: http://www.fitchratings.com, from Fitch Ratings.

★ 1238 ★
Airports (SIC 4581)

Market Shares at Newark International Airport, 2000

Shares are shown based on enplaned passengers.

Continental Airlines 57.0%
Delta Air Lines 7.0
United Airlines 6.0
American Airlines 6.0
Northwest Airlines 4.0
Other 20.0

Source: "U.S. Airlines Passenger Market." Retrieved December 1, 2001 from the World Wide Web: http://www.fitchratings.com, from Fitch Ratings.

★ 1239 ★
Airports (SIC 4581)

Market Shares at Ronald Reagan National Airport, 2000

Shares are shown based on enplaned passengers.

US Airways 30.0%
Delta Air Lines 19.0
American Airlines 13.0
Northwest Airlines 7.0
Continental Airlines 7.0
Other 24.0

Source: "U.S. Airlines Passenger Market." Retrieved December 1, 2001 from the World Wide Web: http://www.fitchratings.com, from Fitch Ratings.

★ 1240 ★
Airports (SIC 4581)

Market Shares at San Antonio International Airport

Shares are shown based on passengers transported.

Southwest Airlines 34.86%
American Airlines 16.12
Delta Airlines 15.61
Continental Airlines 12.33
TWA 5.06
United Airlines 4.41
Northwest Airlines 3.34
America West Airlines 2.45

Source: *San Antonio Business Journal*, November 2, 2001, p. 25.

★ 1241 ★
Airports (SIC 4581)

Market Shares at San Diego International Airport, 2000

Southwest Airlines
United Airlines
American Airlines
Delta Air Lines
Alaska Airlines
Other

Shares are shown based on enplaned passengers.

Southwest Airlines 35.0%
United Airlines 16.0
American Airlines 12.0
Delta Air Lines 9.0
Alaska Airlines 6.0
Other 22.0

Source: "U.S. Airlines Passenger Market." Retrieved December 1, 2001 from the World Wide Web: http://www.fitchratings.com, from Fitch Ratings.

★ 1242 ★
Airports (SIC 4581)

Market Shares at San Francisco Airport

Market shares are shown in percent.

Southwest Airlines 50.2%
United Airlines 7.4
Alaska Airlines 5.2
America Airlines 3.9
America West Airlines 3.2
Other 30.1

Source: *San Francisco Business Times*, June 15, 2001, p. 39.

★ 1243 ★

Airports (SIC 4581)

Market Shares at Spokane International Airport, 2000

Shares are shown based on enplaned passengers.

Southwest Airlines	29.0%
Horizon Air	22.0
United Express	13.0
Alaska Airlines	12.0
Delta Air Lines	9.0
Other	15.0

Source: "U.S. Airlines Passenger Market." Retrieved December 1, 2001 from the World Wide Web: http://www.fitchratings.com, from Fitch Ratings.

★ 1244 ★

Airports (SIC 4581)

Top Airports in the West, 2000

Airports are ranked by number of passengers.

Los Angeles	33.45
Las Vegas	25.70
San Francisco	22.71
Phoenix	21.12
Seattle/Tacoma	19.11
San Diego	14.05
San Jose	11.08
Portland	10.66

Source: *Airports*, July 17, 2001, p. 10.

SIC 47 - Transportation Services

★ 1245 ★
Tourism (SIC 4720)
Where Canadians Like to Visit

In 2000, almost 2 million Canadians visited the coutnry and spent about $1.4 billion. Data show the top U.S. sites.

Florida	33.0%
California	7.7
Other	59.3

Source: *Knight-Ridder/Tribune Business News*, July 9, 2001, p. NA.

★ 1246 ★
Tourism (SIC 4720)
Where Skiers/Snowboarders Like to Vacation

The top vacation destinations are shown, based on a poll of winter sports enthusiasts.

Vail, CO	16.0%
Lake Tahoe/Reno, Nevada	13.0
Europe	13.0
Aspen, CO	13.0
Steamboat Springs, CO	10.0
Park City, Utah	7.0

Source: *PR Newswire*, February 7, 2002, p. NA.

★ 1247 ★
Tourism (SIC 4720)
Where U.S. Travelers Spend Money

The U.S. led the world in spending on tourism, with $65 billion out of the $500 billion industry.

Europe	43.0%
Latin America/Caribbean	15.0
Canada	8.0
Japan	4.0
Australia/New Zealand	3.0
Other	18.0

Source: *USA TODAY*, November 28, 2001, p. 2B, from International Trade Administration.

★ 1248 ★
Tourism (SIC 4720)
Where Vacationers Are Headed

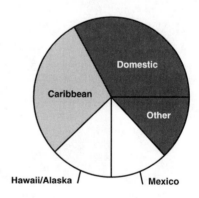

Figures are based on a survey of vacation.com from November - mid December 2001.

Domestic	33.4%
Caribbean	29.1
Hawaii/Alaska	12.5
Mexico	11.8
Other	13.2

Source: *PR Newswire*, January 29, 2002, p. NA, from Vacation.com.

★ 1249 ★
Travel (SIC 4720)

Leisure Travel Spending

Market shares are shown in percent.

	1998	2001
Transportation	23.0%	23.0%
Shopping	18.0	14.0
Hotels/lodging	17.0	20.0
Meals	16.0	16.0
Tour/cruise costs	12.0	13.0
Entertainment	11.0	10.0
Rental car/limo	3.0	4.0

Source: *Travel Agent*, October 8, 2001, p. 18.

★ 1250 ★
Travel (SIC 4720)

Travel Spending by State

| California |
| Florida |
| New York |
| Texas |
| Illinois |
| Nevada |
| Pennsylvania |
| Hawaii |
| Georgia |

Spending is shown in billions of dollars.

California	$ 67.04
Florida	53.60
New York	34.20
Texas	31.45
Illinois	21.10
Nevada	18.72
Pennsylvania	14.21
Hawaii	13.80
Georgia	13.70

Source: *Travel Agent*, April 9, 2001, p. 18, from Travel Industry Association of America.

★ 1251 ★
Travel (SIC 4720)

Who Books Travel in Canada

Figures are based on a survery of 1,500 respondents.

Aircanada.ca	29.0%
Travelocity	11.0
Westjet	6.0
Expedia	5.0
Other	49.0

Source: "Has the Internet Become an Eden." Retrieved April 3, 2002 from the World Wide Web: http://www. etourismnewsletter.com, from Ipsos-Reid.

★ 1252 ★
Travel (SIC 4724)

How We Booked Travel, 2001

Shares are shown based on total bookings.

	($ bil.)	Share
Travel agents	$ 107.1	53.0%
Traditional direct to supplier . . .	69.1	34.0
Travel web sites	15.7	8.0
Supplier web sites	10.1	5.0

Source: *Wall Street Journal*, May 3, 2002, p. A1, from PhoCuswright.

★ 1253 ★
Travel Agencies (SIC 4724)

Largest Travel Agencies

Firms are ranked by gross revenue in billions of dollars.

American Express Travel	$ 14.60
Carlson Wagonlit Travel	12.00
Rosenbluth International	4.80
Worldtravel	4.60
Navigant International	3.80
Travelocity.com	2.50
Expedia	1.79
TQ3 Maritz Travel Solutions	1.66
Liberty Travel	1.39
Satotravel	1.20

Source: *Travel Agent*, June 25, 2001, p. F4.

★ 1254 ★

Travel Agencies (SIC 4724)

Largest Travel Agencies in Silicon Valley, CA

Firms are ranked by sales in millions of dollars.

Associated Travel Service	$ 204.9
Casto Travel Inc.	203.0
Peak Travel Group	52.4
Hunter Travel Manager Inc.	47.0
Peninsula World Travel	40.2
AAA Travel Agency	35.3
Travel Management Corp.	34.0
Cardoza Travel Services Inc.	21.8
Travel Advisors Sunnyvale	16.3

Source: *Silicon Valley/San Jose Business Journal*, November 2, 2001, p. 20.

SIC 48 - Communications

Paging Industry (SIC 4812)

Largest Paging Firms

Firms are ranked by number of subscribers.

Arch Wireless Inc. 11,100
Metrocall Inc. 6,250
Verizon Wireless Messaging Services . . . 3,000
WebLink Wireless Inc. 2,200
SkyTel Communications Inc. 1,800
Cingular Interactive 655

Source: *RCR Wireless News*, June 18, 2001, p. 18.

Telecommunications (SIC 4812)

Mexico's Telecommunications Industry

Figures show share of total revenues.

	2000	2005
Fixed voice	58.0%	39.0%
Internet	22.0	28.0
Mobile voice	8.0	20.0
Pay TV	6.0	7.0
Datacoms	6.0	6.0

Source: *Mexico Telecom*, August 2001, p. 1, from Pyramid Research.

Telecommunications (SIC 4812)

U.S. Telecom Services

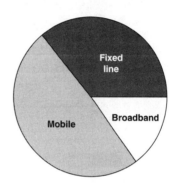

Market shares are shown in percent.

	2001	2006
Fixed line	57.0%	36.2%
Mobile	38.1	49.2
Broadband	4.9	14.6

Source: *Investor's Business Daily*, February 19, 2002, p. A6, from Cellular Telecommunications & Internet Association and Forrester Research.

Wi-Fi Technology (SIC 4812)

Wi-Fi Technology Market Shares

The company has the leading share of public Wi-Fi hot spots. Wi-Fi technology is used in the creation of wireless networks. Market shares in key states: Washington 93%, New York 89%, Texas 77%, California 61%.

HereUare 62.0%
Other 38.0

Source: *PR Newswire*, March 4, 2002, p. NA, from HereUare Communications Inc.

★ 1259 ★
Wi-Fi Technology (SIC 4812)

Wi-Fi Technology Markets

Data show who has the most access points.

San Francisco	257
Seattle	154
New York City	107
Dallas	105
Hosuton	64

Source: *InfoWorld*, March 11, 2002, p. 1, from HereUare Communications Inc.

★ 1260 ★
Wi-Fi Technology (SIC 4812)

Wi-Fi Technology Uses

Wi-Fi technology is used in the creation of wireless networks. San Francisco has the most access points.

Cafes	91.0%
Hotels	8.0
Other	1.0

Source: *Investor's Business Daily*, April 3, 2002, p. A5, from HereUare Communications Inc.

★ 1261 ★
Wireless Services (SIC 4812)

Leading Wireless Service Providers, 2001

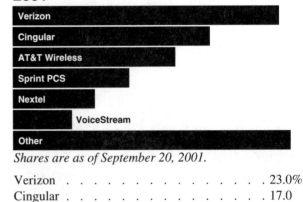

Shares are as of September 20, 2001.

Verizon	23.0%
Cingular	17.0
AT&T Wireless	14.0
Sprint PCS	10.0
Nextel	7.0
VoiceStream	5.0
Other	24.0

Source: *Investor's Business Daily*, January 14, 2002, p. A6, from Merrill Lynch & Co.

★ 1262 ★
Wireless Services (SIC 4812)

Mobile Telephone Market in Mexico

Market shares are shown in percent.

Telemex	78.0%
Other	22.0

Source: *Wall Street Journal*, May 16, 2002, p. A1, from Pyramid Research.

★ 1263 ★
Wireless Services (SIC 4812)

Prepaid Wireless Services

The table shows the growth of the prepaid market in North America.

	1997	1999	2003
Contract/post paid	99.0%	95.0%	72.0%
Prepaid mobile	1.0	5.0	28.0

Source: *America's Network*, November 1, 2001, p. 16.

★ 1264 ★
Wireless Services (SIC 4812)

Top Long Distance Phone Service (Data) Providers in Canada

Market shares are shown based on $4.3 billion in revenue.

Bell Canada	48.6%
Telus	19.3
AT&T Canada	11.4
Sprint Canada	5.9
Aliant	4.2
SaskTel	2.8
Other	7.8

Source: *Marketing Magazine*, May 27, 2002, p. 1, from Yankee Group.

★ 1265 ★
Wireless Services (SIC 4812)

Top States for Broadband Wireless

Figures show number of markets.

California	220
Illinois	207
Texas	141
Minnesota	140
Iowa	88
Florida	82
Indiana	77
Colorado	72
Utah	70

Source: *Telephony*, February 25, 2002, p. 32, from Broadband Wireless Exchange.

★ 1266 ★
Wireless Services (SIC 4812)

Voice Over Broadband Market, 2000

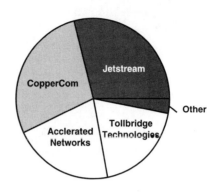

Market shares are shown in percent.

Jetstream	29.0%
CopperCom	28.0
Acclerated Networks	21.0
Tollbridge Technologies	19.0
Other	3.0

Source: *ISP Business*, May 2001, p. 1, from RHK Inc.

★ 1267 ★
Wireless Services (SIC 4812)

Voice Over IP Market Shares

Shares are of voice minutes.

	2000	2005
Circuit-switched networks	94.8%	90.9%
Packet switched networks	5.2	9.1

Source: *Investor's Business Daily*, October 16, 2001, p. A11.

★ 1268 ★
Wireless Services (SIC 4812)

Wireless Data Market

The industry is shown in percent.

Field service	37.0%
Mobile office	34.0
Transportation & logistics	29.0

Source: *M Business*, July 1, 2001, p. 20, from Yankee Group.

★ 1269 ★
Wireless Services (SIC 4812)

Wireless Internet Market Shares

Shares are shown based on subscriptions as of June 2001. TDMA - time division multiple access, CDMA - code division multiple access, GSM - global system for multiple access.

TDMA	39.0%
CDMA	30.0
GSM	7.0
Other	24.0

Source: *Telephony*, September 24, 2001, p. 38, from EMC Database.

★ 1270 ★
Telephone Services (SIC 4813)

Local Phone Market in Anchorage, AK

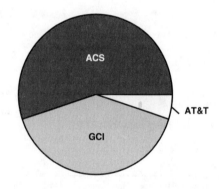

Market shares are estimated in percent. GCI's share is about 35-40%.

ACS	55.0%
GCI	40.0
AT&T	5.0

Source: *Anchorage Daily News*, November 21, 2001, p. E1.

★ 1271 ★
Telephone Services (SIC 4813)

Local Phone Market in California

Market shares are shown in percent.

PacBell	75.2%
Verizon	18.8
Other	6.0

Source: *Los Angeles Times*, December 23, 2001, p. C1, from Federal Communications Commission.

★ 1272 ★
Telephone Services (SIC 4813)

Local Phone Market in Canada

Share are shown for installed lines.

Bell Canada	66.0%
Telus	25.0
Manitoba Telecom	5.0
AT&T Canada	3.0
Other	2.0

Source: *New York Times*, February 28, 2002, p. W1, from AT&T Canada.

★ 1273 ★
Telephone Services (SIC 4813)

Local Phone Market in Colorado

Market shares are shown in percent.

Qwest Communications	92.0%
Other	8.0

Source: *Denver Business Journal*, December 21, 2001, p. 5A.

★ 1274 ★
Telephone Services (SIC 4813)

Local Phone Market in Illinois

Market shares are shown in percent. CLEC stands for competitive local exchange carrier.

SBC Ameritech	90.0%
CLECs	10.0

Source: *Crain's Chicago Business*, February 25, 2002, p. SR4, from FCC.

★ 1275 ★
Telephone Services (SIC 4813)
Local Phone Market in Mexico

Market shares are shown in percent.

Telemex 96.0%
Other 4.0

Source: *Wall Street Journal*, May 16, 2002, p. A1, from
Pyramid Research.

★ 1276 ★
Telephone Services (SIC 4813)
Local Phone Market in Utah

Market shares are shown for residential lines.

Qwest 92.0%
Other 8.0

Source: *Knight-Ridder/Tribune Business News*, April 19,
2002, p. NA.

★ 1277 ★
Telephone Services (SIC 4813)
Long-Distance Market, 2001

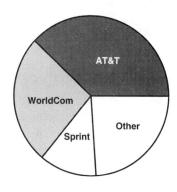

Market shares are shown in percent.

AT&T 38.0%
WorldCom 26.0
Sprint 12.0
Other 24.0

Source: *USA TODAY*, May 29, 2002, p. B3, from Giga Information Group.

★ 1278 ★
Telephone Services (SIC 4813)
Long-Distance Market in Illinois

Market shares are shown for 1999.

AT&T 62.6%
MCI WorldCom 18.1
Sprint 3.1
Other 16.3

Source: *Statistics of the Long-Distance Telecommunications Industry*, January 2001, p. 31, from IAD and TNS
Telecoms.

★ 1279 ★
Telephone Services (SIC 4813)
Long-Distance Market in Kentucky

Market shares are shown for 1999.

AT&T 54.2%
MCI WorldCom 22.8
Sprint 1.6
Other 21.4

Source: *Statistics of the Long-Distance Telecommunications Industry*, January 2001, p. 31, from IAD and TNS
Telecoms.

★ 1280 ★
Telephone Services (SIC 4813)
Long-Distance Market in Maryland

Market shares are shown for 1999.

AT&T 51.9%
MCI WorldCom 24.4
Sprint 9.8
Other 14.0

Source: *Statistics of the Long-Distance Telecommunications Industry*, January 2001, p. 31, from IAD and TNS
Telecoms.

★ 1281 ★
Telephone Services (SIC 4813)

Long-Distance Market in Massachusetts

Market shares are shown for 1999.

AT&T 63.0%
MCI WorldCom 24.9
Sprint 3.2
Other 8.9

Source: *Statistics of the Long-Distance Telecommunications Industry*, January 2001, p. 31, from IAD and TNS Telecoms.

★ 1282 ★
Telephone Services (SIC 4813)

Long-Distance Market in New Jersey

Market shares are shown for 1999.

AT&T 65.8%
MCI WorldCom 20.4
Sprint 2.4
Other 11.4

Source: *Statistics of the Long-Distance Telecommunications Industry*, January 2001, p. 31, from IAD and TNS Telecoms.

★ 1283 ★
Telephone Services (SIC 4813)

Long-Distance Market in New York

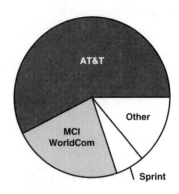

Market shares are shown for 1999.

AT&T 57.9%
MCI WorldCom 22.6
Sprint 5.7
Other 13.8

Source: *Statistics of the Long-Distance Telecommunications Industry*, January 2001, p. 31, from IAD and TNS Telecoms.

★ 1284 ★
Telephone Services (SIC 4813)

Long-Distance Market in Pennsylvania

Market shares are shown for 1999.

AT&T 58.9%
MCI WorldCom 21.8
Sprint 4.3
Other 15.0

Source: *Statistics of the Long-Distance Telecommunications Industry*, January 2001, p. 31, from IAD and TNS Telecoms.

★ 1285 ★

Telephone Services (SIC 4813)

Long-Distance Market in South Carolina

Market shares are shown for 1999.

AT&T 61.6%
MCI WorldCom 19.9
Sprint 4.9
Other 13.5

Source: *Statistics of the Long-Distance Telecommunications Industry*, January 2001, p. 31, from IAD and TNS Telecoms.

★ 1286 ★

Telephone Services (SIC 4813)

Long-Distance Market in Tennessee

Market shares are shown for 1999.

AT&T 56.9%
MCI WorldCom 20.3
Sprint 5.3
Other 17.5

Source: *Statistics of the Long-Distance Telecommunications Industry*, January 2001, p. 31, from IAD and TNS Telecoms.

★ 1287 ★

Telephone Services (SIC 4813)

Long-Distance Market in Texas

Market shares are shown for 1999.

AT&T 49.0%
MCI WorldCom 23.5
Sprint 9.3
Other 18.1

Source: *Statistics of the Long-Distance Telecommunications Industry*, January 2001, p. 31, from IAD and TNS Telecoms.

★ 1288 ★

Telephone Services (SIC 4813)

Long-Distance Market in Virginia

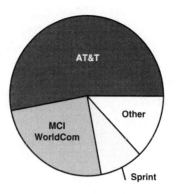

Market shares are shown for 1999.

AT&T 52.6%
MCI WorldCom 25.4
Sprint 9.4
Other 12.6

Source: *Statistics of the Long-Distance Telecommunications Industry*, January 2001, p. 31, from IAD and TNS Telecoms.

★ 1289 ★

Telephone Services (SIC 4813)

U.S. Telephone Service, 2001

Market shares are shown in percent.

Bells 93.5%
Rivals 6.5

Source: *USA TODAY*, November 12, 2001, p. 3B, from Federal Communications Commission.

★ 1290 ★
Distance Learning (SIC 4822)

Distance Learning Degrees

Data show the types of degrees earned in online courses.

Social science and business	20.0%
Computer science	8.0
Vocational education	7.0
Allied health fields	6.0
Nursing	5.0
Other	54.0

Source: *Educational Marketer*, March 18, 2002, p. NA, from Market Data Retrieval.

★ 1291 ★

Electronic Commerce (SIC 4822)

Largest Airlines on the Web

Airlines are ranked by online booking revenue in millions of dollars.

Southwest	$ 2,100
Delta	1,100
American	900
US Airways	705
Northwest	600
United	530
Continental	332
Alaska	311

Source: *USA TODAY*, March 12, 2002, p. 8B, from PhoCusWright.

★ 1292 ★

Electronic Commerce (SIC 4822)

Leading Airline Ticket Sellers

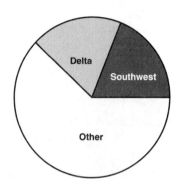

Market shares are shown by airline.

Southwest	19.0%
Delta	19.0
Other	62.0

Source: "Internet Airfare Sales Take Off." Retrieved January 29, 2002 from the World Wide Web: http://www.123Jump.com, from International Data Corp.

★ 1293 ★

Electronic Commerce (SIC 4822)

Leading Government E-Retailers

Agencies generated $3.6 billion in online sales in the year 2000, exceeding sales made by some established Internet firms like Amazon.com. The top sellers are shown, with sales in millions of dollars.

Treasury Department	$ 3,300.0
U.S. Mint	150.0
Amtrak (ticket sales)	62.0
General Services Administration (real estate, property)	43.2
Postal Service (stamps)	27.0
Geological Survey (maps)	7.5
National Park Service	5.4
Government Printing Office	2.0
Smithsonian Institution	1.6

Source: *Christian Science Monitor*, June 12, 2001, p. 20.

★ 1294 ★

Electronic Commerce (SIC 4822)

Online Postage Market

Market shares are shown in percent.

Stamps.com 75.0%
Other 25.0

Source: *Los Angeles Magazine*, October 2001, p. 68.

★ 1295 ★

Electronic Commerce (SIC 4822)

Online Purchasing, 2001

Market shares are shown in percent.

Travel 36.0%
Computer hardware 15.0
Apparel 10.0
Office 8.0
Consumer electronics 6.0
Books 4.0
Event tickets 3.0
Other 18.0

Source: *Internet Wire*, January 16, 2002, p. NA, from comScore Networks.

★ 1296 ★

Electronic Commerce (SIC 4822)

Online Team Market

Active Network is the largest provider of online registration and Web services for individual and team-based sports and recreation.

Active Network 80.0%
Other 20.0

Source: *Business Wire*, November 30, 2001, p. NA.

★ 1297 ★

Electronic Commerce (SIC 4822)

P-to-P Payment Market Shares

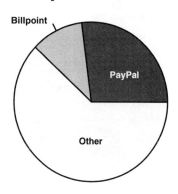

eBay is attempting to buy back stake in Billpoint in order to gain some market share in the person-to person market. PayPal is the dominant company on eBay's own site. Figures show how payments are handled.

PayPal 27.0%
Billpoint 11.0
Other 62.0

Source: *American Banker*, February 22, 2002, p. 1, from Gartner.

★ 1298 ★

Electronic Commerce (SIC 4822)

Top Auction Categories on eBay

Sales are shown in millions of dollars.

Collectibles . . . . $ 25.4
Automobiles 23.7
Sports 18.3
Antiques 11.2
Music, movies, books 9.8
Electronics 9.8
Jewelry 9.4
Computers 7.7

Source: *Fortune*, January 21, 2002, p. 78, from Morgan Stanley.

★ 1299 ★

Electronic Commerce (SIC 4822)

Top Online Auction Firms, 2001

Market shares are shown based on revenues for the first nine months.

eBay.com	69.0%
uBid.com	14.5
Priceline.com	5.2
Amazon.com	3.2
Other	8.1

Source: *Business 2.0*, December 2001, p. 45, from Jupiter Media Metrix.

★ 1300 ★

Electronic Commerce (SIC 4822)

Top Online Book Firms, 2001

Market shares are shown based on revenues for the first nine months.

Amazon.com	44.7%
BarnesandNoble.com	19.1
Half.com	3.9
ChristianBook.com	2.2
eCampus.com	2.1
Other	28.0

Source: *Business 2.0*, December 2001, p. 45, from Jupiter Media Metrix.

★ 1301 ★

Electronic Commerce (SIC 4822)

Top Online Clothing Firms, 2001

Market shares are shown based on revenues for the first nine months.

JCPenney.com	12.1%
VictoriasSecret.com	6.4
LandsEnd.com	5.1
EddieBauer.com	4.4
LLBean.com	4.3
Other	67.7

Source: *Business 2.0*, December 2001, p. 45, from Jupiter Media Metrix.

★ 1302 ★

Electronic Commerce (SIC 4822)

Top Online Computer Hardware Firms, 2001

Market shares are shown based on revenues for the first nine months.

Dell.com	46.1%
Compaq.com	6.1
CDW.com	5.3
TigerDirect.com	3.3
Buy.com	3.0
Staples.com	2.5
eBay.com	2.3
Apple.com	2.2
Other	29.2

Source: *Business 2.0*, December 2001, p. 45, from Jupiter Media Metrix.

★ 1303 ★

Electronic Commerce (SIC 4822)

Top Online Health & Beauty Firms, 2001

Market shares are shown based on revenues for the first nine months.

Quixtar.com	20.5%
Drugstore.com	12.2
Merck-Medco.com	5.7
Other	61.6

Source: *Business 2.0*, December 2001, p. 45, from Jupiter Media Metrix.

★ 1304 ★

Electronic Commerce (SIC 4822)

Top Online Software Firms, 2001

Market shares are shown based on revenues for the first nine months.

CDW.com	10.8%
Macromedia.com	5.8
Symantec.com	5.4
Adobe.com	5.4
Intuit.com	4.9
Dell.com	4.9
Other	62.8

Source: *Business 2.0*, December 2001, p. 45, from Jupiter Media Metrix.

★ 1305 ★

Electronic Commerce (SIC 4822)

Top Online Travel Firms

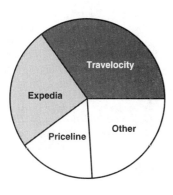

Nearly $13 billion in online travel was conducted during the year. Market shares are shown in percent.

Travelocity	35.0%
Expedia	25.0
Priceline	16.0
Other	24.0

Source: *Investor's Business Daily*, August 30, 2001, p. 1, from PhoCusWright.

★ 1306 ★

Electronic Commerce (SIC 4822)

What Canadians Bought Online

Figures are based on a survey.

Books	37.0%
CDs, tapes or videos	27.0
Clothing	23.0
Toys/games	18.0
Computer software	15.0

Source: *Newsbytes*, February 8, 2002, p. NA, from Ipsos-Reid.

★ 1307 ★

Internet (SIC 4822)

Internet Access Revenues

Figures are in billions of dollars. IP - Internet Protocol. VPN - Virtual Private Network.

	($ bil.)	Share
Private line	$ 12.0	53.33%
Frame relay	8.0	35.56
ATM	2.0	8.89
IP/VPN	0.5	2.22

Source: *Business Communications Review*, January 2002, p. 51, from Vertical Systems Group.

★ 1308 ★

Internet (SIC 4822)

Internet Market in Mexico

Data show market segments. The number of users should hit 2 million in 2000.

	1998 (000)	2000 (000)	Sahre
Business	740	1,777	53.65%
Home	297	1,066	32.19
Educational	154	276	8.33
Government	31	193	5.83

Source: "Internet User Demographics." Retrieved October 2, 2001 from the World Wide Web: http://www.usatrade. gov, from Select-International Data Corp.

★ 1309 ★

Internet (SIC 4822)

Most Wired Households

Figures show percent of households using the Internet.

San Francisco	78.8%
Austin-San Marcos, TX	76.5
Oxnard-Ventura Counties, CA	72.9
Albany-Schnectady-Troy, NY	72.7
Raleigh-Durham-Chapel Hill, NC	71.9
Wilmington-Newark, DE	70.2
Las Vegas, NV	70.1
Columbus, OH	69.1
Washington, D.C.	68.9

Source: *Yahoo! Internet Life*, May 2002, p. 71, from Forrester Research and U.S. Bureau of the Census.

★ 1310 ★
Internet (SIC 4822)

Online Advertising Industry

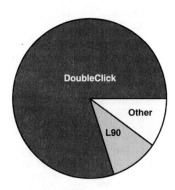

Doubleclick has been buying up smaller companies and rising to prominence in the third party ad market. Their only realistic competition, according to the source, comes from in-house advertising by Yahoo or MSN. Market shares are shown in percent.

DoubleClick 80.0%
L90 . . . . 10.0
Other 10.0

Source: *Interactive Advertising & Branding News*, October 16, 2001, p. NA, from Gartner Research.

★ 1311 ★
Internet (SIC 4822)

Online Job Board Market

Market shares are shown in percent.

Monster.com 44.0%
CareerBuilder/Headhunter.net 15.0
Hotjobs.com 13.0
Other 28.0

Source: *Investor's Business Daily*, December 24, 2001, p. A5, from International Data Corp. and Nielsen/NetRatings.

★ 1312 ★
Internet (SIC 4822)

Search Engine Referrals

Market shares are shown in percent.

Yahoo 38.75%
MSN 15.90
Google 11.29
AOL 7.77
Other 26.29

Source: "Search Engines." Retrieved February 26, 2002 from the World Wide Web: http://www.statmarket.com, from Statmarket.com.

★ 1313 ★
Internet (SIC 4822)

Top Banking Sites

Data show unique visitors for March 2001.

Chase.com 3.55
Wellsfargo.com 2.92
Bankofamerica.com 2.27
Citibank.com 2.11
Netbank.com 1.21

Source: *Upside*, July 2001, p. 59, from Jupiter Media Metrix.

★ 1314 ★
Internet (SIC 4822)

Top Gambling Sites

Online gambling revenues grew from $1 billion in 1999 to $3.5 billion in 2002. Monthly visitors are shown, in millions.

webstakes.com 2.3
kscasino.com 2.3
aceshigh.com 2.1
luckynugget.com 1.7
intercasino.com 1.3
columbuscasino.com 1.2
casino-trade.com 1.1

Source: *USA TODAY*, February 18, 2002, p. 11B, from Jupiter Media Metrix.

★ 1315 ★

Internet (SIC 4822)

Top Music Sites

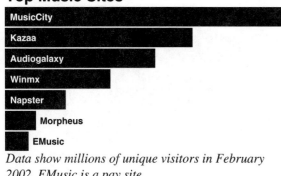

Data show millions of unique visitors in February 2002. EMusic is a pay site.

MusicCity 36.70
Kazaa 24.60
Audiogalaxy 19.70
Winmx 14.00
Napster 7.92
Morpheus 3.89
EMusic 3.49

Source: *Investor's Business Daily*, April 23, 2002, p. A6, from Jupiter Media Metrix Inc., comScore Networks Inc., and Gartner Inc.

★ 1316 ★

Internet (SIC 4822)

Top News Web Sites, 2001

Share of visitors are for September 2001.

CNN.com 24.39%
MSNBC.com 21.82
Time.com 10.12
NYTimes.com 9.51
ABCNews.com 7.38
WashingtonPost.com 6.56
Usatoday.com 6.19
Foxnews.com 4.99
Other 7.81

Source: *Upside*, December 2001- January 2002, p. 17, from Nielsen/NetRatings.

★ 1317 ★

Internet (SIC 4822)

Top Personals Sites

Data show millions of unique visitors in January 2001. Married people make up a sizeable portion of the clientelle.

Match.com 4.69
Yahoo! Personals 4.63
Matchmaker.com 3.16
Dreammates.com 1.58
Friendfinder.com 1.41

Source: *Wall Street Journal*, April 15, 2002, p. R4, from Jupiter Media Metrix.

★ 1318 ★

Internet (SIC 4822)

Top Search Sites

Data show millions of unique visitors in February 2002.

MSN Search 40.5
Yahoo Search 36.2
Google sites 29.0
AOL.com Search 25.2
Ask Jeeves 17.7
LookSmart 9.8
InfoSpace Search 9.0
Netscape Search 8.8
Overture.com 7.4

Source: *New York Times*, April 8, 2002, p. C1, from Jupiter Media Metrix.

★ 1319 ★

Internet (SIC 4822)

Top Web Sites, 2002

Data show unique visitors, in thousands, for January 2002.

AOL Time Warner 80,444
Yahoo! 73,508
MSN 66,176
Microsoft 47,324
Amazon 33,642
About-Primedia 32,410

Continued on next page.

★ 1319 ★ *Continued*

Internet (SIC 4822)

Top Web Sites, 2002

Data show unique visitors, in thousands, for January 2002.

Lycos Network	31,871
Walt Disney Internet Group	26,525
Google	26,303
eBay	25,614

Source: *Business Wire*, February 15, 2002, p. NA, from Nielsen/NetRatings.

★ 1320 ★

Internet (SIC 4822)

Types of Spam

The FTC gets 15,000 complaints a day about Spam.

Financial	25.3%
Products	19.2
Spiritual	16.5
Sex	5.7
Health	4.2
Other	29.1

Source: *BusinessWeek*, April 22, 2002, p. 16, from Brightmail Inc.

★ 1321 ★

Internet Service Providers (SIC 4822)

Dial-Up and Broadband Access

The table shows how the Internet is accessed.

	2002	2003	2004
Dial-up	77.0%	72.0%	67.0%
Broadband	23.0	28.0	33.0

Source: *USA TODAY*, February 21, 2002, p. D1, from Jupiter Media Metrix.

★ 1322 ★

Internet Service Providers (SIC 4822)

ISP Backbone Market

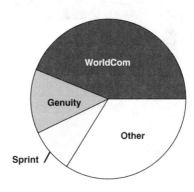

Market shares are shown in percent.

WorldCom	44.0%
Genuity	12.5
Sprint	9.4
Other	34.1

Source: *Rocky Mountain News*, January 28, 2002, p. 12B, from Cahners-Instat.

★ 1323 ★

Internet Service Providers (SIC 4822)

Largest DSL Providers

Market shares are shown in percent.

SBC	33.1%
Verizon	25.0
Qwest	10.6
NellSouth	10.5
Other	20.7

Source: *New York Times*, August 6, 2001, p. C1, from Yankee Group.

★ 1324 ★

Internet Service Providers (SIC 4822)

Largest DSL Subscribers in Canada

Data are as of September 30, 2001.

Bell Canada	625,000
Telus	157,000
Manitoba	26,953

Source: "Cable Modem Stats." Retrieved February 6, 2002 from the World Wide Web: http://www.cabledatacomnews.com, from Kinetic Strategies.

★ 1325 ★

Internet Service Providers (SIC 4822)

Largest High-Speed ISPs in Canada

Market shares are shown based on 2.47 million residential customers.

Shaw	28.0%
Bell	24.0
Rogers	19.0
Videotron	9.0
Telus	9.0
Cogeco	5.0
Aliant	3.0
SaskTel	1.0
MTS	1.0

Source: *Marketing Magazine*, May 27, 2002, p. 1, from Yankee Group.

★ 1326 ★

Internet Service Providers (SIC 4822)

Leading Internet Service Providers, 2001

There were 143 million Americans online in September 2001.

America Online	19.4%
MSN	5.6
United Online	3.9
EarthLink	3.4
Prodigy	2.5
CompuServe	2.1
RoadRunner	1.3
AT&T WorldNet	1.0
AT&T Broadband	1.0
SBC	0.9
Other	58.9

Source: "Top U.S. ISPs." Retrieved April 18, 2002 from the World Wide Web: http://www.isp-planet.com, from *CyberAtlas.*

★ 1327 ★

Internet Service Providers (SIC 4822)

Top Broadband ISPs, 2001

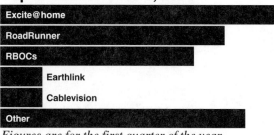

Figures are for the first quarter of the year.

Excite@home	27.0%
RoadRunner	22.0
RBOCs	19.0
Earthlink	4.0
Cablevision	4.0
Other	24.0

Source: *ISP Business*, November 2001, p. 1, from Yankee Group.

★ 1328 ★

Internet Service Providers (SIC 4822)

Top ISPs in Los Angeles, CA

Companies show number of subscribers.

	No.	% of Group
United Online	6,100,000	96.78%
2by2.net	84,234	1.34
Worldkey.net	70,000	1.11
Internet Specialties West Inc.	20,000	0.32
Moon Global Network	7,000	0.11
GUS Network America	5,500	0.09
Anet.net	5,300	0.08
The Loop Internet	5,000	0.08
ISP West	3,000	0.05
AztecaNet Inc.	3,000	0.05

Source: *Los Angeles Business Journal*, December 3, 2001, p. 27.

★ 1329 ★

Radio Broadcasting (SIC 4832)

Largest Radio Groups

Firms are ranked by revenue in millions of dollars.

Clear Channel	$ 3,500
Infinity	2,350

Continued on next page.

★ 1329 ★ *Continued*
Radio Broadcasting (SIC 4832)

Largest Radio Groups

Firms are ranked by revenue in millions of dollars.

Cox Radio	$ 455
ABC Radio	436
Entercom	415
Citadel	349
Radio One	301
Emmis	295
Hispanic Broadcasting	254
Susquehanna	236

Source: *Broadcasting and Cable*, September 3, 2001, p. 30.

★ 1330 ★
Radio Broadcasting (SIC 4832)

Largest Radio Owners in Albuquerque- Santa Fe, NM

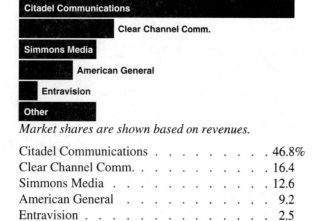

Market shares are shown based on revenues.

Citadel Communications	46.8%
Clear Channel Comm.	16.4
Simmons Media	12.6
American General	9.2
Entravision	2.5
Other	12.5

Source: *Mediaweek*, February 25, 2002, p. 14, from BIA Financial Network.

★ 1331 ★
Radio Broadcasting (SIC 4832)

Largest Radio Owners in Cincinnati, OH

Market shares are shown based on revenue.

Clear Channel Comm.	51.7%
Infinity Broadcasting	28.2
Susquehanna Radio	10.8
Radio One	4.6
Salem Communications	2.3
J4 Broadcasting	1.2

Source: *Mediaweek*, October 8, 2001, p. 16, from BIA Financial Network.

★ 1332 ★
Radio Broadcasting (SIC 4832)

Largest Radio Owners in Harrisburg, PA

Market shares are shown based on revenues.

Cumulus Broadcasting	39.2%
Clear Channel Comm.	33.9
Citadel Communications	16.8
Hepco Communications	3.8
Lebanon Broadcasting	2.6
Other	3.7

Source: *Mediaweek*, January 28, 2002, p. 14, from BIA Financial Network.

★ 1333 ★
Radio Broadcasting (SIC 4832)

Largest Radio Owners in Los Angeles, CA

Market shares are shown in percent.

Clear Channel Communications	30.9%
Infinity Broadcasting	30.8
Hispanic Broadcasting	7.7
Emmis Communications	6.7
ABC Radio	6.5
Radio One	4.7
Liberman Broadcasting	2.5
Spanish Broadcasting	1.7

Source: *Mediaweek*, October 8, 2001, p. 16.

★ 1334 ★

Radio Broadcasting (SIC 4832)

Largest Radio Owners in Oklahoma City, OK

Market shares are shown based on revenue.

Clear Channel Comm.	38.0%
Citadel Communications	29.9
Renda Broadcasting	27.0
Perry Broadcasting	2.8
Tyler Broadcasting	0.9
Other	1.4

Source: *Mediaweek*, February 18, 2002, p. 16, from BIA Financial Network.

★ 1335 ★

Radio Broadcasting (SIC 4832)

Largest Radio Owners in Salt Lake City, Utah

Market shares are shown based on revenues.

Clear Channel Comm.	22.1%
Simmons Media	20.6
Citadel Communications	19.4
Bonneville International	11.3
Mercury Broadcasting	7.5
KSOP Inc.	3.1
John Webb	2.5
Other	13.5

Source: *Mediaweek*, January 28, 2002, p. 14, from BIA Financial Network.

★ 1336 ★

Television Broadcasting (SIC 4833)

HDTV Broadcasting

Data show estimated hours of high-definition television for the week ended February 25 - March 2.

HDNet	119.0
HBO	103.6
Showtime	57.0
NBC	30.0
CBS	22.5
ABC	10.5
PBS	2.0

Source: *Wall Street Journal*, March 7, 2002, p. B5, from *HDTV Magazine* and Consumer Electronics Association.

★ 1337 ★

Television Broadcasting (SIC 4833)

Hispanic Broadcasting Market

Market shares are shown in percent.

Univision	90.0%
Telemundo	10.0

Source: *InfoLatina S.A. de C.V.*, May 15, 2001, p. NA.

★ 1338 ★

Television Broadcasting (SIC 4833)

Largest Television Groups

Groups are ranked by estimated advertising revenue in millions of dollars.

News Corporation	$ 2,310.2
CBS Television Stations Division	1,806.9
NBC/GE	1,480.0
ABC	1,344.2
Tribune Broadcasting	1,243.2
Gannett Company	891.2
Hearst-Argyle TV	828.7
Sinclair Broadcast Group	734.9
Belo Corporation	718.5
Cox Broadcasting	578.9

Source: *Financial Times*, February 21, 2002, p. 13, from BIA's MEDIA Access Pro.

★ 1339 ★
Television Broadcasting (SIC 4833)
Leading Television Firms in Mexico

Market shares are shown for buyers.

Grupo Telvisa 66.0%
Azteca 32.0
Canal 11 . . . . 1.0
Canal 40 . . . . 0.5
Canal 22 . . . . 0.5

Source: *Hollywood Reporter*, October 2, 2001, p. S41, from Mexican Government.

★ 1340 ★
Television Broadcasting (SIC 4833)
Leading TV Broadcasters in Canada

Market shares are shown in percent.

CanWest Global Comm. Corp. 32.0%
CTV Corp. 23.0
Canadian Broadcasting Corp. 16.0
Videotron 11.0
Chum 5.0
Other 13.0

Source: *Hollywood Reporter*, October 2, 2001, p. S30, from CRTC.

★ 1341 ★
Television Broadcasting (SIC 4833)
Top Shows of the Season, 2001-02

Viewers are shown, in millions. Among men 18-49, Monday Night Football was the top show; for women, it was Friends.

Friends 24.5
CSI 23.7
ER 22.1
Survivor: Marquesas 20.8
Survivor: Africa 20.7
Everybody Loves Raymond 20.0
Law & Order 18.7

Will & Grace 17.3
The West Wing 17.2
Monday Night Football 16.8

Source: *USA TODAY*, May 28, 2002, p. D1, from Nielsen Media Research.

★ 1342 ★
Television Broadcasting (SIC 4833)
Top TV Networks

Firms are ranked by revenues in billions of dollars.

NBC . . . . $ 4.3
TNT 4.0
QVC 3.6
CBS 3.4
ABC 3.3
ESPN 2.0
HBO 1.8
Fox 1.8
HSN 1.5

Source: *Broadcasting & Cable*, November 26, 2001, p. 46.

★ 1343 ★
Television Broadcasting (SIC 4833)
TV Viewing Shares

Market shares are shown in percent. Figures run from October 1-September 31 of the following year.

	1997	1998	1999
Broadcast nework affiliates	49.0%	46.0%	44.0%
Basic cable networks	40.0	41.0	46.0
Independent TV stations	12.0	11.0	12.0
Premium cable service	7.0	6.0	11.0
Public TV stations	3.0	3.0	3.0

Source: *Satellite Broadband*, November 2001, p. 40, from Nielsen Media Research.

★ 1344 ★
Television Broadcasting (SIC 4833)

U.S. Television Households

There are 102.2 million TV households.

	(mil.)	Share
Households without cable	32.1	31.38%
Comcast/AT&T Broadband	22.2	21.70
AOL Time Warner	12.7	12.41
Charter	7.0	6.84
Cox	6.2	6.06
Adelphia	5.7	5.57
Other	16.4	16.03

Source: *New York Times*, December 21, 2001, p. C1, from National Cable and Telecommunications Association and Yankee Group.

★ 1345 ★
Television Broadcasting (SIC 4833)

What Adults Most Often Watch on TV

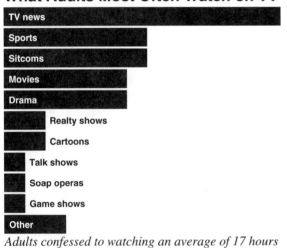

TV news
Sports
Sitcoms
Movies
Drama
Realty shows
Cartoons
Talk shows
Soap operas
Game shows
Other

Adults confessed to watching an average of 17 hours per week. Teenagers averaged 11 hours.

TV news	27.0%
Sports	14.0
Sitcoms	14.0
Movies	12.0
Drama	12.0
Realty shows	4.0
Cartoons	4.0
Talk shows	2.0
Soap operas	2.0
Game shows	2.0
Other	6.0

Source: *PR Newswire*, April 3, 2002, p. NA, from Opinion Research Corporation.

★ 1346 ★
Television Broadcasting (SIC 4833)

What are the Top Morning News Shows

Data show estimated millions of viewers for the last six months.

Today	6.199
Good Morning America	4.780
Early Show	2.700

Source: *Time*, March 18, 2002, p. 74, from Nielsen.

★ 1347 ★
Television Broadcasting (SIC 4833)

What are the Top Nightly News Shows

Data show estimated millions of viewers for the last six months.

Nightly News (NBC)	11.28
World News Tonight (ABC)	10.71
Evening News (CBS)	9.55

Source: *Time*, March 18, 2002, p. 74, from Nielsen.

★ 1348 ★
Television Broadcasting (SIC 4833)

What Are the Top Soap Operas

Data show millions of male and female viewers. The top soap for women is Young and the Restless, except for girls 12 to 17, which is Passions (which is number nine on this list).

The Young and the Restless	7.13
The Bold and the Beautiful	5.42
General Hospital	4.59

Source: *USA TODAY*, June 29, 2001, p. 2E, from NBC and Nielsen Media Research.

★ 1349 ★

Television Broadcasting (SIC 4833)

What are the Top Sunday News Shows

Data show estimated millions of viewers in January 2002.

Meet the Press 4.7
This Week 3.4
Face the Nation 3.1
Fox News Sunday 1.5

Source: *Electronic Media*, February 18, 2002, p. 16.

★ 1350 ★

Television Broadcasting (SIC 4833)

Who has the Most TV Homes, 2001-2

Data are in millions.

New York City 7.3
Los Angeles 5.3
Chicago 3.3
Philadelphia 2.8
San Francisco/Oakland/San Jose 2.4
Boston 2.3
Dallas/Ft. Worth 2.2
Washington D.C. 2.1
Atlanta 1.9

Source: *Multichannel News*, November 12, 2001, p. 6S, from Nielsen Media Research.

★ 1351 ★

Cable Broadcasting (SIC 4841)

Cable TV Market Shares

Market shares are shown in percent.

AT&T Broadband 18.8%
Time Warner Cable 17.4
Comcast Cable 11.7
Cox Communications 8.5
Other 43.6

Source: *Houston Chronicle*, December 23, 2001, p. 3.

★ 1352 ★

Cable Broadcasting (SIC 4841)

Largest Digital Cable Providers

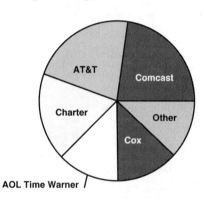

Market shares are shown in percent.

Comcast 23.2%
AT&T 21.6
Charter 17.5
AOL Time Warner 13.2
Cox 12.5
Other 12.0

Source: *Washington Technology*, February 18, 2002, p. 20, from Jupiter Media Metrix.

★ 1353 ★

Cable Broadcasting (SIC 4841)

Leading News Channels

Figures are for second quarter, 8-11 PM.

	1999	2000	2001
CNN	41.0%	33.0%	29.0%
Fox News Channel	13.0	19.0	28.0

Source: *Detroit News*, July 22, 2001, p. A11, from Nielsen ratings.

★ 1354 ★

Cable Broadcasting (SIC 4841)

Leading Sports Channels

Data show share of 1.7 million ratings points.

ESPN 23.3%
CBS 15.5
Fox 14.7
NBC 11.4
ABC Sports 11.4
ESPN2 . . . . 8.2

Continued on next page.

★ 1354 ★ *Continued*
Cable Broadcasting (SIC 4841)
Leading Sports Channels

Data show share of 1.7 million ratings points.

TNT	3.8%
TBS	2.6
Other	9.1

Source: *Electronic Media*, February 4, 2002, p. 7, from
ESPN Communications.

★ 1355 ★
Cable Broadcasting (SIC 4841)
Most Watched Cable Stations

HBO
Turner Broadcasting
USA Network
Lifetime
TNT
Nickelodeon
Cartoon Network
Disney Channel
Discovery Channel
A&E

*Data show average prime time viewers January 1-
May 27, 2001, in millions.*

HBO	2.2
Turner Broadcasting	2.1
USA Network	2.0
Lifetime	2.0
TNT	1.9
Nickelodeon	1.8
Cartoon Network	1.7
Disney Channel	1.5
Discovery Channel	1.4
A&E	1.4

Source: *New York Times*, December 6, 2001, p. C7, from
Nielsen Media Research.

★ 1356 ★
Cable Broadcasting (SIC 4841)
Saturday Morning Market Shares

*Network broadcasters have been losing share to spe-
cialty networks on cable. Shares are for 2-11 year
old viewers.*

Nickelodeon	21.0%
WB	13.0
Fox	9.0
Cartoon Network	9.0
CBS	7.0
NBC	2.0

Source: *Los Angeles Times*, November 29, 2001, p. C1,
from Nielsen Media Research.

★ 1357 ★
Cable Broadcasting (SIC 4841)
Top Cable Providers, 2001

Firms are ranked by basic subscribers, in millions.

AT&T Broadband/Comcast	22.0
Time Warner Cable	12.8
Charter Communications	7.0
Cox Communications	6.2
Adelphia Communications	5.8
Cablevision Systems	3.0
Mediacom	1.6
Insight Communications	1.3
CableOne	0.8
RCN	0.5

Source: *New York Times*, June 25, 2002, p. C7, from
Kagan World Media.

★ 1358 ★
Interactive Broadcasting (SIC 4841)
Interactive Television Industry

*15% of the 105 million households with television
sets will have some kind of interactive service. Data
show millions of households.*

	2001	2002
Enhanced TV	7.5	14.6
Virtual channels	5.3	16.5
Video on demand	3.1	8.5
Viewer participation	0.7	0.6

Source: *New York Times*, April 4, 2002, p. E1, from
Forrester Research.

★ 1359 ★
Pay Per View (SIC 4841)

Top Pay Per View Events, 2001

Events are ranked by revenue in millions of dollars.

Wrestlemania, X-Seven	$ 27.9
Trinidad vs. Hopkins	20.4
Rahman vs. Lewis II	16.2
No Way Out (WWF)	16.1
Trinidad vs. Joppy	15.7
Royal Rumble (WWF)	15.5
Summerslam (WWF)	14.2
Survivor Series (WWF)	13.1
De La Hoya vs. Castillo	12.9

Source: *Electronic Media*, March 4, 2002, p. 13, from Showtime Event Television.

★ 1360 ★
Satellite Broadcasting (SIC 4841)

iTV Subscriber Market Shares

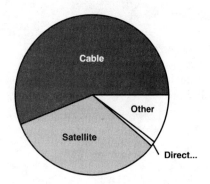

iTV subscribers should grow from 18.4 million in 2002 to 45.5 million in 2005. Shares are by technology.

Cable	56.0%
Satellite	33.0
Direct broadcast	1.0
Other	10.0

Source: *Telephony*, January 7, 2002, p. 24, from Jupiter Media Metrix.

★ 1361 ★
Satellite Broadcasting (SIC 4841)

Sateliite TV Market Shares

Market shares are shown in percent.

	Aug 2000	Aug 2001
DirecTV	65.9%	61.7%
EchoStar	33.1	38.3

Source: *Satellite News*, September 24, 2001, p. NA.

SIC 49 - Electric, Gas, and Sanitary Services

★ 1362 ★
Utilities (SIC 4911)
Electric Utility Market Shares

Share of megawatt-hour sales to customers.

Investor owned	74.10%
Publicly owned	15.42
Cooperatives	8.89
Federal power agencies	1.59

Source: *Energy User News*, June 2001, p. 1.

★ 1363 ★
Utilities (SIC 4911)
Electricity Market in Houston, TX

Market shares are shown in percent.

Reliant	96.0%
Other	4.0

Source: *Knight-Ridder/Tribune Business News*, March 12, 2002, p. NA.

★ 1364 ★
Utilities (SIC 4911)
Largest Gas Marketers in North America, 2001

Companies are ranked by sales in billion cubic feet per day. Data are for the second quarter.

Enron	24.6
Reliant	13.2
Duke Energy	12.8
BP	12.3
Mirant	11.8
Dynergy	10.9

Source: *New York Times*, November 10, 2001, p. C2, from Bloomberg Financial Markets.

★ 1365 ★
Utilities (SIC 4911)
Largest Power Marketers In North America

Companies are ranked by millions of megawatt hours.

Enron	578.8
American Electric	435.1
Duke Energy	283.0
PG&E National	275.3
Reliant Energy	201.9
Aquila Energy	186.7
Mirant	186.0
Edison Mission	180.2
Constellation Power	160.0
Williams Energy	141.3

Source: *Financial Times*, November 9, 2001, p. 19, from Thomson Financial Datastream and Bear Stearns.

★ 1366 ★
Utilities (SIC 4911)
Leading Wholesale Power Sellers, 2000

Firms are ranked by sales in megawatt hours.

Tennessee Valley Authority	$ 125.9
Bonneville Power Administration	74.5
PHI Energy	42.0
Cincinnati Gas & Electric	38.3
PECO Energy Company	38.0
Commonwealth Edison Co.	34.5
New York Power Authority	34.2
PacifiCorp.	29.9
Oglethorpe Power Corp.	29.1
Ohio Power Co.	29.0

Source: *Electric Light & Power*, November 2001, p. 15.

★ 1367 ★
Packaged Gas (SIC 4920)

Packaged Gas Industry

Air Products is planning to sell off most of its business to Airgas. It currently has 3% of the market. The table shows selected shares of the $8 billion industry after the deal. The industry is highly fragmented.

Airgas	19.0%
Air Products	1.0
Other	80.0

Source: *The Morning Call*, January 5, 2002, p. B21.

★ 1368 ★
Solid Waste Disposal (SIC 4953)

Solid Waste Facility Ownership

There were a total of 27,028 private and public firms in 1999. The solid waste industry had revenue of $43.3 billion. MSW - municipal solid waste.

MRFs	22.0%
Transfer stations	20.0
MSW landfills	20.0
Compost facilities	10.0
C&D landfills	10.0
Other	24.0

Source: *Waste Age*, December 2001, p. 60, from R.W. Beck Inc.

★ 1369 ★
Trash Disposal (SIC 4953)

Largest Trash Disposal Firms

Waste Management
Allied Waste Industries Inc.
Republic Services Inc.
Superior Services Inc.
Waste Connections Inc.
Norcal Waste Systems Inc.
Rumpke Consolidated Companies
Waste Holdings Inc.
Caselia Waste Systems Inc.
IESI Corp.

Firms are ranked by revenue in millions of dollars.

Waste Management	$ 11,218.0
Allied Waste Industries Inc.	5,182.4
Republic Services Inc.	1,951.2
Superior Services Inc.	433.2
Waste Connections Inc.	365.0
Norcal Waste Systems Inc.	275.0
Rumpke Consolidated Companies	248.0
Waste Holdings Inc.	242.4
Caselia Waste Systems Inc.	238.7
IESI Corp.	140.2

Source: *Waste News*, June 25, 2001, p. 20.

★ 1370 ★
Trash Disposal (SIC 4953)

Trash Disposal Market in Orange County, FL

Market shares are shown in percent.

Waste Management Inc.	76.0%
Onyx Waste Services of Florida	12.0
Republic Services Inc.	10.0
Florida Recycling Services Inc.	2.0

Source: *Orlando Business Journal*, June 1, 2001, p. 1.

★ 1371 ★

Trash Disposal (SIC 4953)

Trash Disposal Market in Western Kentucky

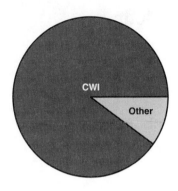

Market shares are estimated in percent.

CWI 90.0%
Other 10.0

Source: *Knight-Ridder/Tribune Business News*, March 6, 2002, p. NA.

SIC 50 - Wholesale Trade - Durable Goods

★ 1372 ★

Wholesale Trade - Office Supplies (SIC 5044)

Leading Office Superstores

Data show number of outlets.

	1997	1999	2001
Staples	685	991	1,283
Officemax	713	946	987
Office Depot	602	825	850

Source: *DSN Retailing Today*, November 5, 2001, p. 25.

★ 1373 ★

Wholesale Trade - Electronics (SIC 5060)

Leading Electrical Goods Distributors

Firms are ranked by revenue in millions of dollars.

Avnet	$ 10,700.0
Arrow Electronics	10,300.0
Future Electronics	2,958.0
Pioneer-Standard	2,474.1
Memec	2,200.0
Bell Microproducts	2,020.0
Premier Farnell	1,130.0
TTI	756.0
Richardson Electronics	437.0
Reptron Electronics	410.0

Source: *Electronic News*, December 3, 2001, p. DT8.

★ 1374 ★

Wholesale Trade - Plumbing & Heating (SIC 5074)

Wholesale Plumbing Supply Market

According to the survey, 80% of firms have fewer than 10 employees. The market is distributed by annual sales range.

$10 to $50 million	29.0%
$500 million or more	19.0
$50 to $500 million	19.0
Less than $10 million	16.0

Source: *Plumbing & Mechanical*, October 2001, p. 64, from Pembroke Consulting.

SIC 51 - Wholesale Trade - Nondurable Goods

★ 1375 ★
Wholesale Trade (SIC 5100)

Largest Industrial Distributors

Firms are ranked by sales in billions of dollars.

Graybar Electric	$ 5.1
W.W. Grainger	4.9
WESCO International	3.8
Hughes Supply	3.3
Motion Industries	2.3
GE Supply	2.2
Applied Industrial Technologies	1.6
Airgas Inc.	1.6
Hagemeyer North America	1.5

Source: *Supply Chain Yearbook*, Annual 2002, p. 87.

★ 1376 ★
Wholesale Trade (SIC 5100)

Leading Wholesale Groups in Canada

Firms are ranked by sales in millions of Canadian dollars.

Rona	$ 1,318.0
Home Hardware	1,250.0
Tim-BR-Mart	533.0
Sodisco-Howden	422.3
Sexton Building Centers	400.0
Castle Building Centres Group	359.0
Homecare Building Centres	234.0
Federated Co-op	232.5
Torbsa	205.0
Groupe BMR	195.0

Source: *National Home Center News*, May 21, 2001, p. 70.

★ 1377 ★
Wholesale Trade - Drugs (SIC 5122)

Largest Drug Wholesalers

Market shares are shown in percent.

McKesson	33.0%
AmerisourceBergen	31.0
Cardinal Health	30.0
Other	6.0

Source: *Chain Drug Review*, November 5, 2001, p. 19, from HDMA Industry Profile and *Healthcare Fact Book*.

★ 1378 ★
Wholesale Trade - Drugs (SIC 5122)

Leading Drug Benefit Managers

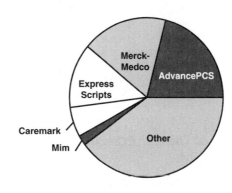

Market shares are shown in percent.

AdvancePCS	21.0%
Merck-Medco	18.0
Express Scripts	13.0
Caremark	6.0
Mim	2.0
Other	40.0

Source: *Investor's Business Daily*, October 17, 2001, p. A12, from company reports and SWS Securities.

★ 1379 ★
Wholesale Trade - Food (SIC 5140)

Largest Convenience Store Wholesalers

Firms are ranked by fiscal year sales in millions of dollars.

McLane Company	$ 16,439
Eby-Brown Company	3,500
Core-Mark International	3,035
H.T. Hackney Co.	2,000
GSC Enterprises	1,170
Miller & Hartman	975
Spartan Stores/Convenience Store Division	941
S. Abraham & Sons	870
Klein Wholesale Distributors	820

Source: *Convenience Store News*, October 21, 2001, p. 97.

★ 1380 ★
Wholesale Trade - Food (SIC 5140)

Leading Foodservice Distributors in Canada, 2002

Figures are estimated as of April 1, 2002.

Sysco	20.0%
Gordon Food Service	11.0
Other	69.0

Source: *Food in Canada*, May 2002, p. 20.

★ 1381 ★
Wholesale Trade - Chemicals (SIC 5160)

Leading Chemical Distributors in North America, 2000

Companies are ranked by sales in millions of dollars.

Vopak	$ 3,030
Ashland Distribution	3,000
Brenntag	1,560
ChemCentral	950
ICC Chemical Distribution	490
JLM Industries	435

GW International	$ 254
Harcros Chemical	244
Canada Colors & Chemicals	209
Helm Distribution	200

Source: *Chemical Week*, November 14, 2001, p. 25, from DistriConsult.

★ 1382 ★
Wholesale Trade - Periodicals (SIC 5192)

Leading Magazine Distributors, 2001

Market shares are shown in percent.

Anderson News Group	37.0%
The News Group	24.0
Chas. Levy Circulation Co.	15.0
Unimag	12.0
Other	12.0

Source: *Folio*, May 1, 2001, p. 51.

★ 1383 ★
Wholesale Trade - Floral Products (SIC 5193)

Largest Wholesale Flower Distributors

Market shares are shown in percent. U.S.A. Floral is selling off parts of its company and will probably soon cease operations.

U.S.A. Floral	25.0%
Dole Fresh Flowers	20.0
Other	55.0

Source: *Daily Business Review*, April 9, 2001, p. A1.

SIC 52 - Building Materials and Garden Supplies

★ 1384 ★

Retailing - Home Improvement (SIC 5211)

Home Improvement Industry

The $212.7 billion industry is shown in percent.

Home centers	63.62%
Discount/dept. stores	9.72
Flooring stores	7.49
Hardware stores	7.34
Nurseries/garden centers	5.20
Paint and wallpaper	4.97
Variety/general	1.66

Source: *National Home Center News*, May 21, 2001, p. 16.

★ 1385 ★

Retailing - Home Improvement (SIC 5211)

Largest Home Improvement Firms in Canada

Market shares are shown in percent.

Home Depot	58.6%
Reno-Depot	15.3
RONA	11.5
Revy	11.5
Kent	3.2
Other	9.9

Source: *Canadian Business*, May 28, 2001, p. 42, from *Hardlines Quarterly Report*.

★ 1386 ★

Retailing - Home Improvement (SIC 5211)

Largest Home Improvement Stores

Firms are ranked by sales in billions of dollars.

Home Depot	$ 11,434.5
Lowe's	3,755.7
Carolina Holdings	2,290.5
Builders FirstSource	1,675.8
84 Lumber	$ 1,420.0
ABC Supply	1,235.0
Lanoga Corp.	959.6
Wickes Lumber	904.6
BMC West Corp.	861.9

Source: *National Home Center News*, June 4, 2001, p. 10.

★ 1387 ★

Retailing - Home Improvement (SIC 5211)

What We Remodel in Our Homes

Data show thousands of households having work done.

Bathrooms	5,543
Carpeting	4,887
Roofing	4,749
Kitchen	4,623
Bedrooms	3,035
Exterior doors	2,736
Vinyl flooring	2,720
Concrete/masonry	2,321
Kitchen countertops	2,317
Kitchen cabinets	2,213

Source: *Research Alert*, September 21, 2001, p. 1, from Unity Marketing and U.S. Bureau of the Census.

★ 1388 ★

Retailing - Hardware (SIC 5251)

Top Hardware Stores in Canada

Market shares are shown in percent. Total sales hit $26.7 billion.

Canadian Tire 19.8%
Home Depot 12.6
Home Hardware 12.0
Rona 10.9
Reno-Depot 2.7
Other 42.0

Source: *Marketing Magazine*, May 27, 2002, p. 1, from *Hardware Merchandising*.

★ 1389 ★

Retailing - Nurseries (SIC 5261)

Florida's Nursery Industry

Total sales reached $8.5 billion. Miami-Dade was the top county with $273 million in sales.

	($ bil.)	Share
Retailers	$ 3.64	42.87%
Landscape businesses	3.11	36.63
Nurseries	1.74	20.49

Source: *American Nurseryman*, February 15, 2002, p. 12, from Florida Nurserymen & Growers Association.

★ 1390 ★

Retailing - Trees (SIC 5261)

Retail Christmas Tree Market

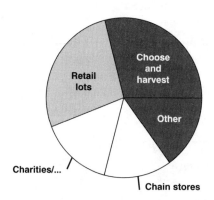

According to a survey, 32.3 million families planned to purchase real Christmas trees this year. 7.3 million planned to buy new artificial trees. 300,000 ordered trees online. The Christmas tree industry has annual revenue over $1 billion. The tableshows where we purchase them.

Choose and harvest farms 29.0%
Retail lots 27.0
Charities/churches 15.0
Chain stores 14.0
Other 15.0

Source: *Traffic World*, December 24, 2001, p. 13, from National Christmas Tree Association and Wirthlin Worldwide survey.

SIC 53 - General Merchandise Stores

★ 1391 ★
Retailing (SIC 5300)

Leading Retailers, 2000

Companies are ranked by 2000 revenue in billions of dollars.

Wal-Mart	$ 191.3
Kroger Co.	49.0
The Home Depot	45.7
Sears	40.9
Kmart	37.0
Target	36.9
Albertson's	36.7
J.C. Penney	32.6
Costco	32.1
Safeway	31.9

Source: *Chain Store Age*, August 2001, p. 4A.

★ 1392 ★
Retailing (SIC 5300)

Retail Market in Canada

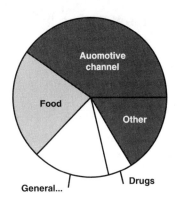

The $277.2 billion industry is shown for the year ended September 2000.

Auomotive channel	40.1%
Food	22.1
General merchandise	16.1
Drugs	4.9
Other	16.1

Source: "Food Processing Ingredients." Retrieved May 1, 2002 from the World Wide Web: http://ffas.usda.gov, from NPD Group.

★ 1393 ★
Retailing (SIC 5300)

U.S. Retailing Industry

Sales are shown in billions of dollars.

Discount department stores	$ 140.1
Supercenters	87.7
Warehouse clubs	65.7
Specialty mass retailers	56.0
Consumer electronics retailers	38.6
Off-price apparel chains	28.3
Office supply superstores	18.5
Automotive aftermarket chains	11.9

Continued on next page.

★ 1393 ★ *Continued*
Retailing (SIC 5300)

U.S. Retailing Industry

Sales are shown in billions of dollars.

PX retailers . . . .$ 10.0
Toy superstores 9.2
Home specialty chains 8.6

Source: *DSN Retailing Today*, July 9, 2001, p. 19.

★ 1394 ★
Department Stores (SIC 5311)

Preferred Department Stores in Milwaukee

Figures are based on a survey.

Kohl's 73.0%
Target 67.0
Kmart 67.0

Source: *Milwaukee Journal Sentinel*, March 21, 2002, p. 1.

★ 1395 ★
Department Stores (SIC 5311)

Top Department Stores

Firms are ranked by sales in millions of dollars.

Sears . . . . $ 29,743.0
Federated 18,407.0
JC Penney 18,397.0
May 14,454.0
Dillard's 8,567.0
Saks 6,581.2
Kohl's 6,151.9
Nordstrom 5,528.5
Mervyn's 4,152.0
Marshall Field's 3,011.0

Source: *Stores*, July 2001, p. S14.

★ 1396 ★
Department Stores (SIC 5311)

Top Department Stores in Canada

Market shares are shown in percent.

Wal-Mart 38.0%
Sears/Eatons 28.0
The Bay 12.0
Other 22.0

Source: *Canadian Business*, March 18, 2002, p. 30, from Dominion Bond Rating Service.

★ 1397 ★
Convenience Stores (SIC 5331)

Convenience Stores by State

Nearly 60,000 of the 119,571 stores are classified as single store operators. Nearly one out of ten are franchisees.

	No.	Share
Texas	12,000	14.89%
California	9,482	11.77
Florida	7,876	9.78
North Carolina	4,892	6.07
New York	4,752	5.90
Other	41,567	51.59

Source: *Confectioner*, October 2001, p. 54, from National Association of Convenience Stores.

★ 1398 ★
Convenience Stores (SIC 5331)

Top Convenience Store Companies

Companies are ranked by total stores.

Equilon Enterprises/Motiva Enterprises . . . 6,530
7-Eleven 5,325

Continued on next page.

★ **1398** ★   *Continued*

Convenience Stores (SIC 5331)

Top Convenience Store Companies

Companies are ranked by total stores.

BP	4,761
Tosco Marketing	3,940
ExxonMobil Corp.	3,603
Chevron Products Co.	2,687
Sinclair Oil	2,370
Speedway SuperAmerica	2,330
Ultramar Diamond	1,500
Clark Retail Enterprises	1,334

Source: *National Petroleum News*, October 2001, p. 76.

★ **1399** ★

Discount Merchandising (SIC 5331)

Largest Discount Merchandisers

Market shares are shown based on sales.

Wal-Mart	25.7%
Target	6.3
Kmart	5.5
Costco	3.4
Sam's Club	2.9
Dollar General	1.3
Family Dollar	0.9
Ames	0.9
Other	53.1

Source: *New York Times*, June 9, 2002, p. 12, from Prudential Securities.

★ **1400** ★

Discount Merchandising (SIC 5331)

Top Discount Chains

Firms are ranked by sales in millions of dollars.

Wal-Mart	$ 121,889.0
Kmart	37,028.0
Costco	32,164.2
Target Stores	29,278.0
Sam's Club	26,798.0
Meijer	10,800.0
BJ's Wholesale	4,828.2
Dollar General	4,551.5
Ames	3,999.9

Source: *Stores*, July 2001, p. S14.

SIC 54 - Food Stores

★ 1401 ★
Grocery Stores (SIC 5411)

Top Discount Grocery Stores in Ontario

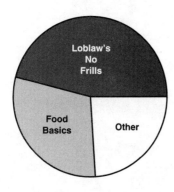

Market shares are shown in percent.

Loblaw's No Frills	46.0%
Food Basics	30.0
Other	24.0

Source: *Supermarket News*, July 9, 2001, p. 1.

★ 1402 ★
Grocery Stores (SIC 5411)

Top Food Retailers, 2001

Total at-home food sales reached $682.3 billion. Market shares are shown in percent.

Wal-Mart Superstores	9.8%
Kroger	7.4
Albertson's	5.6
Safeway	5.0
Ahold USA Retail	3.4
Supervalu	3.1
Costco	3.0
Sam's Clubs	2.7
Fleming	2.3
Publix	2.2

Delhaize America	2.2%
Other	53.3

Source: *Supermarket News*, January 14, 2002, p. 28, from Census Bureau.

★ 1403 ★
Grocery Stores (SIC 5411)

Top Grocery Stores in Athens, GA

Market shares are shown in percent.

Kroger	23.8%
Publix	13.0
BI-LO	12.5
Wal-Mart	11.0
Other	39.7

Source: *Knight-Ridder/Tribune Business News*, July 21, 2001, p. NA, from Trade Dimensions.

★ 1404 ★
Grocery Stores (SIC 5411)

Top Grocery Stores in Atlanta, GA

Market shares are shown in percent.

Kroger	33.5%
Publix	25.2
Ingles	6.4
Winn-Dixie	6.2
Wal-Mart	5.2
Cub Foods	5.1
Harris Teeter	2.8
Harry's	2.5
All American	1.5
Other	11.7

Source: *Knight-Ridder/Tribune Business News*, May 19, 2001, p. NA, from *Shelby Report of the Southeast*.

★ 1405 ★

Grocery Stores (SIC 5411)

Top Grocery Stores in Bergen/ Passaic counties, NJ

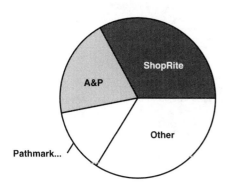

Market shares are shown in percent.

ShopRite	32.5%
A&P	19.9
Pathmark Stores	13.2
Other	34.4

Source: *The Record*, December 30, 2001, p. 36, from Market Scope.

★ 1406 ★

Grocery Stores (SIC 5411)

Top Grocery Stores in Boston/ Lawrence/ Lowell/ Brockton, MA

Data show percent of area volume.

Stop & Shop	26.0%
Shaw's	23.0
DeMoulas	16.0
Other	35.0

Source: *Food Institute Report*, August 13, 2001, p. 5, from *Mass Market Retailers* and *Sales and Marketing Management*.

★ 1407 ★

Grocery Stores (SIC 5411)

Top Grocery Stores in Broward, FL

Market shares are shown in percent.

Publix	61.5%
Winn-Dixie	23.4
Other	15.1

Source: *Daily Business Review*, July 18, 2001, p. A1, from *Market Scope, 2001* and Trade Dimensions.

★ 1408 ★

Grocery Stores (SIC 5411)

Top Grocery Stores in Central Indiana

Market shares are shown in percent.

Marsh-O'Malia	30.5%
Kroger	28.4
Other	41.1

Source: *Knight-Ridder/Tribune Business News*, June 15, 2001, p. NA, from Scarborough Research.

★ 1409 ★

Grocery Stores (SIC 5411)

Top Grocery Stores in Central Pennsylvania

Market shares are shown in percent.

Giant	32.76%
Shurfine	31.52
Weis Markets	20.91
Other	14.81

Source: *Knight-Ridder/Tribune Business News*, July 19, 2001, p. NA, from *Food Trade News*.

★ 1410 ★

Grocery Stores (SIC 5411)

Top Grocery Stores in Chicago, IL

Market shares are shown in percent.

Jewel	39.0%
Dominck's	26.0
Certified Grocers Midwest	10.0
Centrella	5.8
Eagle Food Centers	4.0
Cub Foods	3.9
Other	11.3

Source: *Progressive Grocer*, May 2001, p. 47, from Trade Dimensions.

★ 1411 ★

Grocery Stores (SIC 5411)

Top Grocery Stores in Dallas, TX

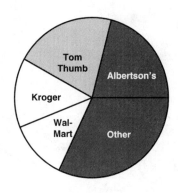

Market shares are shown in percent.

Albertson's	21.0%
Tom Thumb	20.8
Kroger	13.5
Wal-Mart	12.3
Other	32.4

Source: *Knight-Ridder/Tribune Business News*, February 26, 2002, p. NA, from Market Scope.

★ 1412 ★

Grocery Stores (SIC 5411)

Top Grocery Stores in Denver, CO

Data show percent of area volume.

King Scoopers	39.0%
Safeway	21.0
Albertson's	11.0
Other	29.0

Source: *Food Institute Report*, August 13, 2001, p. 5, from *Mass Market Retailers* and *Sales and Marketing Management*.

★ 1413 ★

Grocery Stores (SIC 5411)

Top Grocery Stores in Detroit, MI

Market shares are shown in percent.

Farmer Jack	27.2%
Kroger	22.7
Other	50.1

Source: *Crain's Detroit Business*, May 21, 2001, p. 1.

★ 1414 ★

Grocery Stores (SIC 5411)

Top Grocery Stores in Ft. Worth, TX

Market shares are shown in percent.

Albertson's	22.0%
Winn-Dixie	13.0
Wal-Mart	13.0
Minyard	9.0
Other	43.0

Source: *Dallas Business Journal*, July 20, 2001, p. 8, from Shelby Report.

★ 1415 ★

Grocery Stores (SIC 5411)

Top Grocery Stores in Hampton Roads, Virginia

Market shares are shown in percent.

Food Lion	24.7%
Farm Fresh	17.2
Other	58.1

Source: *Knight-Ridder/Tribune Business News*, June 23, 2001, p. NA, from *Food World*.

★ 1416 ★

Grocery Stores (SIC 5411)

Top Grocery Stores in Houston, TX

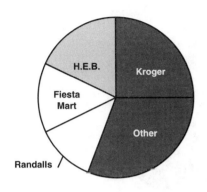

Data show percent of area volume.

Kroger	25.0%
H.E.B.	18.0
Fiesta Mart	14.0
Randalls	12.0
Other	31.0

Source: *Food Institute Report*, August 13, 2001, p. 5, from *Mass Market Retailers* and *Sales and Marketing Management*.

★ 1417 ★

Grocery Stores (SIC 5411)

Top Grocery Stores in Los Angeles/ Long Beach, CA

Data show percent of area volume.

Ralph's	22.0%
Safeway	17.0
Albertson's	14.0
Other	37.0

Source: *Food Institute Report*, August 13, 2001, p. 5, from *Mass Market Retailers* and *Sales and Marketing Management*.

★ 1418 ★

Grocery Stores (SIC 5411)

Top Grocery Stores in Mansfield, TX

Market shares are shown in percent. Figures cover Tarrant, Johnson, Parker and Hood counties.

Albertson's	22.70%
Tom Thumb	13.36
Wal-Mart	13.25
Other	50.69

Source: *Knight-Ridder/Tribune Business News*, September 2, 2001, p. NA, from Southwestern Shelby Report.

★ 1419 ★

Grocery Stores (SIC 5411)

Top Grocery Stores in Memphis, TN

Figures show share of total stores. Data show quarterly figures for March 2002.

Kroger	39.10%
Albertson's	15.19
Wal-Mart	11.61
Sewell Allen James	9.64
Kmart	5.26
Other	19.20

Source: *Commercial Appeal*, March 17, 2002, p. C1, from Shelby Report and Trade Dimensions.

★ 1420 ★

Grocery Stores (SIC 5411)

Top Grocery Stores in Miami-Dade, FL

Market shares are shown in percent.

Publix	45.9%
Winn-Dixie	26.4
Other	27.7

Source: *Daily Business Review*, July 18, 2001, p. A1, from *Market Scope, 2001* and Trade Dimensions.

★ 1421 ★

Grocery Stores (SIC 5411)

Top Grocery Stores in Minneapolis/ St. Paul, MN

Data show percent of area volume.

Super Valu 25.0%
Jerry's 12.0
Lund's 11.0
Other 52.0

Source: *Food Institute Report*, August 13, 2001, p. 5, from *Mass Market Retailers* and *Sales and Marketing Management*.

★ 1422 ★

Grocery Stores (SIC 5411)

Top Grocery Stores in Nashville, TN

The $1.9 billion retail food market is shown in percent.

Kroger 52.0%
Wal-Mart 10.0
Food Lion 9.0
Other 29.0

Source: *Knight-Ridder/Tribune Business News*, June 21, 2002, p. NA, from Shelby Report.

★ 1423 ★

Grocery Stores (SIC 5411)

Top Grocery Stores in Nassau/ Suffolk, NY

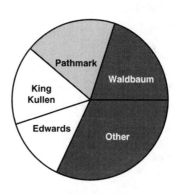

Data show percent of area volume.

Waldbaum 20.0%
Pathmark 19.0
King Kullen 16.0
Edwards 13.0
Other 32.0

Source: *Food Institute Report*, August 13, 2001, p. 5, from *Mass Market Retailers* and *Sales and Marketing Management*.

★ 1424 ★

Grocery Stores (SIC 5411)

Top Grocery Stores in New York, NY

Data show percent of area volume.

Pathmark 16.0%
A&P 9.0
Other 75.0

Source: *Food Institute Report*, August 13, 2001, p. 5, from *Mass Market Retailers* and *Sales and Marketing Management*.

★ 1425 ★

Grocery Stores (SIC 5411)

Top Grocery Stores in North Carolina

Market shares are shown in percent.

Food Lion 35.48%
Harris Teeter 13.42
Wal-Mart 8.54
Lowes Foods 8.19
Winn-Dixie 7.35
Other 27.02

Source: *Winston-Salem Journal*, May 19, 2002, p. D1, from Shelby Report.

★ 1426 ★

Grocery Stores (SIC 5411)

Top Grocery Stores in Philadelphia, PA

Data show percent of area volume.

Acme 24.0%
Pathmark 10.0
Other 66.0

Source: *Food Institute Report*, August 13, 2001, p. 5, from *Mass Market Retailers* and *Sales and Marketing Management*.

★ 1427 ★

Grocery Stores (SIC 5411)

Top Grocery Stores in Phoenix/Mesa, AZ

Data show percent of area sales volume.

Fry's 30.0%
Safeway 12.0
Other 58.0

Source: *Food Institute Report*, August 13, 2001, p. 5, from *Mass Market Retailers* and *Sales and Marketing Management*.

★ 1428 ★

Grocery Stores (SIC 5411)

Top Grocery Stores in Riverside/San Bernardino, CA

Data show percent of area volume.

Stater Bros. 32.0%
Albertson's 15.0
Ralph's 12.0
Safeway 11.0
Other 30.0

Source: *Food Institute Report*, August 13, 2001, p. 5, from *Mass Market Retailers* and *Sales and Marketing Management*.

★ 1429 ★

Grocery Stores (SIC 5411)

Top Grocery Stores in Sacramento, CA

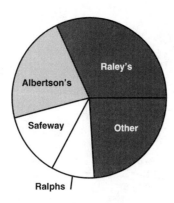

Market shares are shown in percent.

Raley's	32.0%
Albertson's	21.6
Safeway	13.4
Ralphs	8.7
Other	24.3

Source: *Knight-Ridder/Tribune Business News*, July 2, 2001, p. NA, from Market Scope.

★ 1430 ★

Grocery Stores (SIC 5411)

Top Grocery Stores in St. Louis, MO

Data show percent of area volume.

Schnuck Markets	44.0%
Super Valu	12.0
Other	44.0

Source: *Food Institute Report*, August 13, 2001, p. 5, from *Mass Market Retailers* and *Sales and Marketing Management*.

★ 1431 ★

Grocery Stores (SIC 5411)

Top Grocery Stores in Seattle/ Bellevue/ Everett, WA

Data show percent of area volume.

Safeway	26.0%
Quality Food Centers	25.0
Albertson's	11.0
Other	38.0

Source: *Food Institute Report*, August 13, 2001, p. 5, from *Mass Market Retailers* and *Sales and Marketing Management*.

★ 1432 ★

Grocery Stores (SIC 5411)

Top Grocery Stores in Virginia

Market shares are shown in percent.

Ukrop	40.89%
Food Lion	32.28
Wal-Mart	11.12
Other	15.71

Source: *Knight-Ridder/Tribune Business News*, June 20, 2001, p. NA, from *Food World*.

★ 1433 ★

Grocery Stores (SIC 5411)

Top Grocery Stores in Washington D.C.

Shares are for 1999.

Giant Food	41.2%
Safeway	25.6
Shoppers Food Warehouse	12.6
Food Lion	6.2
Other	14.4

Source: *Washington Business Journal*, April 27, 2001, p. 3, from *Food World*.

★ 1434 ★

Retailing - Alcohol (SIC 5411)

Alcohol Sales in Drug Stores

Segments are ranked by sales in millions of dollars.

Liquor	$ 643.1
Beer and ale	584.6
Wine	281.5

Source: *Drug Store News*, May 21, 2001, p. 82, from Information Resources Inc.

★ 1435 ★

Retailing - Alcohol (SIC 5411)

Retail Beer Sales

Sales are shown by channel.

Supermarkets	84.7%
Discounters	11.2
Drug stores	4.1

Source: *MMR*, November 26, 2001, p. 25, from A.C. Nielsen.

★ 1436 ★

Retailing - Food (SIC 5411)

Retail Breakfast Food Sales

Sales are shown by channel.

Supermarkets	83.7%
Discounters	9.3
Drug stores	7.0

Source: *MMR*, November 26, 2001, p. 25, from A.C. Nielsen.

★ 1437 ★

Retailing - Food (SIC 5411)

Retail Food Market

Market shares are shown in percent.

	1999	2004
Superstores	25.2%	27.2%
Conventional supermarkets	20.3	15.4
Food/drug combo	13.7	14.5
Supercenters	8.5	12.3

	1999	2004
Wholesale clubs	7.7%	7.7%
Convenience stores	6.3	5.1
Convenience with gasoline	4.2	4.9
Warehouse stores	2.6	3.0

Source: *Shopping Center World*, October 2001, p. NA, from Willard Bishop Consulting and Competitive Edge.

★ 1438 ★

Retailing - Food (SIC 5411)

Retail Food Market in Canada

Sales are shown in billions of dollars.

	($ bil.)	Share
Warehouse club stores	$ 6.30	36.37%
Mass merchandisers	4.30	24.83
Major banned convenience stores	3.60	20.79
Organic, natural health food stores	1.20	6.93
Online grocers	0.02	0.12
Other	1.90	10.97

Source: "Retail Food Sector." Retrieved May 1, 2002 from the World Wide Web: http://ffas.usda.gov, from A.C. Nielsen.

★ 1439 ★

Retailing - Food (SIC 5411)

Retail Snack Sales

Sales are shown by channel.

Supermarkets	89.3%
Discounters	6.6
Drug stores	4.1

Source: *MMR*, November 26, 2001, p. 25, from A.C. Nielsen.

★ 1440 ★

Retailing - Candy (SIC 5441)

Retail Candy Sales

Sales are shown by channel.

Supermarkets	91.5%
Discounters	7.1
Drug stores	1.4

Source: *MMR*, November 26, 2001, p. 25, from A.C. Nielsen.

SIC 55 - Automotive Dealers and Service Stations

★ 1441 ★
Retailing - Autos (SIC 5511)
Auto Dealer Sales

Used-vehicle sales increased 1 million for a record 42.6 million units and $376 billion in revenue.

Franchised dealers . . . . $ 15,921
Independent dealers 14,414
Private individuals 12,277

Source: *Ward's Dealer Business*, March 2002, p. 20.

★ 1442 ★
Retailing - Autos (SIC 5511)
Largest Auto Dealers in Houston, TX

Data show new vehicle sales.

Sterling McCall Toyota 7,883
Landmark Chevrolet Corp. 7,288
Texan Ford 7,105
Lone Star Ford 6,284
Fred Hass Toyota World 6,174

Source: *Houston Business Journal*, May 4, 2001, p. 28.

★ 1443 ★
Retailing - Auto Parts (SIC 5531)
Largest Auto Parts Chains

Chains are ranked by number of outlets.

AutoZone Inc. 3,019
Advance Auto Parts 2,400
General Parts Inc./CARQUEST 1,232
CSK Auto Corporation 1,154
O'Reilly Auto Parts 850
Genuine Parts/NAPA 734
The Pep Boys 628
Fisher Auto Parts 288
Replacement Parts Inc. 142

Source: *Aftermarket Business*, January 2002, p. 15.

★ 1444 ★
Retailing - Auto Parts (SIC 5531)
Leading Auto Parts Chains

| AutoZone |
| Genuine Parts |
| Pep Boys |
| Advance Auto |
| CSK |
| General Parts |

Chains are ranked by 2000 sales in billions of dollars.

AutoZone . . . . $ 4.48
Genuine Parts 4.16
Pep Boys 2.42
Advance Auto 2.29
CSK 1.45
General Parts 1.20

Source: *Aftermarket Business*, August 2001, p. 8.

★ 1445 ★
Retailing - Auto Supplies (SIC 5531)
Retail Antifreeze Sales

Market shares are shown by type of chain.

Automotive chain 53.0%
Discount chain 43.0
Non-automotive chain 3.0
Department store chain 1.0

Source: *Aftermarket Business*, April 2002, p. 22.

★ 1446 ★
Retailing - Auto Supplies (SIC 5531)

Retail Floor Mat Sales

Market shares are shown by type of chain.

Discount store chains	55.0%
Automotive chains	43.0
Other	2.0

Source: *Aftermarket Business*, April 2002, p. 22.

★ 1447 ★
Retailing Auto Supplies (SIC 5531)

Retail Surface Protectant Sales

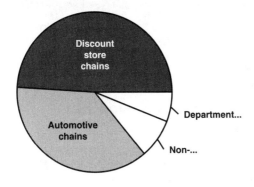

Market shares are shown by type of chain.

Discount store chains	49.0%
Automotive chains	37.0
Non-automotive chains	8.0
Department store chains	6.0

Source: *Aftermarket Business*, April 2002, p. 22.

★ 1448 ★
Retailing - Auto Supplies (SIC 5531)

Retail Tire Inflator Sales

Market shares are shown by type of chain.

Discount store chains	65.0%
Automotive chains	29.0
Non-automotive chains	4.0
Department store chains	2.0

Source: *Aftermarket Business*, April 2002, p. 22.

★ 1449 ★
Retailing - Tires (SIC 5531)

Largest Tire Dealerships

Firms are ranked by retail sales in millions of dollars.

Discount Tire Co.	$ 1,286.0
Les Schwab Tire Centers	813.8
Morgan Tire & Auto	492.0
Penske Auto Centers	298.0
Tire Kingdom	208.4
Merchant's Inc.	157.0
Performacne Management/Winston Tire . . .	137.0
Belle Tire Distributors	105.0
Peerless Tyre	94.7
Kal Tire	80.0

Source: *Tire Business*, October 22, 2001, p. 18.

★ 1450 ★
Retailing - Tires (SIC 5531)

Retail Tire Market

Market shares are shown in percent.

Independent tire dealers	58.5%
Mass merchandisers	16.0
Warehouse clubs	8.5
Tire company stores	8.0
Service stations	4.0
Auto dealerships	3.5
Other outlets	1.5

Source: *Investor's Business Daily*, June 7, 2002, p. A6, from company reports and First Call.

★ 1451 ★
Gas Stations (SIC 5541)

Top Gas Retailers in Chicago, IL

Market shares are shown in percent.

Amoco	23.0%
Shell	20.0
Mobil	14.0
Other	43.0

Source: *Crain's Chicago Business*, July 30, 2001, p. 3, from New Image Marketing Ltd.

★ 1452 ★

Gas Stations (SIC 5541)

Top Gas Retailers in Houston, TX

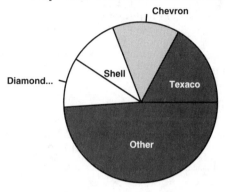

Market shares are shown in percent.

Texaco	16.6%
Chevron	14.3
Shell	10.0
Diamond Shamrock	10.0
Other	49.1

Source: *PR Newswire*, July 3, 2001, p. NA.

★ 1453 ★

Gas Stations (SIC 5541)

Top Gasoline Retailers in Texas

Market shares are shown in percent.

Texaco	16.0%
Chevron	14.1
Exxon	12.3
Shell	10.1
Shamrock	9.7
Other	37.8

Source: *Oil Express*, December 24, 2001, p. 1.

★ 1454 ★

Retailing - Gasoline (SIC 5541)

Leading Gasoline Marketers

There were 175,941 stations in the first quarter, and there are consolidations taking place. The top six firms had 55% of the market. Figures show number of outlets.

Royal Dutch/Shell	22,000
BP	17,500
ConocoPhillips	17,400
Exxon Mobil	16,080
Citgo	13,666
ChevronTexaco	8,055

Source: *Wall Street Journal*, November 20, 2001, p. A2, from *National Petroleum News* and New Energy Information Administration.

★ 1455 ★

Retailing - Boating Equipment (SIC 5551)

Who Sells Boating Supplies

The industry is dominated by mom and pop chains. The figures shown are estimates; West Marine's is less than 10% and the top 3 firms have less than 15% of the $5-6 billion a year industry.

West Marine	10.0%
BoatU.S./Boaters World	5.0
Other	85.0

Source: *Investor's Business Daily*, December 4, 2001, p. A14.

★ 1456 ★

Retailing - Motorcycles (SIC 5571)

Largest Motorcycle Dealers in the Silicon Valley, 2000

Data show unit sales.

Milipitas Motorcycles	1,020
Action Sports	1,000
San Jose Yamaha	792
San Jose Harley-Davidson	728
San Cruz Harley-Davidson	628

Source: *Silicon Valley/San Jose Business Journal*, October 19, 2001, p. 52.

SIC 56 - Apparel and Accessory Stores

★ 1457 ★

Retailing (SIC 5600)

Leading Retailer Market Shares, 1999

Market shares are shown based on general merchandise, apparel and furniture.

Kmart	4.6%
Sears	4.0
Target	3.4
J.C. Penney	2.4
Other	85.6

Source: *Fortune*, December 10, 2001, p. 122, from Bear Stearns.

★ 1458 ★

Retailing (SIC 5600)

Where Students Shop

Figures are based on a survey.

Specialty stores	45.0%
Department stores	23.0
Major chains	15.0

Source: *PR Newswire*, November 6, 2001, p. NA.

★ 1459 ★

Retailing - Apparel (SIC 5611)

Men's Activewear Sales, 2001

Market shares are shown in percent.

Specialty stores	21.4%
Mass merchants	17.1
Sports specialty	14.9
Department stores	14.4
National chains	9.7

Off-price retailers	7.6%
Direct mail/e-tail	4.8
Factory outlets	3.4
Other	6.7

Source: *Sporting Goods Business*, May 2002, p. 18, from NPD Fashionworld.

★ 1460 ★

Retailing - Apparel (SIC 5611)

Men's Underwear Sales

Underwear sales hit $2.8 billion. It is a healthy business for retailers, but highly competitive with consumers overwhelmed by choice: brands, colors and styles.

	($ mil.)	Share
Mass	$ 1,232.4	44.31%
National chains	414.9	14.92
Department stores	385.1	13.85
Specialty stores	280.2	10.07
Other	468.8	16.85

Source: *DNR*, May 13, 2002, p. 28, from NPDFashionworld Consumer.

★ 1461 ★

Retailing - Apparel (SIC 5611)

Top Apparel Retailers for Young Men in Canada

Shares refer to ages 13-19 year old for the first nine months of 2001.

Sears	10.7%
Zellers	6.0
Wal-Mart	5.4
The Bay	3.9
Sport Chek	3.3
Winners	3.2
Moores	3.1

Continued on next page.

★ 1461 ★ *Continued*
Retailing - Apparel (SIC 5611)

Top Apparel Retailers for Young Men in Canada

Shares refer to ages 13-19 year old for the first nine months of 2001.

Tip Top	2.9%
Other	61.5

Source: *Trendex Soft Line Bulletin*, January 2002, p. 4, from Soft Goods Index.

★ 1462 ★
Retailing - Apparel (SIC 5611)

Top Apparel Retailers for Young Women in Canada

Shares refer to ages 13-19 year old for the first nine months of 2001.

Sears	10.1%
Wal-Mart	8.1
Bootlegger	4.8
Suzy Shier	4.7
Bluenotes	3.4
Stitches	3.2
The Bay	3.0
Reitman's	2.9
Other	59.8

Source: *Trendex Soft Line Bulletin*, January 2002, p. 4, from Soft Goods Index.

★ 1463 ★
Retailing - Apparel (SIC 5611)

Top Men's Sports Coat Retailers in Canada

Market shares are shown for October 2000 - September 2001.

Other	36.7%
Moores	35.3
Tip Top Tailors	9.5
Sears	8.6
The Bay	5.5
Harry Rosen	2.9
Jack Fraser	1.6

Source: *Trendex Soft Line Bulletin*, January 2002, p. 5, from Soft Goods Index.

★ 1464 ★
Retailing - Apparel (SIC 5621)

Intimate Apparel Market Shares, 2001

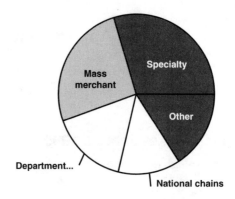

Sales are shown in billions of dollars.

	($ bil.)	Share
Specialty	$ 2.6	29.55%
Mass merchant	2.3	26.14
Department stores	1.4	15.91
National chains	1.1	12.50
Other	1.4	15.91

Source: *Body Fashion Intimate Apparel*, December 2001, p. 10, from NPD Group.

★ 1465 ★
Retailing - Apparel (SIC 5621)

Top Lingerie Retailers in Canada

Market shares are shown for sleepwear for October 2000 - September 2001.

Sears	21.1%
Zellers	15.3
The Bay	11.0
La Senza	10.4
Wal-Mart	9.7
Pennington's	3.5
Other	29.0

Source: *Trendex Soft Line Bulletin*, January 2002, p. 5, from Soft Goods Index.

★ 1466 ★
Retailing - Apparel (SIC 5632)

Apparel Market Shares in Canada

Ontario leads the way in apparel consumer spending, with 40% of the dollars, while Quebec holds onto 25% of the market.

Apparel specialty chains	33.0%
Department stores	26.0
Discount stores	19.0
Independent apparel stores	12.0
Other	10.0

Source: "Apparel Accessories." Retrieved November 6, 2001 from the World Wide Web: http://www.usatrade.gov.

★ 1467 ★
Retailing - Apparel (SIC 5632)

Leading Youth Retailers, 2000

Companies are ranked by 2000 revenue in millions of dollars.

Abercrombie & Fitch	$ 1,237.6
American Eagle Outfitters	1,093.4
Pacific Sunwear of California	589.4
Weat Seal	580.1
Buckle	393.2
Gadzooks	288.4
Urban Outfitters	274.7
Hot Topic	257.1

Source: *Chain Store Age*, August 2001, p. 4A.

★ 1468 ★
Retailing - Apparel (SIC 5641)

Largest Children's Apparel Retailers

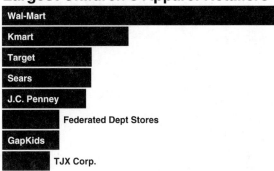

Firms are ranked by sales in millions of dollars.

Wal-Mart	$ 5,851
Kmart	2,666
Target	1,874
Sears	1,864
J.C. Penney	1,753
Federated Dept Stores	1,178
GapKids	1,176
TJX Corp.	977

Source: *Children's Business*, May 2001, p. S2.

★ 1469 ★
Retailing - Shoes (SIC 5661)

Boy's Footwear Market

Market shares are shown in percent.

Discount	25.0%
Self service	15.4
Athletic shoe stores	14.7
High-end shoe stores	14.4
Sporting goods stores	6.4
Sears/J.C. Penney	6.4
Dept. stores	6.1
Moderate price shoe stores	4.9
Apparel specialty stores	2.5

Source: *Children's Business*, July 2001, p. 22, from Footwear Market Insights.

★ 1470 ★

Retailing - Shoes (SIC 5661)

Men's Athletic Shoe Sales, 2001

Market shares are shown in percent.

Athletic specialty	25.0%
Sporting goods	15.1
National chain	12.1
Company store/factory outlet	8.9
Catalog/direct mail	6.5
Discount	6.3
Independents	4.5
Shoe store	3.3
Off-price	3.0
Department stores	2.2
Other	13.1

Source: *Sporting Goods Business*, May 2002, p. 18, from NPD Fashionworld.

★ 1471 ★

Retailing - Shoes (SIC 5661)

Top Sports Shoe Sellers

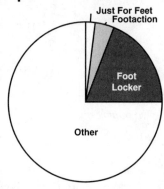

Retail sales hit $13.5 billion. The industry has only recently rebounded from a drop in the 1990s. Market shares are shown in percent.

Foot Locker	19.0%
Footaction	4.0
Just For Feet	2.0
Other	75.0

Source: *Brandweek*, January 21, 2002, p. 18.

★ 1472 ★

Retailing - Shoes (SIC 5661)

Women's Athletic Shoe Sales, 2001

Market shares are shown in percent.

National chain	17.6%
Athletic specialty	15.9
Discount	10.4
Company store/factory outlet	8.8
Sporting goods	8.7
Department stores	6.8
Independents	5.3
Shoe stores	4.9
Off-price	4.7
Other	16.9

Source: *Sporting Goods Business*, May 2002, p. 18, from NPD Fashionworld.

★ 1473 ★

Retailing - Shoes (SIC 5661)

Women's Casual Shoe Sales

Market shares are shown in percent.

Discount stores	17.4%
Department stores	14.5
National chains	11.5
Off-price chains	6.0
Other	50.6

Source: *DSN Retailing Today*, June 4, 2001, p. A18, from NPD Group.

SIC 57 - Furniture and Homefurnishings Stores

★ 1474 ★
Retailing - Furniture (SIC 5712)
Retail Lamp Sales

Market shares are shown in percent.

Lighting specialty stores	30.0%
Mass merchants	18.5
Home improvement stores	18.5
Furniture stores	16.5
Department stores	12.0
Catalogs	4.5

Source: *InFurniture*, June 2001, p. 35.

★ 1475 ★
Retailing - Furniture (SIC 5712)
Top Furniture Retailers

Firms are ranked by sales in millions of dollars.

Ethan Allen	$ 1,014.0
Office Depot	999.0
Heilig-Meyers	983.0
Rooms To Go	957.0
Wal-Mart	930.0
Federated Department Stores	871.0
Berkshire Hathaway	790.0
La-Z-Boy	738.5
Sam's Club	730.0
J.C. Penney	725.0

Source: *Furniture Today*, December 31, 2001, p. 64.

★ 1476 ★
Retailing - Floorcoverings (SIC 5713)
Ceramic Tile Sales

Market shares are shown in percent.

Distributors	41.0%
Contract tile specialty dealers	29.0
Individual floorcovering retailers	15.0
Other	15.0

Source: *Floor Focus*, May 2001, p. NA.

★ 1477 ★
Retailing - Floorcoverings (SIC 5713)
Largest Floor Covering Retailers

Firms are ranked by sales in millions of dollars.

Home Depot	$ 2,500
Lowe's	1,009
Sears	398
Menard	205
Sherwin-Williams	185
Wal-Mart	152
Floors Inc.	142
Federated	141
Coleman Floor	110
Peninsula Floors	105

Source: *Home Channel News*, April 15, 2002, p. 1, from *Floor Covering Weekly*.

★ 1478 ★
Retailing - Floorcoverings (SIC 5713)
Largest Rug Retailers

Total sales jumped from $4.5 billion to $5.1 billion.

Discount stores	42.0%
Home centers	21.0
Specialty chains	11.0
Department stores	9.0
Carpet/floorcovering stores	4.0

Continued on next page.

★ 1478 ★ *Continued*

Retailing - Floorcoverings (SIC 5713)

Largest Rug Retailers

Total sales jumped from $4.5 billion to $5.1 billion.

Warehouse clubs	3.0%
Sears/Ward's	2.0
Individual specialty stores	2.0
Furniture stores	2.0
Catalogs	2.0
Other	2.0

Source: *Home Textiles Today*, August 13, 2001, p. 14.

★ 1479 ★

Retailing - Windowcoverings (SIC 5714)

Leading Window Covering Retailers

Market shares are shown in percent.

Discounters	36.0%
Department stores	16.0
Catalogs	16.0
Specialty stores	13.0
Single-unit specialty stores	7.0
Sears/Montgomery Ward	6.0
Other	6.0

Source: *Home Textiles Today*, June 18, 2001, p. 14.

★ 1480 ★

Retailing - Homefurnishings (SIC 5719)

Cookware Sales by Outlet

Sales are for boxed sets.

Dept. stores	44.0%
Gift/gourmet store	23.9
Cookware/kitchenware	22.3
Specialty foods	17.0

Source: *Gourmet Retailer*, July 2000, p. 98.

★ 1481 ★

Retailing - Homefurnishings (SIC 5719)

Largest Mattress Retailers

Firms are ranked by sales in millions of dollars.

Federated Department Stores	$ 290
Mattress Discounters	275
Select Comfort	270
Mattress Firm	220

Sam's Club	$ 210
Sleepy's	206
Mattress Giant	178
Heilig-Meyers	130

Source: *HFN*, July 16, 2001, p. 34.

★ 1482 ★

Retailing - Homefurnishings (SIC 5719)

Leading Homefurnishings Retailers

Firms are ranked by sales in millions of dollars.

Wal-Mart	$ 8,422
Kmart	3,509
Target	2,447
Sears	1,446
Federated Dept. Stores	1,204
Bed Bath & Beyond	1,080
May Co.	940
Walgreen	816
QVC	700
TruServ	665

Source: *HFN*, October 8, 2001, p. 26.

★ 1483 ★

Retailing - Homefurnishings (SIC 5719)

Leading Kitchen Textile Retailers, 2000

Market shares are shown in percent.

Discount stores	51.0%
Specialty chains	24.0
Department stores	15.0
Warehouse clubs	4.0
Catalogs	2.0
Other	4.0

Source: *Home Textiles Today*, August 13, 2001, p. 14.

★ 1484 ★

Retailing - Homefurnishings (SIC 5719)

Retail Bath Towel Sales

Market shares are shown in percent.

Mass merchants	53.0%
Department stores	19.0
Other	28.0

Source: *HFN*, March 25, 2002, p. 15.

★ 1485 ★
Retailing - Homefurnishings (SIC 5719)

Wall Decor Industry

Sales are shown in percent.

Framed art	41.0%
Mirrors	29.0
Unframed art	6.0
Wall shelves/sconces	3.0
Wall sculpture	3.0
Tapestries/wall hangings	3.0
Dimensional	1.0
Other	14.0

Source: *Home Accents Today*, February 2002, p. 18.

★ 1486 ★
Retailing - Appliances (SIC 5722)

Top Appliance Retailers

Market shares are shown in percent.

	2001	2002
Sears	39.6%	40.7%
Lowe's	8.2	11.4
Best Buy	6.0	6.2
Home Depot	2.6	3.9
Other	43.6	37.8

Source: *Atlanta Journal-Constitution*, May 8, 2002, p. D1, from Stevenson Co.

★ 1487 ★
Retailing - Electronics (SIC 5731)

Leading Digital TV Retailers

Market shares are shown in percent.

Circuit City	21.0%
Best Buy	18.0
Sears	9.5
Good Guys	4.5
Tweeter, etc.	4.0
H.H. Gregg	2.5
Audio King	2.0
Other	45.5

Source: *Dealerscope*, August 2001, p. 1, from NPD Intelect.

★ 1488 ★
Retailing - Electronics (SIC 5731)

Leading DVD Player Sellers

Market shares are shown in percent.

Best Buy	22.3%
Circuit City	16.7
Wal-Mart	11.7
Sears	8.5
Target	3.8
Costco	3.3
Sams	2.6
K-Mart	2.4
Good Guys	1.8
Other	26.9

Source: *Dealerscope*, August 2001, p. 1, from NPD Intelect.

★ 1489 ★
Retailing - Electronics (SIC 5731)

Leading TV Retailers

Market shares are shown in percent.

Wal-Mart	21.3%
Best Buy	13.0
Sears	12.3
Circuit City	11.3
K-Mart	7.0
Montgomery Ward	3.8
Sams	2.5
Other	28.8

Source: *Dealerscope*, August 2001, p. 1, from NPD Intelect.

★ 1490 ★
Retailing - Movies (SIC 5735)

Largest Video/DVD Retailers

Firms are ranked by revenues in millions of dollars.

Blockbuster	$ 3,466
Wal-Mart	1,906
Hollywood Entertainment	1,110
Kmart	774
Target Stores	724
Best Buy	661
Musicland Stores	523

Source: *Video Store*, April 15, 2001, p. 22.

★ 1491 ★
Retailing - Movies (SIC 5735)
Retail VHS/DVD Sales

The table compares the sales of DVDs and VHS movies.

	VHS	DVD
Mass merchants	40.9%	32.9%
Video specialists	19.9	15.7
Warehouse clubs	8.6	4.0
Grocery	7.3	2.3
Consumer electronics stores	5.2	25.0
Clubs	5.1	3.8
Music/video	3.5	4.8
Online	1.8	9.1
Toy stores	1.5	3.8
Other	6.2	1.9

Source: *Video Business*, July 30, 2001, p. 46, from Adams Media Research.

★ 1492 ★
Retailing - Movies (SIC 5735)
Top DVD Retailers, 2001

Market shares are shown in percent.

Best Buy	14.5%
Wal-Mart	12.6
Musicland Stores	7.6
Costco	7.5
Target	7.0
Circuit City	5.0
Suncoast	4.0

Amazon.com	3.5%
Blockbuster	3.1
Kmart	2.7
Other	32.5

Source: *Video Store*, April 28, 2002, p. 28.

★ 1493 ★
Retailing - Movies (SIC 5735)
Top Video Retailers, 2001

Companies are ranked by estimated revenue in millions of dollars.

Blockbuster	$ 5,374
Wal-Mart	2,713
Kmart	2,114
Hollywood Entertainment	1,801
Musicland Stores	1,336
Target	1,055
Circuit City	632
Sam's Club	500
Best Buy	478

Source: *Video Store*, April 28, 2002, p. 28.

★ 1494 ★
Retailing - Movies (SIC 5735)
Video Sell-Through Market, 2001

Market shares are shown in percent.

Wal-Mart	28.0%
Target	9.0
Best Buy	7.9
Costco	6.0
Kmart	5.8
Other	43.3

Source: *Video Store*, April 28, 2002, p. 28.

SIC 58 - Eating and Drinking Places

★ 1495 ★
Foodservice (SIC 5812)

Dining Traffic in Canada

The "food on the go" industry has not developed in many Canadian cities as it has in the United States.

	1995	2000
Off premise	52.8%	56.9%
On premise	47.2	43.1

Source: "Meal Solutions Product." Retrieved November 21, 2001 from the World Wide Web: http://ffas.usda.gov, from NPD.

★ 1496 ★
Foodservice (SIC 5812)

Foodservice Industry in Canada, 2002

Figures are in billions of dollars.

	1996	2001	Share
Retail	$ 38.8	$ 46.8	78.0%
Foodservice	9.9	13.2	22.0

Source: *Food in Canada*, May 2002, p. 20.

★ 1497 ★
Foodservice (SIC 5812)

Leading Foodservice Firms

Firms are ranked by revenue in millions of dollars.

Tricon Global Restaurants Inc.	$ 5.0
McDonald's Corp.	4.8
Aramark Corp.	4.1
Darden Restaurants	3.9
Sodexho Marriott Services	3.8
Compass Group	2.8

Brinker International	$ 2.3
Outback Steakhouses	1.8
Marriott International	1.8
CKE Restaurants	1.6

Source: *Nation's Restaurant News*, June 25, 2001, p. 62.

★ 1498 ★
Foodservice (SIC 5812)

Top Foodservice Leaders, 2001

The $170 billion industry is shown in percent.

Sysco Corp.	14.0%
Royal Ahold's U.S. Foodservice unit	12.0
Other	74.0

Source: *Investor's Business Daily*, June 27, 2002, p. A12.

★ 1499 ★
Foodservice (SIC 5812)

U.S. Foodservice Industry, 2001

Total foodservice sales hit $411.5 billion.

	($ bil.)	Share
Restaurants & bars	$ 251.80	61.2%
Retails hosts	36.86	38.8
Travel & Leisure	27.40	6.7
Business & industry	22.22	5.4
Education	22.12	5.4
Health care	12.43	3.0
Other	38.72	9.4

Source: *Food Institute Report*, November 26, 2001, p. 5, from Technomic.

★ 1500 ★

Restaurants (SIC 5812)

Chicken Market Leaders

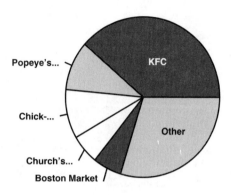

Market shares are shown in percent.

KFC	38.8%
Popeye's Chicken & Biscuits	9.7
Chick-fil-A	9.6
Church's Fried Chicken	6.2
Boston Market	5.5
Other	30.2

Source: *Advertising Age*, April 1, 2002, p. 4, from Technomic and Taylor Nelson Sofres.

★ 1501 ★

Restaurants (SIC 5812)

Eating Place Sales

Sales are shown in millions of dollars.

	($ bil.)	Share
Full-service restaurants	$ 140.3	49.44%
Fast-food restaurants	111.1	39.15
Nonalcoholic beverages, frozen treats, etc.	13.8	4.86
Bars and taverns	12.8	4.51
Social caterers	3.7	1.30
Commercial cafterias	2.1	0.74

Source: *Nation's Restaurant News*, January 7, 2002, p. 1.

★ 1502 ★

Restaurants (SIC 5812)

Fast-Food Industry in Canada

Market shares are shown for the $4 billion industry. Shares are estimated 11-12%.

McDonald's	58.0%
Wendy's	12.0
Burger King	12.0
A&W	12.0
Other	6.0

Source: *Canadian Business*, March 18, 2002, p. 70.

★ 1503 ★

Restaurants (SIC 5812)

Fast-Food Industry in Mexico

The entire industry is made up of 183,782 establishments.

Hamburgers	37.0%
Chicken	30.0
Pizza	24.0
Other	9.0

Source: ''Food Processing Ingredients Sector.'' Retrieved November 19, 2001 from the World Wide Web: http://ffas. usda.gov.

★ 1504 ★

Restaurants (SIC 5812)

Fast-Food Restaurant Activity

Share of traffic is shown as 26 week average.

Burgers	45.5%
Pizza	17.8
Regional chains	13.8
Mexican	8.2
Sandwich	7.8
Chicken	7.6

Source: *Chain Leader*, November 2001, p. 80.

★ 1505 ★

Restaurants (SIC 5812)

Hamburger Market Leaders

Market shares are shown in percent.

McDonald's 43.1%
Burger King 18.8
Wendy 12.7
Hardee's 4.5
JITB 4.4
Other 16.5

Source: *Brandweek*, June 18, 2001, p. 9.

★ 1506 ★

Restaurants (SIC 5812)

Largest Fast Food Chains in Canada, 2000

Firms are ranked by revenues in billions of dollars.

McDonald's . . . . $ 1.38
Tim Hortons 1.23
Tricon 0.71
Subway 0.34
Wendy's 0.28

Source: *Wall Street Journal*, August 23, 2001, p. B1, from Canadian Restaurant and Foodservices Association.

★ 1507 ★

Restaurants (SIC 5812)

Largest Grill Buffet Restaurants

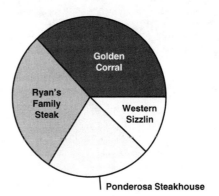

Market shares are shown based on the source's list of the top 100 chains.

Golden Corral 37.41%
Ryan's Family Steak House 28.81
Ponderosa Steakhouse 21.69
Western Sizzlin 12.09

Source: *Nation's Restaurant News*, June 25, 2001, p. 106.

★ 1508 ★

Restaurants (SIC 5812)

Sandwich Market Leaders, 2000

Data show share of $13 billion in sales.

Subway 29.1%
Arby's 18.5
Schlotzsky's Deli 3.2
Blimpie Subs & Salads 2.5
Quizno's Classic Subs 2.0
Other 55.3

Source: *ID: The Information Source for Managers and DSRs*, December 2001, p. 37, from Technomic.

★ 1509 ★

Restaurants (SIC 5812)

Top Asian Restaurants

Firms are ranked by sales in millions of dollars.

Panda Express	$ 287.8
P.F. Chang's China Bistro	234.0
Benihana	207.1
Leeann Chin	75.0
Sizzling Wok	65.0
Yoshinoya Beef Bowl	58.0

Source: *Restaurants & Institutions*, Top 400 Annual Issue, 2001, p. 31.

★ 1510 ★

Restaurants (SIC 5812)

Top Family Dining Restaurants

Firms are ranked by sales in millions of dollars.

Denny's	$ 2,320.0
International House of Pancakes	1,246.2
Cracker Barrel Old Country Store	1,196.7
Perkins Restaurant & Bakery	819.8
Bob Evans	762.2
Big Boy	750.0
Ryan's Steaks, Buffet & Bakery	744.5

Source: *Restaurants & Institutions*, Top 400 Annual Issue, 2001, p. 31.

★ 1511 ★

Restaurants (SIC 5812)

Top Independent Restaurants

Firms are ranked by food & beverage sales in millions of dollars.

Tavern on the Green	$ 31.9
Hilltop Steak House	26.2
Joe's Stone Crab	22.6
Bon Chinn's Crab House	21.5
Sparks Steakhouse	18.5
"21" Club	17.0

Old Ebbitt Grill	$ 15.5
Gibsons	15.1
Fulton's Crab House	15.1

Source: *Restaurants & Institutions*, April 1, 2002, p. 49.

★ 1512 ★

Restaurants (SIC 5812)

Top Mexican Restaurants

Firms are ranked by sales in millions of dollars.

Taco Bell	$ 5,300.0
Del Taco	319.0
Chevys Fresh Mex	310.0
On the Border Mexican Grill & Cantina	298.3
Don Pablo's	297.0
El Torito	236.0
Chi-Chi's	217.5

Source: *Restaurants & Institutions*, Top 400 Annual Issue, 2001, p. 31.

★ 1513 ★

Restaurants (SIC 5812)

Top Pizza Restaurants, 2000

Market shares are shown in percent.

Pizza Hut	20.6%
Domino's	10.9
Papa John's	6.9
Little Caesers	5.3
Other	52.3

Source: *Crain's Detroit Business*, May 28, 2001, p. 3.

★ 1514 ★

Restaurants (SIC 5812)

Top Restaurant Marketers, 2001

Shares are shown based on $269.4 billion in restaurant sales.

McDonald's Corp.	7.8%
Yum Brands	5.4
Diageo	3.2
Wendy's International	2.3
Doctor's Associates	1.7
Darden Restaurants	1.5
Brinker International	1.2

Continued on next page.

★ 1514 ★ *Continued*

Restaurants (SIC 5812)

Top Restaurant Marketers, 2001

Shares are shown based on $269.4 billion in restaurant sales.

Allied Domecq	1.2%
Other	75.7

Source: *Advertising Age*, June 24, 2002, p. S10, from Information Resources Inc.

★ 1515 ★

Restaurants (SIC 5812)

Top Seafood Restaurants

Firms are ranked by sales in millions of dollars.

Red Lobster	$ 2,000.0
Long John Silver's	734.7
Captain D's	495.0
Joe's Crab Shack	290.0
Landry's Seafood House	185.0
McCormick & Schmick's	162.4
Legal Sea Foods	126.5
Shells Seafood Restaurants	100.0

Source: *Restaurants & Institutions*, Top 400 Annual Issue, 2001, p. 31.

★ 1516 ★

Coffee Shops (SIC 5813)

Top Coffee Shops in Canada

TDL Group	
The Second Cup	
Coffee Time Donuts	
Starbucks Coffee	
Country Style Food Services	
Allied-Domecq Retailing	
Afton Food Group	
Timothy's World Coffee	
mmmuffins Canada	
Baker's Dozen Donuts	

Market shares are shown in percent. Total sales hit $2.8 billion.

TDL Group	67.8%
The Second Cup	5.7
Coffee Time Donuts	5.2

Starbucks Coffee	4.7%
Country Style Food Services	4.3
Allied-Domecq Retailing	4.3
Afton Food Group	3.0
Timothy's World Coffee	1.8
mmmuffins Canada	1.6
Baker's Dozen Donuts	1.6

Source: *Marketing Magazine*, May 27, 2002, p. 1, from industry sources.

SIC 59 - Miscellaneous Retail

★ 1517 ★
Drug Stores (SIC 5912)

Top Chains in Pharmacy Sales

Sales are shown in millions of dollars.

CVS	$ 12.6
Walgreen	11.7
Rite Aid	8.6
Eckerd	7.7
Wal-Mart	7.3
Albertson's	5.5
Kroger	3.9
Safeway	2.2
Kmart	1.9

Source: *Drug Store News*, August 20, 2001, p. 19, from Retail Intelligence Group.

★ 1518 ★
Drug Stores (SIC 5912)

Top Drug Store Categories

Sales are shown in millions of dollars.

Medications/remedies	$ 4.06
Tobacco & accessories	2.32
Candy	2.05
Hair care	1.83
Vitamins	1.74
Cosmetics	1.69
Cough & Cold remedies	1.52
Skin care	1.27
Pain remedies	1.14
Beer	1.11

Source: *Retail Merchandiser*, April 2001, p. 54, from ACNielsen.

★ 1519 ★
Drug Stores (SIC 5912)

Top Drug Store Chains

Firms are ranked by sales in millions of dollars.

Walgreen	$ 21,206.9
CVS	20,087.5
Rite Aid	14,516.8
Eckerd	13,088.0
Longs	4,027.1
Phar-Mor	1,292.0
Duane Reade	1,000.0
Brooks	950.0
Drug Emporium	875.0
Marc's	675.0

Source: *Stores*, July 2001, p. S14.

★ 1520 ★
Drug Stores (SIC 5912)

Top Drug Chains in Canada

Companies are ranked by sales in millions of dollars.

Shoppers Drug Mart	$ 3,634
The Katz Group	3,000
The Jean Coutu Group	2,200
London Drugs	1,530
Uniprix	860

Source: *Drug Store News*, April 29, 2002, p. 129.

★ 1521 ★
Drug Stores (SIC 5912)

Top Drug Stores in Atlanta, GA

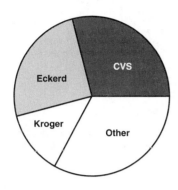

Market shares are shown in percent.

CVS	28.8%
Eckerd	25.2
Kroger	13.0
Other	33.0

Source: *Drug Store News*, March 25, 2002, p. 46, from Metropolitan Statistical Area.

★ 1522 ★
Drug Stores (SIC 5912)

Top Drug Stores in Boston, MA

Shares are shown based on number of outlets in 2000.

CVS	51.2%
Walgreens	17.2
Osco	12.1
Other	19.5

Source: *Drug Store News*, June 25, 2001, p. 96, from *Metro Market Studies 2001 Distribution Guide*.

★ 1523 ★
Drug Stores (SIC 5912)

Top Drug Stores in Chicago, IL

Shares are shown based on number of outlets in 2000.

Walgreens	50.0%
Osco	34.4
Dominick's	2.9
Other	12.7

Source: *Drug Store News*, June 25, 2001, p. 96, from *Metro Market Studies 2001 Distribution Guide*.

★ 1524 ★
Drug Stores (SIC 5912)

Top Drug Stores in Columbus, OH

Market shares are shown in percent.

CVS	34.0%
Rite Aid	10.0
Other	56.0

Source: *Knight-Ridder/Tribune Business News*, January 4, 2002, p. NA.

★ 1525 ★
Drug Stores (SIC 5912)

Top Drug Stores in Dallas, TX

Market shares are shown in percent.

Eckerd	25.4%
Walgreens	21.4
Albertson's	16.7
Other	36.5

Source: *Drug Store News*, March 25, 2002, p. 46, from Metro Market Studies.

★ 1526 ★
Drug Stores (SIC 5912)

Top Drug Stores in Detroit, MI

Market shares are shown in percent.

CVS	36.9%
Rite Aid	23.9
Walgreens	13.1
Other	26.1

Source: *Drug Store News*, March 25, 2002, p. 46, from Metro Market Studies.

★ 1527 ★

Market Share Reporter - 2003

★ 1527 ★

Drug Stores (SIC 5912)

Top Drug Stores in Greensboro/ Winston Salem, NC

Market shares are shown in percent.

CVS 41.0%
Eckerd 28.0
Other 31.0

Source: *Chain Drug Review*, December 10, 2001, p. 50.

★ 1528 ★

Drug Stores (SIC 5912)

Top Drug Stores in Houston, TX

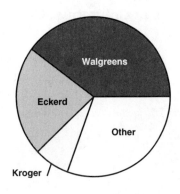

Shares are shown based on number of outlets in 2000.

Walgreens 43.2%
Eckerd 24.0
Kroger 8.0
Other 32.8

Source: *Drug Store News*, June 25, 2001, p. 96, from *Metro Market Studies 2001 Distribution Guide*.

★ 1529 ★

Drug Stores (SIC 5912)

Top Drug Stores in Los Angeles, CA

Shares are shown based on number of outlets in 2000.

Osco/Sav-on 43.5%
Rite Aid 19.9
Albertson's 6.8
Longs 5.5
Other 24.3

Source: *Drug Store News*, June 25, 2001, p. 96, from *Metro Market Studies 2001 Distribution Guide*.

★ 1530 ★

Drug Stores (SIC 5912)

Top Drug Stores in Miami, FL

Market shares are shown in percent.

Walgreens 33.0%
Eckerd 32.0
Other 35.0

Source: *Chain Drug Review*, December 10, 2001, p. 50.

★ 1531 ★

Drug Stores (SIC 5912)

Top Drug Stores in Minneapolis, MN

Shares are shown based on number of outlets in 2000.

Walgreens 47.3%
Snyder's 23.1
Wal-Mart 5.0
Other 24.6

Source: *Drug Store News*, June 25, 2001, p. 96, from *Metro Market Studies 2001 Distribution Guide*.

★ 1532 ★
Drug Stores (SIC 5912)

Top Drug Stores in New York City, NY

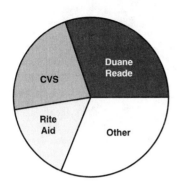

Shares are shown based on number of outlets in 2000.

Duane Reade 30.3%
CVS 22.1
Rite Aid 16.2
Other 31.4

Source: *Drug Store News*, June 25, 2001, p. 96, from *Metro Market Studies 2001 Distribution Guide*.

★ 1533 ★
Drug Stores (SIC 5912)

Top Drug Stores in Philadelphia, PA

Shares are shown based on number of outlets in 2000.

CVS 30.4%
Eckerd 17.4
Rite Aid 16.3
Other 35.9

Source: *Drug Store News*, June 25, 2001, p. 96, from *Metro Market Studies 2001 Distribution Guide*.

★ 1534 ★
Drug Stores (SIC 5912)

Top Drug Stores in Phoenix, AZ

Market shares are shown in percent.

Walgreens 50.9%
Osco 15.4
Fry's Food & Drug 10.2
Other 23.5

Source: *Drug Store News*, March 25, 2002, p. 46, from Metro Market Studies.

★ 1535 ★
Drug Stores (SIC 5912)

Top Drug Stores in Toledo, OH

Market shares are shown in percent.

Rite Aid 25.0%
CVS 11.0
Other 64.0

Source: *Knight-Ridder/Tribune Business News*, January 4, 2002, p. NA.

★ 1536 ★
Retailing - Drugs (SIC 5912)

Where People Shop For OTC Drugs

Supercenters have gained share since 1995, warehouse clubs stayed the same, and the rest lost.

Supermarkets 26.0%
Discount department stores 24.0
Drug stores 22.0
Supercenters 16.0
Warehouse clubs 3.0

Source: *Stores*, April 2002, p. 45, from Retail Forward Inc.

★ 1537 ★
Retailing - Sporting Goods (SIC 5941)

Largest Sports Retailers

Firms are ranked by sales in millions of dollars.

Wal-Mart . . . . $ 5,400.0
Foot Locker 2,912.1
Kmart 2,000.0
The Sports Authority 1,498.8
L.L. Bean 1,107.0

Continued on next page.

★ 1537 ★ *Continued*

Retailing - Sporting Goods (SIC 5941)

Largest Sports Retailers

Firms are ranked by sales in millions of dollars.

Footstar Athletic	$ 927.0
Sears	914.0
Dick's Sporting Goods	893.0
Target Stores	890.0
J.C. Penney Co.	860.0

Source: *Sporting Goods Business*, May 14, 2001, p. 32.

★ 1538 ★

Retailing - Sporting Goods (SIC 5941)

Sporting Goods Market in Seattle, WA

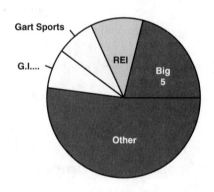

Market shares are shown for the third quarter of 2001.

Big 5	21.0%
REI	11.0
Gart Sports	8.0
G.I. Joe's	8.0
Other	52.0

Source: "Market Research Pinpoints G.I. Joe." Retrieved June 7, 2002 from http://www.gijoes.com, from Scarborough Report.

★ 1539 ★

Retailing - Books (SIC 5942)

Adult Book Sales, 2001

Sales are for the six months of the year. Consumers spent $5.2 billion on 548 million books.

Chain bookstore	22.3%
Book clubs	22.0
Small chains/independents	13.6

Internet	7.5%
Price clubs	6.7
Mass merchandisers	4.6
Mail order	3.3
Used bookstores	3.2
Food/drug	3.0
Other	13.8

Source: *Publishers Weekly*, November 5, 2001, p. 9, from Ipsos-NPD Book Trends Update.

★ 1540 ★

Retailing - Books (SIC 5942)

Book Market in Canada

Chapter is the leading book retailer in the country. The table shows Chapter's share in selected places.

Toronto	83.0%
Ottawa	76.0
Calgary	74.0
Vancouver	70.0

Source: *Publishers Weekly*, July 2, 2001, p. 17, from Association of Canadian Publishers.

★ 1541 ★

Retailing - Books (SIC 5942)

Children's Book Sales, 2001

Sales are for the first six months of the year.

	2000	2001
Book clubs/mail order/book fairs	34.0%	36.0%
Bookstores	25.0	23.0
Mass merchandisers	14.0	13.0
Warehouse/price clubs	4.0	4.0
Variety stores	4.0	4.0
Toy stores	2.0	2.0
Supermarkets	2.0	2.0
Drug stores	2.0	1.0
Dollar stores	2.0	3.0

Source: *Business Wire*, October 24, 2001, p. NA, from NPD-Ipsos.

★ 1542 ★

Retailing - Books (SIC 5942)

Retail Cookbook Sales

The category is growing at a faster pace than the adult segment. Total sales grew from 522 million in 1997 to 530 million in 2000.

Book clubs	27.0%
Large chain bookstores	26.0
Ind. small bookstores	12.0
Private clubs	6.0
Mail order	6.0
Internet	5.0
Discount stores	5.0
Other	13.0

Source: *Publishers Weekly*, July 23, 2001, p. 33, from Ipsos-NPD.

★ 1543 ★

Retailing - Jewelry (SIC 5944)

Online Jewelry Sales

Selected shares are shown in percent. Wal-Mart is the top retailer; Blue Nile is an online firm. Data refer to discounted jewelry; Zales & Tiffany & Co. target different customers.

Wal-Mart	3.5%
Blue Nile	1.0
Other	95.5

Source: *Puget Sound Business Journal*, December 14, 2001, p. 1.

★ 1544 ★

Retailing - Jewelry (SIC 5944)

Where We Buy Jewelry

"Other retailers" include art dealers, gift stores and warehouse clubs.

	($ bil.)	Share
Jewelry stores	$ 21.7	55.0%
Department stores	4.0	10.0
Non-store retailers	3.8	10.0
Discounters/mass	3.0	8.0
Apparel and accessory stores	3.0	8.0
Other general merchandisers	2.9	7.0
Other retailers	1.5	4.0

Source: *National Jeweler*, June 1, 2001, p. 38.

★ 1545 ★

Retailing - Hobbies (SIC 5945)

Retail Craft and Hobby Sales, 2000

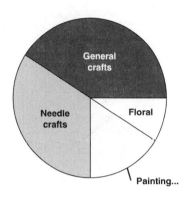

Consumers spent $23 billion on hobbies. Sales are shown by segment. "General crafts" includes cake decorating and candle making.

General crafts	41.0%
Needle crafts	34.0
Painting & finishing	16.0
Floral	9.0

Source: *Christian Science Monitor*, August 27, 2001, p. 12, from Hobby Industry Association.

★ 1546 ★

Retailing - Licensed Merchandise (SIC 5945)

Licensed Merchandise Sales

Sales of licensed products in Canada and the U.S. hit $17.8 billion in 2001.

Discounters	31.0%
Supermarkets/grocery stores	26.0
Specialty stores	13.0
Dealers, wholesalers, distributors	12.0
Department stores	5.0
Mail order	4.0
Other	3.0

Source: *Licensing Letter*, March 4, 2002, p. 3.

★ 1547 ★

Retailing - Toys (SIC 5945)

Largest Toy Chains, 2000

Market shares are shown in percent.

Wal-Mart	19.0%
Toys R Us	16.5

Continued on next page.

★ 1547 ★ *Continued*

Retailing - Toys (SIC 5945)

Largest Toy Chains, 2000

Market shares are shown in percent.

Kmart	7.4%
Target	7.2
KB Toys	4.7
Ames	1.9
J.C. Penney	1.4
Meijers	0.9
Big Lot	0.9

Source: "NPD Reports Top Ten Traditional Toy Retailers. " Retrieved May 16, 2001 from the World Wide Web: http://www.npd.com, from NPD Group.

★ 1548 ★

Retailing - Toys (SIC 5945)

Top Toy Retailers in Canada, 2001

Market shares are shown in percent.

Toys R Us	22.25%
Wal-Mart	21.10
Zellers	15.10
Canadian Tire	8.00
Costco	6.70
Sears Canada	5.40
Bay	3.60
Other	17.85

Source: *Globe and Mail*, December 27, 2001, p. B4, from Kubas Consultants.

★ 1549 ★

Retailing - Photographic Equipment (SIC 5946)

Digital Camera Sales by Outlet

Shares are for the first eight months of the year.

Electronic specialty channel	36.0%
Photo specialty channel	32.0
Computer & office superstores	17.0
Mass merchants	12.0
Other	3.0

Source: *Photo Trade News*, December 2001, p. 24, from NPD Intelect.

★ 1550 ★

Mail Order (SIC 5961)

Inflight Catalog Market

Figures are for North America.

SkyMall	78.0%
Other	22.0

Source: "From In-flight to On-line." Retrieved May 2, 2002 from the World Wide Web: http://www.rayjutkins. com.

★ 1551 ★

Mail Order (SIC 5961)

Largest Apparel/Home Merchandise Catalogers, 2000

Firms are ranked by sales in millions of dollars.

J.C. Penney	$ 3,823
Federated Dept. Stores	1,940
Spiegel	1,711
Brylane	1,400
Land's End	1,355
L.L. Bean	1,110
Intimate Brands	962
Hanover Direct	603
Blair	575
Cornerstone Brands	485
Coldwater Creek	400

Source: *New York Times*, May 14, 2002, p. C10, from *Catalog Age*.

★ 1552 ★

Mail Order (SIC 5961)

Largest Catalogers, 2000

Firms are ranked by sales in millions of dollars.

Dell Computer Corp.	$ 31,890.0
IBM Corp.	7,575.0
W.W. Grainger	4,977.0
Corporate Express	4,054.3
J.C. Penney Co.	3,823.0
CDW Computer Centers	3,800.0
Office Depot	3,600.0
Staples	2,955.0
Micro Warehouse	2,564.8

Source: *Catalog Age*, August 2001, p. 1.

★ 1553 ★

Vending Machines (SIC 5962)

Cold Beverage Sales

Sales are for the four weeks ended October 28, 2001.

Coca-Cola Classic 12-oz.	10.07%
Pepsi-Cola 12-oz.	7.08
Pepsi-Cola 20-oz.	5.85
Diet Coke 12-oz.	5.26
Coke Classic 20-oz.	5.18
Dr. Pepper Original 12-oz.	4.35
Mountain Dew 12-oz.	3.89
Mountain Dew 20-oz.	3.41
Diet Pepsi 20-oz.	2.92
Diet Pepsi 12-oz.	2.66
Other	49.33

Source: *Automatic Merchandiser*, February 2002, p. 12, from Management Science Associates Inc.

★ 1554 ★

Vending Machines (SIC 5962)

Cold Drink Sales by Type, 2000

More cold beverage vending machines have begun to dispense bottles instead of cans. The bottle segment saw growth for the fifth consecutive year.

Can	69.7%
Bottle	12.8
Combination bottle/can	9.6
Can juice	4.6
Cup	2.7
Other	0.6

Source: *Research Alert*, April 19, 2002, p. 3, from Cygnus Business Media.

★ 1555 ★

Vending Machines (SIC 5962)

Popular OCS Companies

Figures show the companies that service single-cup brewers plan or would buy from.

Crane Merchandising Systems	28.3%
Keurig	15.9
Coffee Inn's	9.1
Zanussi (Brio)	8.0
Flavia Beverage Systems	7.4
Gevalia	6.9
Cafection Enterprises	6.3

Source: *Automatic Merchandiser*, February 2002, p. 40, from *Automatic Merchandiser Coffee Service Market Report*.

★ 1556 ★

Vending Machines (SIC 5962)

Vending Machine Product Sales

Dollar shares are shown in percent.

Salty snacks	30.58%
Chocolate	26.36
Cookies	9.66
Crackers	8.25
Non-chocolate	7.82
Pastry	7.79
Nuts & other	3.83

Continued on next page.

★ 1556 ★ *Continued*
Vending Machines (SIC 5962)

Vending Machine Product Sales

Dollar shares are shown in percent.

Gum	2.60%
M/W popcorn	1.31
Mints	1.15
Cereal bars	0.44

Source: *Food Institute Report*, August 27, 2001, p. 5, from InfoVend.

★ 1557 ★
Vending Machines (SIC 5962)

Vending Machine Sales

Data show projected revenue, in millions of dollars.

	($ mil.)	Share
Cold drink sales	$ 7,401.8	28.91%
Bagged chips	2,070.0	8.09
Candy bars	1,720.0	6.72
Pastries	985.0	3.85
Fresh-brew regular coffee	865.7	3.38
Frozen-prepared	534.6	2.09
Milk	461.2	1.80
Bagged/jumbo cookies	413.3	1.61
Bagged/boxed candy	301.7	1.18
Cracker sandwiches	295.2	1.15
Gum/mints	269.0	1.05

Source: *Food Institute Report*, January 28, 2002, p. 9, from *Automatic Merchandiser*.

★ 1558 ★
Retailing - Propane (SIC 5983)

Leading Propane Retailers

Firms are ranked by fiscal year retail sales, in thousands of gallons.

AmeriGas Partners	1,089.0
Ferrellgas Partners	956.7
Cenex Propane Partners	613.2
Suburban Propane Partners	525.0
Heritage Propane Partners	400.0
CornerStone Propane	275.4

Star Gas Propane	136.8
Inergy	117.0
MFA Oil Co.	102.5
Agway Energy Products	98.5

Source: *LP/Gas*, February 2002, p. 24.

★ 1559 ★
Retailing - Flowers (SIC 5992)

Retail Poinsettia Market

Consumers spent $103 million on 13.6 million poinsettias in 2000.

Supermarkets	26.0%
Discount stores	19.0
Garden centers	13.0
Home centers	11.0
Florists	7.0
Other	24.0

Source: *USA TODAY*, December 20, 2001, p. D1, from Consumer Tracking Study collected by Ipsos NPD and American Floral Endowment.

★ 1560 ★
Retailing - Magazines (SIC 5994)

Where Magazines Are Sold

Market shares are shown in percent.

Grocers	45.1%
Mass	16.2
Book stores	10.5
Drug stores	9.0
Terminals	5.8
Convenience stores	5.5
News stands	3.6
Other	4.4

Source: *Supermarket News*, May 21, 2001, p. 62.

★ 1561 ★
Optical Goods Stores (SIC 5995)

Largest Optical Goods Retailers

Firms are ranked by sales in millions of dollars.

LensCrafters	$ 1,253.3
Cole Vision	1,022.0
Wal-Mart Stores	368.5
Eye Care Centers of America	345.5
Vista Eyecare	300.0
Consolidated Vision Group	190.0
Costco Wholesale	189.0
U.S. Vision	147.5
Sterling Vision	119.5
D.O.C. Optics	110.2

Source: *20/20 Magazine*, April 2001, p. 3.

★ 1562 ★
Retailing - Sunglasses (SIC 5995)

Retail Sunglasses Market

Market share is for shopping mall sunglasses market.

Sunglass Hut	90.0%
Other	10.0

Source: "Oakley Sews Red." Retrieved February 8, 2002 from the World Wide Web: http://www.forbes.com.

★ 1563 ★
Retailing - General Merchandise (SIC 5999)

Retail Baby Powder Sales, 2001

Market shares are shown in percent.

Discount stores	38.0%
Food/drug	28.0
Chain drug stores	23.0
Supermarkets	9.0
Other	2.0

Source: *Chain Drug Review*, January 7, 2002, p. 64, from Information Resources Inc.

★ 1564 ★
Retailing - General Merchandise (SIC 5999)

Retail Battery/Flashlight Sales

Sales are shown by percent.

Discounters	53.8%
Drug stores	24.5
Supermarkets	21.7

Source: *MMR*, May 28, 2001, p. 33, from A.C. Nielsen.

★ 1565 ★
Retailing - General Merchandise (SIC 5999)

Retail Broom/Mop Market, 2001

Sales are shown by outlet for the year ended September 2001.

Mass	55.5%
Food	32.1
Drugs	7.4

Source: *Grocery Headquarters*, December 2001, p. 48, from A.C. Nielsen.

★ 1566 ★
Retailing - General Merchandise (SIC 5999)

Retail Candle Sales

Sales are shown by outlet.

Supermarkets	38.3%
Mass	30.3
Drug stores	9.0
Other	22.4

Source: *Progressive Grocer*, October 2001, p. 8, from A.C. Nielsen.

★ 1567 ★
Retailing - General Merchandise (SIC 5999)

Retail Canning Supply Sales

Sales are shown by outlet.

Supermarkets	59.5%
Mass	19.0
Drug stores	1.4
Other	20.1

Source: *Progressive Grocer*, October 2001, p. 8, from A.C. Nielsen.

★ 1568 ★

Retailing - General Merchandise (SIC 5999)

Retail Charcoal Market, 2001

Sales are shown by outlet for the year ended September 2001.

Food 78.0%
Mass 20.1
Drug 1.8

Source: *Grocery Headquarters*, December 2001, p. 48, from A.C. Nielsen.

★ 1569 ★

Retailing - General Merchandise (SIC 5999)

Retail Chewing Tobacco Market, 2001

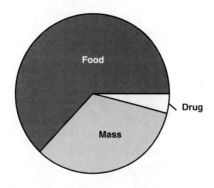

Sales are shown by outlet for the year ended September 2001.

Food 62.7%
Mass 33.4
Drug 3.9

Source: *Grocery Headquarters*, December 2001, p. 48, from A.C. Nielsen.

★ 1570 ★

Retailing - General Merchandise (SIC 5999)

Retail Cigarette Market

Sales are shown by outlet for the year ended September 2001.

Food 64.1%
Drug stores 22.0
Mass 13.8

Source: *Grocery Headquarters*, December 2001, p. 48, from A.C. Nielsen.

★ 1571 ★

Retailing - General Merchandise (SIC 5999)

Retail Condom Sales

Sales are shown by outlet.

	($ mil.)	Share
Drug	$ 151.3	55.26%
Mass	69.7	25.46
Food	52.8	19.28

Source: *Grocery Headquarters*, May 2001, p. 107.

★ 1572 ★

Retailing - General Merchandise (SIC 5999)

Retail Diaper Market

Sales are shown by outlet for the year ended September 2001.

Mass 46.9%
Food 42.6
Drug 10.5

Source: *Grocery Headquarters*, December 2001, p. 48, from A.C. Nielsen.

★ 1573 ★

Retailing - General Merchandise (SIC 5999)

Retail Disposable Dishes Market

Sales are shown by outlet for the year ended September 2001.

Food 66.7%
Mass 29.5
Drug 3.8

Source: *Grocery Headquarters*, December 2001, p. 48, from A.C. Nielsen.

★ 1574 ★

Retailing - General Merchandise (SIC 5999)

Retail Dry Battery Sales

Sales are shown by segment.

	($ mil.)	Share
Mass	$ 1,357.2	52.17%
Food	630.8	24.25
Drug stores	613.4	23.58

Source: *Drug Store News*, September 10, 2001, p. 45, from Information Resources Inc.

★ 1575 ★
Retailing - General Merchandise (SIC 5999)
Retail Fabric Softener Market

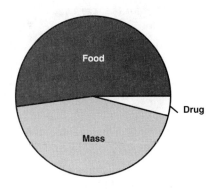

Sales are shown by outlet for the year ended September 2001.

Food	51.8%
Mass	44.4
Drug	3.8

Source: *Grocery Headquarters*, December 2001, p. 48, from A.C. Nielsen.

★ 1576 ★
Retailing - General Merchandise (SIC 5999)
Retail Kitchen Gadget Sales

Sales are shown by outlet.

Supermarkets	38.4%
Mass	33.5
Drug stores	3.5
Other	27.6

Source: *Progressive Grocer*, October 2001, p. 8, from A.C. Nielsen.

★ 1577 ★
Retailing - General Merchandise (SIC 5999)
Retail Laundry/Ironing Aid Market, 2001

Sales are shown by outlet for the year ended September 2001.

Mass	71.1%
Food	18.2
Drug	10.6

Source: *Grocery Headquarters*, December 2001, p. 48, from A.C. Nielsen.

★ 1578 ★
Retailing - General Merchandise (SIC 5999)
Retail Liquid Soap Sales, 2000

Sales are shown by segment.

	($ mil.)	Share
Food	$ 649.0	47.83%
Mass	579.2	42.69
Drug	128.6	9.48

Source: *Drug Store News*, May 21, 2001, p. 51, from Information Resources Inc.

★ 1579 ★
Retailing - General Merchandise (SIC 5999)
Retail Oral Rinse Brands, 2001

Market shares are shown in percent.

Discount	38.0%
Food/drug	26.0
Chain drug stores	22.0
Supermarkets	13.0

Source: *Chain Drug Review*, January 7, 2002, p. 64, from Information Resources Inc.

★ 1580 ★
Retailing - General Merchandise (SIC 5999)
Retail Pet Accessory Market

Sales are shown by outlet for the year ended September 2001.

Mass	29.9%
Food	17.9
Drug	2.2
Other	51.0

Source: *Grocery Headquarters*, December 2001, p. 48, from A.C. Nielsen.

★ 1581 ★

Retailing - General Merchandise (SIC 5999)

Retail Pet Food Sales

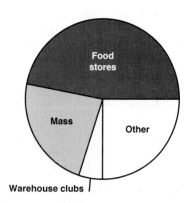

The North American pet food industry is valued at $8.9 billion. Market shares are shown in percent.

Food stores 47.0%
Mass 23.0
Warehouse clubs 5.0
Other 25.0

Source: *Point of Purchase*, September 2001, p. 12, from A. C. Nielsen.

★ 1582 ★

Retailing - General Merchandise (SIC 5999)

Retail Plastic Wrap Market, 2001

Sales are shown by outlet for the year ended September 2001.

Food 74.0%
Mass 23.2
Drug 2.8

Source: *Grocery Headquarters*, December 2001, p. 48, from A.C. Nielsen.

★ 1583 ★

Retailing - General Merchandise (SIC 5999)

Retail Rug Cleaner Market, 2001

Sales are shown by outlet for the year ended September 2001.

Food 49.6%
Mass 45.3
Drug 5.1

Source: *Grocery Headquarters*, December 2001, p. 48, from A.C. Nielsen.

★ 1584 ★

Retailing - General Merchandise (SIC 5999)

Retail Scouring Pad Market, 2001

Sales are shown by outlet for the year ended September 2001.

Food 62.2%
Mass 32.7
Drug 5.2

Source: *Grocery Headquarters*, December 2001, p. 48, from A.C. Nielsen.

★ 1585 ★

Retailing - General Merchandise (SIC 5999)

Retail Tall Kitchen Bags Market, 2001

Sales are shown by outlet for the year ended September 2001.

Food 59.7%
Mass 34.8
Drug 5.8

Source: *Grocery Headquarters*, December 2001, p. 48, from A.C. Nielsen.

★ 1586 ★

Retailing - General Merchandise (SIC 5999)

Retail Toilet Tissue Market

Sales are shown by outlet for the year ended September 2001.

Food 60.4%
Mass 34.8
Drug stores 3.8

Source: *Grocery Headquarters*, December 2001, p. 48, from A.C. Nielsen.

★ 1587 ★

Retailing - Personal Care (SIC 5999)

Retail Arthritis Remedy Sales

Sales include rubs and patches.

Drugs 61.1%
Mass 39.7

Source: *Drug Store News*, December 17, 2001, p. 67, from A.C. Nielsen.

★ 1588 ★

Retailing - Personal Care (SIC 5999)

Retail Ethnic Hair Care Sales

Market shares are shown in percent.

Drug stores 43.9%
Discounters 38.6
Supermarkets 17.5

Source: *MMR*, September 3, 2001, p. 53, from A.C. Nielsen.

★ 1589 ★

Retailing - Personal Care (SIC 5999)

Retail Eye/Lens Care Sales, 2001

Unit shares are for the year ended July 14, 2001.

Discounters 43.3%
Drug stores 31.5
Supermarkets 25.2

Source: *MMR*, September 3, 2001, p. 54, from A.C. Nielsen.

★ 1590 ★

Retailing - Personal Care (SIC 5999)

Retail Foot Care Sales

Sales are shown in millions of dollars.

	($ mil.)	Share
Mass	$ 139.8	39.61%
Drug	139.2	39.44
Food	73.9	20.94

Source: *Grocery Headquarters*, June 2001, p. 67.

★ 1591 ★

Retailing - Personal Care (SIC 5999)

Retail Natural Vitamin Sales

Sales of natural vitamins and minerals hit $430.3 million for the year ended November 2001. Market shares are shown in percent.

Drug 47.1%
Food 33.3
Discount 19.6

Source: *Chain Drug Review*, February 18, 2002, p. 40, from SPINS/A.C. Nielsen.

★ 1592 ★

Retailing - Personal Care (SIC 5999)

Retail Suntan Lotion Sales, 2001

Sales are shown for the year ended March 25, 2001.

	($ mil.)	Share
Mass	$ 213.2	41.46%
Drug	176.4	34.31
Food	124.6	24.23

Source: *Drug Store News*, June 25, 2001, p. 167, from Information Resources Inc.

★ 1593 ★

Retailing - Personal Care (SIC 5999)

U.S. Bath Soap Industry, 2001

Sales are shown for the year ended July 14, 2001.

Discounters 44.1%
Supermarkets 40.0
Drug stores 15.9

Source: *MMR*, September 3, 2001, p. 40, from A.C. Nielsen.

★ 1594 ★

Retailing - Personal Care (SIC 5999)

U.S. Deodorant Industry, 2001

Sales are shown for the year ended July 14, 2001.

Discounters 41.5%
Supermarkets 36.5
Drug stores 22.0

Source: *MMR*, September 3, 2001, p. 40, from A.C. Nielsen.

★ 1595 ★

Retailing - Personal Care (SIC 5999)

Where People Purchased Supplements in Canada

Market shares are shown in percent.

Drug stores 51.0%
Health food retailers 18.0
Grocery stores 9.0
Zellers 6.0
Wal-Mart 6.0
Costco Wholesale Corp. 6.0
Other 4.0

Source: *Globe and Mail*, February 15, 2002, p. 4, from Ipsos-Reid.

SIC 60 - Depository Institutions

★ 1596 ★
Banking (SIC 6020)
Top Banks, 2001

Banks are ranked by deposits, in millions.

Bank of America, National Association	$ 321.7
Chase Manhattan Bank	138.2
First Union National Bank	131.4
Fleet National Bank	108.2
Citibank	76.8
Washington Mutual Bank	74.0
Wells Fargo Bank	69.6
SunTrust Bank	60.2
Bank One, National Association	56.7
Merrill Lynch Bank USA	54.9

Source: *Community Banker*, January 2002, p. 30, from Federal Deposit Insurance Corp.

★ 1597 ★
Banking (SIC 6020)
Top Banks in Alaska

Market shares are shown based on deposits as of June 30, 2000.

National Bank of Alaska	45.61%
First National Bank of Anchorage	20.68
Northrim Bank	10.39
Keybank National Association	9.24
First Bank	5.36
Mt. McKinley Mutual Savings Bank	2.92
Other	5.80

Source: "Market Share Report." Retrieved November 9, 2001 from the World Wide Web: http://www.fdic.gov, from Federal Deposit Insurance Corp.

★ 1598 ★
Banking (SIC 6020)
Top Banks in American Samoa, 2001

Market shares are shown based on deposits for June 30, 2001.

American Samoa Bank	51.09%
Bank of Hawaii	48.91

Source: "Market Share Report." Retrieved March 28, 2002 from the World Wide Web: http://www.fdic.gov, from Federal Deposit Insurance Corp.

★ 1599 ★
Banking (SIC 6020)
Top Banks in Atlanta, GA

Market shares are shown in percent.

Bank of America	15.1%
SunTrust Banks	14.7
First Union	11.5
SouthTrust Bank	6.2
Regions Bank	4.5
Delta Employees Credit Union	2.3
Premier Bank	2.2
Atlanta Postal Credit Union	1.5
Other	42.0

Source: *Atlanta Journal-Constitution*, August 4, 2001, p. 1F, from Sheshunoff Information Services.

★ 1600 ★
Banking (SIC 6020)
Top Banks in Benton County, AK

Market shares are shown based on deposits as of June 30, 2001.

Bank of Bentonville	23.75%
Arvest Bank	19.48
Arkansas National Bank	10.88
First Arvest Bank	7.97

Continued on next page.

351

★ 1600 ★ *Continued*

Banking (SIC 6020)

Top Banks in Benton County, AK

Market shares are shown based on deposits as of June 30, 2001.

Bank of Gravett	6.82%
Regions Bank	6.48
Decatur State Bank	4.88
Other	19.74

Source: *Arkansas Business*, December 17, 2001, p. 21, from Federal Deposit Insurance Corp.

★ 1601 ★

Banking (SIC 6020)

Top Banks in California, 2001

Market shares are shown based on deposits for June 30, 2001.

Bank of America, National Association . . .	22.06%
Wells Fargo Bank, National Association . .	13.93
Washington Mutual Bank	12.14
Union Bank of California, National Association	5.14
California Federal Bank	4.45
World Savings Bank, FSB	3.85
Downey Savings and Loan Association . . .	1.82

Source: ''Market Share Report.'' Retrieved March 28, 2002 from the World Wide Web: http://www.fdic.gov, from Federal Deposit Insurance Corp.

★ 1602 ★

Banking (SIC 6020)

Top Banks in Canada

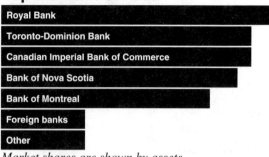

Market shares are shown by assets.

	($ bil.)	Share
Royal Bank	.$ 205.2	19.73%
Toronto-Dominion Bank	187.8	18.06
Canadian Imperial Bank of Commerce	183.5	17.65
Bank of Nova Scotia	179.3	17.24
Bank of Montreal	153.3	14.74
Foreign banks	66.5	6.40
Other	64.2	6.17

Source: *Wall Street Journal*, August 2, 2001, p. A11, from Canadian Bankers Association.

★ 1603 ★

Banking (SIC 6020)

Top Banks in Cecil County, MD

Market shares are shown in percent.

County Banking and Trust Co.	40.0%
Peoples Bank of Elton	14.0
National Bank of Rising Sun	14.0
First National Bank of North East	14.0
Cecil Federal Savings Bank	14.0
Other	4.0

Source: *Baltimore Business Journal*, December 21, 2001, p. 7.

★ 1604 ★

Banking (SIC 6020)

Top Banks in Colorado

Market shares are shown based on deposits as of June 30, 2000.

Wells Fargo Bank West National Association	18.36%
U.S. National Bank Association	10.97

Continued on next page.

★ 1604 ★ *Continued*
Banking (SIC 6020)

Top Banks in Colorado

Market shares are shown based on deposits as of June 30, 2000.

World Savings Bank	5.56%
Bank One, Colorado, National Association . .	5.46
Commercial Federal Bank, a Federal Savings Bank	4.46
Vectra Bank Colorado, National Association .	2.83
Community First National Bank	2.75
Other	49.61

Source: "Market Share Report." Retrieved November 9, 2001 from the World Wide Web: http://www.fdic.gov, from Federal Deposit Insurance Corp.

★ 1605 ★
Banking (SIC 6020)

Top Banks in Delaware

Market shares are shown based on deposits as of June 30, 2000.

MBNA America Bank	31.67%
Greenwood Trust Company	21.44
Chase Manhattan Bank USA, National Association	9.89
First USA Bank, National Association . . .	8.69
Wilmington Trust Company	8.59
PNC Bank, Delaware	3.16
Advanta National Bank	3.11
Other	13.45

Source: "Market Share Report." Retrieved November 9, 2001 from the World Wide Web: http://www.fdic.gov, from Federal Deposit Insurance Corp.

★ 1606 ★
Banking (SIC 6020)

Top Banks in Florida

Market shares are shown in percent.

Lloyds TSB	28.5%
Barclays	20.6
Dresdner	8.3
Banco Bilbao	5.1
ABN-AMRO	4.1
Other	33.4

Source: *Florida Trend*, October 2001, p. 74, from Federal Reserve.

★ 1607 ★
Banking (SIC 6020)

Top Banks in Georgia

Market shares are shown based on deposits for June 30, 2001.

SunTrust Bank	11.87%
Bank of America, National Association . . .	11.62
Wachovia Bank, National Association . . .	9.74
First Union National Bank	7.87
Regions Bank	5.93
SouthTrust Bank	4.84
Branch Banking and Trust Company	4.00
Other	44.13

Source: "Market Share Report." Retrieved March 28, 2002 from the World Wide Web: http://www.fdic.gov, from Federal Deposit Insurance Corp.

★ 1608 ★
Banking (SIC 6020)

Top Banks in Guam, 2001

Market shares are shown based on deposits for June 30, 2001.

Bank of Guam	26.88%
Bank of Hawaii	23.19
First Hawaii	13.25
Citibank N.A.	12.03
Union Bank of California, National Association	8.18
Citizens Security Bank (Guam) Inc.	6.58
Other	90.11

Source: "Market Share Report." Retrieved March 28, 2002 from the World Wide Web: http://www.fdic.gov, from Federal Deposit Insurance Corp.

★ 1609 ★

Banking (SIC 6020)

Top Banks in Hawaii

Market shares are shown based on deposits for June 30, 2001.

First Hawaiian Bank	30.28%
Bank of Hawaii	29.56
American Savings Bank, FSB	19.70
Central Pacific Bank	7.57
City Bank	6.44
Territorial Savings and Loan Association	2.17
Other	4.18

Source: "Market Share Report." Retrieved March 28, 2002 from the World Wide Web: http://www.fdic.gov, from Federal Deposit Insurance Corp.

★ 1610 ★

Banking (SIC 6020)

Top Banks in Idaho

First Security Bank, National Association
U.S. Bank National Association
Keybank National Association
Bank of America, National Association
Wells Fargo Bank, National Association
Washington Federal Savings and Loan Association
Bank of Commerce
Other

Market shares are shown based on deposits as of June 30, 2000.

First Security Bank, National Association	29.94%
U.S. Bank National Association	22.01
Keybank National Association	6.24
Bank of America, National Association	4.15
Wells Fargo Bank, National Association	3.86
Washington Federal Savings and Loan Association	3.83
Bank of Commerce	3.04
Other	26.93

Source: "Market Share Report." Retrieved November 9, 2001 from the World Wide Web: http://www.fdic.gov, from Federal Deposit Insurance Corp.

★ 1611 ★

Banking (SIC 6020)

Top Banks in Ilinois, 2001

Market shares are shown based on deposits for June 30, 2001.

Bank One, National Association	10.76%
LaSalle Bank National Association	9.93
Harris Trust and Savings Bank	3.68
Northern Trust Company	3.65
Citibank, Federal Savings Bank	3.23
Hosuehold Bank, FSB	2.71
American National Bank and Trust Company of Chicago	2.69
Other	63.44

Source: "Market Share Report." Retrieved March 28, 2002 from the World Wide Web: http://www.fdic.gov, from Federal Deposit Insurance Corp.

★ 1612 ★

Banking (SIC 6020)

Top Banks in Indiana, 2001

Market shares are shown based on deposits for June 30, 2001.

Bank One, Indiana, National Association	12.24%
National City Bank of Indiana	10.22
Old National Bank	6.35
Fifth Third Bank, Indiana	5.64
1st Source Bank	3.52
Union Planters Bank, National Association	2.52
Other	59.51

Source: "Market Share Report." Retrieved March 28, 2002 from the World Wide Web: http://www.fdic.gov, from Federal Deposit Insurance Corp.

★ 1613 ★

Banking (SIC 6020)

Top Banks in Indianapolis, MD

Market shares are shown in percent.

National City	24.9%
Bank One	24.1
Union Federal	7.4
Fifth Third	7.1
First Indiana	6.6
Union Planters	3.9
Key Bank	3.1

Continued on next page.

★ 1613 ★ *Continued*
Banking (SIC 6020)

Top Banks in Indianapolis, MD

Market shares are shown in percent.

Huntington National	2.2%
Other	20.7

Source: *Indianapolis Star*, March 25, 2002, p. C1, from Federal Deposit Insurance Corp.

★ 1614 ★
Banking (SIC 6020)

Top Banks in Iowa, 2001

Market shares are shown based on deposits for June 30, 2001.

Wells Fargo Bank Iowa, National Association	13.07%
First Bank, National Association	8.88
Commercial Federal Bank, A Federal Savings Bank	2.90
Bankers Trust Company, National Association	1.94
Principal Bank	1.55
Other	71.66

Source: "Market Share Report." Retrieved March 28, 2002 from the World Wide Web: http://www.fdic.gov, from Federal Deposit Insurance Corp.

★ 1615 ★
Banking (SIC 6020)

Top Banks in Los Angeles, California

Market shares are shown based on deposits for June 30, 2001.

Bank of America, National Association	22.36%
Washington Mutual Bank	12.84
Wells Fargo Bank, National Association	8.91
Union Bank of California, National Association	6.08
California Federal Bank	4.87
City National Bank	3.75
Imperial Bank	3.14

Source: "Market Share Report." Retrieved March 28, 2002 from the World Wide Web: http://www.fdic.gov, from Federal Deposit Insurance Corp.

★ 1616 ★
Banking (SIC 6020)

Top Banks in Maine

Market shares are shown based on deposits as of June 30, 2000.

Peoples Heritage Bank, National Bank	21.26%
Keybank National Association	13.99
Fleet Bank of Maine	9.28
Bangor Savings Bank	7.08
Camden National Bank	3.29
Gardiner Savings Institution	2.54
Kennebunk Savings Bank	2.32
Other	59.76

Source: "Market Share Report." Retrieved November 9, 2001 from the World Wide Web: http://www.fdic.gov, from Federal Deposit Insurance Corp.

★ 1617 ★
Banking (SIC 6020)

Top Banks in Maui, Hawaii

Market shares are shown based on deposits for June 30, 2001.

First Hawaiian Bank	33.92%
Bank of Hawaii	32.94
American Savings Bank	22.10
City Bank	3.26
Territorial Savings and Loan Association	2.40
Other	5.38

Source: "Market Share Report." Retrieved March 28, 2002 from the World Wide Web: http://www.fdic.gov, from Federal Deposit Insurance Corp.

★ 1618 ★

Banking (SIC 6020)

Top Banks in Miami-Dade FL, 2001

Market shares are shown based on deposits for June 30, 2001.

Bank of America, National Association . . . 18.24%
First Union National Bank 13.99
Ocean Bank 7.74
SunTrust Bank 6.68
Union Planters Bank, National Association . . 6.66
Washington Mutual Bank 6.05
Citibank, Federal Savings Bank 4.90
Other 35.74

Source: "Market Share Report." Retrieved March 28, 2002 from the World Wide Web: http://www.fdic.gov, from Federal Deposit Insurance Corp.

★ 1619 ★

Banking (SIC 6020)

Top Banks in Michigan

Market shares are shown based on deposits as of June 30, 2000.

Comerica Bank 15.14%
Bank One, Michigan 14.50
Old Kent Bank 9.02
Standard Federal Bank 8.42
National City Bank of Michigan/Illinois . . . 7.18
Michigan National Bank 7.05
Huntington National Bank 3.62
Other 35.07

Source: "Market Share Report." Retrieved November 9, 2001 from the World Wide Web: http://www.fdic.gov, from Federal Deposit Insurance Corp.

★ 1620 ★

Banking (SIC 6020)

Top Banks in Monterey, CA, 2001

Market shares are shown based on deposits for June 30, 2001.

Washington Mutual Bank 19.38%
Wells Fargo Bank, National Association . . . 16.78
Bank of America, National Association . . . 15.19
Community Bank of Central California . . . 14.37
First National Bank of Central California . . 12.90
World Savings Bank, FSB 9.25
Other 12.13

Source: "Market Share Report." Retrieved March 28, 2002 from the World Wide Web: http://www.fdic.gov, from Federal Deposit Insurance Corp.

★ 1621 ★

Banking (SIC 6020)

Top Banks in Napa, California

Market shares are shown based on deposits for June 30, 2001.

Bank of America, National Association . . . 17.79%
Wells Fargo Bank, National Association . . . 16.58
Vintage Bank 14.08
Westamerica Bank 14.02
California Federal Bank 8.09
World Savings Bank 7.98

Source: "Market Share Report." Retrieved March 28, 2002 from the World Wide Web: http://www.fdic.gov, from Federal Deposit Insurance Corp.

★ 1622 ★
Banking (SIC 6020)

Top Banks in New Jersey

Market shares are shown based on deposits as of June 30, 2000.

Summit Bank	14.27%
First Union National Bank	11.65
Fleet Bank, National Association	8.26
PNC Bank, National Association	7.96
Hudson City Savings Bank	4.37
Sovereign Bank	4.29
Merrill Lynch Bank and Trust Company	3.78
Other	45.42

Source: "Market Share Report." Retrieved November 9, 2001 from the World Wide Web: http://www.fdic.gov, from Federal Deposit Insurance Corp.

★ 1623 ★
Banking (SIC 6020)

Top Banks in Ohio

Market shares are shown based on deposits as of June 30, 2000.

Keybank National Association	11.01%
National City Bank	9.35
Bank One, National Association	8.70
Firstar Bank, National Association	6.65
Huntington National Bank	5.05
Firstmerit National Association	4.51
Provident Bank	4.30
Other	50.43

Source: "Market Share Report." Retrieved November 9, 2001 from the World Wide Web: http://www.fdic.gov, from Federal Deposit Insurance Corp.

★ 1624 ★
Banking (SIC 6020)

Top Banks in Orange County, California

Market shares are shown based on deposits for June 30, 2001.

Bank of America, National Association	19.11%
Washington Mutual Bank, FA	13.53
Wells Fargo Bank, National Association	12.72
Downey Savings and Loan Association	5.42
World Savings Bank	5.18
California Federal Bank	5.05
Other	38.99

Source: "Market Share Report." Retrieved March 28, 2002 from the World Wide Web: http://www.fdic.gov, from Federal Deposit Insurance Corp.

★ 1625 ★
Banking (SIC 6020)

Top Banks in Oregon

Banks are ranked by deposits, in billions.

The Bank of Nova Scotia	$ 8.4
U.S. Bank	7.9
Wells Fargo Bank	3.9
Washington Mutual	3.9
Bank of America	3.3

Source: *Oregon Business*, November 2001, p. 45.

★ 1626 ★
Banking (SIC 6020)

Top Banks in Philadelphia, PA

Market shares are shown based on deposits.

First Union Corp.	23.92%
PNC Bank Corp.	13.23
Mellon Bank	11.24
Commerce Bancorp Inc.	5.83
Summit Bancorp.	4.57
Soverign Bank	3.93
Hudson United Bancorp.	2.17

Continued on next page.

★ 1626 ★ *Continued*
Banking (SIC 6020)

Top Banks in Philadelphia, PA

Market shares are shown based on deposits.

Beneficial Savings Bank	2.04%
Commonwealth Bank	1.68
Other	31.39

Source: *Philadelphia Business Journal*, July 13, 2001, p. 22.

★ 1627 ★
Banking (SIC 6020)

Top Banks in Pulaski County, AK

Market shares are shown based on deposits as of June 30, 2001.

Regions Bank	22.61%
Bank of America	20.71
Firstar Bank	11.45
Metropolitan National Bank	9.49
Pulaski Bank & Trust Co.	5.22
Bank of the Ozarks	4.37
Other	26.15

Source: *Arkansas Business*, December 17, 2001, p. 21, from Federal Deposit Insurance Corp.

★ 1628 ★
Banking (SIC 6020)

Top Banks in Sacramento, CA

Market shares are shown in percent.

Bank of America	21.03%
Wells Fargo Bank	16.22
U.S. Bank	6.94
Bank of the West	5.41

Union Bank of California	2.51%
California Bank and Trust	2.11
Westamerica Bank	1.59
Other	44.19

Source: *Sacramento Business Journal*, June 1, 2001, p. 12.

★ 1629 ★
Banking (SIC 6020)

Top Banks in Santa Barbara, California

Market shares are shown based on deposits for June 30, 2001.

Santa Barbara Bank & Trust	27.42%
Bank of America, National Association	12.94
Washington Mutual Bank	11.29
Mid-State Bank & Trust	10.01
Wells Fargo Bank, National Association	7.93
World Savings Bank, FSB	7.22
Other	23.19

Source: "Market Share Report." Retrieved March 28, 2002 from the World Wide Web: http://www.fdic.gov, from Federal Deposit Insurance Corp.

★ 1630 ★
Banking (SIC 6020)

Top Banks in South Dakota

Market shares are shown based on deposits as of June 30, 2000.

Norwest Bank South Dakota, National Association	14.96%
Citibank	12.41
U.S. Bank National Association	4.45
Home Federal Savings Bank	4.23
First Premier	4.14
Dacotah Bank	3.71
Marquette Bank, National Association	3.18
Other	52.92

Source: "Market Share Report." Retrieved November 9, 2001 from the World Wide Web: http://www.fdic.gov, from Federal Deposit Insurance Corp.

★ 1631 ★
Banking (SIC 6020)

Top Banks in Vermont

Market shares are shown based on deposits as of June 30, 2000.

Chittenden Trust Company	28.33%
Charter One Bank F.S.B.	9.71
Howard Bank, National Association	9.11
Merchants Bank	8.33
First Vermont Bank, National Association	7.40
Keybank National Association	6.27
Northfield Savings Bank	3.92
Other	26.93

Source: "Market Share Report." Retrieved November 9, 2001 from the World Wide Web: http://www.fdic.gov, from Federal Deposit Insurance Corp.

★ 1632 ★
Banking (SIC 6020)

Top Banks in Washington D.C.

Market shares are shown based on deposits as of June 30, 2000.

Riggs Bank, National Association	22.49%
Bank of America, National Association	18.93
First Union National Bank	15.20
Citibank	14.02
SunTrust Bank	10.19
Branch Banking and Trust Company	5.01
Allfirst Bank	2.05
Other	12.11

Source: "Market Share Report." Retrieved November 9, 2001 from the World Wide Web: http://www.fdic.gov, from Federal Deposit Insurance Corp.

★ 1633 ★
Banking (SIC 6020)

Top Banks in Washington State

Market shares are shown in percent.

Suntrust Bank	15.55%
Bank of America	14.77
Chevy Chase Bank	10.75
First Union	9.48

E Trade Bank	6.57%
Riggs Bank	5.70
Capital One Financial	5.42
Other	31.76

Source: *Washington Business Journal*, Annual 2002, p. 24.

★ 1634 ★
Banking (SIC 6020)

Top Banks in Westchester County, NY

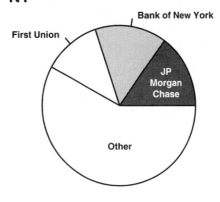

Market shares are shown based on deposits.

JP Morgan Chase	15.0%
Bank of New York	14.7
First Union	12.3
Other	58.0

Source: *Westchester County Business Journal*, May 13, 2002, p. 2, from Union State.

★ 1635 ★
Banking (SIC 6020)

Top Banks in Wisconsin

Market shares are shown based on deposits as of June 30, 2000.

Firstar Bank, National Association	10.87%
M&I Marshall and Ilsley Bank	7.30
Bank One, Wisconsin	5.51
Associated Bank Milwaukee	2.64

Continued on next page.

★ 1635 ★ *Continued*
Banking (SIC 6020)

Top Banks in Wisconsin

Market shares are shown based on deposits as of June 30, 2000.

AnchorBank S.S.B.	2.54%
Norwest Bank Wisconsin	2.40
M&I Bank of Southern Wisconsin	2.24
Other	66.50

Source: "Market Share Report." Retrieved November 9, 2001 from the World Wide Web: http://www.fdic.gov, from Federal Deposit Insurance Corp.

★ 1636 ★
Banking (SIC 6021)

Largest Banks and S&Ls by Assets

Figures are in millions of dollars.

Citigroup	$ 1,068.2
J.P. Morgan Chase & Co.	799.3
Bank of America Corp.	640.1
Wachovia Corp.	325.8
Wells Fargo & Co.	298.1
Bank One Corp.	270.2
MetLife Inc.	251.8
Washington Mutual Inc.	223.6
Taunus Corp.	217.4

Source: *American Banker*, February 26, 2002, p. 7A.

★ 1637 ★
Banking (SIC 6021)

Leading U.S. Thrifts

Banks are ranked by total assets in billions of dollars as of March 2001.

Washington Mutual	$ 246.98
Golden State Bancorp.	61.77
Golden West Financial	56.73
Charter One Financial	35.84
Sovereign Bancorp.	34.05

Source: *Wall Street Journal*, June 26, 2001, p. C1, from SNL Securities and First Manhattan Consulting.

★ 1638 ★
Banking (SIC 6021)

Top Trustee Banks, 2001

Amounts are in billions of dollars.

Bank of New York	$ 36.60
US Bank Corporate Trust Services	16.30
Banc One Capital Markets	13.20
Wells Fargo Bank	12.70
J.P. Morgan Chase & Co.	10.20
State Street Bank & Tust	10.10
Wachovia Securities	7.60
SunTrust Bank	5.20
National City Bank	4.46

Source: *Bond Buyer*, January 2, 2002, p. 1, from Thomson Financial Securities Data.

★ 1639 ★
Credit Unions (SIC 6060)

Credit Union Processing

The number of credit unions has fallen from 21,500 in 1980 to 10,600 in 2000.

Fiserv	23.0%
Fedcomp	14.0
EDS	13.0
Computer Consultants Corp.	7.0
Harland	4.0
ComputerSource Systems	4.0
Jack Henry	3.0
CU Processing	3.0
Other	29.0

Source: *Credit Union Magazine*, October 2001, p. 56, from NCUA and TowerGroup.

★ 1640 ★
Credit Unions (SIC 6060)

Largest Credit Unions

Data show total loans and leases in billions of dollars.

Navy Federal Credit Union	$ 10.0
State Employees Credit Union	6.4
Pentagon Federal Credit Union	3.2
Golden 1 Credit Union	2.5
Boeing Employees Credit Union	2.5
Suncoast Schools Federal Credit Union	2.1
Security Service FCCU	1.9
Orange County Teachers FCU	1.9

Continued on next page.

★ 1640 ★ *Continued*
Credit Unions (SIC 6060)

Largest Credit Unions

Data show total loans and leases in billions of dollars.

Citizens Equity First Credit Union . . . . .$ 1.7
American Airlines Federal Credit Union . . . 1.7

Source: *American Banker*, March 18, 2002, p. 24.

★ 1641 ★
Bankruptcies (SIC 6099)

Bankruptcy Filings by State

Data are for the six months ended August 2001.

Delaware 53.0%
New York 12.5
Other 34.5

Source: *Crain's New York Business*, August 27, 2001, p. 3.

★ 1642 ★
Bonds (SIC 6099)

Government Bond Holders

Nonresidents 34.7%
Central bank 15.5
Insurance companies, pension funds 14.7
Households 8.1
Public sector 7.6
Private banks 5.1
Other 14.3

Source: *Nikkei Weekly*, March 4, 2002, p. 4, from *Nihon Keizai Shimbun*.

★ 1643 ★
Check Processing (SIC 6099)

Check Processing Market Shares

Market shares are shown in percent. There is a wide market for electronic payments, but it only has a 2 percent penetration.

CheckFree Corp. 80.0%
Other 20.0

Source: *San Antonio Business Journal*, October 26, 2001, p. 28, from Legg Mason Wood Walker.

★ 1644 ★
Financial Services (SIC 6099)

Downscale Financial Services Industry

As many as 12 million Americans have no relationship with a bank or credit union. Increasing poverty and immigration has boosted the existence of firms to assist these lower-income groups. Data show fees earned in billions of dollars.

	1999	2002
Money transfer services	$ 2,762	$ 4,173
Payday loan services	1,056	1,876
Check cashing outlets	1,080	1,219

Source: *Research Alert*, May 3, 2002, p. 1, from Marketdata Enterprises.

★ 1645 ★
Payment Transaction Processing (SIC 6099)

Transaction Processing Market Shares

The market refers to all transactions involving credit, debit and other plastic payment cards. Companies house information, ship statements and are involved in similar duties.

In-house 47.0%
First Data 30.0
Total System 19.0
Other 4.0

Source: *Investor's Business Daily*, March 21, 2002, p. A14, from company reports and Legg Mason.

★ 1646 ★
Payment Transaction Processing (SIC 6099)

U.S. Payment Transactions

Although electronic payments are a small part of all payment transactions, they handled 90% of money that changed hands (checks had 11%).

	($ bil.)	Share
Cash transactions	.$ 550.0	82.3%
Check transactions	69.0	10.3
Electronic transactions	49.5	7.4

Source: *Infoworld*, October 22, 2001, p. 52, from National Automated Clearing House Association.

★ 1647 ★

Automated Wire Transfer Business

Market shares are shown in percent.

BankServ	80.0%
Other	20.0

Source: *PR Newswire*, January 31, 2002, p. NA.

SIC 61 - Nondepository Institutions

★ 1648 ★
Credit Cards (SIC 6141)

Credit Card Market, 2001

Shares are shown based on charge volume.

Visa	44.1%
MasterCard	31.3
American Express	16.7
Discover	6.9
Diner's Club	0.9

Source: *Credit Card Management*, May 2002, p. 30.

★ 1649 ★
Credit Cards (SIC 6141)

Leading Credit Card Processors

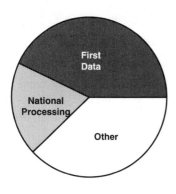

Market shares are shown in percent.

First Data	43.0%
National Processing	19.0
Other	38.0

Source: *Courier Journal*, January 23, 2002, p. 1, from National Processing.

★ 1650 ★
Credit Cards (SIC 6141)

Online Credit Card Market, 2000

Data show share of spending. Forrester Research predicts e-commerce wil reach $6.8 trillion world-wide in 2004.

	($ bil.)	Share
Visa	$ 25.96	50.4%
MasterCard	15.57	30.2
American Express	8.00	15.6
Discover	1.90	3.8

Source: *USA TODAY*, August 13, 2001, p. B1, from The Nilson Report.

★ 1651 ★
Credit Cards (SIC 6141)

Online Credit Card Market by Transactions

Figures are for the third quarter, based on transactions.

Visa	52.9%
Master Card	25.5
American Express	6.4
Discover	4.7
Other	10.5

Source: *Card Marketing*, March 2002, p. 8, from comScore Network.

★ 1652 ★
Credit Cards (SIC 6141)

Top Credit Card Firms in Mexico

Market shares are shown in percent.

BBVA Bancomer	36.0%
Banamex	35.0
Other	29.0

Source: *South American Business Information*, September 3, 2001, p. NA.

★ 1653 ★
Credit Cards (SIC 6141)

Top Credit Card Issuers

Firms are ranked by receivables in billions of dollars.

Citigroup Inc.	$ 103.2
MBNA America	78.1
Bank One Corp/First USA Bank	66.9
Discover Financial Services	47.1
The Chase Manhattan Corp.	36.2
American Express Centurion Bank	31.2
Providian Financial Corp.	27.1
Bank of America	24.2
Capital One Financial Corp.	24.1

Source: *Card Marketing*, October 2001, p. 24.

★ 1654 ★
Debit Cards (SIC 6141)

Debit Card Market

Market shares are shown based on transactions.

Visa Check Card	79.4%
Debit MasterCard	20.6

Source: *ATM & Debit News*, April 25, 2002, p. 2.

★ 1655 ★
Mortgage Loans (SIC 6162)

Top Mortgage Lenders in Baltimore, MD

Market shares are shown in percent.

Bank of America	6.2%
Wells Fargo	5.0
MNC Mortgage	4.1
Countrywide Home Loans	3.7
National City Mortgage Corp.	3.5

Chase Manhattan Mortgage Corp.	3.2%
NVR Mortgage Finance Inc.	2.3
Other	67.0

Source: *Baltimore Business Journal*, October 19, 2001, p. 19.

★ 1656 ★
Mortgage Loans (SIC 6162)

Top Mortgage Loan Providers, 2002

Shares are for the first quarter. Rankings cover the origination of mortgage loans for refinancings and purchases of residential properties.

Wells Fargo Home Mortgage	8.99%
Washington Mutual Bank	8.12
Bank of America	5.32
ABN AMRO Mortgage	2.79
America's Wholesale Lender	2.50
Countrywide Home Loans	2.37
Chase Manhattan Mortgage	2.18
Other	67.73

Source: *Mortgage Banking*, June 2002, p. 95.

★ 1657 ★
Mortgage Loans (SIC 6162)

Top Mortgage Processors in the North Central States

Market shares are shown in percent. Figures are for the first eleven months.

Wells Fargo Home Mortgage	4.52%
ABN AMRO Mortgage	4.27
Third Fed. S&L/Cleveland	1.90
Countrywide Home Loans	1.90
Washington Mutual Bank	1.66
Chase Manhattan Mortgage	1.61
National City Mortgage	1.35
Fifth Third Mortgage	1.28
Charter One Bank	1.25
Firstar Bank	1.22
Other	79.04

Source: *Mortgage Banking*, February 2002, p. 102, from MarketTrac.

★ 1658 ★

Mortgage Loans (SIC 6162)

Top Subprime Mortgage Lenders, 2001

Market shares are shown in percent.

Household Financial	10.5%
CitiFinancial	9.2
Washington Mutual	6.3
Option One	4.9
GMAC	4.5
Countrywide	3.7
New Century	3.6
First Franklin	3.6
Ameriquest	3.5
Bank of America	3.3
Other	46.9

Source: *Investor's Business Daily*, March 25, 2002, p. A10, from company reports, Friedman, Billings, Ramsey & Co., and Inside Mortgage Finance Publications.

★ 1659 ★

Loan Arrangers (SIC 6163)

Largest Commercial and Industrial Loan Providers

Figures are in millions of dollars.

Bank of America Corp.	$ 93.1
Bank One Corp.	50.9
Wachovia Corp.	50.4
FleetBoston Financial Corp.	44.8
Wells Fargo & Co.	42.5
J.P. Morgan Chase & Co.	42.5
Citigroup	41.9
U.S. Bancorp.	35.8
SunTrust Banks Inc.	23.8
Comerica Inc.	22.4

Source: *American Banker*, February 26, 2002, p. 7A.

★ 1660 ★

Loan Arrangers (SIC 6163)

Largest Construction/Land Development Loan Providers

Figures are in millions of dollars.

Bank of America Corp.	$ 12.1
Wells Fargo & Co.	7.9
Bank One Corp.	6.9

U.S. Bancorp.	$ 6.6
Wachovia Corp.	6.1
KeyCorp.	6.0
BB&T Corp.	5.2
SouthTrust Corp.	4.6
Temple-Inland Financial	4.4

Source: *American Banker*, February 26, 2002, p. 7A.

★ 1661 ★

Loan Arrangers (SIC 6163)

Largest Correspondent Lenders

Market shares are shown in percent for the second quarter of the year. Correspondent lending entails the purchase of closed loans.

Chase	20.40%
Washington Mutual	11.26
Other	68.34

Source: *Origination News*, October 2001, p. 1, from Quarterly Data Report.

★ 1662 ★

Loan Arrangers (SIC 6163)

Top Agricultural Banks, 2000

Banks are ranked by total agricultural loans in millions of dollars. Data are for the quarter ended December 31, 2000.

Bank of America	$ 3,162.0
Wells Fargo	2,906.0
US Bank	1,307.9
Firstar	1,031.3
Sanwa Bank California	1,011.4
First Union	838.0
Keybank	826.8
Union Planters	731.5
Regions Bank	722.7
First NB of Omaha	502.3

Source: *Ag Lender*, November 2001, p. 10, from Federal Reserve System.

★ 1663 ★

Loan Arrangers (SIC 6163)

Top Loan Arrangers in Indianapolis, MD

Market shares are shown in percent as of June 30, 2000.

Bank One	45.0%
National City	17.0
Union Federal	6.6
KeyCorp.	5.8
Fifth Third	4.7
Union Planters	3.6
First Indiana	3.6
Huntington	2.5
National Bank of Indianapolis	2.3
Other	8.9

Source: *Indianapolis Business Journal*, August 20, 2001, p. 3B, from SNL Securities.

SIC 62 - Security and Commodity Brokers

★ 1664 ★

Investment Banking (SIC 6211)

401K Investments

Data show where investors have their money.

Employer stock	29.6%
Stable value/bonds	25.2
Large-company stock	22.2
Balanced	9.6
Small/midsize company stock	5.3
Other	8.1

Source: *USA TODAY*, March 7, 2002, p. B1, from Hewitt Associates.

★ 1665 ★

Investment Banking (SIC 6211)

Corporate Securities Underwriting, 2001

Market shares are shown in percent.

Salomon Smith Barney	12.0%
Merrill Lynch	10.6
Credit Suisse First Boston	8.5
J.P. Morgan Chase	7.7
Goldman, Sachs	7.4
Morgan Stanley Dean Witter	6.8
Lehman Brothers	6.4
UBS Warburg	6.2
Deutsche Bank	5.5
Other	28.9

Source: *New York Times*, January 1, 2002, p. C4, from Thomson Financial Securities Data.

★ 1666 ★

Investment Banking (SIC 6211)

Largest Debt And Equity Issuers

Figures include Rule 144A placement.

Citigroup/Salomon Smith Barney	13.9%
Merrill Lynch	12.5
Credit Suisse First Boston	9.5
Goldman Sachs	8.5
J.P. Morgan	8.5
Lehman Brothers	8.0
Morgan Stanley	6.8
UBS Warburg	6.3
Banc of America Securities	5.5
Other	21.5

Source: *Financial Times*, February 22, 2002, p. 2, from Thomson Financial.

★ 1667 ★

Investment Banking (SIC 6211)

Largest Debt and Equity Underwriters, 2001

Market shares are shown bsed on fees.

Citigroup	17.6%
Goldman, Sachs	15.1
Morgan Stanley	14.9
Merrill Lynch	13.0
Credit Suisse First Boston	10.1
Lehman Brothers	6.8
J.P. Morgan Chase	6.0
Banc of America Securities	4.4
UBS Warburg	3.1
Other	9.0

Source: *New York Times*, June 15, 2001, p. C2, from Thomson Financial Securities Data.

★ 1668 ★

Investment Banking (SIC 6211)

Leaders in the Chapter 13 Market

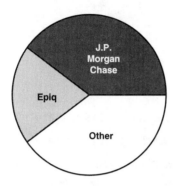

Chapter 13 involves the reorganization of an individual's debt. Market shares are estimated. J.P. Morgan has about 35%-40%.

J.P. Morgan Chase & Co.	40.0%
Epiq	20.0
Other	40.0

Source: *Investor's Business Daily*, November 16, 2001, p. A9.

★ 1669 ★

Investment Banking (SIC 6211)

Leading Bond Counselors

Market shares are shown in percent.

Orrick, Herrington & Sutcliffe	8.3%
Hawkins, Delafield & Wood	5.5
Other	86.2

Source: *Bond Buyer*, January 2, 2002, p. 1.

★ 1670 ★

Investment Banking (SIC 6211)

Leading Euro-Denominated Bond Issuers, 2001

Figures are for the first nine months of the year.

Ford Motor	42.13%
General Motors	22.41
General Electric	5.62
MCI WorldCom	3.18
Hewlett-Packard	3.18
Baxter Travenol Laboratories	2.75
Toys R US	2.12

KPNQwest	2.12%
Other	16.49

Source: *Euromoney*, October 2001, p. 10, from Capital DATA.

★ 1671 ★

Investment Banking (SIC 6211)

Leading Financial Advisers for Bonds

Market shares are shown in percent.

Public Financial Management	8.9%
Public Resources Advisory Group	6.9
First Southwest Co.	3.7
Other	80.5

Source: *Bond Buyer*, January 2, 2002, p. 1.

★ 1672 ★

Investment Banking (SIC 6211)

RMBS Market Shares

Market shares are shown in percent.

UBS	16.4%
Goldman Sachs & Co.	14.3
Bear Stearns & Co.	13.2
Credit Suisse First Boston	11.0
Other	45.1

Source: *Asset Securitization Report*, January 7, 2002, p. 1, from Thomson Financial.

★ 1673 ★

Investment Banking (SIC 6211)

Top Financial Advisors

Firms are ranked by announced deal value, in billions of dollars. Figures are for whole bank and thrift mergers through December 31, 2001.

Credit Suisse First Boston Corp.	$ 24.0
Merrill Lynch & Co.	21.4
Goldman, Sachs & Co.	21.1
Lehman Brothers	9.0
Keefe, Bruyette & Woods Inc.	6.2
Sandler O'Neill & Partners	2.6
J.P. Morgan Chase & Co. Inc.	2.6
Morgan Stanley	2.4

Source: *U.S. Banker*, March 2002, p. 31, from Sheshunoff Information Services.

★ 1674 ★
Investment Banking (SIC 6211)

Top IPO Bookrunners

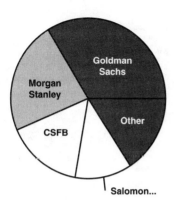

Market shares are shown in percent.

Goldman Sachs	33.5%
Morgan Stanley	23.1
CSFB	15.9
Salomon Smith Barney	11.8
Other	15.8

Source: *Financial Times*, February 26, 2002, p. 20, from Dealogic.

★ 1675 ★
Investment Banking (SIC 6211)

Top IPO Managers, 1999-2000

Market shares are shown in percent.

Goldman Sachs	23.1%
Morgan Stanley	16.0
Credit Suisse First Boston	15.9
Merrill Lynch	9.8
Citigroup/Salomon Smith Barney	7.9
FleetBoston Financial	4.6
J.P. Morgan Chase	3.7
Other	19.0

Source: *Wall Street Journal*, April 25, 2002, p. 1, from Thomson Financial.

★ 1676 ★
Investment Banking (SIC 6211)

Top Mutual Fund Firms in Canada

Market shares are shown based on total assets of $445.3 billion.

Investors Group	9.7%
RBC Funds	8.6
AIM Funds Management	8.4
TD Asset Management	7.8
Mackenzie Financial	7.8
Fidelity Investments Canada	7.6
AGF Management	6.7
CIBC Securities	6.1
C.I. Mutual Funds	4.8
Other	32.5

Source: *Marketing Magazine*, May 27, 2002, p. 1, from Yankee Group.

★ 1677 ★
Investment Banking (SIC 6211)

Top Underwriters of Debt and Equity in Canada

Data show value of deals, in billions.

RBC Dominion Securities	$ 16.9
CIBC World Markets	10.6
Scotia Capital	9.8
BMO Nesbitt Burns	9.5
TD Securities	9.4
National Bank Financial	3.0
Merrill Lynch	3.0
Credit Suisse First Boston	2.3

Source: *Globe and Mail*, January 22, 2002, p. B24, from Bloomberg Financial Services.

★ 1678 ★
Venture Capital (SIC 6211)

Venture Capital Deals by State

Data show number of deals.

California	349
Massachusetts	131
New York	81
Texas	61
Virginia	45
Georgia	44
Washington	36

Continued on next page.

★ 1678 ★ *Continued*
Venture Capital (SIC 6211)

Venture Capital Deals by State

Data show number of deals.

New Jersey 33
Pennsylvania 32

Source: *Business 2.0*, June 26, 2001, p. 76, from Venture Economics and National Venture Capital Association.

★ 1679 ★
Electronic Communication Networks (SIC 6231)

ECN Market Shares

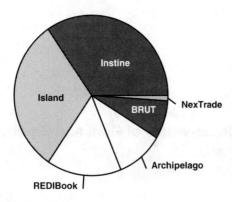

ECN stands for electronic communication networks.

Instine 31.0%
Island 28.0
REDIBook 14.0
Archipelago 9.0
BRUT 7.0
NexTrade 1.0

Source: *Pensions & Investments*, September 3, 2001, p. 24, from Meridien.

★ 1680 ★
Options Industry (SIC 6231)

Who Leads the Options Market, 2001

Shares are shown based on total options traded, as of November 30, 2001.

Chicago Board Options Exchange 39.43%
American Stock Exchange 26.24
Pacific Stock Exchange 13.26
Philadelphia Stock Exchange 13.10
International Securities Exchange 7.97

Source: *New York Times*, December 16, 2001, p. 7, from Options Clearing Corporation.

★ 1681 ★
Securities Exchanges (SIC 6231)

Derivative Exchange Market Shares

Market shares are shown in percent.

Eurex 15.0%
Chicago Board Options Exchange 11.0
Matif 8.0
Chicago Mercantile Exchange 8.0
Chicago Board of Trade 8.0
Other 50.0

Source: *Investor's Business Daily*, June 27, 2001, p. A5, from Celent Communications.

★ 1682 ★
Ratings Services (SIC 6282)

Ratings Service Industry, 2001

Three companies are designated by the Securities and Exchange Commission as nationally recognized statistical ratings organizations.

Standard & Poor's 41.0%
Moody's 38.0
Fitch 14.0
Other 6.0

Source: *New York Times*, April 23, 2002, p. C1, from Moody's.

SIC 63 - Insurance Carriers

★ 1683 ★

Insurance (SIC 6300)

Leading Surplus Line Insurers

Firms are ranked by surplus line premiums written in millions of dollars.

Lexington Insurance	$ 1,242.0
American International Security	1,103.6
Scottsdale Insurance Co.	561.9
Steadfast Insurance	311.2
Evanston Insurance	276.4
General Star Indemnity	270.8
United National Insurance Co.	245.2

Source: *National Underwriter*, September 24, 2001, p. 14.

★ 1684 ★

Insurance (SIC 6300)

Top Supplemental Insurance Firms

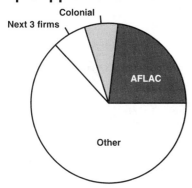

The industry is worth $20 billion.

AFLAC	23.0%
Colonial	7.3
Next 3 firms	6.6
Other	63.1

Source: *Knight-Ridder/Tribune Business News*, November 5, 2001, p. NA.

★ 1685 ★

Life Insurance (SIC 6311)

Top Annuity Insurers in Canada, 2000

Market shares are shown based on premiums. Data are for individuals.

Manufacturers Life	21.68%
Sun Life of Canada	13.75
Clarica Life	13.64
London Life	6.39
Canada Life	6.34
Desjardins-Laurentian	5.69
Industrial Alliance Life	5.34
Transamerica Life Canada	4.13
Other	23.04

Source: *Canadian Insurance*, Statistical Issue, 2001, p. 48.

★ 1686 ★

Life Insurance (SIC 6311)

Top Group Life Insurers in Canada, 2000

Market shares are shown based on premiums.

Clarica Life	11.09%
Sun Life of Canada	10.97
Great-West Life	10.91
Manufacturers Life	10.87
Desjardins-Laurentian	9.42
Canada Life	8.65
Maritime Life	8.39
London Life	4.92
Co-operators Life	3.66
Other	21.13

Source: *Canadian Insurance*, Statistical Issue, 2001, p. 48.

★ 1687 ★

Life Insurance (SIC 6311)

Top Life Insurers in New York State, 2000

Market shares are shown in percent.

Metropolitan Life & Affiliated	32.1%
Hartford Life	9.0
Prudential of America Group	8.9
Aetna Inc. Group	6.0
Cigna Group	4.5
UnumProvident Group	4.2
MassMutual Financial Group	3.3
Other	32.0

Source: *Best's Review*, October 2001, p. 20, from A.M. Best State/Line Reports.

★ 1688 ★

Auto Insurance (SIC 6321)

Top Auto Insurers (Commercial Auto), 2000

Market shares are shown based on premiums.

Zurich/Farmers Group	6.5%
Travelers/Citigroup	6.0
CNA Insurance	4.6
Liberty Mutual	4.1
St. Paul Co.	3.8
CGU Group	3.6
State Farm Group	3.3
Progressive Group	2.8
Nationwide Group	2.5
Amer Intern Group Inc.	2.5
Other	60.3

Source: *Best's Review*, October 2001, p. 76, from A.M. Best & Co.

★ 1689 ★

Auto Insurance (SIC 6321)

Top Auto Insurers in Arizona

Market shares are shown in percent.

Zurich/Farmers Group	16.08%
State Farm Group	15.48
Allstate Insurance Group	12.73
Other	55.71

Source: *A.M. Best Newswire*, February 19, 2002, p. NA, from A.M. Best Co.

★ 1690 ★

Auto Insurance (SIC 6321)

Top Auto Insurers in Florida

Market shares are shown in percent.

State Farm	20.34%
Allstate Insurance	18.75
Berkshire Hathaway	11.57
Progressive Insurance Group	9.37
USAA Group	4.54
Other	35.43

Source: *Best's Review*, November 2001, p. 20, from A.M. Best Statement and Competitive Analysis Report Products.

★ 1691 ★

Auto Insurance (SIC 6321)

Top Auto Insurers in Massachusetts

Market shares are shown in percent.

Commerce Group	22.11%
Arbella Insurance Group	11.81
Safety Group	9.87
MetLife Auto	7.74
Home Group	7.74
Liberty Mutual Insurance Group	7.08
Other	33.65

Source: *A.M. Best Newswire*, October 4, 2001, p. NA, from A.M. Best & Co.

★ 1692 ★

Auto Insurance (SIC 6321)

Top Auto Insurers in New Jersey

Market shares are shown in percent.

State Farm Insurance Cos.	18.0%
Liberty Mutual Insurance	10.8
Allstate Insurance Group	10.5
New Jersey Manufacturers Group	9.6
Prudential of America Group	6.8
Other	44.3

Source: *A.M. Best Newswire*, September 10, 2001, p. NA, from A.M. Best & Co.

★ 1693 ★
Auto Insurance (SIC 6321)

Top Auto Insurers in New York

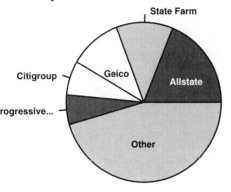

Market shares are shown in percent.

Allstate	18.7%
State Farm	11.6
Geico	11.4
Citigroup	6.6
Progressive Insurance	5.5
Other	46.2

Source: *A.M. Best Newswire*, December 28, 2001, p. NA, from New York Department of Insurance.

★ 1694 ★
Auto Insurance (SIC 6321)

Top Auto Insurers in North Carolina

Market shares are shown in percent.

Nationwide Group	17.2%
State Farm Group	11.4
Allstate Insurance Group	10.0
North Carolina Farm Bureau	8.0
GMAC Insurance Group	7.5
Other	45.9

Source: *A.M. Best Newswire*, December 17, 2001, p. NA, from A.M. Best Co.'s State/Line Group.

★ 1695 ★
Auto Insurance (SIC 6321)

Top Auto Insurers in South Dakota

Market shares are shown in percent.

State Farm	15.77%
American Family Mutual	11.08
Farmers Ins Exchange	5.12

Farmers Mutual	2.89%
Farm Bureau Mutual Ins	2.87
Safeco Ins Co. of America	2.69
American Std Ins	2.60
Mid-Century Ins Co.	2.48
Progressive Northern	2.43
Other	52.07

Source: "Private Passenger Auto Liability." Retrieved January 21, 2002 from the World Wide Web: http://www.state.sd.us.

★ 1696 ★
Auto Insurance (SIC 6321)

Top Auto Insurers in Utah

Market shares are shown in percent for 1999.

State Farm	4.80%
Balboa Insurance	4.54
Great West Casualty	3.83
Travelers Ind.	3.31
National Union Fire	2.87
Truck Ins. Exchange	2.31
Redland Ins. Co.	2.30
Owners Insurance Co.	2.21
Other	73.83

Source: "Marketshare Reports." Retrieved November 7, 2001 from the World Wide Web: http://www.insurance.state.ut.us.

★ 1697 ★
Auto Insurance (SIC 6321)

Top Auto Insurers in West Virginia

Market shares are shown in percent.

State Farm	29.0%
Nationwide	16.7
Erie	8.1
Allstate Insurance Co.	7.9
Shelby Casualty Insurance	2.7
Other	35.6

Source: *Knight-Ridder/Tribune Business News*, April 3, 2002, p. NA.

★ 1698 ★
Auto Insurance (SIC 6321)

Top Auto Insurers (Private Passenger), 2000

Market shares are shown based on premiums.

State Farm Group	17.9%
Allstate Insurance Group	11.8
Zurich/Farmers Group	5.8
Progressive Group	4.7
Berkshire Hathaway	4.7
Nationwide Group	4.6
USAA Group	3.4
Liberty Mutual Insurance Cos.	2.3
Amer Family Insurance Group	2.1
Travelers/Citigroup	2.0
Other	40.7

Source: *Best's Review*, October 2001, p. 76, from A.M. Best & Co.

★ 1699 ★
Health Insurance (SIC 6321)

Largest Accident/Health Insurance Companies in Missouri, 2000

Market shares are shown in percent.

Blue Cross of Missouri	18.68%
Blue Cross and Blue Shield of Kansas City Group	11.96
United Healthcare Insurance Group	6.10
American International Group	4.28
Conseco Group	3.54
Fortis Inc.	3.44
CNA Insurance Group	3.42
UNUM Provident	2.54
Mutual of Omaha	2.30
Principal Financial Group	1.91
Other	41.83

Source: *St. Louis Business Journal*, October 5, 2001, p. 22.

★ 1700 ★
Health Insurance (SIC 6321)

Largest Health Insurers

Firms are ranked by premium revenue in billions of dollars.

United Health	$ 15.4
Aetna	15.0
Kaiser	14.7
Cigna	11.3
WellPoint	8.4

Source: *Baltimore Business Journal*, December 7, 2001, p. 1, from *Modern Healthcare*.

★ 1701 ★
Health Insurance (SIC 6321)

Top Accident/Sickness Insurers in Canada, 2000

Market shares are shown based on premiums.

Great-West Life Assur. Co.	19.93%
Sun Life of Canada	11.10
Manufacturers Life Ins. Co.	10.99
The Maritime Life Assur. Co.	9.59
The Canada Life Assur. Co.	9.18
Clarica Life Ins. Co.	7.82
Desjardins-Laurentian Life	6.26
UNUM: Provident Life	4.66
Other	20.47

Source: *Canadian Underwriter*, Statistical Issue, 2001, p. 67.

★ 1702 ★
Travel Insurance (SIC 6321)

Travel Insurance Industry

Before September 11, the company insured about 6 million travelers annually and had a 40% share. Since the attacks, they insure about 8 million and have a 60% share.

Travel Guard	60.0%
Other	40.0

Source: *Knight-Ridder/Tribune Business News*, June 1, 2002, p. NA.

★ 1703 ★
Health Plans (SIC 6324)

Largest Medicaid HMOs

Market shares are shown in percent.

HealthNet Inc.	5.16%
Blue Cross Blue Shield of Tennessee	4.82
UnitedHealth Group	4.37
WellPoint Health Networks	3.40
Amerigroup	3.24
Other	79.01

Source: *Managed Medicare & Medicaid*, April 22, 2002, p. 7, from *AIS' HMO Directory, 2002.*

★ 1704 ★
Health Plans (SIC 6324)

Largest Medicare HMOs

Market shares are shown in percent.

PacifiCare Inc.	16.0%
Kaiser Foundation Health Plan	13.0
Humana Inc.	7.0
UnitedHealth Group	6.0
Aetna Inc.	4.0
Other	46.0

Source: *Managed Medicare & Medicaid*, April 22, 2002, p. 7, from *AIS' HMO Directory, 2002.*

★ 1705 ★
Health Plans (SIC 6324)

Leading Health Care Providers in Texas

Distribution is shown by company.

HMO Blue	25.7%
Aetna U.S. Healthcare-Prudential	25.6
United Healthcare	8.8
Humana	7.4
Methodist Care	6.7
Pacificare	5.3

Cigna	5.0%
Other	16.0

Source: *Houston Business Journal*, December 7, 2001, p. 2, from Annual HMO statements to the Texas Department of Insurance, Medicaid Managed Care Enrollment Reports from the Dept. of Health, and Quarterly Medicare HMO Enrollment Reports.

★ 1706 ★
Health Plans (SIC 6324)

Leading Medicaid HMOs

Plans are ranked by number of enrolless.

Blue Cross and Blue Shield Association	2,170,134
Health Net	641,867
Humana	616,803
UnitedHealth Group	555,221
Amerigroup	255,568
AmeriChoice Corp.	180,520
Maxicare Health Plans	168,870
Coventry Health Care	164,183
Kaiser Foundation Health Plans	155,371
Aetna	101,588

Source: *Modern Healthcare*, December 24, 2001, p. S11.

★ 1707 ★
Health Plans (SIC 6324)

Top Health Plans in Florida

Market shares are shown in percent.

Blue Cross/Blue Shield Options	28.4%
Prudential	28.0
Aetna Health Plan	17.2
Other	26.4

Source: *The Business Journal - Serving Jacksonville and Northeast Florida*, February 2, 2001, p. 1.

★ 1708 ★
Health Plans (SIC 6324)

Top HMOs in New England

There are 5.4 million enrolled in HMOs.

Blue Cross Blue Shield MA - HMO Blue	17.49%
Anthem Blue Cross Blue Shield	15.72
Harvard Pilgrim	13.70

Continued on next page.

★ 1708 ★   *Continued*
Health Plans (SIC 6324)

Top HMOs in New England

There are 5.4 million enrolled in HMOs.

Tufts	12.75%
Health Net	8.53
CIGNA	6.16
Aetna U.S. Healthcare	5.14
ConnectiCare	4.57
Other	15.94

Source: *Health Care Strategic Management*, February 2002, p. 9, from New England HMO Monitor.

★ 1709 ★
Health Plans (SIC 6324)

Top HMOs in North Carolina

Firms are ranked by membership.

United HealthCare	311,379
Partners	291,076
Cigna Healthcare	236,339
Blue Cross	132,684
Wellpath	78,563
Aetna US Healthcare	67,516
QualChoice	42,672
Coventry	35,565
The Wellness Plan	28,622

Source: *Business North Carolina*, February 2002, p. 42, from North Carolina Department of Insurance.

★ 1710 ★
Health Plans (SIC 6324)

Top HMOs in Sacramento, CA

Data show enrollment.

Kaiser Foundation Health Plan	557,882
Health Net	223,135
Blue Cross of California	120,743
PacificCare/Secure Horizons	110,000
Blue Shield of California	64,350
Western Health Advantage	45,300
Aetna US Healthcare Inc.	21,104

Source: *Sacramento Business Journal*, December 28, 2001, p. 75.

★ 1711 ★
Health Plans (SIC 6324)

Top HMOs in St. Louis, MO

Market shares are as of December 31, 2000.

United Health Care of the Midwest	37.04%
Group Health Plan /Access Sensicare	20.88
Healthcare USA of Missouri LLC/ Healthcare USA	9.75
Health Partners of the Midwest Inc.	8.35
Mercy Health Plans of Missouri	6.69
Prudential Health Care Plan Inc.	6.03
HMO Missouri Inc.	5.32

Source: *St. Louis Business Journal*, October 5, 2001, p. 24.

★ 1712 ★
Homeowners Insurance (SIC 6331)

Top Home Insurers

Market shares are shown in percent.

State Farm	21.4%
Allstate Insurance Group	11.5
Zurich/Farmers Group	8.4
Nationwide Group	4.5
Travelers/Citigroup	3.8
USAA Group	3.6
Chubb Group	2.4
Safeco Insurance	2.2
American Family Insurance Group	2.1
Liberty Mutual	2.0
Other	38.1

Source: *Best's Review*, November 2001, p. 82, from A.M. Best Statement and Competitive Analysis Report Products.

★ 1713 ★
Homeowners Insurance (SIC 6331)

Top Home Insurers in Alaska

Market shares are shown in percent.

State Farm	34.7%
Allstate	30.2
Other	35.1

Source: *Best's Review*, November 2001, p. 82, from A.M. Best Statement and Competitive Analysis Report Products.

★ 1714 ★
Homeowners Insurance (SIC 6331)

Top Home Insurers in California

Market shares are shown in percent.

State Farm Group	22.1%
Zurich/Farmers Group	19.6
Allstate Insurance Group	15.4
California State Auto Group	5.0
USAA Group	4.3
Other	33.6

Source: *A.M. Best Newswire*, December 27, 2001, p. NA, from A.M. Best & Co.

★ 1715 ★
Homeowners Insurance (SIC 6331)

Top Home Insurers in Florida

Market shares are shown in percent.

State Farm	20.40%
HDI	11.59
Allstate Insurance Group	11.42
USAA Group	5.33
Nationwide Group	5.07
Other	46.19

Source: *Best's Review*, November 2001, p. 20, from A.M. Best Statement and Competitive Analysis Report Products.

★ 1716 ★
Homeowners Insurance (SIC 6331)

Top Home Insurers in Georgia

Market shares are shown in percent.

State Farm	32.4%
Allstate	12.3
Other	55.3

Source: *Best's Review*, November 2001, p. 82, from A.M. Best Statement and Competitive Analysis Report Products.

★ 1717 ★
Homeowners Insurance (SIC 6331)

Top Home Insurers in Louisiana, 2000

Market shares are shown in percent.

State Farm	32.8%
Allstate Insurance	17.4
American International Group	7.2
Southern Farm Bureau Group	6.3
Travelers/Citigroup	5.4
Other	30.9

Source: *A.M. Best Newswire*, January 15, 2002, p. NA, from A.M. Best & Co.

★ 1718 ★
Homeowners Insurance (SIC 6331)

Top Home Insurers in Maine

Market shares are shown in percent.

Commercial Union York	20.05%
State Farm Fire & Casualty	9.02
Allstate	8.44
Maine Mutual Fire	6.35
Concord General Mutual	4.91
Other	51.23

Source: *Best's Review*, April 2002, p. 53, from A.M. Best & Co.

★ 1719 ★
Homeowners Insurance (SIC 6331)

Top Home Insurers in Missouri

Market shares are shown in percent.

State Farm Group	24.3%
American Family Insurance Group	19.3
Zurich/Farmers Group	10.4
Shelter Insurance Cos.	6.6
Safeco Insurance Cos.	5.0
Other	34.4

Source: *A.M. Best Newswire*, April 2, 2002, p. NA, from A. M. Best & Co.

★ 1720 ★
Homeowners Insurance (SIC 6331)

Top Home Insurers in New Hampshire

Market shares are shown in percent.

State Farm Fire & Casualty 9.10%
Peerless Insurance 6.65
Concord General Mutual 6.63
Allstate 6.43
Liberty Mutual Fire 4.65
Other 66.54

Source: *Best's Review*, April 2002, p. 53, from A.M. Best & Co.

★ 1721 ★
Homeowners Insurance (SIC 6331)

Top Home Insurers in Oklahoma

Market shares are shown in percent.

State Farm Group 27.4%
Zurich/Farmers Group 25.4
Allstate Insurance Group 9.3
Oklahoma Farm Bureau Group 5.3
USAA Group 3.6
Other 29.0

Source: *A.M. Best Newswire*, February 27, 2002, p. NA, from A.M. Best & Co.

★ 1722 ★
Homeowners Insurance (SIC 6331)

Top Home Insurers in Texas, 2000

Market shares are shown in percent.

State Farm 30.6%
Farmers/Zurich 20.4
Allstate 15.5
USAA 6.8
Travelers 4.4
Nationwide 2.9
SAFECO 2.0

Chubb 1.9%
Southern Farm Bureau 1.5
Other 14.0

Source: "2000 Market Share Report." Retrieved November 9, 2001 from the World Wide Web: http://www.iiaf. org.

★ 1723 ★
Homeowners Insurance (SIC 6331)

Top Home Insurers in Vermont

Market shares are shown in percent.

Co-operatives Insurance Co. 10.82%
Allstate 7.23
Northern Security 6.77
State Farm Fire & Casualty 6.48
Concord General Mutual 6.23
Other 62.47

Source: *Best's Review*, April 2002, p. 53, from A.M. Best & Co.

★ 1724 ★
Property Insurance (SIC 6331)

Home Insurance and Hurricane-Prone States

Market shares are shown in percent.

State Farm 26.5%
Allstate 13.3
Zurich Financial 7.8
Nationwide Group 5.6
USAA Group 5.3
Citigroup 3.9
Liberty Mutual 1.5
Safeco 1.2
Other 34.9

Source: *Business Wire*, July 11, 2001, p. NA.

★ 1725 ★
Property Insurance (SIC 6331)

Largest Fire/Homeowners Insurance in Hawaii

Market shares are shown in percent.

State Farm	16.81%
CNA Insurance	14.45
Ace INA Group	8.24
Island Insurance Group	7.95
Allstate Insurance Group	7.09
Other	45.46

Source: *Best's Review*, October 2001, p. 93, from A.M. Best & Co.

★ 1726 ★
Property Insurance (SIC 6331)

Largest Property/Casualty Insurers

Firms are ranked by directly written premiums in billions of dollars.

State Farm Mutual Auto Insurance	$ 19.93
Allstate Insurance Co.	15.56
Nationwide Mutual Insurance	6.41
State Farm Fire and Casualty	5.67
Farmers Insurance Exchange	3.97
Liberty Mutual Insurance	3.76
Zurich American Insurance	3.70
St. Paul Fire & Marine Insurance	3.58
Government Employees Insurance	3.52

Source: *Small Business Banker*, February 2002, p. 7, from Sheshunoff Information Services.

★ 1727 ★
Property Insurance (SIC 6331)

Largest Property/Casualty Insurers in California

Zurich North America
State Farm Group
American International Group
Allstate Insurance Group
State Comp Insurance Fund of Calif.
California State Auto Group
Interinsurance Exchange of Auto Club
Allianz of America Inc.
Other

Market shares are shown in percent.

Zurich North America	10.4%
State Farm Group	8.0
American International Group	6.7
Allstate Insurance Group	5.7
State Comp Insurance Fund of Calif.	4.7
California State Auto Group	4.2
Interinsurance Exchange of Auto Club	3.5
Allianz of America Inc.	3.0
Other	53.8

Source: *Los Angeles Business Journal*, July 30, 2001, p. 27.

★ 1728 ★
Property Insurance (SIC 6331)

Largest Property/Casualty Insurers in Denver, CO

Market shares are shown in percent.

State Farm Mutual	8.59%
Colorado Compensation Insurance	5.34
Farmers Insurance Exchange	5.10
American Family Mutual Insurance	4.77
Rocky Mountain Hospital & Medicine	4.39
State Farm Fire & Casualty	4.01
Other	67.80

Source: *Denver Business Journal*, December 7, 2001, p. 13A.

★ 1729 ★
Property Insurance (SIC 6331)

Largest Property/Casulty Insurers in Portland, OR

Firms are ranked by direct premiums in millions of dollars.

State Farm	$ 282.2
Farmers Insurance Co. of Oregon	279.2
State Accident Insurance Fund Corp.	219.9
Allstate Insurance Co.	189.3
State Farm Fire & Casualty	140.5
National Union Fire	130.4
Liberty N.W. Insurance Corp.	83.7
Safeco Insurance Co. of Illinois	79.9

Source: *Business Journal-Portland*, November 9, 2001, p. 22.

★ 1730 ★
Earthquake Insurance (SIC 6351)

Top Earthquake Insurers in California

Market shares are shown in percent.

St. Paul Cos.	18.6%
State Farm Group	10.8
Ace INA Group	8.5
Safeco Insurance Cos.	6.0
ICW group	4.9
Other	51.2

Source: *A.M. Best Newswire*, December 18, 2001, p. NA, from A.M. Best & Co.

★ 1731 ★
Fidelity Insurance (SIC 6351)

Leading Fidelity Insurers, 2000

Market shares are shown based on premiums.

Chubb Group of Ins. Cos.	16.3%
Amer Intern Grp Inc.	14.3
Cumis Ins Society	13.6
Travelers/Citigroup	13.2
Zurich/Farmers Group	7.6
Cna Ins Companies	6.1
St. Paul Companies	5.7

Hartford Ins. Group	4.7%
Progressive Group	1.6
Great Amer P&C Group	1.6
Other	15.3

Source: *Best's Review*, September 2001, p. 5, from A.M. Best & Co.

★ 1732 ★
Liability Insurance (SIC 6351)

Leading Liability Insurers

Market shares are shown based on policy count.

Lloyd's	22.0%
AIG	22.0
Chubb	18.0
Great American	5.0
Admiral	5.0
Other	28.0

Source: *Best's Review*, May 2002, p. 65.

★ 1733 ★
Liability Insurance (SIC 6351)

Top Liability Insurers in Canada, 2000

Market shares are shown based on premiums.

CGU Group Canada	8.13%
ING Canada	7.82
Lloyd's Underwriters	6.94
Chubb Ins. Co. of Canada	6.82
American Home Assurance Co.	5.69
Zurich Canada	5.34
Royal Insurance Group	5.19
Motors Ins. Corp.	4.29
Other	49.78

Source: *Canadian Underwriter*, Statistical Issue, 2001, p. 67.

★ 1734 ★
Marine Insurance (SIC 6351)

Top Marine Insurers in Canada, 2000

Market shares are shown based on premiums.

CNA Canada Group	14.75%
Royal Insurance Group	13.98
Allianz Canada	10.07
AXA Canada-Group of Companies	9.20
ING Canada	9.12

Continued on next page.

★ 1734 ★ *Continued*

Marine Insurance (SIC 6351)

Top Marine Insurers in Canada, 2000

Market shares are shown based on premiums.

St. Paul Canada 8.51%
Lloyd's Underwriters 5.62
Gerling Canada Ins. Co.. . . . . 5.21
Other 23.54

Source: *Canadian Underwriter*, Statistical Issue, 2001, p. 67.

★ 1735 ★

Medical Malpractice Insurance (SIC 6351)

Leading Medical Malpractice Firms

Market shares are shown in percent.

St. Paul 9.12%
MLMIC Group 7.93
GE Capital Insurance 5.09
Health Care Indemnity 3.86
CNA Insurance Cos. 3.68
Other 70.32

Source: *A.M. Best Newswire*, August 31, 2001, p. NA, from A.M. Best & Co.

★ 1736 ★

Medical Malpractice Insurance (SIC 6351)

Leading Medical Malpractice Insurers in Minnesota

Market shares are shown in percent.

State Fund Mutual Insurance Co. 10.5%
Liberty Mutual Insurance Co. 8.7
American Compensation Insurance Co. . . . 5.8
CNA Insurance Cos. 5.6
St. Paul Cos. 4.6
Other 64.8

Source: *A.M. Best Newswire*, December 27, 2001, p. NA, from A.M. Best & Co.

★ 1737 ★

Medical Malpractice Insurance (SIC 6351)

Leading Medical Malpractice Insurers in Nevada

Market shares are shown in percent.

St. Paul 39.5%
Health Care Indemnity Inc. 13.9
Doctors Company Insurance Group 11.6
Other 35.0

Source: *A.M. Best Newswire*, March 4, 2002, p. NA, from A.M. Best & Co.

★ 1738 ★

Medical Malpractice Insurance (SIC 6351)

Leading Medical Malpractice Insurers in Pennsylvania

Market shares are shown in percent.

Pennsylvania Medical Society Liability
  Insurance Co. 22.0%
Phico Insurance Co.. . . . . 13.6
Miix Insurance Co. 12.7
Other 51.7

Source: *A.M. Best Newswire*, December 13, 2001, p. NA, from A.M. Best & Co.

★ 1739 ★

Medical Malpractice Insurance (SIC 6351)

Leading Medical Malpractice Insurers in Texas

Market shares are shown in percent.

Health Care Indemnity Inc. 23.1%
GE Capital Insurance Group 15.7
St. Paul Cos. 7.6
Other 53.6

Source: *A.M. Best Newswire*, April 2, 2002, p. NA, from A. M. Best & Co.

★ 1740 ★

Medical Malpractice Insurance (SIC 6351)

Leading Medical Malpractice Insurers in Washington

Market shares are shown in percent.

Washington Physicians Group 50.1%
Washington Casualty Co. 16.7
Doctor's Company Insurance Group 7.6
St. Paul Cos. 6.4
Zurich Farmers Group 5.2
Other 14.0

Source: *A.M. Best Newswire*, April 2, 2002, p. NA, from A. M. Best & Co.

★ 1741 ★

Medical Malpractice Insurance (SIC 6351)

Leading Medical Malpractice Insurers in West Virginia, 2000

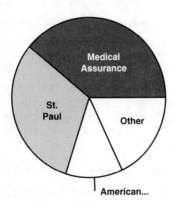

Market shares are shown in percent.

Medical Assurance 39.4%
St. Paul 30.7
American International Group 12.1
Other 17.8

Source: *A.M. Best Newswire*, September 28, 2001, p. NA, from A.M. Best & Co.

★ 1742 ★

Multiple Peril Insurance (SIC 6351)

Leading Commercial Multiple Peril Insurers in Texas, 2000

Market shares are shown in percent.

Travelers 10.8%
Farmers/Zurich 10.2
CNA 8.0
CGU Group 6.0
Hartford 5.7
State Farm 4.4
SAFECO 4.0
Chubb 3.7
Other 47.2

Source: "2000 Market Share Report." Retrieved November 9, 2001 from the World Wide Web: http://www.iiaf. org.

★ 1743 ★

Multiple Peril Insurance (SIC 6351)

Top Multiperil Insurers in California

Market shares are shown in percent.

Allianz of America 11.1%
Zurich/Farmers Group 9.9
Travelers/Citigroup 7.1
Hartford Insurance Group 6.1
Chubb Group of Insurance 5.3
Other 60.5

Source: *A.M. Best Newswire*, January 15, 2002, p. NA, from A.M. Best & Co.

★ 1744 ★

Risk Retention Insurance (SIC 6351)

Risk Retention Marketplace, 2000

Premium is shown in millions of dollars.

Health care . . . . $ 346.3
Professional services 252.2
Government & institutions 88.4
Manufacturing & Commerce 43.8
Property development 36.1
Environmental 24.3
Leisure 2.5

Source: *Risk Retention Reporter*, October 2001, p. NA.

★ 1745 ★

Surety Insurance (SIC 6351)

Leading Surety Insurers, 2000

Market shares are shown based on premiums.

S. Paul Companies	11.5%
CNA Ins Companies	8.5
Travelers/Citigroup	7.9
Zurich/Farmers Group	6.5
Amer Intern Group	6.0
Ace INA Group	3.8
Safeco Ins Cos.	3.7
Liberty Mutual Ins. Cos	3.7
Chubb Group of Ins. Cos.	3.4
Amwest Ins Group	3.2
Other	41.8

Source: *Best's Review*, September 2001, p. 5, from A.M. Best & Co.

★ 1746 ★

Workers Comp Insurance (SIC 6351)

Top Workers Comp Insurers, 2000

Market shares are shown in percent.

Liberty Mutual Insurance Co.	9.1%
State Comp Fund of California	5.5
American International Group	5.0
CNA Insurance	4.8
Zurich/Farmers Group	4.7
Travelers/Citigroup	3.9
Royal & SunAlliance	3.3
Fremont General Group	3.3
Hartford Insurance	3.2
Other	57.2

Source: *Best's Review*, November 2001, p. 91, from A.M. Best & Co.

★ 1747 ★

Workers Comp Insurance (SIC 6351)

Top Workers Comp Insurers in California

Market shares are shown in percent.

State Compensation Insurance Fund of California	28.5%
Fremont General Group	7.2
Liberty Mutual Insurance Co.	6.8
Other	57.5

Source: *A.M. Best Newswire*, March 1, 2002, p. NA, from A.M. Best & Co.

★ 1748 ★

Workers Comp Insurance (SIC 6351)

Top Workers Comp Insurers in Massachusetts

Market shares are shown in percent.

Liberty Mutual	13.27%
Travelers/Citigroup	10.94
Eastern Casualty	9.96
Other	65.83

Source: *A.M. Best Newswire*, September 24, 2001, p. NA, from A.M. Best & Co.

★ 1749 ★

Workers Comp Insurance (SIC 6351)

Top Workers Comp Insurers in New York State, 2000

Market shares are shown in percent.

American International Group	13.6%
Liberty Mutual Insurance Cos.	9.8
Travelers/Citigroup	8.3
CNA Insurance	8.3
Continental Casualty Cos.	7.8
Illinois National Insurance Co.	7.5
Other	44.7

Source: *Best's Review*, October 2001, p. 20, from A.M. Best State/Line Reports.

★ 1750 ★

Title Insurance (SIC 6361)

Leading Title Insurance Firms in Arizona, 2000

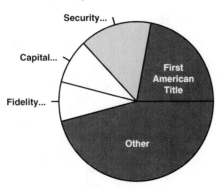

Shares are shown based on number of transactions.

First American Title	22.24%
Security Title Agency	15.05
Capital Title	8.65
Fidelity National Title	7.75
Other	46.31

Source: *The Business Journal - Serving Phoenix & Valley of the Sun*, September 28, 2001, p. 42.

★ 1751 ★

Title Insurance (SIC 6361)

Leading Title Insurance Firms in Colorado

Market shares are shown in percent.

First American Title Insurance Co.	36.14%
Chicago Title Insurance Co.	10.48
Stewart Title Guaranty Co.	9.37
Old Republic National Title Insurance Co.	7.50
Transaction Title Insurance Co.	6.52
Land Title Insurance Corp.	6.50
Lawyers Title Insurance Corp.	5.44
Other	18.05

Source: *Denver Business Journal*, December 21, 2001, p. 11.

★ 1752 ★

Title Insurance (SIC 6361)

Leading Title Insurance Firms in Florida

Market shares are shown in percent.

Attorney's Title Insurance Fund Orlando	25.4%
First American Title Insurance Co. Tallahassee	15.8
Chicago Title Insurance Co. Lake Mary	10.6
Commonwealth Land Title Insurance Co. Orlando	10.2
American Pioneer Title Insurance	8.3
Other	29.7

Source: *Florida Trend*, December 2001, p. S54.

★ 1753 ★

Title Insurance (SIC 6361)

Leading Title Insurance Firms in Missouri, 2000

Market shares are shown in percent.

First American Title Insurance Co.	22.23%
Chicago Title Insurance Co. 2	15.46
Fidelity National Title Insurance Co. 2	11.95
Commonwealth Land Title Insurance Co. 3	10.95
Lawyers Title Insurance Corp. 3	9.83
Stewart Title Guaranty Co.	8.61
Transnation Title Insurance Co. 3	6.67
Other	14.30

Source: *St. Louis Business Journal*, August 3, 2001, p. 20.

★ 1754 ★

Pensions (SIC 6371)

Largest Pension Funds

Assets are shown in billions of dollars.

Calpers	$ 144
New York State Common Retirement Fund	112
California State Teachers	96
General Motors	92
Florida State Retirement System	89

Source: *New York Times*, November 27, 2001, p. C6, from *Pension Funds Reports*.

★ 1755 ★

Hacker Insurance (SIC 6399)

Hacker Insurance Industry

The $75 million in recently written premiums may hit $2.5 billion in 2005.

AIG	70.0%
Other	30.0

Source: *Forbes*, December 24, 2001, p. 42.

★ 1756 ★

Machinery Insurance (SIC 6399)

Top Boiler & Machinery Insurers in Canada, 2000

Market shares are shown based on premiums.

London Guarantee	16.68%
Gerling Canada	9.93
Royal Insurance Group	9.71
Boiler Inspection & Ins. Co.	9.42
ACE INA Insurance	9.06
Factory Mutual Ins. Co.	8.84
CGU Group Canada	5.04
Zurich Canada	4.33
Other	26.99

Source: *Canadian Underwriter*, Statistical Issue, 2001, p. 67.

SIC 64 - Insurance Agents, Brokers, and Service

★ 1757 ★

Reinsurance (SIC 6411)

Leading U.S. Reinsurers, 2000

Market shares are shown in percent.

Swiss Re	30.0%
RGA	11.0
Transmerica Re	11.0
ERC	10.0
ING Re	8.0
Munich Re	8.0
Allianz	5.0
AUL	5.0
Annuity Life & Re	3.0
BMA	3.0
Cologne Re	3.0
Gerling Global	3.0

Source: *National Underwriter*, November 19, 2001, p. NA, from RGA.

SIC 65 - Real Estate

★ 1758 ★
Shopping Centers (SIC 6512)

Largest Shopping Center Managers

Firms are ranked by gross leasable area owned.

Simon Property Group	174.0
General Growth Properties Inc.	127.3
Kimco Realty Corp.	98.0
Jones Lang LaSalle	79.2
Urban Retail Properties	67.0
Westfield	64.5
Trammell Crow	58.0
Developers Diversified Group	57.9
CBL & Associates	56.3
Benderson Development	39.1

Source: *Shopping Center World*, March 2002, p. 81.

★ 1759 ★
Shopping Centers (SIC 6512)

Largest Shopping Center Owners

Firms are ranked by gross leasable area owned.

Simon Property Group	184.0
General Growth Properties	84.3
Westfield Corp. Inc.	64.2
Kimco Realty Corp.	64.0
The Richard E. Jacobs Group	42.3
The Macerich Co.	41.1
Benderson Development Co.	37.0
New Plan Excel Realty Trust	36.5
CBL & Associates Properties	34.0
The Cafaro Co.	33.7

Source: *Shopping Center World*, August 2001, p. 81.

★ 1760 ★
Apartment Buildings (SIC 6513)

Largest Apartment Owners, 2001

Companies are ranked by number of properties.

Apartment Investment and Management Corp.	265,620
Equity Residential Properties Trust	225,466
Related Capital Company	160,860
Lend Lease Real Estate Investments	126,357
Boston Capital	106,000
SunAmerica Affordable Housing Partners	95,000
Whitehall Funds	84,000
United Dominion Realty Trust	79,065
Casden Properties Inc.	71,826
Lefrak Organization	69,000

Source: "Top 50." Retrieved April 1, 2002 from the World Wide Web: http://www.nmhc.org, from National Multi Housing Council.

★ 1761 ★
Office Space (SIC 6531)

Leading Office for Lease (Listing) Brokers

Firms are ranked by total RBA represented, in thousands of square feet.

Newmark & Company Real Estate Inc.	41,122
Insignia/ESG	34,012
Cushman & Wakefield	26,586
Tishman Speyer Companies	17,939
The Mendik Company	15,311
Jones Lang LaSalle Inc.	13,981
Brookfield Financial Properties	12,131

Source: *Wall Street Journal*, July 17, 2001, p. C7, from CoStar Property.

★ 1762 ★

Real Estate (SIC 6531)

Largest Office Property Brokers

Firms are ranked by value of transactions, in millions.

Eastdil . . . . $ 3,700
Cushman & Wakefield 3,415
CB Richard Ellis 2,300
Goldman Sachs 1,900
Jones Land LaSalle 1,700

Source: *Real Estate Alert*, March 6, 2002, p. NA.

★ 1763 ★

Real Estate (SIC 6531)

Largest Real Estate Agents in Indianapolis, MD

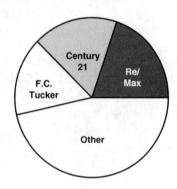

Market shares are shown based on number of homes sold for the first quarter of 2001.

Re/Max 19.8%
Century 21 . . . . 17.7
F.C. Tucker 15.6
Other 46.9

Source: *Indianapolis Business Journal*, June 11, 2001, p. 6.

★ 1764 ★

Real Estate (SIC 6531)

Largest Real Estate Firms

Firms are ranked by number of sides.

NRT 397,049
HomeServices.com Inc. 106,740
Weichert Realtors 85,500
Long & Foster 83,747
Arvida Realty Services 40,377

Source: *Rockford Register Star*, May 28, 2002, p. 1C.

★ 1765 ★

Real Estate (SIC 6531)

Real Estate Market in Arizona

Market shares are shown by type of commercial property. Figures are for the first quarter of 2001.

	No.	Share
Anchored center	458	60.3%
Unanchored strip	147	19.3
Freestanding	65	8.6
Power centers	37	4.9
Regional malls	11	1.4
Other	42	5.5

Source: *The Business Journal-Serving Phoenix & the Valley of the Sun*, June 22, 2001, p. 42.

★ 1766 ★

Cemeteries (SIC 6553)

Who Owns Cemeteries?

Data are for selected firms.

Service Corporation 485
Alderwoods Group 275
Carriage Services 31

Source: "Funeral Industry." Retrieved March 28, 2002 from the World Wide Web: http://www.forbes.com.

SIC 67 - Holding and Other Investment Offices

★ 1767 ★

Bank Holding Companies (SIC 6712)

Largest Bank Holding Companies

Shares are shown based on deposits, as of March 2001.

Bank of America	7.38%
Wells Fargo	3.88
J.P. Morgan Chase	3.37
Bank One	3.31
First Union	3.13
FleetBoston	2.66
U.S. Bancorp.	2.41
Citigroup	2.37
Washington Mutual	2.20
Other	30.71

Source: *American Banker*, June 6, 2001, p. 2.

★ 1768 ★

Trusts (SIC 6730)

Largest Trust Handlers, 2000

Handlers are ranked by total trust assets in billions of dollars.

State Street	$ 5.80
Bank of New York	3.90
Mellon Financial	1.60
Northern Trust	1.50
Wells Fargo	1.10
J.P. Morgan Chase	1.10
Wachovia	0.57
U.S. Bancorp.	0.40
Investors Financial Services	0.28

Source: *U.S. Banker*, February 2002, p. 43, from SNL Securities.

★ 1769 ★

Intellectual Property (SIC 6794)

Digital Rights Management Industry

Share has been estimated at 60-70%.

Reciprocal	70.0%
Other	30.0

Source: *Business First of Buffalo*, May 28, 2001, p. 1.

★ 1770 ★

Patents (SIC 6794)

Internet Trademarks by Year

2000	375,000
1995	175,000
1990	120,000

Source: *USA TODAY*, June 12, 2001, p. A1, from International Trademark Association.

★ 1771 ★

Patents (SIC 6794)

Top Patent Holders, 2000

IBM	3,453
NEC	1,966
Canon	1,877
Micron	1,643
Samsung	1,451
Matsushita	1,447
Sony	1,392
Hitachi	1,283
Mitsubishi	1,210
Fujitsu	1,208

Source: *Investor's Business Daily*, January 23, 2002, p. A5.

SIC 70 - Hotels and Other Lodging Places

★ 1772 ★
Hotels (SIC 7011)

Bed & Breakfasts in the United States

There are about 18,000 B&Bs and country inns.

Northeast	36.0%
West	28.0
South	20.0
Midwest	15.0

Source: *Wall Street Journal*, May 29, 2002, p. B8.

★ 1773 ★
Hotels (SIC 7011)

Casino Hotel Room Market in South Lake Tahoe

Market shares are estimated in percent.

Harrah's/Oasis	53.5%
Other	46.5

Source: *Knight-Ridder/Tribune Business News*, June 27, 2001, p. NA.

★ 1774 ★
Hotels (SIC 7011)

Extended Stay Industry

Figures show room count.

	1999	2000	2001
Midprice	72,494	77,111	82,321
Upscale	60,062	71,320	77,244
Economy	46,737	57,302	61,002

Source: *Hotel & Motel Management*, October 1, 2001, p. 26, from Highland Group.

★ 1775 ★
Hotels (SIC 7011)

Hotel Occupancy Rates in Selected Cities

Figures are for the first nine months of each year. Business consultants expect meetings to be held closer to home or completely eliminated.

	2000	2001
New York City	84.2%	74.0%
Boston	79.5	72.3
Miami	77.3	76.9
Washington D.C.	77.0	72.7

Source: *Travel Agent*, February 25, 2002, p. 18, from Hospitality Research Group of PFK Consulting.

★ 1776 ★
Hotels (SIC 7011)

How Do Hotels Book Rooms

Calls to chain or hotel phone line	57.0%
Travel agencies	27.5
Walk ins	10.0
Hotel branded web sites	3.0
Online travel agencies	2.5

Source: *Wall Street Journal*, June 5, 2002, p. B1, from PhoCusWright.

★ 1777 ★
Hotels (SIC 7011)

Top Hotel Companies

Data show number of guestrooms.

Cendant Corp.	552,879
Six Continents Hotels	500,000
Mariott International	412,000
Choice Hotels International	412,000
Hilton Hotels Corp.	325,605
Best Western International	307,719

Continued on next page.

★ **1777** ★ *Continued*

Hotels (SIC 7011)

Top Hotel Companies

Data show number of guestrooms.

Starwood Hotels & Resorts Worldwide	227,043
VIP International	143,585
Accor Economy Lodging	129,423
Carlson Hospitality Worldwide	128,688

Source: *Hotel & Motel Management*, September 17, 2001, p. 50.

★ **1778** ★

Hotels (SIC 7011)

Top Hotels to the Federal Government

Market shares are shown based on expenses/charges put on government cards.

Holiday Inn	8.6%
Marriott	4.1
Residence Inn	3.7
Hilton Hotels/Inns	3.2
Sheraton	2.8
Best Western	2.7
Embassy Suites	2.5
Comfort Hotel International	2.5
Other	69.9

Source: *Government Executive*, August 1, 2001, p. NA, from General Services Administration's Federal Supply Service.

SIC 72 - Personal Services

★ 1779 ★
Portrait Studios (SIC 7221)

Who Sits For Portraits?

Unsurprisingly, households with young children are the most likely to have professional portraits taken. 86% of portrait sittings were ordered by parents, with 41% being young parents. Data are for 2000.

School photos (K-11)	33.7%
Child/children (nonschool)	16.2
Family portraits	12.2
Sports/team photos	6.9
Event photos (Santa, etc)	5.6
Nursery/day care photos	5.2
Church directory	4.3
High school senior photos	2.8
High school yearbook	2.4
Wedding photos	1.5
High school prom	1.2
Passport	1.0
Cruise ship photo	1.0

Source: *Photo Marketing*, November 2001, p. 17, from *PMA 2001 Professional Portrait Survey*.

★ 1780 ★
Funeral Services (SIC 7261)

Top States for Cremations, 2000

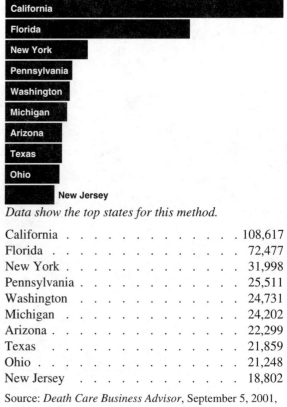

Data show the top states for this method.

California	108,617
Florida	72,477
New York	31,998
Pennsylvania	25,511
Washington	24,731
Michigan	24,202
Arizona	22,299
Texas	21,859
Ohio	21,248
New Jersey	18,802

Source: *Death Care Business Advisor*, September 5, 2001, p. NA.

★ **1781** ★

Weight Loss Clinics (SIC 7299)

Largest Weight Loss Clinics in San Francisco, CA

Data show number of local centers.

Weight Watchers North America	287
Jenny Craig Weight Loss Center	22
Sunrise Health Medical Group	13
Weight Control Medical Clinic	3
Lite for Life	3

Source: *San Francisco Business Times*, October 12, 2001, p. 36.

SIC 73 - Business Services

★ 1782 ★
Advertising (SIC 7311)

Leading Multinational Ad Firms

The top "superagencies" are shown for the U.S., ranked by share of the ad market.

Interpublic Group of Cos.	19.2%
Omnicom Group	14.4
WPP Group	11.9
Havas Advertising	5.7
Publicis Groupe	5.2
Bcom3 Group	4.7
Other	38.9

Source: *Advertising Age*, January 28, 2002, p. 12.

★ 1783 ★
Advertising (SIC 7311)

Top Ad Firms in New England, 2000

Firms are ranked by revenue in millions of dollars.

Arnold	$ 115.3
Hill, Holliday, Connors, Cosmopulos	92.0
Mullen	62.9
Holland Mark	31.0
Allen & Garritsen	12.9

Source: *Adweek*, April 16, 2001, p. 60.

★ 1784 ★
Advertising (SIC 7311)

Top Ad Firms in the East, 2000

Firms are ranked by revenue in millions of dollars.

Grey	$ 477.9
Young & Rubicam	353.2
McCann-Erickson	320.0
Ogilvy & Mather	281.0
BBDO	221.0

Source: *Adweek*, April 16, 2001, p. 60.

★ 1785 ★
Advertising (SIC 7311)

Top Ad Firms in the Midwest, 2000

Firms are ranked by revenue in millions of dollars.

Leo Burnett	$ 428.1
J. Walter Thompson	223.0
Campbell-Ewald	185.0
DDB	157.9
FCB	120.1

Source: *Adweek*, April 16, 2001, p. 60.

★ 1786 ★
Advertising (SIC 7311)

Top Ad Firms in the Northeast, 2000

Firms are ranked by revenue in millions of dollars.

Zimmerman & Partners Advertising	$ 92.8
The Martin Agency	60.2
BBDO South	31.0
J. Walter Thomspon	28.0
McKinney & Silver	26.1

Source: *Adweek*, April 16, 2001, p. 60.

★ 1787 ★
Advertising (SIC 7311)

Top Ad Firms in the Southwest, 2000

Firms are ranked by revenue in millions of dollars.

GSD&M . . . . $ 86.7
The Richards Group 83.5
Temerlin McClain 82.1
Ackerman McQueen 34.5
DDB 29.1

Source: *Adweek*, April 16, 2001, p. 60.

★ 1788 ★
Advertising (SIC 7311)

Top Advertisers, 2001

Spending is shown in millions of dollars. The total hit $135.7 billion.

General Motors . . . . $ 2,188
Procter & Gamble 1,592
AOL/Time Warner 1,553
DaimlerChrysler 1,392
Philip Morris 1,380
Ford Motor 1,249
Walt Disney 1,050
Johnson & Johnson 852
Verizon Communications 843
Pfizer 815

Source: *AdAgeGlobal*, April 2002, p. 18, from Taylor Nelson Sofres and Competitive Media Reporting.

★ 1789 ★
Advertising (SIC 7311)

Top Advertising Categories

Spending is shown in millions of dollars for the first six months of the year.

Automotive . . . . $ 3,912.5
Retailing 2,157.9
Telephone 1,700.6
Financial 1,341.3
Restaurant 1,196.4
Computers 983.2

Drugs . . . . $ 950.0
Food 816.9
Personal care 806.6
Entertainment & media 462.9

Source: *Advertising Age*, November 12, 2001, p. 37, from Competitive Media Reporting.

★ 1790 ★
Advertising (SIC 7311)

Top Advertising Markets by City, 2000

Market shares are shown in percent.

New York City 38.0%
Chicago, IL 10.1
Los Angeles, CA 5.5
Detroit, MI 5.5
San Francisco, CA 3.9
Boston, MA 2.8
Minneapolis, MN 2.4
Dallas, TX 1.6
Other 30.3

Source: *Advertising Age*, September 10, 2001, p. 16.

★ 1791 ★
Advertising (SIC 7312)

Outdoor Advertising in Michigan

Distribution is shown by number of billboards.

	No.	Share
Busienss/consumer services	2,132	20.6%
Retailing	1,993	19.3
Vehicle sales	1,249	12.1
Entertainment/amusements	1,014	9.8

Continued on next page.

★ 1791 ★ *Continued*
Advertising (SIC 7312)

Outdoor Advertising in Michigan

Distribution is shown by number of billboards.

	No.	Share
Travel/hotel/resorts	839	8.1%
Insurance/real estate	778	7.5
Charity/public service	601	5.8
Alcohol	456	4.4

Source: *Detroit News*, February 10, 2002, p. C1, from Outdoor Advertising Association of Michigan.

★ 1792 ★
Advertising (SIC 7319)

Advertising to Hispanics, 2001

Total spending hit $2.2 billion. According to a survey, half of Hispanics read Spanish language materials, the rest read English.

TV	59.0%
Radio	26.0
Newspapers	10.0
Magazines	3.0
Other	3.0

Source: *Wall Street Journal*, May 15, 2002, p. B4, from *Hispanic Business*.

★ 1793 ★
Advertising (SIC 7319)

Business-to-Business Advertising, 2000

The top 100 b-to-b advertisers spent $5.3 billion during the year.

Television	42.1%
Newspapers	17.8
Business publications	16.2
Consumer magazines	13.0
Internet	5.0
Radio	4.3
Outdoor	1.6

Source: *B-to-B*, November 26, 2001, p. 19, from Competitive Media Reporting.

★ 1794 ★
Advertising (SIC 7319)

Computer Publishing Ad Market

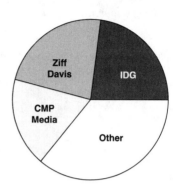

The top 11 firms had $1 billion in revenues. The downturns in ad spending and the tech market have affected this market. Market shares are shown in percent.

IDG	23.2%
Ziff Davis	22.7
CMP Media	18.0
Other	36.1

Source: *Technology Advertising & Branding Report*, April 22, 2002, p. NA.

★ 1795 ★
Advertising (SIC 7319)

Leading Cable TV Advertisers, 2001

Spending is in millions of dollars.

AOL Time Warner	$ 294.0
Procter & Gamble Co.	253.9
General Motors Co.	249.2
AT&T Corp.	158.0
General Mills	150.3
Pfizer	145.6
GlaxoSmithKline	124.2
Walt Disney	122.8

Source: *Electronic Media*, April 29, 2002, p. 12, from Competitive Media Reporting.

★ **1796** ★

Advertising (SIC 7319)

Leading Cigarette Advertisers

Marlboro	
Camel	
Winston	
Virginia Slims	
Doral	
Basic	
Newport	
Salem	

Spending is shown in millions of dollars.

Marlboro	$ 94.1
Camel	44.9
Winston	42.2
Virginia Slims	40.1
Doral	25.1
Basic	24.6
Newport	16.0
Salem	13.1

Source: Brandweek, June 4, 2001, p. S44, from Competitive Media Reporting.

★ **1797** ★

Advertising (SIC 7319)

Leading Credit Card Advertisers

Spending is shown in millions of dollars.

Visa	$ 319.9
MasterCard	215.8
American Express	207.8
Discover	127.2
Diners Club	11.1

Source: Brandweek, June 4, 2001, p. S44, from Competitive Media Reporting.

★ **1798** ★

Advertising (SIC 7319)

Leading Daytime Drama Advertisers

Advertisers are ranked by share of total spending, which was $4.1 billion for January - August 2001.

Procter & Gamble	21.0%
National Amusements	14.0
Sony Corp.	11.0

Pepsico.	10.0%
Walt Disney Co.	9.0
Cadbury Schweppes	9.0
AOL Time Warner	9.0
Castalian Music	7.0
Tracinda Corp.	6.0
Mars	6.0

Source: Electronic Media, December 3, 2001, p. 10, from Cabletelevsion Advertising Bureau.

★ **1799** ★

Advertising (SIC 7319)

Leading Dental Advertisers, 2001

Shares are shown based on total ad spending for the first six months of the year.

Dentsply International	4.22%
Ultradent Products Inc.	3.06
Discus Dental	2.99
Kerr Manufacturing	2.26
Procter & Gamble	1.99
Bisco Dental Products	1.79
Ivoclar North America	1.76
Colgate Palmolive Company	1.71
Other	80.22

Source: Medical Marketing & Media, October 2001, p. 84, from PERQ/HCI.

★ **1800** ★

Advertising (SIC 7319)

Leading Lab Advertisers, 2001

Shares are shown based on total ad spending for the first six months of the year.

Roche Diagnostic Systems	5.70%
Ortho-Clinical Diag./Johnson & Johnson . .	3.01
Abbott Diagnostics	2.82
Inova Diagnostics	2.33
Olympus America	2.16
Beckman Coulter	2.12
Bio-Red	2.06
Other	79.80

Source: Medical Marketing & Media, October 2001, p. 84, from PERQ/HCI.

★ 1801 ★

Advertising (SIC 7319)

Leading Network TV Advertisers, 2001

Spending is in millions of dollars.

General Motors	$ 661.7
Procter & Gamble	527.6
Philip Morris	415.4
Johnson & Johnson	395.9
AOL Time Warner	359.4
Pfizer	343.7
GlaxoSmithKline	335.4
PepsiCo	334.8
Walt Disney	311.3

Source: *Electronic Media*, April 29, 2002, p. 12, from Competitive Media Reporting.

★ 1802 ★

Advertising (SIC 7319)

Leading Optometry Advertisers, 2001

Shares are shown based on total ad spending for the first six months of the year.

Johnson & Johnson	3.42%
CIBA Vision/Wesley Jessen	2.73
Marchon Eyewear	2.59
Bausch & Lomb	2.45
Kenmark Optical	2.29
Safilo Group	2.23
Luxottica Group	2.10
Alcon Laboratories	2.05
Other	80.14

Source: *Medical Marketing & Media*, October 2001, p. 84, from PERQ/HCI.

★ 1803 ★

Advertising (SIC 7319)

Leading Radiology Advertisers, 2001

Shares are shown based on total ad spending for the first six months of the year.

Marconi Medical Systems	4.04%
Siemens Medical Systems Inc.	3.15
Kodak	2.87
GE Medical Systems	2.75
Nycomed Amersham Inc.	2.67
Toshiba	2.44

ATL Ultrasound	2.21%
Other	79.87

Source: *Medical Marketing & Media*, October 2001, p. 84, from PERQ/HCI.

★ 1804 ★

Advertising (SIC 7319)

Liquor Advertising Market, 2000

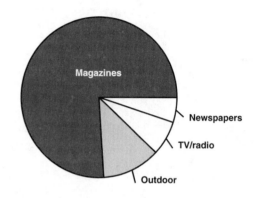

Total spending reached $377 million.

	($ mil.)	Share
Magazines	$ 286.5	76.0%
Outdoor	46.5	12.0
TV/radio	25.1	7.0
Newspapers	18.9	5.0

Source: *Electronic Media*, April 8, 2002, p. 36, from Competitive Media.

★ 1805 ★

Advertising (SIC 7319)

Mobile Internet Advertising

Figures are in millions of dollars.

	2001	2002	2003
Sponsorship	$ 47	$ 111	$ 345
E-commerce related	8	147	510
Other	24	83	284

Source: *M Business*, March 2001, p. 59, from Ovum.

★ 1806 ★

Advertising (SIC 7319)

News Magazine Advertising

Market shares are shown in percent.

Time	37.0%
Newsweek	35.0
U.S. News & World Report	28.0

Source: *New York Times*, May 13, 2002, p. C2, from Publishers Information Bureau.

★ 1807 ★

Advertising (SIC 7319)

Taxi Cab Advertising in New York City

Market shares are shown in percent.

Medallion Media Inc.	90.0%
Other	10.0

Source: "Medallion Financial." Retrieved April 3, 2002 from the World Wide Web: http://www.medallionfinancial.com.

★ 1808 ★

Advertising (SIC 7319)

Top Advertising Market Segments

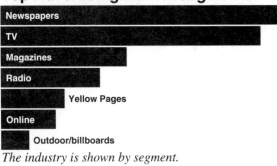

The industry is shown by segment.

Newspapers	30.6%
TV	28.9
Magazines	14.0
Radio	10.6
Yellow Pages	7.2
Online	5.7
Outdoor/billboards	3.0

Source: *USA TODAY*, June 13, 2001, p. 6B.

★ 1809 ★

Advertising (SIC 7319)

Top Advertising Markets in Canada, 2000

Spending is shown in millions of dollars.

Retail	$ 653.3
Automotive	583.2
Financial services	240.4
Food	239.7
Entertainment	228.5
Local automotive dealers	204.9
Telecommunications	184.3
Travel/transportation	158.5
Restaurants	148.4

Source: *AdAgeGlobal*, April 2002, p. 18.

★ 1810 ★

Advertising (SIC 7319)

Top Advertising Markets in Mexico, 2001

Total spending hit $11.3 billion.

	($ mil.)	Share
Terrestrial TV	$ 7,100.0	62.8%
Radio	1,500.0	13.2
Pay TV	1,500.0	13.2
Newspapers	672.5	5.9
Magazines	331.0	2.9
Regional TV	156.5	1.4

Source: *AdAgeGlobal*, February 1, 2002, p. 30.

★ 1811 ★

Advertising (SIC 7319)

Top Advertising Markets in San Jose/ Oakland, CA

Spending is shown in millions of dollars.

	($ mil.)	Share
Spot TV	$ 520.8	37.01%
Local newspapers	467.2	33.21
Spot radio	391.4	27.82
Local magazines	16.0	1.14
Lcoal Sunday supplement	11.6	0.82

Source: *Editor & Publisher*, October 1, 2001, p. 15, from Nielsen Media Plus.

★ 1812 ★
Printing and Duplicating Services (SIC 7334)

Leading Quick Print Shops, 2001

Firms are ranked by sales in millions of dollars.

Superior Group	$ 18.0
Original Impressions	15.7
LazerQuick	14.0
The Fitch Group	13.5
Econoprint	13.3
Catterton Printing	12.0
The JKG Group	11.9
IST Management	11.3
Copy Craft	11.0

Source: *Quick Print Products*, December 2001, p. 13.

★ 1813 ★
Cleaning Services (SIC 7349)

Janitorial Services Industry

Demand for janitorial services and supplies in the U. S. is expected to grow 5.6% annually until hitting $37 billion in 2005. Figures are in millions of dollars.

	2000	2005	Share
Office buildings	$ 9,976	$ 12,870	34.69%
Institutional buildings . . .	9,789	12,800	34.50
Other commercial	3,568	4,480	12.08
Industrial buildings . . .	1,853	2,520	6.79
Residential	1,602	2,470	6.66
Other	1,472	1,960	5.28

Source: *Research Studies - Freedonia Group*, October 29, 2001, p. 3, from Freedonia Group.

★ 1814 ★
Rental Industry (SIC 7350)

Largest Rental Companies

Companies are ranked by revenue in millions of dollars.

United Rentals	$ 2,900
Prime/RSC	1,840
Hertz	1,250
NES	624
Sunbelt	600
NationsRent	600
Neff	225

Source: *Diesel Progress North American Edition*, February 2002, p. 4.

★ 1815 ★
Rental Industry (SIC 7350)

Largest Rental Fleets

Firms are ranked by value of contruction fleet in millions of dollars.

United Rentals	$ 3,200
Rental Service	2,000
Hertz Equipment Rental	1,631
NationsRent	1,100
Sunbelt Rentals	1,000
NES (National Equipment Services)	920
Maxim Crane Works	800
All Erection & Crane Rental	480
Essex Crane Rental	450
Neff	440

Source: *Construction Equipment*, January 2002, p. 15.

★ 1816 ★
Party Rental Firms (SIC 7359)

Leading Party Rental Firms

Firms are ranked by sales in millions of dollars.

Classic Party Rentals	$ 31
Regal Rentals	25
Party Rental Ltd.	25
Broadway Famous Party Rentals	19

Source: *Special Events Magazine*, October 2001, p. NA.

★ 1817 ★
Software (SIC 7372)

Accounting Software Market in Canada

Figures are for the small business market. In the U.S. , QuickBooks has 80%-85% of the market.

Simply Accounting	80.0%
Other	20.0

Source: *San Francisco Business Times*, December 21, 2001, p. S11.

★ 1818 ★
Software (SIC 7372)

AES Vendor Market Shares

AES stands for adverse events tracking and reporting systems. Shares are based on a survey of 96 companies.

Clintrace	46.0%
In-house	13.0
Argus Safety	13.0
ARIS	10.0
EventNet	3.0
eResearch Technology	3.0
Other	22.0

Source: *Applied Clinical Trials*, October 2001, p. 50.

★ 1819 ★
Software (SIC 7372)

ASP Market Shares

Market shares are shown in percent.

Usinternetworking	7.7%
Qwest Cyber.Solutions	7.0
Interliant	3.6
PeopleSoft	2.8
Corio	2.3
eOnline	1.7
Breakaway Solutions	1.4
Agilera	1.4
Surebridge	1.2
Other	70.9

Source: *VAR Business*, July 9, 2001, p. 3, from Dataquest Inc.

★ 1820 ★
Software (SIC 7372)

B2B Software Leaders

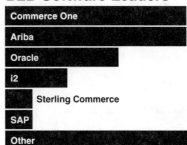

Market shares are shown in percent.

Commerce One	21.0%
Ariba	21.0
Oracle	13.0
i2	7.0
Sterling Commerce	3.0
SAP	3.0
Other	32.0

Source: *Smart Business*, February 2002, p. 49, from AMR Research.

★ 1821 ★
Software (SIC 7372)

CD-Burning Software Industry, 2001

Shares are for the third quarter.

Roxio	61.0%
ValuSoft's Burn & Go	16.0
Stomp's Click 'N Burn	10.0
Other	13.0

Source: *Adweek Magazine's Technology Marketing*, January 2002, p. 21.

★ 1822 ★
Software (SIC 7372)

Content Distribution Market Shares

Web content distribution revenues managed to double in 2001, despite the collapse of the .com industry. Market shares are shown in percent.

Akamai	80.0%
Digital Island	10.0
Other	10.0

Source: *Business Wire*, January 30, 2002, p. NA, from NetsEdge Research Group.

★ 1823 ★

Software (SIC 7372)

Copyright Protection Industry

Macrovision is the leader in VHS and DVD copyright protection. Data show the estimated share for DVDs of Hollywood titles.

Macrovision	90.0%
Other	10.0

Source: *Investor's Business Daily*, August 27, 2001, p. A10.

★ 1824 ★

Software (SIC 7372)

CRM Market Shares

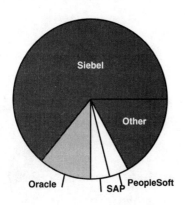

CRM stands for customer relationship management.

Siebel	64.0%
Oracle	11.0
SAP	4.0
PeopleSoft	4.0
Other	17.0

Source: *Investor's Business Daily*, October 22, 2001, p. A8, from Morgan Stanley Dean Witter & Co. and AMR Research.

★ 1825 ★

Software (SIC 7372)

Database Software Market

Market shares are shown in percent.

Oracle	34.0%
IBM	30.0
Microsoft	15.0
Other	21.0

Source: *Infoworld*, November 26, 2001, p. 1, from Dataquest Inc.

★ 1826 ★

Software (SIC 7372)

Dynamic Mechanical System Simulation Market

The software helps in the building and testing of cars, planes and machinery. Market shares are shown in percent.

Mechanical Dynamics	51.0%
Parametric Technology	13.0
CADSI	9.0
MSC Software	8.0
Samtech	4.0
Other	15.0

Source: *Investor's Business Daily*, July 23, 2001, p. A8, from Daratech Inc.

★ 1827 ★

Software (SIC 7372)

Education Internet Filtering Market

Education has roughly 25% of the $215 million filtering market.

N2H2	17.0%
SurfControl	13.0
Other	70.0

Source: *Electronic Education Report*, May 10, 2002, p. NA.

★ 1828 ★
Software (SIC 7372)

Enterprise Portal Software Leaders

Market shares are shown in percent.

Plumtree Software 13.0%
Hummingbird 11.0
Viador 10.0
Citrix Systems 9.0
InfoImage 8.0
Other 49.0

Source: *Smart Business*, February 2002, p. 49, from Delphi Group.

★ 1829 ★
Software (SIC 7372)

ERP Software Market Shares, 2001

ERP stands for enterprise resource planning.

SAP 34.0%
Oracle 16.0
PeopleSoft 10.0
J.D. Edwards 5.0
Geac 3.0
Other 32.0

Source: *Investor's Business Daily*, August 8, 2001, p. A6, from AMR Research Inc.

★ 1830 ★
Software (SIC 7372)

Extraction Market Shares

Market shares are shown in percent.

Avant 28.0%
Ultima Interconnect 12.0
Synopsys 12.0
Simplex Solutions 12.0
Cadence 11.0
Mentor Graphics 10.0
Other 15.0

Source: *Electronic News*, February 4, 2002, p. 24, from Gartner Dataquest.

★ 1831 ★
Software (SIC 7372)

Feed Management Systems in North America

Market shares are shown in percent.

Feed Management Systems 70.0%
Other 30.0

Source: *PR Newswire*, February 26, 2002, p. NA.

★ 1832 ★
Software (SIC 7372)

Firewall Market Shares

Shares are for $1,000-$5,000 firewall appliance market.

WatchGuard Technologies 23.0%
Nokia Corp. 21.0
SonicWall Inc. 18.0
Cisco Systems Inc. 8.0
Other 30.0

Source: *Computerworld*, July 2, 2001, p. 11, from International Data Corp.

★ 1833 ★
Software (SIC 7372)

Game Software Market, 2003

Market shares are shown in percent.

Console software 60.5%
Handheld software 22.6
Personal computer software 16.9

Source: *Investor's Business Daily*, January 28, 2002, p. A6, from J.P. Morgan Securites Inc.

★ 1834 ★
Software (SIC 7372)

Hardware-based/VPN/Firewall Market, 2000

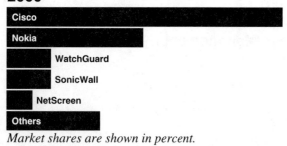

Market shares are shown in percent.

Cisco 45.0%
Nokia 22.0
WatchGuard 7.0
SonicWall 7.0
NetScreen 4.0
Others 15.0

Source: *Investor's Business Daily*, February 27, 2002, p. A6, from International Data Corp.

★ 1835 ★
Software (SIC 7372)

Instant Messaging Market

Sahres are for the general business world.

IBM's SameTime 83.0%
Other 17.0

Source: *Securities Industry News*, April 22, 2002, p. NA.

★ 1836 ★
Software (SIC 7372)

Instructional Software Industry, 2001

Companies are ranked by revenue in millions of dollars. As schools demand increased performance from students, some have turned to software as a teaching tool.

	($ mil.)	Share
NCS Learn	$ 140.3	10.47%
Riverdeep	113.7	8.49
Renaissance Learning	108.4	8.09
Knowledge Adventure	75.2	5.61
McGraw-Hill	65.2	4.87
Other	837.2	62.48

Source: *Electronic Education Report*, December 5, 2001, p. NA, from Simba Information.

★ 1837 ★
Software (SIC 7372)

K-12 Courseware Market

Market shares are shown in percent. Figures are for North America.

The Learning Company 13.0%
NCS Learn 11.6
WRC Media/Compass Learning 10.4
Rennaissance 7.6
Havas 6.1
Plato 5.2
Other 46.1

Source: *Investor's Business Daily*, August 14, 2001, p. A10, from Simba Electronic Media.

★ 1838 ★
Software (SIC 7372)

Largest Software Firms

The software industry is expected to be worth $221.9 billion in 2002, or 2.2% of the GDP. Firms are ranked by revenue in billions of dollars.

Microsoft . . . . $ 25.2
IBM Software 12.5
Oracle 10.8
Computer Associates 4.1

Continued on next page.

★ 1838 ★ *Continued*
Software (SIC 7372)

Largest Software Firms

The software industry is expected to be worth $221.9 billion in 2002, or 2.2% of the GDP. Firms are ranked by revenue in billions of dollars.

Compuware	.$ 2.1
Siebel Systems	1.7
PeopleSoft	1.7
SunGuard Data Systems	1.6

Source: *IEEE Software*, Janaury/February 2002, p. 96.

★ 1839 ★
Software (SIC 7372)

Media Player Use

Data show millions of users. Roughly 42 million people use the player at home (about 16 million at work).

	(mil.)	Share
RealNetworks	25.9	47.35%
Microsoft Windows Media Player	21.5	39.31
Quick Time	7.3	13.35

Source: *Econtent*, September 2001, p. 20.

★ 1840 ★
Software (SIC 7372)

Medical Transcription Device Industry

L&H recently acquired Dictaphone, giving it contol of this $6 billion market.

L&H	.60.0%
Other	.40.0

Source: ''Break Down.'' Retrieved April 23, 2002 from the World Wide Web: http://www.fool.com.

★ 1841 ★
Software (SIC 7372)

Operating Software Market, 2000

Market shares are shown in percent.

Windows	.41.0%
Linux	.27.0
Unix	.13.9
NetWare	.13.8
Other	4.3

Source: *Investor's Business Daily*, January 29, 2002, p. A6, from Gartner Inc. and International Data Corp.

★ 1842 ★
Software (SIC 7372)

Origination Software Industry, 2000

Market shares are shown for mortgage brokers.

Calyx (Point)	.49.0%
Genesis 2000	.13.0
Contour (Loan Handler)	.12.0
Byte	.11.0
Pipeline Solutions	1.0
MortgageFlex Systems	1.0
Loan-Soft	1.0
Interlinq (MortgageWare)	1.0
Other	.11.0

Source: *Mortgage Technology*, December 14, 2001, p. 16.

★ 1843 ★
Software (SIC 7372)

Personal Finance Market

Market shares are shown in percent.

Quicken	.73.0%
Other	.27.0

Source: *Forbes*, May 27, 2002, p. 89.

★ 1844 ★

Software (SIC 7372)

PKI Software and Certification Authority Services

Shares are shown based on an estimated $118 million market.

Entrust	35.0%
VeriSign	19.0
Other	46.0

Source: *Internet Week*, November 26, 2001, p. 52, from Dataquest Inc.

★ 1845 ★

Software (SIC 7372)

Product Life Cycle Software, 2000

Market shares are shown in percent.

SDRC	14.0%
Parametric Technology	14.0
MatrixOne	9.0
Enovia	7.0
Agile Software	5.0
Other	51.0

Source: *Investor's Business Daily*, December 5, 2001, p. A8, from AMR Research and CIMdata Inc.

★ 1846 ★

Software (SIC 7372)

Search Engine Software

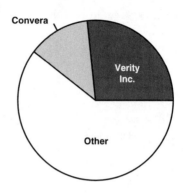

The market is estimated at $352.6 million in the year 2000.

Verity Inc.	27.0%
Convera	12.5
Other	60.5

Source: *Washington Post*, November 22, 2001, p. E5, from International Data Corp.

★ 1847 ★

Software (SIC 7372)

Storage Management Software, 2000

Shares are shown based on new license sales.

EMC	25.5%
Veritas	16.3
IBM	16.1
Computer Associates	11.7
BMC	4.3
Other	26.1

Source: *E Week*, December 17, 2001, p. 9, from Dataquest Inc.

★ 1848 ★
Software (SIC 7372)

System Recovery Software

Market share refers to the retail market. It has about 78% of the retail market for CD recording on Windows computers and 99% on Macintosh computers.

Roxio 91.0%
Other 9.0

Source: *Investor's Business Daily*, April 10, 2002, p. A6.

★ 1849 ★
Software (SIC 7372)

Tax Software Market

Market shares are shown in percent.

TurboTax 78.0%
Other 22.0

Source: *Forbes*, May 27, 2002, p. 89.

★ 1850 ★
Software (SIC 7372)

Top Media Players

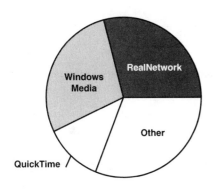

Shares are for April 2002.

RealNetwork 29.0%
Windows Media 28.0
QuickTime 12.0
Other 31.0

Source: *TV Meets the Web*, June 21, 2002, p. NA, from Media Metrix.

★ 1851 ★
Software (SIC 7372)

Virtual Stepper Software

Market shares are shown in percent.

KLA 85.0%
Other 15.0

Source: *Electronic News*, August 13, 2001, p. 2.

★ 1852 ★
Software (SIC 7372)

Web Browser Market

Data are for June 2001.

Microsoft Explorer 75.0%
Netscape 18.0
Other 7.0

Source: *USA TODAY*, August 16, 2001, p. 2B, from Giga Information Group and Jupiter Media Metrix.

★ 1853 ★
Servers (SIC 7373)

Application Server Market

Market shares are shown in percent.

BEA 41.0%
IBM 31.0
iPlanet 13.0
Other 15.0

Source: *Infoworld*, February 4, 2002, p. 22, from Gartner.

★ 1854 ★
Servers (SIC 7373)

Entry Level Server Market

Market shares are shown in percent.

Windows NT 49.9%
Unix 36.2
Linux 6.7
NetWare 5.6
Other 1.6

Source: *USA TODAY*, January 31, 2002, p. 3B, from International Data Corp.

★ 1855 ★

Servers (SIC 7373)

U.S. Server Market

Market shares are shown in percent.

	Units	Share
Dell	399,208	23.4%
Compaq	385,164	22.6
IBM	217,020	12.7
Sun Microsystems	121,402	7.1
Hewlett-Packard	99,708	5.9
Other	480,851	28.2

Source: "Gartner Dataquest Says Worldwide Server Shipments." Retrieved September 4, 2001 from the World Wide Web: http://www.gartner.com, from Dataquest Inc.

★ 1856 ★

Software (SIC 7373)

U.S. Middleware Market

The industry is shown in percent.

	2000	2005
Transaction processing	34.0%	14.0%
Integration software	34.0	50.0
Application servers	20.0	23.0
Message oriented	10.0	12.0
Object request	2.0	1.0

Source: *Investor's Business Daily*, July 17, 2001, p. A6, from Gartner Inc.

★ 1857 ★

Information Technology (SIC 7375)

U.S. Technology Spending, 2002

Spending is shown in millions of dollars. There will be roughly a fall of 2%-5%. Most IT budgets are going to infrastructure development, data centers and operations.

	($ mil.)	Share
Financial services	$ 108.4	13.58%
Manufacturing	74.3	9.31
Health care	59.2	7.42
Retailing	54.5	6.83
Insurance	53.1	6.65
Professional services	52.7	6.60
Banking	47.7	5.98
Media & Entertainment	43.8	5.49

	($ mil.)	Share
Telecommunications	$ 27.1	3.40%
Other	277.2	34.74

Source: *Electronic Commerce World*, December 2001, p. 8, from Meta Group.

★ 1858 ★

Aviation Security (SIC 7381)

Aviation Security Industry

Market shares are shown in percent.

Argenbright Security	40.0%
Huntleigh USA Corp.	20.0
Intl. Total Services	15.0
Globe Aviation Services	10.0
Other	15.0

Source: *Investor's Business Daily*, November 21, 2001, p. A4, from Handelsbanken AP.

★ 1859 ★

Security Services (SIC 7381)

Private Security Demand

Demand has grown 6% a year since 1996, with the highest growth seen in private correctional facilities and consulting. Data are in millions of dollars.

	1996	2001	Share
Guarding	$ 10,000	$ 11,650	34.72%
Alarm monitoring	6,900	11,050	32.94
Private investigations	1,990	2,130	6.35
Pre-employment screening & other	1,900	2,300	6.86
Armored transport	1,490	2,060	6.14
Systems integration	715	1,500	4.47

Continued on next page.

★ 1859 ★ *Continued*
Security Services (SIC 7381)

Private Security Demand

Demand has grown 6% a year since 1996, with the highest growth seen in private correctional facilities and consulting. Data are in millions of dollars.

	1996	2001	Share
Private correctional facilities management	$ 660	$ 1,950	5.81%
Security consulting	525	910	2.71

Source: *Research Alert*, May 17, 2002, p. 10, from Freedonia Group.

★ 1860 ★
Security Services (SIC 7382)

Guarding and Security Industry

Market shares are shown in percent.

Securitas (Pinkerton)	22.0%
Wackenhut Corp.	9.0
Other	69.0

Source: *Wall Street Journal*, April 9, 2002, p. B4.

★ 1861 ★
Security Services (SIC 7382)

Largest Security Firms

Firms are ranked by gross revenue in millions of dollars.

ADT Security Services Inc.	$ 2,000.0
Protection One Alarm Monitoring Inc.	432.0
Brink's Home Security	238.1
Honeywell Security Products	220.8
Slomin's Security	90.4
Edison Security	90.0
Vector Security Inc.	77.0
Bay Alarm Co.	55.0
Sonitrol Management Corp.	48.6
Guardian Alarm Co.	48.0

Source: *SDM*, May 2001, p. 55.

★ 1862 ★
Photofinishing (SIC 7384)

Film Processing by Outlet, 2001

Discount stores	35.6%
Drug stores	23.7
Supermarkets	12.5
Warehouse clubs	10.4
Mail order	7.7
Camera stores	4.3
One-hour labs	2.6
Other	3.2

Source: *Drug Store News*, December 17, 2001, p. 77, from PMA Monthly Processing Surveys.

★ 1863 ★
Career Coaches (SIC 7389)

Certified Coaches by State

Many people have turned to career coaches - people to help them focus their skills and goals. Coaches can become certified by coursework and experience (exact requirements come from several national coaching foundations). The number of "career coaches" is shown for selected states, up from 5,300 in 1998.

	No.	Share
California	533	5.33%
New York	185	1.85
Massachusetts	172	1.72
Illinois	144	1.44
Colorado	140	1.40
Other	8,826	88.26

Source: *Wall Street Journal*, June 26, 2001, p. B6, from MyJobCoach Inc.

★ 1864 ★
Mergers & Acquisitions (SIC 7389)

Leading Industries for Mergers, 2001

Figures show number of deals for third quarter.

	No.	Share
Computer software, supplies, services	108	40.45%
Banking and finance	74	27.72
Drugs, medical supplies and equipment	28	10.49
Brokerages & investments	28	10.49
Other	29	10.86

Source: *Investor's Business Daily*, October 17, 2001, p. A8, from Mergerstat.

★ 1865 ★
Mergers & Acquisitions (SIC 7389)

Top Media Mergers

Acquirers are shown in parentheses. Value is in billions of dollars.

Time Warner (America Online)	$ 181.56
Voicestream Wireless (Deutsche Telekom)	55.06
Liberty Media Group (shareholders)	44.75
Seagram Co. (Vivendi)	42.78
AT&T Wireless (shareholders)	27.40
Network Solutions (VeriSign)	20.78
Canal Plus (Vivendi)	14.11
Infinity Broadcasting (Group Viacom)	13.64
Times Mirror (Tribune Co.)	11.62

Source: *Electronic Media*, April 9, 2001, p. 14.

★ 1866 ★
Stock Photography (SIC 7389)

Stock Photography Industry

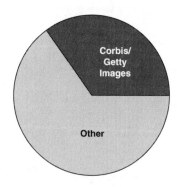

The industry is valued at about $2 billion, with Corbis and Getty Images holding the lead.

Corbis/Getty Images	35.0%
Other	65.0

Source: *Pacific Business News*, August 31, 2001, p. 43.

★ 1867 ★
Trade Shows (SIC 7389)

Largest Trade Show Organizers

Market shares are shown based on square footage of top 200 shows.

Reed Exhibition Companies	8.4%
George Little Management	4.5
Miller Freeman	4.0
VNU Expositions	3.5
Key3Media Group	2.5
Advanstar Communications	2.5
Society of Manufacturing Engineers	2.0
Hall-Erickson	2.0
dmg world media	2.0
Other	68.6

Source: *Tradeshow Week*, April 2001, p. 5.

★ 1868 ★

Trade Shows (SIC 7389)

Largest Trade Shows in Canada

Shows are ranked by number of attendees.

National Petroleum Show 59,997
Canadian Gift & Tableware Association . . 27,115

Source: *Tradeshow Week*, June 18, 2001, p. 1.

★ 1869 ★

Trade Shows (SIC 7389)

Top Sites for Trade Shows, 2002

Data show the top locations.

Las Vegas 161
Toronto 136
Chicago 135
New York City 125
Dallas 101
Atlanta 97
Orlando 83
New Orleans 70
Boston 68
San Francisco 66
San Diego 66

Source: *Tradeshow Week*, December 10, 2001, p. 1.

★ 1870 ★

Translation Services (SIC 7389)

Translation Services In North America

Data show number of professional translators who are members of the American Translators Association by language. The organization is the industry's main professional organization, with 500 of its 8,300 members translation companies or units of majorcorporations.

Spanish 2,217
French 1,189
German 903
Russian 481
Japanese 384
Chinese 154
Arabic 120
Korean 50
Farsi 21
Albanian 7

Source: *New York Times*, October 21, 2001, p. 4, from American Translators Association.

SIC 75 - Auto Repair, Services, and Parking

★ 1871 ★

Auto Rental (SIC 7514)

Body Shop/Insurance Replacement Business

When you get a "loaner" from the mechanic, it is more than likely Enterprise.

Enterprise	63.0%
Other	37.0

Source: *Forbes*, November 26, 2001, p. I60.

★ 1872 ★

Auto Rental (SIC 7514)

Largest Car Rental Companies, 2000

Companies have been trying to reduce fleet size by 20-30% to match diminished demand — in part from less travelers after September 11. Rental rates are also falling. Market shares are shown in percent.

Hertz	29.1%
Avis	22.6
National	15.4
Budget	12.0
Alamo	9.8
Dollar Thrifty	8.9
Other	2.2

Source: *Wall Street Journal*, November 14, 2001, p. B4, from *Auto Rental News*.

★ 1873 ★

Auto Rental (SIC 7514)

Top Car Rental Firms to the Federal Government

Market shares are shown based on expenses/charges put on government cards.

Avis	14.9%
National	12.2
Hertz	10.9
Budget	10.7
Dollar	10.5
Alamo	9.6
Thrifty	9.3
Enterprise	8.9
Other	12.9

Source: *Government Executive*, August 1, 2001, p. NA, from General Services Administration's Federal Supply Service.

★ 1874 ★

Auto Leasing (SIC 7515)

Auto Lease Leaders, 2001

Figures show the percent of autos that were leased in 2001 that sold more than 100,000 units (does not include fleet sales).

Mercedes-Benz	58.3%
BMW	52.1
Volvo	38.7
VW-Audi	37.2
Mitsubishi	36.8
Toyota	31.3
Nissan	29.0
Honda	28.9

Source: *Los Angeles Times*, March 8, 2002, p. C4, from CNW Marketing Research.

★ 1875 ★

Auto Leasing (SIC 7515)

Consumer Vehicle Leasing Market

Market shares are shown for the year to date December 2000.

General Motors Acceptance Corp.	20.20%
Ford Motor Carpet Lease	19.68
Chrysler Financial Corp.	7.45
Toyota Motor Credit Corp.	6.74
Volkswagen Audi	3.21
American Honda Finance Corp.	3.15
Bank of America	3.12
Chase Auto Finance	2.93
Other	33.52

Source: "Consumer Vehicle Lease." Retrieved February 2, 2002 from the World Wide Web: http://www. automotivedigest.com, from R.L. Polk.

★ 1876 ★

Auto Body Repair (SIC 7530)

Types of Parts Used in Collision Shops

Data show the market share of parts used to repair collision damaged vehicles. OEM stands for original equipment manufacturer.

OEM parts	72.0%
Non-certified generics	15.0
Recycled/salvaged parts	10.0
CAPA-certified parts	3.0

Source: *Automotive Body Repair News*, August 2001, p. 24, from Automotive Recyclers Association.

SIC 76 - Miscellaneous Repair Services

★ 1877 ★

Aircraft Repair (SIC 7699)

Civil Aftermarket Business

| Rolls-Royce |
| Other |

In the past five years Rolls-Royce has more than doubled its share of repair and overhaul on its civil engines.

Rolls-Royce 56.0%
Other 44.0

Source: *PR Newswire*, January 30, 2002.

★ 1878 ★

Ship Repair (SIC 7699)

Ship Repair Services on the Great Lakes

Market shares are shown in percent.

Manitowoc 65.0%
Other 35.0

Source: "The Manitowoc Company." Retrieved November 7, 2001 from the World Wide Web: http://www.manitowoc.com.

SIC 78 - Motion Pictures

★ 1879 ★

Home Video (SIC 7812)

Popular Types of Rentals, 2001

Comedy	
Drama	
Action	
Thriller	
Horror	
Animated	
Suspense	
Science fiction	
Family	
Other	

Shares are shown based on active rental turns.

Comedy	35.1%
Drama	23.3
Action	14.7
Thriller	10.2
Horror	3.6
Animated	3.5
Suspense	3.4
Science fiction	2.4
Family	2.1
Other	1.7

Source: *Video Store*, January 13, 2002, p. 24.

★ 1880 ★

Home Video (SIC 7812)

Top Selling Films on DVD

Titles are ranked by rental revenue, in millions.

Shrek	$ 157
Pearl Harbor	144
Dr. Seuss' How the Grinch Stole Christmas	104
Planet of the Apes	101

Cast Away	$ 97
Star Wars Ep. 1 - The Phantom Menace	96
The Godfather Collection	85
The Mummy Returns	79
Jurassic Park III	75
Snow White	74

Source: *Video Business*, January 21, 2002, p. 32, from Video Software Distributors Association VidTrac and studios and retailers.

★ 1881 ★

Home Video (SIC 7812)

Top Selling Films on VHS

Titles are ranked by rental revenue, in millions.

Shrek	$ 228
Dr. Seuss' How the Grinch Stole Christmas	192
Dinosaur	153
Pearl Harbor	119
Lady and the Tramp II	119
The Emperor's New Groove	115
102 Dalmations	93
Remember the Titans	88
Spy Kids	83
The Princess Diaries	80

Source: *Video Business*, January 21, 2002, p. 32, from Video Software Distributors Association VidTrac and studios and retailers.

★ 1882 ★

Home Video (SIC 7812)

Top Fitness Videos, 2001

Shares are for the first quarter.

Artisan	25.4%
Living Arts	16.2
Ventura Distribution	15.7
Anchor Bay	13.0
PPI Ent.	8.2
Sony Music/Wonder	6.9
Other	9.3

Source: *Video Store*, May 20, 2001, p. 12, from VideoScan.

★ 1883 ★

Home Video (SIC 7812)

Top Rental Formats, 2001

VHS rental spending outpaced DVDs by $5.6 billion.

VHS	83.4%
DVDs	16.6

Source: *PR Newswire*, March 27, 2002, p. NA, from Video Software Dealers Association.

★ 1884 ★

Home Video (SIC 7812)

Top Renting Films

Titles are ranked by rental revenue, in millions.

Meet the Parents	$ 115.64
What Women Want	94.86
Cast Away	93.68
Miss Congeniality	90.78
What Lies Beneath	89.77
The Family Man	87.92
Traffic	85.43
Me, Myself & Irene	79.33
Unbreakable	76.11
Remember the Titans	70.11

Source: *Video Business*, January 21, 2002, p. 32, from Video Software Distributors Association VidTrac and studios and retailers.

★ 1885 ★

Home Video (SIC 7812)

Top Selling Films

Titles are ranked by revenues, in millions.

Shrek	$ 385
Dr. Seuss: How the Grinch Stole Christmas	296
Pearl Harbor	263
Dinosaur	198
The Emperor's New Groove	154
Remember the Titans	143
The Mummy Returns	141
Lady and the Tramp II	139
Jurassic Park III	134
The Princess Diaries	133

Source: *Video Business*, January 21, 2002, p. 32, from Video Software Distributors Association VidTrac and studios and retailers.

★ 1886 ★

Home Video (SIC 7812)

Top Videos Of All Time, 2001

The top movies on home-viewing formats, based on the number initially shipped.

The Lion King	28.8
Aladdin	24.0
Shrek	23.8
Titanic	23.5
Snow White and the Seven Dwarfs	21.1
Beauty and the Beast	20.2
Toy Story	19.5
Dr. Seuss' How the Grinch Stole Christmas	17.9
Toy Story 2	17.0

Source: *USA TODAY*, April 2, 2002, p. 3D.

★ 1887 ★

Motion Pictures (SIC 7812)

Blockbuster Weekends of All Time

Films are ranked by opening weekend in millions of dollars.

Spider-Man	$ 114.8
Harry Potter and the Sorcerer's Stone	90.3
The Lost World: Jurassic Park	90.2
Pearl Harbor	75.2
Mission: Impossible 2	70.8

Continued on next page.

★ **1887** ★ *Continued*

Motion Pictures (SIC 7812)

Blockbuster Weekends of All Time

Films are ranked by opening weekend in millions of dollars.

Planet of the Apes	$ 68.5
The Mummy Returns	68.1
Rush Hour 2	67.4
The Lord of the Rings	66.1

Source: *New York Times*, May 7, 2002, p. C6, from ACNielsen EDI.

★ **1888** ★

Motion Pictures (SIC 7812)

Foreign Films on DVD

An estimated 156 foreign films will be released on DVD this year, or 7% of all DVD film releases. Released films are shown by language.

Chinese	38.0%
French	21.0
Japanese	8.0
Italian	7.0
German	6.0
Other	20.0

Source: *Video Store*, July 1, 2001, p. 10.

★ **1889** ★

Motion Pictures (SIC 7812)

Top Films for 2001

The top grossing firms are ranked for the year, as of December 30, 2001. It was a record breaking year, with Exhibitor Relations estimating $8.35 billion spent on movie tickets, beating $7.7 billion in 2000. Harry Potter set a record of $90 million in its first three days.

Harry Potter and the Sorcerer's Stone . .	$ 286.1
Shrek	267.6
Monsters Inc.	236.3
Rush Hour 2	226.1
The Mummy Returns	202.0
Pearl Harbor	198.5
Jurassic Park III	181.2
Planet of the Apes	179.6

Hannibal	$ 165.1
Lord of the Rings: the Fellowship of the Ring	154.5

Source: *New York Times*, December 31, 2001, p. E5, from Exhibitor Relations.

★ **1890** ★

Motion Pictures (SIC 7812)

Top IMAX Films

The top films of all time are ranked by box office, in millions of dollars.

Everest	$ 76.4
Fantasia 2000	60.5
Mysteries of Egypt	40.5
T-Rex: Back to the Cretaceous	38.0
Michael Jordan to the MAX	18.6
Thrill Ride: the Science of Fun	17.1
Across the Sea of Time	15.8
Wings of Courage	14.9
Africa's Elephant Kingdom	13.4
Cirque du Soleil - Journey of Man	12.9

Source: "Top IMAX Movies." Retrieved January 3, 2002 from the World Wide Web: http://www.the-numbers.com.

★ **1891** ★

Motion Pictures (SIC 7812)

Where Movies Are Filmed

The chart shows the locations for production in North America. Some groups have estimated that the country loses $10 billion a year in film and television production to other countries.

Canada	35.0%
California	27.0
New York	12.0
Other	26.0

Source: *Los Angeles Times*, December 13, 2001, p. D1, from Center for Entertainment Industry Research and Data.

★ 1892 ★

Motion Picture Distribution (SIC 7822)

Leading "Niche" Film Marketers

Market shares of art house/independents are shown for year to date.

Newmarket	11.3%
Lions Gate	11.3
Fox Searchlight	8.5
Miramax	8.0
Sony Classics	7.9
Fine Line	7.3
Sony	6.1
U/Focus	3.7
Artisan	3.7
Par Classics	3.3
IDP	3.3
8X Entertainment	3.1
Other	22.6

Source: *Variety*, October 29, 2001, p. 16.

★ 1893 ★

Motion Picture Distribution (SIC 7822)

Top DVD Distributors

Market shares are shown in percent.

Warner	22.8%
Universal	16.4
Buena Vista	15.7
Columbia	12.0
Fox	11.9
Parmount	8.5
MGM	5.4
Artisan	2.3
USA	2.0
Other	3.0

Source: *Video Business*, January 21, 2002, p. 32, from Video Software Distributors Association VidTrac and studios and retailers.

★ 1894 ★

Motion Picture Distribution (SIC 7822)

Top DVD/VHS Distributors

Market shares are shown in percent.

Buena Vista Home Entertainment	19.0%
Warner Home Video	18.9
Universal Studios Home Entertainment	11.8
20th Century Fox Home Entertainment	8.8

Columbia TriStar Home Entertainment	8.6%
Paramount Home Entertainment	7.9
DreamWorks Home Entertainment	5.9
MGM Home Entertainment	4.4
Artisan Home Entertainment	2.6
Other	12.1

Source: *DVD News*, January 21, 2002, p. 1.

★ 1895 ★

Motion Picture Distribution (SIC 7822)

Top Film Distributors, 2002

Market shares are as of April 28, 2002.

New Line	13.8%
Universal	13.6
Buena Vista	13.1
Sony Pictures	12.4
Paramount	11.4
Warner Bros.	10.0
Fox	9.4
Miramax	5.5
Other	10.8

Source: *New York Times*, May 6, 2002, p. C8, from ACNielsen EDI.

★ 1896 ★

Motion Picture Distribution (SIC 7822)

Top VHS Distributors, 2001

Market shares are shown based on revenues.

Warner	19.3%
Buena Vista	16.1
Universal	15.1
Columbia	15.0
Paramount	10.0
Fox	9.1
DreamWorks	5.8

Continued on next page.

★ 1896 ★ *Continued*

Motion Picture Distribution (SIC 7822)

Top VHS Distributors, 2001

Market shares are shown based on revenues.

MGM	3.9%
Artisan	2.9
USA	2.2
Other	6.4

Source: *Video Business*, January 21, 2002, p. 34.

★ 1897 ★

Movie Theaters (SIC 7832)

Drive-Ins by State

The number has fallen from 2,087 in 1987 to 637 in 2000.

	No.	Share
California	59	9.26%
Pennsylvania	55	8.63
Ohio	52	8.16
New York	48	7.54
Indiana	34	5.34
Florida	29	4.55
Michigan	24	3.77
Washington	21	3.30
Missouri	21	3.30
Other	294	46.15

Source: *USA TODAY*, August 31, 2001, p. 2E, from National Association of Theatre Owners.

★ 1898 ★

Movie Theaters (SIC 7832)

Largest Theater Circuits, 2001

Data show screens as of June 1, 2001.

Regal Cinemas	4,067
AMC Entertainment	2,588
Carmike Cinemas	2,431
Loews Cineplex Entertainment	2,323
Cinemark USA Inc.	2,223

Source: "Top 10 Circuits." Retrieved January 8, 2002 from the World Wide Web: http://www.natoonline.org, from National Association of Theater Owners.

★ 1899 ★

Movie Rental Stores (SIC 7841)

Largest Movie Rental Chains

Firms are ranked by number of stores.

Blockbuster	7,800
Hollywood	1,800
Movie Gallery	1,050

Source: *Retail Merchandiser*, February 2002, p. 29.

★ 1900 ★

Movie Rental Stores (SIC 7841)

Top Movie Rental Firms, 2001

Market shares are shown in percent.

Blockbuster	33.3%
Hollywood Entertainment	10.2
Movie Gallery	3.0
Family Video	1.4
Video update	0.9
Other	51.2

Source: *Video Store*, April 28, 2002, p. 28.

★ 1901 ★

Movie Rental Stores (SIC 7841)

Top Video Stores in Mexico

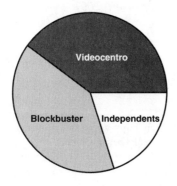

Market shares are shown in percent.

Videocentro	. . . . 40.0%
Blockbuster	. . . . 40.0
Independents	. . . . 20.0

Source: ''Movie Rental Market.'' Retrieved October 2, 2001 from the World Wide Web: http://www.usatrade.gov.

SIC 79 - Amusement and Recreation Services

Dance Schools (SIC 7911)

Who Teaches Us to Dance

Firms are ranked by franchise sales in millions of dollars.

Arthur Murray International . . . . $ 55
Fred Astaire Dance Studios 40

Source: *Knight-Ridder/Tribune Business News*, July 8, 2001, p. NA.

Arenas (SIC 7922)

Largest Entertainment Venues

Facilities are for capacities of 15,000 or more.

Madison Square Garden (NY) . . . . . . $ 73.2
First Union Center (PA) 31.7
FleetCenter (MA) 30.2
Staples Center (CA) 25.2
Palace of Auburn Hills (MI) 24.4
Phillips Arena (GA) 24.1
United Center (IL) 22.0
Continental Airlines Arena (NJ) 21.0
Pepsi Center (CO) 19.1

Source: *Amusement Business*, January 24, 2002, p. 14.

Talent Agencies (SIC 7922)

Largest Talent Agencies

Creative Artists Agency

William Morris Agency

Intl. Creative Management

United Talent Agency

Endeavor

Agencies are ranked by estimated annual revenue in millions of dollars.

Creative Artists Agency . . . . $ 250
William Morris Agency 250
Intl. Creative Management 150
United Talent Agency 100
Endeavor 70

Source: *Wall Street Journal*, February 23, 2002, p. B1.

Concert Promotions (SIC 7929)

Leading Concert Promoters

Data show millions of tickets sold.

Clear Channel Entertainment 27.38
House of Blues Concerts 3.81
Palace Sports & Entertainment 1.40
Jam Productions 1.28
AEG's Concerts West/Goldenvoice 1.24

Source: *Wall Street Journal*, March 29, 2002, p. B4.

Concerts (SIC 7929)

Top Concert Tours, 2001

Artists are ranked by gross concert sales, in millions.

U2 . . . . $ 109.7
'N Sync 86.8

Continued on next page.

★ 1906 ★ *Continued*
Concerts (SIC 7929)

Top Concert Tours, 2001

Artists are ranked by gross concert sales, in millions.

Backstreet Boys	$ 82.1
Dave Matthews Band	60.5
Elton John/Billy Joel	57.2
Madonna	54.7
Aerosmith	49.3
Janet Jackson	42.1
Eric Clapton	38.8
Neil Diamond	35.4

Source: *USA TODAY*, February 18, 2002, p. 2B, from
Pollstar.

★ 1907 ★
Concerts (SIC 7929)

Top Touring Acts

*Acts are ranked by ticket gross for December 11,
2000-September 3, 2001.*

U2	$ 90.4
Backstreet Boys	60.9
Dave Matthews Band	60.6
Billy Joel & Elton John	58.9
'N Sync	55.3
Madonna	40.8
AC/DC	28.2
Ozzfest 2001	19.8

Source: *Amusement Business*, October 22, 2001, p. 5.

★ 1908 ★
Performing Arts (SIC 7929)

Leading Performance Art Organizations in Boston, MA

Figures show attendance.

Boston Symphony Orchestra/Boston Pops .	430,000
Boston Ballet	270,000
Blue Man Group	266,000
Huntington Theatre Co. Inc.	182,660
American Repertory Theatre	99,000
Jose Mateo's Ballet Theatre	70,000
Boston Lyric Opera	61,308

Source: *Boston Business Journal*, November 16, 2001, p.
22.

★ 1909 ★
Bowling Alleys (SIC 7933)

Bowling Alley Industry, 1999

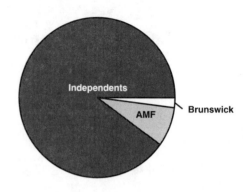

*League play peaked in 1980 with about 9 million
bowlers and has been dropping 3-6% a year. Market
shares are shown in percent.*

Independents	89.5%
AMF	7.5
Brunswick	2.0

Source: *Knight-Ridder/Tribune News Service*, March 19,
2001, p. NA.

★ 1910 ★
Sports (SIC 7941)

Football Teams by Attendance

Teams are ranked by average attendance.

Washington Redskins	80,928
Kansas City Chiefs	78,921
New York Giants	78,010
New York Jets	77,964
Detroit Lions	75,884
Denver Broncos	75,505
Miami Dolphins	73,739
Carolina Panthers	72,936
Cleveland Browns	72,693

Source: "News." Retrieved February 6, 2002 from the
World Wide Web: http://www.sportsvueinc.com, from
Sportsvue Inc.

★ 1911 ★
Sports (SIC 7941)
Largest Sports Events in Atlanta, GA

From 1999-2003, sports pumped $4.5 billion into the local economy. Figures are in billions of dollars.

Atlanta Motor Speedway	$ 2,275
Atlanta Braves	527
Super Bowl XXXIV	250
SEC Football Championship	225
Chick-fil-A Peach Bowl	225
Atlanta Dragway	196
Atlanta Hawks	164
McDonald's Heritage Bowl	75
Atlanta Football Classic	75

Source: *USA TODAY*, March 28, 2002, p. 2B.

★ 1912 ★
Sports (SIC 7941)
Top Earning Athletes

Earnings are shown in millions of dollars. Forbes estimates Tiger Woods has the chance to be the world's first sports billionaire by the end of his career.

Michael Schumacher	$ 59.0
Tiger Woods	53.0
Mike Tyson	48.0
Michael Jordan	37.0
Grant Hill	26.0
Dale Earnhardt	24.5
Shaquille O'Neal	24.0
Oscar De La Hoya	23.0
Lennox Lewis	23.0
Kevin Garnett	21.0

Source: *Christian Science Monitor*, June 8, 2001, p. 12, from *Forbes*.

★ 1913 ★
Horse Racing (SIC 7948)
Horse Track Betting

The two companies have over 50% of the market.

Churchill Downs Inc./Magna Entertainment . .	50.0%
Other	50.0

Source: *BusinessWeek*, May 13, 2002, p. 12.

★ 1914 ★
Health Clubs (SIC 7991)
Fitness Club Membership by Age

30-39	33.0%
40-49	22.0
50-59	17.0
18-29	10.0
60-69	9.0
70+	7.0

Source: *USA TODAY*, December 17, 2001, p. C1, from *American Demographics*.

★ 1915 ★
Health Clubs (SIC 7991)
Fitness Club Memberships by Type

Total members reached 32.8 million, with the largest segment belonging to 35-54 year olds. From 1987 to the present, the 55 and older group grew 379%.

Commercial multipurpose	30.0%
YMCA/JCC	16.0
Commercial fitness	15.0
University based	5.0
Hospital based	5.0
Corporate	5.0
Residential	4.0
Municipal/town	4.0
Military	4.0
Other	12.0

Source: "Statistics." Retrieved February 5, 2002 from the World Wide Web: http://www.ihrsa.org, from International Health & Racquet Club Association.

★ 1916 ★
Spas (SIC 7991)

Favorite Spa Treatments

The day spa industry generates roughly $7.3 billion. The table shows the top treatments for men.

Massage	71.0%
Sauna	27.0
Hydro treatments	20.0

Source: *Cosmetics International*, March 25, 2002, p. 2, from U.S. Day Spa Association.

★ 1917 ★
Golf Courses (SIC 7992)

Alternative Golf Facilities

According to the source, 5,312 of the 5,542 alternative golf facilties are open to the public.

	No.	Share
Driving ranges	2,805	50.61%
Par 3 courses	1,653	29.83
Executive courses	865	15.61
Pitch-and-putt courses	160	2.89
Other	59	1.06

Source: *Golf World*, May 3, 2002, p. S6, from National Golf Foundation.

★ 1918 ★
Slot Machines (SIC 7993)

Slot Machine Industry

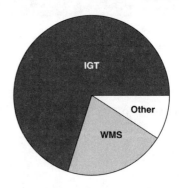

Recent industry trends include machines with better graphics and entertainment value. Market shares are shown in percent.

IGT	70.0%
WMS	21.0
Other	9.0

Source: *Knight-Ridder/Tribune Business News*, May 3, 2001, p. NA.

★ 1919 ★
Amusement Parks (SIC 7996)

Top Amusement Parks

Visitors are shown in millions. Figures are for North America.

The Magic Kingdom	14.7
Disneyland	12.3
EPCOT	9.0
Disney MGM Studios	8.3
Disney's Animal Kingdom	7.7
Universal Studios	7.2
Islands of Adventure	5.5
Seaworld Florida	5.1
Disney's California Adventure	5.0
Universal Studios Hollywood	4.7

Source: *Amusement Business*, December 24, 2001, p. 18.

★ 1920 ★

Amusement Parks (SIC 7996)

Top U.S. Waterparks

Parks are ranked by attendance, in thousands.

Blizzard Beach	1,835
Typhoon Lagoon	1,656
Wet'N Wild (Orlando)	1,326
Schlitterbahn	950
Raging Waters	750
Water Country USA	700
Six Flags Hurricane Harbor	640
Wet'N Wild (Las Vegas)	586
Adventure Island	560

Source: *Amusement Business*, December 24, 2001, p. 28.

★ 1921 ★

Sports (SIC 7997)

Popular Sports for High School Boys

Data show number of participants.

Football	1,012,420
Basketball	539,849
Outdoor track/field	491,420
Baseball	450,513
Soccer	332,850
Wrestling	244,988
Cross country	188,420
Golf	161,757
Tennis	143,650

Source: "Participation Sets Record." Retrieved February 5, 2002 from the World Wide Web: http://www.nfhs.org, from National Federation of State High School Associations.

★ 1922 ★

Sports (SIC 7997)

Popular Sports for High School Girls

Data show number of participants.

Basketball	444,872
Outdoor track and field	415,666
Volleyball	388,518
Fast softball	328,020
Soccer	274,166
Tennis	164,282
Cross country	158,516
Swimming and diving	139,601

Competitive spirits squads	86,336
Field hockey	60,918

Source: "Participation Sets Record." Retrieved February 5, 2002 from the World Wide Web: http://www.nfhs.org, from National Federation of State High School Associations.

★ 1923 ★

Gambling (SIC 7999)

Casino Leaders in Detroit, MI

Market shares are shown based on revenues.

MGM Grand Detroit	36.3%
MotorCity	35.8
Greektown	27.8
Other	9.9

Source: *Knight-Ridder/Tribune Business News*, January 15, 2002, p. NA.

★ 1924 ★

Gambling (SIC 7999)

Colorado's Gaming Industry

The state collected $9.6 million in gaming taxes, with 75% of that from Black Hawk.

Black Hawk	70.0%
Other	30.0

Source: *PR Newswire*, July 6, 2001, p. NA.

★ 1925 ★

Gambling (SIC 7999)

Preferred Casinos in Mississippi

Figures are for the third quarter.

Grand Casino Biloxi 41.0%
Isle of Capri 31.0
Casino Magic Biloxi 30.0

Source: *Knight-Ridder/Tribune News Service*, December 5, 2001, p. NA.

★ 1926 ★

Gambling (SIC 7999)

Top Casino Markets, 2000

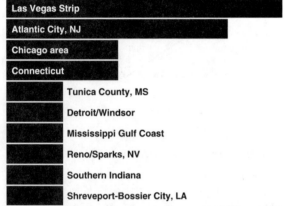

Regions are ranked by gross revenues in billions of dollars. Connecticut refers to Indian casinos; Chicago includes Illinois and northwest Indiana.

Las Vegas Strip . . . . $ 4.80
Atlantic City, NJ 4.30
Chicago area 2.00
Connecticut 1.90
Tunica County, MS 1.20
Detroit/Windsor 1.20
Mississippi Gulf Coast 1.10
Reno/Sparks, NV 1.00
Southern Indiana 0.69
Shreveport-Bossier City, LA 0.68

Source: *Knight-Ridder/Tribune News Service*, January 28, 2002, p. NA, from American Gaming Association.

★ 1927 ★

Lotteries (SIC 7999)

Lottery Market Shares

Market shares are shown in percent.

GTECH 70.0%
Other 30.0

Source: *Knight-Ridder/Tribune Business News*, November 7, 2001, p. NA, from CIBC World Markets.

★ 1928 ★

National Parks (SIC 7999)

Most Visited National Parks, 2000

Roughly 285 million visitors were expected to visit the nation's parks during the summer of 2001, about the same as in 2000. Data show millions of visitors.

Great Smoky Mountains 10.1
Grand Canyon 4.4
Yosemite (AZ) 3.4
Olympic (WA) 3.3
Rocky Mountain (CO) 3.1
Yellowstone 2.8
Grand Teton (WY) 2.5
Acadia (ME) 2.5
Zion (UT) 2.4

Source: *Christian Science Monitor*, June 1, 2001, p. 24.

SIC 80 - Health Services

★ 1929 ★

Health Care (SIC 8000)
Number of Pain Sufferers

| Arthritis |
| Migraine |
| Back and neck pain |
| Repetitive motion injuries |

Data show estimated millions of people who suffer from selected afflictions.

Arthritis 43
Migraine 28
Back and neck pain 27
Repetitive motion injuries 14

Source: *Research Alert*, January 18, 2002, p. 5, from Marketdata Enterprise.

★ 1930 ★

Health Care (SIC 8000)
Personal Health Spending

A total of $1.02 trillion was spent on personal health in 1998.

Hospitals 37.6%
Physician services 22.5
Prescription drugs 12.0
Long term care 11.5
Other 16.5

Source: *Best's Review*, April 2002, p. 75, from Urban Institute.

★ 1931 ★

Health Care (SIC 8011)
Emergency Room Visits

The number of visits grew 14% to 108 million in 2000 from 94.9 million in 1997.

Stomach/abdominal pain, cramps, spasms . . . 6.3%
Chest pain and related symptoms 5.4
Fever 4.1
Headache, pain in head 2.7
Shortness of breath 2.5
Cough 2.4
Back symptoms 2.4
Pain, not referable to specific body system . . 2.2
Other 72.0

Source: *Research Alert*, May 17, 2002, p. 10, from National Center for Health Statistics.

★ 1932 ★

Physicians (SIC 8011)
What Types of Doctors Do We See

Data show percent of office visits.

Family practice 35.0%
Internal medicine 23.0
Pediatrics 18.0
Ob gyn 10.0
Dermatology 8.0
Psychiatry 4.0
Other 3.0

Source: *Family Practice News*, October 1, 2001, p. 1, from National Ambulatory Medical Care Survey and National Center for Health Statistics.

★ 1933 ★

Dentists (SIC 8021)

Largest Dental Firms in Albany, NY

Groups are ranked by number of local dentists.

St. Peter's Hospital	25
1st Advantage Dental	18
St. Clare's Dental	12
Aspen Dental	7
Northeastern Dental PLLC	6
Rose Dental Associates	4
Nothing But the Tooth	4

Source: *The Business Review (Albany, NY)*, December 10, 2001, p. 5B.

★ 1934 ★

Laser Surgery (SIC 8042)

Laser Surgery Performers

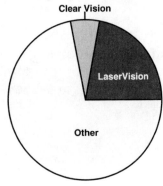

Laser Vision has announced plans to purchase Clear Vision. Market shares are shown in percent.

LaserVision	22.0%
Clear Vision	6.0
Other	72.0

Source: *St. Louis Business Journal*, August 24, 2001, p. 8A, from Market Scope.

★ 1935 ★

Podiatry (SIC 8043)

Common Foot Problems

Figures show the millions of Americans with various feet problems.

	(mil.)	Share
Toenail problems	11.3	20.62%
Infections	11.3	20.62
Corns or calluses	11.2	20.44%
Injuries	5.6	10.22
Flat feet/fallen arches	4.6	8.39
Bunions	4.4	8.03
Arthritis	3.9	7.12
Other joint deformity	2.5	4.56

Source: *USA TODAY*, June 10, 2002, p. 6D, from National Center for Health Statistics.

★ 1936 ★

Alternative Medicine (SIC 8049)

Complementary and Alternative Medicine Market

Total spending hit $30 billion in 2001, or almost 2. 5% of the total of $1.2 trillion in personal health care spending.

Chiropractic	50.0%
Massage therapy	28.0
Tradional Chinese medicine/acupuncture	18.0
Naturopathy	2.0
Homeopathy	2.0

Source: *Research Alert*, April 5, 2002, p. 10, from *Nutrition Business Journal*.

★ 1937 ★

Hospitals (SIC 8060)

Leading Medical Centers in California

Market shares are shown in percent.

Community Medical Centers	46.0%
St. Agnes Medical Centers	29.0
Other	25.0

Source: *Bond Buyer*, July 20, 2001, p. 3.

★ 1938 ★
Surgery (SIC 8060)

Popular Plastic Surgeries

More than 1.3 million went under the knife in 2000, a 198% increase over 1992.

	1992	2000
Eyelid surgery	59,461	172,244
Liposuction	47,212	229,588
Breast implants	32,607	187,755
Tummy tuck	16,810	58,463
Forehead lift	13,501	41,668

Source: *U.S. News & World Report*, June 25, 2001, p. 10, from American Society of Plastic Surgeons.

★ 1939 ★
Surgery (SIC 8060)

Top Nonsurgical Cosmetic Procedures for Men

Botulinum toxin injection
Chemical peel
Laser hair removal
Microdermabrasion
Collagen injection

Data show number of procedures.

Botulinum toxin injection	220,356
Chemical peel	161,320
Laser hair removal	139,461
Microdermabrasion	94,266
Collagen injection	86,119

Source: *Research Alert*, March 1, 2002, p. 1, from American Society for Aesthetic Plastic Surgery.

★ 1940 ★
Surgery (SIC 8060)

Top Nonsurgical Cosmetic Procedures for Women

Data show number of procedures.

Botulinum toxin injection	1,379,890
Chemical peel	1,200,159
Collagen injection	1,012,396
Microdermabrasion	820,457
Laser hair removal	715,121

Source: *Research Alert*, March 1, 2002, p. 1, from American Society for Aesthetic Plastic Surgery.

★ 1941 ★
Surgery (SIC 8060)

U.S. Organ Transplants, 2001

Data show number of surgeries performed.

Kidney	13,041
Liver	4,763
Heart	2,053
Lung	985
Kidney-pancreas	817
Pancreas	421
Intestine	104
Heart-Lung	25

Source: *Wall Street Journal*, March 15, 2002, p. B3, from United Network for Organ Sharing.

★ 1942 ★
Surgery (SIC 8060)

Who Gets Botox Injections, 2000

Figures show users by age range.

35-50	41.0%
51-64	29.0
19-34	17.0
65+	13.0

Source: *Time*, February 18, 2002, p. 59.

★ 1943 ★
Psychiatric Hospitals (SIC 8063)

Largest Psychiatric Hospitals

Hospitals are ranked by number of beds.

South Oaks Hospital (NY)	334
Conifer Park (NY)	225
Caritas Peace Center (NY)	225
Charter Behavioral Health System (KY)	224
Cleo Wallace Centers Hospital (CO)	207
Brentwood Behavioral Health (LA)	200
Friends Hospital (PA)	192
Shepard and Enoch Pratt Hospital (MD)	188
Four Winds Hospital (NY)	175

Source: *Modern Healthcare*, December 24, 2001, p. S11, from Health Forum and *AHA Annual Survey of Hospitals*.

★ 1944 ★

Dialysis Centers (SIC 8092)

Largest Dialysis Centers

Companies show patient count.

Fresenius Medical Care	73,900
DaVita	42,500
Gambro	38,300
Renal Care Group	17,200
Dialysis Clinic Inc.	10,700

Source: *Investor's Business Daily*, October 24, 2001, p. A10, from U.S. Bancorp. Piper Jaffray.

★ 1945 ★

Rehabilitation Hospitals (SIC 8099)

Larget Rehabilitation Hospitals

Hospitals are ranked by number of beds.

Spaulding Rehabilitation Hospital (MA)	333
Kessler Institute for Rehabilitation (NJ)	304
Drake Center (OH)	288
Youville Lifecare (MA)	286
HealthSouth New England Rehabilitation Hospital	273
Villa Maria Hospital (FL)	272
Madonna Rehabilitation Hospital (NB)	252
HealthSouth Harmarville Rehabilitation Hospital	202
HealthSouth Braintree Rehabilitation Hospital (MA)	187

Source: *Modern Healthcare*, December 24, 2001, p. S11, from Health Forum and *AHA Annual Survey of Hospitals*.

SIC 81 - Legal Services

★ 1946 ★

Legal Services (SIC 8111)

Highest-Grossing Law Firms, 2000

Skadden Arps Slate Meagher & Flom	
Baker & McKenzie	
Jones Day Reavis & Pogue	
Latham & Watkins	
Shearman & Sterling	

Firms are ranked by gross revenues in millions of dollars.

Skadden Arps Slate Meagher & Flom . . .	$ 1,154
Baker & McKenzie	940
Jones Day Reavis & Pogue	675
Latham & Watkins	642
Shearman & Sterling	590

Source: *Financial Times*, July 30, 2001, p. 12, from Clifford Chance, *American Lawyer*, and *Legal Business*.

★ 1947 ★

Legal Services (SIC 8111)

Largest Law Firms in Canada

Firms are ranked by number of lawyers.

McCarthy Tetrault	739
Borden Ladner Gervais	611
Gowling Lafleur Henderson	593
Fasken Martineau DuMoulin	509
Fraser Milner Casgrain	507
Blake, Cassels & Graydon	490
Stikeman Elliott	380

Source: *The American Lawyer*, November 2001, p. NA, from Martindale.com.

SIC 82 - Educational Services

★ 1948 ★
Schools (SIC 8211)

Charter Schools by State

Arizona	
California	
Michigan	
Texas	
Florida	

Arizona	336
California	309
Michigan	186
Texas	172
Florida	143

Source: *USA TODAY*, November 14, 2001, p. D1, from The Center for Education Reform.

★ 1949 ★
Schools (SIC 8211)

Districts With the Largest Enrollments

New York City	1,100,000
Los Angeles	736,675
Chicago	435,470
Miami-Dade	368,453
Broward Co, FL	260,000
Clark Co, NV	246,000
Houston	210,000
Philadelphia	198,532
Hawaii	181,299
Hillsborough, FL	169,579

Source: *American School & University*, January 2002, p. 45.

★ 1950 ★
Schools (SIC 8211)

States With the Largest K-12 Spending

Figures are in millions.

California	$ 39.0
New York	29.2
Texas	25.7
Pennsylvania	15.0
Illinois	14.7
Florida	14.5
New Jersey	14.1
Michigan	13.7
Ohio	12.4

Source: *American School & University*, January 2002, p. 45.

★ 1951 ★
Schools (SIC 8211)

Top Boarding Schools in Washington D.C.

Data show number of students.

Episcopal High School	400
Randolph-Macon Academy	397
Woodberry Forest School	387
McDonogh School	192
Massanutten Military Academy	179
Madeira School	163
Saint James School	159
Oldfields School	143

Source: *Washington Business Journal*, Annual 2002, p. 8.

★ 1952 ★

Colleges (SIC 8221)

Colleges With the Most Foreign Students

China, India and Japan are the top countries of origin.

New York University 5,399
University of Southern California 5,321
Columbia University 4,837
Purdue University Main Campus 4,469
Boston University 4,443
University of Texas at Austin 4,320
Ohio State University Main Campus . . . 4,035
University of Michigan Ann Arbor 4,004
University of Wisconsin at Madison . . . 3,938

Source: *New York Times*, January 28, 2002, p. A7, from Institute of International Education.

★ 1953 ★

Colleges (SIC 8221)

Largest College Enrollments

Figures are for Fall 2001.

University of Texas 50,616
Ohio State University 48,447
University of Florida 46,798
University of Minnesota 46,597
Arizona State University 45,693
Texas A&M University 44,618
Michigan State University 44,227
University of Wisconsin 41,000
Pennsylvania State University 40,828

Source: *USA TODAY*, April 29, 2002, p. 3A, from U.S. Department of Education.

★ 1954 ★

Colleges (SIC 8221)

Who Sends the Most Students to the U.S.

China 54,466
Japan 46,872
India 42,337
South Korea 41,191
Taiwan 29,234
Canada 23,544
Indonesia 11,300

Thailand 10,983
Mexico 10,607

Source: *USA TODAY*, July 30, 2001, p. 6A, from Institute for International Education.

★ 1955 ★

Libraries (SIC 8231)

Largest Libraries in the Nation

Data show millions of volumes held.

Library of Congress 24.61
Harvard University 14.19
New York Public Library 10.42
Yale University 10.29
The Public Library of Cincinnati &
   Hamilton County 9.60
University of Illinois - Urbana-Champaign . . 9.30
Chicago Public Library 9.23
Queens Borough Public Library 9.14
University of California - Berkeley 8.90
The Free Library of Philadelphia 8.14

Source: "ALA Fact Sheet." Retrieved February 20, 2002 from the World Wide Web: http://www.ala.org.

★ 1956 ★

Libraries (SIC 8231)

Library Holdings by State

Figures show millions of volumes.

New York 71.8
California 61.1
Texas 49.7
Ohio 44.8
Massachusetts 38.6
Illinois 38.6
New Jersey 28.7
Pennsylvania 27.5
Florida 26.3
Michigan 25.6

Source: *Business North Carolina*, September 2001, p. 64.

SIC 83 - Social Services

★ 1957 ★

Adoption Services (SIC 8322)

Top Nations for Foreign Adoptions

Roughly 19,000 visas were issued for foreign children to be adopted by U.S. citizens. The top nations are shown with their visa counts.

China	4,750
Russia	4,279
Republic of Korea	1,770
Guatemala	1,609
Ukraine	1,246

Source: *USA TODAY*, February 26, 2002, p. D1, from Adoption/MedicalNews.

★ 1958 ★

Child Care (SIC 8351)

Largest Employer Child Care Centers, 2001

Firms are ranked by licensed capacity as of June 1, 2001.

Bright Horizons Family Center	45,000
Knowledge Beginnings	19,565
KinderCare Learning Centers	9,905
Childtime Learning Centers	6,930
The Children's Courtyard	3,818
La Petite Academy	3,782
New Horizons Child Care	3,707
ARAMARK Educational Resources	3,100
Tutor Time	2,880

Source: *Child Care Information Exchange*, September 2001, p. 34.

★ 1959 ★

Child Care (SIC 8351)

Largest For-Profit Child Care Centers

Firms are ranked by licensed capacity.

KinderCare Learning Centers	164,000
La Petite Academy	96,155
Children's World Learning Centers	82,660
Bright Horizons Family Solutions	48,750
Childtime Learning Centers	38,501
Knowledge Learning Communities	35,995
Nobel Learning Communities	28,200
Child Care Network	14,636
New Horizon Child Care	12,737
The Children's Courtyard	12,364

Source: *Child Care Information Exchange*, January 2002, p. 34.

★ 1960 ★

Charities (SIC 8399)

Popular Forms of Volunteering

According to the report, people are, on average, volunteering less time.

Direct service activity	24.0%
Fundraising	16.0
Informal volunteering	15.0
Advice/counseling	11.0
Organizing an event	10.0
Visiting people/offering companionship	9.0

Source: *The Non-Profit Times*, June 1, 2001, p. 5, from *IS Giving and Volunteering in the United States*.

★ 1961 ★

Charities (SIC 8399)

Top Donors to Charity, 2001

Gifts are shown in millions of dollars.

Bill Gates	$ 2,000.0
Jim Stowers	1,110.0
Ted Turner	250.0
Lucille Stewart Beeson	150.0
Henry Melville Fuller	86.0
Jeanne Gaffe	73.3
Peter B. Lewis	60.0

Source: *Knight-Ridder/Tribune Business News*, January 1, 2002, p. NA.

★ 1962 ★

Charities (SIC 8399)

Who Received the Most Private Funds

Amount is shown in millions of dollars.

Salvation Army	$ 1,440.0
Fidelity Charitable Gift Fund	1,087.7
YMCA	812.0
American Cancer Society	746.3
Lutheran Services in America	710.2
American Red Cross	637.6
Gifts in Kind International	601.9
Stanford University	580.7
Harvard University	485.2
Nature Conservancy	445.3

Source: *New York Times*, October 28, 2001, p. A18, from *The Chronicle of Philanthropy*.

SIC 84 - Museums, Botanical, Zoological Gardens

★ 1963 ★

Museums (SIC 8412)

Most Visited Museums

Smithsonian Institution	
	National Air & Space Museum
	National Gallery of Art
	American Museum of Natural History
	Metropolitan Museum of Art

Data show millions of visitors.

Smithsonian Institution	34.0
National Air & Space Museum	9.0
National Gallery of Art	5.1
American Museum of Natural History	5.0
Metropolitan Museum of Art	4.7

Source: *Research Alert*, April 5, 2002, p. 7, from Richard K. Miller & Associates.

★ 1964 ★

Zoos (SIC 8422)

Most Visited Zoos

Data show millions of visitors.

San Diego Zoo	3.40
Lincoln Park Zoo (IL)	3.00
St. Louis Zoological Park	2.78
Smithsonian National Zoological Park	2.70
Conservatory Garden at Bellagio (NV)	2.70

Source: *Research Alert*, April 5, 2002, p. 7, from Richard K. Miller & Associates.

SIC 86 - Membership Organizations

Religious Organizations (SIC 8661)

Largest Religions

| Roman Catholic |
| Southern Baptist Convention |
| United Methodist Church |
| Church of God in Christ |
| Church of Jesus Christ of Latter-day Saints |
| Evangelical Lutheran Church |
| Presbyterian Church |

Membership is shown in millions.

Roman Catholic	62.4
Southern Baptist Convention	15.9
United Methodist Church	8.4
Church of God in Christ	5.5
Church of Jesus Christ of Latter-day Saints	5.2
Evangelical Lutheran Church	5.1
Presbyterian Church	3.6

Source: *USA TODAY*, February 18, 2002, p. A1, from *The World Almanac* and www.adherents.com.

SIC 87 - Engineering and Management Services

Contracting (SIC 8710)

Largest Contractors, 2000

Firms are ranked by construction revenue in billions of dollars.

Bechtel Group Inc.	$ 12.3
Fluor Corp.	7.8
The Turner Corp.	5.7
CENTEX	5.4
Skanska Inc.	5.3
Kellogg Brown & Root	5.2
Peter Kiewit Sons Inc.	4.6
Washington Group International	4.0
Foster Wheeler Corp.	2.8
Bovis Lend Lease	2.8

Source: *ENR*, May 21, 2001, p. 73.

★ 1967 ★
Contracting (SIC 8710)

Leading Power Contractors

The top power plant designers are ranked by revenue in millions of dollars.

Bechtel Group Inc.	$ 3,539.00
Fluor Corp.	1,503.00
Foster Wheeler Corp.	1,453.00
Washington Group International	1,449.00
NEPCO	1,228.56
Black & Veatch	1,225.70
H.B. Zachary Co.	932.45
TIC Holdings Inc.	547.06
The Shaw Group Inc.	519.70
Parsons Corp.	446.10

Source: *ENR*, December 3, 2001, p. 11.

★ 1968 ★
Design Firms (SIC 8710)

Leading Retail Design Firms, 2001

Firms are ranked by design fees, in millions.

Pavlik Design Team	$ 40.8
Callison Architecture Inc.	39.9
Gensler	36.0
Fitch Worldwide	31.5
Carter & Burgess	23.0
Little & Associates Architects	19.6
MCG Architecture	17.0
Design Forum	15.5
Fame	12.0

Source: *VM + SD*, March 2002, p. 44.

★ 1969 ★
Design Firms (SIC 8710)

Top Design Firms, 2001

Firms are ranked by design service revenues in billions of dollars.

URS Corp.	$ 2.0
Bechtel Group Inc.	1.9
AECOM Technology	1.5
Jacobs Engineering Group	1.3
Parsons Corp.	1.1
Fluor Corp.	1.1
Earth Tech	1.1
CH2M Hill	1.1

Source: *ENR*, April 16, 2001, p. 58.

★ 1970 ★

Engineering Services (SIC 8711)

Engineering Industry by Sector

Engineering and construction produced annual revenues of roughly $100 billion.

Petroleum and chemicals	28.0%
Transportation	21.0
Industrial process	16.0
Environmental	11.0
Manufacturing	10.0
Power	8.0
Other	6.0

Source: *Investor's Business Daily*, August 20, 2001, p. A13, from *ENR*.

★ 1971 ★

Accounting Services (SIC 8721)

Largest Accounting Firms in Canada

Firms are ranked by year income in millions of Canadian dollars.

PricewaterhouseCoopers	$ 1,010.0
Deloitte & Touche	895.0
KPMG	727.0
Ernst & Young	554.0
Grant Thorton Canada	270.6
Andersen LLP	230.0
BDO Dunwoody	215.0
Morison International	22.4

Source: *The Accountant*, February 2002, p. 17, from *International Accounting Bulletin*.

★ 1972 ★

Accounting Services (SIC 8721)

Largest Public Accounting Firms

Firms are ranked by revenue in millions of dollars.

PricewaterhouseCoopers	$ 8,058
Deloitte & Touche	6,130

Ernst & Young	$ 4,485
Andersen	4,300
KPMG	3,171
BDO Seidman	420
Grant Thorton	380
McGladrey & Pullen	167

Source: *Wall Street Journal*, March 14, 2002, p. C1, from *Public Accounting Report*.

★ 1973 ★

Accounting Services (SIC 8721)

Leading CPA Firms in the Northeast

Firms are ranked by revenue in 2000 revenue in millions of dollars.

Constantin Associates	$ 88.6
Eisner	72.0
Reznick Fedder & Silverman	56.7
J.H. Cohn	55.0
M.R. Weiser & Co. LLP	53.0

Source: *Practical Accountant*, April 2001, p. 19.

★ 1974 ★

Accounting Services (SIC 8721)

Leading CPA Firms in the Southeast

Firms are ranked by revenue in 2000 revenue in millions of dollars.

Cherry Bekaert & Holland	$ 40.0
Dixon Odom PLLC	34.1
Goodman & Co.	26.0
Crisp Hughes Evans LLP	25.0
Elliott Davis LLP	24.9

Source: *Practical Accountant*, April 2001, p. 19.

★ 1975 ★

Accounting Services (SIC 8721)

Leading Non CPA Firms

Firms are ranked by revenue in 2000 revenue in millions of dollars.

H&R Block	$ 2,100.0
Century Business Services Inc.	436.1
American Express Tax & Business Services	325.0
RSM McGladrey Inc.	210.8
Jackson Hewitt Tax Service	192.8

Source: *Practical Accountant*, April 2001, p. 19.

★ 1976 ★

Research (SIC 8730)

Leading R&D Firms

Firms are ranked by spending is shown in billions of dollars.

Ford Motor	$ 7.63
Motorola	6.00
General Motors	5.54
Cisco	5.30
Microsoft	5.26
Intel	5.16
IBM	4.70
Pfizer	4.70
Pharmacia	3.89

Source: *R&D*, January 2002, p. F3, from Schonfeld & Associates.

★ 1977 ★

Medical Testing (SIC 8732)

Medical Testing Industry

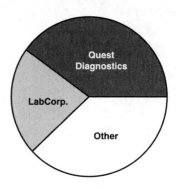

Market shares are shown in percent.

Quest Diagnostics	40.0%
LabCorp.	22.0
Other	38.0

Source: *The Post-Standard*, April 8, 2002, p. 11.

★ 1978 ★

Research (SIC 8733)

Who Provides University Funding, 1998

Total funding reached $27.5 billion.

Federal government	58.2%
Universities	19.6
Industry	7.6
State & local governments	7.3
Other	7.3

Source: *Christian Science Monitor*, June 19, 2001, p. 14, from National Science Foundation.

★ 1979 ★

Laboratories (SIC 8734)

Clinical Laboratory Industry

Market shares are estimated for the $35 billion industry.

Quest Diagnostics	10.0%
LabCorp.	6.0
Other	84.0

Source: *Wall Street Journal*, November 20, 2001, p. A9.

★ 1980 ★

Consulting Services (SIC 8741)

Leading Search Firms

Firms are ranked by revenue per consultant.

Russell Reynolds Associates	$ 1,282,979
Spencer Stuart	1,154,000
Heidrick & Struggles International	1,090,046
Christian & Timbers	1,056,420
Korn/Ferry International	950,833
Ray & Berndtson	782,353
Egon Zehnder International	727,536
TMP Worldwide Executive Search	667,391
DHR International	445,545

Source: *Wall Street Journal*, March 19, 2002, p. B4, from Hunt-Scanlon Advisors.

★ 1981 ★

Public Relations Services (SIC 8743)

Largest Healthcare PR Firms

Firms are ranked by health care income in millions of dollars.

Ketchum	$ 42.0
Porter Novelli International	40.8
Edelmann Public Relations Worldwide	38.8
Ogilvy Public Relations Worldwide	35.6
Fleishman-Hillard	35.0
Ruder Finn	32.1
Manning, Selvage & Lee	28.1
Burson-Marsteller	23.6

Source: *PR Week*, June 25, 2001, p. 19.

★ 1982 ★

Public Relations Services (SIC 8743)

Top PR Firms in Atlanta, GA

Firms are ranked by revenue in millions of dollars.

Ketchum	$ 20.5
Ogilvy PR Worldwide	11.5
CGI Group/APCO Associates	11.3
Duffey Communications	7.2
Cohn & Wolfe	6.4

Fleishman-Hillard	$ 5.9
Manning Selvage & Lee	5.7
Porter Novelli	3.7
Hayslett Sorre	2.9

Source: *PR Week*, December 10, 2001, p. 19, from Council of PR Firms.

★ 1983 ★

Public Relations Services (SIC 8743)

Top PR Firms in New York City, NY

Burson-Marsteller
Ruder Finn
Edelman Public Relations Worldwide
Ketchum
Fleishman-Hillard
BSMG Worldwide
Ogilvy Public Relations Worldwide
Porter Novelli International

Firms are ranked by income in millions of dollars.

Burson-Marsteller	$ 64.9
Ruder Finn	60.9
Edelman Public Relations Worldwide	60.1
Ketchum	34.4
Fleishman-Hillard	34.3
BSMG Worldwide	34.0
Ogilvy Public Relations Worldwide	30.1
Porter Novelli International	29.8

Source: *PR Week*, July 9, 2001, p. 23.

★ 1984 ★

Public Relations Services (SIC 8743)

Top PR Firms in Portland, OR

Firms are ranked by billings in millions of dollars.

Waggener Edstrom	$ 39.5
Young & Roehr Group	32.9
R/H/A/S Advertising & Public Relations	23.0
Robiey Marketing	17.1
KVO Public Relations	8.1

Source: *Business Journal-Portland*, July 6, 2001, p. 1.

★ 1985 ★

Public Relations Services (SIC 8743)

Top PR Firms in Washington D.C.

Firms are ranked by income in millions of dollars.

Weber Shandwick Worldwide . . . . . . $ 60.5
Burson-Marsteller 46.3
Fleishman-Hillard 34.6
Hill & Knowlton 32.3
Ogilvy PR 29.3
Porter Novelli 27.4
Ketchum 26.5
BSMG Worldwide 21.8

Source: *PR Week*, September 3, 2001, p. 23.

★ 1986 ★

School Testing Services (SIC 8748)

Standardized Exam Industry

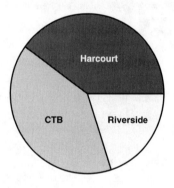

Market shares are estimated in percent.

Harcourt 40.0%
CTB 40.0
Riverside 20.0

Source: *Washington Post*, May 30, 2000, p. A9.

SIC 92 - Justice, Public Order, and Safety

★ 1987 ★
Crime (SIC 9220)

Counterfeit Products Seized

China, Taiwan and Malaysia are the top places of origin.

Music, software and video	$ 7.9
Toys	6.0
Computer hardware	4.4
Apparel	4.3
Cigarettes	4.2
Watches	4.0
Handbags, wallets and purses	1.7
Electronics	1.5
Sunglasses	1.4
Footwear	1.1
Other	8.8

Source: *New York Times*, October 14, 2001, p. 4, from United States Customs Bureau.

★ 1988 ★
Crime (SIC 9220)

Drug Seizures by Customs Agents

Figures are in pounds, except for narcotics, which is for tablets. Data are for October-December 2001, which jumped 17% over the same period in 2000.

Marijuana	361,257
Cocaine	71,210
Heroin	2,071
Methamphetamines	940
Opiate	464
Narcotics	39

Source: *USA TODAY*, April 11, 2002, p. 8A, from U.S. Customs.

★ 1989 ★
Prisons (SIC 9223)

Private Prison Industry

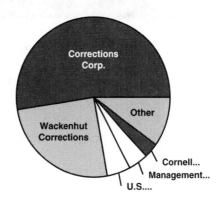

Private corporations now run as many as 6 percent of all U.S. prisons, jails and detention centers. The number of people behind bars rose an average of 7.7 percent each year since 1990 (although last year it dipped to 4.7 percent).

Corrections Corp. of America	52.30%
Wackenhut Corrections	25.11
U.S. Corrections Corp.	5.20
Management & Training Corp.	3.84
Cornell Corrections Inc.	3.37
Other	10.45

Source: "The Booming Prison Business." Retrieved December 11, 2001 from the World Wide Web: http://www.abcnews.go.com.

SIC 93 - Finance, Taxation, and Monetary Policy

★ 1990 ★

Tax Preparation (SIC 9311)

Tax Return Filings

| Paper |
| Electronic |

Over four years, e-filing has increased 78%. Data show millions of returns.

	1999	2000	Share
Paper	190.0	187.4	82.08%
Electronic	34.4	40.9	17.92

Source: *USA TODAY*, February 14, 2002, p. 3B, from General Accounting Office.

★ 1991 ★

Taxation (SIC 9311)

Income Tax Collections, 2001

Data show share of total collections.

Individuals	53.0%
Corporate	8.0
Estate/gift	1.5
Other	37.5

Source: *Wall Street Journal*, April 3, 2002, p. A1, from IRS.

SIC 95 - Environmental Quality and Housing

★ 1992 ★

Hazardous Waste Industry (SIC 9510)

Hazardous Waste Revenues

Facing a tough road to profits, fewer than 200 firms remain in the $3.3 billion industry for the year 2000. The table shows the industry leader, and the revenue category of the other players.

Six large firms $200-$400 million	40.0%
Safety-Kleen	27.0
12 $30-$100 million firms	18.0
150 other firms	15.0

Source: *Hazardous Waste Superfund Week*, June 18, 2001, p. NA.

★ 1993 ★

Land Ownership (SIC 9512)

Where the Government Owns Land

Ownership is shown in selected states.

Nevada	83.0%
Utah	65.0
Idaho	62.0
Alaska	62.0
Oregon	52.0
Wyoming	50.0
Arizona	45.0
California	44.0
Colorado	36.0

Source: *Time*, July 16, 2001, p. 24.

SIC 96 - Administration of Economic Programs

★ 1994 ★

Federal Government (SIC 9611)

U.S. Government Outsourcing

The combined civilian defense markets for outsourcing are expected to grow from $7.8 billion in 2001 to $11.8 billion in 2006. Figures show estimated spending.

	2001	2006
Defense	$ 1,500	$ 3,000
Treasury	445	1,000
Transportation	395	880
Army	378	741
Navy	365	772
NASA	356	638
Air Force	339	667
Justice	266	542

Source: *Washington Technology*, January 7, 2002, p. 7, from Input.

★ 1995 ★

Transportation (SIC 9621)

The Jurisdiction of Public Roads

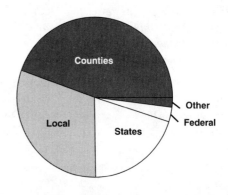

The table shows who controls the 3.9 million miles of public roads. "Local" includes towns, townships and municipalities.

Counties	45.0%
Local	30.6
States	19.6
Federal	3.0
Other	1.8

Source: *USA TODAY*, February 28, 2002, p. A1, from Federal Highway Adminsitration.

★ 1996 ★

U.S. Department of Energy (SIC 9631)

Top Energy Department Purchasers

Market shares are shown based on value of purchases.

University of California System	19.78%
Bechtel Group	12.11
Lockheed Martin	11.84
BNFL Inc.	10.68
Fluor Corp.	6.93
Kaiser Hill	3.88

Continued on next page.

★ 1996 ★ *Continued*

U.S. Department of Energy (SIC 9631)

Top Energy Department Purchasers

Market shares are shown based on value of purchases.

Battelle Memorial Institute	3.87%
Other	30.91

Source: *Government Executive*, August 1, 2001, p. NA.

★ 1997 ★

Technology Spending (SIC 9651)

Federal Technology Spending

Figures are in billions, by agency. The U.S. government is the world's largest consumer of technology. It budgeted $45 billion for tech spending.

Defense Dept.	$ 21.5
Health/Human services	3.9
Treasury	3.0
Transportation Dept.	2.6
NASA	2.0
Justice Dept.	1.6
Agriculture Dept.	1.4
Veterans Affairs	1.2
Energy Dept.	1.1
Commerce Dept.	0.9

Source: *Investor's Business Daily*, February 6, 2002, p. A6, from General Accounting Office.

★ 1998 ★

Space Research (SIC 9661)

Top NASA Contractors

Market shares are shown based on purchases.

Boeing Co.	23.86%
Lockheed Martin Corp.	20.55
California Institute of Technology	12.00
Cordant Technologies Inc.	3.38
Raytheon Co.	3.02
Northrop Grumman Corp.	2.68
United Technologies Corp.	1.54
Other	32.97

Source: *Government Executive*, August 1, 2001, p. NA, from General Services Administration's Federal Supply Service.

SIC 97 - National Security and International Affairs

★ 1999 ★
Military (SIC 9711)

Army National Guard by State

Some units have come under fire for inaccurately stating the size of their troops (some are as high as 20%). Personnel is shown by location.

	No.	Share
Texas	16,359	4.77%
California	16,095	4.69
Pennsylvania	16,069	4.69
Alabama	13,448	3.92
Indiana	12,148	3.54
New York	11,964	3.49
Tennessee	10,580	3.09
Illinois	10,194	2.97
Louisiana	10,066	2.94
Florida	9,961	2.90
Other	216,032	63.00

Source: *USA TODAY*, December 18, 2001, p. 4A, from National Guard Bureau.

★ 2000 ★
Military (SIC 9711)

Our Active Forces

Army	482,170
Navy	373,193
Air Force	355,654
Marines	173,321

Source: *Marines Magazine*, December 15, 2001, p. 42, from Defense Manpower Data Center.

★ 2001 ★
Military (SIC 9711)

Top Army Purchasers

Market shares are shown based on value of purchases.

Lockheed Martin	6.95%
Raytheon Co.	4.97
General Dynamics Corp.	4.00
Boeing Co.	3.70
Carlyle Group	2.32
Northrop Grumman Corp.	2.21
TRW Inc.	1.78
Other	74.07

Source: *Government Executive*, August 1, 2001, p. NA.

★ 2002 ★
Military (SIC 9711)

Top Navy Purchasers

Market shares are shown based on value of purchases.

Lockheed Martin Corp.	9.77%
Boeing Co.	9.58
Northrop Grumman Corp.	7.93
Raytheon Co.	7.18
General Dynamics	5.60
Textron Inc.	2.20

Continued on next page.

★ **2002** ★ *Continued*

Military (SIC 9711)

Top Navy Purchasers

Market shares are shown based on value of purchases.

Newport News Shipbuilding 1.90%
Other 55.84

Source: *Government Executive*, August 1, 2001, p. NA.

★ **2003** ★

Military (SIC 9711)

U.S. Military Abroad

More than 263,000 personnel are stationed abroad.

Army 39.0%
Navy 26.0
Air Force 24.0
Marines 11.0

Source: *USA TODAY*, June 25, 2001, p. A1.

SOURCE INDEX

This index is divided into *primary sources* and *original sources*. Primary sources are the publications where the market shares were found. Original sources are sources cited in the primary sources. Numbers following the sources are entry numbers, arranged sequentially; the first number refers to the first appearance of the source in *Market Share Reporter*. All told, 1009 organizations are listed.

Primary Sources

"1999 North American Diesel Engine Market Share." Retrieved June 1, 2002 from: http://www.corporate-ir.net, 1042-1043

20/20 Magazine, 1117, 1561

"2000 DIS Equipment Survey." Retrieved June 1, 2002 from the World Wide Web: http://www.brooks.af.mil, 1108-1110

"2000 Market Share Report." Retrieved June 1, 2002 from the World Wide Web: http://www.iiaf.org, 1722, 1742

"2001 Registration Statistics." Retrieved June 1, 2002 from the World Wide Web: http://www.aakc.org, 69

Accountant, 1971

AdAgeGlobal, 1788, 1809-1810

Adhesives & Sealants Industry, 605, 770

"Adidas-Salomon." Retrieved June 1, 2002 from the World Wide Web: http://www.bloomberg.com, 787

Advanced Materials & Composites News, 595

Advanced Materials & Processes, 829

Advertising Age, 53, 231, 359, 376, 449, 525, 667, 875, 1029, 1150, 1174-1175, 1500, 1514, 1782, 1789-1790

Adweek, 1783-1787

Adweek Magazine's Technology Marketing, 1821

Aftermarket Business, 1044-1047, 1050, 1443-1448

Ag Lender, 28, 1662

Air Cargo World, 1225, 1227

Air Conditioning, Heating & Refrigeration News, 905

Airport Security Report, 1083

Airports, 1244

"ALA Fact Sheet." Retrieved June 1, 2002 from the World Wide Web: http://www.ala.org, 1955

Aluminum Today, 27

A.M. Best Newswire, 1689, 1691-1694, 1714, 1717, 1719, 1721, 1730, 1735-1741, 1743, 1747-1748

American Banker, 897-898, 1297, 1636, 1640, 1659-1660, 1767

American Ceramic Society Bulletin, 1000, 1089

American Demographics, 1, 57

American Lawyer, 1947

American Metal Market, 821

American Nurseryman, 1389

American Printer, 512

American School & University, 1949-1950

American Shipper, 1188

America's Network, 1263

Amusement Business, 1903, 1907, 1919-1920

Anchorage Daily News, 1270

"Apparel Accessories." Retrieved June 1, 2002 from the World Wide Web: http://www.usatrade.gov, 1466

Appliance, 849-850, 881, 912-913, 916-917, 924-925, 927-929, 932-933, 936-937, 942-944, 948-950, 952, 956, 961-962, 969

Appliance Manufacturer, 851-853, 908-911, 914-915, 923, 926, 930-931, 934-935, 940-941, 945-947, 951, 953-954, 957, 960, 964

Applied Clinical Trials, 1818

"ARG Releases Updated 5 Year Forecast." Retrieved June 1, 2002 from the World Wide Web: http://www.aviationresearch.com, 1054

Arkansas Business, 1600, 1627

Asset Securitization Report, 1672

"Athletic Footwear Sales Climb." Retrieved June 1, 2002 from the World Wide Web: http://www.sgma.com, 788

Atlanta Journal-Constitution, 65, 375, 389-390, 1198, 1486, 1599

ATM & Debit News, 1654

ATM Debit Card News, 902

Audio Week, 959, 970-971, 977

Austin Business Journal, 1129

Automatic Merchandiser, 1553, 1555

Automotive Body Repair News, 1876

Automotive News, 999, 1035-1039, 1041, 1049

AVG, 39-41

Aviation Daily, 1206, 1208-1221

B-to-B, 1793

Source Index: Primary

Original Sources

2001 Annual Sailing Business Review, 1059

A.C. Nielsen, 29, 141-142, 148, 150, 157, 160-161, 167, 169, 185, 192, 211, 220, 222, 298, 341, 363, 381, 392-393, 397, 428, 438, 709, 768, 796, 833, 1435-1436, 1438-1440, 1518, 1564-1570, 1572-1573, 1575-1577, 1580-1589, 1593-1594

A.C. Nielsen EDI, 1887, 1895

A.C. Nielsen for Bush's Baked Beans, 216

A.C. Nielsen Homescan, 217, 228, 265, 269, 294, 537, 1184

A.C. Nielsen MarketTrack, 256, 413

A.C. Nielsen ScanTrack, 611, 938

Adams Handbook, 354, 358, 363-364

Adams Media Research, 1491

Adoption/MedicalNews, 1957

Aerospace Industries Association, 1055

AHA Annual Survey of Hospitals, 1943, 1945

Air Conditioning and Refrigeration Institute, 918, 929

Air Transport Association of America, 1225

Airports Council International, 1227

AIS' HMO Directory, 2002, 1703-1704

Aluminum Association, 827

A.M. Best & Co., 1688-1689, 1691-1692, 1698, 1714, 1717-1721, 1723, 1725, 1730-1731, 1735-1741, 1743, 1745-1748

A.M. Best & Co.'s State/Line Group, 1694

A.M. Best State/Line Reports, 1687, 1749

A.M. Best Statement and Competitive Analysis Report Products, 1690, 1712-1713, 1715-1716

American Association of Railroads, 1189

American Association of Retired Persons, 1

American Demographics, 1914

American Floral Endowment, 58, 1559

American Forest & Paper Association, 518

American Foundry Society, 826

American Gaming Association, 1926

American Greeting Association, 580

American Kennel Association, 69

American Lawyer, 1946

American Society for Aesthetic Plastic Surgery, 1939-1940

American Society of Plastic Surgeons, 1938

American Steel and Iron Institute, 823

American Translators Association, 1870

AMR Research, 1820, 1824, 1829, 1845

ANIQ, 583

Annual HMO statements to the Texas Department of Insurance, 1705

Appliance Magazine, 922

ARC study, 859

Association of Canadian Publishers, 1540

Association of Home Appliance Manufacturers, 923, 932, 949

AT&T Canada, 1272

ATM & Debit News, 900

Audit Bureau of Circulations, 542

Auto Rental News, 1872

Automatic Merchandiser, 1557

Automatic Merchandiser Coffee Service Market Report, 1555

Automotive News, 1029

Automotive News Data Center, 1035-1039

Automotive Recyclers Association, 1876

Aviation Research Group, 1054, 1224

Bear Stearns, 1365, 1457

Beer Marketer's Insights, 356-357

Beverage Digest, 374-375, 390, 394

Beverage Digest/Maxwell, 389, 391

Beverage Digest's Fact Book, 2000, 830

Beverage Marketing Corp., 199, 219, 349-350, 355, 374, 376, 379, 382, 384, 386

BIA Financial Network, 1330-1332, 1334-1335

BIA's MEDIA Access Pro, 1338

Bicycle Products Suppliers Association, 1066

Biomet, 1105

Bloomberg Financial Markets, 1364

Bloomberg Financial Services, 1677

BRG Townsend, 758

Bride's Magazine, 24

Brightmail Inc., 1320

Broadband Wireless Exchange, 1265

The Brookings Institution, 662

Builder, 120

Bureau of Land Management, 589

Bureau of Transportation Statistics, 1205, 1207, 1223

Business & Institutional Furniture Manufacturers Association, 508

Business Communications Co., 143, 596, 606, 659, 811, 1000, 1006, 1020, 1089, 1097

Cabletelevision Advertising Bureau, 1798

CAHA, 763

Cahners In-Stat, 1005, 1322

Canadian Bankers Association, 1602

Canadian Radio and Television Communications, 1340

Canadian Restaurant and Foodservices Association, 1506

Canadian Soft Goods Index, 467

CAP Ventures, 1124

Capital DATA, 1670

Catalog Age, 1551

Cattle Buyers Weekly, 154

CCITriad/Vista home center syndicated scanner data, 955

Celent Communications, 1681

Cellular Telecommunications & Internet Association, 1257

The Center for Education Reform, 1948

The World Almanac, 1965
www.adherents.com, 1965
Yankee Group, 1264, 1268, 1323, 1325, 1327, 1344, 1676
Yengst Associates, 854

PLACE NAMES INDEX

This index shows countries, political entities, states and provinces, regions within countries, parks, airports, and cities. The numbers that follow listings are entry numbers; they are arranged sequentially so that the first mention of a place is listed first. The index shows references to more than 310 places.

PRODUCTS, SERVICES, NAMES, AND ISSUES INDEX

This index shows, in alphabetical order, references to products, services, personal names, and issues covered in *Market Share Reporter*, 13th Edition. More than 2,170 terms are included. Terms include subjects not readily categorized as products and services, including such subjects as *counties* and *crime*. The numbers that follow each term refer to entry numbers and are arranged sequentially so that the first mention is listed first.

Products, Services, Names, and Issues Index

Products, Services, Names, and Issues Index

COMPANY INDEX

The more than 3,570 companies and institutions in this book are indexed here in alphabetical order. Numbers following the terms are entry numbers. They are arranged sequentially; the first entry number refers to the first mention of the company in *Market Share Reporter*. Although most organizations appear only once, some entities are referred to under abbreviations in the sources and these have not always been expanded.

Ahmsa, 821
AHO Construction, 118
Ahold USA Retail, 1402
AIG, 1732, 1755
AIM Funds Management, 1676
Air Liquide America Corp./Airgas Inc., 587
Air Products, 1367
Air Wisconsin, 1213
Airborne Express, 1225
Aircanada.ca, 1251
Airgas Inc., 587, 1367, 1375
Aiwa, 889, 965
AK Steel, 821
Akamai, 1822
Akebono, 1049
Akzo Nobel, 754
Alamo, 1872-1873
Alaska Airlines, 1208, 1221, 1233, 1236, 1241-1243, 1291
Alberto Culver, 719
Albertson's, 1391, 1402, 1411-1412, 1417-1419, 1428-1429, 1431, 1517, 1525, 1529
Alcatel, 992, 998
Alcon Laboratories, 1802
Alcon/Nestle, 698
Alderwoods Group, 1766
Aldila, 1160
Aliant, 1264, 1325
All American, 1404
All Erection & Crane Rental, 1815
All Star Homes Inc., 117
Allen & Garritsen, 1783
Allergan, 698
Allfirst Bank, 1632
Allianz Canada, 1734
Allianz of America Inc., 1727, 1743, 1757
Allied-Domecq Retailing, 1514, 1516
Allied-Domecq Spirits USA, 364
Allied Office Products, 577
Allied Waste Industries Inc., 1369
Allied Worldwide, 1195
Allstate Insurance Group, 1689-1690, 1692-1694, 1697-1698, 1712-1718, 1720-1727, 1729
Allure Home Creation, 484, 492
Almay, 689
Aloha Airlines, 1234
Alpine Electronics, 1008
Amazon.com, 1299-1300, 1319, 1492
AMC Entertainment, 1898
America Online, 1326, 1865
America Online/Time Warner, 10, 1319, 1344, 1352, 1788, 1795, 1798, 1801
America West, 1206, 1208-1209, 1212, 1218, 1240, 1242
American Airlines, 1205-1206, 1208-1210, 1213-1216,

1220, 1222, 1229-1230, 1232, 1235-1236, 1238-1242, 1291
American Airlines Federal Credit Union, 1640
American Bakers Co-op, 280
American Business Forms, 576-577
American Cancer Society, 1962
American Compensation Insurance Co., 1736
American Dairy Brands, 177, 181
American Eagle Outfitters, 1467
American Electric, 1365
American Environmental Corp., 601
American Express, 1648, 1650-1651, 1797
American Express Centurion Bank, 1653
American Express Tax & Business Services, 1975
American Express Travel, 1253
American Family Insurance Group, 1698, 1712, 1719
American Family Mutual Insurance, 1695, 1728
American Freightways, 1194
American General, 1330
American Greetings, 579
American Home Assurance Co., 1733
American Home Products, 647
American Honda Finance Corp., 1875
American International Group Inc., 1688, 1699, 1717, 1727, 1731, 1741, 1745-1746, 1749
American International Security, 1683
American Licorice, 310
American Museum of Natural History, 1963
American National Bank and Trust Company of Chicago, 1611
American Pioneer Title Insurance, 1752
American Plumbing and Mechanical, 129
American Red Cross, 1962
American Repertory Theatre, 1908
American Residential Services/Rescue Rooter, 129
American Safety, 836
American Samoa Bank, 1598
American Savings Bank, 1609, 1617
American Standard (Trane), 910, 913-914
American Standard Insurance, 1695
American Stock Exchange, 1680
American Trans Air, 1217
American Translators Association, 1870
American Water Heater, 917
American West Homes, 108
American Yard Products, 851
America's Wholesale Lender, 1656
AmeriChoice Corp., 1706
AmeriCold Logistics, 1196
AmeriGas Partners, 1558
Amerigroup, 1703, 1706
Ameriquest, 1658
AmerisourceBergen, 1377

Company Index

Company Index

Emmis Communications, 1329, 1333
EMusic, 1315
Encompass Services Corp., 129
Endeavor, 1904
Energizer, 1012
Enfglander, 486
Engineered Sensors/Tedeco, 1088
Engle Homes, 103, 114
Enodis (Delfield), 911
Enovia, 1845
Enron Corp., 513, 1364-1365
Enron Facility Services, 128, 134
Enstrom, 1055
Entercom, 1329
Enterprise, 1871, 1873
Entravision, 1330
Entrust, 1844
eOnline, 1819
Epiq, 1668
Episcopal High School, 1951
Epson, 896
Equilon, 773-774
Equilon Enterprises/Motiva Enterprises, 1398
Equistar, 582, 760
Equity Residential Properties Trust, 1760
ERC, 1757
eResearch Technology, 1818
Ericsson, 984, 997
Erie, 1697
Ernst & Young, 1971-1972
Erpenbeck Co., 97
Escalade Sports, 1171
Esoterix, 658
ESPN, 1342
Essex Crane Rental, 1815
Ethan Allen, 452, 504, 1475
Eureka, 947-948, 952
Eurex, 1681
Evangelical Lutheran Church, 1965
Evanston Insurance, 1683
EventNet, 1818
Evergreen, 1200-1201, 1225
EVTAC, 73
Ex-Cell Home Fashions, 484, 492
Excel Corp., 153-154
Excite@home, 1327
Expedia, 1251, 1253, 1305
Express Scripts, 641, 1378
External PC drives, 886
ExxonMobil, 79, 81, 85, 582, 603, 760, 774, 1398, 1453-1454
Eye Care Centers of America, 1561
F. Menard, 62

Factory Mutual Ins. Co., 1756
Fadal, 858
Fairbult Foods Inc., 39
The Falcon Companies, 452
Falconbridge, 87
Fall Clerk Housing, 500
Fame, 1968
Family Dollar, 1399
Family Video, 1900
Fanuc, 859
Farm Bureau Mutual Ins, 1695
Farm Fresh, 1415
Farmer Jack, 1413
Farmers Insurance Co. of Oregon, 1729
Farmers Insurance Exchange, 1695, 1726, 1728
Farmers Mutual, 1695
Farmers/Zurich, 1722, 1742
Farmland Foods Inc., 156
Farmland Industries, 262
Farmland Management Services, 49
Farmland Refrigerated Foods, 153
Fashion Pillows, 488
Fasken Martineau DuMoulin, 1947
Favorite Brands Intl., 312, 314, 323
F.C. Tucker, 1763
FCB, 1785
Fedcomp, 1639
Fedders, 908, 912
Federal Express, 1195, 1225-1226
Federal-Mogul Corp., 789, 1049
Federated Co-op, 1376
Federated Deparment Stores, 1468
Federated Department Stores, 1395, 1475, 1477, 1481-1482, 1551
Feed Management Systems, 1831
FEMSA, 351
Ferolito, Vultaggio & Sons, 145, 388
Ferrellgas Partners, 1558
Ferrero USA Inc., 300, 327, 329, 333
Ferro, 755
Ferrous Processing & Trading Co., 820
Fidelity Charitable Gift Fund, 1962
Fidelity Investments Canada, 1676
Fidelity National Title, 1750
Fidelity National Title Insurance Co. 2, 1753
Fiesta Mart, 1416
Fifth Third, 1613, 1663
Fifth Third Bank, Indiana, 1612
Fifth Third Mortgage, 1657
Fifty 50, 319
Fine Line, 1892
Fine Painting & Decorating Co. Inc., 130
Fine Products Co. Inc., 318

Grey, 1784
Greystone Homes/Lennar Corp., 113
Greystone Homes/U.S. Home Corp., 116
Grimmway Farms, 41, 43
Gross Builders, 98
Group Health Plan /Access Sensicare, 1711
Groupe BMR, 1376
Groupe Danone, 145
Gruner & Jahr, 549
Grupo Gamesa, 289
Grupo Mexico, 77
Grupo Porcicola Mexicano, 63
Grupo Telvisa, 1339
GSC Enterprises, 1379
GSD&M, 1787
Guardian Alarm Co., 1861
Guide Corp., 600
Guitar Center Inc., 1137
Gulf States Paper, 515
Guptill Farms, 45
GUS Network America, 1328
GW International, 1381
Gwaltney of Smithfield, 156
H&R Block, 841, 1975
Haas, 858, 860
Hachette Filipacchi, 549
Hagemeyer North America, 1375
Haier, 856, 908, 927
Hain Food Group, 319
Haines & Haines, 45
Half.com, 1300
Hall-Erickson, 1867
Hallmark, 579
Hamilton Beach/Proctor-Silex, 940, 942-946
Hamlet Homes, 122
Handspring, 879
Hanjin, 1201
Hannay Reels Inc., 874
Hanover Direct, 1551
Hanover Foods, 246
Hapag-Lloyd, 1200
Harcourt, 1986
Harcourt General, 539
Harcros Chemical, 1381
Hardee's, 1505
Harder Mechanical Contractors, 128
Hardie, 810
Harland, 1639
Harley-Davidson, 1067, 1069
Harmon Inc., 137
Harmon Ltd., 137
HarperCollins, 559
Harrah's/Oasis, 1773

Harris Teeter, 1404, 1425
Harris Trust and Savings Bank, 1611
Harry Rosen, 1463
Harry's, 1404
Hartford, 1742
Hartford Insurance Group, 1731, 1743, 1746
Hartford Life, 1687
The Hartford Roofing Group, 133
Hartung Brothers Inc., 39
Harvard Pilgrim, 1708
Harvard University, 1955, 1962
Havas Advertising, 1782, 1837
Hawaiian Airlines, 1234
Hawkins, Delafield & Wood, 1669
Haworth Inc., 509
Hawthorne Homes Co., 117
Hayslett Sorre, 1982
Hayward Baker Inc., 138
HB Fuller, 755
H.B. Zachary Co., 1967
HBO, 1336, 1342, 1355
HDI, 1715
HDNet, 1336
Health Care Indemnity Inc., 1735, 1737, 1739
Health Net, 1703, 1706, 1708, 1710
Health Partners of the Midwest Inc., 1711
Healthcare USA of Missouri LLC/Healthcare USA, 1711
HealthSouth Braintree Rehabilitation Hospital, 1945
HealthSouth Harmarville Rehabilitation Hospital, 1945
HealthSouth New England Rehabilitation Hospital, 1945
Hearst, 549
Hearst-Argyle TV, 1338
Hearthstone, 500
Heartland Farms Inc., 39
Heartland Homes Inc., 117
Heaven Hill Distilleries, 364
H.E.B., 1416
Hecla Mining Company, 77
Hefty/Pactiv, 520
Heidenhaim, 859
Heidrick & Struggles International, 1980
Heilig-Meyers, 1475, 1481
Heineken, 357
Heinz Co., 214, 227, 241, 278
Heinz Frozen Foods, 246-247
Heinz Pet Products Co., 277
Helen of Troy, 934-935
Helene Curtis, 696, 719, 742
Helm Distribution, 1381
Henry Wurst Inc., 571
Hepco Communications, 1332
HereUare, 1258
Herff Jones Inc., 569

Company Index

Company Index

Company Index

BRANDS INDEX

This index shows more than 1,880 brands—including names of periodicals, television programs, popular movies, and other "brand-equivalent" names. Each brand name is followed by one or more numerals; these are entry numbers; they are arranged sequentially, with the first mention of the brand shown first.

Brands Index

Brands Index

Brands Index

Brands Index

APPENDIX I

SIC COVERAGE

This appendix lists the Standard Industrial Classification codes (SICs) included in *Market Share Reporter*. Page numbers are shown following each SIC category; the page shown indicates the first occurrence of an SIC. *NEC* stands for not elsewhere classified.

2741 Miscellaneous publishing, p. 129
2750 Commercial printing, p. 130
2752 Commercial printing, lithographic, p. 131
2761 Manifold business forms, p. 131
2771 Greeting cards, p. 132

Chemicals and Allied Products

2800 Chemicals and allied products, p. 133
2812 Alkalies and chlorine, p. 134
2813 Industrial gases, p. 134
2819 Industrial inorganic chemicals, nec, p. 135
2821 Plastics materials and resins, p. 136
2824 Organic fibers, noncellulosic, p. 138
2833 Medicinals and botanicals, p. 138
2834 Pharmaceutical preparations, p. 140
2835 Diagnostic substances, p. 149
2836 Biological products exc. diagnostic, p. 149
2841 Soap and other detergents, p. 150
2842 Polishes and sanitation goods, p. 152
2844 Toilet preparations, p. 153
2851 Paints and allied products, p. 169
2865 Cyclic crudes and intermediates, p. 171
2869 Industrial organic chemicals, nec, p. 172
2879 Agricultural chemicals, nec, p. 173
2891 Adhesives and sealants, p. 174
2893 Printing ink, p. 174
2899 Chemical preparations, nec, p. 174

Petroleum and Coal Products

2911 Petroleum refining, p. 175
2952 Asphalt felts and coatings, p. 175
2992 Lubricating oils and greases, p. 175

Rubber and Misc. Plastics Products

3011 Tires and inner tubes, p. 176
3021 Rubber and plastics footwear, p. 177
3050 Hose & belting & gaskets & packing, p. 178
3053 Gaskets, packing and sealing devices, p. 178
3069 Fabricated rubber products, nec, p. 179
3081 Unsupported plastics film & sheet, p. 179
3085 Plastics bottles, p. 179
3088 Plastics plumbing fixtures, p. 179
3089 Plastics products, nec, p. 179

Leather and Leather Products

3131 Footwear cut stock, p. 181
3140 Footwear, except rubber, p. 181
3144 Women's footwear, except athletic, p. 182
3161 Luggage, p. 182

Stone, Clay, and Glass Products

3221 Glass containers, p. 183
3229 Pressed and blown glass, nec, p. 183
3241 Cement, hydraulic, p. 183
3250 Structural clay products, p. 184
3253 Ceramic wall and floor tile, p. 184
3275 Gypsum products, p. 184
3291 Abrasive products, p. 184

Primary Metal Industries

3312 Blast furnaces and steel mills, p. 186
3317 Steel pipe and tubes, p. 187
3320 Iron and steel foundries, p. 187
3334 Primary aluminum, p. 187
3351 Copper rolling and drawing, p. 187
3360 Nonferrous foundries (castings), p. 188

Fabricated Metal Products

3411 Metal cans, p. 189
3421 Cutlery, p. 189
3430 Plumbing and heating, except electric, p. 190
3432 Plumbing fixture fittings and trim, p. 190
3482 Small arms ammunition, p. 191
3489 Ordnance and accessories, nec, p. 191
3499 Fabricated metal products, nec, p. 191

Industry Machinery and Equipment

3511 Turbines and turbine generator sets, p. 193
3519 Internal combustion engines, nec, p. 193
3524 Lawn and garden equipment, p. 193
3531 Construction machinery, p. 194
3532 Mining machinery, p. 194
3536 Hoists, cranes, and monorails, p. 195
3541 Machine tools, metal cutting types, p. 195
3546 Power-driven handtools, p. 196
3549 Metalworking machinery, nec, p. 196
3554 Paper industries machinery, p. 196
3555 Printing trades machinery, p. 196
3556 Food products machinery, p. 197
3559 Special industry machinery, nec, p. 197
3561 Pumps and pumping equipment, p. 197
3565 Packaging machinery, p. 197
3569 General industrial machinery, nec, p. 197
3571 Electronic computers, p. 198
3572 Computer storage devices, p. 200
3575 Computer terminals, p. 201
3577 Computer peripheral equipment, nec, p. 201
3578 Calculating and accounting equipment, p. 202
3579 Office machines, nec, p. 202
3585 Refrigeration and heating equipment, p. 203
3599 Industrial machinery, nec, p. 206

Appendix: SIC Nomenclature

Appendix: SIC Nomenclature

Museums, Botanical, Zoological Gardens

8412 Museums and art galleries, p. 436
8422 Botanical and zoological gardens, p. 436

Membership Organizations

8661 Religious organizations, p. 437

Engineering and Management Services

8710 Engineering & architectural services, p. 438
8711 Engineering services, p. 439
8721 Accounting, auditing, & bookkeeping, p. 439
8730 Research and testing services, p. 440
8732 Commercial nonphysical research, p. 440
8733 Noncommercial research organizations, p. 440
8734 Testing laboratories, p. 440
8741 Management services, p. 441
8743 Public relations services, p. 441
8748 Business consulting, nec, p. 442

Justice, Public Order, and Safety

9220 Public order and safety, p. 443
9223 Correctional institutions, p. 443

Finance, Taxation, and Monetary Policy

9311 Finance, taxation, & monetary policy, p. 444

Environmental Quality and Housing

9510 Environmental quality, p. 445
9512 Land, mineral, wildlife conservation, p. 445

Administration of Economic Programs

9611 Admin. of general economic programs, p. 446
9621 Regulation, admin. of transportation, p. 446
9631 Regulation, admin. of utilities, p. 446
9651 Regulation misc. commercial sectors, p. 447
9661 Space research and technology, p. 447

National Security and International Affairs

9711 National security, p. 448

Appendix: SIC Nomenclature

SIC TO NAICS CONVERSION GUIDE

AGRICULTURE, FORESTRY, & FISHING

0111 Wheat
NAICS 11114   Wheat Farming
0112 Rice
NAICS 11116   Rice Farming
0115 Corn
NAICS 11115   Corn Farming
0116 Soybeans
NAICS 11111   Soybean Farming
0119 Cash Grains, nec
NAICS 11113   Dry Pea & Bean Farming
NAICS 11112   Oilseed Farming
NAICS 11115   Corn Farming
NAICS 111191 Oilseed & Grain Combination Farming
NAICS 111199 All Other Grain Farming
0131 Cotton
NAICS 11192   Cotton Farming
0132 Tobacco
NAICS 11191   Tobacco Farming
0133 Sugarcane & Sugar Beets
NAICS 111991 Sugar Beet Farming
NAICS 11193   Sugarcane Farming
0134 Irish Potatoes
NAICS 111211 Potato Farming
0139 Field Crops, Except Cash Grains, nec
NAICS 11194   Hay Farming
NAICS 111992 Peanut Farming
NAICS 111219 Other Vegetable & Melon Farming
NAICS 111998 All Other Miscellaneous Crop Farming
0161 Vegetables & Melons
NAICS 111219 Other Vegetable & Melon Farming
0171 Berry Crops
NAICS 111333 Strawberry Farming
NAICS 111334 Berry Farming
0172 Grapes
NAICS 111332 Grape Vineyards
0173 Tree Nuts
NAICS 111335 Tree Nut Farming
0174 Citrus Fruits
NAICS 11131   Orange Groves
NAICS 11132   Citrus Groves
0175 Deciduous Tree Fruits
NAICS 111331 Apple Orchards
NAICS 111339 Other Noncitrus Fruit Farming
0179 Fruits & Tree Nuts, nec
NAICS 111336 Fruit & Tree Nut Combination Farming
NAICS 111339 Other Noncitrus Fruit Farming
0181 Ornamental Floriculture & Nursery Products
NAICS 111422 Floriculture Production
NAICS 111421 Nursery & Tree Production
0182 Food Crops Grown under Cover
NAICS 111411 Mushroom Production
NAICS 111419 Other Food Crops Grown under Cover
0191 General Farms, Primarily Crop
NAICS 111998 All Other Miscellaneous Crop Farming
0211 Beef Cattle Feedlots
NAICS 112112 Cattle Feedlots
0212 Beef Cattle, Except Feedlots
NAICS 112111 Beef Cattle Ranching & Farming

0213 Hogs
NAICS 11221   Hog & Pig Farming
0214 Sheep & Goats
NAICS 11241   Sheep Farming
NAICS 11242   Goat Farming
0219 General Livestock, Except Dairy & Poultry
NAICS 11299   All Other Animal Production
0241 Dairy Farms
NAICS 112111 Beef Cattle Ranching & Farming
NAICS 11212   Dairy Cattle & Milk Production
0251 Broiler, Fryers, & Roaster Chickens
NAICS 11232   Broilers & Other Meat-type Chicken
               Production
0252 Chicken Eggs
NAICS 11231   Chicken Egg Production
0253 Turkey & Turkey Eggs
NAICS 11233   Turkey Production
0254 Poultry Hatcheries
NAICS 11234   Poultry Hatcheries
0259 Poultry & Eggs, nec
NAICS 11239   Other Poultry Production
0271 Fur-bearing Animals & Rabbits
NAICS 11293   Fur-bearing Animal & Rabbit Production
0272 Horses & Other Equines
NAICS 11292   Horse & Other Equine Production
0273 Animal Aquaculture
NAICS 112511 Finfish Farming & Fish Hatcheries
NAICS 112512 Shellfish Farming
NAICS 112519 Other Animal Aquaculture
0279 Animal Specialities, nec
NAICS 11291   Apiculture
NAICS 11299   All Other Animal Production
0291 General Farms, Primarily Livestock & Animal Specialties
NAICS 11299   All Other Animal Production
0711 Soil Preparation Services
NAICS 115112 Soil Preparation, Planting & Cultivating
0721 Crop Planting, Cultivating & Protecting
NAICS 48122   Nonscheduled Speciality Air Transportation
NAICS 115112 Soil Preparation, Planting & Cultivating
0722 Crop Harvesting, Primarily by Machine
NAICS 115113 Crop Harvesting, Primarily by Machine
0723 Crop Preparation Services for Market, Except Cotton Ginning
NAICS 115114 Postharvest Crop Activities
0724 Cotton Ginning
NAICS 115111 Cotton Ginning
0741 Veterinary Service for Livestock
NAICS 54194   Veterinary Services
0742 Veterinary Services for Animal Specialties
NAICS 54194   Veterinary Services
0751 Livestock Services, Except Veterinary
NAICS 311611 Animal Slaughtering
NAICS 11521   Support Activities for Animal Production
0752 Animal Specialty Services, Except Veterinary
NAICS 11521   Support Activities for Animal Production
NAICS 81291   Pet Care Services
0761 Farm Labor Contractors & Crew Leaders
NAICS 115115 Farm Labor Contractors & Crew Leaders
0762 Farm Management Services
NAICS 115116 Farm Management Services
0781 Landscape Counseling & Planning
NAICS 54169   Other Scientific & Technical Consulting
               Services
NAICS 54132   Landscape Architectural Services

0782 Lawn & Garden Services
NAICS 56173   Landscaping Services
0783 Ornamental Shrub & Tree Services
NAICS 56173   Landscaping Services
0811 Timber Tracts
NAICS 111421 Nursery & Tree Production
NAICS 11311   Timber Tract Operations
0831 Forest Nurseries & Gathering of Forest Products
NAICS 111998 All Other Miscellaneous Crop
NAICS 11321   Forest Nurseries & Gathering of Forest
            Products
0851 Forestry Services
NAICS 11531   Support Activities for Forestry
0912 Finfish
NAICS 114111 Finfish Fishing
0913 Shellfish
NAICS 114112 Shellfish Fishing
0919 Miscellaneous Marine Products
NAICS 114119 Other Marine Fishing
NAICS 111998 All Other Miscellaneous Crop Farming
0921 Fish Hatcheries & Preserves
NAICS 112511 Finfish Farming & Fish Hatcheries
NAICS 112512 Shellfish Farming
0971 Hunting, Trapping, & Game Propagation
NAICS 11421   Hunting & Trapping

MINING INDUSTRIES

1011 Iron Ores
NAICS 21221   Iron Ore Mining
1021 Copper Ores
NAICS 212234 Copper Ore & Nickel Ore Mining
1031 Lead & Zinc Ores
NAICS 212231 Lead Ore & Zinc Ore Mining
1041 Gold Ores
NAICS 212221 Gold Ore Mining
1044 Silver Ores
NAICS 212222 Silver Ore Mining
1061 Ferroalloy Ores, Except Vanadium
NAICS 212234 Copper Ore & Nickel Ore Mining
NAICS 212299 Other Metal Ore Mining
1081 Metal Mining Services
NAICS 213115 Support Activities for Metal Mining
NAICS 54136   Geophysical Surveying & Mapping Services
1094 Uranium-radium-vanadium Ores
NAICS 212291 Uranium-radium-vanadium Ore Mining
1099 Miscellaneous Metal Ores, nec
NAICS 212299 Other Metal Ore Mining
1221 Bituminous Coal & Lignite Surface Mining
NAICS 212111 Bituminous Coal & Lignite Surface Mining
1222 Bituminous Coal Underground Mining
NAICS 212112 Bituminous Coal Underground Mining
1231 Anthracite Mining
NAICS 212113 Anthracite Mining
1241 Coal Mining Services
NAICS 213114 Support Activities for Coal Mining
1311 Crude Petroleum & Natural Gas
NAICS 211111 Crude Petroleum & Natural Gas Extraction
1321 Natural Gas Liquids
NAICS 211112 Natural Gas Liquid Extraction
1381 Drilling Oil & Gas Wells
NAICS 213111 Drilling Oil & Gas Wells

1382 Oil & Gas Field Exploration Services
NAICS 48122   Nonscheduled Speciality Air Transportation
NAICS 54136   Geophysical Surveying & Mapping Services
NAICS 213112 Support Activities for Oil & Gas Field
            Operations
1389 Oil & Gas Field Services, nec
NAICS 213113 Other Oil & Gas Field Support Activities
1411 Dimension Stone
NAICS 212311 Dimension Stone Mining & Quarry
1422 Crushed & Broken Limestone
NAICS 212312 Crushed & Broken Limestone Mining &
            Quarrying
1423 Crushed & Broken Granite
NAICS 212313 Crushed & Broken Granite Mining &
            Quarrying
1429 Crushed & Broken Stone, nec
NAICS 212319 Other Crushed & Broken Stone Mining &
            Quarrying
1442 Construction Sand & Gravel
NAICS 212321 Construction Sand & Gravel Mining
1446 Industrial Sand
NAICS 212322 Industrial Sand Mining
1455 Kaolin & Ball Clay
NAICS 212324 Kaolin & Ball Clay Mining
1459 Clay, Ceramic, & Refractory Minerals, nec
NAICS 212325 Clay & Ceramic & Refractory Minerals Mining
1474 Potash, Soda, & Borate Minerals
NAICS 212391 Potash, Soda, & Borate Mineral Mining
1475 Phosphate Rock
NAICS 212392 Phosphate Rock Mining
1479 Chemical & Fertilizer Mineral Mining, nec
NAICS 212393 Other Chemical & Fertilizer Mineral Mining
1481 Nonmetallic Minerals Services Except Fuels
NAICS 213116 Support Activities for Non-metallic Minerals
NAICS 54136   Geophysical Surveying & Mapping Services
1499 Miscellaneous Nonmetallic Minerals, Except Fuels
NAICS 212319 Other Crushed & Broken Stone Mining or
            Quarrying
NAICS 212399 All Other Non-metallic Mineral Mining

CONSTRUCTION INDUSTRIES

1521 General Contractors-single-family Houses
NAICS 23321   Single Family Housing Construction
1522 General Contractors-residential Buildings, Other than
   Single-family
NAICS 23332   Commercial & Institutional Building
            Construction
NAICS 23322   Multifamily Housing Construction
1531 Operative Builders
NAICS 23321   Single Family Housing Construction
NAICS 23322   Multifamily Housing Construction
NAICS 23331   Manufacturing & Industrial Building
            Construction
NAICS 23332   Commercial & Institutional Building
            Construction
1541 General Contractors-industrial Buildings & Warehouses
NAICS 23332   Commercial & Institutional Building
            Construction
NAICS 23331   Manufacturing & Industrial Building
            Construction

1542 General Contractors-nonresidential Buildings, Other than Industrial Buildings & Warehouses

NAICS 23332　Commercial & Institutional Building Construction

1611 Highway & Street Construction, Except Elevated Highways

NAICS 23411　Highway & Street Construction

1622 Bridge, Tunnel, & Elevated Highway Construction

NAICS 23412　Bridge & Tunnel Construction

1623 Water, Sewer, Pipeline, & Communications & Power Line Construction

NAICS 23491　Water, Sewer & Pipeline Construction

NAICS 23492　Power & Communication Transmission Line Construction

1629 Heavy Construction, nec

NAICS 23493　Industrial Nonbuilding Structure Construction

NAICS 23499　All Other Heavy Construction

1711 Plumbing, Heating, & Air-conditioning

NAICS 23511　Plumbing, Heating & Air-conditioning Contractors

1721 Painting & Paper Hanging

NAICS 23521　Painting & Wall Covering Contractors

1731 Electrical Work

NAICS 561621　Security Systems Services

NAICS 23531　Electrical Contractors

1741 Masonry, Stone Setting & Other Stone Work

NAICS 23541　Masonry & Stone Contractors

1742 Plastering, Drywall, Acoustical & Insulation Work

NAICS 23542　Drywall, Plastering, Acoustical & Insulation Contractors

1743 Terrazzo, Tile, Marble, & Mosaic Work

NAICS 23542　Drywall, Plastering, Acoustical & Insulation Contractors

NAICS 23543　Tile, Marble, Terrazzo & Mosaic Contractors

1751 Carpentry Work

NAICS 23551　Carpentry Contractors

1752 Floor Laying & Other Floor Work, nec

NAICS 23552　Floor Laying & Other Floor Contractors

1761 Roofing, Siding, & Sheet Metal Work

NAICS 23561　Roofing, Siding, & Sheet Metal Contractors

1771 Concrete Work

NAICS 23542　Drywall, Plastering, Acoustical & Insulation Contractors

NAICS 23571　Concrete Contractors

1781 Water Well Drilling

NAICS 23581　Water Well Drilling Contractors

1791 Structural Steel Erection

NAICS 23591　Structural Steel Erection Contractors

1793 Glass & Glazing Work

NAICS 23592　Glass & Glazing Contractors

1794 Excavation Work

NAICS 23593　Excavation Contractors

1795 Wrecking & Demolition Work

NAICS 23594　Wrecking & Demolition Contractors

1796 Installation or Erection of Building Equipment, nec

NAICS 23595　Building Equipment & Other Machinery Installation Contractors

1799 Special Trade Contractors, nec

NAICS 23521　Painting & Wall Covering Contractors

NAICS 23592　Glass & Glazing Contractors

NAICS 56291　Remediation Services

NAICS 23599　All Other Special Trade Contractors

FOOD & KINDRED PRODUCTS

2011 Meat Packing Plants

NAICS 311611　Animal Slaughtering

2013 Sausages & Other Prepared Meats

NAICS 311612　Meat Processed from Carcasses

2015 Poultry Slaughtering & Processing

NAICS 311615　Poultry Processing

NAICS 311999　All Other Miscellaneous Food Manufacturing

2021 Creamery Butter

NAICS 311512　Creamery Butter Manufacturing

2022 Natural, Processed, & Imitation Cheese

NAICS 311513　Cheese Manufacturing

2023 Dry, Condensed, & Evaporated Dairy Products

NAICS 311514　Dry, Condensed, & Evaporated Milk Manufacturing

2024 Ice Cream & Frozen Desserts

NAICS 31152　Ice Cream & Frozen Dessert Manufacturing

2026 Fluid Milk

NAICS 311511　Fluid Milk Manufacturing

2032 Canned Specialties

NAICS 311422　Specialty Canning

NAICS 311999　All Other Miscellaneous Food Manufacturing

2033 Canned Fruits, Vegetables, Preserves, Jams, & Jellies

NAICS 311421　Fruit & Vegetable Canning

2034 Dried & Dehydrated Fruits, Vegetables, & Soup Mixes

NAICS 311423　Dried & Dehydrated Food Manufacturing

NAICS 311211　Flour Milling

2035 Pickled Fruits & Vegetables, Vegetables Sauces & Seasonings, & Salad Dressings

NAICS 311421　Fruit & Vegetable Canning

NAICS 311941　Mayonnaise, Dressing, & Other Prepared Sauce Manufacturing

2037 Frozen Fruits, Fruit Juices, & Vegetables

NAICS 311411　Frozen Fruit, Juice, & Vegetable Processing

2038 Frozen Specialties, nec

NAICS 311412　Frozen Specialty Food Manufacturing

2041 Flour & Other Grain Mill Products

NAICS 311211　Flour Milling

2043 Cereal Breakfast Foods

NAICS 31192　Coffee & Tea Manufacturing

NAICS 31123　Breakfast Cereal Manufacturing

2044 Rice Milling

NAICS 311212　Rice Milling

2045 Prepared Flour Mixes & Doughs

NAICS 311822　Flour Mixes & Dough Manufacturing from Purchased Flour

2046 Wet Corn Milling

NAICS 311221　Wet Corn Milling

2047 Dog & Cat Food

NAICS 311111　Dog & Cat Food Manufacturing

2048 Prepared Feed & Feed Ingredients for Animals & Fowls, Except Dogs & Cats

NAICS 311611　Animal Slaughtering

NAICS 311119　Other Animal Food Manufacturing

2051 Bread & Other Bakery Products, Except Cookies & Crackers

NAICS 311812　Commercial Bakeries

2052 Cookies & Crackers

NAICS 311821　Cookie & Cracker Manufacturing

NAICS 311919　Other Snack Food Manufacturing

NAICS 311812　Commercial Bakeries

2053 Frozen Bakery Products, Except Bread
NAICS 311813 Frozen Bakery Product Manufacturing
2061 Cane Sugar, Except Refining
NAICS 311311 Sugarcane Mills
2062 Cane Sugar Refining
NAICS 311312 Cane Sugar Refining
2063 Beet Sugar
NAICS 311313 Beet Sugar Manufacturing
2064 Candy & Other Confectionery Products
NAICS 31133　Confectionery Manufacturing from Purchased
　　　　　　Chocolate
NAICS 31134　Non-chocolate Confectionery Manufacturing
2066 Chocolate & Cocoa Products
NAICS 31132　Chocolate & Confectionery Manufacturing from
　　　　　　Cacao Beans
2067 Chewing Gum
NAICS 31134　Non-chocolate Confectionery Manufacturing
2068 Salted & Roasted Nuts & Seeds
NAICS 311911 Roasted Nuts & Peanut Butter Manufacturing
2074 Cottonseed Oil Mills
NAICS 311223 Other Oilseed Processing
NAICS 311225 Fats & Oils Refining & Blending
2075 Soybean Oil Mills
NAICS 311222 Soybean Processing
NAICS 311225 Fats & Oils Refining & Blending
2076 Vegetable Oil Mills, Except Corn, Cottonseed, & Soybeans
NAICS 311223 Other Oilseed Processing
NAICS 311225 Fats & Oils Refining & Blending
2077 Animal & Marine Fats & Oils
NAICS 311613 Rendering & Meat By-product Processing
NAICS 311711 Seafood Canning
NAICS 311712 Fresh & Frozen Seafood Processing
NAICS 311225 Edible Fats & Oils Manufacturing
2079 Shortening, Table Oils, Margarine, & Other Edible Fats & Oils, nec
NAICS 311225 Edible Fats & Oils Manufacturing
NAICS 311222 Soybean Processing
NAICS 311223 Other Oilseed Processing
2082 Malt Beverages
NAICS 31212　Breweries
2083 Malt
NAICS 311213 Malt Manufacturing
2084 Wines, Brandy, & Brandy Spirits
NAICS 31213　Wineries
2085 Distilled & Blended Liquors
NAICS 31214　Distilleries
2086 Bottled & Canned Soft Drinks & Carbonated Waters
NAICS 312111 Soft Drink Manufacturing
NAICS 312112 Bottled Water Manufacturing
2087 Flavoring Extracts & Flavoring Syrups nec
NAICS 31193　Flavoring Syrup & Concentrate Manufacturing
NAICS 311942 Spice & Extract Manufacturing
NAICS 311999 All Other Miscellaneous Food Manufacturing
2091 Canned & Cured Fish & Seafood
NAICS 311711 Seafood Canning
2092 Prepared Fresh or Frozen Fish & Seafoods
NAICS 311712 Fresh & Frozen Seafood Processing
2095 Roasted Coffee
NAICS 31192　Coffee & Tea Manufacturing
NAICS 311942 Spice & Extract Manufacturing
2096 Potato Chips, Corn Chips, & Similar Snacks
NAICS 311919 Other Snack Food Manufacturing

2097 Manufactured Ice
NAICS 312113 Ice Manufacturing
2098 Macaroni, Spaghetti, Vermicelli, & Noodles
NAICS 311823 Pasta Manufacturing
2099 Food Preparations, nec
NAICS 311423 Dried & Dehydrated Food Manufacturing
NAICS 111998 All Other Miscellaneous Crop Farming
NAICS 31134　Non-chocolate Confectionery Manufacturing
NAICS 311911 Roasted Nuts & Peanut Butter Manufacturing
NAICS 311991 Perishable Prepared Food Manufacturing
NAICS 31183　Tortilla Manufacturing
NAICS 31192　Coffee & Tea Manufacturing
NAICS 311941 Mayonnaise, Dressing, & Other Prepared Sauce
　　　　　　Manufacturing
NAICS 311942 Spice & Extract Manufacturing
NAICS 311999 All Other Miscellaneous Food Manufacturing

TOBACCO PRODUCTS

2111 Cigarettes
NAICS 312221 Cigarette Manufacturing
2121 Cigars
NAICS 312229 Other Tobacco Product Manufacturing
2131 Chewing & Smoking Tobacco & Snuff
NAICS 312229 Other Tobacco Product Manufacturing
2141 Tobacco Stemming & Redrying
NAICS 312229 Other Tobacco Product Manufacturing
NAICS 31221　Tobacco Stemming & Redrying

TEXTILE MILL PRODUCTS

2211 Broadwoven Fabric Mills, Cotton
NAICS 31321　Broadwoven Fabric Mills
2221 Broadwoven Fabric Mills, Manmade Fiber & Silk
NAICS 31321　Broadwoven Fabric Mills
2231 Broadwoven Fabric Mills, Wool
NAICS 31321　Broadwoven Fabric Mills
NAICS 313311 Broadwoven Fabric Finishing Mills
NAICS 313312 Textile & Fabric Finishing Mills
2241 Narrow Fabric & Other Smallware Mills: Cotton, Wool, Silk, & Manmade Fiber
NAICS 313221 Narrow Fabric Mills
2251 Women's Full-length & Knee-length Hosiery, Except Socks
NAICS 315111 Sheer Hosiery Mills
2252 Hosiery, nec
NAICS 315111 Sheer Hosiery Mills
NAICS 315119 Other Hosiery & Sock Mills
2253 Knit Outerwear Mills
NAICS 315191 Outerwear Knitting Mills
2254 Knit Underwear & Nightwear Mills
NAICS 315192 Underwear & Nightwear Knitting Mills
2257 Weft Knit Fabric Mills
NAICS 313241 Weft Knit Fabric Mills
NAICS 313312 Textile & Fabric Finishing Mills
2258 Lace & Warp Knit Fabric Mills
NAICS 313249 Other Knit Fabric & Lace Mills
NAICS 313312 Textile & Fabric Finishing Mills
2259 Knitting Mills, nec
NAICS 315191 Outerwear Knitting Mills
NAICS 315192 Underwear & Nightwear Knitting Mills
NAICS 313241 Weft Knit Fabric Mills
NAICS 313249 Other Knit Fabric & Lace Mills

2261 Finishers of Broadwoven Fabrics of Cotton
NAICS 313311 Broadwoven Fabric Finishing Mills
2262 Finishers of Broadwoven Fabrics of Manmade Fiber & Silk
NAICS 313311 Broadwoven Fabric Finishing Mills
2269 Finishers of Textiles, nec
NAICS 313311 Broadwoven Fabric Finishing Mills
NAICS 313312 Textile & Fabric Finishing Mills
2273 Carpets & Rugs
NAICS 31411 Carpet & Rug Mills
2281 Yarn Spinning Mills
NAICS 313111 Yarn Spinning Mills
2282 Yarn Texturizing, Throwing, Twisting, & Winding Mills
NAICS 313112 Yarn Texturing, Throwing & Twisting Mills
NAICS 313312 Textile & Fabric Finishing Mills
2284 Thread Mills
NAICS 313113 Thread Mills
NAICS 313312 Textile & Fabric Finishing Mills
2295 Coated Fabrics, Not Rubberized
NAICS 31332 Fabric Coating Mills
2296 Tire Cord & Fabrics
NAICS 314992 Tire Cord & Tire Fabric Mills
2297 Nonwoven Fabrics
NAICS 31323 Nonwoven Fabric Mills
2298 Cordage & Twine
NAICS 314991 Rope, Cordage & Twine Mills
2299 Textile Goods, nec
NAICS 31321 Broadwoven Fabric Mills
NAICS 31323 Nonwoven Fabric Mills
NAICS 313312 Textile & Fabric Finishing Mills
NAICS 313221 Narrow Fabric Mills
NAICS 313113 Thread Mills
NAICS 313111 Yarn Spinning Mills
NAICS 314999 All Other Miscellaneous Textile Product Mills

APPAREL & OTHER FINISHED PRODUCTS MADE FROM FABRICS & SIMILAR MATERIALS

2311 Men's & Boys' Suits, Coats & Overcoats
NAICS 315211 Men's & Boys' Cut & Sew Apparel Contractors
NAICS 315222 Men's & Boys' Cut & Sew Suit, Coat, & Overcoat Manufacturing
2321 Men's & Boys' Shirts, Except Work Shirts
NAICS 315211 Men's & Boys' Cut & Sew Apparel Contractors
NAICS 315223 Men's & Boys' Cut & Sew Shirt, Manufacturing
2322 Men's & Boys' Underwear & Nightwear
NAICS 315211 Men's & Boys' Cut & Sew Apparel Contractors
NAICS 315221 Men's & Boys' Cut & Sew Underwear & Nightwear Manufacturing
2323 Men's & Boys' Neckwear
NAICS 315993 Men's & Boys' Neckwear Manufacturing
2325 Men's & Boys' Trousers & Slacks
NAICS 315211 Men's & Boys' Cut & Sew Apparel Contractors
NAICS 315224 Men's & Boys' Cut & Sew Trouser, Slack, & Jean Manufacturing
2326 Men's & Boys' Work Clothing
NAICS 315211 Men's & Boys' Cut & Sew Apparel Contractors
NAICS 315225 Men's & Boys' Cut & Sew Work Clothing Manufacturing
2329 Men's & Boys' Clothing, nec
NAICS 315211 Men's & Boys' Cut & Sew Apparel Contractors

NAICS 315228 Men's & Boys' Cut & Sew Other Outerwear Manufacturing
NAICS 315299 All Other Cut & Sew Apparel Manufacturing
2331 Women's, Misses', & Juniors' Blouses & Shirts
NAICS 315212 Women's & Girls' Cut & Sew Apparel Contractors
NAICS 315232 Women's & Girls' Cut & Sew Blouse & Shirt Manufacturing
2335 Women's, Misses' & Junior's Dresses
NAICS 315212 Women's & Girls' Cut & Sew Apparel Contractors
NAICS 315233 Women's & Girls' Cut & Sew Dress Manufacturing
2337 Women's, Misses' & Juniors' Suits, Skirts & Coats
NAICS 315212 Women's & Girls' Cut & Sew Apparel Contractors
NAICS 315234 Women's & Girls' Cut & Sew Suit, Coat, Tailored Jacket, & Skirt Manufacturing
2339 Women's, Misses' & Juniors' Outerwear, nec
NAICS 315999 Other Apparel Accessories & Other Apparel Manufacturing
NAICS 315212 Women's & Girls' Cut & Sew Apparel Contractors
NAICS 315299 All Other Cut & Sew Apparel Manufacturing
NAICS 315238 Women's & Girls' Cut & Sew Other Outerwear Manufacturing
2341 Women's, Misses, Children's, & Infants' Underwear & Nightwear
NAICS 315212 Women's & Girls' Cut & Sew Apparel Contractors
NAICS 315211 Men's & Boys' Cut & Sew Apparel Contractors
NAICS 315231 Women's & Girls' Cut & Sew Lingerie, Loungewear, & Nightwear Manufacturing
NAICS 315221 Men's & Boys' Cut & Sew Underwear & Nightwear Manufacturing
NAICS 315291 Infants' Cut & Sew Apparel Manufacturing
2342 Brassieres, Girdles, & Allied Garments
NAICS 315212 Women's & Girls' Cut & Sew Apparel Contractors
NAICS 315231 Women's & Girls' Cut & Sew Lingerie, Loungewear, & Nightwear Manufacturing
2353 Hats, Caps, & Millinery
NAICS 315991 Hat, Cap, & Millinery Manufacturing
2361 Girls', Children's & Infants' Dresses, Blouses & Shirts
NAICS 315291 Infants' Cut & Sew Apparel Manufacturing
NAICS 315223 Men's & Boys' Cut & Sew Shirt, Manufacturing
NAICS 315211 Men's & Boys' Cut & Sew Apparel Contractors
NAICS 315232 Women's & Girls' Cut & Sew Blouse & Shirt Manufacturing
NAICS 315233 Women's & Girls' Cut & Sew Dress Manufacturing
NAICS 315212 Women's & Girls' Cut & Sew Apparel Contractors
2369 Girls', Children's & Infants' Outerwear, nec
NAICS 315291 Infants' Cut & Sew Apparel Manufacturing
NAICS 315222 Men's & Boys' Cut & Sew Suit, Coat, & Overcoat Manufacturing
NAICS 315224 Men's & Boys' Cut & Sew Trouser, Slack, & Jean Manufacturing
NAICS 315228 Men's & Boys' Cut & Sew Other Outerwear Manufacturing
NAICS 315221 Men's & Boys' Cut & Sew Underwear & Nightwear Manufacturing
NAICS 315211 Men's & Boys' Cut & Sew Apparel Contractors

NAICS 315234 Women's & Girls' Cut & Sew Suit, Coat,
　　　　　　　Tailored Jacket, & Skirt Manufacturing
NAICS 315238 Women's & Girls' Cut & Sew Other Outerwear
　　　　　　　Manufacturing
NAICS 315231 Women's & Girls' Cut & Sew Lingerie,
　　　　　　　Loungewear, & Nightwear Manufacturing
NAICS 315212 Women's & Girls' Cut & Sew Apparel
　　　　　　　Contractors
2371 Fur Goods
NAICS 315292 Fur & Leather Apparel Manufacturing
2381 Dress & Work Gloves, Except Knit & All-leather
NAICS 315992 Glove & Mitten Manufacturing
2384 Robes & Dressing Gowns
NAICS 315231 Women's & Girls' Cut & Sew Lingerie,
　　　　　　　Loungewear, & Nightwear Manufacturing
NAICS 315221 Men's & Boys' Cut & Sew Underwear &
　　　　　　　Nightwear Manufacturing
NAICS 315211 Men's & Boys' Cut & Sew Apparel Contractors
NAICS 315212 Women's & Girls' Cut & Sew Apparel
　　　　　　　Contractors
2385 Waterproof Outerwear
NAICS 315222 Men's & Boys' Cut & Sew Suit, Coat, &
　　　　　　　Overcoat Manufacturing
NAICS 315234 Women's & Girls' Cut & Sew Suit, Coat,
　　　　　　　Tailored Jacket, & Skirt Manufacturing
NAICS 315228 Men's & Boys' Cut & Sew Other Outerwear
　　　　　　　Manufacturing
NAICS 315238 Women's & Girls' Cut & Sew Other Outerwear
　　　　　　　Manufacturing
NAICS 315291 Infants' Cut & Sew Apparel Manufacturing
NAICS 315999 Other Apparel Accessories & Other Apparel
　　　　　　　Manufacturing
NAICS 315211 Men's & Boys' Cut & Sew Apparel Contractors
NAICS 315212 Women's & Girls' Cut & Sew Apparel
　　　　　　　Contractors
2386 Leather & Sheep-lined Clothing
NAICS 315292 Fur & Leather Apparel Manufacturing
2387 Apparel Belts
NAICS 315999 Other Apparel Accessories & Other Apparel
　　　　　　　Manufacturing
2389 Apparel & Accessories, nec
NAICS 315999 Other Apparel Accessories & Other Apparel
　　　　　　　Manufacturing
NAICS 315299 All Other Cut & Sew Apparel Manufacturing
NAICS 315231 Women's & Girls' Cut & Sew Lingerie,
　　　　　　　Loungewear, & Nightwear Manufacturing
NAICS 315212 Women's & Girls' Cut & Sew Apparel
　　　　　　　Contractors
NAICS 315211 Mens' & Boys' Cut & Sew Apparel Contractors
2391 Curtains & Draperies
NAICS 314121 Curtain & Drapery Mills
2392 Housefurnishings, Except Curtains & Draperies
NAICS 314911 Textile Bag Mills
NAICS 339994 Broom, Brush & Mop Manufacturing
NAICS 314129 Other Household Textile Product Mills
2393 Textile Bags
NAICS 314911 Textile Bag Mills
2394 Canvas & Related Products
NAICS 314912 Canvas & Related Product Mills
**2395 Pleating, Decorative & Novelty Stitching, & Tucking for the
　　　Trade**
NAICS 314999 All Other Miscellaneous Textile Product Mills
NAICS 315211 Mens' & Boys' Cut & Sew Apparel Contractors

NAICS 315212 Women's & Girls' Cut & Sew Apparel
　　　　　　　Contractors
**2396 Automotive Trimmings, Apparel Findings, & Related
　　　Products**
NAICS 33636　Motor Vehicle Fabric Accessories & Seat
　　　　　　　Manufacturing
NAICS 315999 Other Apparel Accessories, & Other Apparel
　　　　　　　Manufacturing
NAICS 323113 Commercial Screen Printing
NAICS 314999 All Other Miscellaneous Textile Product Mills
2397 Schiffli Machine Embroideries
NAICS 313222 Schiffli Machine Embroidery
2399 Fabricated Textile Products, nec
NAICS 33636　Motor Vehicle Fabric Accessories & Seat
　　　　　　　Manufacturing
NAICS 315999 Other Apparel Accessories & Other Apparel
　　　　　　　Manufacturing
NAICS 314999 All Other Miscellaneous Textile Product Mills

LUMBER & WOOD PRODUCTS, EXCEPT FURNITURE

2411 Logging
NAICS 11331　Logging
2421 Sawmills & Planing Mills, General
NAICS 321913 Softwood Cut Stock, Resawing Lumber, &
　　　　　　　Planing
NAICS 321113 Sawmills
NAICS 321914 Other Millwork
NAICS 321999 All Other Miscellaneous Wood Product
　　　　　　　Manufacturing
2426 Hardwood Dimension & Flooring Mills
NAICS 321914 Other Millwork
NAICS 321999 All Other Miscellaneous Wood Product
　　　　　　　Manufacturing
NAICS 337139 Other Wood Furniture Manufacturing
NAICS 321912 Hardwood Dimension Mills
2429 Special Product Sawmills, nec
NAICS 321113 Sawmills
NAICS 321913 Softwood Cut Stock, Resawing Lumber, &
　　　　　　　Planing
NAICS 321999 All Other Miscellaneous Wood Product
　　　　　　　Manufacturing
2431 Millwork
NAICS 321911 Wood Window & Door Manufacturing
NAICS 321914 Other Millwork
2434 Wood Kitchen Cabinets
NAICS 337131 Wood Kitchen Cabinet & Counter Top
　　　　　　　Manufacturing
2435 Hardwood Veneer & Plywood
NAICS 321211 Hardwood Veneer & Plywood Manufacturing
2436 Softwood Veneer & Plywood
NAICS 321212 Softwood Veneer & Plywood Manufacturing
2439 Structural Wood Members, nec
NAICS 321913 Softwood Cut Stock, Resawing Lumber, &
　　　　　　　Planing
NAICS 321214 Truss Manufacturing
NAICS 321213 Engineered Wood Member Manufacturing
2441 Nailed & Lock Corner Wood Boxes & Shook
NAICS 32192　Wood Container & Pallet Manufacturing
2448 Wood Pallets & Skids
NAICS 32192　Wood Container & Pallet Manufacturing

2449 Wood Containers, nec
NAICS 32192   Wood Container & Pallet Manufacturing
2451 Mobile Homes
NAICS 321991 Manufactured Home Manufacturing
2452 Prefabricated Wood Buildings & Components
NAICS 321992 Prefabricated Wood Building Manufacturing
2491 Wood Preserving
NAICS 321114 Wood Preservation
2493 Reconstituted Wood Products
NAICS 321219 Reconstituted Wood Product Manufacturing
2499 Wood Products, nec
NAICS 339999 All Other Miscellaneous Manufacturing
NAICS 337139 Other Wood Furniture Manufacturing
NAICS 337148 Other Nonwood Furniture Manufacturing
NAICS 32192   Wood Container & Pallet Manufacturing
NAICS 321999 All Other Miscellaneous Wood Product
      Manufacturing

FURNITURE & FIXTURES

2511 Wood Household Furniture, Except Upholstered
NAICS 337122 Wood Household Furniture Manufacturing
2512 Wood Household Furniture, Upholstered
NAICS 337121 Upholstered Household Furniture
      Manufacturing
2514 Metal Household Furniture
NAICS 337124 Metal Household Furniture Manufacturing
2515 Mattresses, Foundations, & Convertible Beds
NAICS 33791   Mattress Manufacturing
NAICS 337132 Upholstered Wood Household Furniture
      Manufacturing
2517 Wood Television, Radio, Phonograph & Sewing Machine Cabinets
NAICS 337139 Other Wood Furniture Manufacturing
2519 Household Furniture, nec
NAICS 337143 Household Furniture (except Wood & Metal)
      Manufacturing
2521 Wood Office Furniture
NAICS 337134 Wood Office Furniture Manufacturing
2522 Office Furniture, Except Wood
NAICS 337141 Nonwood Office Furniture Manufacturing
2531 Public Building & Related Furniture
NAICS 33636   Motor Vehicle Fabric Accessories & Seat
      Manufacturing
NAICS 337139 Other Wood Furniture Manufacturing
NAICS 337148 Other Nonwood Furniture Manufacturing
NAICS 339942 Lead Pencil & Art Good Manufacturing
2541 Wood Office & Store Fixtures, Partitions, Shelving, & Lockers
NAICS 337131 Wood Kitchen Cabinet & Counter Top
      Manufacturing
NAICS 337135 Custom Architectural Woodwork, Millwork, &
      Fixtures
NAICS 337139 Other Wood Furniture Manufacturing
2542 Office & Store Fixtures, Partitions Shelving, & Lockers, Except Wood
NAICS 337145 Nonwood Showcase, Partition, Shelving, &
      Locker Manufacturing
2591 Drapery Hardware & Window Blinds & Shades
NAICS 33792   Blind & Shade Manufacturing
2599 Furniture & Fixtures, nec
NAICS 339113 Surgical Appliance & Supplies Manufacturing
NAICS 337139 Other Wood Furniture Manufacturing

NAICS 337148 Other Nonwood Furniture Manufacturing

PAPER & ALLIED PRODUCTS

2611 Pulp Mills
NAICS 32211   Pulp Mills
NAICS 322121 Paper Mills
NAICS 32213   Paperboard Mills
2621 Paper Mills
NAICS 322121 Paper Mills
NAICS 322122 Newsprint Mills
2631 Paperboard Mills
NAICS 32213   Paperboard Mills
2652 Setup Paperboard Boxes
NAICS 322213 Setup Paperboard Box Manufacturing
2653 Corrugated & Solid Fiber Boxes
NAICS 322211 Corrugated & Solid Fiber Box Manufacturing
2655 Fiber Cans, Tubes, Drums, & Similar Products
NAICS 322214 Fiber Can, Tube, Drum, & Similar Products
      Manufacturing
2656 Sanitary Food Containers, Except Folding
NAICS 322215 Non-folding Sanitary Food Container
      Manufacturing
2657 Folding Paperboard Boxes, Including Sanitary
NAICS 322212 Folding Paperboard Box Manufacturing
2671 Packaging Paper & Plastics Film, Coated & Laminated
NAICS 322221 Coated & Laminated Packaging Paper &
      Plastics Film Manufacturing
NAICS 326112 Unsupported Plastics Packaging Film & Sheet
      Manufacturing
2672 Coated & Laminated Paper, nec
NAICS 322222 Coated & Laminated Paper Manufacturing
2673 Plastics, Foil, & Coated Paper Bags
NAICS 322223 Plastics, Foil, & Coated Paper Bag
      Manufacturing
NAICS 326111 Unsupported Plastics Bag Manufacturing
2674 Uncoated Paper & Multiwall Bags
NAICS 322224 Uncoated Paper & Multiwall Bag
      Manufacturing
2675 Die-cut Paper & Paperboard & Cardboard
NAICS 322231 Die-cut Paper & Paperboard Office Supplies
      Manufacturing
NAICS 322292 Surface-coated Paperboard Manufacturing
NAICS 322298 All Other Converted Paper Product
      Manufacturing
2676 Sanitary Paper Products
NAICS 322291 Sanitary Paper Product Manufacturing
2677 Envelopes
NAICS 322232 Envelope Manufacturing
2678 Stationery, Tablets, & Related Products
NAICS 322233 Stationery, Tablet, & Related Product
      Manufacturing
2679 Converted Paper & Paperboard Products, nec
NAICS 322215 Non-folding Sanitary Food Container
      Manufacturing
NAICS 322222 Coated & Laminated Paper Manufacturing
NAICS 322231 Die-cut Paper & Paperboard Office Supplies
      Manufacturing
NAICS 322298 All Other Converted Paper Product
      Manufacturing

PRINTING, PUBLISHING, & ALLIED INDUSTRIES

2711 Newspapers: Publishing, or Publishing & Printing
NAICS 51111   Newspaper Publishers
2721 Periodicals: Publishing, or Publishing & Printing
NAICS 51112   Periodical Publishers
2731 Books: Publishing, or Publishing & Printing
NAICS 51223   Music Publishers
NAICS 51113   Book Publishers
2732 Book Printing
NAICS 323117 Book Printing
2741 Miscellaneous Publishing
NAICS 51114   Database & Directory Publishers
NAICS 51223   Music Publishers
NAICS 511199 All Other Publishers
2752 Commercial Printing, Lithographic
NAICS 323114 Quick Printing
NAICS 323110 Commercial Lithographic Printing
2754 Commercial Printing, Gravure
NAICS 323111 Commercial Gravure Printing
2759 Commercial Printing, nec
NAICS 323113 Commercial Screen Printing
NAICS 323112 Commercial Flexographic Printing
NAICS 323114 Quick Printing
NAICS 323115 Digital Printing
NAICS 323119 Other Commercial Printing
2761 Manifold Business Forms
NAICS 323116 Manifold Business Form Printing
2771 Greeting Cards
NAICS 323110 Commercial Lithographic Printing
NAICS 323111 Commercial Gravure Printing
NAICS 323112 Commercial Flexographic Printing
NAICS 323113 Commercial Screen Printing
NAICS 323119 Other Commercial Printing
NAICS 511191 Greeting Card Publishers
2782 Blankbooks, Loose-leaf Binders & Devices
NAICS 323110 Commercial Lithographic Printing
NAICS 323111 Commercial Gravure Printing
NAICS 323112 Commercial Flexographic Printing
NAICS 323113 Commercial Screen Printing
NAICS 323119 Other Commercial Printing
NAICS 323118 Blankbook, Loose-leaf Binder & Device
           Manufacturing
2789 Bookbinding & Related Work
NAICS 323121 Tradebinding & Related Work
2791 Typesetting
NAICS 323122 Prepress Services
2796 Platemaking & Related Services
NAICS 323122 Prepress Services

CHEMICALS & ALLIED PRODUCTS

2812 Alkalies & Chlorine
NAICS 325181 Alkalies & Chlorine Manufacturing
2813 Industrial Gases
NAICS 32512   Industrial Gas Manufacturing
2816 Inorganic Pigments
NAICS 325131 Inorganic Dye & Pigment Manufacturing
NAICS 325182 Carbon Black Manufacturing
2819 Industrial Inorganic Chemicals, nec
NAICS 325998 All Other Miscellaneous Chemical Product
           Manufacturing

NAICS 331311 Alumina Refining
NAICS 325131 Inorganic Dye & Pigment Manufacturing
NAICS 325188 All Other Basic Inorganic Chemical
           Manufacturing
2821 Plastics Material Synthetic Resins, & Nonvulcanizable Elastomers
NAICS 325211 Plastics Material & Resin Manufacturing
2822 Synthetic Rubber
NAICS 325212 Synthetic Rubber Manufacturing
2823 Cellulosic Manmade Fibers
NAICS 325221 Cellulosic Manmade Fiber Manufacturing
2824 Manmade Organic Fibers, Except Cellulosic
NAICS 325222 Noncellulosic Organic Fiber Manufacturing
2833 Medicinal Chemicals & Botanical Products
NAICS 325411 Medicinal & Botanical Manufacturing
2834 Pharmaceutical Preparations
NAICS 325412 Pharmaceutical Preparation Manufacturing
2835 In Vitro & in Vivo Diagnostic Substances
NAICS 325412 Pharmaceutical Preparation Manufacturing
NAICS 325413 In-vitro Diagnostic Substance Manufacturing
2836 Biological Products, Except Diagnostic Substances
NAICS 325414 Biological Product Manufacturing
2841 Soaps & Other Detergents, Except Speciality Cleaners
NAICS 325611 Soap & Other Detergent Manufacturing
2842 Speciality Cleaning, Polishing, & Sanitary Preparations
NAICS 325612 Polish & Other Sanitation Good Manufacturing
2843 Surface Active Agents, Finishing Agents, Sulfonated Oils, & Assistants
NAICS 325613 Surface Active Agent Manufacturing
2844 Perfumes, Cosmetics, & Other Toilet Preparations
NAICS 32562   Toilet Preparation Manufacturing
NAICS 325611 Soap & Other Detergent Manufacturing
2851 Paints, Varnishes, Lacquers, Enamels, & Allied Products
NAICS 32551   Paint & Coating Manufacturing
2861 Gum & Wood Chemicals
NAICS 325191 Gum & Wood Chemical Manufacturing
2865 Cyclic Organic Crudes & Intermediates, & Organic Dyes & Pigments
NAICS 32511   Petrochemical Manufacturing
NAICS 325132 Organic Dye & Pigment Manufacturing
NAICS 325192 Cyclic Crude & Intermediate Manufacturing
2869 Industrial Organic Chemicals, nec
NAICS 32511   Petrochemical Manufacturing
NAICS 325188 All Other Inorganic Chemical Manufacturing
NAICS 325193 Ethyl Alcohol Manufacturing
NAICS 32512   Industrial Gas Manufacturing
NAICS 325199 All Other Basic Organic Chemical
           Manufacturing
2873 Nitrogenous Fertilizers
NAICS 325311 Nitrogenous Fertilizer Manufacturing
2874 Phosphatic Fertilizers
NAICS 325312 Phosphatic Fertilizer Manufacturing
2875 Fertilizers, Mixing Only
NAICS 325314 Fertilizer Manufacturing
2879 Pesticides & Agricultural Chemicals, nec
NAICS 32532   Pesticide & Other Agricultural Chemical
           Manufacturing
2891 Adhesives & Sealants
NAICS 32552   Adhesive & Sealant Manufacturing
2892 Explosives
NAICS 32592   Explosives Manufacturing
2893 Printing Ink
NAICS 32591   Printing Ink Manufacturing

2895 Carbon Black
NAICS 325182 Carbon Black Manufacturing
2899 Chemicals & Chemical Preparations, nec
NAICS 32551 Paint & Coating Manufacturing
NAICS 311942 Spice & Extract Manufacturing
NAICS 325199 All Other Basic Organic Chemical
Manufacturing
NAICS 325998 All Other Miscellaneous Chemical Product
Manufacturing

PETROLEUM REFINING & RELATED INDUSTRIES

2911 Petroleum Refining
NAICS 32411 Petroleum Refineries
2951 Asphalt Paving Mixtures & Blocks
NAICS 324121 Asphalt Paving Mixture & Block Manufacturing
2952 Asphalt Felts & Coatings
NAICS 324122 Asphalt Shingle & Coating Materials
Manufacturing
2992 Lubricating Oils & Greases
NAICS 324191 Petroleum Lubricating Oil & Grease
Manufacturing 2999

RUBBER & MISCELLANEOUS PLASTICS PRODUCTS

3011 Tires & Inner Tubes
NAICS 326211 Tire Manufacturing
3021 Rubber & Plastics Footwear
NAICS 316211 Rubber & Plastics Footwear Manufacturing
3052 Rubber & Plastics Hose & Belting
NAICS 32622 Rubber & Plastics Hoses & Belting
Manufacturing
3053 Gaskets, Packing, & Sealing Devices
NAICS 339991 Gasket, Packing, & Sealing Device
Manufacturing
3061 Molded, Extruded, & Lathe-cut Mechanical Rubber Products
NAICS 326291 Rubber Product Manufacturing for Mechanical
Use
3069 Fabricated Rubber Products, nec
NAICS 31332 Fabric Coating Mills
NAICS 326192 Resilient Floor Covering Manufacturing
NAICS 326299 All Other Rubber Product Manufacturing
3081 Unsupported Plastics Film & Sheet
NAICS 326113 Unsupported Plastics Film & Sheet
Manufacturing
3082 Unsupported Plastics Profile Shapes
NAICS 326121 Unsupported Plastics Profile Shape
Manufacturing
3083 Laminated Plastics Plate, Sheet, & Profile Shapes
NAICS 32613 Laminated Plastics Plate, Sheet, & Shape
Manufacturing
3084 Plastic Pipe
NAICS 326122 Plastic Pipe & Pipe Fitting Manufacturing
3085 Plastics Bottles
NAICS 32616 Plastics Bottle Manufacturing
3086 Plastics Foam Products
NAICS 32615 Urethane & Other Foam Product
Manufacturing
NAICS 32614 Polystyrene Foam Product Manufacturing

3087 Custom Compounding of Purchased Plastics Resins
NAICS 325991 Custom Compounding of Purchased Resin
3088 Plastics Plumbing Fixtures
NAICS 326191 Plastics Plumbing Fixtures Manufacturing
3089 Plastics Products, nec
NAICS 326122 Plastics Pipe & Pipe Fitting Manufacturing
NAICS 326121 Unsupported Plastics Profile Shape
Manufacturing
NAICS 326199 All Other Plastics Product Manufacturing

LEATHER & LEATHER PRODUCTS

3111 Leather Tanning & Finishing
NAICS 31611 Leather & Hide Tanning & Finishing
3131 Boot & Shoe Cut Stock & Findings
NAICS 321999 All Other Miscellaneous Wood Product
Manufacturing
NAICS 339993 Fastener, Button, Needle, & Pin Manufacturing
NAICS 316999 All Other Leather Good Manufacturing
3142 House Slippers
NAICS 316212 House Slipper Manufacturing
3143 Men's Footwear, Except Athletic
NAICS 316213 Men's Footwear Manufacturing
3144 Women's Footwear, Except Athletic
NAICS 316214 Women's Footwear Manufacturing
3149 Footwear, Except Rubber, nec
NAICS 316219 Other Footwear Manufacturing
3151 Leather Gloves & Mittens
NAICS 315992 Glove & Mitten Manufacturing
3161 Luggage
NAICS 316991 Luggage Manufacturing
3171 Women's Handbags & Purses
NAICS 316992 Women's Handbag & Purse Manufacturing
3172 Personal Leather Goods, Except Women's Handbags & Purses
NAICS 316993 Personal Leather Good Manufacturing
3199 Leather Goods, nec
NAICS 316999 All Other Leather Good Manufacturing

STONE, CLAY, GLASS, & CONCRETE PRODUCTS

3211 Flat Glass
NAICS 327211 Flat Glass Manufacturing
3221 Glass Containers
NAICS 327213 Glass Container Manufacturing
3229 Pressed & Blown Glass & Glassware, nec
NAICS 327212 Other Pressed & Blown Glass & Glassware
Manufacturing
3231 Glass Products, Made of Purchased Glass
NAICS 327215 Glass Product Manufacturing Made of
Purchased Glass
3241 Cement, Hydraulic
NAICS 32731 Hydraulic Cement Manufacturing
3251 Brick & Structural Clay Tile
NAICS 327121 Brick & Structural Clay Tile Manufacturing
3253 Ceramic Wall & Floor Tile
NAICS 327122 Ceramic Wall & Floor Tile Manufacturing
3255 Clay Refractories
NAICS 327124 Clay Refractory Manufacturing

3259 Structural Clay Products, nec
NAICS 327123 Other Structural Clay Product Manufacturing

3261 Vitreous China Plumbing Fixtures & China & Earthenware Fittings & Bathroom Accessories
NAICS 327111 Vitreous China Plumbing Fixture & China & Earthenware Fittings & Bathroom Accessories Manufacturing

3262 Vitreous China Table & Kitchen Articles
NAICS 327112 Vitreous China, Fine Earthenware & Other Pottery Product Manufacturing

3263 Fine Earthenware Table & Kitchen Articles
NAICS 327112 Vitreous China, Fine Earthenware & Other Pottery Product Manufacturing

3264 Porcelain Electrical Supplies
NAICS 327113 Porcelain Electrical Supply Manufacturing

3269 Pottery Products, nec
NAICS 327112 Vitreous China, Fine Earthenware, & Other Pottery Product Manufacturing

3271 Concrete Block & Brick
NAICS 327331 Concrete Block & Brick Manufacturing

3272 Concrete Products, Except Block & Brick
NAICS 327999 All Other Miscellaneous Nonmetallic Mineral Product Manufacturing
NAICS 327332 Concrete Pipe Manufacturing
NAICS 32739 Other Concrete Product Manufacturing

3273 Ready-mixed Concrete
NAICS 32732 Ready-mix Concrete Manufacturing

3274 Lime
NAICS 32741 Lime Manufacturing

3275 Gypsum Products
NAICS 32742 Gypsum & Gypsum Product Manufacturing

3281 Cut Stone & Stone Products
NAICS 327991 Cut Stone & Stone Product Manufacturing

3291 Abrasive Products
NAICS 332999 All Other Miscellaneous Fabricated Metal Product Manufacturing
NAICS 32791 Abrasive Product Manufacturing

3292 Asbestos Products
NAICS 33634 Motor Vehicle Brake System Manufacturing
NAICS 327999 All Other Miscellaneous Nonmetallic Mineral Product Manufacturing

3295 Minerals & Earths, Ground or Otherwise Treated
NAICS 327992 Ground or Treated Mineral & Earth Manufacturing

3296 Mineral Wool
NAICS 327993 Mineral Wool Manufacturing

3297 Nonclay Refractories
NAICS 327125 Nonclay Refractory Manufacturing

3299 Nonmetallic Mineral Products, nec
NAICS 32742 Gypsum & Gypsum Product Manufacturing
NAICS 327999 All Other Miscellaneous Nonmetallic Mineral Product Manufacturing

PRIMARY METALS INDUSTRIES

3312 Steel Works, Blast Furnaces , & Rolling Mills
NAICS 324199 All Other Petroleum & Coal Products Manufacturing
NAICS 331111 Iron & Steel Mills

3313 Electrometallurgical Products, Except Steel
NAICS 331112 Electrometallurgical Ferroalloy Product Manufacturing

NAICS 331492 Secondary Smelting, Refining, & Alloying of Nonferrous Metals

3315 Steel Wiredrawing & Steel Nails & Spikes
NAICS 331222 Steel Wire Drawing
NAICS 332618 Other Fabricated Wire Product Manufacturing

3316 Cold-rolled Steel Sheet, Strip, & Bars
NAICS 331221 Cold-rolled Steel Shape Manufacturing

3317 Steel Pipe & Tubes
NAICS 33121 Iron & Steel Pipes & Tubes Manufacturing from Purchased Steel

3321 Gray & Ductile Iron Foundries
NAICS 331511 Iron Foundries

3322 Malleable Iron Foundries
NAICS 331511 Iron Foundries

3324 Steel Investment Foundries
NAICS 331512 Steel Investment Foundries

3325 Steel Foundries, nec
NAICS 331513 Steel Foundries

3331 Primary Smelting & Refining of Copper
NAICS 331411 Primary Smelting & Refining of Copper

3334 Primary Production of Aluminum
NAICS 331312 Primary Aluminum Production

3339 Primary Smelting & Refining of Nonferrous Metals, Except Copper & Aluminum
NAICS 331419 Primary Smelting & Refining of Nonferrous Metals

3341 Secondary Smelting & Refining of Nonferrous Metals
NAICS 331314 Secondary Smelting & Alloying of Aluminum
NAICS 331423 Secondary Smelting, Refining, & Alloying of Copper
NAICS 331492 Secondary Smelting, Refining, & Alloying of Nonferrous Metals

3351 Rolling, Drawing, & Extruding of Copper
NAICS 331421 Copper Rolling, Drawing, & Extruding

3353 Aluminum Sheet, Plate, & Foil
NAICS 331315 Aluminum Sheet, Plate, & Foil Manufacturing

3354 Aluminum Extruded Products
NAICS 331316 Aluminum Extruded Product Manufacturing

3355 Aluminum Rolling & Drawing, nec
NAICS 331319 Other Aluminum Rolling & Drawing,

3356 Rolling, Drawing, & Extruding of Nonferrous Metals, Except Copper & Aluminum
NAICS 331491 Nonferrous Metal Rolling. Drawing, & Extruding

3357 Drawing & Insulating of Nonferrous Wire
NAICS 331319 Other Aluminum Rolling & Drawing
NAICS 331422 Copper Wire Drawing
NAICS 331491 Nonferrous Metal Rolling, Drawing, & Extruding
NAICS 335921 Fiber Optic Cable Manufacturing
NAICS 335929 Other Communication & Energy Wire Manufacturing

3363 Aluminum Die-castings
NAICS 331521 Aluminum Die-castings

3364 Nonferrous Die-castings, Except Aluminum
NAICS 331522 Nonferrous Die-castings

3365 Aluminum Foundries
NAICS 331524 Aluminum Foundries

3366 Copper Foundries
NAICS 331525 Copper Foundries

3369 Nonferrous Foundries, Except Aluminum & Copper
NAICS 331528 Other Nonferrous Foundries

3398 Metal Heat Treating
NAICS 332811 Metal Heat Treating
3399 Primary Metal Products, nec
NAICS 331111 Iron & Steel Mills
NAICS 331314 Secondary Smelting & Alloying of Aluminum
NAICS 331423 Secondary Smelting, Refining & Alloying of Copper
NAICS 331492 Secondary Smelting, Refining, & Alloying of Nonferrous Metals
NAICS 332618 Other Fabricated Wire Product Manufacturing
NAICS 332813 Electroplating, Plating, Polishing, Anodizing, & Coloring

FABRICATED METAL PRODUCTS, EXCEPT MACHINERY & TRANSPORTATION EQUIPMENT

3411 Metal Cans
NAICS 332431 Metal Can Manufacturing
3412 Metal Shipping Barrels, Drums, Kegs & Pails
NAICS 332439 Other Metal Container Manufacturing
3421 Cutlery
NAICS 332211 Cutlery & Flatware Manufacturing
3423 Hand & Edge Tools, Except Machine Tools & Handsaws
NAICS 332212 Hand & Edge Tool Manufacturing
3425 Saw Blades & Handsaws
NAICS 332213 Saw Blade & Handsaw Manufacturing
3429 Hardware, nec
NAICS 332439 Other Metal Container Manufacturing
NAICS 332919 Other Metal Valve & Pipe Fitting Manufacturing
NAICS 33251　Hardware Manufacturing
3431 Enameled Iron & Metal Sanitary Ware
NAICS 332998 Enameled Iron & Metal Sanitary Ware Manufacturing
3432 Plumbing Fixture Fittings & Trim
NAICS 332913 Plumbing Fixture Fitting & Trim Manufacturing
NAICS 332999 All Other Miscellaneous Fabricated Metal Product Manufacturing
3433 Heating Equipment, Except Electric & Warm Air Furnaces
NAICS 333414 Heating Equipment Manufacturing
3441 Fabricated Structural Metal
NAICS 332312 Fabricated Structural Metal Manufacturing
3442 Metal Doors, Sash, Frames, Molding, & Trim Manufacturing
NAICS 332321 Metal Window & Door Manufacturing
3443 Fabricated Plate Work
NAICS 332313 Plate Work Manufacturing
NAICS 33241　Power Boiler & Heat Exchanger Manufacturing
NAICS 33242　Metal Tank Manufacturing
NAICS 333415 Air-conditioning & Warm Air Heating Equipment & Commercial & Industrial Refrigeration Equipment Manufacturing
3444 Sheet Metal Work
NAICS 332322 Sheet Metal Work Manufacturing
NAICS 332439 Other Metal Container Manufacturing
3446 Architectural & Ornamental Metal Work
NAICS 332323 Ornamental & Architectural Metal Work Manufacturing
3448 Prefabricated Metal Buildings & Components
NAICS 332311 Prefabricated Metal Building & Component Manufacturing

3449 Miscellaneous Structural Metal Work
NAICS 332114 Custom Roll Forming
NAICS 332312 Fabricated Structural Metal Manufacturing
NAICS 332321 Metal Window & Door Manufacturing
NAICS 332323 Ornamental & Architectural Metal Work Manufacturing
3451 Screw Machine Products
NAICS 332721 Precision Turned Product Manufacturing
3452 Bolts, Nuts, Screws, Rivets, & Washers
NAICS 332722 Bolt, Nut, Screw, Rivet, & Washer Manufacturing
3462 Iron & Steel Forgings
NAICS 332111 Iron & Steel Forging
3463 Nonferrous Forgings
NAICS 332112 Nonferrous Forging
3465 Automotive Stamping
NAICS 33637　Motor Vehicle Metal Stamping
3466 Crowns & Closures
NAICS 332115 Crown & Closure Manufacturing
3469 Metal Stamping, nec
NAICS 339911 Jewelry Manufacturing
NAICS 332116 Metal Stamping
NAICS 332214 Kitchen Utensil, Pot & Pan Manufacturing
3471 Electroplating, Plating, Polishing, Anodizing, & Coloring
NAICS 332813 Electroplating, Plating, Polishing, Anodizing, & Coloring
3479 Coating, Engraving, & Allied Services, nec
NAICS 339914 Costume Jewelry & Novelty Manufacturing
NAICS 339911 Jewelry Manufacturing
NAICS 339912 Silverware & Plated Ware Manufacturing
NAICS 332812 Metal Coating, Engraving , & Allied Services to Manufacturers
3482 Small Arms Ammunition
NAICS 332992 Small Arms Ammunition Manufacturing
3483 Ammunition, Except for Small Arms
NAICS 332993 Ammunition Manufacturing
3484 Small Arms
NAICS 332994 Small Arms Manufacturing
3489 Ordnance & Accessories, nec
NAICS 332995 Other Ordnance & Accessories Manufacturing 3491
3492 Fluid Power Valves & Hose Fittings
NAICS 332912 Fluid Power Valve & Hose Fitting Manufacturing
3493 Steel Springs, Except Wire
NAICS 332611 Steel Spring Manufacturing
3494 Valves & Pipe Fittings, nec
NAICS 332919 Other Metal Valve & Pipe Fitting Manufacturing
NAICS 332999 All Other Miscellaneous Fabricated Metal Product Manufacturing
3495 Wire Springs
NAICS 332612 Wire Spring Manufacturing
NAICS 334518 Watch, Clock, & Part Manufacturing
3496 Miscellaneous Fabricated Wire Products
NAICS 332618 Other Fabricated Wire Product Manufacturing
3497 Metal Foil & Leaf
NAICS 322225 Laminated Aluminum Foil Manufacturing for Flexible Packaging Uses
NAICS 332999 All Other Miscellaneous Fabricated Metal Product Manufacturing
3498 Fabricated Pipe & Pipe Fittings
NAICS 332996 Fabricated Pipe & Pipe Fitting Manufacturing

Appendix: SIC/NAICS Conversion

3499 Fabricated Metal Products, nec
NAICS 337148 Other Nonwood Furniture Manufacturing
NAICS 332117 Powder Metallurgy Part Manufacturing
NAICS 332439 Other Metal Container Manufacturing
NAICS 33251 Hardware Manufacturing
NAICS 332919 Other Metal Valve & Pipe Fitting
Manufacturing
NAICS 339914 Costume Jewelry & Novelty Manufacturing
NAICS 332999 All Other Miscellaneous Fabricated Metal
Product Manufacturing

INDUSTRIAL & COMMERCIAL MACHINERY & COMPUTER EQUIPMENT

3511 Steam, Gas, & Hydraulic Turbines, & Turbine Generator Set Units
NAICS 333611 Turbine & Turbine Generator Set Unit
Manufacturing
3519 Internal Combustion Engines, nec
NAICS 336399 All Other Motor Vehicle Parts Manufacturing
NAICS 333618 Other Engine Equipment Manufacturing
3523 Farm Machinery & Equipment
NAICS 333111 Farm Machinery & Equipment Manufacturing
NAICS 332323 Ornamental & Architectural Metal Work
Manufacturing
NAICS 332212 Hand & Edge Tool Manufacturing
NAICS 333922 Conveyor & Conveying Equipment
Manufacturing
3524 Lawn & Garden Tractors & Home Lawn & Garden Equipment
NAICS 333112 Lawn & Garden Tractor & Home Lawn &
Garden Equipment Manufacturing
NAICS 332212 Hand & Edge Tool Manufacturing
3531 Construction Machinery & Equipment
NAICS 33651 Railroad Rolling Stock Manufacturing
NAICS 333923 Overhead Traveling Crane, Hoist, & Monorail
System Manufacturing
NAICS 33312 Construction Machinery Manufacturing
3532 Mining Machinery & Equipment, Except Oil & Gas Field Machinery & Equipment
NAICS 333131 Mining Machinery & Equipment Manufacturing
3533 Oil & Gas Field Machinery & Equipment
NAICS 333132 Oil & Gas Field Machinery & Equipment
Manufacturing
3534 Elevators & Moving Stairways
NAICS 333921 Elevator & Moving Stairway Manufacturing
3535 Conveyors & Conveying Equipment
NAICS 333922 Conveyor & Conveying Equipment
Manufacturing
3536 Overhead Traveling Cranes, Hoists & Monorail Systems
NAICS 333923 Overhead Traveling Crane, Hoist & Monorail
System Manufacturing
3537 Industrial Trucks, Tractors, Trailers, & Stackers
NAICS 333924 Industrial Truck, Tractor, Trailer, & Stacker
Machinery Manufacturing
NAICS 332999 All Other Miscellaneous Fabricated Metal
Product Manufacturing
NAICS 332439 Other Metal Container Manufacturing
3541 Machine Tools, Metal Cutting Type
NAICS 333512 Machine Tool Manufacturing
3542 Machine Tools, Metal Forming Type
NAICS 333513 Machine Tool Manufacturing

3543 Industrial Patterns
NAICS 332997 Industrial Pattern Manufacturing
3544 Special Dies & Tools, Die Sets, Jigs & Fixtures, & Industrial Molds
NAICS 333514 Special Die & Tool, Die Set, Jig, & Fixture
Manufacturing
NAICS 333511 Industrial Mold Manufacturing
3545 Cutting Tools, Machine Tool Accessories, & Machinists' Precision Measuring Devices
NAICS 333515 Cutting Tool & Machine Tool Accessory
Manufacturing
NAICS 332212 Hand & Edge Tool Manufacturing
3546 Power-driven Handtools
NAICS 333991 Power-driven Hand Tool Manufacturing
3547 Rolling Mill Machinery & Equipment
NAICS 333516 Rolling Mill Machinery & Equipment
Manufacturing
3548 Electric & Gas Welding & Soldering Equipment
NAICS 333992 Welding & Soldering Equipment Manufacturing
NAICS 335311 Power, Distribution, & Specialty Transformer
Manufacturing
3549 Metalworking Machinery, nec
NAICS 333518 Other Metalworking Machinery Manufacturing
3552
3553 Woodworking Machinery
NAICS 33321 Sawmill & Woodworking Machinery
Manufacturing
3554 Paper Industries Machinery
NAICS 333291 Paper Industry Machinery Manufacturing
3555 Printing Trades Machinery & Equipment
NAICS 333293 Printing Machinery & Equipment
Manufacturing
3556 Food Products Machinery
NAICS 333294 Food Product Machinery Manufacturing
3559 Special Industry Machinery, nec
NAICS 33322 Rubber & Plastics Industry Machinery
Manufacturing
NAICS 333319 Other Commercial & Service Industry
Machinery Manufacturing
NAICS 333295 Semiconductor Manufacturing Machinery
NAICS 333298 All Other Industrial Machinery Manufacturing
3561 Pumps & Pumping Equipment
NAICS 333911 Pump & Pumping Equipment Manufacturing
3562 Ball & Roller Bearings
NAICS 332991 Ball & Roller Bearing Manufacturing
3563 Air & Gas Compressors
NAICS 333912 Air & Gas Compressor Manufacturing
3564 Industrial & Commercial Fans & Blowers & Air Purification Equipment
NAICS 333411 Air Purification Equipment Manufacturing
NAICS 333412 Industrial & Commercial Fan & Blower
Manufacturing
3565 Packaging Machinery
NAICS 333993 Packaging Machinery Manufacturing
3566 Speed Changers, Industrial High-speed Drives, & Gears
NAICS 333612 Speed Changer, Industrial High-speed Drive, &
Gear Manufacturing
3567 Industrial Process Furnaces & Ovens
NAICS 333994 Industrial Process Furnace & Oven
Manufacturing
3568 Mechanical Power Transmission Equipment, nec
NAICS 333613 Mechanical Power Transmission Equipment
Manufacturing

3569 General Industrial Machinery & Equipment, nec
NAICS 333999 All Other General Purpose Machinery
  Manufacturing
3571 Electronic Computers
NAICS 334111 Electronic Computer Manufacturing
3572 Computer Storage Devices
NAICS 334112 Computer Storage Device Manufacturing
3575 Computer Terminals
NAICS 334113 Computer Terminal Manufacturing
3577 Computer Peripheral Equipment, nec
NAICS 334119 Other Computer Peripheral Equipment
  Manufacturing
**3578 Calculating & Accounting Machines, Except Electronic
Computers**
NAICS 334119 Other Computer Peripheral Equipment
  Manufacturing
NAICS 333313 Office Machinery Manufacturing
3579 Office Machines, nec
NAICS 339942 Lead Pencil & Art Good Manufacturing
NAICS 334518 Watch, Clock, & Part Manufacturing
NAICS 333313 Office Machinery Manufacturing
3581 Automatic Vending Machines
NAICS 333311 Automatic Vending Machine Manufacturing
3582 Commercial Laundry, Drycleaning, & Pressing Machines
NAICS 333312 Commercial Laundry, Drycleaning, & Pressing
  Machine Manufacturing
**3585 Air-conditioning & Warm Air Heating Equipment &
Commercial & Industrial Refrigeration Equipment**
NAICS 336391 Motor Vehicle Air Conditioning Manufacturing
NAICS 333415 Air Conditioning & Warm Air Heating
  Equipment & Commercial & Industrial
  Refrigeration Equipment Manufacturing
3586 Measuring & Dispensing Pumps
NAICS 333913 Measuring & Dispensing Pump Manufacturing
3589 Service Industry Machinery, nec
NAICS 333319 Other Commercial and Service Industry
  Machinery Manufacturing
3592 Carburetors, Pistons, Piston Rings & Valves
NAICS 336311 Carburetor, Piston, Piston Ring & Valve
  Manufacturing
3593 Fluid Power Cylinders & Actuators
NAICS 333995 Fluid Power Cylinder & Actuator
  Manufacturing
3594 Fluid Power Pumps & Motors
NAICS 333996 Fluid Power Pump & Motor Manufacturing
3596 Scales & Balances, Except Laboratory
NAICS 333997 Scale & Balance Manufacturing
3599 Industrial & Commercial Machinery & Equipment, nec
NAICS 336399 All Other Motor Vehicle Part Manufacturing
NAICS 332999 All Other Miscellaneous Fabricated Metal
  Product Manufacturing
NAICS 333319 Other Commercial & Service Industry
  Machinery Manufacturing
NAICS 33271 Machine Shops
NAICS 333999 All Other General Purpose Machinery
  Manufacturing

ELECTRONIC & OTHER ELECTRICAL EQUIPMENT & COMPONENTS, EXCEPT COMPUTER EQUIPMENT

3612 Power, Distribution, & Specialty Transformers
NAICS 335311 Power, Distribution, & Specialty Transformer
  Manufacturing
3613 Switchgear & Switchboard Apparatus
NAICS 335313 Switchgear & Switchboard Apparatus
  Manufacturing
3621 Motors & Generators
NAICS 335312 Motor & Generator Manufacturing
3624 Carbon & Graphite Products
NAICS 335991 Carbon & Graphite Product Manufacturing
3625 Relays & Industrial Controls
NAICS 335314 Relay & Industrial Control Manufacturing
3629 Electrical Industrial Apparatus, nec
NAICS 335999 All Other Miscellaneous Electrical Equipment
  & Component Manufacturing
3631 Household Cooking Equipment
NAICS 335221 Household Cooking Appliance Manufacturing
3632 Household Refrigerators & Home & Farm Freezers
NAICS 335222 Household Refrigerator & Home Freezer
  Manufacturing
3633 Household Laundry Equipment
NAICS 335224 Household Laundry Equipment Manufacturing
3634 Electric Housewares & Fans
NAICS 335211 Electric Housewares & Fan Manufacturing
3635 Household Vacuum Cleaners
NAICS 335212 Household Vacuum Cleaner Manufacturing
3639 Household Appliances, nec
NAICS 335212 Household Vacuum Cleaner Manufacturing
NAICS 333298 All Other Industrial Machinery Manufacturing
NAICS 335228 Other Household Appliance Manufacturing
3641 Electric Lamp Bulbs & Tubes
NAICS 33511 Electric Lamp Bulb & Part Manufacturing
3643 Current-carrying Wiring Devices
NAICS 335931 Current-carrying Wiring Device Manufacturing
3644 Noncurrent-carrying Wiring Devices
NAICS 335932 Noncurrent-carrying Wiring Device
  Manufacturing
3645 Residential Electric Lighting Fixtures
NAICS 335121 Residential Electric Lighting Fixture
  Manufacturing
**3646 Commercial, Industrial, & Institutional Electric Lighting
Fixtures**
NAICS 335122 Commercial, Industrial, & Institutional Electric
  Lighting Fixture Manufacturing
3647 Vehicular Lighting Equipment
NAICS 336321 Vehicular Lighting Equipment Manufacturing
3648 Lighting Equipment, nec
NAICS 335129 Other Lighting Equipment Manufacturing
3651 Household Audio & Video Equipment
NAICS 33431 Audio & Video Equipment Manufacturing 3652
NAICS 51222 Integrated Record Production/distribution
3661 Telephone & Telegraph Apparatus
NAICS 33421 Telephone Apparatus Manufacturing
NAICS 334416 Electronic Coil, Transformer, & Other Inductor
  Manufacturing
NAICS 334418 Printed Circuit/electronics Assembly
  Manufacturing

3663 Radio & Television Broadcasting & Communication Equipment
NAICS 33422 Radio & Television Broadcasting & Wireless Communications Equipment Manufacturing
3669 Communications Equipment, nec
NAICS 33429 Other Communication Equipment Manufacturing
3671 Electron Tubes
NAICS 334411 Electron Tube Manufacturing
3672 Printed Circuit Boards
NAICS 334412 Printed Circuit Board Manufacturing
3674 Semiconductors & Related Devices
NAICS 334413 Semiconductor & Related Device Manufacturing
3675 Electronic Capacitors
NAICS 334414 Electronic Capacitor Manufacturing
3676 Electronic Resistors
NAICS 334415 Electronic Resistor Manufacturing
3677 Electronic Coils, Transformers, & Other Inductors
NAICS 334416 Electronic Coil, Transformer, & Other Inductor Manufacturing
3678 Electronic ConNECtors
NAICS 334417 Electronic ConNECtor Manufacturing
3679 Electronic Components, nec
NAICS 33422 Radio & Television Broadcasting & Wireless Communications Equipment Manufacturing
NAICS 334418 Printed Circuit/electronics Assembly Manufacturing
NAICS 336322 Other Motor Vehicle Electrical & Electronic Equipment Manufacturing
NAICS 334419 Other Electronic Component Manufacturing
3691 Storage Batteries
NAICS 335911 Storage Battery Manufacturing
3692 Primary Batteries, Dry & Wet
NAICS 335912 Dry & Wet Primary Battery Manufacturing
3694 Electrical Equipment for Internal Combustion Engines
NAICS 336322 Other Motor Vehicle Electrical & Electronic Equipment Manufacturing
3695 Magnetic & Optical Recording Media
NAICS 334613 Magnetic & Optical Recording Media Manufacturing
3699 Electrical Machinery, Equipment, & Supplies, nec
NAICS 333319 Other Commercial & Service Industry Machinery Manufacturing
NAICS 333618 Other Engine Equipment Manufacturing
NAICS 334119 Other Computer Peripheral Equipment Manufacturing Classify According to Function
NAICS 335129 Other Lighting Equipment Manufacturing
NAICS 335999 All Other Miscellaneous Electrical Equipment & Component Manufacturing

TRANSPORTATION EQUIPMENT

3711 Motor Vehicles & Passenger Car Bodies
NAICS 336111 Automobile Manufacturing
NAICS 336112 Light Truck & Utility Vehicle Manufacturing
NAICS 33612 Heavy Duty Truck Manufacturing
NAICS 336211 Motor Vehicle Body Manufacturing
NAICS 336992 Military Armored Vehicle, Tank, & Tank Component Manufacturing
3713 Truck & Bus Bodies
NAICS 336211 Motor Vehicle Body Manufacturing

3714 Motor Vehicle Parts & Accessories
NAICS 336211 Motor Vehicle Body Manufacturing
NAICS 336312 Gasoline Engine & Engine Parts Manufacturing
NAICS 336322 Other Motor Vehicle Electrical & Electronic Equipment Manufacturing
NAICS 33633 Motor Vehicle Steering & Suspension Components Manufacturing
NAICS 33634 Motor Vehicle Brake System Manufacturing
NAICS 33635 Motor Vehicle Transmission & Power Train Parts Manufacturing
NAICS 336399 All Other Motor Vehicle Parts Manufacturing
3715 Truck Trailers
NAICS 336212 Truck Trailer Manufacturing
3716 Motor Homes
NAICS 336213 Motor Home Manufacturing
3721 Aircraft
NAICS 336411 Aircraft Manufacturing
3724 Aircraft Engines & Engine Parts
NAICS 336412 Aircraft Engine & Engine Parts Manufacturing
3728
NAICS 336413 Other Aircraft Part & Auxiliary Equipment Manufacturing
3731 Ship Building & Repairing
NAICS 336611 Ship Building & Repairing
3732 Boat Building & Repairing
NAICS 81149 Other Personal & Household Goods Repair & Maintenance
NAICS 336612 Boat Building
3743 Railroad Equipment
NAICS 333911 Pump & Pumping Equipment Manufacturing
NAICS 33651 Railroad Rolling Stock Manufacturing
3751 Motorcycles, Bicycles, & Parts
NAICS 336991 Motorcycle, Bicycle, & Parts Manufacturing
3761 Guided Missiles & Space Vehicles
NAICS 336414 Guided Missile & Space Vehicle Manufacturing
3764
3769 Guided Missile Space Vehicle Parts & Auxiliary Equipment, nec
NAICS 336419 Other Guided Missile & Space Vehicle Parts & Auxiliary Equipment Manufacturing
3792 Travel Trailers & Campers
NAICS 336214 Travel Trailer & Camper Manufacturing
3795 Tanks & Tank Components
NAICS 336992 Military Armored Vehicle, Tank, & Tank Component Manufacturing
3799 Transportation Equipment, nec
NAICS 336214 Travel Trailer & Camper Manufacturing
NAICS 332212 Hand & Edge Tool Manufacturing
NAICS 336999 All Other Transportation Equipment Manufacturing

MEASURING, ANALYZING, & CONTROLLING INSTRUMENTS

3812 Search, Detection, Navigation, Guidance, Aeronautical, & Nautical Systems & Instruments
NAICS 334511 Search, Detection, Navigation, Guidance, Aeronautical, & Nautical System & Instrument Manufacturing
3821 Laboratory Apparatus & Furniture
NAICS 339111 Laboratory Apparatus & Furniture Manufacturing

3822 Automatic Controls for Regulating Residential & Commercial Environments & Appliances
NAICS 334512 Automatic Environmental Control Manufacturing for Regulating Residential, Commercial, & Appliance Use

3823 Industrial Instruments for Measurement, Display, & Control of Process Variables & Related Products
NAICS 334513 Instruments & Related Product Manufacturing for Measuring Displaying, & Controlling Industrial Process Variables

3824 Totalizing Fluid Meters & Counting Devices
NAICS 334514 Totalizing Fluid Meter & Counting Device Manufacturing

3825 Instruments for Measuring & Testing of Electricity & Electrical Signals
NAICS 334416 Electronic Coil, Transformer, & Other Inductor Manufacturing
NAICS 334515 Instrument Manufacturing for Measuring & Testing Electricity & Electrical Signals

3826 Laboratory Analytical Instruments
NAICS 334516 Analytical Laboratory Instrument Manufacturing

3827 Optical Instruments & Lenses
NAICS 333314 Optical Instrument & Lens Manufacturing

3829 Measuring & Controlling Devices, nec
NAICS 339112 Surgical & Medical Instrument Manufacturing
NAICS 334519 Other Measuring & Controlling Device Manufacturing

3841 Surgical & Medical Instruments & Apparatus
NAICS 339112 Surgical & Medical Instrument Manufacturing

3842 Orthopedic, Prosthetic, & Surgical Appliances & Supplies
NAICS 339113 Surgical Appliance & Supplies Manufacturing
NAICS 334510 Electromedical & Electrotherapeutic Apparatus Manufacturing

3843 Dental Equipment & Supplies
NAICS 339114 Dental Equipment & Supplies Manufacturing

3844 X-ray Apparatus & Tubes & Related Irradiation Apparatus
NAICS 334517 Irradiation Apparatus Manufacturing

3845 Electromedical & Electrotherapeutic Apparatus
NAICS 334517 Irradiation Apparatus Manufacturing
NAICS 334510 Electromedical & Electrotherapeutic Apparatus Manufacturing

3851 Ophthalmic Goods
NAICS 339115 Ophthalmic Goods Manufacturing

3861 Photographic Equipment & Supplies
NAICS 333315 Photographic & Photocopying Equipment Manufacturing
NAICS 325992 Photographic Film, Paper, Plate & Chemical Manufacturing

3873 Watches, Clocks, Clockwork Operated Devices & Parts
NAICS 334518 Watch, Clock, & Part Manufacturing

MISCELLANEOUS MANUFACTURING INDUSTRIES

3911 Jewelry, Precious Metal
NAICS 339911 Jewelry Manufacturing
3914 Silverware, Plated Ware, & Stainless Steel Ware
NAICS 332211 Cutlery & Flatware Manufacturing
NAICS 339912 Silverware & Plated Ware Manufacturing
3915 Jewelers' Findings & Materials, & Lapidary Work
NAICS 339913 Jewelers' Material & Lapidary Work Manufacturing

3931 Musical Instruments
NAICS 339992 Musical Instrument Manufacturing
3942 Dolls & Stuffed Toys
NAICS 339931 Doll & Stuffed Toy Manufacturing
3944 Games, Toys, & Children's Vehicles, Except Dolls & Bicycles
NAICS 336991 Motorcycle, Bicycle & Parts Manufacturing
NAICS 339932 Game, Toy, & Children's Vehicle Manufacturing
3949 Sporting & Athletic Goods, nec
NAICS 33992 Sporting & Athletic Good Manufacturing
3951 Pens, Mechanical Pencils & Parts
NAICS 339941 Pen & Mechanical Pencil Manufacturing
3952 Lead Pencils, Crayons, & Artist's Materials
NAICS 337139 Other Wood Furniture Manufacturing
NAICS 337139 Other Wood Furniture Manufacturing
NAICS 325998 All Other Miscellaneous Chemical Manufacturing
NAICS 339942 Lead Pencil & Art Good Manufacturing
3953 Marking Devices
NAICS 339943 Marking Device Manufacturing
3955 Carbon Paper & Inked Ribbons
NAICS 339944 Carbon Paper & Inked Ribbon Manufacturing
3961 Costume Jewelry & Costume Novelties, Except Precious Metals
NAICS 339914 Costume Jewelry & Novelty Manufacturing
3965 Fasteners, Buttons, Needles, & Pins
NAICS 339993 Fastener, Button, Needle & Pin Manufacturing
3991 Brooms & Brushes
NAICS 339994 Broom, Brush & Mop Manufacturing
3993 Signs & Advertising Specialties
NAICS 33995 Sign Manufacturing
3995 Burial Caskets
NAICS 339995 Burial Casket Manufacturing
3996 Linoleum, Asphalted-felt-base, & Other Hard Surface Floor Coverings, nec
NAICS 326192 Resilient Floor Covering Manufacturing
3999 Manufacturing Industries, nec
NAICS 337148 Other Nonwood Furniture Manufacturing
NAICS 321999 All Other Miscellaneous Wood Product Manufacturing
NAICS 31611 Leather & Hide Tanning & Finishing
NAICS 335121 Residential Electric Lighting Fixture Manufacturing
NAICS 325998 All Other Miscellaneous Chemical Product Manufacturing
NAICS 332999 All Other Miscellaneous Fabricated Metal Product Manufacturing
NAICS 326199 All Other Plastics Product Manufacturing
NAICS 323112 Commercial Flexographic Printing
NAICS 323111 Commercial Gravure Printing
NAICS 323110 Commercial Lithographic Printing
NAICS 323113 Commercial Screen Printing
NAICS 323119 Other Commercial Printing
NAICS 332212 Hand & Edge Tool Manufacturing
NAICS 339999 All Other Miscellaneous Manufacturing

TRANSPORTATION, COMMUNICATIONS, ELECTRIC, GAS, & SANITARY SERVICES

4011 Railroads, Line-haul Operating
NAICS 482111 Line-haul Railroads
4013 Railroad Switching & Terminal Establishments
NAICS 482112 Short Line Railroads
NAICS 48821   Support Activities for Rail Transportation
4111 Local & Suburban Transit
NAICS 485111 Mixed Mode Transit Systems
NAICS 485112 Commuter Rail Systems
NAICS 485113 Bus & Motor Vehicle Transit Systems
NAICS 485119 Other Urban Transit Systems
NAICS 485999 All Other Transit & Ground Passenger
          Transportation
4119 Local Passenger Transportation, nec
NAICS 62191   Ambulance Service
NAICS 48541   School & Employee Bus Transportation
NAICS 48711   Scenic & Sightseeing Transportation , Land
NAICS 485991 Special Needs Transportation
NAICS 485999 All Other Transit & Ground Passenger
          Transportation
NAICS 48532   Limousine Service
4121 Taxicabs
NAICS 48531   Taxi Service
4131 Intercity & Rural Bus Transportation
NAICS 48521   Interurban & Rural Bus Transportation
4141 Local Bus Charter Service
NAICS 48551   Charter Bus Industry
4142 Bus Charter Service, Except Local
NAICS 48551   Charter Bus Industry
4151 School Buses
NAICS 48541   School & Employee Bus Transportation
4173 Terminal & Service Facilities for Motor Vehicle Passenger Transportation
NAICS 48849   Other Support Activities for Road
          Transportation
4212 Local Trucking Without Storage
NAICS 562111 Solid Waste Collection
NAICS 562112 Hazardous Waste Collection
NAICS 562119 Other Waste Collection
NAICS 48411   General Freight Trucking, Local
NAICS 48421   Used Household & Office Goods Moving
NAICS 48422   Specialized Freight Trucking, Local
4213 Trucking, Except Local
NAICS 484121 General Freight Trucking, Long-distance,
          Truckload
NAICS 484122 General Freight Trucking, Long-distance, less
          than Truckload
NAICS 48421   Used Household & Office Goods Moving
NAICS 48423   Specialized Freight Trucking, Long-distance
4214 Local Trucking with Storage
NAICS 48411   General Freight Trucking, Local
NAICS 48421   Used Household & Office Goods Moving
NAICS 48422   Specialized Freight Trucking, Local
4215 Couriers Services Except by Air
NAICS 49211   Couriers
NAICS 49221   Local Messengers & Local Delivery
4221 Farm Product Warehousing & Storage
NAICS 49313   Farm Product Storage Facilities
4222 Refrigerated Warehousing & Storage
NAICS 49312   Refrigerated Storage Facilities

4225 General Warehousing & Storage
NAICS 49311   General Warehousing & Storage Facilities
NAICS 53113   Lessors of Miniwarehouses & Self Storage
          Units
4226 Special Warehousing & Storage, nec
NAICS 49312   Refrigerated Warehousing & Storage Facilities
NAICS 49311   General Warehousing & Storage Facilities
NAICS 49319   Other Warehousing & Storage Facilities
4231 Terminal & Joint Terminal Maintenance Facilities for Motor Freight Transportation
NAICS 48849   Other Support Activities for Road
          Transportation
4311 United States Postal Service
NAICS 49111   Postal Service
4412 Deep Sea Foreign Transportation of Freight
NAICS 483111 Deep Sea Freight Transportation
4424 Deep Sea Domestic Transportation of Freight
NAICS 483113 Coastal & Great Lakes Freight Transportation
4432 Freight Transportation on the Great Lakes - St. Lawrence Seaway
NAICS 483113 Coastal & Great Lakes Freight Transportation
4449 Water Transportation of Freight, nec
NAICS 483211 Inland Water Freight Transportation
4481 Deep Sea Transportation of Passengers, Except by Ferry
NAICS 483112 Deep Sea Passenger Transportation
NAICS 483114 Coastal & Great Lakes Passenger
          Transportation
4482 Ferries
NAICS 483114 Coastal & Great Lakes Passenger
          Transportation
NAICS 483212 Inland Water Passenger Transportation
4489 Water Transportation of Passengers, nec
NAICS 483212 Inland Water Passenger Transportation
NAICS 48721   Scenic & Sightseeing Transportation, Water
4491 Marine Cargo Handling
NAICS 48831   Port & Harbor Operations
NAICS 48832   Marine Cargo Handling
4492 Towing & Tugboat Services
NAICS 483113 Coastal & Great Lakes Freight Transportation
NAICS 483211 Inland Water Freight Transportation
NAICS 48833   Navigational Services to Shipping
4493 Marinas
NAICS 71393   Marinas
4499 Water Transportation Services, nec
NAICS 532411 Commercial Air, Rail, & Water Transportation
          Equipment Rental & Leasing
NAICS 48831   Port & Harbor Operations
NAICS 48833   Navigational Services to Shipping
NAICS 48839   Other Support Activities for Water
          Transportation
4512 Air Transportation, Scheduled
NAICS 481111 Scheduled Passenger Air Transportation
NAICS 481112 Scheduled Freight Air Transportation
4513 Air Courier Services
NAICS 49211   Couriers
4522 Air Transportation, Nonscheduled
NAICS 62191   Ambulance Services
NAICS 481212 Nonscheduled Chartered Freight Air
          Transportation
NAICS 481211 Nonscheduled Chartered Passenger Air
          Transportation
NAICS 48122   Nonscheduled Speciality Air Transportation
NAICS 48799   Scenic & Sightseeing Transportation , Other

4581 Airports, Flying Fields, & Airport Terminal Services
NAICS 488111 Air Traffic Control
NAICS 488112 Airport Operations, Except Air Traffic Control
NAICS 56172 Janitorial Services
NAICS 48819 Other Support Activities for Air Transportation

4612 Crude Petroleum Pipelines
NAICS 48611 Pipeline Transportation of Crude Oil

4613 Refined Petroleum Pipelines
NAICS 48691 Pipeline Transportation of Refined Petroleum Products

4619 Pipelines, nec
NAICS 48699 All Other Pipeline Transportation

4724 Travel Agencies
NAICS 56151 Travel Agencies

4725 Tour Operators
NAICS 56152 Tour Operators

4729 Arrangement of Passenger Transportation, nec
NAICS 488999 All Other Support Activities for Transportation
NAICS 561599 All Other Travel Arrangement & Reservation Services

4731 Arrangement of Transportation of Freight & Cargo
NAICS 541618 Other Management Consulting Services
NAICS 48851 Freight Transportation Arrangement

4741 Rental of Railroad Cars
NAICS 532411 Commercial Air, Rail, & Water Transportation Equipment Rental & Leasing
NAICS 48821 Support Activities for Rail Transportation

4783 Packing & Crating
NAICS 488991 Packing & Crating

4785 Fixed Facilities & Inspection & Weighing Services for Motor Vehicle Transportation
NAICS 48839 Other Support Activities for Water Transportation
NAICS 48849 Other Support Activities for Road Transportation

4789 Transportation Services, nec
NAICS 488999 All Other Support Activities for Transportation
NAICS 48711 Scenic & Sightseeing Transportation, Land
NAICS 48821 Support Activities for Rail Transportation

4812 Radiotelephone Communications
NAICS 513321 Paging
NAICS 513322 Cellular & Other Wireless Telecommunications
NAICS 51333 Telecommunications Resellers

4813 Telephone Communications, Except Radiotelephone
NAICS 51331 Wired Telecommunications Carriers
NAICS 51333 Telecommunications Resellers

4822 Telegraph & Other Message Communications
NAICS 51331 Wired Telecommunications Carriers

4832 Radio Broadcasting Stations
NAICS 513111 Radio Networks
NAICS 513112 Radio Stations

4833 Television Broadcasting Stations
NAICS 51312 Television Broadcasting

4841 Cable & Other Pay Television Services
NAICS 51321 Cable Networks
NAICS 51322 Cable & Other Program Distribution

4899 Communications Services, nec
NAICS 513322 Cellular & Other Wireless Telecommunications
NAICS 51334 Satellite Telecommunications
NAICS 51339 Other Telecommunications

4911 Electric Services
NAICS 221111 Hydroelectric Power Generation
NAICS 221112 Fossil Fuel Electric Power Generation
NAICS 221113 Nuclear Electric Power Generation

NAICS 221119 Other Electric Power Generation
NAICS 221121 Electric Bulk Power Transmission & Control
NAICS 221122 Electric Power Distribution

4922 Natural Gas Transmission
NAICS 48621 Pipeline Transportation of Natural Gas

4923 Natural Gas Transmission & Distribution
NAICS 22121 Natural Gas Distribution
NAICS 48621 Pipeline Transportation of Natural Gas

4924 Natural Gas Distribution
NAICS 22121 Natural Gas Distribution

4925 Mixed, Manufactured, or Liquefied Petroleum Gas Production And/or Distribution
NAICS 22121 Natural Gas Distribution

4931 Electric & Other Services Combined
NAICS 221111 Hydroelectric Power Generation
NAICS 221112 Fossil Fuel Electric Power Generation
NAICS 221113 Nuclear Electric Power Generation
NAICS 221119 Other Electric Power Generation
NAICS 221121 Electric Bulk Power Transmission & Control
NAICS 221122 Electric Power Distribution
NAICS 22121 Natural Gas Distribution

4932 Gas & Other Services Combined
NAICS 22121 Natural Gas Distribution

4939 Combination Utilities, nec
NAICS 221111 Hydroelectric Power Generation
NAICS 221112 Fossil Fuel Electric Power Generation
NAICS 221113 Nuclear Electric Power Generation
NAICS 221119 Other Electric Power Generation
NAICS 221121 Electric Bulk Power Transmission & Control
NAICS 221122 Electric Power Distribution
NAICS 22121 Natural Gas Distribution

4941 Water Supply
NAICS 22131 Water Supply & Irrigation Systems

4952 Sewerage Systems
NAICS 22132 Sewage Treatment Facilities

4953 Refuse Systems
NAICS 562111 Solid Waste Collection
NAICS 562112 Hazardous Waste Collection
NAICS 56292 Materials Recovery Facilities
NAICS 562119 Other Waste Collection
NAICS 562211 Hazardous Waste Treatment & Disposal
NAICS 562212 Solid Waste Landfills
NAICS 562213 Solid Waste Combustors & Incinerators
NAICS 562219 Other Nonhazardous Waste Treatment & Disposal

4959 Sanitary Services, nec
NAICS 488112 Airport Operations, Except Air Traffic Control
NAICS 56291 Remediation Services
NAICS 56171 Exterminating & Pest Control Services
NAICS 562998 All Other Miscellaneous Waste Management Services

4961 Steam & Air-conditioning Supply
NAICS 22133 Steam & Air-conditioning Supply

4971 Irrigation Systems
NAICS 22131 Water Supply & Irrigation Systems

WHOLESALE TRADE

5012 Automobiles & Other Motor Vehicles
NAICS 42111 Automobile & Other Motor Vehicle Wholesalers

5013 Motor Vehicle Supplies & New Parts
NAICS 44131   Automotive Parts & Accessories Stores - Retail
NAICS 42112   Motor Vehicle Supplies & New Part
Wholesalers

5014 Tires & Tubes
NAICS 44132   Tire Dealers - Retail
NAICS 42113   Tire & Tube Wholesalers

5015 Motor Vehicle Parts, Used
NAICS 42114   Motor Vehicle Part Wholesalers

5021 Furniture
NAICS 44211   Furniture Stores
NAICS 42121   Furniture Wholesalers

5023 Home Furnishings
NAICS 44221   Floor Covering Stores
NAICS 42122   Home Furnishing Wholesalers

5031 Lumber, Plywood, Millwork, & Wood Panels
NAICS 44419   Other Building Material Dealers
NAICS 42131   Lumber, Plywood, Millwork, & Wood Panel
Wholesalers

5032 Brick, Stone & Related Construction Materials
NAICS 44419   Other Building Material Dealers
NAICS 42132   Brick, Stone & Related Construction Material
Wholesalers

5033 Roofing, Siding, & Insulation Materials
NAICS 42133   Roofing, Siding, & Insulation Material
Wholesalers

5039 Construction Materials, nec
NAICS 44419   Other Building Material Dealers
NAICS 42139   Other Construction Material Wholesalers

5043 Photographic Equipment & Supplies
NAICS 42141   Photographic Equipment & Supplies
Wholesalers

5044 Office Equipment
NAICS 42142   Office Equipment Wholesalers

5045 Computers & Computer Peripheral Equipment & Software
NAICS 42143   Computer & Computer Peripheral Equipment
& Software Wholesalers
NAICS 44312   Computer & Software Stores - Retail

5046 Commercial Equipment, nec
NAICS 42144   Other Commercial Equipment Wholesalers

5047 Medical, Dental, & Hospital Equipment & Supplies
NAICS 42145   Medical, Dental & Hospital Equipment &
Supplies Wholesalers
NAICS 446199 All Other Health & Personal Care Stores -
Retail

5048 Ophthalmic Goods
NAICS 42146   Ophthalmic Goods Wholesalers

5049 Professional Equipment & Supplies, nec
NAICS 42149   Other Professional Equipment & Supplies
Wholesalers
NAICS 45321   Office Supplies & Stationery Stores - Retail

5051 Metals Service Centers & Offices
NAICS 42151   Metals Service Centers & Offices

5052 Coal & Other Minerals & Ores
NAICS 42152   Coal & Other Mineral & Ore Wholesalers

5063 Electrical Apparatus & Equipment Wiring Supplies, & Construction Materials
NAICS 44419   Other Building Material Dealers
NAICS 42161   Electrical Apparatus & Equipment, Wiring
Supplies & Construction Material Wholesalers

5064 Electrical Appliances, Television & Radio Sets
NAICS 42162   Electrical Appliance, Television & Radio Set
Wholesalers

5065 Electronic Parts & Equipment, Not Elsewhere Classified
NAICS 42169   Other Electronic Parts & Equipment
Wholesalers

5072 Hardware
NAICS 42171   Hardware Wholesalers

5074 Plumbing & Heating Equipment & Supplies
NAICS 44419   Other Building Material Dealers
NAICS 42172   Plumbing & Heating Equipment & Supplies
Wholesalers

5075 Warm Air Heating & Air-conditioning Equipment & Supplies
NAICS 42173   Warm Air Heating & Air-conditioning
Equipment & Supplies Wholesalers

5078 Refrigeration Equipment & Supplies
NAICS 42174   Refrigeration Equipment & Supplies
Wholesalers

5082 Construction & Mining Machinery & Equipment
NAICS 42181   Construction & Mining Machinery &
Equipment Wholesalers

5083 Farm & Garden Machinery & Equipment
NAICS 42182   Farm & Garden Machinery & Equipment
Wholesalers
NAICS 44421   Outdoor Power Equipment Stores - Retail

5084 Industrial Machinery & Equipment
NAICS 42183   Industrial Machinery & Equipment Wholesalers

5085 Industrial Supplies
NAICS 42183   Industrial Machinery & Equipment Wholesalers
NAICS 42184   Industrial Supplies Wholesalers
NAICS 81131   Commercial & Industrial Machinery &
Equipment Repair & Maintenence

5087 Service Establishment Equipment & Supplies
NAICS 42185   Service Establishment Equipment & Supplies
Wholesalers
NAICS 44612   Cosmetics, Beauty Supplies, & Perfume Stores

5088 Transportation Equipment & Supplies, Except Motor Vehicles
NAICS 42186   Transportation Equipment & Supplies
Wholesalers

5091 Sporting & Recreational Goods & Supplies
NAICS 42191   Sporting & Recreational Goods & Supplies
Wholesalers

5092 Toys & Hobby Goods & Supplies
NAICS 42192   Toy & Hobby Goods & Supplies Wholesalers

5093 Scrap & Waste Materials
NAICS 42193   Recyclable Material Wholesalers

5094 Jewelry, Watches, Precious Stones, & Precious Metals
NAICS 42194   Jewelry, Watch , Precious Stone, & Precious
Metal Wholesalers

5099 Durable Goods, nec
NAICS 42199   Other Miscellaneous Durable Goods
Wholesalers

5111 Printing & Writing Paper
NAICS 42211   Printing & Writing Paper Wholesalers

5112 Stationery & Office Supplies
NAICS 45321   Office Supplies & Stationery Stores
NAICS 42212   Stationery & Office Supplies Wholesalers

5113 Industrial & Personal Service Paper
NAICS 42213   Industrial & Personal Service Paper
Wholesalers

5122 Drugs, Drug Proprietaries, & Druggists' Sundries
NAICS 42221   Drugs, Drug Proprietaries, & Druggists'
Sundries Wholesalers

5131 Piece Goods, Notions, & Other Dry Goods
NAICS 313311 Broadwoven Fabric Finishing Mills
NAICS 313312 Textile & Fabric Finishing Mills
NAICS 42231 Piece Goods, Notions, & Other Dry Goods
Wholesalers
5136 Men's & Boys' Clothing & Furnishings
NAICS 42232 Men's & Boys' Clothing & Furnishings
Wholesalers
5137 Women's Children's & Infants' Clothing & Accessories
NAICS 42233 Women's, Children's, & Infants' Clothing &
Accessories Wholesalers
5139 Footwear
NAICS 42234 Footwear Wholesalers
5141 Groceries, General Line
NAICS 42241 General Line Grocery Wholesalers
5142 Packaged Frozen Foods
NAICS 42242 Packaged Frozen Food Wholesalers
5143 Dairy Products, Except Dried or Canned
NAICS 42243 Dairy Products Wholesalers
5144 Poultry & Poultry Products
NAICS 42244 Poultry & Poultry Product Wholesalers
5145 Confectionery
NAICS 42245 Confectionery Wholesalers
5146 Fish & Seafoods
NAICS 42246 Fish & Seafood Wholesalers
5147 Meats & Meat Products
NAICS 311612 Meat Processed from Carcasses
NAICS 42247 Meat & Meat Product Wholesalers
5148 Fresh Fruits & Vegetables
NAICS 42248 Fresh Fruit & Vegetable Wholesalers
5149 Groceries & Related Products, nec
NAICS 42249 Other Grocery & Related Product Wholesalers
5153 Grain & Field Beans
NAICS 42251 Grain & Field Bean Wholesalers
5154 Livestock
NAICS 42252 Livestock Wholesalers
5159 Farm-product Raw Materials, nec
NAICS 42259 Other Farm Product Raw Material Wholesalers
5162 Plastics Materials & Basic Forms & Shapes
NAICS 42261 Plastics Materials & Basic Forms & Shapes
Wholesalers
5169 Chemicals & Allied Products, nec
NAICS 42269 Other Chemical & Allied Products Wholesalers
5171 Petroleum Bulk Stations & Terminals
NAICS 454311 Heating Oil Dealers
NAICS 454312 Liquefied Petroleum Gas Dealers
NAICS 42271 Petroleum Bulk Stations & Terminals
5172 Petroleum & Petroleum Products Wholesalers, Except Bulk Stations & Terminals
NAICS 42272 Petroleum & Petroleum Products Wholesalers
5181 Beer & Ale
NAICS 42281 Beer & Ale Wholesalers
5182 Wine & Distilled Alcoholic Beverages
NAICS 42282 Wine & Distilled Alcoholic Beverage
Wholesalers
5191 Farm Supplies
NAICS 44422 Nursery & Garden Centers - Retail
NAICS 42291 Farm Supplies Wholesalers
5192 Books, Periodicals, & Newspapers
NAICS 42292 Book, Periodical & Newspaper Wholesalers
5193 Flowers, Nursery Stock, & Florists' Supplies
NAICS 42293 Flower, Nursery Stock & Florists' Supplies
Wholesalers
NAICS 44422 Nursery & Garden Centers - Retail

5194 Tobacco & Tobacco Products
NAICS 42294 Tobacco & Tobacco Product Wholesalers
5198 Paint, Varnishes, & Supplies
NAICS 42295 Paint, Varnish & Supplies Wholesalers
NAICS 44412 Paint & Wallpaper Stores
5199 Nondurable Goods, nec
NAICS 54189 Other Services Related to Advertising
NAICS 42299 Other Miscellaneous Nondurable Goods
Wholesalers

RETAIL TRADE

5211 Lumber & Other Building Materials Dealers
NAICS 44411 Home Centers
NAICS 42131 Lumber, Plywood, Millwork & Wood Panel
Wholesalers
NAICS 44419 Other Building Material Dealers
5231 Paint, Glass, & Wallpaper Stores
NAICS 42295 Paint, Varnish & Supplies Wholesalers
NAICS 44419 Other Building Material Dealers
NAICS 44412 Paint & Wallpaper Stores
5251 Hardware Stores
NAICS 44413 Hardware Stores
5261 Retail Nurseries, Lawn & Garden Supply Stores
NAICS 44422 Nursery & Garden Centers
NAICS 453998 All Other Miscellaneous Store Retailers
NAICS 44421 Outdoor Power Equipment Stores
5271 Mobile Home Dealers
NAICS 45393 Manufactured Home Dealers
5311 Department Stores
NAICS 45211 Department Stores
5331 Variety Stores
NAICS 45299 All Other General Merchandise Stores
5399 Miscellaneous General Merchandise Stores
NAICS 45291 Warehouse Clubs & Superstores
NAICS 45299 All Other General Merchandise Stores
5411 Grocery Stores
NAICS 44711 Gasoline Stations with Convenience Stores
NAICS 44511 Supermarkets & Other Grocery Stores
NAICS 45291 Warehouse Clubs & Superstores
NAICS 44512 Convenience Stores
5421 Meat & Fish Markets, Including Freezer Provisioners
NAICS 45439 Other Direct Selling Establishments
NAICS 44521 Meat Markets
NAICS 44522 Fish & Seafood Markets
5431 Fruit & Vegetable Markets
NAICS 44523 Fruit & Vegetable Markets
5441 Candy, Nut, & Confectionery Stores
NAICS 445292 Confectionary & Nut Stores
5451 Dairy Products Stores
NAICS 445299 All Other Specialty Food Stores
5461 Retail Bakeries
NAICS 722213 Snack & Nonalcoholic Beverage Bars
NAICS 311811 Retail Bakeries
NAICS 445291 Baked Goods Stores
5499 Miscellaneous Food Stores
NAICS 44521 Meat Markets
NAICS 722211 Limited-service Restaurants
NAICS 446191 Food Supplement Stores
NAICS 445299 All Other Specialty Food Stores
5511 Motor Vehicle Dealers
NAICS 44111 New Car Dealers

5521 Motor Vehicle Dealers
NAICS 44112 Used Car Dealers
5531 Auto & Home Supply Stores
NAICS 44132 Tire Dealers
NAICS 44131 Automotive Parts & Accessories Stores
5541 Gasoline Service Stations
NAICS 44711 Gasoline Stations with Convenience Store
NAICS 44719 Other Gasoline Stations
5551 Boat Dealers
NAICS 441222 Boat Dealers
5561 Recreational Vehicle Dealers
NAICS 44121 Recreational Vehicle Dealers
5571 Motorcycle Dealers
NAICS 441221 Motorcycle Dealers
5599 Automotive Dealers, nec
NAICS 441229 All Other Motor Vehicle Dealers
5611 Men's & Boys' Clothing & Accessory Stores
NAICS 44811 Men's Clothing Stores
NAICS 44815 Clothing Accessories Stores
5621 Women's Clothing Stores
NAICS 44812 Women's Clothing Stores
5632 Women's Accessory & Specialty Stores
NAICS 44819 Other Clothing Stores
NAICS 44815 Clothing Accessories Stores
5641 Children's & Infants' Wear Stores
NAICS 44813 Children's & Infants' Clothing Stores
5651 Family Clothing Stores
NAICS 44814 Family Clothing Stores
5661 Shoe Stores
NAICS 44821 Shoe Stores
5699 Miscellaneous Apparel & Accessory Stores
NAICS 315 Included in Apparel Manufacturing Subsector Based on Type of Garment Produced
NAICS 44819 Other Clothing Stores
NAICS 44815 Clothing Accessories Stores
5712 Furniture Stores
NAICS 337133 Wood Household Furniture, Except Upholstered, Manufacturing
NAICS 337131 Wood Kitchen Cabinet & Counter Top Manufacturing
NAICS 337132 Upholstered Household Furniture Manufacturing
NAICS 44211 Furniture Stores
5713 Floor Covering Stores
NAICS 44221 Floor Covering Stores
5714 Drapery, Curtain, & Upholstery Stores
NAICS 442291 Window Treatment Stores
NAICS 45113 Sewing, Needlework & Piece Goods Stores
NAICS 314121 Curtain & Drapery Mills
5719 Miscellaneous Homefurnishings Stores
NAICS 442291 Window Treatment Stores
NAICS 442299 All Other Home Furnishings Stores
5722 Household Appliance Stores
NAICS 443111 Household Appliance Stores
5731 Radio, Television, & Consumer Electronics Stores
NAICS 443112 Radio, Television, & Other Electronics Stores
NAICS 44131 Automotive Parts & Accessories Stores
5734 Computer & Computer Software Stores
NAICS 44312 Computer & Software Stores
5735 Record & Prerecorded Tape Stores
NAICS 45122 Prerecorded Tape, Compact Disc & Record Stores

5736 Musical Instrument Stores
NAICS 45114 Musical Instrument & Supplies Stores
5812 Eating & Drinking Places
NAICS 72211 Full-service Restaurants
NAICS 722211 Limited-service Restaurants
NAICS 722212 Cafeterias
NAICS 722213 Snack & Nonalcoholic Beverage Bars
NAICS 72231 Foodservice Contractors
NAICS 72232 Caterers
NAICS 71111 Theater Companies & Dinner Theaters
5813 Drinking Places
NAICS 72241 Drinking Places
5912 Drug Stores & Proprietary Stores
NAICS 44611 Pharmacies & Drug Stores
5921 Liquor Stores
NAICS 44531 Beer, Wine & Liquor Stores
5932 Used Merchandise Stores
NAICS 522298 All Other Non-depository Credit Intermediation
NAICS 45331 Used Merchandise Stores
5941 Sporting Goods Stores & Bicycle Shops
NAICS 45111 Sporting Goods Stores
5942 Book Stores
NAICS 451211 Book Stores
5943 Stationery Stores
NAICS 45321 Office Supplies & Stationery Stores
5944 Jewelry Stores
NAICS 44831 Jewelry Stores
5945 Hobby, Toy, & Game Shops
NAICS 45112 Hobby, Toy & Game Stores
5946 Camera & Photographic Supply Stores
NAICS 44313 Camera & Photographic Supplies Stores
5947 Gift, Novelty, & Souvenir Shops
NAICS 45322 Gift, Novelty & Souvenir Stores
5948 Luggage & Leather Goods Stores
NAICS 44832 Luggage & Leather Goods Stores
5949 Sewing, Needlework, & Piece Goods Stores
NAICS 45113 Sewing, Needlework & Piece Goods Stores
5961 Catalog & Mail-order Houses
NAICS 45411 Electronic Shopping & Mail-order Houses
5962 Automatic Merchandising Machine Operator
NAICS 45421 Vending Machine Operators
5963 Direct Selling Establishments
NAICS 72233 Mobile Caterers
NAICS 45439 Other Direct Selling Establishments
5983 Fuel Oil Dealers
NAICS 454311 Heating Oil Dealers
5984 Liquefied Petroleum Gas Dealers
NAICS 454312 Liquefied Petroleum Gas Dealers
5989 Fuel Dealers, nec
NAICS 454319 Other Fuel Dealers
5992 Florists
NAICS 45311 Florists
5993 Tobacco Stores & Stands
NAICS 453991 Tobacco Stores
5994 News Dealers & Newsstands
NAICS 451212 News Dealers & Newsstands
5995 Optical Goods Stores
NAICS 339117 Eyeglass & Contact Lens Manufacturing
NAICS 44613 Optical Goods Stores
5999 Miscellaneous Retail Stores, nec
NAICS 44612 Cosmetics, Beauty Supplies & Perfume Stores
NAICS 446199 All Other Health & Personal Care Stores
NAICS 45391 Pet & Pet Supplies Stores

NAICS 45392   Art Dealers
NAICS 443111 Household Appliance Stores
NAICS 443112 Radio, Television & Other Electronics Stores
NAICS 44831   Jewelry Stores
NAICS 453999 All Other Miscellaneous Store Retailers

FINANCE, INSURANCE, & REAL ESTATE

6011 Federal Reserve Banks
NAICS 52111   Monetary Authorities-central Banks
6019 Central Reserve Depository Institutions, nec
NAICS 52232   Financial Transactions Processing, Reserve, &
              Clearing House Activities
6021 National Commercial Banks
NAICS 52211   Commercial Banking
NAICS 52221   Credit Card Issuing
NAICS 523991 Trust, Fiduciary & Custody Activities
6022 State Commercial Banks
NAICS 52211   Commercial Banking
NAICS 52221   Credit Card Issuing
NAICS 52219   Other Depository Intermediation
NAICS 523991 Trust, Fiduciary & Custody Activities
6029 Commercial Banks, nec
NAICS 52211   Commercial Banking
6035 Savings Institutions, Federally Chartered
NAICS 52212   Savings Institutions
6036 Savings Institutions, Not Federally Chartered
NAICS 52212   Savings Institutions
6061 Credit Unions, Federally Chartered
NAICS 52213   Credit Unions
6062 Credit Unions, Not Federally Chartered
NAICS 52213   Credit Unions
6081 Branches & Agencies of Foreign Banks
NAICS 522293 International Trade Financing
NAICS 52211   Commercial Banking
NAICS 522298 All Other Non-depository Credit
              Intermediation
6082 Foreign Trade & International Banking Institutions
NAICS 522293 International Trade Financing
6091 Nondeposit Trust Facilities
NAICS 523991 Trust, Fiduciary, & Custody Activities
6099 Functions Related to Deposit Banking, nec
NAICS 52232   Financial Transactions Processing, Reserve, &
              Clearing House Activities
NAICS 52313   Commodity Contracts Dealing
NAICS 523991 Trust, Fiduciary, & Custody Activities
NAICS 523999 Miscellaneous Financial Investment Activities
NAICS 52239   Other Activities Related to Credit
              Intermediation
6111 Federal & Federally Sponsored Credit Agencies
NAICS 522293 International Trade Financing
NAICS 522294 Secondary Market Financing
NAICS 522298 All Other Non-depository Credit
              Intermediation
6141 Personal Credit Institutions
NAICS 52221   Credit Card Issuing
NAICS 52222   Sales Financing
NAICS 522291 Consumer Lending
**6153 Short-term Business Credit Institutions, Except
    Agricultural**
NAICS 52222   Sales Financing
NAICS 52232   Financial Transactions Processing, Reserve, &
              Clearing House Activities

NAICS 522298 All Other Non-depository Credit
              Intermediation
6159 Miscellaneous Business Credit Institutions
NAICS 52222   Sales Financing
NAICS 532   Included in Rental & Leasing Services
              Subsector by Type of Equipment & Method of
              Operation
NAICS 522293 International Trade Financing
NAICS 522298 All Other Non-depository Credit
              Intermediation
6162 Mortgage Bankers & Loan Correspondents
NAICS 522292 Real Estate Credit
NAICS 52239   Other Activities Related to Credit
              Intermediation
6163 Loan Brokers
NAICS 52231   Mortgage & Other Loan Brokers
6211 Security Brokers, Dealers, & Flotation Companies
NAICS 52311   Investment Banking & Securities Dealing
NAICS 52312   Securities Brokerage
NAICS 52391   Miscellaneous Intermediation
NAICS 523999 Miscellaneous Financial Investment Activities
6221 Commodity Contracts Brokers & Dealers
NAICS 52313   Commodity Contracts Dealing
NAICS 52314   Commodity Brokerage
6231 Security & Commodity Exchanges
NAICS 52321   Securities & Commodity Exchanges
6282 Investment Advice
NAICS 52392   Portfolio Management
NAICS 52393   Investment Advice
**6289 Services Allied with the Exchange of Securities or
    Commodities, nec**
NAICS 523991 Trust, Fiduciary, & Custody Activities
NAICS 523999 Miscellaneous Financial Investment Activities
6311 Life Insurance
NAICS 524113 Direct Life Insurance Carriers
NAICS 52413   Reinsurance Carriers
6321 Accident & Health Insurance
NAICS 524114 Direct Health & Medical Insurance Carriers
NAICS 52519   Other Insurance Funds
NAICS 52413   Reinsurance Carriers
6324 Hospital & Medical Service Plans
NAICS 524114 Direct Health & Medical Insurance Carriers
NAICS 52519   Other Insurance Funds
NAICS 52413   Reinsurance Carriers
6331 Fire, Marine, & Casualty Insurance
NAICS 524126 Direct Property & Casualty Insurance Carriers
NAICS 52519   Other Insurance Funds
NAICS 52413   Reinsurance Carriers
6351 Surety Insurance
NAICS 524126 Direct Property & Casualty Insurance Carriers
NAICS 52413   Reinsurance Carriers
6361 Title Insurance
NAICS 524127 Direct Title Insurance Carriers
NAICS 52413   Reinsurance Carriers
6371 Pension, Health, & Welfare Funds
NAICS 52392   Portfolio Management
NAICS 524292 Third Party Administration for Insurance &
              Pension Funds
NAICS 52511   Pension Funds
NAICS 52512   Health & Welfare Funds
6399 Insurance Carriers, nec
NAICS 524128 Other Direct Insurance Carriers

6411 Insurance Agents, Brokers, & Service
NAICS 52421   Insurance Agencies & Brokerages
NAICS 524291 Claims Adjusters
NAICS 524292 Third Party Administrators for Insurance &
              Pension Funds
NAICS 524298 All Other Insurance Related Activities
6512 Operators of Nonresidential Buildings
NAICS 71131   Promoters of Performing Arts, Sports & Similar
              Events with Facilities
NAICS 53112   Lessors of Nonresidential Buildings
6513 Operators of Apartment Buildings
NAICS 53111   Lessors of Residential Buildings & Dwellings
6514 Operators of Dwellings Other than Apartment Buildings
NAICS 53111   Lessors of Residential Buildings & Dwellings
6515 Operators of Residential Mobile Home Sites
NAICS 53119   Lessors of Other Real Estate Property
6517 Lessors of Railroad Property
NAICS 53119   Lessors of Other Real Estate Property
6519 Lessors of Real Property, nec
NAICS 53119   Lessors of Other Real Estate Property
6531 Real Estate Agents & Managers
NAICS 53121   Offices of Real Estate Agents & Brokers
NAICS 81399   Other Similar Organizations
NAICS 531311 Residential Property Managers
NAICS 531312 Nonresidential Property Managers
NAICS 53132   Offices of Real Estate Appraisers
NAICS 81222   Cemeteries & Crematories
NAICS 531399 All Other Activities Related to Real Estate
6541 Title Abstract Offices
NAICS 541191 Title Abstract & Settlement Offices
6552 Land Subdividers & Developers, Except Cemeteries
NAICS 23311   Land Subdivision & Land Development
6553 Cemetery Subdividers & Developers
NAICS 81222   Cemeteries & Crematories
6712 Offices of Bank Holding Companies
NAICS 551111 Offices of Bank Holding Companies
6719 Offices of Holding Companies, nec
NAICS 551112 Offices of Other Holding Companies
6722 Management Investment Offices, Open-end
NAICS 52591   Open-end Investment Funds
6726 Unit Investment Trusts, Face-amount Certificate Offices, &
**   Closed-end Management Investment Offices**
NAICS 52599   Other Financial Vehicles
6732 Education, Religious, & Charitable Trusts
NAICS 813211 Grantmaking Foundations
6733 Trusts, Except Educational, Religious, & Charitable
NAICS 52392   Portfolio Management
NAICS 523991 Trust, Fiduciary, & Custody Services
NAICS 52519   Other Insurance Funds
NAICS 52592   Trusts, Estates, & Agency Accounts
6792 Oil Royalty Traders
NAICS 523999 Miscellaneous Financial Investment Activities
NAICS 53311   Owners & Lessors of Other Non-financial
              Assets
6794 Patent Owners & Lessors
NAICS 53311   Owners & Lessors of Other Non-financial
              Assets
6798 Real Estate Investment Trusts
NAICS 52593   Real Estate Investment Trusts
6799 Investors, nec
NAICS 52391   Miscellaneous Intermediation
NAICS 52392   Portfolio Management
NAICS 52313   Commodity Contracts Dealing
NAICS 523999 Miscellaneous Financial Investment Activities

SERVICE INDUSTRIES

7011 Hotels & Motels
NAICS 72111   Hotels & Motels
NAICS 72112   Casino Hotels
NAICS 721191 Bed & Breakfast Inns
NAICS 721199 All Other Traveler Accommodation
7021 Rooming & Boarding Houses
NAICS 72131   Rooming & Boarding Houses
7032 Sporting & Recreational Camps
NAICS 721214 Recreational & Vacation Camps
7033 Recreational Vehicle Parks & Campsites
NAICS 721211 Rv & Campgrounds
7041 Organization Hotels & Lodging Houses, on Membership
**   Basis**
NAICS 72111   Hotels & Motels
NAICS 72131   Rooming & Boarding Houses
7211 Power Laundries, Family & Commercial
NAICS 812321 Laundries, Family & Commercial
7212 Garment Pressing, & Agents for Laundries
NAICS 812391 Garment Pressing & Agents for Laundries
7213 Linen Supply
NAICS 812331 Linen Supply
7215 Coin-operated Laundry & Drycleaning
NAICS 81231   Coin-operated Laundries & Drycleaners
7216 Drycleaning Plants, Except Rug Cleaning
NAICS 812322 Drycleaning Plants
7217 Carpet & Upholstery Cleaning
NAICS 56174   Carpet & Upholstery Cleaning Services
7218 Industrial Launderers
NAICS 812332 Industrial Launderers
7219 Laundry & Garment Services, nec
NAICS 812331 Linen Supply
NAICS 81149   Other Personal & Household Goods Repair &
              Maintenance
NAICS 812399 All Other Laundry Services
7221 Photographic Studios, Portrait
NAICS 541921 Photographic Studios, Portrait
7231 Beauty Shops
NAICS 812112 Beauty Salons
NAICS 812113 Nail Salons
NAICS 611511 Cosmetology & Barber Schools
7241 Barber Shops
NAICS 812111 Barber Shops
NAICS 611511 Cosmetology & Barber Schools
7251 Shoe Repair Shops & Shoeshine Parlors
NAICS 81143   Footwear & Leather Goods Repair
7261 Funeral Services & Crematories
NAICS 81221   Funeral Homes
NAICS 81222   Cemeteries & Crematories
7291 Tax Return Preparation Services
NAICS 541213 Tax Preparation Services
7299 Miscellaneous Personal Services, nec
NAICS 62441   Child Day Care Services
NAICS 812191 Diet & Weight Reducing Centers
NAICS 53222   Formal Wear & Costume Rental
NAICS 812199 Other Personal Care Services
NAICS 81299   All Other Personal Services
7311 Advertising Agencies
NAICS 54181   Advertising Agencies
7312 Outdoor Advertising Services
NAICS 54185   Display Advertising

7313 Radio, Television, & Publishers' Advertising Representatives
NAICS 54184   Media Representatives
7319 Advertising, nec
NAICS 481219 Other Nonscheduled Air Transportation
NAICS 54183   Media Buying Agencies
NAICS 54185   Display Advertising
NAICS 54187   Advertising Material Distribution Services
NAICS 54189   Other Services Related to Advertising
7322 Adjustment & Collection Services
NAICS 56144   Collection Agencies
NAICS 561491 Repossession Services
7323 Credit Reporting Services
NAICS 56145   Credit Bureaus
7331 Direct Mail Advertising Services
NAICS 54186   Direct Mail Advertising
7334 Photocopying & Duplicating Services
NAICS 561431 Photocopying & Duplicating Services
7335 Commercial Photography
NAICS 48122   Nonscheduled Speciality Air Transportation
NAICS 541922 Commercial Photography
7336 Commercial Art & Graphic Design
NAICS 54143   Commercial Art & Graphic Design Services
7338 Secretarial & Court Reporting Services
NAICS 56141   Document Preparation Services
NAICS 561492 Court Reporting & Stenotype Services
7342 Disinfecting & Pest Control Services
NAICS 56172   Janitorial Services
NAICS 56171   Exterminating & Pest Control Services
7349 Building Cleaning & Maintenance Services, nec
NAICS 56172   Janitorial Services
7352 Medical Equipment Rental & Leasing
NAICS 532291 Home Health Equipment Rental
NAICS 53249   Other Commercial & Industrial Machinery & Equipment Rental & Leasing
7353 Heavy Construction Equipment Rental & Leasing
NAICS 23499   All Other Heavy Construction
NAICS 532412 Construction, Mining & Forestry Machinery & Equipment Rental & Leasing
7359 Equipment Rental & Leasing, nec
NAICS 53221   Consumer Electronics & Appliances Rental
NAICS 53231   General Rental Centers
NAICS 532299 All Other Consumer Goods Rental
NAICS 532412 Construction, Mining & Forestry Machinery & Equipment Rental & Leasing
NAICS 532411 Commercial Air, Rail, & Water Transportation Equipment Rental & Leasing
NAICS 562991 Septic Tank & Related Services
NAICS 53242   Office Machinery & Equipment Rental & Leasing
NAICS 53249   Other Commercial & Industrial Machinery & Equipment Rental & Leasing
7361 Employment Agencies
NAICS 541612 Human Resources & Executive Search Consulting Services
NAICS 56131   Employment Placement Agencies
7363 Help Supply Services
NAICS 56132   Temporary Help Services
NAICS 56133   Employee Leasing Services
7371 Computer Programming Services
NAICS 541511 Custom Computer Programming Services
7372 Prepackaged Software
NAICS 51121   Software Publishers
NAICS 334611 Software Reproducing

7373 Computer Integrated Systems Design
NAICS 541512 Computer Systems Design Services
7374 Computer Processing & Data Preparation & Processing Services
NAICS 51421   Data Processing Services
7375 Information Retrieval Services
NAICS 514191 On-line Information Services
7376 Computer Facilities Management Services
NAICS 541513 Computer Facilities Management Services
7377 Computer Rental & Leasing
NAICS 53242   Office Machinery & Equipment Rental & Leasing
7378 Computer Maintenance & Repair
NAICS 44312   Computer & Software Stores
NAICS 811212 Computer & Office Machine Repair & Maintenance
7379 Computer Related Services, nec
NAICS 541512 Computer Systems Design Services
NAICS 541519 Other Computer Related Services
7381 Detective, Guard, & Armored Car Services
NAICS 561611 Investigation Services
NAICS 561612 Security Guards & Patrol Services
NAICS 561613 Armored Car Services
7382 Security Systems Services
NAICS 561621 Security Systems Services
7383 News Syndicates
NAICS 51411   New Syndicates
7384 Photofinishing Laboratories
NAICS 812921 Photo Finishing Laboratories
NAICS 812922 One-hour Photo Finishing
7389 Business Services, nec
NAICS 51224   Sound Recording Studios
NAICS 51229   Other Sound Recording Industries
NAICS 541199 All Other Legal Services
NAICS 81299   All Other Personal Services
NAICS 54137   Surveying & Mapping Services
NAICS 54141   Interior Design Services
NAICS 54142   Industrial Design Services
NAICS 54134   Drafting Services
NAICS 54149   Other Specialized Design Services
NAICS 54189   Other Services Related to Advertising
NAICS 54193   Translation & Interpretation Services
NAICS 54135   Building Inspection Services
NAICS 54199   All Other Professional, Scientific & Technical Services
NAICS 71141   Agents & Managers for Artists, Athletes, Entertainers & Other Public Figures
NAICS 561422 Telemarketing Bureaus
NAICS 561432 Private Mail Centers
NAICS 561439 Other Business Service Centers
NAICS 561491 Repossession Services
NAICS 56191   Packaging & Labeling Services
NAICS 56179   Other Services to Buildings & Dwellings
NAICS 561599 All Other Travel Arrangement & Reservation Services
NAICS 56192   Convention & Trade Show Organizers
NAICS 561591 Convention & Visitors Bureaus
NAICS 52232   Financial Transactions, Processing, Reserve & Clearing House Activities
NAICS 561499 All Other Business Support Services
NAICS 56199   All Other Support Services
7513 Truck Rental & Leasing, Without Drivers
NAICS 53212   Truck, Utility Trailer & Rv Rental & Leasing

7514 Passenger Car Rental
NAICS 532111 Passenger Cars Rental
7515 Passenger Car Leasing
NAICS 532112 Passenger Cars Leasing
7519 Utility Trailer & Recreational Vehicle Rental
NAICS 53212 Truck, Utility Trailer & Rv Rental & Leasing
7521 Automobile Parking
NAICS 81293 Parking Lots & Garages
7532 Top, Body, & Upholstery Repair Shops & Paint Shops
NAICS 811121 Automotive Body, Paint, & Upholstery Repair
& Maintenance
7533 Automotive Exhaust System Repair Shops
NAICS 811112 Automotive Exhaust System Repair
7534 Tire Retreading & Repair Shops
NAICS 326212 Tire Retreading
NAICS 811198 All Other Automotive Repair & Maintenance
7536 Automotive Glass Replacement Shops
NAICS 811122 Automotive Glass Replacement Shops
7537 Automotive Transmission Repair Shops
NAICS 811113 Automotive Transmission Repair
7538 General Automotive Repair Shops
NAICS 811111 General Automotive Repair
7539 Automotive Repair Shops, nec
NAICS 811118 Other Automotive Mechanical & Electrical
Repair & Maintenance
7542 Carwashes
NAICS 811192 Car Washes
7549 Automotive Services, Except Repair & Carwashes
NAICS 811191 Automotive Oil Change & Lubrication Shops
NAICS 48841 Motor Vehicle Towing
NAICS 811198 All Other Automotive Repair & Maintenance
7622 Radio & Television Repair Shops
NAICS 811211 Consumer Electronics Repair & Maintenance
NAICS 443112 Radio, Television & Other Electronics Stores
7623 Refrigeration & Air-conditioning Services & Repair Shops
NAICS 443111 Household Appliance Stores
NAICS 81131 Commercial & Industrial Machinery &
Equipment Repair & Maintenance
NAICS 811412 Appliance Repair & Maintenance
7629 Electrical & Electronic Repair Shops, nec
NAICS 443111 Household Appliance Stores
NAICS 811212 Computer & Office Machine Repair &
Maintenance
NAICS 811213 Communication Equipment Repair &
Maintenance
NAICS 811219 Other Electronic & Precision Equipment
Repair & Maintenance
NAICS 811412 Appliance Repair & Maintenance
NAICS 811211 Consumer Electronics Repair & Maintenance
7631 Watch, Clock, & Jewelry Repair
NAICS 81149 Other Personal & Household Goods Repair &
Maintenance
7641 Reupholster & Furniture Repair
NAICS 81142 Reupholstery & Furniture Repair
7692 Welding Repair
NAICS 81149 Other Personal & Household Goods Repair &
Maintenance
7694 Armature Rewinding Shops
NAICS 81131 Commercial & Industrial Machinery &
Equipment Repair & Maintenance
NAICS 335312 Motor & Generator Manufacturing
7699 Repair Shops & Related Services, nec
NAICS 561622 Locksmiths
NAICS 562991 Septic Tank & Related Services

NAICS 56179 Other Services to Buildings & Dwellings
NAICS 48839 Other Supporting Activities for Water
Transportation
NAICS 45111 Sporting Goods Stores
NAICS 81131 Commercial & Industrial Machinery &
Equipment Repair & Maintenance
NAICS 11521 Support Activities for Animal Production
NAICS 811212 Computer & Office Machine Repair &
Maintenance
NAICS 811219 Other Electronic & Precision Equipment
Repair & Maintenance
NAICS 811411 Home & Garden Equipment Repair &
Maintenance
NAICS 811412 Appliance Repair & Maintenance
NAICS 81143 Footwear & Leather Goods Repair
NAICS 81149 Other Personal & Household Goods Repair &
Maintenance
7812 Motion Picture & Video Tape Production
NAICS 51211 Motion Picture & Video Production
7819 Services Allied to Motion Picture Production
NAICS 512191 Teleproduction & Other Post-production
Services
NAICS 56131 Employment Placement Agencies
NAICS 53222 Formal Wear & Costumes Rental
NAICS 53249 Other Commercial & Industrial Machinery &
Equipment Rental & Leasing
NAICS 541214 Payroll Services
NAICS 71151 Independent Artists, Writers, & Performers
NAICS 334612 Prerecorded Compact Disc , Tape, & Record
Manufacturing
NAICS 512199 Other Motion Picture & Video Industries
7822 Motion Picture & Video Tape Distribution
NAICS 42199 Other Miscellaneous Durable Goods
Wholesalers
NAICS 51212 Motion Picture & Video Distribution
7829 Services Allied to Motion Picture Distribution
NAICS 512199 Other Motion Picture & Video Industries
NAICS 51212 Motion Picture & Video Distribution
7832 Motion Picture Theaters, Except Drive-ins.
NAICS 512131 Motion Picture Theaters, Except Drive-in
7833 Drive-in Motion Picture Theaters
NAICS 512132 Drive-in Motion Picture Theaters
7841 Video Tape Rental
NAICS 53223 Video Tapes & Disc Rental
7911 Dance Studios, Schools, & Halls
NAICS 71399 All Other Amusement & Recreation Industries
NAICS 61161 Fine Arts Schools
7922 Theatrical Producers & Miscellaneous Theatrical Services
NAICS 56131 Employment Placement Agencies
NAICS 71111 Theater Companies & Dinner Theaters
NAICS 71141 Agents & Managers for Artists, Athletes,
Entertainers & Other Public Figures
NAICS 71112 Dance Companies
NAICS 71131 Promoters of Performing Arts, Sports, &
Similar Events with Facilities
NAICS 71132 Promoters of Performing Arts, Sports, &
Similar Events Without Facilities
NAICS 51229 Other Sound Recording Industries
NAICS 53249 Other Commercial & Industrial Machinery &
Equipment Rental & Leasing
7929 Bands, Orchestras, Actors, & Other Entertainers & Entertainment Groups
NAICS 71113 Musical Groups & Artists
NAICS 71151 Independent Artists, Writers, & Performers

NAICS 71119   Other Performing Arts Companies
7933 Bowling Centers
NAICS 71395   Bowling Centers
7941 Professional Sports Clubs & Promoters
NAICS 711211 Sports Teams & Clubs
NAICS 71141   Agents & Managers for Artists, Athletes,
Entertainers , & Other Public Figures
NAICS 71132   Promoters of Arts, Sports & Similar Events
Without Facilities
NAICS 71131   Promoters of Arts, Sports, & Similar Events
with Facilities
NAICS 711219 Other Spectator Sports
7948 Racing, Including Track Operations
NAICS 711212 Race Tracks
NAICS 711219 Other Spectator Sports
7991 Physical Fitness Facilities
NAICS 71394   Fitness & Recreational Sports Centers
7992 Public Golf Courses
NAICS 71391   Golf Courses & Country Clubs
7993 Coin Operated Amusement Devices
NAICS 71312   Amusement Arcades
NAICS 71329   Other Gambling Industries
NAICS 71399   All Other Amusement & Recreation Industries
7996 Amusement Parks
NAICS 71311   Amusement & Theme Parks
7997 Membership Sports & Recreation Clubs
NAICS 48122   Nonscheduled Speciality Air Transportation
NAICS 71391   Golf Courses & Country Clubs
NAICS 71394   Fitness & Recreational Sports Centers
NAICS 71399   All Other Amusement & Recreation Industries
7999 Amusement & Recreation Services, nec
NAICS 561599 All Other Travel Arrangement & Reservation
Services
NAICS 48799   Scenic & Sightseeing Transportation, Other
NAICS 71119   Other Performing Arts Companies
NAICS 711219 Other Spectator Sports
NAICS 71392   Skiing Facilities
NAICS 71394   Fitness & Recreational Sports Centers
NAICS 71321   Casinos
NAICS 71329   Other Gambling Industries
NAICS 71219   Nature Parks & Other Similar Institutions
NAICS 61162   Sports & Recreation Instruction
NAICS 532292 Recreational Goods Rental
NAICS 48711   Scenic & Sightseeing Transportation, Land
NAICS 48721   Scenic & Sightseeing Transportation, Water
NAICS 71399   All Other Amusement & Recreation Industries
8011 Offices & Clinics of Doctors of Medicine
NAICS 621493 Freestanding Ambulatory Surgical &
Emergency Centers
NAICS 621491 Hmo Medical Centers
NAICS 621112 Offices of Physicians, Mental Health Specialists
NAICS 621111 Offices of Physicians
8021 Offices & Clinics of Dentists
NAICS 62121   Offices of Dentists
8031 Offices & Clinics of Doctors of Osteopathy
NAICS 621111 Offices of Physicians
NAICS 621112 Offices of Physicians, Mental Health Specialists
8041 Offices & Clinics of Chiropractors
NAICS 62131   Offices of Chiropractors
8042 Offices & Clinics of Optometrists
NAICS 62132   Offices of Optometrists
8043 Offices & Clinics of Podiatrists
NAICS 621391 Offices of Podiatrists

8049 Offices & Clinics of Health Practitioners, nec
NAICS 62133   Offices of Mental Health Practitioners
NAICS 62134   Offices of Physical, Occupational, & Speech
Therapists & Audiologists
NAICS 621399 Offices of All Other Miscellaneous Health
Practitioners
8051 Skilled Nursing Care Facilities
NAICS 623311 Continuing Care Retirement Communities
NAICS 62311   Nursing Care Facilities
8052 Intermediate Care Facilities
NAICS 623311 Continuing Care Retirement Communities
NAICS 62321   Residential Mental Retardation Facilities
NAICS 62311   Nursing Care Facilities
8059 Nursing & Personal Care Facilities, nec
NAICS 623311 Continuing Care Retirement Communities
NAICS 62311   Nursing Care Facilities
8062 General Medical & Surgical Hospitals
NAICS 62211   General Medical & Surgical Hospitals
8063 Psychiatric Hospitals
NAICS 62221   Psychiatric & Substance Abuse Hospitals
8069 Specialty Hospitals, Except Psychiatric
NAICS 62211   General Medical & Surgical Hospitals
NAICS 62221   Psychiatric & Substance Abuse Hospitals
NAICS 62231   Specialty Hospitals
8071 Medical Laboratories
NAICS 621512 Diagnostic Imaging Centers
NAICS 621511 Medical Laboratories
8072 Dental Laboratories
NAICS 339116 Dental Laboratories
8082 Home Health Care Services
NAICS 62161   Home Health Care Services
8092 Kidney Dialysis Centers
NAICS 621492 Kidney Dialysis Centers
8093 Specialty Outpatient Facilities, nec
NAICS 62141   Family Planning Centers
NAICS 62142   Outpatient Mental Health & Substance Abuse
Centers
NAICS 621498 All Other Outpatient Care Facilities
8099 Health & Allied Services, nec
NAICS 621991 Blood & Organ Banks
NAICS 54143   Graphic Design Services
NAICS 541922 Commercial Photography
NAICS 62141   Family Planning Centers
NAICS 621999 All Other Miscellaneous Ambulatory Health
Care Services
8111 Legal Services
NAICS 54111   Offices of Lawyers
8211 Elementary & Secondary Schools
NAICS 61111   Elementary & Secondary Schools
8221 Colleges, Universities, & Professional Schools
NAICS 61131   Colleges, Universities & Professional Schools
8222 Junior Colleges & Technical Institutes
NAICS 61121   Junior Colleges
8231 Libraries
NAICS 51412   Libraries & Archives
8243 Data Processing Schools
NAICS 611519 Other Technical & Trade Schools
NAICS 61142   Computer Training
8244 Business & Secretarial Schools
NAICS 61141   Business & Secretarial Schools
8249 Vocational Schools, nec
NAICS 611513 Apprenticeship Training
NAICS 611512 Flight Training
NAICS 611519 Other Technical & Trade Schools

8299 Schools & Educational Services, nec
NAICS 48122 Nonscheduled speciality Air Transportation
NAICS 611512 Flight Training
NAICS 611692 Automobile Driving Schools
NAICS 61171 Educational Support Services
NAICS 611691 Exam Preparation & Tutoring
NAICS 61161 Fine Arts Schools
NAICS 61163 Language Schools
NAICS 61143 Professional & Management Development
                Training Schools
NAICS 611699 All Other Miscellaneous Schools & Instruction
8322 Individual & Family Social Services
NAICS 62411 Child & Youth Services
NAICS 62421 Community Food Services
NAICS 624229 Other Community Housing Services
NAICS 62423 Emergency & Other Relief Services
NAICS 62412 Services for the Elderly & Persons with
                Disabilities
NAICS 624221 Temporary Shelters
NAICS 92215 Parole Offices & Probation Offices
NAICS 62419 Other Individual & Family Services
8331 Job Training & Vocational Rehabilitation Services
NAICS 62431 Vocational Rehabilitation Services
8351 Child Day Care Services
NAICS 62441 Child Day Care Services
8361 Residential Care
NAICS 623312 Homes for the Elderly
NAICS 62322 Residential Mental Health & Substance Abuse
                Facilities
NAICS 62399 Other Residential Care Facilities
8399 Social Services, nec
NAICS 813212 Voluntary Health Organizations
NAICS 813219 Other Grantmaking & Giving Services
NAICS 813311 Human Rights Organizations
NAICS 813312 Environment, Conservation & Wildlife
                Organizations
NAICS 813319 Other Social Advocacy Organizations
8412 Museums & Art Galleries
NAICS 71211 Museums
NAICS 71212 Historical Sites
8422 Arboreta & Botanical or Zoological Gardens
NAICS 71213 Zoos & Botanical Gardens
NAICS 71219 Nature Parks & Other Similar Institutions
8611 Business Associations
NAICS 81391 Business Associations
8621 Professional Membership Organizations
NAICS 81392 Professional Organizations
8631 Labor Unions & Similar Labor Organizations
NAICS 81393 Labor Unions & Similar Labor Organizations
8641 Civic, Social, & Fraternal Associations
NAICS 81341 Civic & Social Organizations
NAICS 81399 Other Similar Organizations
NAICS 92115 American Indian & Alaska Native Tribal
                Governments
NAICS 62411 Child & Youth Services
8651 Political Organizations
NAICS 81394 Political Organizations
8661 Religious Organizations
NAICS 81311 Religious Organizations
8699 Membership Organizations, nec
NAICS 81341 Civic & Social Organizations
NAICS 81391 Business Associations
NAICS 813312 Environment, Conservation, & Wildlife
                Organizations

NAICS 561599 All Other Travel Arrangement & Reservation
                Services
NAICS 81399 Other Similar Organizations
8711 Engineering Services
NAICS 54133 Engineering Services
8712 Architectural Services
NAICS 54131 Architectural Services
8713 Surveying Services
NAICS 48122 Nonscheduled Air Speciality Transportation
NAICS 54136 Geophysical Surveying & Mapping Services
NAICS 54137 Surveying & Mapping Services
8721 Accounting, Auditing, & Bookkeeping Services
NAICS 541211 Offices of Certified Public Accountants
NAICS 541214 Payroll Services
NAICS 541219 Other Accounting Services
8731 Commercial Physical & Biological Research
NAICS 54171 Research & Development in the Physical
                Sciences & Engineering Sciences
NAICS 54172 Research & Development in the Life Sciences
8732 Commercial Economic, Sociological, & Educational
     Research
NAICS 54173 Research & Development in the Social Sciences
                & Humanities
NAICS 54191 Marketing Research & Public Opinion Polling
8733 Noncommercial Research Organizations
NAICS 54171 Research & Development in the Physical
                Sciences & Engineering Sciences
NAICS 54172 Research & Development in the Life Sciences
NAICS 54173 Research & Development in the Social Sciences
                & Humanities
8734 Testing Laboratories
NAICS 54194 Veterinary Services
NAICS 54138 Testing Laboratories
8741 Management Services
NAICS 56111 Office Administrative Services
NAICS 23   Included in Construction Sector by Type of
                Construction
8742 Management Consulting Services
NAICS 541611 Administrative Management & General
                Management Consulting Services
NAICS 541612 Human Resources & Executive Search Services
NAICS 541613 Marketing Consulting Services
NAICS 541614 Process, Physical, Distribution & Logistics
                Consulting Services
8743 Public Relations Services
NAICS 54182 Public Relations Agencies
8744 Facilities Support Management Services
NAICS 56121 Facilities Support Services
8748 Business Consulting Services, nec
NAICS 61171 Educational Support Services
NAICS 541618 Other Management Consulting Services
NAICS 54169 Other Scientific & Technical Consulting
                Services
8811 Private Households
NAICS 81411 Private Households
8999 Services, nec
NAICS 71151 Independent Artists, Writers, & Performers
NAICS 51221 Record Production
NAICS 54169 Other Scientific & Technical Consulting
                Services
NAICS 51223 Music Publishers
NAICS 541612 Human Resources & Executive Search
                Consulting Services
NAICS 514199 All Other Information Services

NAICS 54162   Environmental Consulting Services

PUBLIC ADMINISTRATION

9111 Executive Offices
NAICS 92111   Executive Offices
9121 Legislative Bodies
NAICS 92112   Legislative Bodies
9131 Executive & Legislative Offices, Combined
NAICS 92114   Executive & Legislative Offices, Combined
9199 General Government, nec
NAICS 92119   All Other General Government
9211 Courts
NAICS 92211   Courts
9221 Police Protection
NAICS 92212   Police Protection
9222 Legal Counsel & Prosecution
NAICS 92213   Legal Counsel & Prosecution
9223 Correctional Institutions
NAICS 92214   Correctional Institutions
9224 Fire Protection
NAICS 92216   Fire Protection
9229 Public Order & Safety, nec
NAICS 92219   All Other Justice, Public Order, & Safety
9311 Public Finance, Taxation, & Monetary Policy
NAICS 92113   Public Finance
9411 Administration of Educational Programs
NAICS 92311   Administration of Education Programs
9431 Administration of Public Health Programs
NAICS 92312   Administration of Public Health Programs
9441 Administration of Social, Human Resource & Income Maintenance Programs
NAICS 92313   Administration of Social, Human Resource & Income Maintenance Programs
9451 Administration of Veteran's Affairs, Except Health Insurance
NAICS 92314   Administration of Veteran's Affairs
9511 Air & Water Resource & Solid Waste Management
NAICS 92411   Air & Water Resource & Solid Waste Management
9512 Land, Mineral, Wildlife, & Forest Conservation
NAICS 92412   Land, Mineral, Wildlife, & Forest Conservation
9531 Administration of Housing Programs
NAICS 92511   Administration of Housing Programs
9532 Administration of Urban Planning & Community & Rural Development
NAICS 92512   Administration of Urban Planning & Community & Rural Development
9611 Administration of General Economic Programs
NAICS 92611   Administration of General Economic Programs
9621 Regulations & Administration of Transportation Programs
NAICS 488111 Air Traffic Control
NAICS 92612   Regulation & Administration of Transportation Programs
9631 Regulation & Administration of Communications, Electric, Gas, & Other Utilities
NAICS 92613   Regulation & Administration of Communications, Electric, Gas, & Other Utilities
9641 Regulation of Agricultural Marketing & Commodity
NAICS 92614   Regulation of Agricultural Marketing & Commodity

9651 Regulation, Licensing, & Inspection of Miscellaneous Commercial Sectors
NAICS 92615   Regulation, Licensing, & Inspection of Miscellaneous Commercial Sectors
9661 Space Research & Technology
NAICS 92711   Space Research & Technology
9711 National Security
NAICS 92811   National Security
9721 International Affairs
NAICS 92812   International Affairs
9999 Nonclassifiable Establishments
NAICS 99999   Unclassified Establishments

Appendix: SIC/NAICS Conversion

NAICS TO SIC CONVERSION GUIDE

AGRICULTURE, FORESTRY, FISHING, & HUNTING

11111 Soybean Farming
SIC 0116 Soybeans
11112 Oilseed Farming
SIC 0119 Cash Grains, nec
11113 Dry Pea & Bean Farming
SIC 0119 Cash Grains, nec
11114 Wheat Farming
SIC 0111 Wheat
11115 Corn Farming
SIC 0115 Corn
SIC 0119 Cash Grains, nec
11116 Rice Farming
SIC 0112 Rice
111191 Oilseed & Grain Combination Farming
SIC 0119 Cash Grains, nec
111199 All Other Grain Farming
SIC 0119 Cash Grains, nec
111211 Potato Farming
SIC 0134 Irish Potatoes
111219 Other Vegetable & Melon Farming
SIC 0161 Vegetables & Melons
SIC 0139 Field Crops Except Cash Grains
11131 Orange Groves
SIC 0174 Citrus Fruits
11132 Citrus Groves
SIC 0174 Citrus Fruits
111331 Apple Orchards
SIC 0175 Deciduous Tree Fruits
111332 Grape Vineyards
SIC 0172 Grapes
111333 Strawberry Farming
SIC 0171 Berry Crops
111334 Berry Farming
SIC 0171 Berry Crops
111335 Tree Nut Farming
SIC 0173 Tree Nuts
111336 Fruit & Tree Nut Combination Farming
SIC 0179 Fruits & Tree Nuts, nec
111339 Other Noncitrus Fruit Farming
SIC 0175 Deciduous Tree Fruits
SIC 0179 Fruit & Tree Nuts, nec
111411 Mushroom Production
SIC 0182 Food Crops Grown Under Cover
111419 Other Food Crops Grown Under Cover
SIC 0182 Food Crops Grown Under Cover
111421 Nursery & Tree Production
SIC 0181 Ornamental Floriculture & Nursery Products
SIC 0811 Timber Tracts
111422 Floriculture Production
SIC 0181 Ornamental Floriculture & Nursery Products
11191 Tobacco Farming
SIC 0132 Tobacco
11192 Cotton Farming
SIC 0131 Cotton
11193 Sugarcane Farming
SIC 0133 Sugarcane & Sugar Beets

11194 Hay Farming
SIC 0139 Field Crops, Except Cash Grains, nec
111991 Sugar Beet Farming
SIC 0133 Sugarcane & Sugar Beets
111992 Peanut Farming
SIC 0139 Field Crops, Except Cash Grains, nec
111998 All Other Miscellaneous Crop Farming
SIC 0139 Field Crops, Except Cash Grains, nec
SIC 0191 General Farms, Primarily Crop
SIC 0831 Forest Products
SIC 0919 Miscellaneous Marine Products
SIC 2099 Food Preparations, nec
112111 Beef Cattle Ranching & Farming
SIC 0212 Beef Cattle, Except Feedlots
SIC 0241 Dairy Farms
112112 Cattle Feedlots
SIC 0211 Beef Cattle Feedlots
11212 Dairy Cattle & Milk Production
SIC 0241 Dairy Farms
11213 Dual Purpose Cattle Ranching & Farming
No SIC equivalent
11221 Hog & Pig Farming
SIC 0213 Hogs
11231 Chicken Egg Production
SIC 0252 Chicken Eggs
11232 Broilers & Other Meat Type Chicken Production
SIC 0251 Broiler, Fryers, & Roaster Chickens
11233 Turkey Production
SIC 0253 Turkey & Turkey Eggs
11234 Poultry Hatcheries
SIC 0254 Poultry Hatcheries
11239 Other Poultry Production
SIC 0259 Poultry & Eggs, nec
11241 Sheep Farming
SIC 0214 Sheep & Goats
11242 Goat Farming
SIC 0214 Sheep & Goats
112511 Finfish Farming & Fish Hatcheries
SIC 0273 Animal Aquaculture
SIC 0921 Fish Hatcheries & Preserves
112512 Shellfish Farming
SIC 0273 Animal Aquaculture
SIC 0921 Fish Hatcheries & Preserves
112519 Other Animal Aquaculture
SIC 0273 Animal Aquaculture
11291 Apiculture
SIC 0279 Animal Specialties, nec
11292 Horse & Other Equine Production
SIC 0272 Horses & Other Equines
11293 Fur-Bearing Animal & Rabbit Production
SIC 0271 Fur-Bearing Animals & Rabbits
11299 All Other Animal Production
SIC 0219 General Livestock, Except Dairy & Poultry
SIC 0279 Animal Specialties, nec
SIC 0291 General Farms, Primarily Livestock & Animal
   Specialties;
11311 Timber Tract Operations
SIC 0811 Timber Tracts
11321 Forest Nurseries & Gathering of Forest Products
SIC 0831 Forest Nurseries & Gathering of Forest Products
11331 Logging
SIC 2411 Logging

114111 Finfish Fishing
 SIC 0912 Finfish
114112 Shellfish Fishing
 SIC 0913 Shellfish
114119 Other Marine Fishing
 SIC 0919 Miscellaneous Marine Products
11421 Hunting & Trapping
 SIC 0971 Hunting & Trapping, & Game Propagation;
115111 Cotton Ginning
 SIC 0724 Cotton Ginning
115112 Soil Preparation, Planting, & Cultivating
 SIC 0711 Soil Preparation Services
 SIC 0721 Crop Planting, Cultivating, & Protecting
115113 Crop Harvesting, Primarily by Machine
 SIC 0722 Crop Harvesting, Primarily by Machine
115114 Other Postharvest Crop Activities
 SIC 0723 Crop Preparation Services For Market, Except Cotton
  Ginning
115115 Farm Labor Contractors & Crew Leaders
 SIC 0761 Farm Labor Contractors & Crew Leaders
115116 Farm Management Services
 SIC 0762 Farm Management Services
11521 Support Activities for Animal Production
 SIC 0751 Livestock Services, Except Veterinary
 SIC 0752 Animal Specialty Services, Except Veterinary
 SIC 7699 Repair Services, nec
11531 Support Activities for Forestry
 SIC 0851 Forestry Services

MINING

211111 Crude Petroleum & Natural Gas Extraction
 SIC 1311 Crude Petroleum & Natural Gas
211112 Natural Gas Liquid Extraction
 SIC 1321 Natural Gas Liquids
212111 Bituminous Coal & Lignite Surface Mining
 SIC 1221 Bituminous Coal & Lignite Surface Mining
212112 Bituminous Coal Underground Mining
 SIC 1222 Bituminous Coal Underground Mining
212113 Anthracite Mining
 SIC 1231 Anthracite Mining
21221 Iron Ore Mining
 SIC 1011 Iron Ores
212221 Gold Ore Mining
 SIC 1041 Gold Ores
212222 Silver Ore Mining
 SIC 1044 Silver Ores
212231 Lead Ore & Zinc Ore Mining
 SIC 1031 Lead & Zinc Ores
212234 Copper Ore & Nickel Ore Mining
 SIC 1021 Copper Ores
212291 Uranium-Radium-Vanadium Ore Mining
 SIC 1094 Uranium-Radium-Vanadium Ores
212299 All Other Metal Ore Mining
 SIC 1061 Ferroalloy Ores, Except Vanadium
 SIC 1099 Miscellaneous Metal Ores, nec
212311 Dimension Stone Mining & Quarrying
 SIC 1411 Dimension Stone
212312 Crushed & Broken Limestone Mining & Quarrying
 SIC 1422 Crushed & Broken Limestone
212313 Crushed & Broken Granite Mining & Quarrying
 SIC 1423 Crushed & Broken Granite

212319 Other Crushed & Broken Stone Mining & Quarrying
 SIC 1429 Crushed & Broken Stone, nec
 SIC 1499 Miscellaneous Nonmetallic Minerals, Except Fuels
212321 Construction Sand & Gravel Mining
 SIC 1442 Construction Sand & Gravel
212322 Industrial Sand Mining
 SIC 1446 Industrial Sand
212324 Kaolin & Ball Clay Mining
 SIC 1455 Kaolin & Ball Clay
212325 Clay & Ceramic & Refractory Minerals Mining
 SIC 1459 Clay, Ceramic, & Refractory Minerals, nec
212391 Potash, Soda, & Borate Mineral Mining
 SIC 1474 Potash, Soda, & Borate Minerals
212392 Phosphate Rock Mining
 SIC 1475 Phosphate Rock
212393 Other Chemical & Fertilizer Mineral Mining
 SIC 1479 Chemical & Fertilizer Mineral Mining, nec
212399 All Other Nonmetallic Mineral Mining
 SIC 1499 Miscellaneous Nonmetallic Minerals, Except Fuels
213111 Drilling Oil & Gas Wells
 SIC 1381 Drilling Oil & Gas Wells
213112 Support Activities for Oil & Gas Operations
 SIC 1382 Oil & Gas Field Exploration Services
 SIC 1389 Oil & Gas Field Services, nec
213113 Other Gas & Field Support Activities
 SIC 1389 Oil & Gas Field Services, nec
213114 Support Activities for Coal Mining
 SIC 1241 Coal Mining Services
213115 Support Activities for Metal Mining
 SIC 1081 Metal Mining Services
**213116 Support Activities for Nonmetallic Minerals, Except
  Fuels**
 SIC 1481 Nonmetallic Minerals Services, Except Fuels

UTILITIES

221111 Hydroelectric Power Generation
 SIC 4911 Electric Services
 SIC 4931 Electric & Other Services Combined
 SIC 4939 Combination Utilities, nec
221112 Fossil Fuel Electric Power Generation
 SIC 4911 Electric Services
 SIC 4931 Electric & Other Services Combined
 SIC 4939 Combination Utilities, nec
221113 Nuclear Electric Power Generation
 SIC 4911 Electric Services
 SIC 4931 Electric & Other Services Combined
 SIC 4939 Combination Utilities, nec
221119 Other Electric Power Generation
 SIC 4911 Electric Services
 SIC 4931 Electric & Other Services Combined
 SIC 4939 Combination Utilities, nec
221121 Electric Bulk Power Transmission & Control
 SIC 4911 Electric Services
 SIC 4931 Electric & Other Services Combined
 SIC 4939 Combination Utilities, NEC
221122 Electric Power Distribution
 SIC 4911 Electric Services
 SIC 4931 Electric & Other Services Combined
 SIC 4939 Combination Utilities, nec
22121 Natural Gas Distribution
 SIC 4923 Natural Gas Transmission & Distribution
 SIC 4924 Natural Gas Distribution

SIC 4925 Mixed, Manufactured, or Liquefied Petroleum Gas Production and/or Distribution

SIC 4931 Electronic & Other Services Combined

SIC 4932 Gas & Other Services Combined

SIC 4939 Combination Utilities, nec

22131 Water Supply & Irrigation Systems

SIC 4941 Water Supply

SIC 4971 Irrigation Systems

22132 Sewage Treatment Facilities

SIC 4952 Sewerage Systems

22133 Steam & Air-Conditioning Supply

SIC 4961 Steam & Air-Conditioning Supply

CONSTRUCTION

23311 Land Subdivision & Land Development

SIC 6552 Land Subdividers & Developers, Except Cemeteries

23321 Single Family Housing Construction

SIC 1521 General contractors-Single-Family Houses

SIC 1531 Operative Builders

23322 Multifamily Housing Construction

SIC 1522 General Contractors-Residential Building, Other Than Single-Family

SIC 1531 Operative Builders

23331 Manufacturing & Industrial Building Construction

SIC 1531 Operative Builders

SIC 1541 General Contractors-Industrial Buildings & Warehouses

23332 Commercial & Institutional Building Construction

SIC 1522 General Contractors-Residential Building Other than Single-Family

SIC 1531 Operative Builders

SIC 1541 General Contractors-Industrial Buildings & Warehouses

SIC 1542 General Contractor-Nonresidential Buildings, Other than Industrial Buildings & Warehouses

23411 Highway & Street Construction

SIC 1611 Highway & Street Construction, Except Elevated Highways

23412 Bridge & Tunnel Construction

SIC 1622 Bridge, Tunnel, & Elevated Highway Construction

2349 Other Heavy Construction

23491 Water, Sewer, & Pipeline Construction

SIC 1623 Water, Sewer, Pipeline, & Communications & Power Line Construction

23492 Power & Communication Transmission Line Construction

SIC 1623 Water, Sewer, Pipelines, & Communications & Power Line Construction

23493 Industrial Nonbuilding Structure Construction

SIC 1629 Heavy Construction, nec

23499 All Other Heavy Construction

SIC 1629 Heavy Construction, nec

SIC 7353 Construction Equipment Rental & Leasing

23511 Plumbing, Heating & Air-Conditioning Contractors

SIC 1711 Plumbing, Heating & Air-Conditioning

23521 Painting & Wall Covering Contractors

SIC 1721 Painting & Paper Hanging

SIC 1799 Special Trade Contractors, nec

23531 Electrical Contractors

SIC 1731 Electrical Work

23541 Masonry & Stone Contractors

SIC 1741 Masonry, Stone Setting & Other Stone Work

23542 Drywall, Plastering, Acoustical & Insulation Contractors

SIC 1742 Plastering, Drywall, Acoustical, & Insulation Work

SIC 1743 Terrazzo, Tile, Marble & Mosaic work

SIC 1771 Concrete Work

23543 Tile, Marble, Terrazzo & Mosaic Contractors

SIC 1743 Terrazzo, Tile, Marble, & Mosaic Work

23551 Carpentry Contractors

SIC 1751 Carpentry Work

23552 Floor Laying & Other Floor Contractors

SIC 1752 Floor Laying & Other Floor Work, nec

23561 Roofing, Siding & Sheet Metal Contractors

SIC 1761 Roofing, Siding, & Sheet Metal Work

23571 Concrete Contractors

SIC 1771 Concrete Work

23581 Water Well Drilling Contractors

SIC 1781 Water Well Drilling

23591 Structural Steel Erection Contractors

SIC 1791 Structural Steel Erection

23592 Glass & Glazing Contractors

SIC 1793 Glass & Glazing Work

SIC 1799 Specialty Trade Contractors, nec

23593 Excavation Contractors

SIC 1794 Excavation Work

23594 Wrecking & Demolition Contractors

SIC 1795 Wrecking & Demolition Work

23595 Building Equipment & Other Machinery Installation Contractors

SIC 1796 Installation of Erection of Building Equipment, nec

23599 All Other Special Trade Contractors

SIC 1799 Special Trade Contractors, nec

FOOD MANUFACTURING

311111 Dog & Cat Food Manufacturing

SIC 2047 Dog & Cat Food

311119 Other Animal Food Manufacturing

SIC 2048 Prepared Feeds & Feed Ingredients for Animals & Fowls, Except Dogs & Cats

311211 Flour Milling

SIC 2034 Dehydrated Fruits, Vegetables & Soup Mixes

SIC 2041 Flour & Other Grain Mill Products

311212 Rice Milling

SIC 2044 Rice Milling

311213 Malt Manufacturing

SIC 2083 Malt

311221 Wet Corn Milling

SIC 2046 Wet Corn Milling

311222 Soybean Processing

SIC 2075 Soybean Oil Mills

SIC 2079 Shortening, Table Oils, Margarine, & Other Edible Fats & Oils, nec

311223 Other Oilseed Processing

SIC 2074 Cottonseed Oil Mills

SIC 2079 Shortening, Table Oils, Margarine & Other Edible Fats & Oils, nec

SIC 2076 Vegetable Oil Mills, Except Corn, Cottonseed, & Soybean

311225 Edible Fats & Oils Manufacturing

SIC 2077 Animal & Marine Fats & Oil, nec

SIC 2074 Cottonseed Oil Mills

SIC 2075 Soybean Oil Mills

SIC 2076 Vegetable Oil Mills, Except Corn, Cottonseed, &
Soybean
SIC 2079 Shortening, Table Oils, Margarine, & Other Edible
Fats & Oils, nec
31123 Breakfast Cereal Manufacturing
SIC 2043 Cereal Breakfast Foods
311311 Sugarcane Mills
SIC 2061 Cane Sugar, Except Refining
311312 Cane Sugar Refining
SIC 2062 Cane Sugar Refining
311313 Beet Sugar Manufacturing
SIC 2063 Beet Sugar
**31132 Chocolate & Confectionery Manufacturing from Cacao
Beans**
SIC 2066 Chocolate & Cocoa Products
31133 Confectionery Manufacturing from Purchased Chocolate
SIC 2064 Candy & Other Confectionery Products
31134 Non-Chocolate Confectionery Manufacturing
SIC 2064 Candy & Other Confectionery Products
SIC 2067 Chewing Gum
SIC 2099 Food Preparations, nec
311411 Frozen Fruit, Juice & Vegetable Processing
SIC 2037 Frozen Fruits, Fruit Juices, & Vegetables
311412 Frozen Specialty Food Manufacturing
SIC 2038 Frozen Specialties, NEC
311421 Fruit & Vegetable Canning
SIC 2033 Canned Fruits, Vegetables, Preserves, Jams, & Jellies
SIC 2035 Pickled Fruits & Vegetables, Vegetable Sauces, &
Seasonings & Salad Dressings
311422 Specialty Canning
SIC 2032 Canned Specialties
311423 Dried & Dehydrated Food Manufacturing
SIC 2034 Dried & Dehydrated Fruits, Vegetables & Soup
Mixes
SIC 2099 Food Preparation, nec
311511 Fluid Milk Manufacturing
SIC 2026 Fluid Milk
311512 Creamery Butter Manufacturing
SIC 2021 Creamery Butter
311513 Cheese Manufacturing
SIC 2022 Natural, Processed, & Imitation Cheese
311514 Dry, Condensed, & Evaporated Milk Manufacturing
SIC 2023 Dry, Condensed & Evaporated Dairy Products
31152 Ice Cream & Frozen Dessert Manufacturing
SIC 2024 Ice Cream & Frozen Desserts
311611 Animal Slaughtering
SIC 0751 Livestock Services, Except Veterinary
SIC 2011 Meat Packing Plants
SIC 2048 Prepared Feeds & Feed Ingredients for Animals &
Fowls, Except Dogs & Cats
311612 Meat Processed from Carcasses
SIC 2013 Sausages & Other Prepared Meats
SIC 5147 Meat & Meat Products
311613 Rendering & Meat By-product Processing
SIC 2077 Animal & Marine Fats & Oils
311615 Poultry Processing
SIC 2015 Poultry Slaughtering & Processing
311711 Seafood Canning
SIC 2077 Animal & Marine Fats & Oils
SIC 2091 Canned & Cured Fish & Seafood
311712 Fresh & Frozen Seafood Processing
SIC 2077 Animal & Marine Fats & Oils
SIC 2092 Prepared Fresh or Frozen Fish & Seafood

311811 Retail Bakeries
SIC 5461 Retail Bakeries
311812 Commercial Bakeries
SIC 2051 Bread & Other Bakery Products, Except Cookies &
Crackers
SIC 2052 Cookies & Crackers
311813 Frozen Bakery Product Manufacturing
SIC 2053 Frozen Bakery Products, Except Bread
311821 Cookie & Cracker Manufacturing
SIC 2052 Cookies & Crackers
**311822 Flour Mixes & Dough Manufacturing from Purchased
Flour**
SIC 2045 Prepared Flour Mixes & Doughs
311823 Pasta Manufacturing
SIC 2098 Macaroni, Spaghetti, Vermicelli & Noodles
31183 Tortilla Manufacturing
SIC 2099 Food Preparations, nec
311911 Roasted Nuts & Peanut Butter Manufacturing
SIC 2068 Salted & Roasted Nuts & Seeds
SIC 2099 Food Preparations, nec
311919 Other Snack Food Manufacturing
SIC 2052 Cookies & Crackers
SIC 2096 Potato Chips, Corn Chips, & Similar Snacks
31192 Coffee & Tea Manufacturing
SIC 2043 Cereal Breakfast Foods
SIC 2095 Roasted Coffee
SIC 2099 Food Preparations, nec
31193 Flavoring Syrup & Concentrate Manufacturing
SIC 2087 Flavoring Extracts & Flavoring Syrups
**311941 Mayonnaise, Dressing & Other Prepared Sauce
Manufacturing**
SIC 2035 Pickled Fruits & Vegetables, Vegetable Seasonings, &
Sauces & Salad Dressings
SIC 2099 Food Preparations, nec
311942 Spice & Extract Manufacturing
SIC 2087 Flavoring Extracts & Flavoring Syrups
SIC 2095 Roasted Coffee
SIC 2099 Food Preparations, nec
SIC 2899 Chemical Preparations, nec
311991 Perishable Prepared Food Manufacturing
SIC 2099 Food Preparations, nec
311999 All Other Miscellaneous Food Manufacturing
SIC 2015 Poultry Slaughtering & Processing
SIC 2032 Canned Specialties
SIC 2087 Flavoring Extracts & Flavoring Syrups
SIC 2099 Food Preparations, nec

BEVERAGE & TOBACCO PRODUCT
MANUFACTURING

312111 Soft Drink Manufacturing
SIC 2086 Bottled & Canned Soft Drinks & Carbonated Water
312112 Bottled Water Manufacturing
SIC 2086 Bottled & Canned Soft Drinks & Carbonated Water
312113 Ice Manufacturing
SIC 2097 Manufactured Ice
31212 Breweries
SIC 2082 Malt Beverages
31213 Wineries
SIC 2084 Wines, Brandy, & Brandy Spirits
31214 Distilleries
SIC 2085 Distilled & Blended Liquors

31221 Tobacco Stemming & Redrying
SIC 2141 Tobacco Stemming & Redrying
312221 Cigarette Manufacturing
SIC 2111 Cigarettes
312229 Other Tobacco Product Manufacturing
SIC 2121 Cigars
SIC 2131 Chewing & Smoking Tobacco & Snuff
SIC 2141 Tobacco Stemming & Redrying

TEXTILE MILLS

313111 Yarn Spinning Mills
SIC 2281 Yarn Spinning Mills
SIC 2299 Textile Goods, nec
313112 Yarn Texturing, Throwing & Twisting Mills
SIC 2282 Yarn Texturing, Throwing, Winding Mills
313113 Thread Mills
SIC 2284 Thread Mills
SIC 2299 Textile Goods, NEC
31321 Broadwoven Fabric Mills
SIC 2211 Broadwoven Fabric Mills, Cotton
SIC 2221 Broadwoven Fabric Mills, Manmade Fiber & Silk
SIC 2231 Broadwoven Fabric Mills, Wool
SIC 2299 Textile Goods, nec
313221 Narrow Fabric Mills
SIC 2241 Narrow Fabric & Other Smallware Mills: Cotton,
　　　　 Wool, Silk & Manmade Fiber
SIC 2299 Textile Goods, nec
313222 Schiffli Machine Embroidery
SIC 2397 Schiffli Machine Embroideries
31323 Nonwoven Fabric Mills
SIC 2297 Nonwoven Fabrics
SIC 2299 Textile Goods, nec
313241 Weft Knit Fabric Mills
SIC 2257 Weft Knit Fabric Mills
SIC 2259 Knitting Mills nec
313249 Other Knit Fabric & Lace Mills
SIC 2258 Lace & Warp Knit Fabric Mills
SIC 2259 Knitting Mills nec
313311 Broadwoven Fabric Finishing Mills
SIC 2231 Broadwoven Fabric Mills, Wool
SIC 2261 Finishers of Broadwoven Fabrics of Cotton
SIC 2262 Finishers of Broadwoven Fabrics of Manmade Fiber
　　　　 & Silk
SIC 2269 Finishers of Textiles, nec
SIC 5131 Piece Goods & Notions
313312 Textile & Fabric Finishing Mills
SIC 2231 Broadwoven Fabric Mills, Wool
SIC 2257 Weft Knit Fabric Mills
SIC 2258 Lace & Warp Knit Fabric Mills
SIC 2269 Finishers of Textiles, nec
SIC 2282 Yarn Texturizing, Throwing, Twisting, & Winding
　　　　 Mills
SIC 2284 Thread Mills
SIC 2299 Textile Goods, nec
SIC 5131 Piece Goods & Notions
31332 Fabric Coating Mills
SIC 2295 Coated Fabrics, Not Rubberized
SIC 3069 Fabricated Rubber Products, nec

TEXTILE PRODUCT MILLS

31411 Carpet & Rug Mills
SIC 2273 Carpets & Rugs
314121 Curtain & Drapery Mills
SIC 2391 Curtains & Draperies
SIC 5714 Drapery, Curtain, & Upholstery Stores
314129 Other Household Textile Product Mills
SIC 2392 Housefurnishings, Except Curtains & Draperies
314911 Textile Bag Mills
SIC 2392 Housefurnishings, Except Curtains & Draperies
SIC 2393 Textile Bags
314912 Canvas & Related Product Mills
SIC 2394 Canvas & Related Products
314991 Rope, Cordage & Twine Mills
SIC 2298 Cordage & Twine
314992 Tire Cord & Tire Fabric Mills
SIC 2296 Tire Cord & Fabrics
314999 All Other Miscellaneous Textile Product Mills
SIC 2299 Textile Goods, nec
SIC 2395 Pleating, Decorative & Novelty Stitching, & Tucking
　　　　 for the Trade
SIC 2396 Automotive Trimmings, Apparel Findings, & Related
　　　　 Products
SIC 2399 Fabricated Textile Products, nec

APPAREL MANUFACTURING

315111 Sheer Hosiery Mills
SIC 2251 Women's Full-Length & Knee-Length Hosiery,
　　　　 Except socks
SIC 2252 Hosiery, nec
315119 Other Hosiery & Sock Mills
SIC 2252 Hosiery, nec
315191 Outerwear Knitting Mills
SIC 2253 Knit Outerwear Mills
SIC 2259 Knitting Mills, nec
315192 Underwear & Nightwear Knitting Mills
SIC 2254 Knit Underwear & Nightwear Mills
SIC 2259 Knitting Mills, nec
315211 Men's & Boys' Cut & Sew Apparel Contractors
SIC 2311 Men's & Boys' Suits, Coats, & Overcoats
SIC 2321 Men's & Boys' Shirts, Except Work Shirts
SIC 2322 Men's & Boys' Underwear & Nightwear
SIC 2325 Men's & Boys' Trousers & Slacks
SIC 2326 Men's & Boys' Work Clothing
SIC 2329 Men's & Boys' Clothing, nec
SIC 2341 Women's, Misses', Children's, & Infants' Underwear
　　　　 & Nightwear
SIC 2361 Girls', Children's, & Infants' Dresses, Blouses &
　　　　 Shirts
SIC 2369 Girls', Children's, & Infants' Outerwear, nec
SIC 2384 Robes & Dressing Gowns
SIC 2385 Waterproof Outerwear
SIC 2389 Apparel & Accessories, nec
SIC 2395 Pleating, Decorative & Novelty Stitching, & Tucking
　　　　 for the Trade
315212 Women's & Girls' Cut & Sew Apparel Contractors
SIC 2331 Women's, Misses', & Juniors' Blouses & Shirts
SIC 2335 Women's, Misses' & Juniors' Dresses
SIC 2337 Women's, Misses', & Juniors' Suits, Skirts, & Coats
SIC 2339 Women's, Misses', & Juniors' Outerwear, nec

SIC 2341 Women's, Misses', Children's, & Infants' Underwear & Nightwear

SIC 2342 Brassieres, Girdles, & Allied Garments

SIC 2361 Girls', Children's, & Infants' Dresses, Blouses, & Shirts

SIC 2369 Girls', Children's, & Infants' Outerwear, nec

SIC 2384 Robes & Dressing Gowns

SIC 2385 Waterproof Outerwear

SIC 2389 Apparel & Accessories, nec

SIC 2395 Pleating, Decorative & Novelty Stitching, & Tucking for the Trade

315221 Men's & Boys' Cut & Sew Underwear & Nightwear Manufacturing

SIC 2322 Men's & Boys' Underwear & Nightwear

SIC 2341 Women's, Misses', Children's, & Infants' Underwear & Nightwear

SIC 2369 Girls', Children's, & Infants' Outerwear, nec

SIC 2384 Robes & Dressing Gowns

315222 Men's & Boys' Cut & Sew Suit, Coat & Overcoat Manufacturing

SIC 2311 Men's & Boys' Suits, Coats, & Overcoats

SIC 2369 Girls', Children's, & Infants' Outerwear, nec

SIC 2385 Waterproof Outerwear

315223 Men's & Boys' Cut & Sew Shirt Manufacturing

SIC 2321 Men's & Boys' Shirts, Except Work Shirts

SIC 2361 Girls', Children's, & Infants' Dresses, Blouses, & Shirts

315224 Men's & Boys' Cut & Sew Trouser, Slack & Jean Manufacturing

SIC 2325 Men's & Boys' Trousers & Slacks

SIC 2369 Girls', Children's, & Infants' Outerwear, NEC

315225 Men's & Boys' Cut & Sew Work Clothing Manufacturing

SIC 2326 Men's & Boys' Work Clothing

315228 Men's & Boys' Cut & Sew Other Outerwear Manufacturing

SIC 2329 Men's & Boys' Clothing, nec

SIC 2369 Girls', Children's, & Infants' Outerwear, nec

SIC 2385 Waterproof Outerwear

315231 Women's & Girls' Cut & Sew Lingerie, Loungewear & Nightwear Manufacturing

SIC 2341 Women's, Misses', Children's, & Infants' Underwear & Nightwear

SIC 2342 Brassieres, Girdles, & Allied Garments

SIC 2369 Girls', Children's, & Infants' Outerwear, nec

SIC 2384 Robes & Dressing Gowns

SIC 2389 Apparel & Accessories, NEC

315232 Women's & Girls' Cut & Sew Blouse & Shirt Manufacturing

SIC 2331 Women's, Misses', & Juniors' Blouses & Shirts

SIC 2361 Girls', Children's, & Infants' Dresses, Blouses & Shirts

315233 Women's & Girls' Cut & Sew Dress Manufacturing

SIC 2335 Women's, Misses', & Juniors' Dresses

SIC 2361 Girls', Children's, & Infants' Dresses, Blouses & Shirts

315234 Women's & Girls' Cut & Sew Suit, Coat, Tailored Jacket & Skirt Manufacturing

SIC 2337 Women's, Misses', & Juniors' Suits, Skirts, & Coats

SIC 2369 Girls', Children's, & Infants' Outerwear, nec

SIC 2385 Waterproof Outerwear

315238 Women's & Girls' Cut & Sew Other Outerwear Manufacturing

SIC 2339 Women's, Misses', & Juniors' Outerwear, nec

SIC 2369 Girls', Children's, & Infants' Outerwear, nec

SIC 2385 Waterproof Outerwear

315291 Infants' Cut & Sew Apparel Manufacturing

SIC 2341 Women's, Misses', Children's, & Infants' Underwear & Nightwear

SIC 2361 Girls', Children's, & Infants' Dresses, Blouses, & Shirts

SIC 2369 Girls', Children's, & Infants' Outerwear, nec

SIC 2385 Waterproof Outerwear

315292 Fur & Leather Apparel Manufacturing

SIC 2371 Fur Goods

SIC 2386 Leather & Sheep-lined Clothing

315299 All Other Cut & Sew Apparel Manufacturing

SIC 2329 Men's & Boys' Outerwear, nec

SIC 2339 Women's, Misses', & Juniors' Outerwear, nec

SIC 2389 Apparel & Accessories, nec

315991 Hat, Cap & Millinery Manufacturing

SIC 2353 Hats, Caps, & Millinery

315992 Glove & Mitten Manufacturing

SIC 2381 Dress & Work Gloves, Except Knit & All-Leather

SIC 3151 Leather Gloves & Mittens

315993 Men's & Boys' Neckwear Manufacturing

SIC 2323 Men's & Boys' Neckwear

315999 Other Apparel Accessories & Other Apparel Manufacturing

SIC 2339 Women's, Misses', & Juniors' Outerwear, nec

SIC 2385 Waterproof Outerwear

SIC 2387 Apparel Belts

SIC 2389 Apparel & Accessories, nec

SIC 2396 Automotive Trimmings, Apparel Findings, & Related Products

SIC 2399 Fabricated Textile Products, nec

LEATHER & ALLIED PRODUCT MANUFACTURING

31611 Leather & Hide Tanning & Finishing

SIC 3111 Leather Tanning & Finishing

SIC 3999 Manufacturing Industries, nec

316211 Rubber & Plastics Footwear Manufacturing

SIC 3021 Rubber & Plastics Footwear

316212 House Slipper Manufacturing

SIC 3142 House Slippers

316213 Men's Footwear Manufacturing

SIC 3143 Men's Footwear, Except Athletic

316214 Women's Footwear Manufacturing

SIC 3144 Women's Footwear, Except Athletic

316219 Other Footwear Manufacturing

SIC 3149 Footwear Except Rubber, NEC

316991 Luggage Manufacturing

SIC 3161 Luggage

316992 Women's Handbag & Purse Manufacturing

SIC 3171 Women's Handbags & Purses

316993 Personal Leather Good Manufacturing

SIC 3172 Personal Leather Goods, Except Women's Handbags & Purses

316999 All Other Leather Good Manufacturing

SIC 3131 Boot & Shoe Cut Stock & Findings

SIC 3199 Leather Goods, nec

WOOD PRODUCT MANUFACTURING

321113 Sawmills
SIC 2421 Sawmills & Planing Mills, General
SIC 2429 Special Product Sawmills, nec
321114 Wood Preservation
SIC 2491 Wood Preserving
321211 Hardwood Veneer & Plywood Manufacturing
SIC 2435 Hardwood Veneer & Plywood
321212 Softwood Veneer & Plywood Manufacturing
SIC 2436 Softwood Veneer & Plywood
321213 Engineered Wood Member Manufacturing
SIC 2439 Structural Wood Members, nec
321214 Truss Manufacturing
SIC 2439 Structural Wood Members, nec
321219 Reconstituted Wood Product Manufacturing
SIC 2493 Reconstituted Wood Products
321911 Wood Window & Door Manufacturing
SIC 2431 Millwork
321912 Hardwood Dimension Mills
SIC 2426 Hardwood Dimension & Flooring Mills
321913 Softwood Cut Stock, Resawing Lumber, & Planing
SIC 2421 Sawmills & Planing Mills, General
SIC 2429 Special Product Sawmills, nec
SIC 2439 Structural Wood Members, nec
321914 Other Millwork
SIC 2421 Sawmills & Planing Mills, General
SIC 2426 Hardwood Dimension & Flooring Mills
SIC 2431 Millwork
32192   Wood Container & Pallet Manufacturing
SIC 2441 Nailed & Lock Corner Wood Boxes & Shook
SIC 2448 Wood Pallets & Skids
SIC 2449 Wood Containers, NEC
SIC 2499 Wood Products, nec
321991 Manufactured Home Manufacturing
SIC 2451 Mobile Homes
321992 Prefabricated Wood Building Manufacturing
SIC 2452 Prefabricated Wood Buildings & Components
321999 All Other Miscellaneous Wood Product Manufacturing
SIC 2426 Hardwood Dimension & Flooring Mills
SIC 2499 Wood Products, nec
SIC 3131 Boot & Shoe Cut Stock & Findings
SIC 3999 Manufacturing Industries, nec
SIC 2421 Sawmills & Planing Mills, General
SIC 2429 Special Product Sawmills, nec

PAPER MANUFACTURING

32211   Pulp Mills
SIC 2611 Pulp Mills
322121 Paper Mills
SIC 2611 Pulp Mills
SIC 2621 Paper Mills
322122 Newsprint Mills
SIC 2621 Paper Mills
32213   Paperboard Mills
SIC 2611 Pulp Mills
SIC 2631 Paperboard Mills
322211 Corrugated & Solid Fiber Box Manufacturing
SIC 2653 Corrugated & Solid Fiber Boxes
322212 Folding Paperboard Box Manufacturing
SIC 2657 Folding Paperboard Boxes, Including Sanitary

322213 Setup Paperboard Box Manufacturing
SIC 2652 Setup Paperboard Boxes
322214 Fiber Can, Tube, Drum, & Similar Products Manufacturing
SIC 2655 Fiber Cans, Tubes, Drums, & Similar Products
322215 Non-Folding Sanitary Food Container Manufacturing
SIC 2656 Sanitary Food Containers, Except Folding
SIC 2679 Converted Paper & Paperboard Products, NEC
322221 Coated & Laminated Packaging Paper & Plastics Film Manufacturing
SIC 2671 Packaging Paper & Plastics Film, Coated & Laminated
322222 Coated & Laminated Paper Manufacturing
SIC 2672 Coated & Laminated Paper, nec
SIC 2679 Converted Paper & Paperboard Products, nec
322223 Plastics, Foil, & Coated Paper Bag Manufacturing
SIC 2673 Plastics, Foil, & Coated Paper Bags
322224 Uncoated Paper & Multiwall Bag Manufacturing
SIC 2674 Uncoated Paper & Multiwall Bags
322225 Laminated Aluminum Foil Manufacturing for Flexible Packaging Uses
SIC 3497 Metal Foil & Leaf
322231 Die-Cut Paper & Paperboard Office Supplies Manufacturing
SIC 2675 Die-Cut Paper & Paperboard & Cardboard
SIC 2679 Converted Paper & Paperboard Products, nec
322232 Envelope Manufacturing
SIC 2677 Envelopes
322233 Stationery, Tablet, & Related Product Manufacturing
SIC 2678 Stationery, Tablets, & Related Products
322291 Sanitary Paper Product Manufacturing
SIC 2676 Sanitary Paper Products
322292 Surface-Coated Paperboard Manufacturing
SIC 2675 Die-Cut Paper & Paperboard & Cardboard
322298 All Other Converted Paper Product Manufacturing
SIC 2675 Die-Cut Paper & Paperboard & Cardboard
SIC 2679 Converted Paper & Paperboard Products, NEC

PRINTING & RELATED SUPPORT ACTIVITIES

323110 Commercial Lithographic Printing
SIC 2752 Commercial Printing, Lithographic
SIC 2771 Greeting Cards
SIC 2782 Blankbooks, Loose-leaf Binders & Devices
SIC 3999 Manufacturing Industries, nec
323111 Commercial Gravure Printing
SIC 2754 Commercial Printing, Gravure
SIC 2771 Greeting Cards
SIC 2782 Blankbooks, Loose-leaf Binders & Devices
SIC 3999 Manufacturing Industries, nec
323112 Commercial Flexographic Printing
SIC 2759 Commercial Printing, NEC
SIC 2771 Greeting Cards
SIC 2782 Blankbooks, Loose-leaf Binders & Devices
SIC 3999 Manufacturing Industries, nec
323113 Commercial Screen Printing
SIC 2396 Automotive Trimmings, Apparel Findings, & Related Products
SIC 2759 Commercial Printing, nec
SIC 2771 Greeting Cards
SIC 2782 Blankbooks, Loose-leaf Binders & Devices
SIC 3999 Manufacturing Industries, nec

323114 Quick Printing
SIC 2752 Commercial Printing, Lithographic
SIC 2759 Commercial Printing, nec
323115 Digital Printing
SIC 2759 Commercial Printing, nec
323116 Manifold Business Form Printing
SIC 2761 Manifold Business Forms
323117 Book Printing
SIC 2732 Book Printing
323118 Blankbook, Loose-leaf Binder & Device Manufacturing
SIC 2782 Blankbooks, Loose-leaf Binders & Devices
323119 Other Commercial Printing
SIC 2759 Commercial Printing, nec
SIC 2771 Greeting Cards
SIC 2782 Blankbooks, Loose-leaf Binders & Devices
SIC 3999 Manufacturing Industries, nec
323121 Tradebinding & Related Work
SIC 2789 Bookbinding & Related Work
323122 Prepress Services
SIC 2791 Typesetting
SIC 2796 Platemaking & Related Services

PETROLEUM & COAL PRODUCTS MANUFACTURING

32411   Petroleum Refineries
SIC 2911 Petroleum Refining
324121 Asphalt Paving Mixture & Block Manufacturing
SIC 2951 Asphalt Paving Mixtures & Blocks
324122 Asphalt Shingle & Coating Materials Manufacturing
SIC 2952 Asphalt Felts & Coatings
324191 Petroleum Lubricating Oil & Grease Manufacturing
SIC 2992 Lubricating Oils & Greases
324199 All Other Petroleum & Coal Products Manufacturing
SIC 2999 Products of Petroleum & Coal, nec
SIC 3312 Blast Furnaces & Steel Mills

CHEMICAL MANUFACTURING

32511   Petrochemical Manufacturing
SIC 2865 Cyclic Organic Crudes & Intermediates, & Organic
         Dyes & Pigments
SIC 2869 Industrial Organic Chemicals, nec
32512   Industrial Gas Manufacturing
SIC 2813 Industrial Gases
SIC 2869 Industrial Organic Chemicals, nec
325131 Inorganic Dye & Pigment Manufacturing
SIC 2816 Inorganic Pigments
SIC 2819 Industrial Inorganic Chemicals, nec
325132 Organic Dye & Pigment Manufacturing
SIC 2865 Cyclic Organic Crudes & Intermediates, & Organic
         Dyes & Pigments
325181 Alkalies & Chlorine Manufacturing
SIC 2812 Alkalies & Chlorine
325182 Carbon Black Manufacturing
SIC 2816 Inorganic pigments
SIC 2895 Carbon Black
325188 All Other Basic Inorganic Chemical Manufacturing
SIC 2819 Industrial Inorganic Chemicals, nec
SIC 2869 Industrial Organic Chemicals, nec

325191 Gum & Wood Chemical Manufacturing
SIC 2861 Gum & Wood Chemicals
325192 Cyclic Crude & Intermediate Manufacturing
SIC 2865 Cyclic Organic Crudes & Intermediates & Organic
         Dyes & Pigments
325193 Ethyl Alcohol Manufacturing
SIC 2869 Industrial Organic Chemicals
325199 All Other Basic Organic Chemical Manufacturing
SIC 2869 Industrial Organic Chemicals, nec
SIC 2899 Chemical & Chemical Preparations, nec
325211 Plastics Material & Resin Manufacturing
SIC 2821 Plastics Materials, Synthetic & Resins, &
         Nonvulcanizable Elastomers
325212 Synthetic Rubber Manufacturing
SIC 2822 Synthetic Rubber
325221 Cellulosic Manmade Fiber Manufacturing
SIC 2823 Cellulosic Manmade Fibers
325222 Noncellulosic Organic Fiber Manufacturing
SIC 2824 Manmade Organic Fibers, Except Cellulosic
325311 Nitrogenous Fertilizer Manufacturing
SIC 2873 Nitrogenous Fertilizers
325312 Phosphatic Fertilizer Manufacturing
SIC 2874 Phosphatic Fertilizers
325314 Fertilizer Manufacturing
SIC 2875 Fertilizers, Mixing Only
32532   Pesticide & Other Agricultural Chemical Manufacturing
SIC 2879 Pesticides & Agricultural Chemicals, nec
325411 Medicinal & Botanical Manufacturing
SIC 2833 Medicinal Chemicals & Botanical Products
325412 Pharmaceutical Preparation Manufacturing
SIC 2834 Pharmaceutical Preparations
SIC 2835 In-Vitro & In-Vivo Diagnostic Substances
325413 In-Vitro Diagnostic Substance Manufacturing
SIC 2835 In-Vitro & In-Vivo Diagnostic Substances
325414 Biological Product Manufacturing
SIC 2836 Biological Products, Except Diagnostic Substance
32551   Paint & Coating Manufacturing
SIC 2851 Paints, Varnishes, Lacquers, Enamels & Allied
         Products
SIC 2899 Chemicals & Chemical Preparations, nec
32552   Adhesive & Sealant Manufacturing
SIC 2891 Adhesives & Sealants
325611 Soap & Other Detergent Manufacturing
SIC 2841 Soaps & Other Detergents, Except Specialty Cleaners
SIC 2844 Toilet Preparations
325612 Polish & Other Sanitation Good Manufacturing
SIC 2842 Specialty Cleaning, Polishing, & Sanitary Preparations
325613 Surface Active Agent Manufacturing
SIC 2843 Surface Active Agents, Finishing Agents, Sulfonated
         Oils, & Assistants
32562   Toilet Preparation Manufacturing
SIC 2844 Perfumes, Cosmetics, & Other Toilet Preparations
32591   Printing Ink Manufacturing
SIC 2893 Printing Ink
32592   Explosives Manufacturing
SIC 2892 Explosives
325991 Custom Compounding of Purchased Resin
SIC 3087 Custom Compounding of Purchased Plastics Resin
**325992 Photographic Film, Paper, Plate & Chemical
         Manufacturing**
SIC 3861 Photographic Equipment & Supplies

325998 All Other Miscellaneous Chemical Product Manufacturing
SIC 2819 Industrial Inorganic Chemicals, nec
SIC 2899 Chemicals & Chemical Preparations, nec
SIC 3952 Lead Pencils & Art Goods
SIC 3999 Manufacturing Industries, nec

PLASTICS & RUBBER PRODUCTS MANUFACTURING

326111 Unsupported Plastics Bag Manufacturing
SIC 2673 Plastics, Foil, & Coated Paper Bags
326112 Unsupported Plastics Packaging Film & Sheet Manufacturing
SIC 2671 Packaging Paper & Plastics Film, Coated, & Laminated
326113 Unsupported Plastics Film & Sheet Manufacturing
SIC 3081 Unsupported Plastics Film & Sheets
326121 Unsupported Plastics Profile Shape Manufacturing
SIC 3082 Unsupported Plastics Profile Shapes
SIC 3089 Plastics Product, nec
326122 Plastics Pipe & Pipe Fitting Manufacturing
SIC 3084 Plastics Pipe
SIC 3089 Plastics Products, nec
32613 Laminated Plastics Plate, Sheet & Shape Manufacturing
SIC 3083 Laminated Plastics Plate, Sheet & Profile Shapes
32614 Polystyrene Foam Product Manufacturing
SIC 3086 Plastics Foam Products
32615 Urethane & Other Foam Product Manufacturing
SIC 3086 Plastics Foam Products
32616 Plastics Bottle Manufacturing
SIC 3085 Plastics Bottles
326191 Plastics Plumbing Fixture Manufacturing
SIC 3088 Plastics Plumbing Fixtures
326192 Resilient Floor Covering Manufacturing
SIC 3069 Fabricated Rubber Products, nec
SIC 3996 Linoleum, Asphalted-Felt-Base, & Other Hard Surface Floor Coverings, nec
326199 All Other Plastics Product Manufacturing
SIC 3089 Plastics Products, nec
SIC 3999 Manufacturing Industries, nec
326211 Tire Manufacturing
SIC 3011 Tires & Inner Tubes
326212 Tire Retreading
SIC 7534 Tire Retreading & Repair Shops
32622 Rubber & Plastics Hoses & Belting Manufacturing
SIC 3052 Rubber & Plastics Hose & Belting
326291 Rubber Product Manufacturing for Mechanical Use
SIC 3061 Molded, Extruded, & Lathe-Cut Mechanical Rubber Goods
326299 All Other Rubber Product Manufacturing
SIC 3069 Fabricated Rubber Products, nec

NONMETALLIC MINERAL PRODUCT MANUFACTURING

327111 Vitreous China Plumbing Fixture & China & Earthenware Fittings & Bathroom Accessories Manufacturing
SIC 3261 Vitreous China Plumbing Fixtures & China & Earthenware Fittings & Bathroom Accessories

327112 Vitreous China, Fine Earthenware & Other Pottery Product Manufacturing
SIC 3262 Vitreous China Table & Kitchen Articles
SIC 3263 Fine Earthenware Table & Kitchen Articles
SIC 3269 Pottery Products, nec
327113 Porcelain Electrical Supply Manufacturing
SIC 3264 Porcelain Electrical Supplies
327121 Brick & Structural Clay Tile Manufacturing
SIC 3251 Brick & Structural Clay Tile
327122 Ceramic Wall & Floor Tile Manufacturing
SIC 3253 Ceramic Wall & Floor Tile
327123 Other Structural Clay Product Manufacturing
SIC 3259 Structural Clay Products, nec
327124 Clay Refractory Manufacturing
SIC 3255 Clay Refractories
327125 Nonclay Refractory Manufacturing
SIC 3297 Nonclay Refractories
327211 Flat Glass Manufacturing
SIC 3211 Flat Glass
327212 Other Pressed & Blown Glass & Glassware Manufacturing
SIC 3229 Pressed & Blown Glass & Glassware, nec
327213 Glass Container Manufacturing
SIC 3221 Glass Containers
327215 Glass Product Manufacturing Made of Purchased Glass
SIC 3231 Glass Products Made of Purchased Glass
32731 Hydraulic Cement Manufacturing
SIC 3241 Cement, Hydraulic
32732 Ready-Mix Concrete Manufacturing
SIC 3273 Ready-Mixed Concrete
327331 Concrete Block & Brick Manufacturing
SIC 3271 Concrete Block & Brick
327332 Concrete Pipe Manufacturing
SIC 3272 Concrete Products, Except Block & Brick
32739 Other Concrete Product Manufacturing
SIC 3272 Concrete Products, Except Block & Brick
32741 Lime Manufacturing
SIC 3274 Lime
32742 Gypsum & Gypsum Product Manufacturing
SIC 3275 Gypsum Products
SIC 3299 Nonmetallic Mineral Products, nec
32791 Abrasive Product Manufacturing
SIC 3291 Abrasive Products
327991 Cut Stone & Stone Product Manufacturing
SIC 3281 Cut Stone & Stone Products
327992 Ground or Treated Mineral & Earth Manufacturing
SIC 3295 Minerals & Earths, Ground or Otherwise Treated
327993 Mineral Wool Manufacturing
SIC 3296 Mineral Wool
327999 All Other Miscellaneous Nonmetallic Mineral Product Manufacturing
SIC 3272 Concrete Products, Except Block & Brick
SIC 3292 Asbestos Products
SIC 3299 Nonmetallic Mineral Products, nec

PRIMARY METAL MANUFACTURING

331111 Iron & Steel Mills
SIC 3312 Steel Works, Blast Furnaces , & Rolling Mills
SIC 3399 Primary Metal Products, nec
331112 Electrometallurgical Ferroalloy Product Manufacturing
SIC 3313 Electrometallurgical Products, Except Steel

33121 Iron & Steel Pipes & Tubes Manufacturing from Purchased Steel
SIC 3317 Steel Pipe & Tubes

331221 Cold-Rolled Steel Shape Manufacturing
SIC 3316 Cold-Rolled Steel Sheet, Strip & Bars

331222 Steel Wire Drawing
SIC 3315 Steel Wiredrawing & Steel Nails & Spikes

331311 Alumina Refining
SIC 2819 Industrial Inorganic Chemicals, nec

331312 Primary Aluminum Production
SIC 3334 Primary Production of Aluminum

331314 Secondary Smelting & Alloying of Aluminum
SIC 3341 Secondary Smelting & Refining of Nonferrous Metals
SIC 3399 Primary Metal Products, nec

331315 Aluminum Sheet, Plate & Foil Manufacturing
SIC 3353 Aluminum Sheet, Plate, & Foil

331316 Aluminum Extruded Product Manufacturing
SIC 3354 Aluminum Extruded Products

331319 Other Aluminum Rolling & Drawing
SIC 3355 Aluminum Rolling & Drawing, nec
SIC 3357 Drawing & Insulating of Nonferrous Wire

331411 Primary Smelting & Refining of Copper
SIC 3331 Primary Smelting & Refining of Copper

331419 Primary Smelting & Refining of Nonferrous Metal
SIC 3339 Primary Smelting & Refining of Nonferrous Metals, Except Copper & Aluminum

331421 Copper Rolling, Drawing & Extruding
SIC 3351 Rolling, Drawing, & Extruding of Copper

331422 Copper Wire Drawing
SIC 3357 Drawing & Insulating of Nonferrous Wire

331423 Secondary Smelting, Refining, & Alloying of Copper
SIC 3341 Secondary Smelting & Refining of Nonferrous Metals
SIC 3399 Primary Metal Products, nec

331491 Nonferrous Metal Rolling, Drawing & Extruding
SIC 3356 Rolling, Drawing & Extruding of Nonferrous Metals, Except Copper & Aluminum
SIC 3357 Drawing & Insulating of Nonferrous Wire

331492 Secondary Smelting, Refining, & Alloying of Nonferrous Metal
SIC 3313 Electrometallurgical Products, Except Steel
SIC 3341 Secondary Smelting & Reining of Nonferrous Metals
SIC 3399 Primary Metal Products, nec

331511 Iron Foundries
SIC 3321 Gray & Ductile Iron Foundries
SIC 3322 Malleable Iron Foundries

331512 Steel Investment Foundries
SIC 3324 Steel Investment Foundries

331513 Steel Foundries,
SIC 3325 Steel Foundries, nec

331521 Aluminum Die-Castings
SIC 3363 Aluminum Die-Castings

331522 Nonferrous Die-Castings
SIC 3364 Nonferrous Die-Castings, Except Aluminum

331524 Aluminum Foundries
SIC 3365 Aluminum Foundries

331525 Copper Foundries
SIC 3366 Copper Foundries

331528 Other Nonferrous Foundries
SIC 3369 Nonferrous Foundries, Except Aluminum & Copper

FABRICATED METAL PRODUCT MANUFACTURING

332111 Iron & Steel Forging
SIC 3462 Iron & Steel Forgings

332112 Nonferrous Forging
SIC 3463 Nonferrous Forgings

332114 Custom Roll Forming
SIC 3449 Miscellaneous Structural Metal Work

332115 Crown & Closure Manufacturing
SIC 3466 Crowns & Closures

332116 Metal Stamping
SIC 3469 Metal Stampings, nec

332117 Powder Metallurgy Part Manufacturing
SIC 3499 Fabricated Metal Products, nec

332211 Cutlery & Flatware Manufacturing
SIC 3421 Cutlery
SIC 3914 Silverware, Plated Ware, & Stainless Steel Ware

332212 Hand & Edge Tool Manufacturing
SIC 3423 Hand & Edge Tools, Except Machine Tools & Handsaws
SIC 3523 Farm Machinery & Equipment
SIC 3524 Lawn & Garden Tractors & Home Lawn & Garden Equipment
SIC 3545 Cutting Tools, Machine Tools Accessories, & Machinist Precision Measuring Devices
SIC 3799 Transportation Equipment, nec
SIC 3999 Manufacturing Industries, nec

332213 Saw Blade & Handsaw Manufacturing
SIC 3425 Saw Blades & Handsaws

332214 Kitchen Utensil, Pot & Pan Manufacturing
SIC 3469 Metal Stampings, nec

332311 Prefabricated Metal Building & Component Manufacturing
SIC 3448 Prefabricated Metal Buildings & Components

332312 Fabricated Structural Metal Manufacturing
SIC 3441 Fabricated Structural Metal
SIC 3449 Miscellaneous Structural Metal Work

332313 Plate Work Manufacturing
SIC 3443 Fabricated Plate Work

332321 Metal Window & Door Manufacturing
SIC 3442 Metal Doors, Sash, Frames, Molding & Trim
SIC 3449 Miscellaneous Structural Metal Work

332322 Sheet Metal Work Manufacturing
SIC 3444 Sheet Metal Work

332323 Ornamental & Architectural Metal Work Manufacturing
SIC 3446 Architectural & Ornamental Metal Work
SIC 3449 Miscellaneous Structural Metal Work
SIC 3523 Farm Machinery & Equipment

33241 Power Boiler & Heat Exchanger Manufacturing
SIC 3443 Fabricated Plate Work

33242 Metal Tank Manufacturing
SIC 3443 Fabricated Plate Work

332431 Metal Can Manufacturing
SIC 3411 Metal Cans

332439 Other Metal Container Manufacturing
SIC 3412 Metal Shipping Barrels, Drums, Kegs, & Pails
SIC 3429 Hardware, nec
SIC 3444 Sheet Metal Work
SIC 3499 Fabricated Metal Products, nec
SIC 3537 Industrial Trucks, Tractors, Trailers, & Stackers

33251 Hardware Manufacturing
SIC 3429 Hardware, nec
SIC 3499 Fabricated Metal Products, nec

332611 Steel Spring Manufacturing
SIC 3493 Steel Springs, Except Wire

332612 Wire Spring Manufacturing
SIC 3495 Wire Springs

332618 Other Fabricated Wire Product Manufacturing
SIC 3315 Steel Wiredrawing & Steel Nails & Spikes
SIC 3399 Primary Metal Products, nec
SIC 3496 Miscellaneous Fabricated Wire Products

33271 Machine Shops
SIC 3599 Industrial & Commercial Machinery & Equipment, nec

332721 Precision Turned Product Manufacturing
SIC 3451 Screw Machine Products

332722 Bolt, Nut, Screw, Rivet & Washer Manufacturing
SIC 3452 Bolts, Nuts, Screws, Rivets, & Washers

332811 Metal Heat Treating
SIC 3398 Metal Heat Treating

332812 Metal Coating, Engraving , & Allied Services to Manufacturers
SIC 3479 Coating, Engraving, & Allied Services, nec

332813 Electroplating, Plating, Polishing, Anodizing & Coloring
SIC 3399 Primary Metal Products, nec
SIC 3471 Electroplating, Plating, Polishing, Anodizing, & Coloring

332911 Industrial Valve Manufacturing
SIC 3491 Industrial Valves

332912 Fluid Power Valve & Hose Fitting Manufacturing
SIC 3492 Fluid Power Valves & Hose Fittings
SIC 3728 Aircraft Parts & Auxiliary Equipment, nec

332913 Plumbing Fixture Fitting & Trim Manufacturing
SIC 3432 Plumbing Fixture Fittings & Trim

332919 Other Metal Valve & Pipe Fitting Manufacturing
SIC 3429 Hardware, nec
SIC 3494 Valves & Pipe Fittings, nec
SIC 3499 Fabricated Metal Products, nec

332991 Ball & Roller Bearing Manufacturing
SIC 3562 Ball & Roller Bearings

332992 Small Arms Ammunition Manufacturing
SIC 3482 Small Arms Ammunition

332993 Ammunition Manufacturing
SIC 3483 Ammunition, Except for Small Arms

332994 Small Arms Manufacturing
SIC 3484 Small Arms

332995 Other Ordnance & Accessories Manufacturing
SIC 3489 Ordnance & Accessories, nec

332996 Fabricated Pipe & Pipe Fitting Manufacturing
SIC 3498 Fabricated Pipe & Pipe Fittings

332997 Industrial Pattern Manufacturing
SIC 3543 Industrial Patterns

332998 Enameled Iron & Metal Sanitary Ware Manufacturing
SIC 3431 Enameled Iron & Metal Sanitary Ware

332999 All Other Miscellaneous Fabricated Metal Product Manufacturing
SIC 3291 Abrasive Products
SIC 3432 Plumbing Fixture Fittings & Trim
SIC 3494 Valves & Pipe Fittings, nec
SIC 3497 Metal Foil & Leaf
SIC 3499 Fabricated Metal Products, NEC
SIC 3537 Industrial Trucks, Tractors, Trailers, & Stackers
SIC 3599 Industrial & Commercial Machinery & Equipment, nec
SIC 3999 Manufacturing Industries, nec

MACHINERY MANUFACTURING

333111 Farm Machinery & Equipment Manufacturing
SIC 3523 Farm Machinery & Equipment

333112 Lawn & Garden Tractor & Home Lawn & Garden Equipment Manufacturing
SIC 3524 Lawn & Garden Tractors & Home Lawn & Garden Equipment

33312 Construction Machinery Manufacturing
SIC 3531 Construction Machinery & Equipment

333131 Mining Machinery & Equipment Manufacturing
SIC 3532 Mining Machinery & Equipment, Except Oil & Gas Field Machinery & Equipment

333132 Oil & Gas Field Machinery & Equipment Manufacturing
SIC 3533 Oil & Gas Field Machinery & Equipment

33321 Sawmill & Woodworking Machinery Manufacturing
SIC 3553 Woodworking Machinery

33322 Rubber & Plastics Industry Machinery Manufacturing
SIC 3559 Special Industry Machinery, nec

333291 Paper Industry Machinery Manufacturing
SIC 3554 Paper Industries Machinery

333292 Textile Machinery Manufacturing
SIC 3552 Textile Machinery

333293 Printing Machinery & Equipment Manufacturing
SIC 3555 Printing Trades Machinery & Equipment

333294 Food Product Machinery Manufacturing
SIC 3556 Food Products Machinery

333295 Semiconductor Machinery Manufacturing
SIC 3559 Special Industry Machinery, nec

333298 All Other Industrial Machinery Manufacturing
SIC 3559 Special Industry Machinery, nec
SIC 3639 Household Appliances, nec

333311 Automatic Vending Machine Manufacturing
SIC 3581 Automatic Vending Machines

333312 Commercial Laundry, Drycleaning & Pressing Machine Manufacturing
SIC 3582 Commercial Laundry, Drycleaning & Pressing Machines

333313 Office Machinery Manufacturing
SIC 3578 Calculating & Accounting Machinery, Except Electronic Computers
SIC 3579 Office Machines, nec

333314 Optical Instrument & Lens Manufacturing
SIC 3827 Optical Instruments & Lenses

333315 Photographic & Photocopying Equipment Manufacturing
SIC 3861 Photographic Equipment & Supplies

333319 Other Commercial & Service Industry Machinery Manufacturing
SIC 3559 Special Industry Machinery, nec
SIC 3589 Service Industry Machinery, nec
SIC 3599 Industrial & Commercial Machinery & Equipment, nec
SIC 3699 Electrical Machinery, Equipment & Supplies, nec

333411 Air Purification Equipment Manufacturing
SIC 3564 Industrial & Commercial Fans & Blowers & Air Purification Equipment

333412 Industrial & Commercial Fan & Blower Manufacturing
SIC 3564 Industrial & Commercial Fans & Blowers & Air Purification Equipment

333414 Heating Equipment Manufacturing
SIC 3433 Heating Equipment, Except Electric & Warm Air Furnaces

SIC 3634 Electric Housewares & Fans
**333415 Air-Conditioning & Warm Air Heating Equipment &
Commercial & Industrial Refrigeration Equipment
Manufacturing**
SIC 3443 Fabricated Plate Work
SIC 3585 Air-Conditioning & Warm Air Heating Equipment &
Commercial & Industrial Refrigeration Equipment
333511 Industrial Mold Manufacturing
SIC 3544 Special Dies & Tools, Die Sets, Jigs & Fixtures, &
Industrial Molds
333512 Machine Tool Manufacturing
SIC 3541 Machine Tools, Metal Cutting Type
333513 Machine Tool Manufacturing
SIC 3542 Machine Tools, Metal Forming Type
**333514 Special Die & Tool, Die Set, Jig & Fixture
Manufacturing**
SIC 3544 Special Dies & Tools, Die Sets, Jigs & Fixtures, &
Industrial Molds
333515 Cutting Tool & Machine Tool Accessory Manufacturing
SIC 3545 Cutting Tools, Machine Tool Accessories, &
Machinists' Precision Measuring Devices
333516 Rolling Mill Machinery & Equipment Manufacturing
SIC 3547 Rolling Mill Machinery & Equipment
333518 Other Metalworking Machinery Manufacturing
SIC 3549 Metalworking Machinery, nec
333611 Turbine & Turbine Generator Set Unit Manufacturing
SIC 3511 Steam, Gas, & Hydraulic Turbines, & Turbine
Generator Set Units
**333612 Speed Changer, Industrial High-Speed Drive & Gear
Manufacturing**
SIC 3566 Speed Changers, Industrial High-Speed Drives, &
Gears
**333613 Mechanical Power Transmission Equipment
Manufacturing**
SIC 3568 Mechanical Power Transmission Equipment, nec
333618 Other Engine Equipment Manufacturing
SIC 3519 Internal Combustion Engines, nec
SIC 3699 Electrical Machinery, Equipment & Supplies, nec
333911 Pump & Pumping Equipment Manufacturing
SIC 3561 Pumps & Pumping Equipment
SIC 3743 Railroad Equipment
333912 Air & Gas Compressor Manufacturing
SIC 3563 Air & Gas Compressors
333913 Measuring & Dispensing Pump Manufacturing
SIC 3586 Measuring & Dispensing Pumps
333921 Elevator & Moving Stairway Manufacturing
SIC 3534 Elevators & Moving Stairways
333922 Conveyor & Conveying Equipment Manufacturing
SIC 3523 Farm Machinery & Equipment
SIC 3535 Conveyors & Conveying Equipment
**333923 Overhead Traveling Crane, Hoist & Monorail System
Manufacturing**
SIC 3536 Overhead Traveling Cranes, Hoists, & Monorail
Systems
SIC 3531 Construction Machinery & Equipment
**333924 Industrial Truck, Tractor, Trailer & Stacker Machinery
Manufacturing**
SIC 3537 Industrial Trucks, Tractors, Trailers, & Stackers
333991 Power-Driven Hand Tool Manufacturing
SIC 3546 Power-Driven Handtools
333992 Welding & Soldering Equipment Manufacturing
SIC 3548 Electric & Gas Welding & Soldering Equipment

333993 Packaging Machinery Manufacturing
SIC 3565 Packaging Machinery
333994 Industrial Process Furnace & Oven Manufacturing
SIC 3567 Industrial Process Furnaces & Ovens
333995 Fluid Power Cylinder & Actuator Manufacturing
SIC 3593 Fluid Power Cylinders & Actuators
333996 Fluid Power Pump & Motor Manufacturing
SIC 3594 Fluid Power Pumps & Motors
333997 Scale & Balance Manufacturing
SIC 3596 Scales & Balances, Except Laboratory
333999 All Other General Purpose Machinery Manufacturing
SIC 3599 Industrial & Commercial Machinery & Equipment,
nec
SIC 3569 General Industrial Machinery & Equipment, nec

COMPUTER & ELECTRONIC PRODUCT MANUFACTURING

334111 Electronic Computer Manufacturing
SIC 3571 Electronic Computers
334112 Computer Storage Device Manufacturing
SIC 3572 Computer Storage Devices
334113 Computer Terminal Manufacturing
SIC 3575 Computer Terminals
334119 Other Computer Peripheral Equipment Manufacturing
SIC 3577 Computer Peripheral Equipment, nec
SIC 3578 Calculating & Accounting Machines, Except
Electronic Computers
SIC 3699 Electrical Machinery, Equipment & Supplies, nec
33421 Telephone Apparatus Manufacturing
SIC 3661 Telephone & Telegraph Apparatus
**33422 Radio & Television Broadcasting & Wireless
Communications Equipment Manufacturing**
SIC 3663 Radio & Television Broadcasting & Communication
Equipment
SIC 3679 Electronic Components, nec
33429 Other Communications Equipment Manufacturing
SIC 3669 Communications Equipment, nec
33431 Audio & Video Equipment Manufacturing
SIC 3651 Household Audio & Video Equipment
334411 Electron Tube Manufacturing
SIC 3671 Electron Tubes
334412 Printed Circuit Board Manufacturing
SIC 3672 Printed Circuit Boards
334413 Semiconductor & Related Device Manufacturing
SIC 3674 Semiconductors & Related Devices
334414 Electronic Capacitor Manufacturing
SIC 3675 Electronic Capacitors
334415 Electronic Resistor Manufacturing
SIC 3676 Electronic Resistors
**334416 Electronic Coil, Transformer, & Other Inductor
Manufacturing**
SIC 3661 Telephone & Telegraph Apparatus
SIC 3677 Electronic Coils, Transformers, & Other Inductors
SIC 3825 Instruments for Measuring & Testing of Electricity &
Electrical Signals
334417 Electronic Connector Manufacturing
SIC 3678 Electronic Connectors
334418 Printed Circuit/Electronics Assembly Manufacturing
SIC 3679 Electronic Components, nec
SIC 3661 Telephone & Telegraph Apparatus

334419 Other Electronic Component Manufacturing
SIC 3679 Electronic Components, nec
334510 Electromedical & Electrotherapeutic Apparatus Manufacturing
SIC 3842 Orthopedic, Prosthetic & Surgical Appliances & Supplies
SIC 3845 Electromedical & Electrotherapeutic Apparatus
334511 Search, Detection, Navigation, Guidance, Aeronautical, & Nautical System & Instrument Manufacturing
SIC 3812 Search, Detection, Navigation, Guidance, Aeronautical, & Nautical Systems & Instruments
334512 Automatic Environmental Control Manufacturing for Residential, Commercial & Appliance Use
SIC 3822 Automatic Controls for Regulating Residential & Commercial Environments & Appliances
334513 Instruments & Related Products Manufacturing for Measuring, Displaying, & Controlling Industrial Process Variables
SIC 3823 Industrial Instruments for Measurement, Display, & Control of Process Variables; & Related Products
334514 Totalizing Fluid Meter & Counting Device Manufacturing
SIC 3824 Totalizing Fluid Meters & Counting Devices
334515 Instrument Manufacturing for Measuring & Testing Electricity & Electrical Signals
SIC 3825 Instruments for Measuring & Testing of Electricity & Electrical Signals
334516 Analytical Laboratory Instrument Manufacturing
SIC 3826 Laboratory Analytical Instruments
334517 Irradiation Apparatus Manufacturing
SIC 3844 X-Ray Apparatus & Tubes & Related Irradiation Apparatus
SIC 3845 Electromedical & Electrotherapeutic Apparatus
334518 Watch, Clock, & Part Manufacturing
SIC 3495 Wire Springs
SIC 3579 Office Machines, nec
SIC 3873 Watches, Clocks, Clockwork Operated Devices, & Parts
334519 Other Measuring & Controlling Device Manufacturing
SIC 3829 Measuring & Controlling Devices, nec
334611 Software Reproducing
SIC 7372 Prepackaged Software
334612 Prerecorded Compact Disc , Tape, & Record Reproducing
SIC 3652 Phonograph Records & Prerecorded Audio Tapes & Disks
SIC 7819 Services Allied to Motion Picture Production
334613 Magnetic & Optical Recording Media Manufacturing
SIC 3695 Magnetic & Optical Recording Media

ELECTRICAL EQUIPMENT, APPLIANCE, & COMPONENT MANUFACTURING

33511 Electric Lamp Bulb & Part Manufacturing
SIC 3641 Electric Lamp Bulbs & Tubes
335121 Residential Electric Lighting Fixture Manufacturing
SIC 3645 Residential Electric Lighting Fixtures
SIC 3999 Manufacturing Industries, nec
335122 Commercial, Industrial & Institutional Electric Lighting Fixture Manufacturing
SIC 3646 Commercial, Industrial, & Institutional Electric Lighting Fixtures

335129 Other Lighting Equipment Manufacturing
SIC 3648 Lighting Equipment, nec
SIC 3699 Electrical Machinery, Equipment, & Supplies, nec
335211 Electric Housewares & Fan Manufacturing
SIC 3634 Electric Housewares & Fans
335212 Household Vacuum Cleaner Manufacturing
SIC 3635 Household Vacuum Cleaners
SIC 3639 Household Appliances, nec
335221 Household Cooking Appliance Manufacturing
SIC 3631 Household Cooking Equipment
335222 Household Refrigerator & Home Freezer Manufacturing
SIC 3632 Household Refrigerators & Home & Farm Freezers
335224 Household Laundry Equipment Manufacturing
SIC 3633 Household Laundry Equipment
335228 Other Household Appliance Manufacturing
SIC 3639 Household Appliances, nec
335311 Power, Distribution & Specialty Transformer Manufacturing
SIC 3548 Electric & Gas Welding & Soldering Equipment
SIC 3612 Power, Distribution, & Speciality Transformers
335312 Motor & Generator Manufacturing
SIC 3621 Motors & Generators
SIC 7694 Armature Rewinding Shops
335313 Switchgear & Switchboard Apparatus Manufacturing
SIC 3613 Switchgear & Switchboard Apparatus
335314 Relay & Industrial Control Manufacturing
SIC 3625 Relays & Industrial Controls
335911 Storage Battery Manufacturing
SIC 3691 Storage Batteries
335912 Dry & Wet Primary Battery Manufacturing
SIC 3692 Primary Batteries, Dry & Wet
335921 Fiber-Optic Cable Manufacturing
SIC 3357 Drawing & Insulating of Nonferrous Wire
335929 Other Communication & Energy Wire Manufacturing
SIC 3357 Drawing & Insulating of Nonferrous Wire
335931 Current-Carrying Wiring Device Manufacturing
SIC 3643 Current-Carrying Wiring Devices
335932 Noncurrent-Carrying Wiring Device Manufacturing
SIC 3644 Noncurrent-Carrying Wiring Devices
335991 Carbon & Graphite Product Manufacturing
SIC 3624 Carbon & Graphite Products
335999 All Other Miscellaneous Electrical Equipment & Component Manufacturing
SIC 3629 Electrical Industrial Apparatus, nec
SIC 3699 Electrical Machinery, Equipment, & Supplies, nec

TRANSPORTATION EQUIPMENT MANUFACTURING

336111 Automobile Manufacturing
SIC 3711 Motor Vehicles & Passenger Car Bodies
336112 Light Truck & Utility Vehicle Manufacturing
SIC 3711 Motor Vehicles & Passenger Car Bodies
33612 Heavy Duty Truck Manufacturing
SIC 3711 Motor Vehicles & Passenger Car Bodies
336211 Motor Vehicle Body Manufacturing
SIC 3711 Motor Vehicles & Passenger Car Bodies
SIC 3713 Truck & Bus Bodies
SIC 3714 Motor Vehicle Parts & Accessories
336212 Truck Trailer Manufacturing
SIC 3715 Truck Trailers

336213 Motor Home Manufacturing
SIC 3716 Motor Homes
336214 Travel Trailer & Camper Manufacturing
SIC 3792 Travel Trailers & Campers
SIC 3799 Transportation Equipment, nec
336311 Carburetor, Piston, Piston Ring & Valve Manufacturing
SIC 3592 Carburetors, Pistons, Piston Rings, & Valves
336312 Gasoline Engine & Engine Parts Manufacturing
SIC 3714 Motor Vehicle Parts & Accessories
336321 Vehicular Lighting Equipment Manufacturing
SIC 3647 Vehicular Lighting Equipment
336322 Other Motor Vehicle Electrical & Electronic Equipment Manufacturing
SIC 3679 Electronic Components, nec
SIC 3694 Electrical Equipment for Internal Combustion Engines
SIC 3714 Motor Vehicle Parts & Accessories
33633 Motor Vehicle Steering & Suspension Components Manufacturing
SIC 3714 Motor Vehicle Parts & Accessories
33634 Motor Vehicle Brake System Manufacturing
SIC 3292 Asbestos Products
SIC 3714 Motor Vehicle Parts & Accessories
33635 Motor Vehicle Transmission & Power Train Parts Manufacturing
SIC 3714 Motor Vehicle Parts & Accessories
33636 Motor Vehicle Fabric Accessories & Seat Manufacturing
SIC 2396 Automotive Trimmings, Apparel Findings, & Related Products
SIC 2399 Fabricated Textile Products, nec
SIC 2531 Public Building & Related Furniture
33637 Motor Vehicle Metal Stamping
SIC 3465 Automotive Stampings
336391 Motor Vehicle Air-Conditioning Manufacturing
SIC 3585 Air-Conditioning & Warm Air Heating Equipment & Commercial & Industrial Refrigeration Equipment
336399 All Other Motor Vehicle Parts Manufacturing
SIC 3519 Internal Combustion Engines, nec
SIC 3599 Industrial & Commercial Machinery & Equipment, NEC
SIC 3714 Motor Vehicle Parts & Accessories
336411 Aircraft Manufacturing
SIC 3721 Aircraft
336412 Aircraft Engine & Engine Parts Manufacturing
SIC 3724 Aircraft Engines & Engine Parts
336413 Other Aircraft Part & Auxiliary Equipment Manufacturing
SIC 3728 Aircraft Parts & Auxiliary Equipment, nec
336414 Guided Missile & Space Vehicle Manufacturing
SIC 3761 Guided Missiles & Space Vehicles
336415 Guided Missile & Space Vehicle Propulsion Unit & Propulsion Unit Parts Manufacturing
SIC 3764 Guided Missile & Space Vehicle Propulsion Units & Propulsion Unit Parts
336419 Other Guided Missile & Space Vehicle Parts & Auxiliary Equipment Manufacturing
SIC 3769 Guided Missile & Space Vehicle Parts & Auxiliary Equipment
33651 Railroad Rolling Stock Manufacturing
SIC 3531 Construction Machinery & Equipment
SIC 3743 Railroad Equipment
336611 Ship Building & Repairing
SIC 3731 Ship Building & Repairing

336612 Boat Building
SIC 3732 Boat Building & Repairing
336991 Motorcycle, Bicycle, & Parts Manufacturing
SIC 3944 Games, Toys, & Children's Vehicles, Except Dolls & Bicycles
SIC 3751 Motorcycles, Bicycles & Parts
336992 Military Armored Vehicle, Tank & Tank Component Manufacturing
SIC 3711 Motor Vehicles & Passenger Car Bodies
SIC 3795 Tanks & Tank Components
336999 All Other Transportation Equipment Manufacturing
SIC 3799 Transportation Equipment, nec

FURNITURE & RELATED PRODUCT MANUFACTURING

337121 Upholstered Household Furniture Manufacturing
SIC 2512 Wood Household Furniture, Upholstered
SIC 2515 Mattress, Foundations, & Convertible Beds
SIC 5712 Furniture
337122 Nonupholstered Wood Household Furniture Manufacturing
SIC 2511 Wood Household Furniture, Except Upholstered
SIC 5712 Furniture Stores
337124 Metal Household Furniture Manufacturing
SIC 2514 Metal Household Furniture
337125 Household Furniture Manufacturing
SIC 2519 Household Furniture, NEC
337127 Institutional Furniture Manufacturing
SIC 2531 Public Building & Related Furniture
SIC 2599 Furniture & Fixtures, nec
SIC 3952 Lead Pencils, Crayons, & Artist's Materials
SIC 3999 Manufacturing Industries, nec
337129 Wood Television, Radio, & Sewing Machine Cabinet Manufacturing
SIC 2517 Wood Television, Radio, Phonograph, & Sewing Machine Cabinets
337131 Wood Kitchen & Counter Top Manufacturing
SIC 2434 Wood Kitchen Cabinets
SIC 2541 Wood Office & Store Fixtures, Partitions, Shelving, & Lockers
SIC 5712 Furniture Stores
337132 Upholstered Wood Household Furniture Manufacturing
SIC 2515 Mattresses, Foundations, & Convertible Beds
SIC 5712 Furniture Stores
337133 Wood Household Furniture
SIC 5712 Furniture Stores
337134 Wood Office Furniture Manufacturing
SIC 2521 Wood Office Furniture
337135 Custom Architectural Woodwork, Millwork, & Fixtures
SIC 2541 Wood Office & Store Fixtures, Partitions, Shelving, and Lockers
337139 Other Wood Furniture Manufacturing
SIC 2426 Hardwood Dimension & Flooring Mills
SIC 2499 Wood Products, nec
SIC 2517 Wood Television, Radio, Phonograph, & Sewing Machine Cabinets
SIC 2531 Public Building & Related Furniture
SIC 2541 Wood Office & Store Fixtures, Partitions., Shelving, & Lockers
SIC 2599 Furniture & Fixtures, nec
SIC 3952 Lead Pencils, Crayons, & Artist's Materials

337141 Nonwood Office Furniture Manufacturing
SIC 2522 Office Furniture, Except Wood
337143 Household Furniture Manufacturing
SIC 2519 Household Furniture, NEC
337145 Nonwood Showcase, Partition, Shelving, & Locker Manufacturing
SIC 2542 Office & Store Fixtures, Partitions, Shelving, & Lockers, Except Wood
337148 Other Nonwood Furniture Manufacturing
SIC 2499 Wood Products, NEC
SIC 2531 Public Building & Related Furniture
SIC 2599 Furniture & Fixtures, nec
SIC 3499 Fabricated Metal Products, nec
SIC 3952 Lead Pencils, Crayons, & Artist's Materials
SIC 3999 Manufacturing Industries, nec
337212 Custom Architectural Woodwork & Millwork Manufacturing
SIC 2541 Wood Office & Store Fixtures, Partitions, Shelving, & Lockers
337214 Nonwood Office Furniture Manufacturing
SIC 2522 Office Furniture, Except Wood
337215 Showcase, Partition, Shelving, & Locker Manufacturing
SIC 2542 Office & Store Fixtures, Partitions, Shelving & Lockers, Except Wood
SIC 2541 Wood Office & Store Fixtures, Partitions, Shelving, & Lockers
SIC 2426 Hardwood Dimension & Flooring Mills
SIC 3499 Fabricated Metal Products, nec
33791 Mattress Manufacturing
SIC 2515 Mattresses, Foundations & Convertible Beds
33792 Blind & Shade Manufacturing
SIC 2591 Drapery Hardware & Window Blinds & Shades

MISCELLANEOUS MANUFACTURING

339111 Laboratory Apparatus & Furniture Manufacturing
SIC 3829 Measuring & Controlling Devices, nec
339112 Surgical & Medical Instrument Manufacturing
SIC 3841 Surgical & Medical Instruments & Apparatus
SIC 3829 Measuring & Controlling Devices, nec
339113 Surgical Appliance & Supplies Manufacturing
SIC 2599 Furniture & Fixtures, nec
SIC 3842 Orthopedic, Prosthetic, & Surgical Appliances & Supplies
339114 Dental Equipment & Supplies Manufacturing
SIC 3843 Dental Equipment & Supplies
339115 Ophthalmic Goods Manufacturing
SIC 3851 Opthalmic Goods
SIC 5995 Optical Goods Stores
339116 Dental Laboratories
SIC 8072 Dental Laboratories 339117 Eyeglass & Contact Lens Manufacturing
SIC 5995 Optical Goods Stores
339911 Jewelry Manufacturing
SIC 3469 Metal Stamping, nec
SIC 3479 Coating, Engraving, & Allied Services, nec
SIC 3911 Jewelry, Precious Metal
339912 Silverware & Plated Ware Manufacturing
SIC 3479 Coating, Engraving, & Allied Services, nec
SIC 3914 Silverware, Plated Ware, & Stainless Steel Ware
339913 Jewelers' Material & Lapidary Work Manufacturing
SIC 3915 Jewelers' Findings & Materials, & Lapidary Work

339914 Costume Jewelry & Novelty Manufacturing
SIC 3479 Coating, Engraving, & Allied Services, nec
SIC 3499 Fabricated Metal Products, nec
SIC 3961 Costume Jewelry & Costume Novelties, Except Precious Metal
33992 Sporting & Athletic Goods Manufacturing
SIC 3949 Sporting & Athletic Goods, nec
339931 Doll & Stuffed Toy Manufacturing
SIC 3942 Dolls & Stuffed Toys
339932 Game, Toy, & Children's Vehicle Manufacturing
SIC 3944 Games, Toys, & Children's Vehicles, Except Dolls & Bicycles
339941 Pen & Mechanical Pencil Manufacturing
SIC 3951 Pens, Mechanical Pencils, & Parts
339942 Lead Pencil & Art Good Manufacturing
SIC 2531 Public Buildings & Related Furniture
SIC 3579 Office Machines, nec
SIC 3952 Lead Pencils, Crayons, & Artists' Materials
339943 Marking Device Manufacturing
SIC 3953 Marking Devices
339944 Carbon Paper & Inked Ribbon Manufacturing
SIC 3955 Carbon Paper & Inked Ribbons
33995 Sign Manufacturing
SIC 3993 Signs & Advertising Specialties
339991 Gasket, Packing, & Sealing Device Manufacturing
SIC 3053 Gaskets, Packing, & Sealing Devices
339992 Musical Instrument Manufacturing
SIC 3931 Musical Instruments
339993 Fastener, Button, Needle & Pin Manufacturing
SIC 3965 Fasteners, Buttons, Needles, & Pins
SIC 3131 Boat & Shoe Cut Stock & Findings
339994 Broom, Brush & Mop Manufacturing
SIC 3991 Brooms & Brushes
SIC 2392 Housefurnishings, Except Curtains & Draperies
339995 Burial Casket Manufacturing
SIC 3995 Burial Caskets
339999 All Other Miscellaneous Manufacturing
SIC 2499 Wood Products, NEC
SIC 3999 Manufacturing Industries, nec

WHOLESALE TRADE

42111 Automobile & Other Motor Vehicle Wholesalers
SIC 5012 Automobiles & Other Motor Vehicles
42112 Motor Vehicle Supplies & New Part Wholesalers
SIC 5013 Motor Vehicle Supplies & New Parts
42113 Tire & Tube Wholesalers
SIC 5014 Tires & Tubes
42114 Motor Vehicle Part Wholesalers
SIC 5015 Motor Vehicle Parts, Used
42121 Furniture Wholesalers
SIC 5021 Furniture
42122 Home Furnishing Wholesalers
SIC 5023 Homefurnishings
42131 Lumber, Plywood, Millwork & Wood Panel Wholesalers
SIC 5031 Lumber, Plywood, Millwork, & Wood Panels
SIC 5211 Lumber & Other Building Materials Dealers - Retail
42132 Brick, Stone & Related Construction Material Wholesalers
SIC 5032 Brick, Stone, & Related Construction Materials
42133 Roofing, Siding & Insulation Material Wholesalers
SIC 5033 Roofing, Siding, & Insulation Materials

42139 Other Construction Material Wholesalers
SIC 5039 Construction Materials, nec

42141 Photographic Equipment & Supplies Wholesalers
SIC 5043 Photographic Equipment & Supplies

42142 Office Equipment Wholesalers
SIC 5044 Office Equipment

42143 Computer & Computer Peripheral Equipment & Software Wholesalers
SIC 5045 Computers & Computer Peripherals Equipment & Software

42144 Other Commercial Equipment Wholesalers
SIC 5046 Commercial Equipment, nec

42145 Medical, Dental & Hospital Equipment & Supplies Wholesalers
SIC 5047 Medical, Dental & Hospital Equipment & Supplies

42146 Ophthalmic Goods Wholesalers
SIC 5048 Ophthalmic Goods

42149 Other Professional Equipment & Supplies Wholesalers
SIC 5049 Professional Equipment & Supplies, nec

42151 Metal Service Centers & Offices
SIC 5051 Metals Service Centers & Offices

42152 Coal & Other Mineral & Ore Wholesalers
SIC 5052 Coal & Other Mineral & Ores

42161 Electrical Apparatus & Equipment, Wiring Supplies & Construction Material Wholesalers
SIC 5063 Electrical Apparatus & Equipment, Wiring Supplies & Construction Materials

42162 Electrical Appliance, Television & Radio Set Wholesalers
SIC 5064 Electrical Appliances, Television & Radio Sets

42169 Other Electronic Parts & Equipment Wholesalers
SIC 5065 Electronic Parts & Equipment, nec

42171 Hardware Wholesalers
SIC 5072 Hardware

42172 Plumbing & Heating Equipment & Supplies Wholesalers
SIC 5074 Plumbing & Heating Equipment & Supplies

42173 Warm Air Heating & Air-Conditioning Equipment & Supplies Wholesalers
SIC 5075 Warm Air Heating & Air-Conditioning Equipment & Supplies

42174 Refrigeration Equipment & Supplies Wholesalers
SIC 5078 Refrigeration Equipment & Supplies

42181 Construction & Mining Machinery & Equipment Wholesalers
SIC 5082 Construction & Mining Machinery & Equipment

42182 Farm & Garden Machinery & Equipment Wholesalers
SIC 5083 Farm & Garden Machinery & Equipment

42183 Industrial Machinery & Equipment Wholesalers
SIC 5084 Industrial Machinery & Equipment
SIC 5085 Industrial Supplies

42184 Industrial Supplies Wholesalers
SIC 5085 Industrial Supplies

42185 Service Establishment Equipment & Supplies Wholesalers
SIC 5087 Service Establishment Equipment & Supplies Wholesalers

42186 Transportation Equipment & Supplies Wholesalers
SIC 5088 Transportation Equipment and Supplies, Except Motor Vehicles

42191 Sporting & Recreational Goods & Supplies Wholesalers
SIC 5091 Sporting & Recreational Goods & Supplies

42192 Toy & Hobby Goods & Supplies Wholesalers
SIC 5092 Toys & Hobby Goods & Supplies

42193 Recyclable Material Wholesalers
SIC 5093 Scrap & Waste Materials

42194 Jewelry, Watch, Precious Stone & Precious Metal Wholesalers
SIC 5094 Jewelry, Watches, Precious Stones, & Precious Metals

42199 Other Miscellaneous Durable Goods Wholesalers
SIC 5099 Durable Goods, nec
SIC 7822 Motion Picture & Video Tape Distribution

42211 Printing & Writing Paper Wholesalers
SIC 5111 Printing & Writing Paper

42212 Stationary & Office Supplies Wholesalers
SIC 5112 Stationery & Office Supplies

42213 Industrial & Personal Service Paper Wholesalers
SIC 5113 Industrial & Personal Service Paper

42221 Drug, Drug Proprietaries & Druggists' Sundries Wholesalers
SIC 5122 Drugs, Drug Proprietaries, & Druggists' Sundries

42231 Piece Goods, Notions & Other Dry Goods Wholesalers
SIC 5131 Piece Goods, Notions, & Other Dry Goods

42232 Men's & Boys' Clothing & Furnishings Wholesalers
SIC 5136 Men's & Boys' Clothing & Furnishings

42233 Women's, Children's, & Infants' & Accessories Wholesalers
SIC 5137 Women's, Children's, & Infants' Clothing & Accessories

42234 Footwear Wholesalers
SIC 5139 Footwear

42241 General Line Grocery Wholesalers
SIC 5141 Groceries, General Line

42242 Packaged Frozen Food Wholesalers
SIC 5142 Packaged Frozen Foods

42243 Dairy Product Wholesalers
SIC 5143 Dairy Products, Except Dried or Canned

42244 Poultry & Poultry Product Wholesalers
SIC 5144 Poultry & Poultry Products

42245 Confectionery Wholesalers
SIC 5145 Confectionery

42246 Fish & Seafood Wholesalers
SIC 5146 Fish & Seafoods

42247 Meat & Meat Product Wholesalers
SIC 5147 Meats & Meat Products

42248 Fresh Fruit & Vegetable Wholesalers
SIC 5148 Fresh Fruits & Vegetables

42249 Other Grocery & Related Products Wholesalers
SIC 5149 Groceries & Related Products, nec

42251 Grain & Field Bean Wholesalers
SIC 5153 Grain & Field Beans

42252 Livestock Wholesalers
SIC 5154 Livestock

42259 Other Farm Product Raw Material Wholesalers
SIC 5159 Farm-Product Raw Materials, nec

42261 Plastics Materials & Basic Forms & Shapes Wholesalers
SIC 5162 Plastics Materials & Basic Forms & Shapes

42269 Other Chemical & Allied Products Wholesalers
SIC 5169 Chemicals & Allied Products, nec

42271 Petroleum Bulk Stations & Terminals
SIC 5171 Petroleum Bulk Stations & Terminals

42272 Petroleum & Petroleum Products Wholesalers
SIC 5172 Petroleum & Petroleum Products Wholesalers, Except Bulk Stations & Terminals

42281 Beer & Ale Wholesalers
SIC 5181 Beer & Ale

42282 Wine & Distilled Alcoholic Beverage Wholesalers
SIC 5182 Wine & Distilled Alcoholic Beverages
42291 Farm Supplies Wholesalers
SIC 5191 Farm Supplies
42292 Book, Periodical & Newspaper Wholesalers
SIC 5192 Books, Periodicals, & Newspapers
42293 Flower, Nursery Stock & Florists' Supplies Wholesalers
SIC 5193 Flowers, Nursery Stock, & Florists' Supplies
42294 Tobacco & Tobacco Product Wholesalers
SIC 5194 Tobacco & Tobacco Products
42295 Paint, Varnish & Supplies Wholesalers
SIC 5198 Paints, Varnishes, & Supplies
SIC 5231 Paint, Glass & Wallpaper Stores
42299 Other Miscellaneous Nondurable Goods Wholesalers
SIC 5199 Nondurable Goods, nec

RETAIL TRADE

44111 New Car Dealers
SIC 5511 Motor Vehicle Dealers, New and Used
44112 Used Car Dealers
SIC 5521 Motor Vehicle Dealers, Used Only
44121 Recreational Vehicle Dealers
SIC 5561 Recreational Vehicle Dealers
441221 Motorcycle Dealers
SIC 5571 Motorcycle Dealers
441222 Boat Dealers
SIC 5551 Boat Dealers
441229 All Other Motor Vehicle Dealers
SIC 5599 Automotive Dealers, NEC
44131 Automotive Parts & Accessories Stores
SIC 5013 Motor Vehicle Supplies & New Parts
SIC 5731 Radio, Television, & Consumer Electronics Stores
SIC 5531 Auto & Home Supply Stores
44132 Tire Dealers
SIC 5014 Tires & Tubes
SIC 5531 Auto & Home Supply Stores
44211 Furniture Stores
SIC 5021 Furniture
SIC 5712 Furniture Stores
44221 Floor Covering Stores
SIC 5023 Homefurnishings
SIC 5713 Floor Coverings Stores
442291 Window Treatment Stores
SIC 5714 Drapery, Curtain, & Upholstery Stores
SIC 5719 Miscellaneous Homefurnishings Stores
442299 All Other Home Furnishings Stores
SIC 5719 Miscellaneous Homefurnishings Stores
443111 Household Appliance Stores
SIC 5722 Household Appliance Stores
SIC 5999 Miscellaneous Retail Stores, nec
SIC 7623 Refrigeration & Air-Conditioning Service & Repair Shops
SIC 7629 Electrical & Electronic Repair Shops, nec
443112 Radio, Television & Other Electronics Stores
SIC 5731 Radio, Television, & Consumer Electronics Stores
SIC 5999 Miscellaneous Retail Stores, nec
SIC 7622 Radio & Television Repair Shops
44312 Computer & Software Stores
SIC 5045 Computers & Computer Peripheral Equipment & Software
SIC 7378 Computer Maintenance & Repair '
SIC 5734 Computer & Computer Software Stores

44313 Camera & Photographic Supplies Stores
SIC 5946 Camera & Photographic Supply Stores
44411 Home Centers
SIC 5211 Lumber & Other Building Materials Dealers
44412 Paint & Wallpaper Stores
SIC 5198 Paints, Varnishes, & Supplies
SIC 5231 Paint, Glass, & Wallpaper Stores
44413 Hardware Stores
SIC 5251 Hardware Stores
44419 Other Building Material Dealers
SIC 5031 Lumber, Plywood, Millwork, & Wood Panels
SIC 5032 Brick, Stone, & Related Construction Materials
SIC 5039 Construction Materials, nec
SIC 5063 Electrical Apparatus & Equipment, Wiring Supplies, & Construction Materials
SIC 5074 Plumbing & Heating Equipment & Supplies
SIC 5211 Lumber & Other Building Materials Dealers
SIC 5231 Paint, Glass, & Wallpaper Stores
44421 Outdoor Power Equipment Stores
SIC 5083 Farm & Garden Machinery & Equipment
SIC 5261 Retail Nurseries, Lawn & Garden Supply Stores
44422 Nursery & Garden Centers
SIC 5191 Farm Supplies
SIC 5193 Flowers, Nursery Stock, & Florists' Supplies
SIC 5261 Retail Nurseries, Lawn & Garden Supply Stores
44511 Supermarkets & Other Grocery Stores
SIC 5411 Grocery Stores
44512 Convenience Stores
SIC 5411 Grocery Stores
44521 Meat Markets
SIC 5421 Meat & Fish Markets, Including Freezer Provisioners
SIC 5499 Miscellaneous Food Stores
44522 Fish & Seafood Markets
SIC 5421 Meat & Fish Markets, Including Freezer Provisioners
44523 Fruit & Vegetable Markets
SIC 5431 Fruit & Vegetable Markets
445291 Baked Goods Stores
SIC 5461 Retail Bakeries
445292 Confectionery & Nut Stores
SIC 5441 Candy, Nut & Confectionery Stores
445299 All Other Specialty Food Stores
SIC 5499 Miscellaneous Food Stores
SIC 5451 Dairy Products Stores
44531 Beer, Wine & Liquor Stores
SIC 5921 Liquor Stores
44611 Pharmacies & Drug Stores
SIC 5912 Drug Stores & Proprietary Stores
44612 Cosmetics, Beauty Supplies & Perfume Stores
SIC 5087 Service Establishment Equipment & Supplies
SIC 5999 Miscellaneous Retail Stores, nec
44613 Optical Goods Stores
SIC 5995 Optical Goods Stores
446191 Food Supplement Stores
SIC 5499 Miscellaneous Food Stores
446199 All Other Health & Personal Care Stores
SIC 5047 Medical, Dental, & Hospital Equipment & Supplies
SIC 5999 Miscellaneous Retail Stores, nec
44711 Gasoline Stations with Convenience Stores
SIC 5541 Gasoline Service Station
SIC 5411 Grocery Stores
44719 Other Gasoline Stations
SIC 5541 Gasoline Service Station

44811 Men's Clothing Stores
SIC 5611 Men's & Boys' Clothing & Accessory Stores
44812 Women's Clothing Stores
SIC 5621 Women's Clothing Stores
44813 Children's & Infants' Clothing Stores
SIC 5641 Children's & Infants' Wear Stores
44814 Family Clothing Stores
SIC 5651 Family Clothing Stores
44815 Clothing Accessories Stores
SIC 5611 Men's & Boys' Clothing & Accessory Stores
SIC 5632 Women's Accessory & Specialty Stores
SIC 5699 Miscellaneous Apparel & Accessory Stores
44819 Other Clothing Stores
SIC 5699 Miscellaneous Apparel & Accessory Stores
SIC 5632 Women's Accessory & Specialty Stores
44821 Shoe Stores
SIC 5661 Shoe Stores
44831 Jewelry Stores
SIC 5999 Miscellaneous Retailer, nec
SIC 5944 Jewelry Stores
44832 Luggage & Leather Goods Stores
SIC 5948 Luggage & Leather Goods Stores
45111 Sporting Goods Stores
SIC 7699 Repair Shops & Related Services, NEC
SIC 5941 Sporting Goods Stores & Bicycle Shops
45112 Hobby, Toy & Game Stores
SIC 5945 Hobby, Toy, & Game Stores
45113 Sewing, Needlework & Piece Goods Stores
SIC 5714 Drapery, Curtain, & Upholstery Stores
SIC 5949 Sewing, Needlework, & Piece Goods Stores
45114 Musical Instrument & Supplies Stores
SIC 5736 Musical Instruments Stores
451211 Book Stores
SIC 5942 Book Stores
451212 News Dealers & Newsstands
SIC 5994 News Dealers & Newsstands
45122 Prerecorded Tape, Compact Disc & Record Stores
SIC 5735 Record & Prerecorded Tape Stores
45211 Department Stores
SIC 5311 Department Stores
45291 Warehouse Clubs & Superstores
SIC 5399 Miscellaneous General Merchandise Stores
SIC 5411 Grocery Stores
45299 All Other General Merchandise Stores
SIC 5399 Miscellaneous General Merchandise Stores
SIC 5331 Variety Stores
45311 Florists
SIC 5992 Florists
45321 Office Supplies & Stationery Stores
SIC 5049 Professional Equipment & Supplies, nec
SIC 5112 Stationery & Office Supplies
SIC 5943 Stationery Stores
45322 Gift, Novelty & Souvenir Stores
SIC 5947 Gift, Novelty, & Souvenir Shops
45331 Used Merchandise Stores
SIC 5932 Used Merchandise Stores
45391 Pet & Pet Supplies Stores
SIC 5999 Miscellaneous Retail Stores, NEC
45392 Art Dealers
SIC 5999 Miscellaneous Retail Stores, nec
45393 Manufactured Home Dealers
SIC 5271 Mobile Home Dealers

453991 Tobacco Stores
SIC 5993 Tobacco Stores & Stands
453999 All Other Miscellaneous Store Retailers
SIC 5999 Miscellaneous Retail Stores, nec
SIC 5261 Retail Nurseries, Lawn & Garden Supply Stores
45411 Electronic Shopping & Mail-Order Houses
SIC 5961 Catalog & Mail-Order Houses
45421 Vending Machine Operators
SIC 5962 Automatic Merchandise Machine Operators
454311 Heating Oil Dealers
SIC 5171 Petroleum Bulk Stations & Terminals
SIC 5983 Fuel Oil Dealers
454312 Liquefied Petroleum Gas Dealers
SIC 5171 Petroleum Bulk Stations & Terminals
SIC 5984 Liquefied Petroleum Gas Dealers
454319 Other Fuel Dealers
SIC 5989 Fuel Dealers, nec
45439 Other Direct Selling Establishments
SIC 5421 Meat & Fish Markets, Including Freezer Provisioners
SIC 5963 Direct Selling Establishments

TRANSPORTATION & WAREHOUSING

481111 Scheduled Passenger Air Transportation
SIC 4512 Air Transportation, Scheduled
481112 Scheduled Freight Air Transportation
SIC 4512 Air Transportation, Scheduled
481211 Nonscheduled Chartered Passenger Air Transportation
SIC 4522 Air Transportation, Nonscheduled
481212 Nonscheduled Chartered Freight Air Transportation
SIC 4522 Air Transportation, Nonscheduled
481219 Other Nonscheduled Air Transportation
SIC 7319 Advertising, nec
48122 Nonscheduled Speciality Air Transportation
SIC 0721 Crop Planting, Cultivating, & Protecting
SIC 1382 Oil & Gas Field Exploration Services
SIC 4522 Air Transportation, Nonscheduled
SIC 7335 Commercial Photography
SIC 7997 Membership Sports & Recreation Clubs
SIC 8299 Schools & Educational Services, nec
SIC 8713 Surveying Services
482111 Line-Haul Railroads
SIC 4011 Railroads, Line-Haul Operating
482112 Short Line Railroads
SIC 4013 Railroad Switching & Terminal Establishments
483111 Deep Sea Freight Transportation
SIC 4412 Deep Sea Foreign Transportation of Freight
483112 Deep Sea Passenger Transportation
SIC 4481 Deep Sea Transportation of Passengers, Except by Ferry
483113 Coastal & Great Lakes Freight Transportation
SIC 4424 Deep Sea Domestic Transportation of Freight
SIC 4432 Freight Transportation on the Great Lakes - St. Lawrence Seaway
SIC 4492 Towing & Tugboat Services
483114 Coastal & Great Lakes Passenger Transportation
SIC 4481 Deep Sea Transportation of Passengers, Except by Ferry
SIC 4482 Ferries
483211 Inland Water Freight Transportation
SIC 4449 Water Transportation of Freight, nec
SIC 4492 Towing & Tugboat Services

483212 Inland Water Passenger Transportation
SIC 4482 Ferries
SIC 4489 Water Transportation of Passengers, nec

48411 General Freight Trucking, Local
SIC 4212 Local Trucking without Storage
SIC 4214 Local Trucking with Storage

484121 General Freight Trucking, Long-Distance, Truckload
SIC 4213 Trucking, Except Local

484122 General Freight Trucking, Long-Distance, Less Than Truckload
SIC 4213 Trucking, Except Local

48421 Used Household & Office Goods Moving
SIC 4212 Local Trucking Without Storage
SIC 4213 Trucking, Except Local
SIC 4214 Local Trucking With Storage

48422 Specialized Freight Trucking, Local
SIC 4212 Local Trucking without Storage
SIC 4214 Local Trucking with Storage

48423 Specialized Freight Trucking, Long-Distance
SIC 4213 Trucking, Except Local

485111 Mixed Mode Transit Systems
SIC 4111 Local & Suburban Transit

485112 Commuter Rail Systems
SIC 4111 Local & Suburban Transit

485113 Bus & Motor Vehicle Transit Systems
SIC 4111 Local & Suburban Transit

485119 Other Urban Transit Systems
SIC 4111 Local & Suburban Transit

48521 Interurban & Rural Bus Transportation
SIC 4131 Intercity & Rural Bus Transportation

48531 Taxi Service
SIC 4121 Taxicabs

48532 Limousine Service
SIC 4119 Local Passenger Transportation, nec

48541 School & Employee Bus Transportation
SIC 4151 School Buses
SIC 4119 Local Passenger Transportation, nec

48551 Charter Bus Industry
SIC 4141 Local Charter Bus Service
SIC 4142 Bus Charter Services, Except Local

485991 Special Needs Transportation
SIC 4119 Local Passenger Transportation, nec

485999 All Other Transit & Ground Passenger Transportation
SIC 4111 Local & Suburban Transit
SIC 4119 Local Passenger Transportation, nec

48611 Pipeline Transportation of Crude Oil
SIC 4612 Crude Petroleum Pipelines

48621 Pipeline Transportation of Natural Gas
SIC 4922 Natural Gas Transmission
SIC 4923 Natural Gas Transmission & Distribution

48691 Pipeline Transportation of Refined Petroleum Products
SIC 4613 Refined Petroleum Pipelines

48699 All Other Pipeline Transportation
SIC 4619 Pipelines, nec

48711 Scenic & Sightseeing Transportation, Land
SIC 4119 Local Passenger Transportation, nec
SIC 4789 Transportation Services, nec
SIC 7999 Amusement & Recreation Services, nec

48721 Scenic & Sightseeing Transportation, Water
SIC 4489 Water Transportation of Passengers, nec
SIC 7999 Amusement & Recreation Services, nec

48799 Scenic & Sightseeing Transportation, Other
SIC 4522 Air Transportation, Nonscheduled
SIC 7999 Amusement & Recreation Services, nec

488111 Air Traffic Control
SIC 4581 Airports, Flying Fields, & Airport Terminal Services
SIC 9621 Regulation & Administration of Transportation Programs

488112 Airport Operations, except Air Traffic Control
SIC 4581 Airports, Flying Fields, & Airport Terminal Services
SIC 4959 Sanitary Services, nec

488119 Other Airport Operations
SIC 4581 Airports, Flying Fields, & Airport Terminal Services
SIC 4959 Sanitary Services, nec

48819 Other Support Activities for Air Transportation
SIC 4581 Airports, Flying Fields, & Airport Terminal Services

48821 Support Activities for Rail Transportation
SIC 4013 Railroad Switching & Terminal Establishments
SIC 4741 Rental of Railroad Cars
SIC 4789 Transportation Services, nec

48831 Port & Harbor Operations
SIC 4491 Marine Cargo Handling
SIC 4499 Water Transportation Services, nec

48832 Marine Cargo Handling
SIC 4491 Marine Cargo Handling

48833 Navigational Services to Shipping
SIC 4492 Towing & Tugboat Services
SIC 4499 Water Transportation Services, nec

48839 Other Support Activities for Water Transportation
SIC 4499 Water Transportation Services, nec
SIC 4785 Fixed Facilities & Inspection & Weighing Services for Motor Vehicle Transportation
SIC 7699 Repair Shops & Related Services, nec

48841 Motor Vehicle Towing
SIC 7549 Automotive Services, Except Repair & Carwashes

48849 Other Support Activities for Road Transportation
SIC 4173 Terminal & Service Facilities for Motor Vehicle Passenger Transportation
SIC 4231 Terminal & Joint Terminal Maintenance Facilities for Motor Freight Transportation
SIC 4785 Fixed Facilities & Inspection & Weighing Services for Motor Vehicle Transportation

48851 Freight Transportation Arrangement
SIC 4731 Arrangement of Transportation of Freight & Cargo

488991 Packing & Crating
SIC 4783 Packing & Crating

488999 All Other Support Activities for Transportation
SIC 4729 Arrangement of Passenger Transportation, nec
SIC 4789 Transportation Services, nec

49111 Postal Service
SIC 4311 United States Postal Service

49211 Couriers
SIC 4215 Courier Services, Except by Air
SIC 4513 Air Courier Services

49221 Local Messengers & Local Delivery
SIC 4215 Courier Services, Except by Air

49311 General Warehousing & Storage Facilities
SIC 4225 General Warehousing & Storage
SIC 4226 Special Warehousing & Storage, nec

49312 Refrigerated Storage Facilities
SIC 4222 Refrigerated Warehousing & Storage
SIC 4226 Special Warehousing & Storage, nec

49313 Farm Product Storage Facilities
SIC 4221 Farm Product Warehousing & Storage

49319 Other Warehousing & Storage Facilities
SIC 4226 Special Warehousing & Storage, nec

INFORMATION

51111 Newspaper Publishers
SIC 2711 Newspapers: Publishing or Publishing & Printing
51112 Periodical Publishers
SIC 2721 Periodicals: Publishing or Publishing & Printing
51113 Book Publishers
SIC 2731 Books: Publishing or Publishing & Printing
51114 Database & Directory Publishers
SIC 2741 Miscellaneous Publishing
511191 Greeting Card Publishers
SIC 2771 Greeting Cards
511199 All Other Publishers
SIC 2741 Miscellaneous Publishing
51121 Software Publishers
SIC 7372 Prepackaged Software
51211 Motion Picture & Video Production
SIC 7812 Motion Picture & Video Tape Production
51212 Motion Picture & Video Distribution
SIC 7822 Motion Picture & Video Tape Distribution
SIC 7829 Services Allied to Motion Picture Distribution
512131 Motion Picture Theaters, Except Drive-Ins.
SIC 7832 Motion Picture Theaters, Except Drive-In
512132 Drive-In Motion Picture Theaters
SIC 7833 Drive-In Motion Picture Theaters
512191 Teleproduction & Other Post-Production Services
SIC 7819 Services Allied to Motion Picture Production
512199 Other Motion Picture & Video Industries
SIC 7819 Services Allied to Motion Picture Production
SIC 7829 Services Allied to Motion Picture Distribution
51221 Record Production
SIC 8999 Services, nec
51222 Integrated Record Production/Distribution
SIC 3652 Phonograph Records & Prerecorded Audio Tapes & Disks
51223 Music Publishers
SIC 2731 Books: Publishing or Publishing & Printing
SIC 2741 Miscellaneous Publishing
SIC 8999 Services, nec
51224 Sound Recording Studios
SIC 7389 Business Services, nec
51229 Other Sound Recording Industries
SIC 7389 Business Services, nec
SIC 7922 Theatrical Producers & Miscellaneous Theatrical Services
513111 Radio Networks
SIC 4832 Radio Broadcasting Stations
513112 Radio Stations
SIC 4832 Radio Broadcasting Stations
51312 Television Broadcasting
SIC 4833 Television Broadcasting Stations
51321 Cable Networks
SIC 4841 Cable & Other Pay Television Services
51322 Cable & Other Program Distribution
SIC 4841 Cable & Other Pay Television Services
51331 Wired Telecommunications Carriers
SIC 4813 Telephone Communications, Except Radiotelephone
SIC 4822 Telegraph & Other Message Communications
513321 Paging
SIC 4812 Radiotelephone Communications
513322 Cellular & Other Wireless Telecommunications
SIC 4812 Radiotelephone Communications
SIC 4899 Communications Services, nec

51333 Telecommunications Resellers
SIC 4812 Radio Communications
SIC 4813 Telephone Communications, Except Radiotelephone
51334 Satellite Telecommunications
SIC 4899 Communications Services, NEC
51339 Other Telecommunications
SIC 4899 Communications Services, NEC
51411 News Syndicates
SIC 7383 News Syndicates
51412 Libraries & Archives
SIC 8231 Libraries
514191 On-Line Information Services
SIC 7375 Information Retrieval Services
514199 All Other Information Services
SIC 8999 Services, nec
51421 Data Processing Services
SIC 7374 Computer Processing & Data Preparation & Processing Services

FINANCE & INSURANCE

52111 Monetary Authorities - Central Bank
SIC 6011 Federal Reserve Banks
52211 Commercial Banking
SIC 6021 National Commercial Banks
SIC 6022 State Commercial Banks
SIC 6029 Commercial Banks, nec
SIC 6081 Branches & Agencies of Foreign Banks
52212 Savings Institutions
SIC 6035 Savings Institutions, Federally Chartered
SIC 6036 Savings Institutions, Not Federally Chartered
52213 Credit Unions
SIC 6061 Credit Unions, Federally Chartered
SIC 6062 Credit Unions, Not Federally Chartered
52219 Other Depository Credit Intermediation
SIC 6022 State Commercial Banks
52221 Credit Card Issuing
SIC 6021 National Commercial Banks
SIC 6022 State Commercial Banks
SIC 6141 Personal Credit Institutions
52222 Sales Financing
SIC 6141 Personal Credit Institutions
SIC 6153 Short-Term Business Credit Institutions, Except Agricultural .
SIC 6159 Miscellaneous Business Credit Institutions
522291 Consumer Lending
SIC 6141 Personal Credit Institutions
522292 Real Estate Credit
SIC 6162 Mortgage Bankers & Loan Correspondents
522293 International Trade Financing
SIC 6081 Branches & Agencies of Foreign Banks
SIC 6082 Foreign Trade & International Banking Institutions
SIC 6111 Federal & Federally-Sponsored Credit Agencies
SIC 6159 Miscellaneous Business Credit Institutions
522294 Secondary Market Financing
SIC 6111 Federal & Federally Sponsored Credit Agencies
522298 All Other Nondepository Credit Intermediation
SIC 5932 Used Merchandise Stores
SIC 6081 Branches & Agencies of Foreign Banks
SIC 6111 Federal & Federally-Sponsored Credit Agencies
SIC 6153 Short-Term Business Credit Institutions, Except Agricultural
SIC 6159 Miscellaneous Business Credit Institutions

Appendix: NAICS/SIC Conversion

52231 Mortgage & Other Loan Brokers
SIC 6163 Loan Brokers
52232 Financial Transactions Processing, Reserve, & Clearing House Activities
SIC 6019 Central Reserve Depository Institutions, nec
SIC 6099 Functions Related to Depository Banking, nec
SIC 6153 Short-Term Business Credit Institutions, Except Agricultural
SIC 7389 Business Services, nec
52239 Other Activities Related to Credit Intermediation
SIC 6099 Functions Related to Depository Banking, nec
SIC 6162 Mortgage Bankers & Loan Correspondents
52311 Investment Banking & Securities Dealing
SIC 6211 Security Brokers, Dealers, & Flotation Companies
52312 Securities Brokerage
SIC 6211 Security Brokers, Dealers, & Flotation Companies
52313 Commodity Contracts Dealing
SIC 6099 Functions Related to depository Banking, nec
SIC 6799 Investors, nec
SIC 6221 Commodity Contracts Brokers & Dealers
52314 Commodity Brokerage
SIC 6221 Commodity Contracts Brokers & Dealers
52321 Securities & Commodity Exchanges
SIC 6231 Security & Commodity Exchanges
52391 Miscellaneous Intermediation
SIC 6211 Securities Brokers, Dealers, & Flotation Companies
SIC 6799 Investors, nec
52392 Portfolio Management
SIC 6282 Investment Advice
SIC 6371 Pension, Health, & Welfare Funds
SIC 6733 Trust, Except Educational, Religious, & Charitable
SIC 6799 Investors, nec
52393 Investment Advice
SIC 6282 Investment Advice
523991 Trust, Fiduciary & Custody Activities
SIC 6021 National Commercial Banks
SIC 6022 State Commercial Banks
SIC 6091 Nondepository Trust Facilities
SIC 6099 Functions Related to Depository Banking, nec
SIC 6289 Services Allied With the Exchange of Securities or Commodities, nec
SIC 6733 Trusts, Except Educational, Religious, & Charitable
523999 Miscellaneous Financial Investment Activities
SIC 6099 Functions Related to Depository Banking, nec
SIC 6211 Security Brokers, Dealers, & Flotation Companies
SIC 6289 Services Allied With the Exchange of Securities or Commodities, nec
SIC 6799 Investors, nec
SIC 6792 Oil Royalty Traders
524113 Direct Life Insurance Carriers
SIC 6311 Life Insurance
524114 Direct Health & Medical Insurance Carriers
SIC 6324 Hospital & Medical Service Plans
SIC 6321 Accident & Health Insurance
524126 Direct Property & Casualty Insurance Carriers
SIC 6331 Fire, Marine, & Casualty Insurance
SIC 6351 Surety Insurance
524127 Direct Title Insurance Carriers
SIC 6361 Title Insurance
524128 Other Direct Insurance Carriers
SIC 6399 Insurance Carriers, nec
52413 Reinsurance Carriers
SIC 6311 Life Insurance
SIC 6321 Accident & Health Insurance

SIC 6324 Hospital & Medical Service Plans
SIC 6331 Fire, Marine, & Casualty Insurance
SIC 6351 Surety Insurance
SIC 6361 Title Insurance
52421 Insurance Agencies & Brokerages
SIC 6411 Insurance Agents, Brokers & Service
524291 Claims Adjusters
SIC 6411 Insurance Agents, Brokers & Service
524292 Third Party Administration for Insurance & Pension Funds
SIC 6371 Pension, Health, & Welfare Funds
SIC 6411 Insurance Agents, Brokers & Service
524298 All Other Insurance Related Activities
SIC 6411 Insurance Agents, Brokers & Service
52511 Pension Funds
SIC 6371 Pension, Health, & Welfare Funds
52512 Health & Welfare Funds
SIC 6371 Pension, Health, & Welfare Funds
52519 Other Insurance Funds
SIC 6321 Accident & Health Insurance
SIC 6324 Hospital & Medical Service Plans
SIC 6331 Fire, Marine, & Casualty Insurance
SIC 6733 Trusts, Except Educational, Religious, & Charitable
52591 Open-End Investment Funds
SIC 6722 Management Investment Offices, Open-End
52592 Trusts, Estates, & Agency Accounts
SIC 6733 Trusts, Except Educational, Religious, & Charitable
52593 Real Estate Investment Trusts
SIC 6798 Real Estate Investment Trusts
52599 Other Financial Vehicles
SIC 6726 Unit Investment Trusts, Face-Amount Certificate Offices, & Closed-End Management Investment Offices

REAL ESTATE & RENTAL & LEASING

53111 Lessors of Residential Buildings & Dwellings
SIC 6513 Operators of Apartment Buildings
SIC 6514 Operators of Dwellings Other Than Apartment Buildings
53112 Lessors of Nonresidential Buildings
SIC 6512 Operators of Nonresidential Buildings
53113 Lessors of Miniwarehouses & Self Storage Units
SIC 4225 General Warehousing & Storage
53119 Lessors of Other Real Estate Property
SIC 6515 Operators of Residential Mobile Home Sites
SIC 6517 Lessors of Railroad Property
SIC 6519 Lessors of Real Property, nec
53121 Offices of Real Estate Agents & Brokers
SIC 6531 Real Estate Agents Managers
531311 Residential Property Managers
SIC 6531 Real Estate Agents & Managers
531312 Nonresidential Property Managers
SIC 6531 Real Estate Agents & Managers
53132 Offices of Real Estate Appraisers
SIC 6531 Real Estate Agents & Managers
531399 All Other Activities Related to Real Estate
SIC 6531 Real Estate Agents & Managers
532111 Passenger Car Rental
SIC 7514 Passenger Car Rental
532112 Passenger Car Leasing
SIC 7515 Passenger Car Leasing

53212 Truck, Utility Trailer, & RV Rental & Leasing
SIC 7513 Truck Rental & Leasing Without Drivers
SIC 7519 Utility Trailers & Recreational Vehicle Rental
53221 Consumer Electronics & Appliances Rental
SIC 7359 Equipment Rental & Leasing, nec
53222 Formal Wear & Costume Rental
SIC 7299 Miscellaneous Personal Services, nec
SIC 7819 Services Allied to Motion Picture Production
53223 Video Tape & Disc Rental
SIC 7841 Video Tape Rental
532291 Home Health Equipment Rental
SIC 7352 Medical Equipment Rental & Leasing
532292 Recreational Goods Rental
SIC 7999 Amusement & Recreation Services, nec
532299 All Other Consumer Goods Rental
SIC 7359 Equipment Rental & Leasing, nec
53231 General Rental Centers
SIC 7359 Equipment Rental & Leasing, nec
**532411 Commercial Air, Rail, & Water Transportation
        Equipment Rental & Leasing**
SIC 4499 Water Transportation Services, nec
SIC 4741 Rental of Railroad Cars
SIC 7359 Equipment Rental & Leasing, nec
**532412 Construction, Mining & Forestry Machinery &
        Equipment Rental & Leasing**
SIC 7353 Heavy Construction Equipment Rental & Leasing
SIC 7359 Equipment Rental & Leasing, nec
53242 Office Machinery & Equipment Rental & Leasing
SIC 7359 Equipment Rental & Leasing
SIC 7377 Computer Rental & Leasing
**53249 Other Commercial & Industrial Machinery &
        Equipment Rental & Leasing**
SIC 7352 Medical Equipment Rental & Leasing
SIC 7359 Equipment Rental & Leasing, nec
SIC 7819 Services Allied to Motion Picture Production
SIC 7922 Theatrical Producers & Miscellaneous Theatrical
        Services
53311 Owners & Lessors of Other Nonfinancial Assets
SIC 6792 Oil Royalty Traders
SIC 6794 Patent Owners & Lessors

PROFESSIONAL, SCIENTIFIC, & TECHNICAL SERVICES

54111 Offices of Lawyers
SIC 8111 Legal Services
541191 Title Abstract & Settlement Offices
SIC 6541 Title Abstract Offices
541199 All Other Legal Services
SIC 7389 Business Services, nec
541211 Offices of Certified Public Accountants
SIC 8721 Accounting, Auditing, & Bookkeeping Services
541213 Tax Preparation Services
SIC 7291 Tax Return Preparation Services
541214 Payroll Services
SIC 7819 Services Allied to Motion Picture Production
SIC 8721 Accounting, Auditing, & Bookkeeping Services
541219 Other Accounting Services
SIC 8721 Accounting, Auditing, & Bookkeeping Services
54131 Architectural Services
SIC 8712 Architectural Services

54132 Landscape Architectural Services
SIC 0781 Landscape Counseling & Planning
54133 Engineering Services
SIC 8711 Engineering Services
54134 Drafting Services
SIC 7389 Business Services, nec
54135 Building Inspection Services
SIC 7389 Business Services, nec
54136 Geophysical Surveying & Mapping Services
SIC 8713 Surveying Services
SIC 1081 Metal Mining Services
SIC 1382 Oil & Gas Field Exploration Services
SIC 1481 Nonmetallic Minerals Services, Except Fuels
54137 Surveying & Mapping Services
SIC 7389 Business Services, nec
SIC 8713 Surveying Services
54138 Testing Laboratories
SIC 8734 Testing Laboratories
54141 Interior Design Services
SIC 7389 Business Services, nec
54142 Industrial Design Services
SIC 7389 Business Services, nec
54143 Commercial Art & Graphic Design Services
SIC 7336 Commercial Art & Graphic Design
SIC 8099 Health & Allied Services, nec
54149 Other Specialized Design Services
SIC 7389 Business Services, nec
541511 Custom Computer Programming Services
SIC 7371 Computer Programming Services
541512 Computer Systems Design Services
SIC 7373 Computer Integrated Systems Design
SIC 7379 Computer Related Services, nec
541513 Computer Facilities Management Services
SIC 7376 Computer Facilities Management Services
541519 Other Computer Related Services
SIC 7379 Computer Related Services, nec
**541611 Administrative Management & General Management
        Consulting Services**
SIC 8742 Management Consulting Services
**541612 Human Resources & Executive Search Consulting
        Services**
SIC 8742 Management Consulting Services
SIC 7361 Employment Agencies
SIC 8999 Services, nec
541613 Marketing Consulting Services
SIC 8742 Management Consulting Services
**541614 Process, Physical, Distribution & Logistics Consulting
        Services**
SIC 8742 Management Consulting Services
541618 Other Management Consulting Services
SIC 4731 Arrangement of Transportation of Freight & Cargo
SIC 8748 Business Consulting Services, nec
54162 Environmental Consulting Services
SIC 8999 Services, nec
54169 Other Scientific & Technical Consulting Services
SIC 0781 Landscape Counseling & Planning
SIC 8748 Business Consulting Services, nec
SIC 8999 Services, nec
**54171 Research & Development in the Physical Sciences &
        Engineering Sciences**
SIC 8731 Commercial Physical & Biological Research
SIC 8733 Noncommercial Research Organizations

54172 Research & Development in the Life Sciences
SIC 8731 Commercial Physical & Biological Research
SIC 8733 Noncommercial Research Organizations
54173 Research & Development in the Social Sciences & Humanities
SIC 8732 Commercial Economic, Sociological, & Educational Research
SIC 8733 Noncommercial Research Organizations
54181 Advertising Agencies
SIC 7311 Advertising Agencies
54182 Public Relations Agencies
SIC 8743 Public Relations Services
54183 Media Buying Agencies
SIC 7319 Advertising, nec
54184 Media Representatives
SIC 7313 Radio, Television, & Publishers' Advertising Representatives
54185 Display Advertising
SIC 7312 Outdoor Advertising Services
SIC 7319 Advertising, nec
54186 Direct Mail Advertising
SIC 7331 Direct Mail Advertising Services
54187 Advertising Material Distribution Services
SIC 7319 Advertising, NEC
54189 Other Services Related to Advertising
SIC 7319 Advertising, nec
SIC 5199 Nondurable Goods, nec
SIC 7389 Business Services, nec
54191 Marketing Research & Public Opinion Polling
SIC 8732 Commercial Economic, Sociological, & Educational Research
541921 Photography Studios, Portrait
SIC 7221 Photographic Studios, Portrait
541922 Commercial Photography
SIC 7335 Commercial Photography
SIC 8099 Health & Allied Services, nec
54193 Translation & Interpretation Services
SIC 7389 Business Services, NEC
54194 Veterinary Services
SIC 0741 Veterinary Services for Livestock
SIC 0742 Veterinary Services for Animal Specialties
SIC 8734 Testing Laboratories
54199 All Other Professional, Scientific & Technical Services
SIC 7389 Business Services

MANAGEMENT OF COMPANIES & ENTERPRISES

551111 Offices of Bank Holding Companies
SIC 6712 Offices of Bank Holding Companies
551112 Offices of Other Holding Companies
SIC 6719 Offices of Holding Companies, nec
551114 Corporate, Subsidiary, & Regional Managing Offices
No SIC equivalent

ADMINISTRATIVE & SUPPORT, WASTE MANAGEMENT & REMEDIATION SERVICES

56111 Office Administrative Services
SIC 8741 Management Services

56121 Facilities Support Services
SIC 8744 Facilities Support Management Services
56131 Employment Placement Agencies
SIC 7361 Employment Agencies
SIC 7819 Services Allied to Motion Pictures Production
SIC 7922 Theatrical Producers & Miscellaneous Theatrical Services
56132 Temporary Help Services
SIC 7363 Help Supply Services
56133 Employee Leasing Services
SIC 7363 Help Supply Services
56141 Document Preparation Services
SIC 7338 Secretarial & Court Reporting
561421 Telephone Answering Services
SIC 7389 Business Services, nec
561422 Telemarketing Bureaus
SIC 7389 Business Services, nec
561431 Photocopying & Duplicating Services
SIC 7334 Photocopying & Duplicating Services
561432 Private Mail Centers
SIC 7389 Business Services, nec
561439 Other Business Service Centers
SIC 7334 Photocopying & Duplicating Services
SIC 7389 Business Services, nec
56144 Collection Agencies
SIC 7322 Adjustment & Collection Services
56145 Credit Bureaus
SIC 7323 Credit Reporting Services
561491 Repossession Services
SIC 7322 Adjustment & Collection
SIC 7389 Business Services, nec
561492 Court Reporting & Stenotype Services
SIC 7338 Secretarial & Court Reporting
561499 All Other Business Support Services
SIC 7389 Business Services, NEC
56151 Travel Agencies
SIC 4724 Travel Agencies
56152 Tour Operators
SIC 4725 Tour Operators
561591 Convention & Visitors Bureaus
SIC 7389 Business Services, nec
561599 All Other Travel Arrangement & Reservation Services
SIC 4729 Arrangement of Passenger Transportation, nec
SIC 7389 Business Services, nec
SIC 7999 Amusement & Recreation Services, nec
SIC 8699 Membership Organizations, nec
561611 Investigation Services
SIC 7381 Detective, Guard, & Armored Car Services
561612 Security Guards & Patrol Services
SIC 7381 Detective, Guard, & Armored Car Services
561613 Armored Car Services
SIC 7381 Detective, Guard, & Armored Car Services
561621 Security Systems Services
SIC 7382 Security Systems Services
SIC 1731 Electrical Work
561622 Locksmiths
SIC 7699 Repair Shops & Related Services, nec
56171 Exterminating & Pest Control Services
SIC 4959 Sanitary Services, NEC
SIC 7342 Disinfecting & Pest Control Services
56172 Janitorial Services
SIC 7342 Disinfecting & Pest Control Services
SIC 7349 Building Cleaning & Maintenance Services, nec
SIC 4581 Airports, Flying Fields, & Airport Terminal Services

56173   Landscaping Services
SIC 0782 Lawn & Garden Services
SIC 0783 Ornamental Shrub & Tree Services
56174   Carpet & Upholstery Cleaning Services
SIC 7217 Carpet & Upholstery Cleaning
56179   Other Services to Buildings & Dwellings
SIC 7389 Business Services, nec
SIC 7699 Repair Shops & Related Services, nec
56191   Packaging & Labeling Services
SIC 7389 Business Services, nec
56192   Convention & Trade Show Organizers
SIC 7389 Business Services, NEC
56199   All Other Support Services
SIC 7389 Business Services, nec
562111 Solid Waste Collection
SIC 4212 Local Trucking Without Storage
SIC 4953 Refuse Systems
562112 Hazardous Waste Collection
SIC 4212 Local Trucking Without Storage
SIC 4953 Refuse Systems
562119 Other Waste Collection
SIC 4212 Local Trucking Without Storage
SIC 4953 Refuse Systems
562211 Hazardous Waste Treatment & Disposal
SIC 4953 Refuse Systems
562212 Solid Waste Landfill
SIC 4953 Refuse Systems
562213 Solid Waste Combustors & Incinerators
SIC 4953 Refuse Systems
562219 Other Nonhazardous Waste Treatment & Disposal
SIC 4953 Refuse Systems
56291   Remediation Services
SIC 1799 Special Trade Contractors, nec
SIC 4959 Sanitary Services, nec
56292   Materials Recovery Facilities
SIC 4953 Refuse Systems
562991 Septic Tank & Related Services
SIC 7359 Equipment Rental & Leasing, nec
SIC 7699 Repair Shops & Related Services, nec
562998 All Other Miscellaneous Waste Management Services
SIC 4959 Sanitary Services, nec

EDUCATIONAL SERVICES

61111   Elementary & Secondary Schools
SIC 8211 Elementary & Secondary Schools
61121   Junior Colleges
SIC 8222 Junior Colleges & Technical Institutes
61131   Colleges, Universities & Professional Schools
SIC 8221 Colleges, Universities, & Professional Schools
61141   Business & Secretarial Schools
SIC 8244 Business & Secretarial Schools
61142   Computer Training
SIC 8243 Data Processing Schools
61143   Professional & Management Development Training Schools
SIC 8299 Schools & Educational Services, nec
611511 Cosmetology & Barber Schools
SIC 7231 Beauty Shops
SIC 7241 Barber Shops
611512 Flight Training
SIC 8249 Vocational Schools, nec
SIC 8299 Schools & Educational Services, nec

611513 Apprenticeship Training
SIC 8249 Vocational Schools, nec
611519 Other Technical & Trade Schools
SIC 8249 Vocational Schools, NEC
SIC 8243 Data Processing Schools
61161   Fine Arts Schools
SIC 8299 Schools & Educational Services, nec
SIC 7911 Dance Studios, Schools, & Halls
61162   Sports & Recreation Instruction
SIC 7999 Amusement & Recreation Services, nec
61163   Language Schools
SIC 8299 Schools & Educational Services, nec
611691 Exam Preparation & Tutoring
SIC 8299 Schools & Educational Services, nec
611692 Automobile Driving Schools
SIC 8299 Schools & Educational Services, nec
611699 All Other Miscellaneous Schools & Instruction
SIC 8299 Schools & Educational Services, nec
61171   Educational Support Services
SIC 8299 Schools & Educational Services nec
SIC 8748 Business Consulting Services, nec

HEALTH CARE & SOCIAL ASSISTANCE

621111 Offices of Physicians
SIC 8011 Offices & Clinics of Doctors of Medicine
SIC 8031 Offices & Clinics of Doctors of Osteopathy
621112 Offices of Physicians, Mental Health Specialists
SIC 8011 Offices & Clinics of Doctors of Medicine
SIC 8031 Offices & Clinics of Doctors of Osteopathy
62121   Offices of Dentists
SIC 8021 Offices & Clinics of Dentists
62131   Offices of Chiropractors
SIC 8041 Offices & Clinics of Chiropractors
62132   Offices of Optometrists
SIC 8042 Offices & Clinics of Optometrists
62133   Offices of Mental Health Practitioners
SIC 8049 Offices & Clinics of Health Practitioners, nec
62134   Offices of Physical, Occupational & Speech Therapists & Audiologists
SIC 8049 Offices & Clinics of Health Practitioners, nec
621391 Offices of Podiatrists
SIC 8043 Offices & Clinics of Podiatrists
621399 Offices of All Other Miscellaneous Health Practitioners
SIC 8049 Offices & Clinics of Health Practitioners, nec
62141   Family Planning Centers
SIC 8093 Speciality Outpatient Facilities, NEC
SIC 8099 Health & Allied Services, nec
62142   Outpatient Mental Health & Substance Abuse Centers
SIC 8093 Specialty Outpatient Facilities, nec
621491 HMO Medical Centers
SIC 8011 Offices & Clinics of Doctors of Medicine
621492 Kidney Dialysis Centers
SIC 8092 Kidney Dialysis Centers
621493 Freestanding Ambulatory Surgical & Emergency Centers
SIC 8011 Offices & Clinics of Doctors of Medicine
621498 All Other Outpatient Care Centers
SIC 8093 Specialty Outpatient Facilities, nec
621511 Medical Laboratories
SIC 8071 Medical Laboratories
621512 Diagnostic Imaging Centers
SIC 8071 Medical Laboratories

62161 Home Health Care Services
SIC 8082 Home Health Care Services
62191 Ambulance Services
SIC 4119 Local Passenger Transportation, nec
SIC 4522 Air Transportation, Nonscheduled
621991 Blood & Organ Banks
SIC 8099 Health & Allied Services, nec
621999 All Other Miscellaneous Ambulatory Health Care Services
SIC 8099 Health & Allied Services, nec
62211 General Medical & Surgical Hospitals
SIC 8062 General Medical & Surgical Hospitals
SIC 8069 Specialty Hospitals, Except Psychiatric
62221 Psychiatric & Substance Abuse Hospitals
SIC 8063 Psychiatric Hospitals
SIC 8069 Specialty Hospitals, Except Psychiatric
62231 Specialty Hospitals
SIC 8069 Specialty Hospitals, Except Psychiatric
62311 Nursing Care Facilities
SIC 8051 Skilled Nursing Care Facilities
SIC 8052 Intermediate Care Facilities
SIC 8059 Nursing & Personal Care Facilities, nec
62321 Residential Mental Retardation Facilities
SIC 8052 Intermediate Care Facilities
62322 Residential Mental Health & Substance Abuse Facilities
SIC 8361 Residential Care
623311 Continuing Care Retirement Communities
SIC 8051 Skilled Nursing Care Facilities
SIC 8052 Intermediate Care Facilities
SIC 8059 Nursing & Personal Care Facilities, nec
623312 Homes for the Elderly
SIC 8361 Residential Care
62399 Other Residential Care Facilities
SIC 8361 Residential Care
62411 Child & Youth Services
SIC 8322 Individual & Family Social Services
SIC 8641 Civic, Social, & Fraternal Organizations
62412 Services for the Elderly & Persons with Disabilities
SIC 8322 Individual & Family Social Services
62419 Other Individual & Family Services
SIC 8322 Individual & Family Social Services
62421 Community Food Services
SIC 8322 Individual & Family Social Services
624221 Temporary Shelters
SIC 8322 Individual & Family Social Services
624229 Other Community Housing Services
SIC 8322 Individual & Family Social Services
62423 Emergency & Other Relief Services
SIC 8322 Individual & Family Social Services
62431 Vocational Rehabilitation Services
SIC 8331 Job Training & Vocational Rehabilitation Services
62441 Child Day Care Services
SIC 8351 Child Day Care Services
SIC 7299 Miscellaneous Personal Services, nec

ARTS, ENTERTAINMENT, & RECREATION

71111 Theater Companies & Dinner Theaters
SIC 5812 Eating Places
SIC 7922 Theatrical Producers & Miscellaneous Theatrical Services

71112 Dance Companies
SIC 7922 Theatrical Producers & Miscellaneous Theatrical Services
71113 Musical Groups & Artists
SIC 7929 Bands, Orchestras, Actors, & Entertainment Groups
71119 Other Performing Arts Companies
SIC 7929 Bands, Orchestras, Actors, & Entertainment Groups
SIC 7999 Amusement & Recreation Services, nec
711211 Sports Teams & Clubs
SIC 7941 Professional Sports Clubs & Promoters
711212 Race Tracks
SIC 7948 Racing, Including Track Operations
711219 Other Spectator Sports
SIC 7941 Professional Sports Clubs & Promoters
SIC 7948 Racing, Including Track Operations
SIC 7999 Amusement & Recreation Services, nec
71131 Promoters of Performing Arts, Sports & Similar Events with Facilities
SIC 6512 Operators of Nonresidential Buildings
SIC 7922 Theatrical Procedures & Miscellaneous Theatrical Services
SIC 7941 Professional Sports Clubs & Promoters
71132 Promoters of Performing Arts, Sports & Similar Events without Facilities
SIC 7922 Theatrical Producers & Miscellaneous Theatrical Services
SIC 7941 Professional Sports Clubs & Promoters
71141 Agents & Managers for Artists, Athletes, Entertainers & Other Public Figures
SIC 7389 Business Services, nec
SIC 7922 Theatrical Producers & Miscellaneous Theatrical Services
SIC 7941 Professional Sports Clubs & Promoters
71151 Independent Artists, Writers, & Performers
SIC 7819 Services Allied to Motion Picture Production
SIC 7929 Bands, Orchestras, Actors, & Other Entertainers & Entertainment Services
SIC 8999 Services, nec
71211 Museums
SIC 8412 Museums & Art Galleries
71212 Historical Sites
SIC 8412 Museums & Art Galleries
71213 Zoos & Botanical Gardens
SIC 8422 Arboreta & Botanical & Zoological Gardens
71219 Nature Parks & Other Similar Institutions
SIC 7999 Amusement & Recreation Services, nec
SIC 8422 Arboreta & Botanical & Zoological Gardens
71311 Amusement & Theme Parks
SIC 7996 Amusement Parks
71312 Amusement Arcades
SIC 7993 Coin-Operated Amusement Devices
71321 Casinos
SIC 7999 Amusement & Recreation Services, nec
71329 Other Gambling Industries
SIC 7993 Coin-Operated Amusement Devices
SIC 7999 Amusement & Recreation Services, nec
71391 Golf Courses & Country Clubs
SIC 7992 Public Golf Courses
SIC 7997 Membership Sports & Recreation Clubs
71392 Skiing Facilities
SIC 7999 Amusement & Recreation Services, nec
71393 Marinas
SIC 4493 Marinas

71394 Fitness & Recreational Sports Centers
SIC 7991 Physical Fitness Facilities
SIC 7997 Membership Sports & Recreation Clubs
SIC 7999 Amusement & Recreation Services, nec
71395 Bowling Centers
SIC 7933 Bowling Centers
71399 All Other Amusement & Recreation Industries
SIC 7911 Dance Studios, Schools, & Halls
SIC 7993 Amusement & Recreation Services, nec
SIC 7997 Membership Sports & Recreation Clubs
SIC 7999 Amusement & Recreation Services, nec

ACCOMMODATION & FOODSERVICES

72111 Hotels & Motels
SIC 7011 Hotels & Motels
SIC 7041 Organization Hotels & Lodging Houses, on
    Membership Basis
72112 Casino Hotels
SIC 7011 Hotels & Motels
721191 Bed & Breakfast Inns
SIC 7011 Hotels & Motels
721199 All Other Traveler Accommodation
SIC 7011 Hotels & Motels
721211 RV Parks & Campgrounds
SIC 7033 Recreational Vehicle Parks & Campgrounds
721214 Recreational & Vacation Camps
SIC 7032 Sporting & Recreational Camps
72131 Rooming & Boarding Houses
SIC 7021 Rooming & Boarding Houses
SIC 7041 Organization Hotels & Lodging Houses, on
    Membership Basis
72211 Full-Service Restaurants
SIC 5812 Eating Places
722211 Limited-Service Restaurants
SIC 5812 Eating Places
SIC 5499 Miscellaneous Food Stores
722212 Cafeterias
SIC 5812 Eating Places
722213 Snack & Nonalcoholic Beverage Bars
SIC 5812 Eating Places
SIC 5461 Retail Bakeries
72231 Foodservice Contractors
SIC 5812 Eating Places
72232 Caterers
SIC 5812 Eating Places
72233 Mobile Caterers
SIC 5963 Direct Selling Establishments
72241 Drinking Places
SIC 5813 Drinking Places

OTHER SERVICES

811111 General Automotive Repair
SIC 7538 General Automotive Repair Shops
811112 Automotive Exhaust System Repair
SIC 7533 Automotive Exhaust System Repair Shops
811113 Automotive Transmission Repair
SIC 7537 Automotive Transmission Repair Shops

**811118 Other Automotive Mechanical & Electrical Repair &
    Maintenance**
SIC 7539 Automotive Repair Shops, nec
**811121 Automotive Body, Paint & Upholstery Repair &
    Maintenance**
SIC 7532 Top, Body, & Upholstery Repair Shops & Paint
    Shops
811122 Automotive Glass Replacement Shops
SIC 7536 Automotive Glass Replacement Shops
811191 Automotive Oil Change & Lubrication Shops
SIC 7549 Automotive Services, Except Repair & Carwashes
811192 Car Washes
SIC 7542 Carwashes
811198 All Other Automotive Repair & Maintenance
SIC 7534 Tire Retreading & Repair Shops
SIC 7549 Automotive Services, Except Repair & Carwashes
811211 Consumer Electronics Repair & Maintenance
SIC 7622 Radio & Television Repair Shops
SIC 7629 Electrical & Electronic Repair Shops, nec
811212 Computer & Office Machine Repair & Maintenance
SIC 7378 Computer Maintenance & Repair
SIC 7629 Electrical & Electronic Repair Shops, nec
SIC 7699 Repair Shops & Related Services, nec
811213 Communication Equipment Repair & Maintenance
SIC 7622 Radio & Television Repair Shops
SIC 7629 Electrical & Electronic Repair Shops, nec
**811219 Other Electronic & Precision Equipment Repair &
    Maintenance**
SIC 7629 Electrical & Electronic Repair Shops, nec
SIC 7699 Repair Shops & Related Services, NEC
**81131 Commercial & Industrial Machinery & Equipment
    Repair & Maintenance**
SIC 7699 Repair Shops & Related Services, nec
SIC 7623 Refrigerator & Air-Conditioning Service & Repair
    Shops
SIC 7694 Armature Rewinding Shops
811411 Home & Garden Equipment Repair & Maintenance
SIC 7699 Repair Shops & Related Services, nec
811412 Appliance Repair & Maintenance
SIC 7623 Refrigeration & Air-Conditioning Service & Repair
    Shops
SIC 7629 Electrical & Electronic Repair Shops, NEC
SIC 7699 Repairs Shops & Related Services, nec
81142 Reupholstery & Furniture Repair
SIC 7641 Reupholstery & Furniture Repair
81143 Footwear & Leather Goods Repair
SIC 7251 Shoe Repair & Shoeshine Parlors
SIC 7699 Repair Shops & Related Services
**81149 Other Personal & Household Goods Repair &
    Maintenance**
SIC 3732 Boat Building & Repairing
SIC 7219 Laundry & Garment Services, nec
SIC 7631 Watch, Clock, & Jewelry Repair
SIC 7692 Welding Repair
SIC 7699 Repair Shops & Related Services, nec
812111 Barber Shops
SIC 7241 Barber Shops
812112 Beauty Salons
SIC 7231 Beauty Shops
812113 Nail Salons
SIC 7231 Beauty Shops
812191 Diet & Weight Reducing Centers
SIC 7299 Miscellaneous Personal Services, nec

812199 Other Personal Care Services
SIC 7299 Miscellaneous Personal Services, nec,

81221 Funeral Homes
SIC 7261 Funeral Services & Crematories

81222 Cemeteries & Crematories
SIC 6531 Real Estate Agents & Managers
SIC 6553 Cemetery Subdividers & Developers
SIC 7261 Funeral Services & Crematories

81231 Coin-Operated Laundries & Drycleaners
SIC 7215 Coin-Operated Laundry & Drycleaning

812321 Laundries, Family & Commercial
SIC 7211 Power Laundries, Family & Commercial

812322 Drycleaning Plants
SIC 7216 Drycleaning Plants, Except Rug Cleaning

812331 Linen Supply
SIC 7213 Linen Supply
SIC 7219 Laundry & Garment Services, nec,

812332 Industrial Launderers
SIC 7218 Industrial Launderers

812391 Garment Pressing, & Agents for Laundries
SIC 7212 Garment Pressing & Agents for Laundries

812399 All Other Laundry Services
SIC 7219 Laundry & Garment Services, NEC

81291 Pet Care Services
SIC 0752 Animal Speciality Services, Except Veterinary

812921 Photo Finishing Laboratories
SIC 7384 Photofinishing Laboratories

812922 One-Hour Photo Finishing
SIC 7384 Photofinishing Laboratories

81293 Parking Lots & Garages
SIC 7521 Automobile Parking

81299 All Other Personal Services
SIC 7299 Miscellaneous Personal Services, nec
SIC 7389 Miscellaneous Business Services

81311 Religious Organizations
SIC 8661 Religious Organizations

813211 Grantmaking Foundations
SIC 6732 Educational, Religious, & Charitable Trust

813212 Voluntary Health Organizations
SIC 8399 Social Services, nec

813219 Other Grantmaking & Giving Services
SIC 8399 Social Services, NEC

813311 Human Rights Organizations
SIC 8399 Social Services, nec

813312 Environment, Conservation & Wildlife Organizations
SIC 8399 Social Services, nec
SIC 8699 Membership Organizations, nec

813319 Other Social Advocacy Organizations
SIC 8399 Social Services, NEC

81341 Civic & Social Organizations
SIC 8641 Civic, Social, & Fraternal Organizations
SIC 8699 Membership Organizations, nec

81391 Business Associations
SIC 8611 Business Associations
SIC 8699 Membership Organizations, nec

81392 Professional Organizations
SIC 8621 Professional Membership Organizations

81393 Labor Unions & Similar Labor Organizations
SIC 8631 Labor Unions & Similar Labor Organizations

81394 Political Organizations
SIC 8651 Political Organizations

81399 Other Similar Organizations
SIC 6531 Real Estate Agents & Managers
SIC 8641 Civic, Social, & Fraternal Organizations

SIC 8699 Membership Organizations, nec
81411 Private Households
SIC 8811 Private Households

PUBLIC ADMINISTRATION

92111 Executive Offices
SIC 9111 Executive Offices

92112 Legislative Bodies
SIC 9121 Legislative Bodies

92113 Public Finance
SIC 9311 Public Finance, Taxation, & Monetary Policy

92114 Executive & Legislative Offices, Combined
SIC 9131 Executive & Legislative Offices, Combined

92115 American Indian & Alaska Native Tribal Governments
SIC 8641 Civic, Social, & Fraternal Organizations

92119 All Other General Government
SIC 9199 General Government, nec

92211 Courts
SIC 9211 Courts

92212 Police Protection
SIC 9221 Police Protection

92213 Legal Counsel & Prosecution
SIC 9222 Legal Counsel & Prosecution

92214 Correctional Institutions
SIC 9223 Correctional Institutions

92215 Parole Offices & Probation Offices
SIC 8322 Individual & Family Social Services

92216 Fire Protection
SIC 9224 Fire Protection

92219 All Other Justice, Public Order, & Safety
SIC 9229 Public Order & Safety, nec

92311 Administration of Education Programs
SIC 9411 Administration of Educational Programs

92312 Administration of Public Health Programs
SIC 9431 Administration of Public Health Programs

92313 Administration of Social, Human Resource & Income Maintenance Programs
SIC 9441 Administration of Social, Human Resource & Income Maintenance Programs

92314 Administration of Veteran's Affairs
SIC 9451 Administration of Veteran's Affairs, Except Health Insurance

92411 Air & Water Resource & Solid Waste Management
SIC 9511 Air & Water Resource & Solid Waste Management

92412 Land, Mineral, Wildlife, & Forest Conservation
SIC 9512 Land, Mineral, Wildlife, & Forest Conservation

92511 Administration of Housing Programs
SIC 9531 Administration of Housing Programs

92512 Administration of Urban Planning & Community & Rural Development
SIC 9532 Administration of Urban Planning & Community & Rural Development

92611 Administration of General Economic Programs
SIC 9611 Administration of General Economic Programs

92612 Regulation & Administration of Transportation Programs
SIC 9621 Regulations & Administration of Transportation Programs

92613 Regulation & Administration of Communications, Electric, Gas, & Other Utilities
SIC 9631 Regulation & Administration of Communications, Electric, Gas, & Other Utilities

92614 Regulation of Agricultural Marketing & Commodities
SIC 9641 Regulation of Agricultural Marketing & Commodities

92615 Regulation, Licensing, & Inspection of Miscellaneous Commercial Sectors
SIC 9651 Regulation, Licensing, & Inspection of Miscellaneous Commercial Sectors

92711 Space Research & Technology
SIC 9661 Space Research & Technology

92811 National Security
SIC 9711 National Security

92812 International Affairs
SIC 9721 International Affairs

99999 Unclassified Establishments
SIC 9999 Nonclassifiable Establishments

APPENDIX III

ANNOTATED SOURCE LIST

The following listing provides the names, publishers, addresses, telephone and fax numbers (if available), and frequency of publications for the primary sources used in *Market Share Reporter*.

20/20 Magazine, Jobson Publishing Corp., 100 Avenue of the Americas, 9th Floor, New York, NY 10013, *Telephone:* (212) 274-7000, *Fax:* (212) 431-0500, *Published:* monthly.

The Accountant, Lafferty Publications Ltd., IDA Tower, Pearse Street, Dublin 2, Ireland, *Telephone:* (353-1) 671-8022, *Fax:* (353-1) 671-8520, *Published:* monthly.

AdAgeGlobal, Crain Communications, Inc., 220 E. 42nd St., New York, NY 10017, *Telephone:* (212) 210-0725, *Fax:* (212) 210-0111.

Adhesive & Sealants Industry, Communication Channels Inc., 6255 Barfield Rd., Atlanta, GA 30328, *Telephone:* (404) 256-9800, *Fax:* (404) 256-3116, *Published:* monthly.

Advanced Materials & Composites News, Composites Worldwide, 991C Lomas Santa Fe Drive, MS409, Solana Beach, CA 92075-2198, *Telephone:* (1 858) 755-1372, *Fax:* (1 858) 755-5271.

Advanced Materials & Processes, ASM International, 9639 Kinsman Rd., Materials Park, OH 44073-0002, *Telephone*: (216) 338-5151, *Fax:* (216) 338-4634, *Published*: monthly.

Advertising Age, Crain Communications, Inc., 220 E. 42nd St., New York, NY 10017, *Telephone:* (212) 210-0725, *Fax:* (212) 210-0111, *Published:* weekly.

Adweek, BPI Communications, Merchandise Mart, Suite 396, Chicago, IL 60654, *Telephone:* (800) 722-6658, *Fax*: (312) 464-8540, *Published*: weekly.

Adweek Magazine's Technology Marketing, BPI Communications, Merchandise Mart, Suite 396, Chicago, IL 60654, *Telephone:* (800) 722-6658, *Fax:* (312) 464-8540.

Aftermarket Business, Advanstar Communications, Inc., 7500 Old Oak Blvd., Cleveland, OH 44130-3343, *Published*: monthly.

Ag Lender, 11701 BoormanDrive, St. Louis, MO 63146, *Telephone:* (800) 535-2342.

Air Cargo World, Journal of Commerce Inc., 1230 National Press Building, Washington D.C. 20045, *Telphone*: (202) 783-1148, *Published*: monthly.

Air Conditioning, Heating and Refrigeration News, Business News Publishing Co., P.O. Box 2600, Troy, MI 48007, *Telephone:* (313) 362-3700, *Fax:* (313) 362-0317.

Airport Security Report, PBI Media, 1201 Seven Locks Road, Suite 300, Potomac, MD 20854, *Telephone:* (301) 354-2000.

Airports, Airport Council International, P.O. Box 16, 1215 Geneva 15, Switzerland, *Telephone:* (41 22) 717 8585, *Fax:* (41 22) 717 88 88.

Aluminum Today, DMG World Media, Queensway House, 2 Queensway, Redhill, Surrey RH1 1QS, United Kingdom, *Telephone:* 44 (0) 1737 768-611, *Fax:* 44 (0) 1737 761-685.

American Banker, American Banker Inc., 1 State St, New York, NY 10023, *Telephone:* (212) 408-1480, *Fax:* (212) 943-2984, *Published:* Mon. - Fri.

American Ceramic Society Bulletin, American Ceramic Society, 735 Ceramic Place, Westerville, OH 43081-8720, *Published:* monthly, *Price:* $50 per year for nonmembers and libraries.

American Demographics, Media Central, 470 Park Avenue South, 8th Floor, New York, NY 10016, *Telephone:* (800) 529-7502, *Published:* monthly, Price: $89 a year; $99 Canada.

American Lawyer, 600 3rd Avenue, New York 10016, *Telephone:* (212) 973-2800, *Fax:* (212) 972-6258, *Published:* monthly, with combined issues, *Price:* $135, $265, home; $525 office.

American Metal Market, Capital Cities Media Inc., 825 7th Avenue, New York, NY 10019, *Telephone:* (800) 360-7600, *Published:* daily, except Saturdays, Sundays, and holidays, *Price:* $560 per year (U.S., Canada, and Mexico).

American Nurseryman, American Nurseryman Publishing Co., 77 W. Washington St., Ste. 2100, Chicago, IL 60602-2801, *Telephone:* (312) 782-5505, *Fax:* (312) 782-3232.

American Printer, Maclean Hunter Publishing Co., 29 N. Wacker Dr., Chicago, IL 60606. *Published:* monthly.

American School & University, North American Publishing Co., 401 N. Broad St., Philadelphia, PA 19106, *Telephone:* (215) 238-4200, *Fax:* (215) 238-4227, *Published:* monthly.

American Shipper, Howard Publications Inc., 33 South Hogan Street, P.O. Box 4728, Jacksonville, FL

32201, *Telephone:* (904) 365-2601, *Telephone:* (904) 365-2601, *Published:* monthly, *Price:* $35 per year.

America's Network, Advanstar Communications, 201 Sandepointe Ave., Ste 600, Santa Ana, CA 92707, *Telephone:* (714) 513-8614, *Fax:* (714) 513-8634.

Amusement Business, BPI Communications Inc., Box 24970, Nashville, TN 37202, *Telephone:* (615)321-4250, *Fax:* (615) 327-1575. *Published:* weekly.

Anchorage Daily News, P.O. Box 149001, Anchorage, Alaska 99514-9001.

Appliance, Dana Chase Publications Inc., 1110 Jorie Blvd., CS 9019, Ste. 203, Hinsdale, IL 60521, *Telephone:* (708) 990 - 3484, *Fax:* (708) 990 - 0078, *Published:* monthly, *Price:* $60.

Applied Clinical Trials, 859 Williamette St, Eugene, OR 97401, *Telephone:* (541) 343-1200, *Fax:* (984) 5250.

Appliance Manufacturer, Business News Publishing Co., 755 W. Big Beaver Rd., Ste. 1000, Troy, MI 48084-4900, *Telephone:* (313) 362-3700, *Fax:* (313) 244-6439, *Published:* monthly.

Arkansas Business, 201 E. Markham, P.O. Box 3686, Little Rock, AR 72203, *Telephone:* (501)372-1443 Fax: (501) 375-3623, *Published:* weekly, *Price:* $38 per year.

Asset Securitization Report, Lewtan Technologies Inc., 300 Fifth Avenue, Waltham, MA 02451, *Telephone:* (781) 895-9800, *Fax:* (781) 890-3684.

Atlanta Journal-Constitution, 72 Marietta St., NW Atlanta, GA 30303, *Telephone:* (404) 526 - 5151, *Published:* daily.

ATM & Debit News, One State Street Plaza, New York, NY 10004, *Telephone:* (800) 221-1809, *Fax:* (800) 235-5552.

ATM Debit Card News, One State Street Plaza, New York, NY 10004, *Telephone:* (800) 221-1809, *Fax:* (800) 235-5552.

Audioweek, Waaren Communications News, 2115 Ward CT, NW, Washington D.C. 20037.

Austin Business Journal, Austin Business Journal Inc., 1301 Capital of Texas Hwy, C-200, Austin, TX 78746, *Telephone:* (512) 328-0180, *Fax:* (512) 328-7304, *Published:* weekly

Automatic Merchandiser, Johnson Hill Press Inc., 1233 Janesville Ave., Fort Atkinson, WI 53538, *Telephone:* (414) 563-6388, *Fax:* (414) 563-1699, *Published:* monthly.

Automotive Body Repair News, Capital Cities/ABC/Chilton,. Chilton Way, Radnor, PA 19089, *Telephone:* (215) 964-4000, *Fax:* (215) 964-4981.

Automotive News, Crain Communications Inc., 380 Woodbridge, Detroit, MI 48207, *Telephone:* (313) 446-6000, *Fax:* (313) 446-0347.

AVG, Meister Publishing Co., 37733 Euclid Ave., Willoughby, OH 44094-5992, *Telephone:* (216) 942-2000, *Fax:* (216) 942-0662, *Published:* monthly.

Aviation Daily, McGraw Hill Inc., 1221 Avenue of the Americas, New York, NY 10020, *Telephone:* (212) 512-2294, *Fax:* (212) 869-7799, *Published:* weekly.

B-to-B, Crain Communications Inc., 220 E 42nd St., New York, NY 10017, *Telephone:* (202) 210-0725, *Fax:* (212) 210-0111, *Published:* weekly.

Baking & Snack, Sosland Publishing Co., 4800 Main St., Ste 100, Kansas City, MO 64112, *Telephone:* (816) 756-1000.

Baltimore Business Journal, American City Business Journals, 117 Water St., Baltimore, MD 21202, *Tele-*

phone: (410) 576-1161, *Fax:* (301) 383-321, *Published:* weekly.

Bank Systems & Technology, Miller Freeman Inc., 1515 Broadway, New York, NY 10036, *Telephone:* (212) 869-1300.

Barron's, Dow Jones & Company Inc., 200 Liberty St., New York, NY 10281, *Telephone:* (212) 416-2700, *Fax:* (212) 749-6531.

Beer Handbook, Jobson Publishing, 100 Avenue of the Americas, 9th Floor, New York, NY 10013, *Telephone:* (212) 274-7000, *Fax:* (212) 431-0500.

Bellingham Business Journal, 1321 King Street, Ste. 4, Bellingham WA 98226, *Telephone:* (360) 647-8805.

Best's Review, A.M. Best Co. Inc., Ambest Rd., Oldwick, NJ 08858, *Telephone:* (908) 439-2200, *Fax:* (908) 439-3363, *Published:* monthly.

Beverage Aisle, Advanstar Communications, Inc., 7500 Old Oak Blvd., Cleveland OH 44130.

Beverage Dynamics, Jobson Publishing Corp., 100 Avenues of the Americas, 9th Floor, New York, NY 10013, *Telephone:* (212) 274-7000, *Fax:* (212) 431-0500.

Beverage Industry, Advanstar Communications, Inc., 7500 Old Oak Blvd., Cleveland OH 44130, *Telephone:* (216) 243-8100, *Fax:* (216) 891-2651, *Published:* monthly, *Price:* $40 per year.

Beverage World, Keller International Publishing Corp., 150 Great Neck Rd., Great Neck, NY 11021, *Telephone:* (516) 829-9210, *Fax:* (516) 829-5414, *Published:* monthly.

Beverage World International, Keller International Publishing Corp., 150 Great Neck Rd., Great Neck, NY 11021, *Telephone:* (516) 829-9210, *Fax:* (516) 829-5414, *Published:* monthly.

Bicycle Retailer & Industry News, 502 W. Cordova Rd., Santa Fe, NM 87501, *Telephone:* (505) 988-5099, *Fax:* (505) 988-7224, *Published:* monthly.

Billboard, BPI Communications, 1515 Broadway, 14th FL, New York, NY 10036, *Telephone*: (212) 764-7300, *Fax:* (212) 536-5358.

Biomedical Market Newsletter, 3237 Idaho Place, Costa Mesa, CA 92626-2207, *Telephone:* (714) 434-9500, *Fax:* (714) 434-9755.

Bobbin, Bobbin Blenheim Media Corp., 1110 Shop Rd, Columbia, SC 29202.

Body Fashions and Intimate Apparel, Advanstar Communications, 7500 Old Oak Blvd, Cleveland, OH 44130, Telephone: (212) 826-2839, Fax: (212) 891-2726.

Bond Buyer, American Banker Inc., 1 State St, New York, NY 10023.

Boston Business Journal, MCP Inc., 200 High St., Boston, MA 02110, Telephone: (617) 330-1000, Fax: (617) 330-1016, Published: weekly, Price: $54.

BP Report, Primedia, P.O. Box 4234, 11 River Bend Drive South, Stamford, CT 06907-0234, *Telephone:* (203) 358-4100, *Fax:* (203) 358-5824.

Brandweek, Adweek L.P., 1515 Broadway, New York, NY 10036, *Telephone:* (212) 536-5336. *Published:* weekly, except no issue in the last week of Dec.

Broadcasting & Cable, Cahners Publishing Co., 1705 DeSales Street, N.W., Washington, DC 20036, *Telephone:* (800) 554-5729 or (202) 659-2340, *Fax:* (202) 331-1732.

Builder, Hanley-Wood Inc., 655 15th St. N.W., Ste. 475, Washington, D.C. 20005, *Telephone:* (202) 737-0717, *Fax:* (202) 737-2439, *Published:* monthly.

Business 2.0, 5 Thomas Mellon Circle, Suite 305, San Francisco, CA 94134.

Business Communications Review, BCR Enterprises, Inc., 950 York Rd., Hinsdale, IL 60521, *Telephone:* (800) 227-1324, *Published:* monthly.

Business First Columbus, 200 E. Rich St., Columbus, OH 43215, *Telephone:* (614) 461-4040.

Business First of Buffalo, 472 Delaware St., Buffalo, NY 14202.

Business Forms, Labels & Systems, North American Publishing Co., 401 N Broad Street, Philadelphia, PA 19108, *Telephone:* (215) 238-5300, *Fax:* (215) 238-5457, *Published:* 2x/mo, *Price:* $24.

The Business Journal - Serving Jacksonville and Northeast Florida, 1200 Gulf Life Drive, Number 501, Jacksonville, FL 32207-1802, *Telephone:* (904) 396-3502, *Fax:* (904) 396-5706, *Published:* weekly.

The Business Journal - Portland, 851 SW Sizth Ave., Ste 500,Nertland, OR 97204.

The Business Journal - Serving Phoenix and the Valley of the Sun, 3737 N. 7th St., Ste. 200, Phoenix, AZ 85014, *Telephone:* (602) 230-8400, *Fax:* (602) 230-0955, *Published:* weekly, *Cost:* $46.

Business Mexico, American Chamber of Commerce, A.C., Lucerna 78, Col. Juarez, DEL. Cuahtemoc, Mexico City, Mexico, *Telephone:* 705-0995, *Published:* monthly.

Business North Carolina, 5435 77 Center Dr., No. 50, Charlotte, NC 28217-0711 *Telephone:* (704) 523-6987 *Published:* monthly.

Business Review (Albany, NY), P.O. Box 15081, Albany, NY 12212-5081, *Telephone:* (518) 437-9855, *Fax:* (518) 437-0764, *Published:* weekly, *Price:* $45.

BusinessWeek, McGraw-Hill Inc., 1221 Avenue of the Americas, New York, NY 10020. *Published:* weekly, *Price:* U.S.: $46.95 per year; Canada: $69 CDN per year.

C&EN, American Chemical Society, Dept. L-0011, Columbus, OH 43210, *Telephone:* (800) 333-9511 or (614) 447-3776. *Published:* weekly, except last week in December, *Price:* U.S.: $100 per year, $198 for 2 years; elsewhere: $148 per year, $274 for 2 years.

CableFAX, Media Business Corp., 1786 Platte St., Denver, CO 80202, *Telephone:* (303) 964-8400, *Fax:* (303) 964-8405.

The Calgary Sun, 2615 12th St., NE, Calgary, AB, Canada T2E 7W9, *Telephone:* (403) 250-4200, *Fax:* (403) 291-4242, *Published:* daily, *Price:* $104.

Canadian Business, CB Media Limited, 70 Esplanade, Second Floor, Toronto MSE IR2 Canada, *Telephone:* (416) 364-4266, *Fax:* (416) 364-2783. *Published:* monthly, *Price:* Canada: $24 per year, $60 for 3 years; Elsewhere: $40 per year, $100 for 3 years.

Canadian Insurance, Stone & Cox, 111 Peter St., Ste 202, Toronto, ON, Canada M5V 2H1, *Telephone:* (416) 599-0772, *Fax:* (416) 599-0867, *Published:* monthly.

Canadian Machinery and Metalworking, Maclean Hunter, 777 Bay St., Toronto, ON Canada, *Telephone:* (416) 596-5772, *Fax:* (416) 593-3162, *Published:* monthly.

Canadian Mining Journal, Southern Business Communications, 1450 Don Mills Rd., Don Mills, ON Canada M3B 2X7, *Telephone:* (416) 445-6641.

Canadian Underwriter, Southern Business Communications, 1450 Don Mills Rd., Don Mills, ON Canada M3B 2X7, *Telephone:* (416) 445-6641.

Candy Industry, Advanstar Communications Inc., 7500 Old Oak Blvd, Cleveland, OH 44130, *Telephone:* (216) 891-2612, *Fax:* (216) 891-2651, *Published:* monthly.

Capital Times, Penn State Univ., Penn State, Middletown, PA 17057, *Telephone:* (717) 944-0461, *Fax:* (717) 944-3107.

Capper's, 1503 S.W. 42nd St., Topeka, KS 66609-1265, *Telephone:* (800) 678-4883.

Card Marketing, Faulkner & Grey, Eleven Penn Plaza, 17th Floor, New York, NY 10001, *Telephone:* (800)535-8403.

Catalog Age, Cowles Business Media, 911 Hope St., Six River Bend Center, P.O. Box 4949, Stanford, CT 06907-0949, *Telephone:* (203) 358-9900, *Published:* monthly.

Ceramic Industry, Business News Publishing Co., 5900 Harper Road, Suite 109, Solon, OH 44139, *Telephone:* (216) 498-9214, *Fax:* (216) 498-9121. *Published:* monthly, *Price:* U.S.: $53 per year; Mexico: $63; Canada: $66.71 (includes postage & GST).

Chain Drug Review, Racher Press, 220 5th Ave, New York, NY 10001, *Telephone:* (212) 213-6000, *Fax:* (212) 725-3961.

Chain Leader, Attn: Reader Services, 1350 E. Touhy Ave, PO Box 5080, Des Plaines, IL 60017-5080.

Chain Store Age, Lebhar-Friedman Inc., 425 Park Ave., New York, NY 10022, *Telephone:* (212) 371-9400, *Fax:* (212) 319-4129. *Published:* monthly.

Cheers, Jobson Publishing, 100 Avenue of the Americas, 9th Floor, New York, NY 10013, *Telephone:* (212) 274-7000, *Fax:* (212) 431-0500.

Chemical Engineering, McGraw-Hill, 1221 Avenue of the Americas, New York, NY 10020, *Telephone:* (212) 512-2921, *Fax:* (212) 512-4762, *Published:* bi-weekly, Price: $27.50.

Chemical Market Reporter, Schnell Publishing Co., Inc., 80 Broad St., New York, NY 1004-2203, *Telephone:* (212) 248-4177, *Fax:* (212) 248-4903, *Published:* weekly.

Chemical Specialties, CNI, Ste. 300, 3730 Kirby Drive, Houston, TX 77098, *Telephone:* (713) 525-2653.

Chemical Week, Chemical Week Associates, P.O. Box 7721, Riverton, NJ 08077-7721, *Telephone:* (609) 786-0401, *Published:* weekly, except four combination issues (total of 49 issues), *Price:* U.S.: $99 per year; Canada: $129 per year. Single copies $8 in U.S. and $10 elsewhere.

The Chicago Tribune, 435 N. Michigan Ave., Chicago, IL 60611, *Telephone:* (312) 222-3232. *Published:* daily.

Child Care Information Exchange, Exchange Press Inc., P.O. 2890, Redmond, WA 98073, *Telephone:* (800) 221-2864, *Published:* bimonthly, *Price:* $35 per year.

Children's Business, Fairchild Publications, 7 W 34th St., New York, NY 10001, *Telephone:* (212) 630-4520, *Fax:* (212) 630-4511.

The Christian Science Monitor, Christian Science Publishing Society, One Norway St., Boston, MA 02115, *Telephone:* (800) 456-2220, *Published:* daily, except weekends and holidays.

CircuiTree, BNP, 755 West Big Beaver, Ste 100, Troy, MI 48084, *Telephone:* (248)362-3700.

Clinical Lab Products, MWC/Allied Healthcare Group, 295 Promenade Street, Suite 2, Providence, RI 02908-5720, *Telephone:* (401) 455-0555, *Fax:* (401) 455-1555.

Club Management, Finian Publishing, 107 W. Pacific Ave., St. Louis, MO *Telephone:* 63119-3776, *Fax:* (314) 961-6644.

Coatings World, 70 Hilltop Road, Ramsey, NJ 07446.

Collections & Credit Risk, Faulkner & Grey, Eleven Penn Plaza, 17th Floor, New York, NY 10001, *Telephone:* (800)535-8403.

Columbus Dispatch, 34 S. Third Street, Columbus, OH 43215.

Comic Buyer's Guide, Krause Publications Inc., 700 E State St., Iola, WI 54990-0001, *Telephone:* (715) 445-2214, *Fax:* (715) 445-4087, *Published:* weekly, *Price:* $38.95 a year.

Commercial Appeal, Memphis Publishing Co., 495 Union Ave., Memphis, TN 38103, *Telephone:* (901) 529-2211, *Fax:* (901) 529-2522, *Published:* daily.

Commercial Carrier Journal, Capital Cities/ABC/Chilton Co., Chilton Way, Radnor, PA 19089, *Telephone:* (215) 964-4000, *Fax:* (215) 964-4981.

Community Banker, 5704 71st Street, Lubbock, TX 79424.

Computerworld, P.O. Box 2043, Marion, OH 43305-2403, *Telephone:* (800) 669-1002, *Published:* weekly.

Computing Canada, Plesman Publications Ltd., 2005 Sheppard Ave. E., 4th Fl., Willowsdale, ON, Canada M2J 5B1, *Telephone:* (416) 497-9562, *Fax:* (416) 497-9427. *Published:* biweekly.

Confectioner, American Publishing Corp., 17400 Dallas Pkway, Number 121, Dallas, TX 752-7305, *Telephone:* (214) 250-3630, *Fax:* (214) 250-3733.

Construction Equipment, Cahners PublishingCo., 1350 E. Touhy Ave., Des Plaines, IL 60018, *Telephone:* (708) 635-8800, *Fax:* (708) 390-2690.

Consumer Electronics, CEA, 2500 Wilson Blvd., Arlington, VA 22201-3834.

Contracting Business, Penton Publishing, 1100 Suprior Ave., Cleveland, OH 44114, Telephone: (216) 696-7000, Fax: (216) 696-7932.

Contractor, Cahners Publishing Co., 44 Cook St., Denver, CO. 80206-5800, *Telephone:* (708) 390-2676, *Fax:* (708) 390-2690, *Published:* monthly.

Contractor's Business Management Report, IOMA, 29 West 35th Street, New York, NY 10001-2299.

Convenience Store News, BMT Publications Inc., 7 Penn Plaza, New York, NY 10001-3900, *Telephone:* (212) 594-4120, *Fax:* (212) 714-0514, *Published:* 16x/yr.

Converting, Delta Communications, 455 N. Cityfront Plaza Drive, Chicago, IL 60614, *Telephone:* (312) 222-2000, *Fax:* (312) 222-2026, *Published:* monthly, *Price:* $25 per year.

Cosmetics International, 307 Linen Hall, 162/' 168 Regent Street, London, W1R 5TB, United Kingdom, *Telephone:* (020) 7434-1530, *Fax:* (020) 7437-0915.

Courier Journal, 525 W Broadway, P.O. Box 740031, Louisville, KY 40201-7431, *Telephone:* (502) 582-4011.

Crain's Chicago Business, Crain Communications Inc., 740 N. Rush St., Chicago, IL 60611, *Telephone:* (312) 649-5411.

Crain's Detroit Business, Crain Communications Inc., 1400 Woodbridge, Detroit, MI 48207-3187, *Telephone:* (313) 446-6000. *Published:* weekly, except semiweekly the fourth week in May.

Crain's New York Business, Crain Communications, Inc., 220 E. 42nd St., New York, NY 10017, *Telephone:* (212) 210-0100, *Fax:* (212) 210-0799. *Published:* weekly.

Credit Card Management, Faulkner & Gray Inc., 11 Penn Plaza, 17th FL, New York, NY 10001, *Telephone:* (212) 766-7800, *Fax:* (212) 766-0142.

Credit Union Magazine, CUNA, P.O. Box 431, Madison, WI 53701, *Telephone:* (608) 231-4000, *Fax:* (608) 231-4370.

Daily Business Review, 330 Clematis Street, Via Jardin, Suite 114, West Palm Beach, FL 33401, *Telephone:* (561) 820-2060, *Fax:* (561) 820-2077.

Dairy Field, Stagnito Communications Inc., 155 Pfingsten Road, Suite 205, Deerfield, IL 60015, *Telephone:* (847) 205-5660, *Fax:* (847) 205-5680.

Dairy Foods, Gorman Publishing Co., 8750 W. Bryn Mawr Ave., Chicago, IL 60062, *Telephone:* (312) 693-3200. *Published:* monthly, except semimonthly in Aug.

Dairy Herd Management, Miller Publishing, 12400 Whitewater Dr., Minnetonka, MD 55345.

Dallas Business Journal, 4131 N. Central Expwy., Ste. 310, Dallas, TX 75204, *Telephone:* (214) 520-1010, *Fax:* (214) 522-5606, *Published:* weekly, *Price:* $46.

Datamonitor Industry Market Research, Datamonitor USA, 1 Park Avenue, 14th Floor, New York, NY 10016-5802.

Dealernews, Advanstar Communications Inc., 1700 E Dyer Rd., Ste. 250, Santa Ana, CA 92705, *Telephone:* (714) 252-5300, *Fax:* (714) 261-9790, *Published:* monthly.

Dealerscope, North American Publishing Co., 401 N Broad St, Philadelphia, PA 19108.

Death Care Business Advisor, LRP Publications, 360 Hiatt Drive, Palm Beach Gardens, FL 33418, *Telephone:* (561) 622-6520, *Fax:* (561) 622-0757.

Delaney Report, 149 Fifth Ave., New York, NY 10010, *Telephone:* (212) 979-7881.

Denver Business Journal, 1700 Broadway, Ste. 515, Denver, CO 80290, Telephone: (303) 837-3500, Fax: (303) 837-3535, *Published:* weekly.

Design News, McGraw-Hill, Two Penn Plaza, New York, NY 10121-2298, *Telephone:* (212) 904-2000, *Published:* quarterly.

Detroit Free Press, Knight-Ridder, Inc., 1 Herald Plaza, Miami, FL 33132, *Telephone:* (305) 376-3800, *Published:* daily.

Detroit News, Detroit News Inc., 615 Lafayette, Detroit, MI 48226, *Telephone:* (313) 222-2300, *Published:* daily.

Diagnostics Imaging, 600 Harrison St, San Francisco, CA 94107.

Diesel Progress, Diesel & Gas Turbine Publications, 13555 Bishop Ct., Brookfield, WI 53005-6286.

DNR, Cahners Publishing Co., 275 Washington St., Newton, MA 02158, *Telephone:* (617) 558-4243, *Fax:* (617) 558-4759, *Published:* 2x/mo.

Do-It-Yourself-Retailing, National Retail Hardware Assn., 5822 W. 74th St., Indianapolis, IN 46278-1756, *Telephone:* (317) 297-1190, *Fax:* (317) 328-4354, *Published:* monthly, *Price: $8; $2 single issue.*

Drug Store News, Lehbhar-Friedman Inc., 425 Park Ave, New York, NY 10022, *Telephone:* (212) 756-5000, *Fax:* (212) 838-9487, *Published:* 2x/mo.

DSN Retailing Today, Lebharr-Friedmann Inc., 425 Park Ave., New York, NY 10022, *Telephone:* (212) 756-5100, *Fax:* (212) 756-5125.

DVD News, PBI Media, 1201 Seven Locks Road, Suite 300, Potomac, MD 20854.

E&MJ, Maclean Hunter Publishing Co., 29 Wacker Dr., Chicago, IL 60606, *Fax:* (312) 726-2574, *Published:* monthly.

E Week, 10 Presidents Landing, Medford, MA 02155, *Telephone:* (781) 393-3700.

The Economist, The Economist Bldg, 111 W. 57th St., New York, NY 10019, *Telephone:* (212) 541-5730, *Fax:* (212) 541-9378, *Published:* weekly, *Cost:* $110; $3.50 per single issue.

Econtent, Online Inc., 213 Danbury Rd., Wilton, CT 06897-4007, *Telephone:* (203) 761-1466, *Fax:* (203) 761-1444.

Editor & Publisher, Editor & Publisher Co., 11 W 19th St., New York, NY 10011, *Telephone:* (212) 675-4380, *Fax:* (212) 929-1259, *Published*: weekly.

EDP Weekly's IT Monitor, Millin Publishing, 714 Church St., Alexandria, VA 22314, *Telephone:* (703) 739-8500, *Fax:* (703) 739-8505.

Education Week, Editorial Projects for Education, Sutie 100, 6935 Arlington Road, Bethesda, MD 20814-5233, *Telephone:* (800) 346-1834, *Fax:* (301) 280-3200.

Educational Marketer, Simba Information, PO Box 4234, 11 River Bend Drive South, Stamford, CT 06907-0234.

Egg Industry, Watt Publishing Co., 122 S. Wesley Ave., Mount Morris, IL 61054-1497, *Telephone:* (815) 734-4171, *Fax:* (815) 734-4201, *Published:* bi-monthly.

Electric Light & Power, 1421 S Sheridan Road, Tulsa, OK 74112, *Telephone:* (918) 832-9249, *Fax:* (918) 831-9875, *Published:* monthly.

Electrical Wholesaling, Intertec Publishing Corp., 9800 Metcalf, Overland Park, KS 66212-2215, *Telephone:* (913) 341-1300, *Fax:* (913) 967-1898, *Published:* monthly, *Price:* $10.

Electronic Business, Cahners Publishing Co., 275 Washington, Newton, MA 02158-1630, *Telephone:* (617) 964-3030, *Fax:* (617) 558-4470.

Electronic Commerce World, EC Media Group, Thomson Financial, 300 S Wacker Drive, 18th Floor, Chciago, IL 60606, *Telephone:* (312) 913-1334, *Fax:* (312) 913-1959.

Electronic Education Report, Simba Information, PO Box 4234, 11 River Bend Drive South, Stamford, CT 06907-0234.

Electronic Media, 488 Madison Ave., New York, NY 10022.

Electronic News, Electronic News Publishing Corp., 488 Madison Ave., New York, NY 10022, *Telephone:* (212) 909-5924, *Published:* weekly, except last week of Dec.

Employee Benefit News, Enterprise Communications, 1483 Chain Bridge Rd., Ste 202, McLean, VA 22101-4599, *Telephone:* (703) 448-0322, *Fax:* (703) 827-0720, *Published:* monthly, *Price:* $56; $62 in Canada and Mexico.

Energy User News, Capital Cities/ABC/Chilton Co., Chilton Way, Radnor, PA 19089, *Telephone:* (215) 964-4000, *Fax:* (215) 964-4647.

ENR , McGraw-Hill Inc., Fulfillment Manager, ENR, P.O. Box 518, Highstown, NJ 08520, *Telephone:* (609) 426-7070 or (212) 512-3549, *Fax:* (212) 512-3150, *Published:* weekly, *Price:* U.S.: $89 per year; Canada: $75 per year. Single copies $5 in U.S.

Euromoney, Euromoney Publications, Nestor House, Playhouse Yard, London EC4V 5EX UK, *Published:* monthly.

Family Practice News, International Medical News Group, 770 Lexington Ave., New York, NY 10021, *Telephone:* (212) 888-3232, *Fax:* (212) 421-0106, *Published:* 2x/mo. *Price:* $96.

Feedstuffs, Miller Publishing Co., 12400 Whitewater Dr., Ste. 1600, Minnetonka, MN 55343, *Telephone:* (612) 931-0211.

Fiber Optics Magazine, IGI Publishing, 214 Harvard Ave., Boston, MA 02134, *Telephone:* (617) 232-3111, Fax: (617) 734-8562, *Published:* 9x/yr. *Price:* $45 U.S. Canada; free to qualified subscribers.

Financial Times, FT Publications Inc., 14 East 60th Street, New York, NY 21002, *Telephone:* (212) 752-4500, *Fax:* (212) 319-0704, *Published:* daily, except for Sundays and holidays, *Price:* $425.

Flight International, Reed Elsevier, PO Box 302, Haywards Heath, West Sussex England, RH 16 3YY.

Floor Focus, 28 Old Stone Hill, Pound Ridge, NY 10576, *Telephone:* (914) 764-0556, *Fax:* (914) 764-0560.

Florida Trend, Trend Magazines, PO Box 611, Saint Petersburg, FL 33731.

Folio, Cowles Business Media, 911 Hope St, PO Box Stamford, CT 06907-0949, *Telephone:* (203) 358-9900.

Food in Canada, Rogers Media Inc., 777 Bay Street, 6th Floor, Toronto, Ontario, Canada M5W 1A7, *Published:* monthly.

Food Institute Report, Food Insitute, Elwood Park, New Jersey.

Food Processing, Putnam Media, 555 W Pierce Road, Ste. 301, Itasca, IL 60143.

Footwear News, Fairchild Publications, 7 W. 34th Street, New York, NY 10001, *Telephone:* (212) 630-4000, *Published:* weekly.

Forbes, Forbes, Inc., P.O. Box 10048, Des Moines, IA 50340-0048, *Telephone:* (800) 888-9896, *Published:* 27 issues per year, *Price:* U.S.: $54 per year; Canada: $95 per year (includes GST).

Forging, Penton Industries, Penton Media Building, 1300 E 9th St, Cleveland, OH 44114, *Telephone:* (216) 931-9141, *Fax:* (216) 931-9678.

Fortune, Time Inc., Time & Life Building, Rockefeller Center, New York, NY 10020-1393, *Published:* twice monthly, except two issues combined into a single issue at year-end, *Price:* U.S.: $57 per year; Canada: $65 per year.

Fresno Bee, McClatchy Newspapers, 1626 E St., Fresno, CA 93786-0001, *Telephone:* (209) 441-6111, *Fax:* (209) 441-6436, *Published:* daily.

Frozen Food Age, Maclean Hunter, 4 Stamford Four, Stamford, CT 06901-1201, *Telephone:* (203) 325-3500, *Published:* weekly.

Frozen Fruit Digest, 271 Madison Ave, New York, NY 10016.

Fruit Grower, Meister Publishing Co., 37733 Euclid Ave., Willoughsby, OH 44094-5992.

FSB, Forbes, Inc., P.O. Box 10048, Des Moines, IA 50340-0048, *Telephone:* (800) 888-9896.

Fuel Oil News, Hunter Publishing, 950 Lee St., Des Plaines, IL 60016, *Telephone:* (708) 296-0770, *Fax:* (708) 296-8821, *Published:* monthly.

Furniture Today, Cahners Publishing Co., 200 S. Main St., P.O. Box 2754, High Point, NC 27261, *Telephone:* (919) 889-0113, *Published:* weekly.

Gases & Welding Distributor, Penton Media, P.O. Box 901979, Cleveland, OH 44190-1979.

Globe and Mail, 444 Front St. W., Toronto, ON, Canada M5V 2S9, *Telephone:* (416) 585-5000, *Fax:* (416) 585-5085, *Published:* Mon.-Sat. (Morn.).

Golf World, 5520 Park Ave, Trumbull, CT 06611.

Golf World Business, 5520 Park Ave., Trumbull, CT 06611.

Gourmet Retailer, 3301 Ponce de Leon, Suite 300, Coral Gables, FL 33134.

Government Executive, National Journal Inc., 1730 M. NW, Ste 1100, Washington D.C. 20036, *Telephone:* (202) 862-0600.

Grand Rapids Press, Booth Newspapers Inc., 155 Michigan St., NW, Grand Rapids, MI 49503, *Telephone:* (616) 459-1567, *Publlished:* daily.

Graphic Arts Monthly, Cahners Publishing Company, 44 Cook St., Denver, CO 80206-5800, *Telephone:* (800) 637-6089.

Greater Baton Rouge Business Report, Louisiana Business, P.O. Box 1949, Baton Rouge, LA 70821, *Telephone:* (504) 928-1700, *Fax:* (504) 923-3448, *Published:* biweekly, *Price:* $24; free to qualified subscribers.

Green Bay Press-Gazette, 435 E. Walnut, P.O. Box 19430, Green Bay, WI 54307-9430, *Telephone:* (414) 435-4411, *Fax:* (414) 431-8499, *Published:* daily.

Grocery Headquarters, Delta Communications Inc., 455 N. Cityfront Plaza Drive, Chicago, IL 60611, *Telephone:* (312) 222-2000, *Fax:* (312) 222-2026, *Published:* monthly.

H&HN, Chilton Co., 737 North Michigan Ave., Suite 700, Chicago, IL 60611, *Telephone:* (312) 440-6836, *Published:* monthly.

Hazardous Waste/Superfund Week, Business Publishers, 8737 Colesville Rd., Suite 1100, Silver Spring, MD 20910-3925, *Telephone:* (301) 589-5103, *Fax:* (301) 587-4530.

Health Care Strategic Management, 5353 S Roslyn St., number 400, Englewood, CO 80111-2111, *Published:* monthly, *Price:* $187.

Health Products Business, Cygnus Publishing, P.O. Box 803, Ft. Atkinson, WI 53538-0803.

Healthcare Purchasing News, Nelson Publishing, 2500 Tamiami Trial, Nokomis, FL 34275.

Hearing Journal, The Laux Company Inc., 63 Great Rd., Maynard, MA 01754-2025, *Telephone:* (508) 897-5552, *Fax:* (508) 897-6824, *Published:* monthly.

HFN, 7 E. 12th St., New York, NY 10003. *Published:* weekly.

Hollywood Reporter, 5055 Wilshire Blvd, 6th Fl, Los Angeles, CA 90036, *Telephone:* (213) 525-2000, *Fax:* (213) 525-2377, *Published:* weekdays.

Home Accents Today, 1350 E. Touhy Ave, PO Box 5080, Des Plaines, IL 60017-5080.

Home Channel News, Lebhar-Friedman Inc., 425 Park Avenue, New York, NY 10022, *Telephone:* (212) 756-5228, *Published:* 22x/yr.

Home Textiles Today, Cahners Publishing Co., 249 W 17th St., New York, NY 10011, *Telephone:* (212) 337-6900.

Hospital Materials Management, Aspen Publishers, 200 Orchard Ridge Dr., Ste. 200, Gaithersburg, MD 20878, Telephone: (301) 417-7500, Fax: (301) 417-7550.

Hotel & Motel Management, Advanstar Communications, Inc., 7500 Old Oak Blvd., Clcvcland, OII 44130, *Telephone:* (216) 826-2839.

Household and Personal Products Industry, Rodman Publishing, 17 S. Franklin Turnpike, Box 555, Ramsey, NJ 07446, *Telephone:* (201) 825-2552, *Fax:* (201) 825-0553, *Published:* monthly.

Houston Business Journal, 1 W. Loop S, Ste. 650, Houston, TX 77027-9009, *Telephone:* (713) 688-8811, *Fax:* (713) 963-0482, *Published:* weekly, *Price:* $36.

Houston Chronicle, 801 Texas Ave., Houston, TX 77002, *Telephone:* (713) 220-7171, *Fax:* (713) 220-6677.

ID, Magazine Publications, 250 W 57th St., Ste. 215, New York, NY 10107-0001, *Telephone:* (212)956-0535, *Published:* 6x/yr.

IEEE Software, Institute of Electrical and Electronics engineers, 345 E 47th St., New York, NY 10017, *Telephone:* (212) 705-7555, *Fax:* (212) 705-7589, *Published:* monthly.

Indianapolis Business Journal, IBJ Corp., 431 N Pennsylvania St., Indianapolis, IN 46204, *Telephone:* (317) 634-6200, Fax: (317) 263-5060, *Published:* weekly, *Price:* $54.

The Indianapolis Star, Indianapolis Newspapers Inc., 307 N. Pennsylvania St., Indianapolis, IN 46204, *Telephone:* (317) 633-1157, *Fax:* (317) 633-1174.

Industrial Bioprocessing, Techncial Insights, San Jose, TX, *Telephone:* (877) 463-7678, *Fax:* (888) 690-3329.

Industrial Ceramics, Cahners Publishing, 275 Washington, Newton, MA 02158.

Industrial Distribution, Cahners Publishing Company, 275 Washington Street, Newton, MA 02158, *Telephone:* (617) 964-3030, *Published:* monthly.

Infoworld, Infoworld Publishing Co., 155 Bovet Rd., Ste. 800, San Mateo, CA 94402, *Telephone:* (415) 572-7341, *Published:* weekly.

InFurniture, 7 West 34th Street, New York, NY 10001, *Telephone:* (212) 630-4000, *Published:* monthly.

Ink World, 70 Hilltop Road, Ramsey NJ 07446.

Inside Business, 601 West 26th Street, 13th Floor, New York, NY 10001.

Interactive Advertising & Branding News, Simba Information, PO Box 4234, 11 River Bend Drive South, Stamford, CT 06907-0234.

Internetweek, CMP Media, 600 Community Drive, Manhasset, NY 11030.

Investor's Business Daily, P.O. Box 661750, Los Angeles, CA 90066-8950, *Published:* daily, except weekends and holidays, *Price:* $128 per year.

Journal of Commerce, Journal of Commerce Inc., Two World Trade Center, 27th Floor, New York, NY 10048, Telephone: (800) 331-1341, Fax: (973) 848-7259.

Landscape Management, Advanstar Communications, 7500 Old Oak Blvd, Cleveland, OH 44130, *Telephone:* (216) 243-8100, *Fax:* (216) 891-2675.

Latin Trade, Freedom Communications Inc., 200 South Bicauyne Blvd., Suite 1150, Miami, FL 33131, *Published:* monthly.

LI Business News, 2150 Smithtown Ave., Ronkonkoma, New York 11779.

Library Journal, Cahners Publishing, 249 W 17th St., New York, NY 10010, *Telephone:* (212) 463-6822, *Fax:* (212) 463-6734.

Licensing Letter, EPM Communications, 160 Mercer Street, 3rd Floor, New York, NY 10012.

Los Angeles Business Journal, Los Angeles, CA 92005-0001, *Telephone:* (800) 404-5225.

Los Angeles Magazine, 1888 Century Park E., Ste. 920, Los Angeles, CA 90067, *Telephone:* (310) 557-7569, *Fax:* (310) 277-9087.

Los Angeles Times, The Times Mirror Company, Times Mirror Square, Los Angeles, CA 90053, *Telephone:* (800) LA TIMES.

LP/GAS, Advanstar Communications, 131 West First Street, Duluth, MN 55802-2065, *Published:* monthly, *Price:* $40.

Lubricants World, Chemical Week Associates, 110 William Street, New York, NY 10138, *Telephone:* (212) 621-4900, *Fax:* (212) 621-4949.

M Business, CMP Media, 600 Harrison St., San Francisco, CA 94107, *Telephone:* (415) 905-2200.

Macleans, 7th Floor, 777 Bay Street, Toronto, ON M5W 1A7.

Managed Medicare & Medicaid, AIS, 1100 17th St., NW Ste 300, Washington D.C., 20036.

The Manufacturing Confectioner, The Manufacturing Confectioner Publishing Company, 175 Rock Rd., Glen Rock, NJ 07452, *Telephone:* (201) 652-2655, *Fax:* (201) 652-3419, *Published:* 12 times per year, *Price:* $25 per year, single copies $10 each, except $25 for April and July issues.

Marines, Division of Public Affairs, Media Branch, HQMC, 2 Navy Annex, Washington D.C.

Marketing Magazine, Maclean Hunter Canadian Publishing, P.O. Box 4541, Buffalo, NY 14240-4541, *Telephone:* (800) 567-0444, *Fax:* (416) 946-1679, *Price:* Canada: $59.50 per year, $98.50 for 2 years, $125 for 3 years; U.S.: $90 per year.

Mediaweek, Adweek, LP, PO Box 1976, Danbury, CT 06813-1976, *Telephone:* (800) 722-6658, *Published:* weekly.

Medical Devices & Surgical Technology News, NewsRX, P.O. Box 5528, Atlanta, GA 31107-0528, *Telephone:* (770) 507-7777.

Medical Marketing & Media, CPS Communications, 7200 West Camino Real, Ste. 215, Boca Raton, FL 33433, *Telephone:* (407) 368-9301, *Fax:* (407) 368-7870, *Published:* monthly, *Price:* $75 per year.

Mergers & Acquisitions, 195 Broadway, 10th Floor, New York, NY 10007, Telephone: (646) 822-2000.

Metalworking Marketer, P.O. Box 107, Larchmont, NY 10538, *Telephone:* (914) 834-7035, *Fax:* (914) 834-7035, *Published:* 24x/yr.

Metro Magazine, Bobit Publishing, 2512 Artesia Blvd, Redondo Beach,CA 90278, *Telephone:* (310) 376-8788, *Fax:* (310) 376-9043, *Published:* 7x/yr., *Price:* $12.

Mexico Telecom, Information Gatekeepers, 214 Harvard Avenue, Boston, MA 02134, *Telephone:* (617) 738-8088.

Milling & Baking News, Sosland Publishing Co., 4800 Main St., Ste. 100, Kansas City, MO 64112, Telephone: (816) 756-1000, Fax: (816) 756-0494.

Milwaukee Journal-Sentinel, Journal/Sentinel Inc., P.O. Box 371, 53201, *Telephone:* (414) 224-2000, *Published:* Mon-Sat.

Minneapolis-St. Paul CityBusiness, 527 Marquette Avenue, Suite 300, Minneapolis, MN 55402, *Telephone:* (612) 288-2100, *Fax:* (612) 288-1212.

MMR, Racher Press, 220 5th Ave., New York, NY 1001, *Telephone:* (212) 213-6000, *Fax:* (212) 213-6101, *Published:* biweekly.

Modern Healthcare, Crain Communications, 740 N Rush, Chicago, IL 60611-2590, *Telephone:* (312) 649-5350, *Fax:* (312) 280-3189.

Modern Plastics, McGraw-Hill, P.O. Box 481, Highstown, NJ 08520, *Telephone:* (800) 525-5003, *Published:* monthly.

Modern Tire Dealer, Bill Communications Inc., PO Box 3599, Akron, OH 44309-3599, *Telephone:* (216) 867-4401, *Fax:* (216) 867-0019, *Published:* 14x/yr.

The Morning Call, 101 N. 6th St., Allentown, PA 18105, *Telephone:* (215) 820-6646, *Published:* daily.

Mortgage Banking, Mortgage Bankers Assn of America, 1125 15th St. NW, Washington D.C. 20005, *Telephone:* (202) 861-6500, *Fax:* (202) 872-0186, *Published:* monthly.

Mortgage Technology, One Station Place, Stamford, CT 06902, *Telephone:* (203) 969-8700, *Fax:* (203) 977-8354.

Motor Trend, Peterson Publishing, 8490 Sunset Blvd, Los Angeles, CA 90069, Telephone: (213) 854-2222.

Motion Systems Distributor, Penton Media, 1300 E 9th Street, Cleveland, OH 44114.

Multichannel News, 360 Park Ave S, New York, NY 10010, *Telephone:* (646) 746-6400.

Music Trades, P.O. Box 432, 80 West St., Englewood, NJ 07631, *Telephone:* (201) 871-1965, *Fax:* (201) 871-0455, *Published:* monthly.

National Defense, 2111 Wilson Boulevard, Suite 400, Arlington VA 2201-3061, *Telephone:* (703) 522-1820, *Fax:* (703) 522-1885.

National Home Center News, Lebhar-Friedman Inc., 425 Park Ave., New York, NY 10022, *Telephone:* (212) 756-5151, Fax: (212) 756-5295, *Published:* 2x/mo.

National Jeweler, Miller Freeman, 1515 Broadway, New York, NY 10036, *Telephone:* (212) 626-2380, *Fax:* (212) 944-7164, *Published:* 2x/mo.

National Petroleum News, Hunter Publishing, 950 Lee St., Des Plaines, IL 60016, *Telephone:* (708) 296-0770, *Fax:* (708) 296-8821, *Published:* monthly.

National Provisioner, 15 W. Huron St., Chicago, IL 60610, *Telephone:* (312) 944-3380, *Fax:* (312) 944-3709.

National Underwriter, The National Underwriter Co., 505 Gest St., Cincinnati, OH 45203, *Telephone:* (800) 543-0874, *Fax:* (800) 874-1916, *Published:* weekly, except last week in December, *Price:* U.S.: $77 per year, $130 for 2 years; Canada: $112 per year, $130 for 2 years.

Nation's Restaurant News, Lebhar-Friedman, Inc., Subscription Dept., P.O. Box 31179, Tampa, FL 33631-3179, *Telephone:* (800) 447-7133. *Published:* weekly on Mondays, except the first Monday in July and the last Monday in December, *Price:* $34.50 per year and $55 for 2 years for professionals in the field; $89 per year for those allied to field.

Natural Foods Merchandiser, 1401 Pearl Street, Boulder, CO 80302.

New Steel , Chilton Publishing, 191 S. Gary Ave, Carol Stream, IL 60188, *Telephone:* (708) 462-2282, *Fax:* (708) 462-2862, *Published:* monthly.

The New York Times, New York Times Co., 229 W. 43rd St., New York, NY 10036, *Telephone:* (212) 556-1234. *Published:* daily.

Nikkei Weekly, 1-9-5 Otemachi, Chiyoda-ku, Tokyo, 100-66 Japan.

Non-Profit Times, 120 Littleton Road, Sutie 120, Parsippany, NJ 07054-1803, *Telephone:* (973) 394-1800, *Fax:* (973) 394-2888, *Published:* 24x/yr.

Nonwoven Industry, Rodman Publishing, 17 S. Franklin Turnpike, P.O. Box 555, Ramsey, NJ 07446, *Telephone:* (201) 825-2552, *Fax:* (201) 825-0553, *Published:* monthly, *Price:* $48, or free to qualified subscribers.

North County Times, 207 Escondido Avenue, Vista, CA 92083, *Telephone:* (760) 631-6600.

Nutraceuticals World, 70 Hilltop Road, Ramsey, NJ 07446, *Telephone:* (201) 825-2552, *Fax:* (201) 825-0553.

Offshore, 500 Victory Road, Marina Bay, North Quincy, MA 02171, *Telephone:* (617) 221-1400, *Fax:* (617) 847-1871.

Oil & Gas Journal, PennWell Publishing CO., PO Box 2002, Tulsa, OK 74101, *Telephone:* (800) 633-1656, *Published:* weekly.

Oil Express, PennWell Publishing CO., PO Box 2002, Tulsa, OK 74101.

Oregon Business, 921 SW Morrison St., number 407, Portland, OR 97205-2722, *Telephone:* (503) 223-0304, *Fax:* (503) 221-6544, *Published:* monthly, *Price:* $24, free to qualified subscribers.

Origination News, Thomas Financial Mortgage Publications.

Orlando Business Journal, 1221 W Colonial Dr., Ste. 101, Orlando, FL 32804, *Telephone:* (407) 649-8470, *Fax:* (407) 649-8469, *Published:* weekly, *Price:* $39.

Outdoor Retailer, Miller Freeman, 600 Harrison St., San Francisco, CA 94107, *Telephone:* (415) 905-2200, *Fax:* (714) 499-5554, *Published:* monthly.

Pacific Business News, Cross roads Press, P.O. Box 833, Honolulu, HI 96808, *Telephone:* (808) 521-0021, *Fax:* (808) 526-3273.

Packaging Digest, Delta Communications, 455 N. CityFront Plaza Drive, Chicago, IL 60611, *Telephone:* (312) 222-2000, *Fax:* (312) 222-2026, *Published:* monthly, *Price:* $75.

Packaging Strategies, 901 South Bolmar St., Suite P, West Chester, PA 19382-4550, *Telephone:* (800) 524-7225, *Fax:* (610) 436-6277, *Published:* monthly.

Paint & Coatings Industry, 755 W Big Bewaver Rd, Ste. 1000, Troy, MI 48083.

Paperboard Packaging, Advanstar Communications Inc., 131 West First Street, Duluth, MN 55802, *Telephone:* (218) 723-9477, *Fax:* (218) 723-9437, *Published:* monthly, *Price:* U.S.: $39 per year, $58 for 2 years; Canada: $59 per year, $88 for 2 years.

Pensions & Investments, Crain Communications, 220 E 42nd St., New York, NY 10017, *Telephone:* (212) 210-0227, *Fax:* (212) 210-0117, *Published:* biweekly.

Performance Materials, P.O. Box 201009, Houston, TX 77216-1009.

Philadelphia Business Journal, 718 Arch St., Ste. 6N, Philadelphia, PA 19106-1505, *Telephone:* (215) 238-1450, *Fax:* (215) 238-1466, *Published:* weekly, *Price:* $52.

Photo Marketing, Photo Marketing Association International, 3000 Picture Place, Jackson, MI 49201, *Telephone:* (517) 788-8100, *Fax:* (517) 788-8371. *Published:* monthly, *Price:* U.S.: $35 per year/with Newsline $50, $55 for 2 years/$65 with Newsline; Canada: $35 per year/$50 with Newsline, $55 for 2 years/$70 with Newsline (payable in Canadian funds plus GST).

Photo Trade News, 445 Broad Hollow Road, Suite 21, Melville, NY 11747, *Telephone:* (631) 845-2700.

Pit & Quarry, Edgell Communications, 7500 Old Oak Blvd, Cleveland, OH 44130, *Telephone:* (216) 243-8100, *Fax:* (216) 891-2726, *Published:* monthly.

Pittsburgh Business Times, MCP Inc., 2313 E Carson St., Pittsburgh, PA 15203, *Telephone:* (412) 481-6397, *Fax:* (412) 481-9956, *Published:* weekly.

Plastics News, Crain Communications, 965 E. Jefferson, Detroit, MI 48207-3185, *Published:* weekly.

Playthings, Geyer-McAllister Publications, Inc., 51 Madison Ave., New York, NY 10010, *Telephone:* (212) 689-4411, *Fax:* (212) 683-7929, *Published:* monthly, except semimonthly in May.

Plumbing & Mechanical, Horton Publishing, 1350 E Touhy Ave, 100 E, Rosemont, IL 60018, *Published:* monthly.

Point of Purchase, VNU Media, 770 Broadway, 6th Floor, New York, NY 10003.

Pool & Spa Marketing, Hubbard Marketing & Publishing, 46 Crockford Blvd, Scarborough, ON, Canada M1R 3C3, *Telephone:* (416) 752-2500, *Fax:* (416) 752-2748, *Published:* monthly, *Price:* $20.

Post-Standard, Syracuse Newspapers, Clinton Square, P.O. Box 4915, Syracuse, NY 13221, *Telephone:* (315) 470-0011, *Fax:* (315) 470-3081, *Published:* Mon-Sat.

PR Week, PR Publications Ltd., 220 Fifth Ave., New York, NY 10001, *Telephone:* (212) 532-9200, *Fax:* (212) 532-9200, *Published:* 49x/yr.

Practical Accountant, Faulkner & Gray, Inc., 11 Penn Plaza, 17th Floor, New York, NY 10001, *Telephone:* (800) 535-8403 or (212) 967-7060, *Published:* monthly, *Price:* U.S.: $60 per year; Elsewhere: $79 per year.

Prepared Foods, Cahners Publishing Company, 44 Cook St., Denver, CO 80217-3377, *Telephone:* (303) 388-4511, *Published:* monthly.

Presentations, VNU Media, 770 Broadway, New York, NY 10003.

Printing Impressions, North American Publishing Co., 401 N Broad St., Philadelphia, PA 19108, *Telephone*: (215) 238-5300, *Fax:* (215) 238-5457.

Printing News, Cahners Publishing, 245 W 17th St., New York, NY 10011, *Telephone:* (212) 463-6730, Fax: (212) 463-6733, *Published:* weekly, *Price:* $24.95.

Private Label Buyer, Stagnito Communications Inc., 155 Pfingsten Road, Suite 205, Deerfield, IL 60015, *Telephone:* (847) 205-5660, *Fax:* (847) 205-5680.

Professional Builder, Cahners Publishing, 1350 E Touhy Ave, Des Plaines, IL 60018, *Telephone:* (708) 635-8800, *Fax:* (708) 635-9950.

Professional Candy Buyer, Adams Business Media, 2101 S. Arlington Heights Rd., Arlington Heights, IL 60005-4142.

Progressive Grocer, 263 Tresser Blvd., Stamford, CT 06901, *Telephone:* (203) 325-3500, *Published:* monthly, *Price:* U.S.: $75 per year; Canada: $86 per year; single copies $9 each.

Publishers Weekly, Cahners Publishing Company, ESP Computer Services, 19110 Van Ness Ave., Torrance, CA 90501-1170, *Telephone:* (800) 278-2991, *Published:* weekly, *Price:* U.S.: $129 per year; Canada: $177 per year (includes GST).

Puget Sound Business Journal, 101 Yesler Way, Ste. 200, Seattle, WA 98104, *Telephone:* (206) 583-0701, *Fax:* (206) 447-8510, *Published:* weekly, *Price:* $48.

Pulp & Paper, Miller Freeman Inc., P.O. Box 1065, Skokie, IL 60076-8065, *Telephone:* (800) 682-8297, *Published:* monthly, *Price:* free to those in pulp, paper, and board manufacturing and paper converting firms; Others in U.S.: $100 per year.

Purchasing, Cahners Publishing Company, 44 Cook St., Denver, CO 80217-3377, *Telephone:* (303)

388-4511. *Published:* semimonthly, except monthly in January, February, July, August, December, and one extra issue in March and September, *Price:* U.S.: $84.95 per year; Canada: $133.95 per year; Mexico: $124.95 per year.

Quick Frozen Foods International, EW Williams Publishing Co., 2125 Center Ave., Ste. 305, Fort Lee, NJ 07024, *Telephone:* (201) 592-7007, *Fax:* (201) 592-7171, *Published:* monthly.

Quick Print Products, Reed Business, 360 Park Ave., New York, NY 10010, *Telephone:* (646) 746-6400.

R&D Magazine, Cahners Publishing Company, 275 Washington St, Newton, MA 02158, Telephone: (708) 635-8800, Fax: (708) 390-2618, Published: monthly.

Railway Age, Simmons-Boardman Publishing, 345 Hudson St., New York, NY 10014, *Telephone:* (212) 620-7200, *Fax:* (212) 633-1165, *Published:* monthly.

RCR, RCR Publications, 777 East Speer Blvd., Denver, CO 80203.

Real Estate Alert, 5 Marine View Plaza, Ste. 301, Hoboken, NJ 07030-5795, *Telephone:* (201) 659-1700, *Fax:* (201) 659-4141.

The Record, 150 River St., Hackensack, NJ 07601.

Recycling Today, 4012 Bridge Avenue, Cleveland, OH 44113, *Telephone:* (800) 456-0707, *Fax:* (216) 961-0365.

Refrigerated & Frozen Foods, Stagnito Communications, 1935 Sherman Rd., Northbrook, IL 60062, *Telephone:* (847) 205-5660, *Fax:* (847) 205-5680, *Published:* monthly.

The Register-Guard, P.O. Box 10188, Eugene, OR 97440-2188, *Telephone:* (541) 485-1234, *Fax:* (541) 683-7631.

Reinforced Plastics, United Kingdom, *Telephone*: (44) 0 1865-843-208, *Fax:* (440) 1865-843-973.

Report/ Magazine (Alberta Edition), 17327, 106A, Edmonton, Alberta, CA.

Research Alert, EPM Communications, 160 Mercer Street, 3rd Floor, New York, NY 10012.

Research Studies, BCC Inc., 25 Van Zant, Norwalk, CT 06855-1781.

Research Studies, Freedonia Group, 767 Beta Drive, Cleveland, OH 44143, Telephone: (440) 684-9600.

Restaurants & Institutions, Cahners Publishing Co., 1350 Touhy Ave., Cahners Plaza, Des Plaines, IL 60017-5080, *Telephone:* (312) 635-8800.

Retail Merchandiser, Schwartz Publications, 233 Park Ave, New York, NY 1003, *Telephone:* (212) 979-4860.

Risk Retention Reporter, P.O Box 50147, Pasadena, CA 91115, *Telephone:* (626)796-4972, *Fax:* (626) 796-2363.

Rockford Register Star, 99 E. State St., Rockford, IL 61104.

Rocky Mountain News, 400 West Colfax, Denver, CO 80204.

Rubber & Plastics News, Crain Communications, 1725 Merriman Road, Ste. 300, Akron, OH 44313, *Telephone:* (330) 836-9180, *Fax:* (33) 836-1005, *Published:* weekly.

Rubber World, P.O. Box 5451, 1867 W. Market St., Akron, OH 44313-6901, *Telephone:* (330) 864-2122, *Fax:* (330) 864-5298.

Rural Cooperatives, USDA, Superintendents of Documents, USGPO, Washington D.C.

RV Business, P.O. Box 17126, North Hollywood, CA 91615-9925, *Published:* monthly.

Sacramento Business Journal, 1401 21st St., Sacramento, CA 95814-5221, *Telephone:* (916) 447-7661, *Fax:* (916) 444-7779, *Published:* weekly.

St. Louis Business Journal, American City Business Journals, 1 Metropolitan Square, PO Box 647, Saint Louis, MO 63188, *Telephone:* (314) 421-6200, *Fax:* (314) 621-5031.

St. Louis Post Dispatch, 400 South 4th Street, Ste 1200, St. Louis, MO 63102.

San Antonio Business Journal, American City Business Journal, 82001H 10 W, Ste. 300, San Antonio, TX 78230-4819, *Telephone:* (512) 341-3202.

San Diego Business Journal, 4909 Murphy Canyon, number 200, San Diego, CA 92123, *Telephone:* (619) 277-6359, *Fax:* (619) 571-3628.

San Francisco Business Times, 275 Battery St., 940, San Francisco, CA 94111, *Telephone:* (415) 989-2522, *Fax:* (415) 398-2494.

San Francisco Chronicle, Chroncile Publishing Co., 901 Mission St., San Francisco, CA 94103-2988, *Telephone:* (415) 777-1111, *Fax:* (415) 512-8196.

San Jose Mercury News, Knight-Ridder Inc., 1 Herald Plaza, Miami, Fl 33132, *Published:* daily.

Sarasota Herald-Tribune, 801 S. Tamiami Trail, Sarasota, FL 34236, *Telephone:* (813) 953-7755, *Fax:* (813) 957-5235.

Satellite Broadband, Primedia Business, 1440 Broadway, New York, NY 10018, *Published:* monthly.

Satellite News, 800 Siesta Way, Sonoma, CA 95476, *Telephone:* (707) 939-9306, *Fax:* (707) 939-9235.

Science World, Scholastic Inc., 730 Broadway, New York, NY 10003, *Telephone:* (212) 505-3000, *Published:* 18x/yr.

Screen Digest, EMAP Media, 33-39 Bowling Green Lane, London EC1R ODA, *Telephone:* 44 (0)171 396-8000, *Published:* weekly.

SDM, Cahners Publishing Co., 1350 E. Touhy Ave., Des Plaines, IL 60018, *Telephone:* (708) 635-8800, *Fax:* (708) 299-8622.

Seafood Business, Journal Publications, P.O. Box 98, Rockland, ME 04841, *Telephone:* (207) 594-6222, *Fax:* (207) 594-8978, *Published:* 6x/yr.

Securities Industry News, One State Street, 27th Floor, New York, NY 10004, *Telephone:* (888) 280-4820, *Fax:* (301) 545-4836.

Shooting Industry, Publishers Development Corp., 591 Camino de la Reina, Ste. 200, San Diego, CA 92108, *Telephone:* (619) 297-8520, *Fax:* (619) 297-5353, *Published:* monthly, *Price:* $25.

Shopping Center World, Communications Channels, Inc., 6255 Barfield Rd., Altanta, GA 30328, *Telephone:* (404) 256-9800.

Silicon Valley/San Jose Business Journal, 96 N. Third Street, Suite 100, San Jose, CA 95112, *Telephone:* (408) 295-3800, *Fax:* (408) 295-5028.

Skillings Mining Review, 11 E Superior St., Ste. 514, Duluth, MN 55802.

Small Business Banker, American Banker Inc., 1 State St, New York, NY 10023, *Telephone:* (212) 408-1480, *Fax:* (212) 943-2984.

Smart Business, ZDNet, 650 Townsend Street, San Francisco, CA 94103.

Snack Food & Wholesale Bakery, Stagnito Publishing Co., 1935 Shermer Rd., Ste. 100, Northbrook, IL 60062-5354, *Telephone:* (708) 205-5660, *Fax:* (708) 205-5680, *Published:* monthly, *Price:* free to qualified subscribers; $45 per year to all others.

Soap & Cosmetics, 455 Broad Hollow Road, Melville, NY 11747-4722, *Published:* monthly.

South Florida Business Journal, American City Business Journals, 7950 NW 53 St., Ste. 210, Miami, FL 33166, *Telephone:* (305) 594-2100, *Fax:* (305) 594-1892.

Special Events Magazine, Miramar Publishing, 6133 Bristol Pkway, Culver City, CA 90230, *Telephone:* (310) 337-9717, *Fax:* (310) 337-1041, *Published:* monthly.

Sporting Goods Business, Gralla Publications, Inc., 1515 Broadway, New York, NY 10036, *Telephone:* (212) 869-1300.

Sporting Goods Dealer, Times Mirror, 2 Park Ave, New York, NY 10016, *Telephone:* (212) 779-5000, *Fax:* (212) 213-3540, *Published:* monthly.

Star Tribune, 425 Portland Ave., Minneapolis, MN 55488, *Telephone:* (612) 673-4000.

Statistics of the Long-Distance Industry, USDA, Superintendents of Documents, USGPO, Washington D.C.

Stone World, Tradeline Publishing, 320 Kinderkamack Rd., Oradell, NJ 07649-2102, *Telephone:* (201) 599-0136, *Fax:* (201) 599-2378, *Published:* monthly, *Price:* $55.

Stores, NRF Enterprises Inc., 100 West 31st St., New York, NY 10001, *Published:* monthly, *Price:* U.S./Canada: $49 per year, $80 for 2 years, $120 for 3 years.

Successful Farming, Meredith Corp., 1716 Locust St., Des Moines, IA 50309, *Telephone:* (515) 284-3000, *Fax:* (515) 284-2700, *Published:* monthly.

Supermarket Business, Howfrey Communications, Inc., 1086 Teaneck Rd., Teaneck, NJ 07666, *Telephone:* (201) 833-1900, *Published:* monthly.

Supermarket News, Fairchild Publications, 7 W. 34th St., New York, NY 10001, *Telephone:* (212) 630-4750, *Fax:* (212) 630-4760.

Supply Chain Yearbook, 275 Washington, Newton, MA 02458.

Supply House Times, Horton Publishing, 1350 Touhy Ave, Ste. 100E, Rosemont, IL 60018-3358.

Swimming Pool/Spa Age, Communications Channels, 6255 Rd, Atlanta, GA 30328, *Telephone:* (404) 256-9800, *Fax:* (404) 256-3116, *Published:* monthly.

Tape-Disc Business, PBI Media, 1201 Seven Locks Road, Suite 300, Potomac, MD 20854, *Telephone:* (301) 354-2000.

Tea & Coffee Trade Journal, Lockwood Trade Journal, 130 W 42nd St., Ste 2200, New York, NY 10036-7802, *Telephone:* (212) 391-2060, *Fax:* (212) 827-0945, *Published:* monthly, *Price:* $29.

Technology Advertising & Branding Report, Simba Information, PO Box 4234, 11 River Bend Drive South, Stamford, CT 06907-0234.

Telephony, Intersec Publishing Corp., 9800 Metcalf, Overland Park, KS 66282-2960, *Published:* monthly.

Textile World, Maclean Hunter Publishing Co., Circulation Dept., 29 N. Wacker Dr., Chicago, IL 60606, *Price:* U.S./Canada: $45 per year, $75 for 2 years, $105 for 3 years.

Time, Time, Inc., Time & Life Bldg., Rockefeller Center, New York, NY 10020-1393, *Telephone:* (800) 843-8463, *Published:* weekly.

Tire Business, Crain Communcations, Inc., 1725 Merriman Rd., Ste. 300, Akron, OH 44313-5251, *Telephone:* (216) 836-9180, *Fax:* (216) 836-1005.

Tradeshow Week, 5700 Wilshire Blvd, Ste 120, Los Angeles, CA 90036, *Telephone:* (323) 965-2437, *Fax:* (323) 965-2407.

Traffic World, New York, NY 10048, *Published:* monthly.

Trains Magazine, Kalmbach Publishing, P.O. Box 1612, Waukesha, WI 53187-1612.

Transportation & Distribution, Penton Publishing, 1100 Superior Ave., Cleveland, OH 44114-2543, *Telephone:* (216) 696-7000, *Fax:* (216) 696-4135, *Published:* monthly, *Price:* $45.

Travel Agent, Advanstar, 545 Boylston St., Boston, MA 02116, *Telephone:* (617) 267-6500, *Fax:* (617) 267-6900.

Trendex Soft Line, 3454 Oak Alley Court, Suite 302, Toledo, OH 43606.

TV Meets the Web, Van Dusseldorp & Partners, De Ruyterkade 128, 1011 AC Amsterdam, Netherlands, *Telephone:* (3120) 623-1530, *Fax:* (3120) 623-1522.

U.S. Banker, Kalo Communications, 60 E. 42nd St., Ste. 3810, New York, NY 10165, Telephone: (212) 599-3310.

U.S. News & World Report, 2400 N. St. NW, Washington, D.C. 20037, *Telephone:* (202) 955-2000, *Published:* weekly.

Upholstery Design & Management, 380 Northwest Highway, Des Plaines, IL 60016-2208, *Telephone:* (847) 390-6700, *Fax:* (847) 390-7100.

Upside, Upside Media Inc., 2015 Pioneer Court, San Mateo, CA 94403, *Telephone:* (650) 377-0950, *Fax:* (650) 377-1962, *Published:* monthly.

Urethane Technology, Crain Communications Inc., 1725 Merriman Rd., Ste. 300, Akron, OH 44313-5251, *Telephone:* (216) 836-9180, *Fax:* (216) 836-1005, *Published:* 6x/yr, Price: $83.

USA TODAY, Gannett Co., Inc., 1000 Wilson Blvd., Arlington, VA 22229, *Telephone:* (703) 276-3400. *Published:* Mon.-Fri.

Utah Agriculture, Utah Agricultural Statistics Service, P.O. Box 25007, Salt Lake City, UT

84125-0007, *Telephone:* (801) 524-5003, Published: semi-monthly.

Utility Automation, 1421 S. Sheridan Road, Tulsa, OK 74112, *Telephone:* (918) 832-9249, *Fax:* (918) 831-9875.

VAR Business, CMP Media Inc., 1 Jericho Plaza A, Jericho NY 11753, *Telephone:* (516) 733-6700, *Published:* weekly.

Variety, 475 Park Ave., South, New York, NY 10016, *Telephone:* (212) 779-1100, *Fax:* (212) 779-0026. *Published:* weekly.

Video Business, Capital Cities/ABC/Chilton CO., Chilton Way, Radnor, PA 19089, *Telephone:* (215) 964-4000, *Fax:* (215) 964-4285, *Published:* weekly.

Video Store, Advanstar Communications Inc., 1700 E. Dyer Rd., Ste 250, Santa Ana, CA 92705, *Telephone:* (714) 252-5300.

VM+SD, ST Publications, 407 Gilbert Ave., Cincinnati, OH 45202, *Telephone:* (513) 421-2050, *Published:* monthly, *Price:* $39.

Wall Street Journal, Dow Jones & Co. Inc., 200 Liberty St., New York, NY 10281, *Telephone:* (212) 416-2000. *Published:* Mon.-Fri.

WARD's Auto World, Ward's Communications, 28 W. Adams, Detroit, MI 48226, *Telephone:* (313) 962-4456. *Published:* monthly.

WARD's Dealer Business, Ward's Communications, 28 W. Adams, Detroit, MI 48226, *Telephone:* (313) 962-4456. *Published:* monthly.

Washington Business Journal, American City Business Journals, 2000 14th St, Ste. 500, Arlington, VA 22201.

The Washington Post, The Washington Post, 1150 15th St., N.W., Washington, DC 20071, *Published:* weekly.

Washington Technology, Tech News Inc., 1953 Gallows Road, Ste. 130, Vienna, VA 22182.

Waste Age, National Solid Waste Management Assn, 1730 Rhode Island Ave., NW, Ste. 100, Washington D.C. 20036.

Waste News, 1725 Merriman Road, Akron, OH 44313.

WattPoultryUSA, WATT Publishing, 122 S. Wesley Ave., Mt. Morris, IL 61054, *Telephone:* (815) 734-4171, *Fax:* (815) 734-4201.

WC&P Magazine, 2800 E Ft. Lowell Road, Tucson, Arizona 85716, *Telephone:* (520) 323-6144, *Fax:* (520) 323-7412.

Wearable Business, Intertec Publishing, 707 Westchester, White Plains, NY, *Published:* monthly.

Westchester County Business Journal, Westfair Communications, 3 Gannett Drive, White Plains, New York 10604, *Telephone:* (914) 694-3600, *Fax:* (914) 694-3699.

Wine Handbook, Jobson Publishing, 100 Avenue of the Americas, 9th Floor, New York, NY 10013, *Telephone:* (212) 274-7000, *Fax:* (212) 431-0500.

Wines & Vines, Hiaring Co., 1800 Lincoln Ave., San Rafael, CA 94901-1298, *Telephone:* (415) 453-9700, *Fax:* (415) 453-2517, *Published:* monthly, *Price:* $32

per year without directory; $77.50 per year including directory.

Winston-Salem Journal, Piedmont Publishing, P.O. Box 3159, Winston-Salem, NC 27102-3159, *Telephone:* (919) 727-7211, *Fax:* (919) 727-7315.

Wood & Wood Products, Vance Publishing Corp., 400 Knightsbridge Pkway., Lincolnshire, IL 60069, *Telephone:* (708) 634-4347, *Fax:* (708) 634-4379, Published: monthly, except semimonthly in March.

Wood Digest, Johnson Hill Press, 1233 Janesville Ave., Fort Atkinson, WI 53538, *Telephone:* (414) 563-6388, *Fax:* (414) 563-1702.

World Oil, Gulf Publishing, 3301 Allen Pkway, PO Box 2608, Houston, TX 77242, *Telephone:* (713) 529-4301, *Fax:* (713) 520-4433.

World Poultry, Misset International, P.O. Box 4, 7000BA, Doetinchem, the Netherlands, *Telephone:* (31) 8340-49562, *Price:* $79.

WWD, Fairchild Publications, 7 E. 12th St., New York, NY 10003, *Telephone:* (212) 741-4000, *Fax:* (212) 337-3225. *Published:* weekly.

Yahoo!Internet Life, Ziff Davis Inc., Ona Park Ave., New York, NY 10016, *Published:* monthly.